CW00923820

RUSSIAN PISTON AERO ENGINES

RUSSIAN PISTON AERO ENGINES

Vladimir Kotelnikov

THE CROWOOD PRESS

First published in 2005 by
The Crowood Press Ltd
Ramsbury, Marlborough
Wiltshire SN8 2HR

www.crowood.com

British Library Cataloguing-in-Publication Data
A catalogue record for this book is available from the British Library.

ISBN 1 86126 702 9

Acknowledgements

The author would like to thank all of his friends and colleagues for their assistance in the preparation of this book, among them E. Arsenyev, V. Bakurskiy, S. Balakin, M. Baryatinskiy, N. Eastaway, D. Khazanov, V. Kulikov, M. Maslov, A. Medved, V. Mikheev, M. Orlov, B. Osetinskiy, G. Petrov, V. Rigmant, G. Sloutski, N. Valuev, A. Yurgenson and V. Zolotov.

Designed and typeset by Focus Publishing, Sevenoaks, Kent

Printed and bound in Great Britain by CPI Bath

Contents

Introduction 7
Abbreviations 11

Part 1

1 State Control Over the Aero-engine Industry 13
2 The Planning of the Research and Development Works, and Preparation and Approval of Engine Specifications 15
3 The Organization of Aero-engine Development and Prototype Manufacturing 18
4 Engine Testing and Acceptance 22
5 Aero-engine Designations 24
6 Aero-engine Factories 27

Part 2

1 Aero-engines in Russia Before October 1917 33
2 Tsarist Heritage 42
3 Eight-cylinder Hispano-Suiza Engines 45
4 RAM – the first Soviet High-powered Aero-engine 48
5 Soviet-built Liberty Engines 49
6 The Engines of the GAZ No. 2 Ikar Factory and Their Evolution 55
7 The High-powered Aero-engines Developed at NAMI 59
8 MK – *Motor Kireeva* (Kireev's Engine) 62
9 The Engines Built at the Bolshevik Factory in Leningrad 63
10 The Contest for Aero-engines for Training Aircraft, and Further Evolution of the M-11 64
11 The History of the M-17 73
12 Jupiter Engines from Zaporozhye 78
13 A Family of Air-cooled Engines Developed at Factory No. 24 83
14 The FED Engines 86
15 The First Engines of the IAM 88
16 Engines of Unusual Layout Developed During 1923–32 91

17 Unfulfilled Orders 93
18 Amateur Designs of the 1920s and 1930s 94
19 The M-56 and MGM Engines 95
20 The Low-powered TsIAM Engines 96
21 Automobile Engines Modified for Use in Aircraft 97
22 The Engines of A.A. Mikulin 98
23 The Engines of A.D. Shvetsov 117
24 The Engines of V.Ya. Klimov 133
25 Gnome-Rhône – the Last Attempt 147
26 The Engines of M.A. Kossov, and Other Attempts to Create a Low-powered Engine Based on the M-11 157
27 Voronezh-built Renault Engines 163
28 The Last Piston Engines Developed at the TsIAM 167
29 Diesel Aero-engines 169
30 Projects for H-shaped Engines by A.P. Ro 181
31 The Engines of A.M. Dobrotvorskiy 182
32 The Engines of S.D. Kolosov 183
33 The Conrod-free Engines of S.S. Balandin 185
34 Lesser-known Projects of 1939–47 190
35 The Engines of G.S. Skubachevskiy and I.V. Dobrynin 192
36 The Engines of A.G. Ivchenko and their Evolution 196
37 The Engines of the Voronezh Engine-building Design Bureau 204
38 Wankel-type Engines 207
39 The Engines of the Samara Machine-Building Design Bureau 210
40 The Engines of the Kazan Engine-Building Production Enterprise (KMPO) 213
41 The Engines Developed at the Rybinskie Motory Enterprise During the 1980s–1990s 214
42 Engines for Ultralight Aircraft, Based on Motorcycle Engines 215
43 Postwar Homebuilt Engines 217
44 Foreign Piston Aero-engines in Russia 218

Appendix I Engine Characteristics 240
Appendix II Russian Aircraft and Their Piston Engines 266
Select Bibliography 268
Index 269

Introduction

This book covers the evolution of piston aero-engines in Russia, from the first efforts to create aircraft powerplants in the second half of the nineteenth century to modern low-powered designs.

Russian aero-engine development had its ups and downs, its share of great optimism and pessimism. In the late nineteenth century, as in other countries, Russian enthusiasts and engineers attempted to build both lighter-than-air and heavier-than-air craft. These needed light and sufficiently powerful engines, the development of which had begun at that time. However, series production of aero-engines in Russia did not start until 1910, under a licence for a US-designed engine which had been acquired in Germany. Although the mass-production of aero-engines in Russia was undertaken during the First World War, only foreign-designed engines or improved copies were built. While engine production in Russia grew rapidly, it still lagged behind the aero-engine industry of the UK, France and Germany, both with respect to quality and production rates. During the four years of the First World War the Russian factories delivered almost fifteen times fewer engines than France in 1917 alone. Because the quantities produced were not sufficient to satisfy the needs of the indigenous aircraft manufacturers, a great number of engines had to be imported.

Two successive revolutions inflicted a heavy blow on Russia's aviation industry. Political chaos, economic recession and the Civil War caused an almost total standstill in aero-engine production. It was only in 1921 that the Soviet factories managed to exceed an output of 100 engines per year; a drop in the ocean for such a large country.

After the Civil War drew to an end, the Soviet Government began to restore the Red Air Fleet (later on renamed *Voenno-Vozdushnie Sili Raboche-Krestyanskoy Krasnoy Armii*, or the Air Force of the Workers' and Peasants' Red Army, VVS RKKA), and this fleet urgently needed aeroplanes and aero-engines. At first the authorities relied upon the importation of cheap surplus equipment left over from the First World War. At the same time, the order was given to arrange production of aero-engines under licences acquired as far back as the Tsarist times but not implemented until then. A further step was the copying and setting up of series production of the Liberty and Hispano-Suiza engines captured from the White Guard during the Civil War. The Soviet version of the Liberty, designated M-5, was the most widely used aero-engine in the VVS RKKA in the 1920s.

Development of the first original Soviet aero-engines began in 1922. When Soviet Russia became the Union of Soviet Socialist Republics (USSR, or Soviet Union), the expansion and modernization of heavy industry (including aviation) was set as the primary task for the country. The air force development plan, as well as the plans for the construction of experimental aircraft and aero-engines, were issued simultaneously with the first five-year plan for developing the country's economy. However, the aviation industry's growth was hindered by limited financial resources, shortages of skilled specialists and considerable delay in the metallurgy and electrotechnical industries. The country produced only one type of aluminium alloy (so-called *kolchugoalyuminiy*), while there were no magnesium alloys at all. Soviet aero-engine manufacturers had to import certain steel alloys, bearings, spark plugs, magnetos, ignition cables, fuel and oil pumps. Considerable harm was caused by over-ambitious planning which did not take into account the real capabilities of the industry. More-or-less realistic plans were rejected as deliberate delay or even sabotage.

In the mid-1920s three main directions of evolution were simultaneously taken by the Soviet aero-engine industry. The first envisioned modernization of the M-5 engine and development of a unified engine family based upon it; the second consisted of designing new engines employing certain design solutions featured in Western powerplants; and the third one was aimed at creating totally original engines, including those having unconventional layouts. However, none of these directions yielded any significant results. Within the first five years forty new engine types were designed in Russia, and seventeen of these were completely or partly built as prototypes. However, only one, the 100hp M-11 radial engine (an original design), was launched into series production. This heavy and inefficient engine was none-the-less insensitive to variations in fuel and oil quality, as well as to harsh operating conditions. These features ensured its long service life, and in different versions the M-11 remained in production for almost thirty years.

However, the M-11 was designed to equip training aeroplanes, and Soviet engineers did not succeed in creating a satisfactory powerplant for combat aircraft in the 1920s. The aviation industry authorities tried to resolve the problem by purchasing manufacturing licences for the German BMW VI (M-17), and French GR 9Aq (M-22) engines. When these types were introduced into series production the Air Force and the Civil Air Fleet (*Grazhdanskiy Vozdushniy Flot*, GVF) were provided with sufficient quantities of aero-engines, and the practice of importing aero-engines was discontinued from 1931. However, while Soviet factories were arranging the M-17 and M-22 production, these engines became somewhat obsolete.

Initially, it was planned that the M-17 and M-22 would be interim, 'transitional' types, to be replaced by modern Soviet engines in a short time, and an ambitious programme to develop more than thirty various aero-engine types was started in 1928-33. However, the plans were totally at variance with reality. Only the M-34, designed by A.A. Mikulin, could be considered a success. This formed the basis for a large family of engines produced until the mid-1950s, but the powerful and heavy

There was a popular saying in the USSR in the early 1930s: 'Soviet pilot, Soviet aeroplane, Soviet engine!'. This picture shows a Soviet pilot, a Soviet aeroplane (an R-5 reconnaissance aircraft of Polikarpov design, which was built in Moscow), and a Soviet engine (M-17, built in Rybinsk, but under German licence).

M-34 was suitable for bombers but not for fighters.

When foreign designers were striving to improve the high-altitude performance of aero-engines by fitting them with superchargers, Soviet engineers made similar efforts but did not achieve success. Superchargers became the Achilles' heel of many Soviet aero-engine prototypes. A decree of the Revolutionary Military Council (*Revvoensovet*, RVS), issued in June 1933, stated: 'While almost all foreign air fleets have started employing high-altitude aero-engines, which considerably increase the speed of an aircraft at high altitudes, its climb rate and service ceiling, the Soviet industry has not created a single aero-engine with a supercharger so far, not even a prototype for State testing ...'. Once again Soviet authorities decided to purchase manufacturing licences from abroad. Licenses for the Wright R-1820 Cyclone and Curtiss V-1800 were acquired from the USA, and for the Hispano-Suiza 12Ybrs and Gnome-Rhône 14K and 9K engines from France. Later they were followed by a licence to produce a family of Renault air-cooled in-line engines. However, only the Wright, Hispano-Suiza and 14-cylinder Gnome-Rhône types went into mass production in the USSR. They formed the basis for three main families of aero-engines which powered Soviet aircraft in the late 1930s and the 1940s. The licensed types were not considered to be temporary, but, on the contrary, they enjoyed the status of primary powerplants. It was planned to put these engines into series production in the shortest time, with the modernization and development of new versions expected to follow soon. The authorities believed it would take the industry three to four years to bridge the gap related to purchasing the licences for engine types that had already been introduced into series production in the West. It was too risky to acquire licences for prototype engines; moreover, Western manufacturers were less eager to grant them.

As a result, four aero-engine families were in mass production in the USSR during the pre-Second World War period: those designed by V.Ya. Klimov (based on the Hispano-Suiza); engines designed by A.D. Shvetsov (Wright-based); engines manufactured at Factory No. 29 (Gnome-Rhône); and engines designed by A.A. Mikulin (based on the M-34). The first three families were extensive modifications of their respective prototypes, and often had no direct equivalents in the companies that had sold the licences. Soviet engineers introduced multi-speed geared centrifugal superchargers (GCS), turbo-supercharging, float-less carburettors and direct injection. However, Soviet engines still lagged a year or two behind their foreign counterparts with respect to specific power rating, altitude characteristics and, first and foremost, times between scheduled overhauls. The M-11 remained dominant in the training sphere, and the temperamental Renaults did not succeed in replacing it. Another direction in aero-engine development was the work on diesel engines actively carried out in the Soviet Union.

At this stage the Soviet aviation industry was receiving sufficient quantities of contemporary powerplants to allow the country to expand both its military and civil aviation. In 1935 aero-engine production in the USSR exceeded 10,000 units per year, and the introduction of new engine types forced the allied industries to catch up. Almost no engine parts were imported from abroad, ball and roller bearings being the only exception, Soviet ones being of considerably inferior quality.

The new powerplants required better fuel, and the quality of aviation fuel improved constantly. In the late 1930s the air force turned from the benzine-benzole mixture to leaded fuel, the octane number of which was being raised constantly. This enabled supercharging and compression ratios to be boosted.

The Second World War was approaching, and in 1939-40 the aero-engine industry once again came into into the Soviet Government spotlight. Although the USSR produced lots of engines, their quality left much to be desired and they still lagged behind their Western contemporaries. For instance, while Klimov's M-103A was basically comparable to its 'cousin', the Hispano-Suiza 12Y51 (the difference in their maximum power rating was just 10 per cent), the M-87A was considerably inferior to the French Gnome-Rhône 14N50. The performance of the Soviet M-62 was similar to that of the R-1820-G103 of 1936, but it had a 200hp lower maximum power rating compared with the latest versions of the Wright Cyclone. The time between scheduled overhauls of most Soviet engines was 100-150hr, while for the German engines it was 200-300hr, and for British and American engines it was up to 400-600hr. One of the decrees of 1940 stated: 'The main cause of the lag is the fact that the Soviet aero-engine industry is oriented and based primarily on licence-built engines, and does not pay due attention to scientific research and experimental works which lay the foundation for developing new indigenous engines'.

The industry again faced the task of 'catching up and outpacing the West'. Much emphasis was put on developing high-powered engines for military aircraft. Engines with power ratings of up to 3,500hp and featuring different types of cooling were expected to be introduced into series production by 1942. Various approaches were envisioned for this task. On the one hand, multi-block structures based on the existing powerplants were being developed, while, on the other, designers were creating completely new engine types. At the same time, Soviet representatives started negotiations to

A line of Pe-2 dive-bombers powered by M-105PF engines, photographed in 1944. The development of the Soviet aero-engine industry was a major factor in the Soviet contribution to victory in the Second World War.

acquire production licences and examples of modern engines from abroad; in France, the USA, the UK, Italy and, later, Germany. However, the intent was not to put the Western engines into series production in the USSR, but to incorporate successful design solutions into new Soviet powerplants. In July 1940 a programme for experimental aero-engine-building until the year of 1943 was issued, with the intended aim that Soviet aero-engines would match the contemporary Western level by 1943.

Certain goals had been achieved. New AM-35 and AM-38, M-82 and M-105 engines were introduced into series production, and the large-scale programme of diesel engine development, started as far back as 1930, finally yielded results in early 1941, series production of the M-30 and M-40 diesels being arranged. These significantly increased the range of bombers, and would allow the Soviet industry to expand its capacities for aviation fuel production. However, these powerplants never achieved reliability comparable to that of engines operating on light fuel. Consequently, diesel engines were not widely used in the VVS RKKA.

The Great Patriotic War, which broke out on 22 June 1941, interfered with fulfilment of the Soviet aero-engine programme. From the outset of combat operations priority was given to increasing series production, research and development work being reduced to a minimum. Later, this situation was further aggravated by the heavy losses of the first year of the war. Plans to cease production of obsolete engine types, and also the programme for the refinement and setting-up of series production of new powerplants were rejected. The number of series engine types was reduced to a minimum by removing some types and versions from production. All the designers had to do was carry out gradual and smooth modernization, which did not threaten production rates.

As a result, Soviet aero-engines were inferior to their foreign counterparts, and this had an impact on the aircraft manufacture. For instance, the lack of high-powered liquid-cooled engines considerably limited the scope of Soviet fighter designers. The insufficient thrust-to-weight ratio had to be offset by thorough reductions in weight and strict limitations with respect to aircraft equipment and armament. In addition, Soviet designers failed to bring indigenous turbo-superchargers to satisfactory levels of reliability.

Unlike the UK, the Soviet Union did not accept the practice of equipping its indigenous aeroplanes with imported engines, though development of such versions was undertaken. British and American engines were supplied under the Lend-Lease programme, either as parts of aeroplanes or as spares. Soviet designers, as well as flight and ground personnel, gained much useful information by studying them. Some of the design solutions seen on Western types were incorporated in indigenous engines put into series production at the end of the war or immediately after it.

At the end of the Second World War Soviet aviation had basically the same primary types of aero-engines as at the war's outbreak, though certain modifications and improvements had been introduced. At the same time, the engine production rate was considerably higher. For instance, Soviet industry built over 21,000 engines in 1940, and in 1945 the output reached almost 45,000.

Intensive preparations for post-war aviation modernization started in the Soviet Union as early as 1944, and numerous programmes of aircraft and engine development were under way. However, this stage also had its peculiarities. Towards the end of the war the Germans, closely followed by the British, began to introduce jet aircraft into combat. While in 1945-46 new piston-engined fighters were still being developed in parallel with jet-powered equivalents, from 1947 the jet fighter began to predominate, and a year or two later even tactical bombers were beginning to be powered by jet engines. Trainers, sports aircraft, passenger aircraft, military transports and heavy bombers were still fitted with piston engines. The latter types employed very-high-powered engines; multi-block in-line or multi-row radial engines with forced cooling. In the end Soviet designers mastered turbo-supercharging, and created compound engines in which the exhaust gases rotated turbines, the additional power from the turbines being delivered to the propeller shaft via reduction gearing. Helicopters became a new 'eco-niche' for piston engines; a programme for developing special helicopter versions of the engines, with various power ratings, was started in Soviet Union in 1946-47.

Already in 1947 a number of piston aero-engine types were excluded from the development plans, because the engine design bureaux were busy developing jets. Later on, both series production and new piston engine development were cancelled. Starting from 1953-54, work was carried out only on new engines for light aeroplanes and helicopters, apart from modernization of series-production powerplants. By 1962 just one factory producing piston aero-engines remained in the USSR.

The interest in piston-engined flight was rapidly decreasing. In the 1970s only one piston aero-engine, the M-14, was being produced in the USSR. Helicopter designers turned to the turboshaft engines, while air force flying schools had adopted ab initio jet training. Piston engines were used only in sports and agricultural aviation, as well as on the short-haul passenger aircraft working in remote regions of the Soviet Union.

The early 1980s saw some revival in the interest in piston engines. The Soviet armed forces wanted to add a small unmanned aerial vehicle (UAV) to their inventory, and this required a small piston engine. Several design bureaux embarked on the development of such engine, and several types were eventually built and tested, some even being introduced into series production.

After the collapse of the Soviet Union the large country's aviation industry plunged into a deep recession. There were almost no orders from the Ministry of Defence, the Government owed large debts to the factories, passenger traffic in civil aviation decreased, the network of sports aeroclubs (which had been financed by the State) disintegrated, and agricultural aviation was brought to a standstill because the collective farms could no longer pay for the work. In this environment many specialists considered privately-owned small piston-engined aircraft to be a way out of the crisis. Designers received some work to do, while some factories began arranging series production of piston aero-engines. However, up to the present time the number of firm orders for such aircraft has not increased drastically, though the Russian economy has bottomed out and has recently been showing a growth trend. Russian piston engines may soon enter a new stage of their evolution. We must hope for the best.

Abbreviations

Aviakhim (*Aviatsiya i Khimiya*) – Aviation and Chemistry (society)
Aviatrest (*Gosudarstvenniy Trest Aviatsionnoy Promishlennosti*) – State Aviation Industry Trust
GAZ (*Gosudarstvenniy Aviatsionniy Zavod*) – State Aircraft Factory
GCS – geared centrifugal supercharger
GEEI (*Gosudarstvenniy Elektro-Energeticheskiy Institut*) – State Institute of Electricity and Energy
GKAT (*Gosudarstvenniy Komitet po Aviatsionnoy Tekhnike*) – State Committee of Aviation Equipment
GKO (*Gosudarstvenniy Komitet Oboroni*) – State Defence Committee
Glavkoavia (*Glavnoe Pravlenie Ob'edinennikh Aviapromishlennikh Zavodov*) – Chief Directorate of United Aviation Industry Factories
GOST (*Gosudarstvenniy Standart*) – State Standard
GUAP (*Glavnoe Upravlenie Aviatsionnoy Promishlennosti*) – Chief Directorate of the Aviation Industry
GU GVF (*Glavnoe Upravlenie Grazhdanskogo Vozdushnogo Flota*) – Chief Directorate of the Civil Air Fleet
GUVP (*Glavnoe Upravlenie Voennoy Promishlennosti*) – Chief Directorate of Military Industry
GVF (*Grazhdanskiy Vozdushniy Flot*) – Civil Air Fleet
IAM (*Institut Aviatsionnogo Motorostroeniya*) – Aviation Motor Construction Institute
IPE (*Institut Promishlennoy Energetiki*) – Institute of Industrial Power Engineering
KhAI (*Kharkovskiy Aviatsionniy Institut*) – Kharkov Aviation Institute
KhTZ (*Kharkovskiy Traktorniy Zavod*) – Kharkov Tractor Factory
KMPO (*Kazanskoe Motorostroitelnoe Proizvodsvennoe Ob'edinenie*) – Kazan Engine-Building Production Enterprise
KO (*Komitet Oboroni*) – Defence Committee
MAI (*Moskovskiy Aviatsionniy Institut*) – Moscow Aviation Institute
MAP (*Ministerstvo Aviatsionnoy Promishlennosti*) – Ministry of the Aviation Industry
NAL (*Nauchno—Avtomobilnaya Laboratoriya*) – Scientific Automobile Laboratory
NAMI (*Nauchniy Avtomotorniy Institut*) – Scientific Automotor Institute
NII AD GVF (*Nauchno-Issledovatelskiy Institut Aviadvigateley Grazhdanskogo Vozdushnogo Flota*) – Civil Air Fleet Scientific Research Institute for Aviation Engines
NII DVS (*Nauchno-Issledovatelskiy Institut Dvigateley Vnutrennego Sgoraniya*) – Scientific Research Institute for Internal Combustion Engines
NII GVF (*Nauchno-Issledovatelskiy Institut Grazhdanskogo Vozdushnogo Flota*) – Scientific Research Institute for the Civil Air Fleet
NII VVS (*Nauchno-Ispitatelniy Institut Voenno-Vozdushnikh Sil*) – Scientific Testing Institute of the Air Force
NK/NTK UVVS (*Nauchniy Komitet/Nauchno-Tekhnicheskiy Komitet Upravleniya Voenno-Vozdushnikh Sil*) – Scientific Committee/Scientific Technical Committee of the Air Force Directorate
NKAP (*Narodniy Komissariat Aviatsionnoy Promishlennosti*) – People's Commissariat of the Aviation Industry
NKOP (*Narodniy Komissariat Oboronnoy Promishlennosti*) – People's Commissariat of the Defence Industry
NKTP (*Narodniy Komissariat Tyazheloy Promishlennosti*) – People's Commissariat of Heavy Industry
NKVD (*Narodniy Komissariat Vnutrennikh Del*) – People's Commissariat of Internal Affairs
NKVM (*Narodniy Komissariat po Voennim i Morskim Delam*) – People's Commissariat of Military and Naval Affairs
NKVT (*Narodniy Komissariat Vneshney Torgovli*) – People's Commissariat of Foreign Trade
NOA (*Nauchno-Opitniy Aerodrom*) – Scientific Experimental Airfield
NPO (*Nauchno-Proizvodstvennoe Ob'edinenie*) – Scientific Production Enterprise
OGPU (*Ob'edinyonnoe Glavnoe Politicheskoe Upravlenie*) – United Chief Political Directorate
ODVF (*Obshchestvo Druzey Vozdushnogo Flota*) – Society of Friends of the Air Fleet
OKB (*Opitno-Konstruktorskoe Byuro*) – Experimental Design Bureau
OKBM, early abbreviation (*Opitno-Konstruktorskoe Byuro Mashinostroeniya*) – Experimental Design Bureau for Machine Construction
OKBM, modern abbreviation (*Opitno-Konstruktorskoe Byuro Motorostroeniya*) – Experimental Design Bureau for Motor Construction
OMO (*Opitno-Motorniy Otdel*) – Experimental-Motor Department
OND (*Otdel Neftyanikh Dvigateley*) – Department of Crude-Oil Engines
Osoaviakhim (*Obshchestvo Sodeystviya Aviatsii i Khimii*) – Society of Assistance to Aviation and Chemistry
OTB (*Osoboe Tekhnicheskoe Byuro*) – Special Technical Bureau
Promvoensovet (*Sovet Voennoy Promishlennosti*) – Council of the Defence Industry
RAM (*Russkiy Aviatsionniy Motor*) – Russian Aviation Motor
RBVZ (*Russko-Baltiyskiy Vagonniy Zavod*) – Russo-Baltic Railroad Wagon Factory
RKKVF (*Vozdushniy Flot Raboche-Krestyanskoy Krasnoy Armii*) – Air Fleet of the Workers' and Peasants' Red Army
RVS (*Revolyutsionniy Voenniy Sovet*, or *Revvoensovet*) – Revolutionary Military Council
SKB (*Seriyno-Konstruktorskoe Byuro*) – Series Production Design Bureau
SKB RPD VAZ (*Spetsialnoe Konstruktorskoe Byuro Rotorno-Porshnevikh Dvigateley Volzhskogo Avtomobilnogo Zavoda*) – Special

Design Bureau for Wankel-type Engines of the Volga Automobile Factory
Sovnarkhoz (*Sovet Narodnogo Khozyaystva*) – Council of National Economy
Sovnarkom (*Sovet Narodnikh Komissarov*) – Council of People's Commissars
STO (*Sovet Truda i Oboroni*) – Council of Labour and Defence
TO EKU of OGPU (*Tekhnicheskiy Otdel Ekonomicheskogo Upravleniya OGPU*) – Technical Department of the Economic Directorate of OGPU
TsAGI (*Tsentralniy Aero-Gidrodinamicheskiy Institut*) – Central Aero-Hydrodynamic Institute
TsIAM (*Tsentralniy Institut Aviatsionnogo Motorostroeniya*) – Central Institute of Aviation Motor Construction
TsKB (*Tsentralnoe Konstruktorskoe Byuro*) – Central Design Bureau
TsNIDI (*Tsentralniy Nauchno-Issledovatelskiy Dizelniy Institut*) – Central Scientific Research Diesel Institute
UAV – unmanned aerial vehicle
UIDVS (*Ukrainskiy Institut Dvigateley Vnutrennego Sgoraniya*) – Ukrainian Institute of Internal Combustion Engines
UNIADI (*Ukrainskiy Nauchno-Issledovatelskiy Aviadizelniy Institut*) – Ukrainian Scientific Research Aviation Diesel Institute
UVVF (*Upravlenie Voenno-Vozdushnogo Flota*) – Directorate of the Military Air Fleet
UVVS (*Upravlenie Voenno-Vozdushnikh Sil*) – Air Force Directorate
VAO (*Vsesoyuznoe Aviatsionnoe Ob'edinenie*) – All-Union Aviation Association
VMO (*Vintomotorniy Otdel*) – Propeller-Motor Department
VNIDI (*Vsesoyuzniy Nauchno-Issledovatelskiy Dizelniy Institut*) – All-Union Scientific Research Diesel Institute
VNIImotoprom (*Vsesoyuzniy Naucho-Issledovatelskiy Institut Motornoy Promishlennosti*) – All-Union Scientific Research Institute of the Engine Industry
VSNKh (*Visshiy Sovet Narodnogo Khozyaystva*) – Supreme Council of the People's Economy
VVS RKKA (*Voenno-Vozdushnie Sili Raboche-Krestyanskoy Krasnoy Armii*) – Air Force of the Workers' and Peasants' Red Army
ZOK (*Zavod Opitnikh Konstruktsiy*) – Factory of Experimental Designs

PART ONE

CHAPTER ONE

State Control Over the Aero-engine Industry

Before the October Revolution of 1917 there had been no State authorities controlling the aero-engine industry in Russia. All factories were privately owned, and the State role was limited to placing orders for engine deliveries to the Military Ministry, preparing engine specifications, and paying for the delivered powerplants. Later, the State authorities were involved in the acquisition of series production licences from Western companies, and the granting of loans to Russian engine manufacturers.

The First All-Russian Aviation Congress, held in August 1917, elected the All-Russian Aviation Council (Aviasovet). However, this was basically a society, and its decisions were not mandatory for the industry. This situation prevailed until 1 August 1918, when the Bolsheviks established the Commission on Aviation Industry Organization as part of the defence industry section of the Metal Department of the Supreme Council of the People's Economy (*Visshiy Sovet Narodnogo Khozyaystva*, VSNKh). A transition to a State-controlled economy then started. After completion of the aircraft factories' nationalization, in December 1918 they were united to form the Chief Directorate of United Aviation Industry Factories (*Glavnoe Pravlenie Ob'edinennikh Aviapromishlennikh Zavodov*, Glavkoavia).

The Civil War in Russia grew in scale, on 22 December 1919 Glavkoavia was transferred to Council of Defence Industry (*Sovet Voennoy Promishlennosti*, Promvoensovet), which was responsible for deliveries of arms and military materiel to the Red Army. All aircraft factories were declared to be a part of the defence industry, and their personnel were treated as though they had been mobilized.

As the Civil War drew to an end in most parts of Russia, on 17 March 1921 the Glavkoavia was returned to VSNKh structure as part of the 5th (Aviation) Department of the Chief Directorate of Military Industry (*Glavnoe Upravlenie Voennoy Promishlennosti*, GUVP). The Soviet Government then embraced the new economic policy, which slightly relaxed the tough centralized control, and on 28 January 1925 Glavkoavia was converted into a self-supporting trust, called the State Aviation Industry Trust (*Gosudarstvenniy Trest Aviatsionnoy Promishlennosti*, Aviatrest). The enterprises subordinate to the Aviatrest were devoid of any economic independence. The Trust was controlled collectively, in the same way as the separate factories of which it was formed. From early 1926 M.G. Uryvaev was chairman of the Aviatrest board, and the chief engineer for engine construction, M.P. Makaruk, was also included the Trust's board.

In the mid-1920s aero-engine manufacture was also carried on outside Aviatrest's scope. The Bolshevik factory in Leningrad, which belonged to the Ordnance-Armoury Trust, built the engines for aircraft. This factory also attempted to conduct independent research and development on the engines. The VSNKh was responsible for co-ordinating the efforts of the two trusts.

However, the trend of militarizing the Soviet economy and making it subject to directive planning soon resulted in a new reshuffle of the aviation industry structure. In 1927 Aviatrest was subordinated to the Defence Industry Directorate of the VSNKh, and on 15 April 1930 Aviatrest was annulled and replaced by the All-Union Aviation Association (*Vsesoyuznoe Aviatsionnoe Ob'edinenie*, VAO). The Association was headed by the aforementioned Uryvaev, who was succeeded by P.I. Baranov. At first the VAO was supervised by the Chief Directorate of the Metal Industry of the VSNKh. However as early as 28 July 1930 a decree was issued, transferring the VAO to the People's Commissariat of Military and Naval Affairs (*Narodniy Komissariat po Voennim i Morskim Delam*, NKVM). Although the military were the VAO's primary customer, the act of assigning the aircraft factories to the NKVM did not yield positive results. On 7 February 1931 the Association was returned to VSNKh structure.

In early 1932 the VSNKh was annulled and divided into separate people's commissariats, including the People's Commissariat of Heavy Industry (*Narodniy Komissariat Tyazheloy Promishlennosti*, NKTP), headed by G.K. Ordzhonikidze. The VAO was included in the NKTP structure as the Chief Directorate of the Aviation Industry (*Glavnoe Upravlenie Aviatsionnoy Promishlennosti*, GUAP). Unlike the VAO, which had been a self-supporting entity, the GUAP was a purely budgetary organization, operating strictly along the guidelines of the People's Commissariat. The GUAP comprised four trusts, one of them being the aero-engine trust. However, in 1933 these interim links were considered redundant, and the aero-engine trust was annulled. Aircraft factories became subordinate directly to the GUAP.

This structure of the industry had lasted for quite a long time. Following the death of P.I. Baranov in aircraft accident, the GUAP was headed by G.N. Korolev, and M.M. Kaganovich succeeded him in late 1935.

The leadership of the Chief Directorate

A contemporary photograph of the group of NKAP (later MAP) buildings in downtown Moscow. For decades this was a control centre of the Soviet aviation industry. It now accommodates the offices of a variety of private companies, state-owned enterprises and government departments.

of the Civil Air Fleet (*Glavnoe Upravlenie Grazhdanskogo Vozdushnogo Flota*, GU GVF) was not pleased that the aviation industry was primarily oriented to satisfying air force needs (in line with the State policy), and in the early 1930s they started establishing their own aero-engine factories and research and development institutes. These entities operated independently until 1939, when they were merged into the aero-engine industry.

The United Chief Political Directorate (*Ob'edinyonnoe Glavnoe Politicheskoe Upravlenie*, OGPU) became involved in solving the problems of aero-engine development from 1929, and established a design bureau manned by imprisoned engineers. Supervised by the Technical Department of the Economic Directorate (*Tekhnicheskiy Otdel Ekonomicheskogo Upravleniya*, TO EKU) of OGPU, this bureau operated for several years without yielding any significant results. The system was revived in 1938, but before that the so-called *sharagas* (the nickname for design bureaux manned by imprisoned specialists) were supervised by the People's Commissariat of Internal Affairs (*Narodniy Komissariat Vnutrennikh Del*, NKVD). The aero-engine *sharagas* existed until 1945. However, the volume of work carried out in GVF and OGPU/NKVD structures was much less than in the GUAP and the organizations that succeeded it.

As the number of supervised enterprises constantly increased during the active growth of the Soviet aviation industry, the NKTP leadership began to experience difficulties in controlling them. Consequently the NKTP was divided into several People's Commissariats. From December 1936 the aviation industry was supervised by the People's Commissariat of Defence Industry (*Narodniy Komissariat Oboronnoy Promishlennosti*, NKOP), and its First Chief Directorate was responsible for controlling the aviation industry. In February 1938 this directorate was further subdivided into two directorates: the First (aircraft construction) Directorate, and the Eighteenth (aero-engine construction) Directorate. In some documents the latter was named the Chief Directorate of Aero-Engine Construction.

On 11 January 1939 the NKOP was in its turn divided into several People's Commissariats, one of them being the People's Commissariat of the Aviation Industry (*Narodniy Komissariat Aviatsionnoy Promishlennosti*, NKAP). It was initially headed by M.M. Kaganovich, who was replaced by A.I. Shakhurin in January 1940, and in December 1945 the post was taken by M.V. Khrunichev. The Commissariat included two Chief Engine-Building Directorates: the Series Production Engine-Building Directorate, and the Experimental Engine-Building Directorate. Aero-engine construction was supervised by the Deputy People's Commissar, the post at first occupied by V.P. Balandin and, from January 1942, by A.A. Zavitaev.

When the People's Commissariats were renamed as Ministries after the war, the Ministry of the Aviation Industry (*Ministerstvo Aviatsionnoy Promishlennosti*, MAP) was established in March 1946. It included the Chief Directorate, which supervised aero-engine construction. However, starting from late 1945 the work on piston engines was gradually run down, and in the early 1950s it was considered to be a secondary task.

In 1957 N.S. Khrushchev tried to replace the vertical (industrial) structural control of the economy with a horizontal (territorial) one. Most ministries, including the Ministry of the Aviation Industry, were liquidated, and the factories then came under the supervision of regional Councils of National Economy (*Sovet Narodnogo Khozyaystva*, Sovnarkhoz). However, since the aviation industry was considered to be one of the most important ones, the functions of the former ministry were now taken over by the State Committee of Aviation Equipment (*Gosudarstvenniy Komitet po Aviatsionnoy Tekhnike*, GKAT).

This system collapsed very soon after Khrushchev's resignation, and in 1964 various ministries, including the MAP, were restored. After these events the aviation industry control structure lasted for more than twenty years without any considerable changes.

When the Ministry of the Aviation Industry was liquidated during the rule of M.S. Gorbachev, some of its functions were transferred to the Department of the Aviation Industry of the Ministry of Economy, though this did not survive for a long, either. When Russia returned to the market economy, aircraft factories became economically independent. At present there is no State structure in Russia to supervise the development and production of piston aero-engines.

CHAPTER TWO

The Planning of the Research and Development Works, and Preparation and Approval of Engine Specifications

Before the October Revolution a standard procedure for issuing aero-engine specifications did not exist in Russia. At best, a specification for the development of an engine was couched in very general terms. For instance, it might require the copying of a foreign engine of a specific power rating. More detailed characteristics were indicated in the delivery terms for series production engines, but even these documents specified only the most critical requirements, such as power rating, weight, and, at a later stage, fuel and oil consumption, as well as the installation of additional engine units. The delivery terms were usually prepared by the Directorate of the Military Air Fleet (*Upravlenie Voenno-Vozdushnogo Flota*, UVVF) or by customer representatives (of aircraft factories). State plans for the development of experimental engine construction did not exist.

During the early post-Revolution years the country's new leaders paid no attention to aero-engine development. Designers kept working on their own initiative, submitting their projects to the Headquarters of the Red Air Fleet, but the realization of such projects was considered untimely.

It was not until 1923 that the development of new indigenous aero-engines was started. At first the designers based their efforts on the available projects, which had reached various degrees of completeness. These projects progressed through the process of evaluation and approval, carried out by the GUVP Technical Committee, and later by the Scientific (later renamed Scientific-Technical) Committee of the Air Force Directorate (*Nauchniy Komitet / Nauchno-Tekhnicheskiy Komitet Upravleniya Voenno-Vozdushnikh Sil*, NK/NTK UVVS). At that time the military was the only customer for new aero-engines. Once a project had been evaluated, a report was produced to assess whether it would be expedient to build the engine. Then a specification for the engine was developed, listing the characteristics that had been found realistic and capable of meeting needs of the Air Force. After that, the enterprise tasked with building the engine submitted cost estimates for the manufacture of a prototype (or prototypes).

In 1923 the first prospective plans for research and development in the sphere of aero-engine construction for the period 1923-25 were issued. There were two such plans, one by the UVVS and the other prepared by Aviatrest. The former was based on a rather unrealistic approach, but the latter took into account the real capabilities of the aviation industry, with some level of reserve. The military wanted three new types of indigenous engines to be brought to the first stage of development: a 100hp 'training' engine, a 180-200hp 'interim' engine, and a 600-700hp high-powered 'combat' engine. The last two were to be water-cooled. At the same time work was started on a short-term programme aimed at modernization of the available M-5 engine (the Soviet variant of the Liberty) to increase its power to 450-500hp.

The NK UVVS prepared specifications for these new engine types that were very concise, taking just one typed page, and defined the following features and characteristics: type of of cooling system, engine layout, number of cylinders (not in every case), power rating, compression ratio, maximum weight, types of fuel and oil, consumption rates, presence or absence of reduction gear, and the list of necessary engine components. At that time only the nominal power rating was specified, and its relation to the operating modes or altitude was not defined.

In some cases a very generalized preliminary specification was issued, which was clarified in detail later on. At the same time the requirements of such a clarified specification might became more stringent. However, there were some occasions when the specified engine weight was increased, taking into account the preliminary calculations. Such weight increase was usually demanded by engine designers who declared the air force requirements unrealistic. Mandatory requirements were that the engine was made from materials available within the country, and that there were few or no imported components. A specification always had to be reviewed at meetings of the NK/NTK and be approved by them, after which it was signed by the head of the UVVS.

Various design bureaux might propose different engine projects based on an engine specification, the best one being selected after competitive evaluation.

At the time, a certain economic independence of Aviatrest enabled it to avoid working on specifications that were considered unrealistic, and this flexibility also enabled the trust to finance the development of engine types rejected by the air force but considered promising by the trust's leadership. The Ordnance-Armoury Trust, which only partly co-ordinated its development efforts with the air force's plans, operated in a similar manner.

The next plan for aero-engine development was a two-year one, embracing the 1925-26 period. Since the goals specified in the previous plan had not been met, all of them were included in the new plan. Significant features of this plan were the introduction of a chapter devoted to diesel engines (at that time as experimental units), and a considerable expansion of efforts to develop air-cooled engines (with power ratings up to 600hp). For the first time there was a requirement to develop a unified family of air-cooled engines having different numbers of cylinders.

The first five-year plan of Soviet economical development, covering the period 1928-33, was accompanied by a corresponding plan from the VVS RKKA. The Air Force Directorate boldly prepared a long list of water- and air-cooled engines for various-purposes. For instance, in 1931 alone the design bureaux and factories were to produce eighteen types of new and modernized aero-engines for testing. A period of co-ordinating the air force plan with the VAO followed, when the VAO's specialists managed to remove several especially risky projects from the plan. In fact, the VAO prepared its own variant of the plan, which specified less-ambitious engine characteristics than those given in the UVVS document, and a three- to four-year-longer development schedule. This plan was severely criticized as 'dooming the industry to lagging behind'.

The Council of Labour and Defence (*Sovet Truda i Oboroni*, STO) and Revvoensovet, which were approving the development plan, supported the air force approach. This is explained by the lack of experience in planning. Senior Soviet officials were party-promoted persons who had neither proper education nor special knowledge in the sphere they were appointed to head. They believed it was possible to catch up with and surpass the technologies of the developed Western countries using only the mere 'enthusiasm of the masses', without proper funding and the necessary equipment, specialists or materials.

As a result, the ambitious plan for the development of thirty-four engine types within five years was approved. The plan itself listed only the most important characteristics of the aero-engines (number of cylinders, layout, cooling system type, power rating, and weight), as well as deadlines for the beginning of factory and State (official) testing. Using the characteristics listed in the plan, the UVVS prepared more-detailed specifications. The most important difference between these specifications and the earlier ones lay in the fact that they defined the engine power rating with respect to altitude, and two operating modes were specified, at ground level and at a rated altitude. The list of required components was also broadened to include starters and electric generators. The engine weight was specified with respect to a certain powerplant configuration.

The unrealistic nature of this ambitious plan became clear immediately after its approval. For the sake of propaganda, a rumour of 'sabotage' was spread, but even the UVVS admitted that the allocated financial assets and the available engineering and production capacities were insufficient to realize the plan.

Being a governmental entity, the VAO could not refuse to fulfil the plan approved by higher authorities, but neither was it eager to discharge the most complicated tasks, justifying the delays by the lack of capacities and assets. The Government was finally forced to reduce the plan's scope to focus industry efforts on the most crucial aero-engine types. A number of projects were removed from the plan, while the most important types were given priority. The new revision of the plan was approved by the RVS on 3 December 1930. Later, another revision was carried out, and under a decree of the Defence Committee (*Komitet Oboroni*, KO) dated 4 July 1932 priority was assigned to the M-32, M-38, M-44, and FED engines, as well as new versions of the M-34, which were considered to be the most readily available for series production.

The above-mentioned plan was related only to engines of interest to military. The Civil Air Fleet prepared its own plans and issued its own specifications, approved by the Chief of the GU GVF, with further approval by the very same STO. The structure of the specifications was similar to those issued by the air force. Moreover, both the plans and specifications of the GVF had to be approved by the military.

In some cases, public organizations such as defence-sport societies became customers for new aero-engine development. The first was the Society of Friends of the Air Fleet (*Obshchestvo Druzey Vozdushnogo Flota*, ODVF), then the Aviakhim (*Aviatsiya i Khimiya*, or Aviation and Chemistry) and Osoaviakhim (*Obshchestvo Sodeystviya Aviatsii i Khimii*, Society of Assistance to Aviation and Chemistry). These organizations submitted specifications and announced contests for developing low-powered engines for training and sports aeroplanes, such specifications usually being less detailed than those of the UVVS.

However, priority was always given to projects carried out by the aviation industry to meet air force requirements. The plans succeeded each other regularly, becoming increasingly detailed, while specifications became more thorough. Starting from 1930-31 the engine power rating was specified with respect to the engine operational mode and flight altitude. Much attention was paid to an engine's critical altitudes, and the specifications began to indicate the presence or absence of a supercharger, plus the number of its stages and their speeds. The acceptable levels of fuel and oil consumption for various engine operating modes were also specified in detail, these figures being based on statistical analyses of the characteristics of modern Western aero-engines.

A specific feature of the plan of experimental engine construction for 1932-33 was the introduction of a separate programme for crude-oil engines (diesels). From 1934 until 1939 the plans became concentrated on improving the four established families of Soviet aero-engines. After 1939 the development of new aero-engine designs once again attracted the interest of the industry authorities.

This interest was reflected in the large-scale pre-war programme of aero-engine development, prepared in July 1940 and covering the 1941-43 period. This required that, by early 1943, the engines created by the Soviet industry were to match the characteristics of modern American, British and German types. The programme envisioned the development of engines having ratings of up to 3,000hp.

However, the war interfered with the programme's realization. When Germany invaded the Soviet Union the aero-engine industry was reoriented to concentrate on increasing series production. The development of new aero-engines was cancelled, but the creation of improved versions of series engines was stepped up.

From 1944 greater attention was paid to jet-powered flight, but in 1945-46 Soviet designers once again embarked on the development of new piston aero-engines. The form of engine specification remained unchanged from the pre-war period, though the requirements were obviously raised.

From the mid-1950s the development of new piston aero-engines in the Soviet Union ceased, and production was constantly reduced. Then, in the early 1980s, the Ministry of Defence issued specifications for an engine to power UAVs, and the Ministry of Aviation Industry prepared a programme for the development of such an engine. These were the official 'specifications', as this term had been introduced into the system of State Standards (*Gosudarstvenniy Standart*, GOST) in 1973, and for the first time they included cost estimates.

After the collapse of the USSR, when the whole Russian industry plunged into a deep recession, separate factories and design bureaux kept working at their own risk, trying to find customers for their products. At that time the engine performance requirements were defined by developers and manufacturers, while there appeared new, consumer-oriented characteristics such as noise and pollution levels.

At present there is no State programme for piston aero-engine development in Russia. However, certain private companies finance the development of new powerplants and the production of prototypes. The Russian Ministry of Defence evinces some interest in piston engines for UAVs, while the military continues to discuss the possibility of returning to the practice of using piston-engined aircraft for *ab initio* pilot training. If a positive decision is made, specifications might be issued for a new aeroplane type and its piston engine.

CHAPTER THREE

The Organization of Aero-engine Development and Prototype Manufacturing

Before the October Revolution aero-engines in Russia had primarily been designed by individual enthusiasts, who often built their own prototypes as well. Within the existing engine-building enterprises, only the Motor factory as well as two factories of the RBVZ company (*Russko-Baltiyskiy Vagonniy Zavod*, or Russo-Baltic Railroad Wagon Factory) had teams of engine designers and specially assigned workers. Later, a similar team was established at the Dyuflon & Konstantinovich (DEKA) factory. However, those teams were not organized as separate departments, and most of their members discharged other responsibilities in addition to engineering work. Neither did these groups have officially appointed heads. The specialists heading the teams were simultaneously engaged in series production or administrative work. No special workshops or factory areas were allocated for the manufacture of prototype engines. Most parts were built on production lines, and only the final assembly and adjustment of the protrotype engines involved participation of experienced workers. The enterprises, which belonged to foreign companies such as Gnome-Rhône and Salmson, produced engines strictly in compliance with foreign documentation and did not carry out any independent research or development. This situation remained the same during the rule of the Provisional Government.

These small design teams disappeared in the first few years after the October Revolution. Most experts emigrated, but some perished during the Civil War or changed the their spheres of interest. Only the Motor factory, evacuated from Riga to Moscow, and the Moscow-based Ikar factory (the former Gnome-Rhône factory) retained small teams of engineers and technicians, who for the most part were more involved in maintaining the production rather than in any engineering work.

After the Civil War the new government applied considerable efforts to restoring and modernizing the country's military aviation. Development of new aero-engines was started as early as the beginning of 1923. All this work was co-ordinated by the Design Sub-Department of the GUVP Aviation Department.

At that time in Russia there were three centres of experimental aero-engine-building. The largest team worked at the Scientific Auto-Motor Institute (*Nauchniy Avtomotorniy Institut*, NAMI). This institute had been created on the basis of the Scientific Automobile Laboratory (*Nauchno-Avtomobilnaya Laboratoriya*, NAL) in 1921. In 1923-24 the institute established a design bureau, tasked with developing various engine types including aircraft powerplants. In late 1923 NAMI prepared the first preliminary design of a 100hp aero-engine. The second centre was a small design bureau headed by A.A. Bessonov at the Ikar factory. Another design bureau, which did not even have a head (it was supervised by chief engineer A.D. Shvetsov), was operating at the Motor factory.

In 1925 a small bureau was established at the Zaporozhye-based Bolshevik factory (former DEKA), but it existed for less than a year, after which it was shut down. A group of enthusiasts, not registered officially, worked at another Bolshevik factory (Leningrad-based).

In addition to these teams and design bureaux, which belonged to the series-production factories, a practice of contracting independent designers was also customary at that time. The nature of such designers' employment could have been quite different. In some cases a designer might be officially contracted by the factory with a fixed salary and for the period of time required to design and build the engine prototype. He might also be assigned a team of assistants and promised a certain reward in the event of a successful outcome. In other cases the cost estimates for employing assistants, renting workshops, etc. were defined in course of negotiations with a designer, and he was held fully responsible for meeting these cost estimates. The allocated finances were usually inadequate, additional funds having to be earmarked.

The development work was usually carried under the limits of UVVS orders. The military approved cost estimates submitted by a factory, then allocated the funds from the NKVM budget. The engines designed under the initiative of the factories were financed by the factories themselves. Some powerplants were created using Aviatrest financing.

The engine projects were reviewed by the GUVP Technical Committee, which examined them at its councils, as well as by the NK (later NTK) UVVS. If a contest was held, the competing projects were considered by a specially appointed inter-departmental commission, which included representatives of Aviatrest, the air force and various scientific organizations. From the early 1930s engine project evaluations were carried out by the Propeller-Motor Department of the NII VVS (*Nauchno-Ispitatelniy Institut Voenno-Vozdushnikh Sil*, or Scientific Testing Institute of the Air Force), which issued a written report on the project after its deliberations. The decision on whether or not to build a prototype was made in the form of a resolution of the GUVP board, or as the Aviatrest order (if the engine in question was funded by and built on the initiative of Aviatrest). From one to three engine prototypes were usually ordered.

When prototypes were built under air force order, Aviatrest and the UVVS prepared an agreement defining the engine's major characteristics, the materials and parts to be used, and the deadlines.

The prototypes were manufactured at series-production factories. If an engine was designed at a factory, the factory was responsible for building the prototype. If a powerplant was developed by an independent designer, Aviatrest issued an order for manufacture of the prototype. The engine parts and assemblies could be ordered at different factories, and an leading enterprise was appointed to carry out final assembly. Series-production factories were not interested in such insignificant outside orders, and agreed to fulfil them only under pressure from Aviatrest. Lack of interest usually caused delays in prototype manufacture.

Experimental engine-building had slightly expanded by May 1929, but there were still too few design teams, and they were quite small. Aero-engine development was carried out by the following organizations: NAMI, Central Aero-Hydrodynamic Institute (*Tsentralniy Aero-Gidrodinamicheskiy Institut*, TsAGI) where the Propeller-Motor Department (Vintomotorniy Otdel, VMO), initially headed by B.S. Stechkin, was established in 1926; Factory No. 24 in Moscow (a result of the merger of the Ikar and Motor factories); Factory No. 29 in Zaporozhye; and the Leningrad-based Bolshevik factory. At Factory No. 24 only twenty employees worked on developing new aero-engines. NAMI put thirty people on the task, while the Bolshevik factory assigned fifteen designers (plus thirty workers). The Bolshevik factory was the only enterprise to set up a special prototype-engine workshop. On 17 November 1929 a Government Commission headed by V.S. Unshlikht proposed that design bureaux should be established at all engine-building factories 'in order to support series production and modernization' of the engines. In November 1930 a relatively complete design bureau, comprising thirty-eight people, existed only at Factory No. 24; there were also small teams of designers at Factories No. 26 (eleven specialists) and No. 29 (six people). Given the ambitious State plans, this contradiction resulted in regular overtime for designers. The USSR spent ten to fifteen times less on the development of new types of aero-engines than the USA and Great Britain. If the investments of the Western private companies are taken into account, this imbalance looks even greater.

The STO, which reviewed the state of experimental aircraft- and aero-engine construction in early 1930, declared the following in its resolution: 'It should be stated that the experimental-construction facilities of the Air Fleet (the number of factories involved in the manufacture of experimental types, the condition of their equipment, the status of the design bureaux, funding, etc.), especially with respect to ... aero-engines, are absolutely inadequate to the interests of the country's defence and do not follow the Government Decree which ordered the industry to catch up with and outpace leading capitalist countries'.

As a result it was decided to intensify experimental engine construction by restructuring the engineering works, and to concentrate them under a single authority. In the initial stage VAO transferred control over its designers to the Central Design Bureau (*Tsentralnoe Konstruktorskoe Byuro*, TsKB) and set up the Experimental-Motor Department (*Opitno-Motorniy Otdel*, OMO) which was based at Factory No. 24. At that time TsKB operated under the then-popular brigade system, which resembled a conveyer belt. Each brigade discharged a certain task, while the engine programmes did not have leading designers responsible for each specific type, the head of the OMO being held responsible for the overall development of all powerplant types. As a result, the development process was not properly co-ordinated, and the scattering of effort created a situation where most of the projects became stuck at a point where responsibilities were transferred from one brigade to the other. As early as May 1930 suggestions had been made that specific designers should be held responsible for developing certain engine types. Maryamov, the head of VMO TsAGI (he had replaced Stechkin, who had been arrested), even worked out a plan for such assignments.

One of the major problems faced by the Soviet industry was the lack of specialists. At the same time, many outstanding engineers with pre-revolution educational background and vast experience were imprisioned in jails and prison camps. Many leading aero-engine designers were arrested in connection with the 'Industrial Party' case. However, it was decided that they should not waste their potential in mines or lumber camps, and in 1929 the OGPU Design Bureau, manned by imprisoned engineers, was set up at Factory No. 24. The bureau was headed by high-ranking OGPU officers who did not have any professional education (however, all they had to do was supervise designers). Motivations to encourage the engineers to produce better work included possible shortening of their sentences. However, the bureau's efficiency proved inadequate, and in 1932 it was shut down and most of its employees were released.

In some cases educational institutes (such as the Kharkov Aviation Institute) or scientific research organizations became involved in aero-engine development. For instance, the diesel engine development programme saw participation by the Leningrad-based All-Union Scientific-Research Diesel Institute (*Vsesoyuzniy Nauchno-Issledovatelskiy Dizelniy Institut*, VNIDI).

In late 1930 the next step in concentrating design efforts was taken when the Aviation Motor-Building Institute (*Institut Aviatsionnogo Motorostroeniya*, IAM) was founded. Specialists from the VMO TsAGI, NAMI, and OMO TsKB were transferred to the IAM, which at first was basically a large design bureau, the Design Department having the largest number of employees in the Institute. A number of uncompleted engine projects and several unrealized programmes were given to the department. At the same time the workload of the designers, who remained at Factory No. 24, decreased. All of the OGPU Design Bureau projects were also transferred to the expanding IAM. In June 1933 it employed 3,600 people, including 1,000 engineers and designers. The institute had its own workshops and, later, an experimental factory. At the same time, the factories retained their own small design departments.

However, the idea of concentrating design efforts did not yield significant results. Because of the large number of engine types under development and the lack of personal responsibility, only a few powerplants were sufficiently refined to go into series production. Only four of the ten engine types stipulated in the plan for

1931 were built, and just one of them was introduced into the air force inventory. Only five of fourteen types listed in the plan for 1932 reached the prototype-building stage.

Faced with this problem, the authorities decided to adopt a different approach. One of the clauses in the STO decree of March 1934 was related to establishing series production of the engines for which licences had been purchased from the USA and France. For this purpose, design departments were to be established at Factories No. 26 and No. 19, which would be tasked with improving the acquired engines. Such design departments were soon organized at the other factories. The post of chief designer was introduced at aero-engine enterprises from 1 April 1934.

As the IAM (renamed the Central Institute of Aviation Motor-Building, *Tsentralniy Institut Aviatsionnogo Motorostroeniya*, TsIAM, on 29 June 1933) gradually relinquished its role as a design organization, the major burden of engine development was shouldered by the factories' design departments, and the numbers of their employees was constantly increasing. From January 1935 such departments were renamed the Experimental Design Bureaux (*Opitno-Konstruktorskoe Byuro*, OKB).

The OKBs specialized in certain powerplant types, gradually developing them into engine families. Leading designers, who co-ordinated the development efforts, were appointed to supervise the creation of specific engine types. The engine prototypes were manufactured in special workshops and production areas.

Design organizations of the GVF were operating in parallel with the OKBs, which were initially assigned to the NKTP and then to the NKOP structure. The Scientific Research Institute of Civil Air Fleet (*Nauchno-Issledovatelskiy Institut Grazhdanskogo Vozdushnogo Flota*, NII GVF), founded in 1930, was divided into three institutes by a decree of 4 July 1932, including the Civil Air Fleet Scientific Research Institute of Aviation Engines (*Nauchno-Issledovatelskiy Institut Aviadvigateley Grazhdanskogo Vozdushnogo Flota*, NII AD GVF). The NII AD GVF had under its supervision (as an affiliate institute) the Ukrainian Scientific Research Aviation Diesel Institute (*Ukrainskiy Nauchno-Issledovatelskiy Aviadizelniy Institut*, or UNIADI, which had been initially named *Ukrainskiy Nauchno-Issledovatelskiy Institut Dvigateley Vnutrennego Sgoraniya*, or Ukrainian Scientific-Research Institute of Internal Combustion Engines, Ukrainian NII DVS), which had been established earlier and was based in Kharkov. In the late 1930s the NII AD GVF was reintegrated into the NII GFV structure, and all its development work on new aero-engines was cancelled. About a year earlier UNIADI had been transferred to come under the supervision of Factory No. 75 and was converted to tank diesel engine development.

Osoaviakhim did not have any of its own engineering organizations, but it participated in funding the development work on low-powered engines. Such work was often documented as unplanned, and was carried out by employees of various organizations (the TsIAM, for instance). Labour agreements were signed by each participant for each development stage, the salary usually being paid after completion of each stage. When working with organizations, Osoaviakhim made an agreement covering the unplanned work and then transferred the amounts required.

In the late 1930s the State security authorities once again participated in aero-engine development, following the same pattern as before. Many aero-engine engineers were arrested in 1937-38, accused of being 'saboteurs', 'people's enemies' and 'foreign spies'. They were gathered at the Special Technical Bureau (*Osoboe Tekhnicheskoe Byuro*, OTB) of the NKVD Special Technical Department. The OTB was soon divided into two bureaux: one at Factory No. 82, based in Tushino and tasked with diesel engine development, and the other at Factory No. 27 in Kazan, which was developing X-configuration powerplants based on the M-105 engine. The designers were released as they attained certain levels of success in the creation of the engines, but the prison design bureau system existed until 1946.

In November 1937 it was decided to concentrate all development efforts on diesel engines, including aviation diesels, at Factory No. 183 in Kharkov. The UNIADI was to act as the factory design bureau, and a special decree of the Council of People's Commissars (*Sovet Narodnikh*

Part of the PB experimental engine on the NII VVS test bench, 1938.

The VK-108 engine prototype before State testing, August 1945.

Komissarov, Sovnarkom) was issued to this end. However, this decision was not brought to fruition.

The number of aero-engine factories in the USSR increased considerably in the late 1930s. The same powerplant type or several types of the same family were produced simultaneously at several factories. One of these factories was regarded as the leading one, and hosted the design bureau, while the others accommodated Series Production Design Bureaux (*Seriyno-Konstruktorskoe Byuro*, SKB). The SKBs were tasked with developing production techniques for their factory, taking into account the available equipment, as well as introducing minor improvements in the engine design.

In 1939 five engine-building OKBs existed. One person could act as chief designer at several factories. For instance, in 1943 Mikulin occupied such a post at Factories No. 24, No. 45, and No. 300, all of which were producing engines of his design. It was prohibited to introduce any changes to the engine drawings without the OKB's consent. Later it became necessary to obtain permission from the People's Commissariat for any such changes, while from October 1940 this had to be co-ordinated with Sovnarkom.

This structure of design and development works remained in place throughout the war years. The only difference was the appearance of special experimental factories, some of which began to host design bureaux. The first factory of this type, No. 300, was established in Moscow in 1943 to accommodate the OKB of A.A. Mikulin. Such factories did not carry out series production, but built the prototypes and small batches of aero-engines.

The OKBs and SKBs were designated by the numbers of their respective factories. For instance, OKB-19 was situated at Factory No. 19, based in Molotov (nowadays Perm). If there was more than one design bureau per factory, they were differentiated by additional Roman numerals; for instance, OKB-500-I and OKB-500-II. When a design bureau was transferred to another factory, it received a new designation. For example, in May 1944 OKB-154 was transferred from Factory No. 154 in Andizhan to Moscow-based Factory No. 41, where it received the new designation OKB-41.

From 1945 the number of design bureaux working on piston aero-engine development was constantly decreasing,

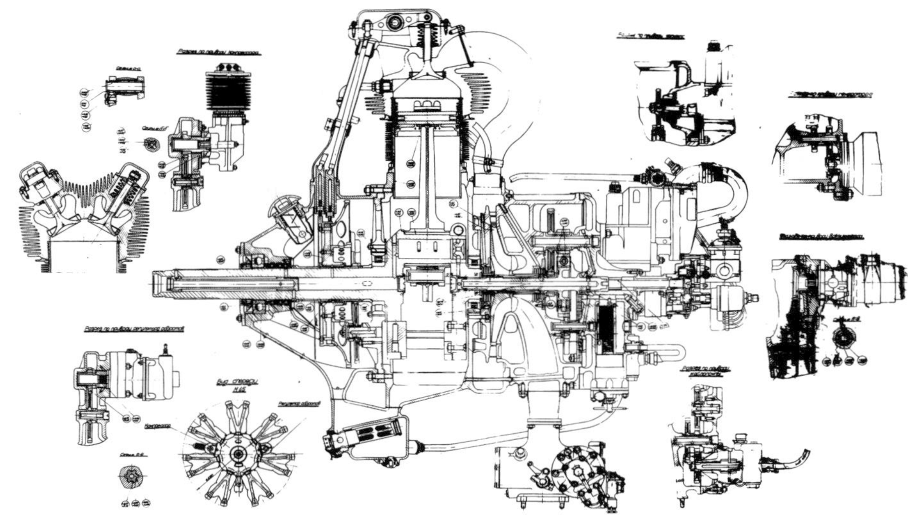

The M-13FN engine project, developed by the OKB-41 in Moscow in 1948.

and the larger OKBs switched to jet engines.

In 1948 only Molotov-based OKB-19, Omsk-based OKB-29, Zaporozhye-based OKB-478 and Moscow-based OKB-500-I and OKB-500-II were working on piston aero-engines. A year later, in the process of reducing defence equipment production, some OKBs were modified into SKBs and others were closed or diverted to different products.

By the mid-1950s only three OKBs working on piston aero-engines remained, in Zaporozhye, Voronezh and Perm. Moreover, they did not carry out development of conceptually new engines, but were creating modifications of proven powerplants. Later the Perm-based OKB was fully converted to turbojets, while the design bureau in Zaporozhye focused its efforts on turboprops.

In the early 1960s the OKB in Voronezh was the only remaining design bureau specializing in piston aero-engines. It had been established in 1950 on the basis of the Design Department of Factory No. 154, which had earlier merged with OKB-41 (which had been closed in Moscow). At that time this design bureau was called the Experimental Design Bureau of Machine-Building (*Opitno-Konstruktorskoe Byuro Mashinostroeniya*, OKBM). In 1953 it was turned into an affiliate of the Zaporozhye-based OKB of A.G. Ivchenko, and in 1960 it was once again made independent. In 1994 the OKBM evolved into a joint stock company, the control stock being held by the state. The abbreviation now stood for Experimental Design Bureau of Motor-Building (*Opitno-Konstruktorskoe Byuro Motorostroeniya*, OKBM). Today this design bureau remains the leading Russian enterprise developing piston aero-engines.

In the early 1980s, in light of emerging UAVs, the Machine-Building Design Bureau in Kuibyshev became involved in the development of low-powered piston aero-engines.

From the early 1990s the interest in low-powered piston aero-engines increased. The Special Design Bureau of Wankel-type Engines of the Volga Automobile Factory enterprise (*Spetsialnoe Konstruktorskoe Byuro Rotorno-Porshnevikh Dvigateley Volzhskogo Avtomobilnogo Zavoda*, SKB RPD VAZ) started working in the aero-engine field. The Kazan Scientific-Production Enterprise (*Kazanskoe Nauchno-Proizvodstvennoe Ob'edinenie*, KNPO), with the assistance of the Voronezh-based OKBM, embarked on developing a family of horizontally-opposed aero-engines. At the same time there appeared a whole range of small design organizations (not organized in any kind of centralized structure) which develop piston engines for ultra-light aircraft. Such teams often use motorcycle and snowmobile engines.

From the late 1990s, according to State regulations, all aviation engineering organizations have to be licensed and meet certain requirements with respect to personnel, professional skills, equipment, etc.

CHAPTER FOUR

Engine Testing and Acceptance

In the pre-October Revolution era no definite system for aero-engine testing existed in Russia. Each manufacturer defined its own methods for testing engine prototypes. The conditions and methodologies for testing for series production engines, built to UVVF orders, were stipulated in the relevant contracts with the factories. Usually the engine was tested on a simple bench, being run at nominal power rating for an hour. The acceptances were carried out according to UVVF commissions, while the acceptance procedures were limited to an external inspection of the engine, attendance at the tests, and the completion of paperwork. Later an engine weight check was added, and from 1916 fuel and oil consumption had to be verified.

The same approach was used throughout the Civil War years. From 1923 engine prototype testing was divided into factory, state, and joint testing. The first was conducted at the stage of prototype initial refinements, on the test benches of the manufacturing factory or the developing enterprise. State testing was similar to the procedure of certification testing used in Western countries. Engines capable of operating without overhaul for no less than 100hr were released to State testing. (In the 1920s it was acceptable to conduct testing in two 50hr stages, with a break for adjustment and small repairs.)

Specific test programmes were prepared for each engine type, and were approved by the NTK UVVS. Before the tests, the engine was weighed and disassembled for its major components to be measured. In the course of State testing, the engine's nominal and maximum power ratings, and fuel and oil consumption, were defined. After completion of the tests the powerplant was usually disassembled again and its components re-measured to determine the rate of wear. If there were any failures, the broken parts were submitted for examination to determine the cause of failure. At first, the State tests were conducted at the same location as the factory tests, but were attended by a commission made up of representatives of the air force and aviation industry. Later the Propeller-Motor Department of the NII VVS, which built its own test benches, specialized in the State testing of engines.

As a result of State testing a powerplant was deemed to have 'passed satisfactorily' or to have 'failed'. However, the third and most common assessment stated that the engine had 'passed the tests with shortcomings', and it was demanded that the shortcomings revealed during testing should be rectified in series-production engines. An engine that was reported to have passed the tests 'satisfactorily' was designated as the pattern powerplant for series production. If it was reported to have 'passed with shortcomings', a specification was prepared for the pattern powerplant based on the existing engine, including a list of required changes to be introduced into the series engines. In some cases the shortcomings had to be rectified gradually, and the authorities defined specific series (batches) in which one or another correction was to be introduced.

An engine could only be launched into series production after it had passed State testing. In reality, however, this provision was frequently violated. After the first or second failure, a powerplant that was considered promising was introduced into series production, and later a series-production engine (usually not the first one built) was submitted for State testing. There were cases when a powerplant type

The first workshop for engine testing at Factory No. 26 in Rybinsk, 1928.

The M-17 engine during State tests on the NII VVS test bench, 1930.

Taken at Factory No. 26, Ufa, in November 1943, this photograph shows M-105P engines undergoing cold running before the delivery tests.

The simple roll-out engine demonstration benches at the MAI. An M-11G is on the left and an M-105R on the right.

was transferred to State testing up to six or seven times.

Sometimes State testing was replaced by joint testing, carried out at a factory with the air force representatives in attendance. This usually happened when the engine type had to be introduced into series production in the shortest possible time, or when a new version of an existing engine type was tested.

In the early 1930s the programme of State testing became more sophisticated owing to the introduction of a requirement for operating on the maximum, nominal and cruise power ratings for a specified period of time. An assessment of the engine's acceleration time was also required.

Starting from the early 1930s all series-production engines underwent a standard 3hr test programme. The NII VVS sometimes carried out check testing of sample series engines, using a programme similar to that of State testing, to assess whether production quality had improved or deteriorated. Engines were selected at random from a current batch.

The acceptance of aero-engines for the air force was carried out by acceptance inspectors serving in the armed force and usually having a technical school or institute background. All factory-built engines had to pass the acceptance procedure, and an engine was not shipped or paid for by the UVVS unless it had been approved by the military acceptance inspector. When production quality deteriorated, the UVVS ordered the acceptance procedure to be carried out at subassembly and even at component level, the military acceptance inspectors examining and measuring certain subassemblies and most crucial parts. No component or subassembly could be sent for further assembly unless authorised by the military acceptance inspector.

From the mid-1930s the military acceptance inspectors (also called 'military representatives') were also responsible for monitoring design and development work at the factories. Thus the UVVS received first-hand information, bypassing Aviatrest and the People's Commissariat, which were interested in concealing drawbacks and presenting only the positive aspects.

Until 1930 the military acceptance commissions also checked powerplants for the Civil Air Fleet, Osoaviakhim, and other authorities. However, due to the acute shortage of aero-engines the GU GVF agreed to take powerplants rejected by the military, or falling under the category of 'training engine'. The latter were cheaper, had lower power ratings due to increased tolerances, and shorter service lives. In the spring of 1930 the GU GVF, which had less-stringent quality requirements than those of the air force, established its own system of engine acceptance. Later the NII GVF began State testing of engine types in which the military were not interested. In 1938 the naval aviation acceptance system was separated from that of the air force.

By the late 1930s a streamlined system of aero-engine testing and acceptance had been established in the Soviet Union. Standard programmes for testing new and repaired engines had been prepared and adopted. The powerplants were tested with different types of fuel and oil, as well as with special cooling mixtures for experimental purposes. For high-altitude testing, a system of mobile test beds, mounted on automobile chassis, was built and transported to the Pamirs area.

Such testing and acceptance systems existed until the early 1990s with only minor changes. When both the manufacturers and purchasers of aero-engines became partially state-owned or fully private, State testing was replaced by certification testing in accordance with the Western practices.

A test bench for investigating the heating rate of the ACh-30B.

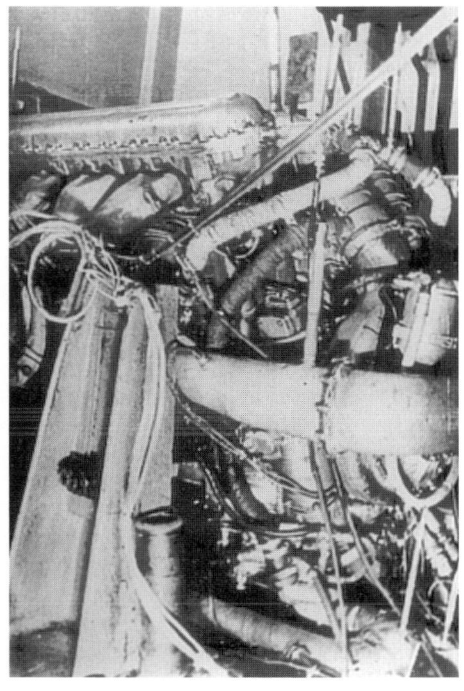

CHAPTER FIVE

Aero-engine Designations

Until the early 1920s imported or licence-built engines used in Russia retained their original designations. More frequently, however, peculiar 'hybrid' designations were used, combining the name of the Western company which had created the engine, and its power rating. For instance, the widely used French 50hp Gnome Omega rotary engine was named *Gnom-50*. Sometimes the designation was written as *Gnom 50HP*.

Foreign aero-engine types manufactured in Russia were sometimes designated with the appendage *Russkiy* (Russian), such as *Russkiy Reno* (Russian Renault) and *Russkiy Ispano* (Russian Hispano). On the other hand, Sunbeam engines produced by the Ilyin factory in Moscow were still called Sunbeams, despite the fact that they were not exact copies of the British powerplant.

Aero-engines developed by Russian designers received designations indicating the manufacturer and certain parameters of the powerplant. For instance, two factories of the RBVZ enterprise built MRB-6 (*Motor Russko-Baltiyskiy*, or Russo-Baltic engine) and RBVZ-6 engines (both of which had six cylinders). The Dyuflon & Konstantinovich (DEKA) factory was arranging production of 100hp DEKA M-100 engines.

Engine prototype designations were more varied and usually included the initials of the designer(s). For example, the AMBS engine was created by Aleksandr Mikulin and Boris Stechkin.

This inconsistency survived until the end of the Civil War. In 1921 the UVVF, jointly with Glavkoavia, introduced a new system of aero-engine designation. The designation now included letter 'M' (for *Motor* – engine) and a number (for instance, M-5). The first numbers were given to engines already in service. The RBVZ-6 became the M-1, and the *Ron-120* (Le Rhône Jb) became the M-2. Subsequent numbers were assigned in the same order as the engine specifications were issued. Initially, therefore, the designation was related to the specification rather than to the engine project or prototype. However, several projects could be under development under the same specification. For instance, IAM was preparing three different projects with different configurations and different numbers of cylinders to meet the M-35 specification.

Designations allotted to specifications that were not brought to fruition might later be reassigned to other specifications for different engine types. After the Second World War the designations that had been given to earlier engine prototypes were repeatedly used for new powerplant types.

In the 1920s and early 1930s the engine designations also included the power rating, for instance M-5-400 (400hp M-5 engine). Starting from the mid-1930s, designations were assigned on the engine family principle, and the designations of types evolved from a common original powerplant had successive numbers. As a case in point, the M-85, M-86, M-87, M-88 and M-89 engines all originated from the Gnome-Rhône 14K.

The engine development enterprises

Two engine types given the same designation; the M-9 experimental engine of L.I. Starostin ...

... and the modern M9F produced by the Voronezh Mechanical Factory.

often assigned their own designations. For instance, the widely known M-11 was initially designated M-100 (it had a 100hp power rating) by the Motor factory, and the 65hp M-23 developed by NAMI was named NAMI-65. The Bolshevik factory in Leningrad designated its powerplants with the initial letters 'AB', for *Aviamotori Bolshevika* (Aviation Motors of the Bolshevik factory). In some cases the engine developers included their own initials in designations. For instance, A.A. Mikulin called the M-20 engine the AM-20 in some documents, while the engine project proposed by Kireev for a for a contest in 1925 was simply designated 'MK', which stood for *Motor Kireeva* (Kireev's engine).

The engine designation formed a part of the official designation of the aircraft it powered. For instance, R3-M5 or R-3M5 meant 'Reconnaissance aeroplane -3 with the M-5 engine'. If an aeroplane had more than one engine, the number of engines was indicated in front of the engine type designation. So TB3-4M17 or TB-3-4M-17 stood for 'Heavy Bomber -3 with four M-17 engines'. In the late 1930s the type and number of engines no longer formed a part of the aircraft designation.

Starting from the late 1920s, the engine designation also included a reference to its version. At first, the reference letter was based the form of modification. For instance, in the designation M-27R the 'R' stood for the reduction gear (*Reduktor*) fitted to the engine. The letter 'N' stood for a supercharger (*Nagnetatel'*), while a combination of both letters (RN) indicated the presence of both reduction gear and supercharger. The letter 'F' denoted a boosted engine (*Forsirovanniy*).

In the mid-1930s OKB-19 used letter 'D' to designate two-row radial engines (*Dvukhryadniy*, two-row) based on single-row radials. For instance, the M-70 was initially designated M-25D18, indicating that it was an 18-cylinder two-row engine with cylinders from the M-25. There was a case when letter 'D' was used to designate a diesel version of an engine using light fuel (M-87D). In the early 1940s 'N' often stood for direct injection (*Neposredsvenniy vprysk*), while 'TK' denoted a turbo-supercharger (*Turbokompressor*).

The letter 'G', when placed in front of an 'M', as in GM-13, denoted a marine version of an aero-engine. In the late 1920s and early 1930s the second variant of an engine prototype, which had considerable design differences, might have an additional figure '2' in front of letter 'M', as in 2M-15. However, this held true only for the prototype, as the engine was designated M-15 when added to the air force inventory.

The M-34RN. This designation, typical of the 1930s, had the following meaning: 'M' – *Motor*, '34' – the number of the specification; 'R' – *Reduktorniy*, or geared; 'N' – *Nagnetatel'*, or supercharger.

From the early 1930s engine version designations started to use successive letters of the Russian alphabet, and experimental versions of engines were also included in the same sequence, for instance M-11A, M-11B, M-11V, M-11G and M-11D. In some cases both systems were used in combination. For instance, in the designation M-34FRNB the first three letters denoted a boosted engine with reduction gear and supercharger (*Forsirovanniy, Reduktorniy, s Nadduvom*), while the last letter denoted the version ('B' = second version).

Foreign engines acquired for the VVS RKKA retained their original designations, which were usually written in Cyrillic. However, powerplants manufactured under licence by Soviet factories received new designations in compliance with the existing system. For example, the Gnome-Rhône 9Aq was designated M-22.

The French Renault engines produced under licence in Voronezh were an exception, being designated by the letters 'MV'. The meaning of this designation is not clear; it might have stood for air-cooled engine (*Motor Vozdushnogo okhlazhdeniya*), or for Voronezh-built engine (*Motor Voronezhskiy*).

Designations starting with 'M' were given only to engines ordered by the air force. It was prohibited to use this designation system for engines developed on the initiative of Aviatrest (and, later, VAO and GUAP initiative) or by the factories. The variants of such types' designations were quite different. There were some occasions when Roman rather than Russian letters were used. For instance, W18 denoted an 18-cylinder W-shaped (three-row) engine. In the early 1930s the OGPU design bureau designated all its engines FED, the initials of Feliks Edmundovich Dzerzhinskiy, the founder of the All-Russian Emergency Commission (*Vserossiyskaya Chrezvichaynaya Komissiya*, VChK – a predecessor of the OGPU).

At first the 'M' designations were used

ASh-82FN engine (previously designated M-82FN). The engine's designation stands for: 'ASh' – initials of OKB-19 chief designer Arkadiy Shvetsov; '82' – the next number in sequence to the engine types of this design bureau (following the M-80 and M-81 prototypes); 'F' – *Forsirovanniy*, or boosted; 'N' – *Neposredstvenniy vprysk*, or direct injection.

for engines using light fuels, and it was suggested that diesel engines should be designated by the letter 'N' (1, or working on crude oil); N-1, N-2, and so on. Later on the designation changed to 'AN' (*Aviatsionniy Neftyanoy*, or aero-engine working on crude oil), although diesel engines used solar oil or kerosene, rather than crude oil. From 1940 diesels were designated in compliance with the existing system, using the letter 'M' (M-30, M-40).

Engines developed and built within the GVF system were distinguished by an additional letter 'G' (*Grazhdanskiy*, or civil), such as MG-11 and MG-21. However, the air-cooled diesel produced at Factory No. 82 was designated simply D-11 (or MD-11).

In the late 1930s and early 1940s the OTB of NKVD worked on a family of MB engines, 'MB' standing for block-type engine (*Motor Blochniy*). These engines used cylinder blocks from the powerplants developed by V.Ya. Klimov.

The 'M-number' designation was not applied to steam aero-engines, steam turbines or gas turbines.

On 9 August 1936, due to the extensive contribution of A.A. Mikulin to the development of Soviet aero-engines, the M-34 engine was redesignated AM-34 (using the designer's initials). All further types created under Mikulin's leadership were similarly designated (AM-35, AM-36, and so on). However, the existing designation system was still applied to new aero-engines, though the Mikulin types were frequently referred to by their old names in daily usage.

In December 1940 the whole system of aircraft and aero-engine designation was changed. Aircraft were now designated by the first two or three letters of their designers' surnames (for example, Pe-2, Yak-1, Ar-2). This system was not applied to types no longer in production, which retained their old designations. The approach to aero-engine designations was similar, but used the initials of designers, in the same manner as applied to Mikulin types. The M-62 became the ASh-62, while the M-105 was redesignated VK-105.

However, the new system was used only with respect to powerplants developed by famous designers such as A.D. Shvetsov and V.Ya. Klimov. It was decided to retain the designations of the engines created in Zaporozhye, probably, because it was very difficult to determine their designers, there having been a succession of chief designers over a short period of time. (Besides, there were two 'public enemies' among them.) The redesignation system was not applied retrospectively to older engine types, which retained their original names/designations. A new engine type officially received its designation when entering the air force inventory; until then it was named under the old system, in compliance with the specification. However, some designers used the new type of designation in documentation relating to experimental engines. Thus two systems were in use simultaneously.

During the Second World War and in the early postwar years the engine designation system was slightly expanded. A.D. Charomskiy merited the honour of having his engines designated by his own initials in 1944, and in 1948 the same honour was extended to A.G. Ivchenko and V.A. Dobrynin.

From the mid-1950s and for quite a long time thereafter the Soviet Union did not develop new piston aero-engines. The designations of engine types still in series production remained unchanged, with the sole exception of the AI-14 (originally M-14), which was redesignated M-14 after modernization.

A number of piston engine prototypes produced in Voronezh in the 1980s and later also received 'M-number' designations, often duplicating the designations of engines that had been in production before the war.

The design bureau in Kuibyshev (nowadays Samara) designated its low-powered engines using the letter 'P' (*Porshnevoy*, or piston) plus their maximum rated horsepower: P-020, P-032, and so on. Similar designations were later used by Kazan designers, but the figures after the dash were rough estimates. The Wankel-type engines designed by SKB RPD VAZ were designated using the traditional designations for this factory, such as VAZ-430, in which the numbers stood for the version and modification (in this particular example '0' means the baseline version).

At the present time, the numerous small design organizations that develop engines for ultralight aircraft do not adhere to any common system of engine designation.

CHAPTER SIX

Aero-engine Factories

The first Russian enterprise to undertake the series production of aero-engines was the Motor factory in Riga. The first engines were assembled there in the summer of 1910, and by early 1914 the factory was producing thirteen or fourteen engines a month.

The French Gnome company established a factory in Moscow in 1912, and this began producing engines in April 1913. A year later it was building seven to ten engines per month.

After the outbreak of the First World War, aero-engine production rates started to rise rapidly. In 1915 the Gnome factory assembled an average of twenty-three engines a month. That same year, after the Gnome and Le Rhône companies merged, the factory was renamed Gnome-Rhône. In late 1916 the factory employed more than 100 people, and in early 1917 it was building forty engines a month, the number of employees having reached 235.

The Motor factory received huge orders after the outbreak of war, but in 1915 it had to be relocated to Moscow as German troops advanced towards Riga. The factory resumed production at the new location, manufacturing about twenty engines per month. By early 1917 it employed 330 persons.

In July 1915 another factory, belonging to the French Salmson company, was set up in Moscow, and from April 1916 it was assembling aero-engines from imported parts. By early 1917 it employed about 300 workers, and its output had reached up to 100 engines per month, the highest production rate in Russia at that time.

In 1916 the Carriage-Automobile Factory of P. Ilyin in Moscow also started building aero-engines, but made only a few. In July that year the Automobile-Carriage Repair Workshops of the Russkiy Reno enterprise in Petrograd began assembling Renault engines from imported French parts.

Two engine-building factories of the RBVZ enterprise were operating in Petrograd. One of them, the Motorniy factory, was founded on the basis of equipment and personnel evacuated from the RBVZ factory in Riga. In 1914 this factory was preparing for series production of the RBVZ-6 engine, but the plans were disrupted by advancing German forces. As a result, RBVZ-6 production was started in Petrograd. The second RBVZ plant, the Mekhanicheskiy factory, was building MRB-6 engines.

Using State loans, the Dyuflon & Konstantinovich Joint Stock Company acquired an incomplete factory in Aleksandrovsk (now Zaporozhye) in August 1915. It was planned that, after expansion, this factory would become the largest aero-engine-building enterprise in Russia.

In compliance with the decision taken in February 1916, State loans were allocated for the building of new automobile factories, some of which were planned to produce piston aero-engines as well. These plants included the Aksay factory in Nakhichevan, 'Kuznetsov, Ryabushinskiy and Co.' (AMO) and the RBVZ factories near Moscow, the Russkiy Reno in Rybinsk, and the factory of the V.A. Lebedev Aeronautical Joint Stock Company in Yaroslavl. One of the factories of A.A. Anatra was also preparing to produce aero-engines. All of these companies, as well as those mentioned earlier, were private.

However, by the autumn of 1917 none of the new factories had become operational. The period of political instability

Assembly of a Gnome rotary engine, 1915.

The engine workshop of the Dux factory, Moscow, 1916.

following the abdication of Tsar Nikolay II, as well as large military contracts that stretched the country's economy to the limit, resulted in an economic recession. By the autumn of 1917 the production rate of aero-engines in Russia had decreased about three-fold compared with that of 1916.

The October Revolution paralysed the aviation industry. Owing to the disruption of the supply system and the lack of financing, factories were shut down one after another, and the construction new factories was suspended. At first, the new government paid no particular attention to the aviation industry. On 12 June 1918 the VSNKh placed the aircraft factories to the fourth (last) category with regard to the supply of required material and equipment, and the importation of engine components was halted. After the outbreak of the Civil War, some of the factory workers and employees were recruited, while others tried to find new jobs.

As early as the beginning of 1918 the Soviet Government started to nationalize various enterprises. In January the DEKA factory was nationalized, followed in December of the same year by the Motor and Gnome-Rhône factories (the latter was renamed Ikar in 1922). These two Moscow factories were the last ones capable of delivering engines. The DEKA factory was ruined during the Civil War when the eighteen different governments, which successively came into power in this region during a three-year period, completely destroyed the plant while trying to evacuate it to various locations.

Factory No. 26 in Rybinsk, August 1928.

Factory No. 26 under construction in the late 1930s.

The Salmson factory was destroyed by heavy gunfire in early 1918, and all of the factories in Petrograd were shut down.

Escalation of the Civil War made the Sovnarkom reconsider its attitude towards the aviation industry. The White Guard and intervention forces had already captured more than half of Russian territory. In March 1919 the employees of aero-engine factories were declared mobilized, and from then on they were no longer conscripted. On 16 June 1920, in accordance with STO decree, these factories were considered the 'spearhead' of the defence industry, and were given priority in receiving supplies and manpower.

During that time only the GAZ No. 2 Ikar and GAZ No. 4 Motor factories (GAZ, *Gosudarstvenniy Aviatsionniy Zavod*, or State Aircraft Factory) were operational; GAZ No. 6 (Amstro, formerly Salmson) was under reconstruction. In 1923 the Amstro factory became part of the GAZ No. 4. The Bolshevik factory in Petrograd (formerly the Obukhovskiy factory) was converted to the production of aero-engines in 1923. In 1925 the DEKA factory in Zaporozhye was restored and renamed GAZ No. 9 Bolshevik. Under the STO decree of 17 July 1925, the uncompleted Russkiy Reno factory in Rybinsk was reactivated and named GAZ No. 6. At first it served as a repair factory, but from 1928 it began arranging production of the German BMW VI (M-17) engine.

These factories became the backbone of the Soviet aero-engine industry in the 1920s and early 1930s. On 21 March 1927 GAZ No. 2 and GAZ No. 4 were merged to form a single enterprise with a peculiar name: 'Joint State Aircraft Factory No. 2 and No. 4 named after Frunze'. On 1 October that year all factories received new designations. The Joint Factory became Factory No. 24, GAZ No. 6 became Factory No. 26, and GAZ No. 9 became Factory No. 29.

In the early 1930s the new Factory No. 19 was founded in Perm, and in 1932 Factory No. 27 was established in Kazan. Factory No. 19, named after Stalin, set up its first production line in November 1932. At first it operated as a pure assembly factory, producing M-22 engines from parts produced by Factory No. 29, but a year later it began arranging the production of the American Wright Cyclone engine. It was initially estimated that the funds allocated for purchasing the licence

The M-17 engine crankcase assembly area in Factory No. 26 in the first half of the 1930s.

The assembly line for M-34RN engines at Factory No. 24 in Moscow, 1936.

would be sufficient to acquire production equipment for the new factory in Gorkiy (now Nizhniy Novgorod), but the costs were higher than expected and Factory No. 19 had to be converted to Cyclone production.

In 1934 Factory No. 16 in Voronezh, originally set up for aircraft production, was converted for engine building. The production of all types of low-powered engines was transferred to this factory from Factory No. 29 (named after Baranov). In the late 1930s Factory No. 154 was formed on the basis of Factory No. 16. The new enterprise started producing M-11s, while Factory No. 16 was responsible for the 'more important' M-105.

It took a long time to complete Factory No. 27, and it was only in the late 1930s that it started assembling M-25Vs from parts built by Factory No. 19.

The Civil Air Fleet also improved its engine-building capabilities. In accordance with an STO decree of 5 December 1931, 1.5 million roubles were allocated for building Factory No. 63, which became operational in 1933 (under the new designation No. 82).

The Soviet aero-engine industry underwent rapid growth before the outbreak of the Second World War. In compliance with a Defence Committee decree of 11 June 1939, seven new factories were founded, while the existing ones underwent modernization. In addition, some factories that had specialized in other products were converted to the production of aero-engines in 1938. For instance, Factory No. 234 in Leningrad was founded in 1938 by merging the Krasniy Oktyabr factory (piano manufacture), the Pishmash factory (typewriter manufacture) and a gramophone factory. It is noteworthy that the Krasniy Oktyabr factory had been established at the workshops of the Russkiy Reno, which assembled aero-engines during the First World War. In July 1940 the People's Commissariat of Medium Machine-Building transferred the Ufa Engine-Building Factory, which had been manufacturing combine-harvester engines, to the People's Commissariat of the Aviation Industry, the factory receiving the new designation No. 384. In July 1939 GVF Factory No. 82 was also transferred to the NKAP.

Arrangements were also made for aero-engine production at factories of other People's Commissariats. In 1941 the manufacture of M-40 diesels started at the Leningrad-based Factory of Lifting and Transportation Equipment (named after Kirov). Factory No. 75 in Kharkov, which manufactured tank diesels, was also preparing to build the M-40. In October 1940 the Gorkiy Automobile Factory (*Gorkovskiy Avtomobilniy Zavod*, GAZ) established a special workshop (Workshop No. 10) to manufacture M-105s, and in March 1942 this workshop was transferred to the NKAP as Factory No. 466.

An aerial view of Factory No. 16 in Voronezh in the early 1940s.

Workshop No. 25 (non-ferrous casting) of the factory in Rybinsk after a German bombing raid in the spring of 1942.

Factory No. 29 after evacuation to Omsk, 1944.

The former cotton warehouse that accommodated Workshop No. 13 of Factory No. 154 after evacuation from Voronezh, November 1941.

The inside of the same warehouse before the production machinery was installed.

LEFT: **Building a new mechanical workshop in Andizhan, 29 August 1942.**

RIGHT: **The main assembly line of Factory No. 26 in Ufa, 1943.**

Such efforts resulted in a considerable increase in aero-engine production on the eve of the war, and created conditions for further growth. New factories under construction in the country's inland regions became very important when, in September-October 1941, the evacuation of older factories from the Ukraine and western Russia to Trans-Volga regions and Siberia started. Factory No. 29 was evacuated to Omsk, Factory No. 26 to Ufa, Factory No. 24 to Kuibyshev and Factory No. 16 to Kazan. Factory No. 154 was transferred to Central Asia (Andizhan) and accommodated in barns designed to store cotton; absolutely unsuitable for engine production.

In some cases several factories arrived at the same site, which had been occupied by a local factory. In such a situation the factories were usually merged, and the top management of the largest recently-arrived enterprise was put in control of the newly created factory. For instance, Factories No. 234 and No. 451 were merged with Factory No. 26 in Ufa (fortunately they all produced engines of the M-105 family) and were accommodated at the premises of Factory No. 384. Part of Factory No. 219 was also evacuated there. On 17 December 1941 this conglomerate was turned into Factory No. 26. Factories No. 16 and No. 82 were merged with local Factory No. 27 in Kazan.

A worker attaches a pan to the M-105P engine, using a pneumatic nut wrench. Ufa, November 1943.

Cargo trains carrying the equipment and personnel of the evacuated factories often arrived at unfinished sites. Factories were built at the same time as equipment was installed, and lathes were turned on when there was still no roof, canvas providing temporary cover. There were no window panes and workshops were not heated, and this was during the cold winter of 1941-42.

Despite these hardships, factories quickly recovered from the enforced shutdowns. For instance, Factory No. 29 had reached its pre-war production rate as early as February 1942, Factory No. 24 achieved this goal in May, Factories No. 16 and No. 154 in July, and Factory No. 26 in August.

The factory workshops abandoned in the west of the country were used as repair

Manufacturing engine crankcases at Factory No. 19 in Perm, July 1944.

Machining cylinders for ASh-82FN engines at Factory No. 19, 1944.

The workshop for non-ferrous metal parts at Factory No. 36, February 1945.

Assembling crankcases for ASh-73TK engines at Rybinsk in the first half of the 1950s.

workshops. However, as early as 1942 the issue of restoring fully-fledged factories at these locations was raised. By that time the evacuated factories had become fully operational in their new locations, and it seemed unreasonable to interrupt their output during the war. So new factories were established at the old premises. They were provided with equipment taken from less-important enterprises, as well as with new machinery, including that received under the Lend-Lease programme.

In February 1942 Factory No. 45 emerged at the site previously occupied by Factory No. 24 in Moscow, and in April of that year Factory No. 500 was established on the premises of Factory No. 82 in Tushino, near Moscow. In the latter case, some workers and equipment of Factory No. 82 were returned to their old location in March 1942. The question of returning Factory No. 26 to Rybinsk was raised, but the proposal was rejected in light of enemy bombing raids, and in November 1943 the new Factory No. 36 was founded there.

When Zaporozhye was liberated from the Germans in autumn 1943, Factory No. 478 was set up on the former premises of Factory No. 29. The evacuated Factory No. 20 was replaced in Moscow by Factory No. 41, which in 1942 produced its first batch of M-11 engines. In late 1942 the experimental Factory No. 300, which was to become the basis of the A.A. Mikulin Design Bureau (OKB-300), was accommodated in workshops of the Orgaviaprom factory, which had been evacuated to the eastern part of the Soviet Union.

After the war's end the factories' locations were left unchanged. Only Factory No. 154 was returned to Voronezh in 1946, while Factory No. 466 had been transferred to Leningrad a year before to occupy the premises of evacuated Factory No. 234. In 1946 experimental Factory No. 117, the basis of the V.Ya. Klimov Design Bureau (OKB-117), was separated from Factory No. 466.

No more factories for piston aero-engine manufacture were established in the USSR, as jet engines were gradually taking over the production lines. As early as 1945 Factory No. 45 ceased production of piston engines, and a year later Factories Nos. 16, 26, 41, and 500 followed suit. In 1954 the last AM-42 was assembled at Factory No. 24 in Kuibyshev, and a year later Factory No. 19 transferred production of Shvetsov piston engines to other enterprises. In 1957 the last ASh-73TK was built at Factory No. 36 in Rybinsk, though Factory No. 478 assembled piston engines until 1962. After that, Factory No. 154 in Voronezh remained the only large enterprise mass-producing piston aero-engines in the Soviet Union. From 1963 it was called the Voronezh Mechanical Factory. Nowadays, and it is still Russia's largest manufacturer of piston aero-engines.

In the 1980s the factory in Kuibyshev built small batches of two-stroke engines for UAVs. One of the factories of the Rybinskie Motory enterprise manufactured *Buran-Avia* engines in the 1980s and 1990s. At present there are no other companies in Russia undertaking the mass production of piston aero-engines. Several small workshops are converting motorcycle and automobile engines for aviation use, but these products are primarily intended for home-built ultralight aircraft.

PART TWO

CHAPTER ONE

Aero-engines in Russia Before October 1917

As in other countries, Russia had enthusiasts striving to achieve powered flight. These devotees developed and built various aircraft powered by different types of engine; steam, electric, jet, and so on. Probably the first Russian internal-combustion aero-engine was the project developed in 1879 by a naval engineer Capt A.K. Mozhaiskiy. Mozhaiskiy's 'gas-fired machine' was a modified Brayton-system engine employing ignition from a Ruhmkorff's coil and using mineral oil as fuel. However, Mozhaiskiy calculated that this engine would be too heavy and bulky, and decided not to use it on his aircraft, which was built during 1882-84. Instead he installed two steam engines manufactured in Britain to his requirements.

Another project completed almost at the same time as Mozhaiskiy's achieved realization. In 1879 O.S. Kostovich proposed to build an 80hp engine with electric ignition for installation in an airship. This 8-cylinder engine was to use light fuel and featured an original mechanism, having four pairs of horizontally-opposed cylinders with pistons moving in opposite directions. Each cylinder pair had a common combustion chamber with inlet and outlet valves. Connecting rods rotated the crankshaft with the help of large rockers, and the camshaft was turned by the crankshaft through chain gear. The engine structure looked rather bulky.

In 1880 Kostovich built a smaller 2-cylinder engine with this layout, and tested it on a boat at the beginning of 1881. He also planned to install it on his aircraft, which was being developed in 1881-83. In August 1882 construction of the 8-cylinder engine was started. The prototype was completed in 1884, and it achieved the calculated power rating of 80hp during ground testing.

In later attempts to build powered aircraft, Russian designers used imported automobile or marine four-stroke light fuel engines. For example, a French 10hp Buchet was installed in E.S. Fyodorov's quintuplane, which was built in 1897-1903 but not flown. The hydroplane built by V.V. Kress had a German 35hp Daimler engine. It was built in 1901 in Vienna, but during testing it was capsized by a gust of wind and sank.

Foreign engines were also imported for installation in Russian airships. In 1893 an in-line, four-stroke, watercooled Daimler engine was acquired from Germany for the all-metal Schwarz airship, which was being built secretly in Russia. The 10hp engine weighed 298kg (657lb), while the total weight of the powerplant exceeded 500kg (1,100lb). The Daimler engine's specific power rating of was lower than that of contemporary steam engines. Schwarz's airship was not completed.

In 1907 the Lessner factory in St Petersburg received an order for two 50hp engines, intended for installation on *Krechet* (Merlin) airship. The company's engineers developed a 4-cylinder, four-stroke, watercooled light fuel engine, and a prototype was built and tested in the spring of 1908. After two hours of running the oil overheated, the crankshaft seized and the nose section of the crankcase cracked. Refinement work lasted several

O.S. Kostovich's engine, intended for installation in an airship, is now exhibited at Russian Air Force Museum in Monino.

months but was unsuccessful. Instead, two 85hp Panhard-Levasseur engines were purchased in France in October 1908.

Later, different engine types were acquired in France and Germany for installation in Russian military airships: 150-180hp Clement-Bayard, 110hp NAG, 180hp Maybach, 200hp Chenu, 64hp ENV, 75hp Kerting, 100hp De Dion-Bouton, 60hp Dancelle, 50hp Harleu.

Theodore (Fyodor Grigoryevich) Kalep (1866-1913) was the first to arrange specialized aero-engine production in Russia. Kalep was Estonian, but worked in Riga, Latvia. (At that time the whole territory of the Baltic States was a province of the Russian Empire, and its industry functioned as a part of the Russian industry. The author therefore considers it appropriate to mention Kalep as a Russian engineer and industrialist.)

Kalep was a director of the Motor factory in Riga, which at that time manufactured lathe transmissions, and in March 1910 he purchased from the German Flugmaschine Wright company a Wright Type A biplane powered by an in-line, 4-cylinder, water-cooled 30hp Wright aero-engine. Kalep wrote: 'Having ascertained in the need to produce aero-engines for Russian-built aircraft, in 1910 we started to manufacture an automobile-type aero-engine at our factory in Riga-Sassenhoff, which had been established in 1889…'. Kalep introduced a number of improvements in the design that increased its power rating to 35hp. The Motor factory manufactured the first Wright engine (sometimes called Wright-Riga engines) in the summer of 1910. In January 1911 the first engine was flight tested on a modified biplane based on the Wright design. A number of flights were carried out with this powerplant, but by that time the characteristics of the Wright engine did not suit the demands of the industry, especially with regard to power rating. At the end of that year Kalep developed and built a 4-cylinder, two-stroke engine of his own design, but this remained only a prototype.

In December 1910 Lt Col S.A. Ulyanin, an aircraft designer and the head of the Aviation Department of the Aeronautical School, was sent to France. The Engineering Department of the Russian Army had charged him with the task of finding out which aero-engines would be best to manufacture in Russia. In his report Ulyanin wrote: 'My personal opinion … is the following: we should start production of Gnome engines…'.

As a result of this recommendation, Kalep opened negotiations with the Gnome company with the aim of acquiring a licence for production of the 7-cylinder air-cooled, 50hp Gnome Omega rotary engine. However, the French company imposed unacceptable conditions that meant that the Motor factory had to relinquish up to two-thirds of its net profit. Consequently, Kalep decided to adopt an alternative approach. Several engines were purchased in France and thoroughly examined in Riga, and a new version, differing considerably from the original, was created with the Omega as its basis. Kalep himself and engineer Schuchgalter worked on the design. Aluminium pistons replaced the cast-iron units, and an improved carburettor facilitated engine operation in the severe conditions of a Russian winter. The cylinders were attached in the crankcase via a threaded connection, which replaced the original arrangement using split rings and rods. The crankcase design was changed considerably. In general, Kalep and Schuchgalter simplified the engine's structure; it had eighty-five fewer parts. The crankshaft and connecting rods were now made of higher-quality steel, and the exhaust valves had a longer service life. On the whole, the Omega, manufactured at the Motor factory was lighter, weighing only 68kg (150lb), it had a maximum power rating of 60hp due to increased rpm, and the period between scheduled maintenance was increased to 50hr, compared with 15-20hr for the French original. To distinguish the Riga-built engines from the French ones, they were called *Kalep-Gnom* or merely *Kalep*. Later, a figure denoting nominal power rating was added to the name.

By February 1912 the Motor factory had manufactured five such engines, and carried out comparison tests with the original French engines. The *Kalep* demonstrated complete superiority. On 12 February Kalep sent a report to the Council of Ministers, describing the results, and offered his engines for use by the Russian Army and Navy. A specimen engine was transferred for testing to Sevastopol Aviation School, and another to the Laboratory of Aeronautical and Automobile Engines at the St Petersburg

Left **This Wright engine, produced by the Motor factory, is now displayed in the Monino museum.**

Right **The *Kalep-80* rotary engine was an improved version of the Gnome Lambda.**

The engine stockroom of the Moscow Aeronautical Society, 1914. Most of the engines are Gnome rotaries.

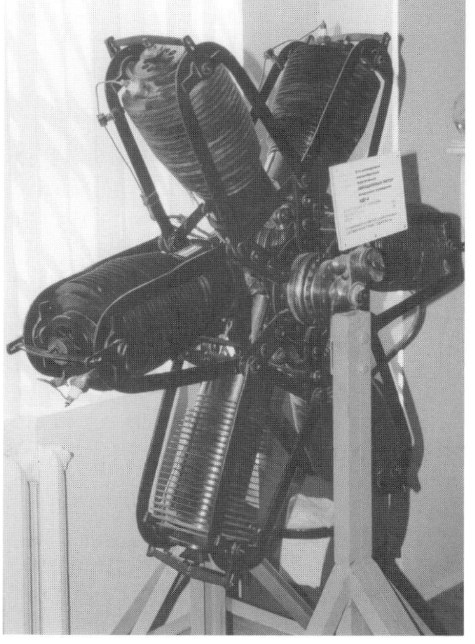

The ADU-4 engine designed by Ufimtsev.

Polytechnic Institute, headed by Professor Lebedev. The testing of these engines proved the high quality of the Motor-built engines, their only shortcoming being an insufficiently reliable ignition system, revealed after several hours of continuous running.

A *Kalep* was installed in a monoplane of Dybovskiy design that participated in the Military Aeroplane Contest of 1913 and flew successfully. Also that year a *Kalep* was installed in the *Severnaya Lastochka* (northern swallow) prototype aeroplane built by A.Y. Villish in Revel (Tallinn), tested in July 1913. In 1914 at the RBVZ factory a *Kalep* was installed in an S-XVI scout designed by I.I. Sikorsky.

Although the superiority of the Russian-built engine over the French one was evident, the Military Ministry's first order for 50 Gnomes was placed with the French company. Russian aviation historian P.D. Duz has written that bribes accepted by Ministry officials from representatives of the Gnome company affected this decision.

Nevertheless, the Motor factory was gradually turning to aero-engines as its primary product. The workshops were re-equipped and new facilities built. In 1913 the company introduced into production three more Gnome types of different power ratings: 60, 80 and 100hp. They underwent a modernization process similar to that applied to the Omega engine (in particular, the power rating was increased by 5-10 per cent). The engine based on the Gnome Lambda, designated *Kalep*-80, was built in the greatest numbers. Its compression ratio was increased to 4.0:1, comparing with 3.8:1 for the prototype, yet it weighed 7kg (15lb) less and was rated at 85hp instead of the original 80hp. According to the records of the commission of the Chief Engineering Department of the Army, which inspected the factory in 1913, the company was able to build 500 to 1,000 engines per year. Other sources give more conservative estimates of up to 300 engines per year. However, because of the shortage of military orders, the actual production rate of the Motor factory was 13-14 engines per month in 1914. In addition, the factory also manufactured spare parts for Gnomes.

By then, several other aero-engine factories had been set up in Russia. In 1912 the French Gnome company established a branch in Moscow. The staff of this small factory, which was almost a workshop, initially consisted of sixteen persons, the sole Russian worker being a yard-keeper. On 19 April 1913 the factory built its first engine of the Lambda type. It did not have its own designers, all the work being performed in accordance with drawings received from France. Unlike Kalep's engines, the Moscow-built Gnomes were identical to those manufactured in France, the only difference being their Russian markings. The enterprise gradually expanded, and by 1914 its production rate had increased from seven to ten engines per month.

Russian designers persisted in their attempts to create an indigenous aero-engine. Self-taught mechanic and an inventor A.G. Ufimtsev worked on engine development in Kursk. Ufimtsev was developing and building an original type of aircraft (the Sferoplan, which had a circular wing), and engines for it. He designed his first engine in 1908 and built it a year later. It was a rotary, 2-cylinder, two-stroke 20hp engine. In the summer 1909 a Sferoplan with this engine made high-speed runs in a field, but failed to take off. In the same year Ufimtsev built an improved version of his engine.

In 1910-11 the inventor turned to a contrarotating rotary engine, several years earlier than the designers of the Siemens company in Germany. In such engines the crankshaft and crankcase rotated in opposite directions, reducing the loadings on the bearings and eliminating the effect of gyroscopic moment. Initially, Ufimtsev designed a 4-cylinder, 35-40hp 'birotary' engine (43hp according to some sources),

The 100hp Gnome Monosoupape.

followed this with a 6-cylinder 60hp engine. The former type was built in 1910 at the Shchetinin factory in St Petersburg, and underwent testing in June-July of that year. Weighing 50kg (110lb), the engine achieved 25hp during bench testing. In 1911 it was used in the Kostovich seaplane project, and in September 1911 Ufimtsev was granted a patent for his design. In November that year he submitted a new patent application for the engine, which could now operate both as a conventional rotary and as a 'birotary'. In its contrarotating form the engine drove two propellers in opposite directions, and had an estimated power of 80-90hp. Ufimtsev's application of was under consideration for a long time, and he was finally granted a patent for this engine in 1913.

A prototype of Ufimtsev's 6-cylinder engine was also built and bench tested. His engines did not have valves and solid crankcases, but had a load-bearing truss structure. In 1917 a group of enthusiasts at the Locomotive Factory in Bryansk built a 40hp engine of Ufimtsev's design, but none of these 'birotary' engines was installed on an aircraft.

In Kharkov, S.V. Grizodubov created a copy of the well-known Esnault-Pelterie (REP) engine, and then developed and built on his own 40hp engine (or 30hp according to some sources). This was an in-line, 4-cylinder, watercooled engine, which featured a rather short piston stroke. No information about this design has yet been found, but it is known that the engine drove two propellers through a chain drive, and that it weighed about 112kg (247lb). All the components of the engine except for cylinders were built by Grizodubov in his home workshop. In 1910-11 this engine was successively tested on three aeroplanes, but no one of them managed to take off.

In 1909 Russian engineer B.G. Lutskoy, working in Germany, built an aeroplane, *Lutskoy-1*, powered by two engines of his own design, known to be in-line, 50-60hp water-cooled units. The aircraft was tested in the fall of 1909.

In 1914 the management of the Dux aircraft factory in Moscow decided to embark on the production of aero-engines. Y.A. Meller, the factory's director, invited military engineer A.V. Nesterov to design an engine, and he produced the *Hypocycle* 7-cylinder, radial, watercooled engine. A unique feature of its design resulted from Nesterov's decision to reject the usual combination of master and articulated connecting rods. All of the *Hypocycle*'s connecting rods were equal in action, and were placed one after the other on the same journal of the crankshaft; thus all of the cylinders were positioned in different planes. This configuration increased the lengths of both crankshaft and engine. During testing, the engine reached 120hp, but one of its cylinders broke away after several hours of running. The *Hypocycle* was repaired, but as it did not promise any advantages over the other aero-engines available in Russia, it was preserved but no further work was carried out.

By the middle of 1914 not one Russian-designed aero-engine had reached a stage at which it was suitable for series production. At that time, however, foreign-designed engines and their variants were built in Russia in small quantities. Consequently the Russian aircraft industry was heavily dependant upon imported engines.

During the pre-war period mainly French and German engines were brought into Russia, but Italian, British and American powerplants also came into the country. In 1910-12 Russian aeroplanes were usually equipped with watercooled 55hp Renault and aircooled 30hp Anzani engines. However, 30hp Antoinette and 50hp Oerlikon engines were also purchased. Later, the in-line, watercooled Argus engines of 50, 80 and 100hp were imported from Germany. In 1913-14 these types were most frequently installed on Russian-built aeroplanes. The Argus engines, in particular, powered the first Sikorsky *Ilya Muromets* bombers. The Russian Military Ministry favoured the French Gnome engines, requiring their use on aeroplanes supplied to the Army. This choice was disputed by many specialists, as Gnomes were expensive, had low reliability and were inferior in many ways to German engines. For example, a 50hp Gnome cost 7,000 roubles and had 50hr period between major overhauls (actually, a maximum of 30hr), whereas a 100hp Argus cost 4,000 roubles and its real period between major overhauls was 100hr. Moreover, the French engines had considerably higher oil consumption and used castor oil, while the German engines used cheaper mineral oil. The political situation prevailing in the prewar period should be taken into consideration. Russia was an ally of France and Great Britain, and treated Germany as one of its main potential enemies, therefore the preference for the French engines is quite understandable.

In addition to purchasing seaplanes and flying-boats from the Curtiss Aeroplane and Motor Corporation in the USA, the Russian Navy acquired several engine batches produced by this company. In 1912-13 the Black Sea Fleet had seaplanes powered by 8-cylinder, watercooled 75hp Vee engines. It soon transpired that these engines suffered from cracking of the crankcase front section. In 1913 the Navy received twelve Curtiss flying-boats powered by 100hp Curtiss OX engines, and similar engines were purchased for installation in the aeroplanes built at the Shchetinin factory.

The First World War gave a strong impetus to the development of the Russian aero-engine industry, the Military Ministry issuing large-scale orders for engines. In 1915 the average monthly production rate of the Gnome factory in Moscow reached twenty-three engines. At the end of the year the 100hp Gnome Monosoupape became the primary type produced by the factory, and about forty such engines were produced in the first ten months of 1916. Next, the factory began to prepare for series production of the 110hp Le Rhône J rotary engine. By the fall of 1916 several tens of such engines had been assembled there. At the end of 1916 (after Gnome and Le Rhône had merged in 1915) the Moscow branch of the company employed more than 100 workers. At the beginning of 1917 the factory's monthly output reached forty engines and the number of staff had risen to 235.

With the coming of war the Motor factory at last received large-scale military orders. Engine production grew quickly, and *Kalep-80s* were installed on the Farman XVI biplanes widely used in Russia. However, in 1915, when German troops were approaching Riga, the factory was evacuated to Moscow, all lathes, reserve stocks of parts and subassemblies, engineering staff and some skilled workers being moved to the new location. The production department of the Motor factory in Moscow was headed by A.D. Shvetsov, destined to become a famous Soviet engine designer. After evacuation the factory continued to produce the well-proven *Kalep-80* at the rate of about twenty units per month, while preparations were begun for building the 120hp Le Rhône Jb. By the beginning of 1917 the factory had about 330 employees.

New engine-building enterprises appeared in Russia at this time. In July 1915 the French Salmson company opened a factory in Moscow, established under agreement between the company and the Chief Military-Technical Department of the Russian Military Ministry. The factory undertook assembly of three types of 9-cylinder watercooled radial engines from imported parts: the 130hp M.9, 150hp P.9 and 160hp R.9. The first engines were delivered in April 1916. About 300 employees worked at Salmson at the beginning of 1917, the factory's engineering-technical personnel mainly being French. By that time production of some engine accessories had been arranged inside Russia, and the factory built 50 to 100 engines per month.

In 1916 the Carriage-Automobile Factory of P. Ilyin in Moscow, which had been established eight years earlier, also turned to aero-engine production. The factory manufactured the British Beardmore engine, a high-rpm, geared engine of contemporary block-type layout. No information has been found to show whether the engines were fully manufactured at the Ilyin factory, or whether some components were imported from Britain.

ABOVE: **One of two Morane Monocoque monoplanes built in the Dux factory and powered by the 110hp Le Rhône engine, seen in the factory yard in 1917.**

ABOVE RIGHT: **This VI (Voisin of Ivanov) biplane, powered by Salmson engine, was built at the Anatra factory in Odessa.**

RIGHT: **A Russian-assembled Salmson engine.**

FAR RIGHT: **Salmson engines of different versions were installed in some variants of the *Ilya Muromets* heavy bomber.**

The factory probably built nearly all of the components, as even such sophisticated parts as crankshafts were manufactured in Russia at that time, being delivered from a factory in Sormovo. During 1916-17 a total of 25 Beardmores (20 according to another source) were produced in Russia. In 1917 the Ilyin factory planned to start manufacturing of 200hp Hispano-Suiza engines, but not one of the 200 engines ordered by the Military Ministry was built.

From July 1916 the Automobile-Carriage Repair Workshops of the Russkiy Reno company in Petrograd (renamed from St Petersburg after the beginning of the First World War) started assembling watercooled, 220hp vee Renault WC engines from imported parts. By September 1917 the company had assembled 98 engines of the batch of 150 units ordered by Military Ministry. It was planned to produce an improved version with pistons of aluminium instead of cast-iron and the power increased to 280hp.

After the beginning of the war the RBVZ also started producing aero-engines. One of a largest companies in Russia, it specialized in transport, building not only railway cars but also *Russobalt* automobiles and trucks and the famous *Ilya Muromets* bombers. The RBVZ factory in Riga manufactured automobile engines, while Argus aero-engines for Ilya Muromets were imported from Germany.

When Germany and Russia became enemies the importation of Argus engines was discontinued, and it became necessary to find an alternative powerplant for the *Ilya Muromets*. In the autumn of 1914 Shydlovskiy, head of RBVZ board, announced a contest for an indigenous aero-engine to replace the Argus. Two groups took part in the contest. One, under the leadership of V.V. Kireev, worked at the RBVZ factory in Riga, while the other, under the direct leadership of I.I. Sikorsky, was based at the RBVZ Mekhanicheskiy factory in Petrograd.

The Sikorsky engine, designated MRB-6 (*Motor Russko-Baltiyskiy-6*, or Russo-Baltic Engine 6), was a copy of the 140hp Argus. The RBVZ-6 engine designed by Kireev was based on the 150hp Benz engine. Both were 6-cylinder, in-line, watercooled engines. However, neither were exact copies of their foreign prototypes, as the Russian designers adapted them to enable the use of materials, components and production equipment available in Russia.

Kireev's engine was considered the better, and preparations were made for series production in Riga. Only five prototypes were built there, as in 1915 the factory was evacuated to Petrograd before Riga was surrendered to Germans. Some of the production equipment was left in Riga, and because the trains carrying the lathes impeded troop trains attempting to reach the front, they were derailed. As a result, the factory almost disappeared.

Consequently, the MRB-6 was introduced into series production at the Mekhanicheskiy factory in Petrograd as a transient type until series production of the RBVZ-6 was begun. An order for sixty-eight MRB-6s was received, and by August 1917 thirty-four had been assembled. In total about forty MRB-6s were built.

The MRB-6 was slightly lighter and shorter than the RBVZ-6, and was lower powered and less reliable. Moreover, the Mekhanicheskiy factory was hardly adhereing to the weights and power ratings specified by the Military Ministry.

To arrange production of the RBVZ-6, the RBVZ Motorniy factory was established in Petrograd, on a rented site of former wine warehouses. The personnel and equipment of the Riga-based factory that reached Petrograd formed the core of the new enterprise. In July 1916 the RBVZ Motorniy factory manufactured another batch of five engine prototypes, and then started to fulfil the order for the Russian Air Fleet. By March 1917 a total twenty-five engines had been built, and by September the number had risen to thirty-nine units. In total, the factory in Petrograd manufactured forty-five RBVZ-6s. These engines received favourable comments from the mechanics of the Squadron of Flying Ships (operating *Ilya Muromets* heavy bombers), who called them *Russobalt*.

In August 1915 the Duflon & Konstantinovich (DEKA) Joint Stock Company, with the support of the Military Ministry, received a State loan and acquired an uncompleted factory in Aleksandrovsk. Having invested huge resources into re-equipping the factory and building new facilities, in a year the company possessed the largest engine factory in Russia. Although the company had already received orders from the Air Fleet, it was not fully ready for series production.

Although the number of engine manufacturers was increasing, they could not keep pace with the demands of the aviation industry and armed forces. By 1 May 1916 the aircraft factories had received 461 Russian-built engines, which constituted only about 35 per cent of the quantity required.

As early as February 1916 the Russian

The MRB-6 engine.

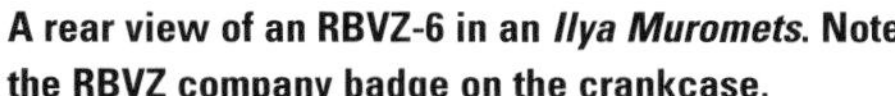

A rear view of an RBVZ-6 in an *Ilya Muromets*. Note the RBVZ company badge on the crankcase.

The *Ilya Muromets* series V was powered by four RBVZ-6s.

Government adopted a whole programme of automobile- and engine-building development. It was planned to establish five major enterprises to manufacture automobiles and engines, using loans provided by state. These factories were also to manufacture aero-engines, and the production plans for them had already been issued.

The Aksai factory was established in Nakhichevan, but it did not produce an engine before October 1917. Two factories were being erected at the same time in the outskirts of Moscow. The 'Kuznetsov, Ryabushinskiy, and Co.' had the support of the Italian Fiat company, but it did not start production before the October revolution, and the first AMO trucks left its workshops only in the 1920s. Aero-engines were never produced there. Today it is the AMO-ZIL automobile factory.

The RBVZ established a multi-purpose factory in Fili (Moscow region), which included automobile, engine and aircraft manufacture. It was planned to transfer RBVZ-6 engine production to this factory from Petrograd. Assembly of these engines, using Petrograd-built parts, began there in the summer of 1917, and about twenty units were completed. After the end of Russian Civil War the Fili factory was given as a concession to the Junkers company, and it later became the well-known Aircraft Factory No. 22, but no more engines were built there. It is now the Khrunichev Factory, which develops space systems.

The V.A. Lebedev Aeronautical Joint Stock Company built a factory in Yaroslavl, but this, too, was not finished before the Revolution. From the beginning of the 1930s it was the Yaroslavl Automobile Factory, and it then became the Yaroslavl Engine Factory. It manufactured trucks and tractors, and then diesel engines for these vehicles, but not for aircraft.

The fifth factory in this group was the Russkiy Reno enterprise in Rybinsk. By the middle of 1917 two of the four buildings planned had been erected, and the workshops started operating in April 1918, repairing automobiles and armoured cars. From 1928 the factory was converted to aero-engine construction, and today it is a parent enterprise of the Lyulka-Saturn company.

Neither DEKA nor the five factories laid up in 1916 managed to contribute to the production of aero-engines in Russia. Plans to set up the production of 200hp Hispano-Suizas at one of the A.A. Anatra factories in Odessa or Simferopol, in the south of Russia, also remained unfulfilled. In 1917 Anatra received an order for 200 such engines, but built none.

In 1916 negotiations were carried out with Glenn Curtiss regarding establishing a factory in Russia for aero-engine building and repair. The negotiations ceased following the crash of a Curtiss H-7TB flying-boat in Sevastopol, in which American pilot A. Jannus perished.

At the beginning of 1916 the Russian Air Fleet authorities turned their attention to the quality of aero-engines produced in Russia. Rotary engines were approaching the limit of their capabilities. Due to the high centrifugal forces, which loaded the cylinder attachment points, it was difficult to increase engine revolutions any further, and the impossibility of recycling oil from the rotating crankcase resulted in excessive oil consumption. Stationary in-line and radial engines with fixed crankcases and rotating crankshafts had no such disadvantages, and by that time in-line watercooled engines were in widespread use outside Russia. It was therefore decided to use the German 6-cylinder Mercedes engine, which had shown sufficient reliability and relative simplicity of production, as a basis for new type. A number of such engines had been captured on the Russo-German Front, and these were used as patterns.

Three Russian manufacturers, Motor, DEKA and Aksai, were tasked with arranging production of the Mercedes engines. Moscow-based Motor was to manufacture the 100hp and 168hp models, the 100hp, 129hp and 168hp engines were to be built by DEKA in Aleksandrovsk, and a 168hp engine was the responsibility of Aksai in Nakhichevan.

In fact, only two companies reached the stages of prototype manufacture and testing. The DEKA specialists, working under

A Sopwith 1½-Strutter reconnaissance aeroplane, powered by a 110hp Le Rhône engine, in service with the Red Air Fleet.

the leadership of engineer Vorobyov, created the DEKA M-100 (or DEKA M-101), a version of 100hp Mercedes. Engineering documentation was prepared by examining and measuring captured units. Trainee V.Ya. Klimov, later to became a famous engine designer, participated in the work on this engine. The M-100 prototype was built in August-September 1916, and attained 101hp (hence its second designation, M-101) during bench testing. According to records, the only such engine that had been accepted by the Military Ministry in 1916 was installed on the *Lebed* (Swan) biplane, but no information regarding its flight testing have been found. Series production of the M-100 had not begun before the October Revolution. Some development work was carried out on the other two engines, but the prototypes were not built.

The Motor factory in Moscow built a prototype batch of five 100hp Mercedes engines, but all were rejected by the military owing to various defects. On 14 May 1917, in the period of Provisional Government, the Air Fleet authorities cancelled Motor factory order and suggested replacing it with an additional batch of Le Rhône rotary engines.

As for totally original Russian engines of 1915-16 period, only the AMBS-1 created by A.A. Mikulin and B.S. Stechkin (both of whom later became prominent engine designers) is worthy of note. Developed during January-August 1915, this was a two-stroke 300hp engine of unusual layout, its cylinders being placed in parallel with each other. Each cylinder had two pistons moving in opposite directions, lateral movement being converted into rotary motion via two inclined discs placed on both sides of the engine. The fuel was supplied to combustion chambers via direct-injection nozzles. According to some sources, it might be concluded that the work was financed by the Duflon & Konstantinovich company.

In September 1915 the Osh & Weser factory in Moscow started manufacturing an AMBS-1 prototype, its assembly being completed in November 1916. A month later the engine was set up on a test bench in a shed at the Moscow Emperor's Technical High School, but ran for only three minutes before its piston rods bent. Up to February 1917 attempts were made to repair the AMBS-1 and proceed with testing, but they proved unsuccessful.

In conclusion, it is evident that all aero-engines in series production in Russia during the First World War were copies or variants of foreign engines. The output of Russia's aero-engine factories was insufficient to meet the demands of aircraft manufacturers, let alone the need for spare engines for the Air Fleet. This shortage was partly compensated for by importing Western powerplants.

During the war Russia imported aero-engines for Russian-manufactured aircraft from France and Great Britain, and later from Italy. Deliveries from France started in 1915, initially in small quantities. However, they had increased a year later, and were at their peak in the middle of 1917. The following French companies supplied engines to Russia: Gnome, Le Rhône, Salmson, Renault, Hispano-Suiza and Clerget (in smaller numbers). Different Gnome types were installed in Blériots and Nieuports produced at the Dux factory, in Farmans and Voisins built at the Shchetinin and Anatra factories, in *Lebed-VII* reconnaissance aeroplanes manufactured at the Lebedev factory, in the S-XVI fighters of the RBVZ factory, and in other aircraft types. Le Rhône engines powered Farman XX biplanes, *Lebed-X* reconnaissance aircraft and S-XX fighters. Salmsons were installed in the *Lebed-XII* and *Lebed-XIII*, *Anasal*, *Anatra DSS* and some B-type *Ilya Muromets* bombers. Renaults mainly powered G2-type Ilya Muromets.

Engine deliveries from Britain began in the autumn of 1916. Compared with the quantities supplied from France, they were not large. The engines were mainly of the

The Nieuport XVI fighter, built at the Dux factory in Moscow, was powered by the 80hp *Ron-80*.

The Moska MBbis had an 80hp *Ron-80* engine.

Sunbeam and Rolls-Royce Eagle types. The Sunbeams were supplied to the RBVZ for installation on B- and G-typ *Ilya Muromets* bombers, and they also powered some indigenous aeroplanes built in small quantities or as prototypes. The Eagle was not installed on Russian series-production aircraft.

The Italian-built Fiat 100hp A.10 and 200hp A.12, the 200hp SPA 6A, and the 100hp and 200hp Isotta-Fraschini powered Voisin, *Lebed-XIIbis* and *Anadis* landplanes and M-15 flying-boats. Aero-engines were also delivered together with imported aircraft.

The Russian Navy continued purchasing flying-boats and engines from the USA. In April-September 1915 about 100 160hp engines were imported (including two VX types), and 161 Curtiss engines were delivered to Russia.

The quantities of Russian orders quite often exceeded the capabilities of foreign engine manufacturers, leading to numerous delays in deliveries. For example, the Russian Military Attache in Rome, Duke Golitsin, ordered a total of 1,642 engines, but only 400 arrived in Russia. There are known cases when engines were delivered incomplete and could not be used. For instance, a large batch of engines was supplied from France without magnetos, and there was a shortage of these in Russia. Moreover, governments of the countries in which the engines were built sometimes commandeered them for their own use.

The delivery of cargoes to Russia during the First World War presented considerable difficulties. The route across the Baltic Sea was blockaded by the Germans, and across the Black Sea by the Turks. The remaining route lay across the White Sea (which freezes in winter) to Arkhangelsk. A single-track, narrow-gauge railway of low traffic capacity ran from Arkhangelsk to Vologda. In 1916 this railway was reconstructed to the standard gauge size. During the war another port, Nikolaevsk-on-Murman (now Murmansk), was brought into service and was connected with Petrograd by a single-track railway. The problems of cargo transportation from the ports resulted in crated engines being stored for long periods at the wharfs, where they gradually became unserviceable.

According to the estimates of the former Military Attache in Paris, Count A.A. Ignatyev, more than 4,000 engines were actually delivered to Russia. Some were transported from the Northern ports to the central part of Russia after the October Revolution.

The aero-engine shortage inevitably led to the use of captured units. Some 150 German aero-engines of different types were taken from the Front, both with aeroplanes and separately. Most were in-line watercooled engines such as the 100hp and 150hp Mercedes, 120hp, 140hp and 150hp Benz, and 160hp Maybach. In particular, these were used by the Lebedev factory in Petrograd, being installed in *Lebed-XI* two-seat reconnaissance aircraft. Maybach engines were installed in the *Svyatogor* bomber prototype, but turned out to be damaged and were intended to be replaced by Rolls-Royce Eagles (which, in their turn, were not received in time).

After the February Revolution of 1917 and demise of Tsar Nikolai II, Russia entered a period of political instability. Mutinies, and the dual power of the Provisional Government and the Soviets led to a complete collapse of the country's economy, which had been overheated by the war. Production began to fall sharply, and there was a downturn in the aero-engine industry. In the autumn of 1917 the total factory area and the number of workers in this industry were at their peak, there being 1,870 employees. But production had decreased approximately three times when compared with the level of 1916. Russian-built engines could cover at most only 5 per cent of the demand of the aircraft factories. Although it had placed orders for 2,290 aircraft, the Military Ministry received only 525 engines by October 1917, including imported units. In particular, the Dux factory received only twenty engines for sixty SPAD fighters being built there. In 1917 Russian factories assembled only between a quarter and a third of the planned number of aero-engines. For instance, the Gnome-Rhône factory delivered sixty-nine Le Rhône engines of 200 ordered, and sixty-one of 150 Monosoupapes, while the Salmson factory supplied 271 engines of 900 ordered.

The Provisional Government made attempts to remedy the situation by placing orders abroad. Negotiations with the US Government were carried out in July 1917, but not one engine ordered in this period was delivered to Russia.

The October Revolution paralyzed Russia's aviation industry to an even greater extent.

CHAPTER TWO

Tsarist Heritage

The powerplants considered to be the first Soviet aero-engines do not pertain to the Soviet period, as they had been introduced into series production before the February Revolution, in the time of Tsar Nikolai II. The orders placed by the Military Ministry of the Tsarist Government were formally valid both under the Provisional Government and, later, under the Bolsheviks during the first months of their rule. Despite the collapse of the country's transportation system, the breakdown of its economy and the total uncertainty of the political prospects, some enterprises continued to function, though production rates decreased sharply. However, in February-March 1918 industrial activity finally came to a halt.

Later, the engine types that had been built at the end of 1917 and the beginning of 1918 were included in the designation system for Soviet-built engines established in the 1920s. There were only three such engines.

An RBVZ-6 (M-1) engine in an *Ilya Muromets* bomber.

The first was the RBVZ-6 designed by V.V. Kireev. The RBVZ factory in Petrograd continued production of this type until March 1918. According to another source, the order for 150 engines was cancelled on 25 January 1918. The RBVZ-6 engines were successfully used on *Ilya Muromets* bombers in service in the Squadron of Flying Ships, and had a good reputation for their high reliability (for those days). The RBVZ-6 is considered the first Soviet piston aero-engine to be given the M-1 designation.

The second type was the French 110hp Le Rhône J rotary engine, which was in production at the Moscow Gnome-Rhône factory from August 1916. Manufacture of the improved version of this engine, the 120hp Le Rhône Jb, was being arranged at the Motor factory after its transfer from Riga to Moscow. The factory was given an order for 300 of these engines, but not one was assembled there before the October Revolution. Production at this factory ceased in August 1917.

In the Red Air Fleet the Le Rhône was designated M-2, and its assembly was resumed in December 1918; it was the first engine type actually built in Soviet Russia. It remained in production until 1930, by which time it had become completely obsolete. The M-2 was produced in large quantities because it was installed in the U-1 (a copy of the Avro 504), a primary training aircraft of the time.

The third engine, designated M-3, was also French; the 220hp Renault. This was assembled from imported parts at the Automobile-Carriage Workshops of the Russkiy Reno Joint Stock Company in Petrograd, which had received an order for 150. In his report to the RVS, made at the beginning of 1929, P.I. Baranov, the head of the UVVS, noted that this engine was in production from July 1916 to January 1918. However, other documents show that assembly was stopped in October

A rear view of an M-2 engine in storage in the Russian Air Force museum in Monino.

The U-1 trainer (the Soviet copy of the Avro 504) was powered by the M-2 engine.

The U-1 was also built in a floatplane version, designated MU-1.

1917, after the delivery of 98 engines. It is quite possible that the M-3 was not manufactured during the Soviet period, but only used and repaired.

M-1

The designation M-1 was assigned in the Soviet period to the RBVZ-6, manufactured by the RBVZ Motorniy factory in Petrograd. By March 1917 twenty-five had been built, and by September thirty-nine. A total of forty-five RBVZ-6s was built in Petrograd. According to Russian historian V. Mikheev, another twenty were later assembled in Fili.

The RBVZ-6 was installed in V- and G-series *Ilya Muromets* bombers.

Characteristics

6-cylinder, in-line vee, watercooled, direct-drive engine

Power rating	150hp
Bore/stroke	130/180mm (5.12/7.09in)
Volume	8.61 litres (525cu in)
Weight	292kg (644lb)

M-2

This was a copy of the French Le Rhône J engine, a production licence having been acquired during the period of Tsarist Government. The M-2 was manufactured during July-August 1919 at the GAZ No. 2 factory in Moscow, and series production started in 1925. Production ceased in 1930. About 2,000 engines of this type were built, including 1,014 in the post-revolution period.

The engine was manufactured in two versions:

M2-110 – a copy of Le Rhône J engine with cast-iron pistons. Power rating, 110hp.

M2-120 – a copy of Le Rhône Jb engine with aluminium pistons. Power rating, 120hp.

The M-2 was installed in the U-1 and MU-1 series production aeroplanes, the MUR-1 and MUR-2 prototypes, the KASKR-1 autogyro prototype, and on the TsAGI 1-EA, TsAGI 3-EA and TsAGI 5-EA helicopter prototypes.

Characteristics

9-cylinder, radial rotary, four-stroke, direct-drive, air-cooled engine

Bore/stroke	112/170mm (4.41/6.69in)
Volume	15.07 litres (920cu in)
Compression ratio	4.5:1.
Weight	145kg (320lb) (M-2-120 version)

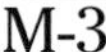

M-3

The French Renault WC engines were assembled from imported parts by the Automobile-Carriage Workshops of the Russkiy Reno company in Petrograd. A *Reno-220* designation was also used for this engine type. By September 1917 ninety-eight of the ordered batch of 150 had been built. Later it was planned to arrange production of the improved version of the engine with aluminium pistons instead of the cast iron ones, with power rating increased up to 280hp.

The M-3 was installed in V- and G-series *Ilya Muromets* bombers, and in the prototype GASN torpedo bomber.

Characteristics

12-cylinder, in-line vee, direct-drive engine

Power rating	220/225hp
Bore/stroke	125/150mm (4.92/5.91in)
Weight	367kg (809lb)

Renault WC (M-3) engines were installed in a prototype of the GASN torpedo bomber designed by D.P. Grigorovich.

CHAPTER THREE

Eight-cylinder Hispano-Suiza Engines

The French Hispano-Suiza engines, which were of quite advanced design (introducing cast cylinder blocks for the first time), had attracted the interest of Russian aircraft manufacturers before the October Revolution of 1917. In 1916 the Carriage-Automobile Factory of P. Ilyin in Moscow started aero-engine production by assembling British Sunbeam engines. From December that year this factory was also arranging production of the 200hp Hispano-Suiza 8Ab, but, according to UVVF data, none had been completed there by April 1918. The Odessa-based Anatra factory also received an order for 200 such engines, but it is unlikely that production was started there.

In December 1918 the Command of the Air Fleet of the Workers' and Peasants' Red Army (*Vozdushniy Flot Raboche-Krestyanskoy Krasnoy Armii*, RKKVF) placed an order with the Motor factory in Moscow for 100 Hispano-Suiza engines, given the name *Russkiy Ispano* (Russian Hispano). In fact, the first engine, also designated M-4, was not completed until July 1920, by which time the M-4 had become rather outdated. Fewer than forty engines of this type were built, and in 1922 it was phased out of production.

In 1923 specialists at the Ikar factory in Moscow prepared the drawings of a 300hp Hispano-Suiza 8Fb based on a specimen engine purchased in France. However, series production of this type, under the designation M-6, was transferred to the GAZ No. 9 Bolshevik factory (former DEKA) in Zaporozhye. Preparations for production were begun there as early as April 1923, but the factory itself was in an incomplete state (it had also been partly destroyed during the Civil War). Setting up engine production took a long time, and GAZ No. 9 did not manufacture its first batch of ten M-6s until April 1925. By then the engine was quite unsuitable for aircraft manufacturers, but it nevertheless remained in series production until 1930.

In 1925 plans of further modernization of the M-6 were considered. Factory specialists suggested that a unified family of engines based on the type be created, including 4-cylinder, 8-cylinder (M-6), and 12-cylinder engines using, respectively, one, two and three cylinder blocks from the M-6. A project for a 150hp 4-cylinder engine, using up to 90 per cent of the parts of the basic powerplant, had been prepared by September 1925. The 12-cylinder, W-configuration, three-block 150hp engine, designated in documents merely as the *Ispano W*, was under development in April-June 1926.

However the Aviatrest had its own plans for Hispano-Suiza engines. In June 1925 the GAZ No. 9 factory was ordered to copy a new 450hp Vee engine produced by the French company. To do this, a small design bureau headed by engineer B.S. Andrykhevich was established at the factory by 1 October. The new engine was to be installed in the 2IN-1 fighter, but in January 1926 the order was cancelled and the design bureau closed down. The project, designated M-6A, was not completed.

The M-4 engine.

An M-4 displayed in the Polytechnic Museum in Moscow.

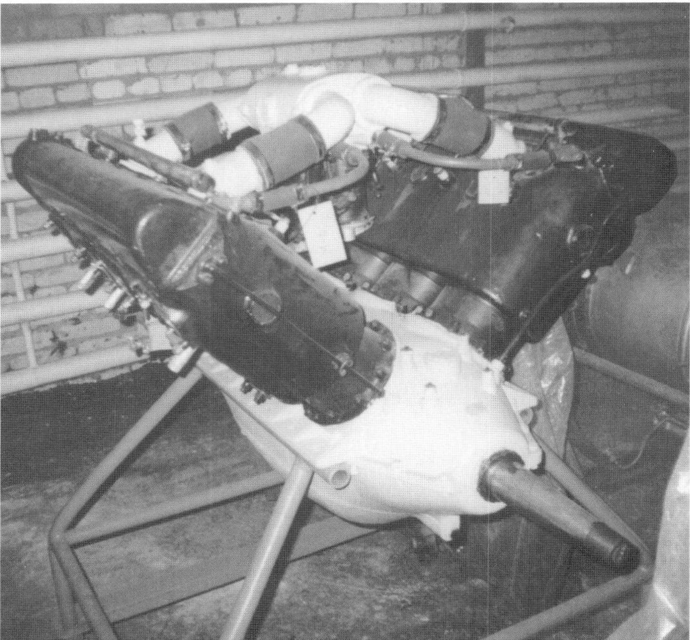

The M-6 engine on display in the Monino museum.

Another direction in M-6 modernization was taken at the NAMI. During May-October 1928 A.A. Mikulin prepared a project to convert the engine to air cooling. Designated M-21, the prototype was built in February 1929 at the Bolshevik (former Obukhovskiy) factory in Leningrad. No information on its testing has yet been traced.

Production of the M-6 aero-engine ceased in 1930, but another application was found for it, a derated M-6T12 version with lower compression ratio being built for installation in Soviet tanks. These engines remained in series production at Zaporozhye until 1932.

M-4

The M-4 was a copy of the French Hispano-Suiza 8Ab, the production licence for which was acquired in 1916. Initially, the engine was named *Russkiy Ispano*.

An order for 100 engines was issued in December 1918. The manufacture of production plant and the mastering of production technology took the whole of 1919. The first engine was completed in July 1920 at the Ikar factory in Moscow, and it completed bench testing on 24 March 1921. Thirty-six engines were built up to 1922, when the now-outdated M-4 was phased out of production.

The M-4s were used as replacements for Hispano-Suiza engines on Western aeroplanes in Russian service.

Characteristics

8-cylinder, in-line vee, four-stroke, watercooled, geared engine

Power rating	200/300hp
Bore/stroke	120/130mm (4.72/5.12in)
Volume	11.76 litres (718cu in)
Compression ratio	5.3:1
Weight	240kg (529lb)

M-6

This was a copy of the French Hispano-Suiza 8Fb. The production drawings, based on a sample purchased in France, were prepared in 1923 at the Ikar factory. Initially the engine was designated *Ispano-300*.

Production was being arranged at GAZ No. 9 factory in Aleksandrovsk from 1924. The first series-built engine passed State testing in May 1925, and the type was in production until 1932. In all, 331 were built.

The following versions of the M-6 are known:

M-6: aero-engine. Compression ratio – 5.35:1-5.45:1. Weight – 275kg (606lb).

M-6T12: tank version with modified pistons and cylinder-heads. Compression ratio – 4.75:1.

The M-6 was installed as a replacement of the original French engines in Fokker D.XI and Martinsyde F.4 aircraft, and also in series-built P-2 aircraft and the K-4 prototype. The M-6T12 was installed in T-12 light tanks.

Characteristics

8-cylinder, in-line vee, four-stroke, watercooled, direct-drive engine

Power rating	300/340hp
Bore/stroke	140/150mm (5.51/5.91in)
Volume	18.48 litres (1,128cu in)

M-6A

This project, based on the 450hp Hispano-Suiza, was under development from June 1925 until January 1926 at the design bureau of the GAZ No. 9 factory, under the leadership of B.S. Andrykhevich. The prototype engine was not completed.

Characteristics

8-cylinder, in-line vee, four-stroke, watercooled engine

Power rating	450hp

ISPANO I

This project, for a single-row engine using one block from the M-6, was developed at the GAZ No. 9 factory. Development was completed in September 1925, but the prototype was not built.

Characteristics

4-cylinder, in-line, four-stroke, watercooled, direct-drive engine

Power rating	150/170hp
Bore/stroke	140/150mm (5.51/5.91in)
Volume	9.24 litres (564cu in)
Compression ratio	5.35:1

ISPANO W

This project for a W-configuration engine using three M-6 cylinder blocks was being developed at the GAZ No. 9 factory in April-June 1926. The prototype was not built.

Characteristics

12-cylinder, in-line W-shaped, four-stroke, watercooled, direct-drive engine

Power rating	450/510hp
Bore/stroke	140/150mm (5.51/5.91in)
Volume	27.72 litres (1,692cu in)
Compression ratio	5.35:1.

The T-24 tank, built in small series, was powered by the M-6T12.

M-21

This was a modification of the M-6, introducing of air-cooling and using the cylinders from the M-12 (described later). The project was completed at NAMI by A.A. Mikulin in May-October 1928. The prototype engine was built in February 1929 at the Bolshevik factory in Leningrad. No information on its testing has been found.

Characteristics

8-cylinder, in-line vee, four-stroke, air-cooled, direct-drive engine

Bore/stroke	140/150mm (5.51/5.91in)
Volume	18.48 litres (1,128cu in)

BELOW: **An M-6 installed in a Fokker D.XI fighter.**

CHAPTER FOUR

RAM: the First Soviet High-powered Aero-engine

The GAZ No.4 Motor factory in Moscow had a small design department that actively supported the growth of the young Soviet state's aero-engine industry. This department carried out the work of adapting the French Hispano-Suiza 8Ab and 8Fb engines to use available materials and production equipment. The department also refined the M-5, and started development of the M-100 (M-11) 'trainer' engine.

As early as September 1923 the design department of the Motor factory began creating the first Soviet high-powered aero-engine, designated RAM (an abbreviation of *Russkiy Aviatsionniy Motor*, or Russian Aero Engine). The development work on this 12-cylinder, watercooled vee engine was headed by A.D. Shvetsov and P.A. Moisheev. On 26 October 1923 the preliminary project was approved by the NK UVVS, and the manufacture of components was started at the end of the year. In parallel, more accurate calculations were made and revised drawings issued. The project was completed in July 1924, and by the beginning of November 1924 about a half of the parts had been manufactured and almost all forgings and castings were prepared. Engine assembly was delayed by relocation of the factory, and then by defects in the forgings.

Assembly of the RAM, designated M-8 by the UVVS, was completed in January 1926. During cold running several failures occurred, and full-scale testing did not begin until July. The M-8 underwent bench testing for almost a year, and a range of defects were revealed, including burnt-though pistons.

During the three years that elapsed before development was completed, the engine became outdated. As it was also overweight and had poor reliability, the M-8 was no longer of interest to the UVVS.

In 1925 an improved RAM-2 version was being developed, but no information about manufacture of the prototype has been found.

M-8 (RAM)

Developed in 1923-24 at the Motor factory in Moscow under the leadership of A.D. Shvetsov and P.A. Moisheev. The prototype underwent testing from July 1926, but failed owing to burnt-through pistons and detonation in the cylinders.

The following versions of the engine are known:

RAM – original version. Single prototype built.

RAM-2 – a project of 1925. No details of this version have been found.

Characteristics

12-cylinder, in-line vee, four-stroke, watercooled, direct-drive engine

Power rating	750/750hp
Bore/stroke	165/200mm (6.50/7.87in)
Volume	51.0 litres (3,112cu in)
Compression ratio	5.4:1
Weight	760kg (1,675lb)

CHAPTER FIVE

Soviet-built Liberty Engines

The quite successful Ford A12-400 Liberty engine, introduced into series production in the USA in 1917, aroused interest in Russia even before the October Revolution of 1917. However, a thorough examination of this engine took place only during the Civil War. In the South of Russia the Red Army captured from the White Russians several Liberty powered Airco (de Havilland) D.H.9A reconnaissance aeroplanes. One of these aircraft was transported to Moscow, and in 1920 it was tested at the Scientific Experimental Airfield (*Nauchno-Opitniy Aerodrom*, NOA).

After the First World War the young Soviet State purchased from Great Britain a number of D.H.9A airframes which were now surplus to RAF requirements. These aircraft were to equip the Red Air Fleet, but the Soviets did not have suitable engines, and at first the Daimler engines that had been purchased earlier were used. These were later supplemented by British-built Siddeley Puma engines. At the same time, production of the D.H.9A (designated R-1) was being set up in Moscow using engineering drawings received before the October Revolution.

The Moscow-based Ikar factory was tasked with copying the Liberty and arranging its series production. From June 1922 the factory began to prepare the necessary documentation, and as early as November 1922 the first engines (designated M-5) were assembled. Unlike their American-built counterparts and the British license-built copies, which were manufactured to Imperial dimensions, the Soviet engines were built to metric dimensions, with an applicable system of tolerances and fits. In the meantime, negotiations were carried out with Junkers regarding the possibility of Liberty production at the factory in Fili, which was offered to Germans on concession basis.

The Bolshevik factory in Leningrad (the former Obukhovskiy factory) also started to build the M-5, using drawings received from the Ikar factory. It is notable that the Bolshevik factory had never been an aircraft-building factory, and belonged not to the Aviatrest but to the Ordnance-Armoury Trust. The engines from Moscow and Leningrad were different, as the Ikar factory was introducing changes to the design. Some of these improvements were copied from American engines built after the war (these engines were being obtained from the USA up to 1930). By September 1925 680 M-5s had been built in Moscow.

The Bolshevik factory tried to follow in Ikar's footsteps, and was also attempting to introduce the changes into the design, but was considerably behind schedule. Consequently, many parts and units built at these factories were not interchangeable.

Fuel pumps, fuel system components and the complete ignition system for the M-5 were imported from abroad. The ignition system was imported because of its unusual nature. In spite of its high power rating the Liberty had an automobile-type ignition system (though it was provided with two spark-plugs per cylinder), and nothing of this type had been produced in Russia. Some of the engines also received American-built crankshafts purchased from the Atlas and Packard companies. For instance, a complete engine series, 'Zh', built at Moscow factory, was fitted with such crankshafts. This forced the factories to produce engines using mixed metric/Imperial systems.

Rather primitive production technology resulted in considerable variations of engine weight (from 410 to 420kg (904 to

The M-5 engine built at the Bolshevik factory in Leningrad.

The R-1 light bomber and reconnaissance aircraft, powered by the M-5, was a Soviet-designed version of the British D.H.9A. The R-1 was the most numerous aircraft in service with the VVS RKKA at the end of the 1920s.

926lb)), compression ratio (the engines built in Moscow up to the series 'Z' had compression ratios from 5.25:1 to 5.3:1, while in later series it was increased to levels from 5.35:1 to 5.45:1), and nominal power rating.

In 1925-26 only three types of aero-engine were in series production in the Soviet Union, the M-2, M-5 and M-6, the M-5 being the mass-produced type. However, these engines, which had been developed during the First World War, became obsolete and required modernization.

As early as 1923, work on the creation of Soviet versions of the Liberty (as well as new types based upon it) had been started. Soviet designers carried out the development in two main directions: to modify the engine's structure to suit the capabilities of the indigenous aviation industry, and to increase the engine's power rating. The idea of developing the Liberty did not gain overall support. There were also suggestions to start building other foreign-designed aero-engines, such as the Napier Lion, Wright T3 or Lorraine-Dietrich 12E, or to concentrate all effort on the development of original indigenous powerplants. However, in 1925, when production of the M-5 was in full swing and it had become the primary engine in service with the VVS RKKA, development of an engine family based on the Liberty was officially recognized by Aviatrest and the UVVS as the primary approach. The NAMI, Ikar (GAZ No. 2) and Bolshevik factories were given orders to develop boosted versions of the M-5 with power ratings of 500-600hp. As a result, development of a Liberty-based engine family was started.

The basic M-5 engine, retaining the initial 400hp power rating, was to be given a traditional aviation-type ignition system with magneto. The cylinders' vee angle was to change to 60°, as this had been found to be more efficient for the engine's balance. A specification for the 'M-5 with 60° vee angle' (later designated M-10) was issued in 1924. At the end of that year the Aviatrest administration approved the project for such modifications, to be carried out at the Ikar factory. The prototype was to be ready as early as 1925, but by 1 January 1926 it was only half-completed. By that time production of the ignition system components for the M-5 had been arranged in the USSR, so the modified engine now seemed unnecessary, and it was excluded from the plan of work for 1926. However, in August 1926 assembly of the M-10 was completed, and the engine passed its testing programme in September-December of that year.

Later, the idea of the M-5 modification was revived. In February 1928 the State Institute of Electricity and Energy (*Gosudarstvenniy Elektro-Energeticheskiy Institut*, GEEI) and Factory No. 24 (the merged Ikar and Motor factories) proposed a project for an 'M-5 with magneto'. In November 1928 a prototype of such an engine was built, and during December 1928-November 1929 it underwent factory testing. By that time M-5 manufacture had ceased, and the new version was not put into production.

The designers' major efforts were concentrated on boosting the engine's power. Three methods were used to achieve this: quantitative (increasing the number of cylinders while adhereing to the main parameters of Liberty engine operation), qualitative (retaining the general layout while increasing the rpm, compression ratio and supercharging), and using different combinations of the two previous methods.

Work on the quantitative method started earliest. Under a decree of the Aviatrest Technical Committee issued on 10 November 1923, creation of 16-cylinder X-shaped engine useing the cylinders from the Liberty was started. The work was carried out under the leadership of G.M. Gorokhov, and the main calculations were done at the NAMI. On 3 April 1924 the UVVS Scientific Committee approved the preliminary project. Development had been completed by September 1925, and the engine was designated M-9. However, the prototype was not built, as the design was considered too sophisticated.

This R-1, powered by an M-5 fitted with a General Electric turbo-supercharger, was tested at the NII VVS.

The designers at Factory No.24 chose the qualitative method of M-5 development, and created the M-14 engine. The group included such specialists as A.D. Shvetsov and V.A. Dobrynin, later to become famous for their engine work. The M-14 retained the main design features of the Liberty, but was goven bored and shortened cylinders, a new crankshaft (contrary to the specification, which required that the most complex parts of the Liberty be retained), and a second fuel pump. Using the experience gained during previous work (first of all on the M-10), the designers introduced a 60° angle between the cylinder blocks and an ignition system using magnetos. Compared with the M-5, the engine's rpm and compression ratio were increased.

It was intended that the M-14 would form the basis of a whole family, including the M-14P inverted-vee engine and the M-16 single-row engine, a 'half M-14' for conversion-training aeroplanes. However,

An M-5 on display in the Monino museum.

An M-5 in an R-3M5 reconnaissance aeroplane. Only Soviet-built engines were permitted to be installed in this aircraft type, as the original Liberty, being lighter, caused a dangerous change in the aircraft's centre of gravity.

development of these two powerplants was not completed.

The M-14 prototype was assembled in May 1928 and passed bench tests under the factory and State testing programmes. The State testing ended with a failure. A broken pin flew out, ricocheted off the testing control cabin and smashed into the rotating wooden drag propeller (used to create the necessary resistance when the engine was running). Refinement of the M-14 lasted for a whole year, but it was not introduced into production.

Almost the same approach to Liberty modernization was chosen by the engineers of the NAMI, where specialists N.R. Brilling and Aleksandrov prepared a project to boost the M-5 to 450hp. The main friction bearings were to be replaced by roller bearings, the crankshaft cranks widened and the crankcase strengthened. This remained a paper project, but a number of its innovations were included in the project for the V18-I engine (which was also designated W18, and for some time M-14). This engine had three, instead of two, rows of cylinders in W configuration. As a result, its power was increased half as much again compared with the M-5. In addition to the changes stipulated in the earlier project it featured lug suspension of the crankshaft, shortened pistons (the M-5's pistons were too long for an aero-engine), articulated connecting rods of circular cross-section, and magneto ignition. N.R. Brilling and V.M. Yakovlev participated in the creation of the V18-I. As more refinements were introduced, fewer components remained from the original M-5, and in the end this engine became an almost completely different powerplant.

By the end of the 1920s all work on M-5 modernization had ceased, and production of this engine type was gradually being reduced. The Bolshevik factory in Leningrad began to convert the earlier M-5s into tank engines, and also carried out overhaul and modification of the used engines that had been purchased in the USA. Tank versions of the M-5 engine were installed on the Soviet BT-2 and BT-5 tanks.

In 1930 the M-5 was phased out of production (production in Leningrad was stopped in 1929), though some UWS officials considered such a decision untimely, as flying schools were still equipped with a large number of R-1 biplanes powered by the engine. As a result of persistent requests, production was resumed for short time in 1932, and 80 M-5s were built.

In 1935 an M-5 engine was fitted with American turbo-supercharger produced by General Electric, and underwent flight testing at the NII VVS. These were the first flights of a turbo-supercharged engine in the Soviet Union. During July-October 1935 the R-1 powered by this engine performed 17 flights. However the M-5 was used for this experiment only because it was suitable for the supercharger type, and the interest lay in the turbo-supercharger and its capabilities.

The M-5 was used in flying schools until the second half of the 1930s.

M-5

This was a copy of Ford A12-400 Liberty engine. The engineering drawings for the M-5 were being prepared from June 1922, based on a captured American Liberty. The powerplant's development and introduction into series production was carried out under the leadership of A.A. Bessonov and M.P. Makaruk.

The order for the engine's series production was issued in September 1922. The first engines were built in November at GAZ Factory No. 2, the prototype passed State tests in December 1923, and the first series batch was accepted in 1924. The M-5 was in series production at the GAZ No. 2 factory in Moscow and at the Bolshevik factory in Leningrad until 1930. In total 2,829 engines were built (480 of them at the Bolshevik factory); it was produced in greater numbers than any other Soviet aero-engine of the1920s.

Later-series engines had tulip-shaped valves, a modified design of synchronization mechanism, a strengthened gas-distribution mechanism and a higher number of parts made from light alloys.

In December 1926 two types of starter for the M-5 were developed at the TsKB Department of Land-based Aircraft Development, under the leadership of N.N. Polikarpov; the Type III hand-starter and an inertia starter of Aeromarine type.

The M-5 powered the following aircraft types: R-1, MR-1, R-3M5, Fokker C.IV,

A BT-2 high-speed tank powered by an M-5.

The tank version of the M-5 had a forced-air-cooling fan.

I-2bis and R-4 (prototype). It was also used in the 3BL-3, 4BL-3, 2B-L2 and L-2 aircraft projects.

A tank version of this engine, equipped with a forced-air-cooling fan, was built and installed on BT-2 (later series), BT-5 and BT-5A tanks.

In the summer of 1935 an M-5 was fitted with a General Electric turbo-supercharger in the workshops of the NII VVS, under the leadership of P.N. Pavlyuchuk. This powerplant underwent flight testing in July-October 1935.

The M-5 formed the basis of a number of experimental designs and unrealized projects. Some of its components were used in the design of other Soviet powerplants.

Characteristics

12-cylinder, in-line vee, four-stroke, direct-drive, water-cooled engine

Power rating	400/440hp
Bore/stroke	127/178mm (5.00/7.01in)
Volume	27.01 litres (1,648cu in)
Compression ratio	5.4:1 (early series – 5.25:1 to 5.35:1)
Weight	410-420kg (904-926lb)

M-9 (Liberty X)

For some time the designation M-9 was used for the engine developed by Starostin. Later it was transferred to a projected X-shaped 16-cylinder engine developed by G.M. Gorokhov and using components and units of the mass-produced M-5.

Work on the M-9 project was carried out under a decree of the Aviatrest Technical Committee issued on 10 November 1923. The preliminary project was approved by the Scientific Committee on 3 April 1924.

The engineering development was carried out between November 1924 and September 1925, and the main calculations were made at the NAMI. However, the engine was considered too sophisticated, and the prototype was not built.

Characteristics

16-cylinder, in-line X-shaped, four-stroke, watercooled, direct-drive engine

Power rating	500/530hp
Bore/stroke	127/178mm (5.00/7.01in)
Compression ratio	5.4:1

M-10

This was a modification of the M-5 with a 60° angle between cylinder blocks and an ignition system using a magneto. A specification for 'the M-5 with 60° vee angle' was issued in 1924. The preliminary project was developed under the leadership of A.A. Bessonov at the Ikar factory and approved at the end of 1924. Engineering development was carried out during January-August 1925, and the prototype was built from September 1925 to August 1926 (according to the plan, it was to be completed in 1925). The engine passed bench testing in September-December 1926, but was not introduced into series production.

Characteristics

12-cylinder, in-line vee, direct-drive, four-stroke, water-cooled engine

Power rating	400/440hp.
Bore/stroke	127/178mm (5.00/7.01in)
Volume	27.01 litres (1,648cu in)
Compression ratio	5.4:1

M-14

This engine, a further development of the M-5 and M-10, was developed under the leadership of A.A. Bessonov and V.A. Dobrynin at the GAZ No.4 factory (and later at OMO TsKB) from July 1926. On 26 March 1927 the NK UVVS approved the general layout of the engine. The engineering development was carried out from May to September 1927. Compared with the M-5, the M-14 had higher rpm, its cylinders were shorter and of increased bore, the cylinders' vee angle was 60° (instead of 45°), the crankshaft was strengthened and shortened (not in accordance with specification), and a new magneto ignition system was introduced. Initially, a GCS installation was also planned. The M-14 was expected to become the main rival of the V12 engine developed at NAMI. During manufacture the cover of the distribution mechanism was modified, and a Farman-type powder self-starter introduced. Two M-14 prototypes were built In October 1927-April 1928, the second having increased compression ratio.

Factory testing of the prototypes was carried out from March 1928. In September-November the first prototype underwent testing at the NII VVS, but this ended when the engine broke down. Water leaks, bearing spalling and broken pins were noted, and the engine was returned to the factory for repair and refinement. The second prototype was submitted for acceptance testing on 4 March 1929, and passed in March-April. For the years 1928-29 Factory No. 24 was instructed to manufacture a prototype batch of twenty M-14s, but in December 1928 it was proposed that all work on the

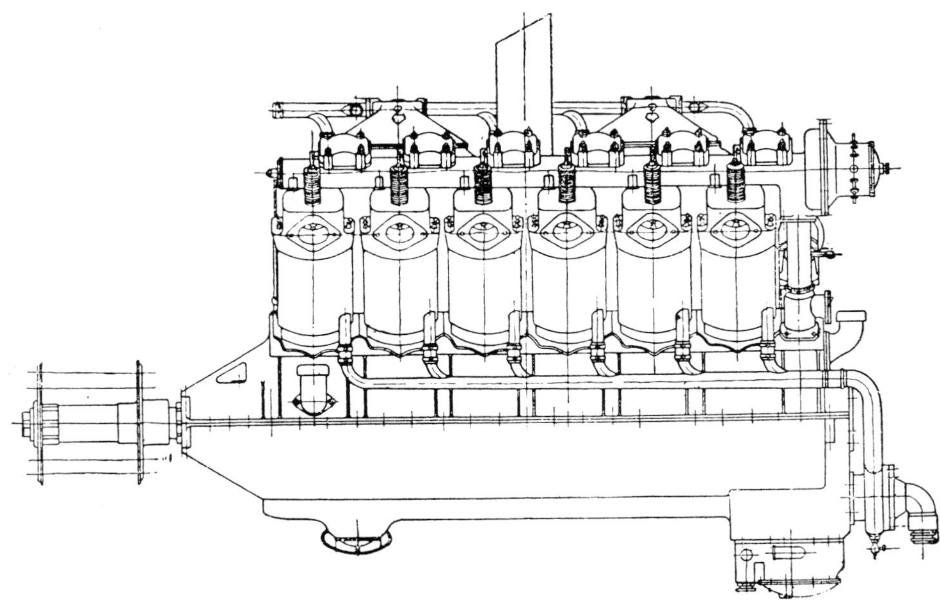

A side elevation of the M-14 engine.

Cadets of the RKKA Academy of Mechanization and Motorization study the M-5 engine of a BT-5 tank.

engine be cancelled, and it did not enter series production.

It was planned to install the M-14 in the MRT-1, L-2 and K-5 aeroplanes.

Characteristics

12-cylinder, in-line vee, direct-drive, four-stroke, water-cooled engine

Power rating	450/480hp (450/500hp according to the project)
Bore/stroke	130/170mm (5.12/6.69in) (according to the project, 130/178mm (5.12/7.01in))
Volume	27.1 litres (1,654cu in) (according to the initial project, 28.2 litres (1,721cu in))
Compression ratio	6.0:1 (initially 5.4:1, and 6.25:1 for the second prototype)
Weight	415kg (915lb) (later improved to 407kg (897lb))

M-14P

This was an inverted version of the M-14. The project was to be completed as early as 1926, but owing to insufficient financing it was not finished until March 1928 at the OMO TsKB of Factory No. 24. According to the plan, the prototype engine was to be built by 1 November 1928, but its manufacture was not started.

Characteristics

12-cylinder, in-line inverted-vee, direct-drive, four-stroke, watercooled engine

Power rating	450/500hp
Bore/stroke	130/170mm (5.12/6.69in)
Volume	27.1 litres (1,654cu in)
Compression ratio	6.0:1

M-16 (Liberty I)

This projected engine, using one block of cylinders from the M-14, was intended for installation on conversion-training aeroplanes. The project was completed in February-May 1928 at the OMO TsKB of Factory No. 24. No information about prototype manufacture has been found.

Characteristics

6-cylinder in-line, direct-drive, four-stroke, watercooled engine

Power rating	200/250hp
Bore/stroke	130/170mm (5.12/6.69in)
Compression ratio	6.0:1
Weight	250kg (551lb) (according to the specification)

M-5 equipped with magneto

This was a modification of the M-5 incorporating an ignition system using a magneto. It was developed by Factory No. 24 in co-operation with the GEEI during September 1927-February 1928. The prototype engine was under construction from March to November 1928, and underwent testing from December 1928 to February 1929. This version was not introduced into series production.

Characteristics

12-cylinder in-line vee, direct-drive, four-stroke, water-cooled engine

Power rating	400/440hp
Bore/stroke	127/178mm (5.00/7.01in)
Volume	27.01 litres (1,648cu in)
Compression ratio	5.4:1
Weight	420kg (926lb)

Project of Brilling and Aleksandrov

In 1924-25 designers N.R. Brilling and Aleksandrov, working at the NAMI, prepared a project for an improved M-5, boosted in rpm to a nominal power rating of 450hp. Unlike the standard M-5 it had main roller bearings, wider cranks in the crankshaft, a strengthened crankcase and three carburettors instead of two. The prototype was not built, but some elements of its design were later used in the V18-1 engine project.

Characteristics

12-cylinder in-line vee, direct-drive, four-stroke, water-cooled engine

Nominal power rating	450hp
Bore/stroke	127/178mm (5.00/7.01in)
Volume	27.01 litres (1,648cu in)
Compression ratio	5.4:1

Liberty W18 (V18-I)

The V18-I engine was being developed at the NAMI from May 1925 under the leadership of N.R. Brilling and V.M. Yakovlev. The preliminary project was completed in October 1925 and approved by the UVVS Scientific Committee and Aviatrest. The engineering development was carried out from December 1925 to May 1926. The Aviatrest excluded the project from the plan for 1926 because of funding shortfall, and the development was continued at NAMI under the institute's own initiative. The engine had a crankshaft on roller bearings with lug suspension, shortened pistons, magneto ignition and articulated connecting rods of circular cross-section. After the project refinement, the only remaining components of the original M-5 design were the upper part of the cylinders and a part of the gas-distribution mechanism.

In September 1926 the NAMI made an attempt to conclude an agreement with the GAZ No. 4 (Ikar) factory for building the engine prototype, but this proved in vain.

Characteristics

18-cylinder in-line W-shaped, direct-drive, four-stroke, watercooled engine

Power rating	600/700hp
Bore/stroke	127/178mm (5.00/7.01in)
Compression ratio	5.4:1.

The Engines of the GAZ No. 2 Ikar Factory and Their Evolution

Apparently the first original engine developed at the Ikar factory was a small one designed by A.A. Bessonov in 1923-24. On 5 May 1923 the UVVS issued an order for a 20hp engine, designated M-7. To meet this requirement Bessonov designed a 2-cylinder, two-stroke engine with port-slot gas-distribution.

Manufacture of the prototype engine was started in May 1924. By the end of October the M-7 was assembled, but the resolution of minor defects took about two weeks more. On 11 October the engine was shown to the UVVS Commission, and after that it underwent factory testing. The M-7 was under test until mid-1925, and was then handed over to the Air Force Academy as a teaching aid.

During November 1925-February 1926 Bessonov designed an improved version of this engine rated at 30hp, but it type did not attract any customer interest.

On 23 March 1925 the UVVS Scientific Committee approved a specification for a new high-powered engine intended for air force use. The power rating of this water-cooled engine was set at 600-700hp, its compression ratio was to be 5.4:1-6.6:1 (depending on available fuel), and it was to have not more than six cylinders per row. A carburettor was required. In June the Scientific Committee issued an official order to Aviatrest for the development of an engine able to meet these requirements.

The NAMI, GAZ No. 4 Motor and GAZ No. 2 Ikar factories entered the competition to fulfil this requirement. Already, by May 1925, the Ikar factory's design department had started to evaluate a three-row W-shaped 18-cylinder engine with cylinder blocks similar to those of the Curtiss D.12. A example of this American engine was acquired in the USA, and underwent testing at the Ikar factory. The work on engine development was carried out under the leadership of A.A. Bessonov.

The cylinder block of the new engine was not quite the same as that of the D.12. Cylinder displacement was decreased, and the cylinders had spherical bottoms (an alternative conical version also existed) and were screwed into the block. The valves had direct drive, and their axes were not parallel. The cylinder blocks were positioned at an angle of 40° to each other.

Bessonov planned to create a unified family of three engines. Initially they were named *Kertis I* (single-row, 600-700hp), *Kertis V* (V-shaped, 450hp), and *Kertis W* (W-shaped, 600-700hp). All of them had the same cylinder blocks and cylinder-piston group, but they had different crankcases, conrods and crankshafts.

On 12-14 October 1925 a meeting was held at which the three competing manufacturers' projects were reviewed: the NAMI M-600, the Ikar factory's *Kertis W* and the MK-14 of Kireev's group. The M-600 was selected as being the simplest from the production technology viewpoint, as well as the cheapest (according to the estimates). The UVVS designated this engine M-13, and a prototype was planned to be built. As a reserve in case of failure, a prototype of Bessonov's engine, designated M-14, was also ordered.

That same month the GAZ No. 2 factory's designers began the thorough development of all three versions of their engine. The project completion deadline, defined by the Aviatrest administration, was 1 January 1926.

However, in December 1925, owing to a reduction in financing, Aviatrest excluded the M-14 from the plan. Despite this, the factory continued work at its own expense,

The prototype of the W18.

but because of the lack of funds the development period lengthened considerably. The project for the 6-cylinder *Kertis I* was completed in May 1926. Its potential buyer, the UVVS, evinced no interest in the engine, and all work on it was stopped.

On 3 September 1926 M.P. Makaruk, the chief engineer of the GAZ No. 2 factory, sent a letter to the Aviatrest administration, saying he thought the decision regarding further improvement of the M-5 (Liberty) engine a mistake. He believed that the modernization of this obviously outdated engine led to a dead end, and, as an alternative, he offered a family of engines based on the Curtiss D.12. Makaruk believed that the *Kertis W* should to be built in parallel with the M-13, and that selection of the better engine should be based on the test results.

Whether Makaruk's letter yielded results is not known, but the manufacture of M-14 components began in October. Aviatrest refused to finance the work, and on 16 September officially redesignated the M-14 the W18, as designations prefixed 'M' were given only to engines included into the State plan for development work, and the W18 was being built merely at the factory's initiative.

The factory had few funds to allocate to the project, and the W18 prototype was not assembled until March 1928. The engine's refinement took the whole of April, and in May it was put on the bench and the testing begun. The tests attracted the attention of the air force, and the engine then received semi-official status and the new designation M-18.

By that time ideas for W18 and V12 modernization had arisen. Starting from September 1928 the M-27 engine, based on the former type, was being developed. This powerplant was included into the UVVS plan for development work, and Aviatrest gave the factory an official order for creation of the M-27, which was to be installed on bombers and was to be rated at 700/800hp. Compared with the W18, cylinder diameter was increased and the cylinder design was changed (the cylinder liner bottom was rejected). A combustion chamber was then created between the cylinder and the head, and range of other changes was also introduced.

In June 1929 the Soviet Navy showed interest in the M-27. On 27 June an official order was issued for the development of a marine version of the engine, equipped with a reversing clutch.

Development of the M-19 engine, based on the V12, was begun in October 1928. It was linked with the M-27 by its dimensions and cylinder design. Initially it was not equipped with a supercharger, but early in 1929 it was decided to equip the M-19 with a single-speed GCS. This version was designated M-19K (K for *Kompressor*, or compressor) in some documents, but soon the letter 'K' was dropped, as all M-19 prototypes were built with superchargers.

In the meantime, in October 1928, the V12 prototype was completed, and in November it was run on the factory bench. Testing of the W18 continued until 4 October, when it suffered a failure of the cylinderhead block. To enable testing to continue, small batches of both engine types were built; five of each. Testing was completed by the end of 1929.

The work of testing and refining the V12 continued until June 1930. By that time it had become clear that the design was outdated. Both the UVVS and the Propeller-Engine Department of TsAGI repeatedly declared that the powerplant was useless, and the V12 is not mentioned in records after 1930.

As for the W18, it was transferred to State testing twice, first in December 1929 and again in April 1930. Although it became the first high-powered soviet-built engine to pass the 100hr running test, it suffered from water and oil leakage and excessive fuel consumption. In April 1930 cracks were found in the crankcase. It was concluded that the W18 offered no advantages over the M-17, which was already in series production.

Further work was carried out only on the M-19 and M-27 engines at the Factory No. 24 (the merged GAZ No. 2 and GAZ No. 4 factories). The factory managed to begin testing the M-19 in January 1930. A lot of effort was applied to resolving the problem of cracking of the cylinder cooling jackets, and in the end corrugated jackets were introduced. Other problems included breakages of the main bearings and piston rods, cracking of the crankshaft on several occasions, and excessive abrasion of the valve plates and piston pins. In November 1930 the M-19 was transferred to State testing, but on 4 December it was destroyed when its con rod tore off. The second prototype was run for 100hr, but the GCS impeller was replaced twice during this period.

In spite of the failure during State tests, the engine was flight-tested on an R-5 biplane, which made several flights in May-June 1931. However, the characteristics of the M-19-powered R-5 were inferior to those of the M-17-powered version, and the production order for fifty M-19s, planned for 1931, was cancelled.

The IAM was instructed to carry out further refinement of the M-19, and from May 1931 the institute proceeded with the development of the M-19a version, boosted to 650hp. This engine differed in having a new cylinder block and a modified GCS drive, but work on the M-19 was cancelled in 1931, and the M-19a was not built.

The first M-27 prototype was under test from September 1930. The second prototype was also transferred to testing in the beginning of December, and on 30 December the engine went for State testing, two being used for this. The 900hp maximum power rating was not reached, the registered maximum rating being 828hp. Moreover, the engine was over the weight stipulated in the specification.

It was planned to fit the M-27 with a gear and supercharger. Specialists at Factory No. 24 also evaluated the possibility of boosting it to 1,000hp without the use of supercharging. The M-27N version, equipped with a supercharger, was excluded from the IAM work plan in 1931, but development of the geared M-27R was completed at IAM in May 1931. The institute also developed a reverse clutch for the GM-27, but neither the M-27R nor the GM-27 was built. At the end of 1931 all work on the engine was cancelled, as the M-27 offered no great advantages over the series-built M-17, or, more importantly, over the new M-34.

In 1932 the M-27 was revived for the last time. Two M-27s were used in a version of a powerplant intended for installation in the G-1 (*Gigant*) aeroplane, driving common angle gears. Testing of the powerplant with coupled M-27s took place in March-April 1933.

M-7 (AB-20)

The engine was developed at the Motor factory in Moscow under the leadership of A.A. Bessonov, in accordance with a UVVS specification issued on 5 May 1923. Work on the project was completed in September 1924, and a single prototype was built and underwent testing from

A front view of the V12 prototype.

A rear view of the V12 engine.

November of the same year. The prototype reached only 15hp instead of estimated 20hp.

A project existed for an improved version, planned to deliver 30hp.

Characteristics

2-cylinder, two-stroke, direct-drive engine

Power rating	15hp

V12 (*KERTIS V*)

Developed at Factory No. 24, Moscow, in 1925-27, this engine used components from the Curtiss D.12. In the course of its development a GCS was introduced. The project was completed in July 1927, and the first prototype was assembled in October 1928. Refinement of the GCS was protracted. All work on the engine was cancelled in the middle of 1930, as it was not powerful enough for air force requirements. Six prototypes were built.

The type formed the basis for development of the M-19.

Characteristics

12-cylinder in-line vee, four-stroke, watercooled, direct-drive engine with GCS

Power rating	450/610hp
Bore/stroke	125/160mm (4.92/6.30in)
Volume	23.55 litres (1,437cu in)
Compression ratio	5.5:1
Weight	510kg (1,124lb)

W18 (*KERTIS W*, M-14, M-18)

This was a W-shaped engine, created at Factory No. 24, Moscow, in 1925-26, under the leadership of A.A. Bessonov, and its design was unified with that of the V12. The first prototype was built in March 1930, and the engine was transferred to State testing twice, in December 1929 and in April 1930. When being run for the second time the engine successfully operated for 100hr, but it was not introduced into series production. Six prototypes were built.

The W18 served as the basis for development of the M-27.

Characteristics

18-cylinder in-line W-shaped, block-type (cylinder blocks positioned at 40° angle), four-stroke, watercooled, direct-drive engine

Power rating (project figure)	670/800hp (601/735hp was achieved during testing)
Bore/stroke	125/160mm (4.92/6.30in)
Volume	35.4 litres (2,160cu in)
Compression ratio	6.35:1 (first prototype, 5.5:1)
Weight	575kg (1,268lb) (first prototype, 560kg (1,235lb))

KERTIS I

This 6-cylinder engine, developed in association with the V12 and W18, was developed in 1925-26 at Factory No. 24, under the leadership of A.A. Bessonov. Development was completed in May 1926, but a prototype was not built.

Characteristics

6-cylinder in-line, four-stroke, watercooled, direct-drive engine

Power rating	250hp (according to the project).
Bore/stroke	125-160mm (4.92/6.30in)
Compression ratio	5.5:1

M-19

This engine, which was under development from October 1928 at Factory No. 24, under the leadership of A.A. Bessonov, was a further evolution of the V12, with cylinders of increased diameter. Unlike its predecessor, the M-19 used bottomless cylinders, which were screwed in into a common block of cylinder heads. The heads were of two-valve type, and the conrods were side-articulated. The engine had cylinders and pistons in common with those of the M-27. Development was completed in 1929, and three prototypes were built. The M-19 was bench tested from January 1930, and in January-December 1930 it passed State testing, but the results were unsatisfactory. In May-June 1931 the prototype was flight tested in an R-5, but the engine was not introduced into series production owing to the unreliability of the GCS.

The following versions of the M-19 are known:

M-19 (M-19K) The main version, rated at 500/600hp (525/600hp registered). Three prototypes were built and tested.

M-19a An improved 600/650hp version developed in 1931 at the IAM. It had a new cylinder head block and modified mechanism for the GCS drive. The prototype was not built.

The M-19 was installed in one of the R-5 prototypes, and was also intended for the DI-4 fighter.

Characteristics

12-cylinder in-line vee, four-stroke, watercooled, direct-drive engine with a single-speed GCS

Power rating	depending on version
Bore/stroke	135/160mm (5.31/6.30in)
Volume	27.47 litres (1,493cu in)
Compression ratio	6.4:1
Weight	475kg (1,047lb) (without propeller hub, synchronizing gear and fuel pump)

M-27

This 18-cylinder engine, related to the M-19, was created at Factory No. 24 in Moscow under the leadership of A.A. Bessonov, and was intended for installation in bombers. It was a further development of the W18, with cylinders of increased diameter. Like to the M-19, the engine had bottomless cylinder liners. The master conrods were removable. Development was begun in September 1928, and two prototypes were manufactured at Factory No. 24. The first underwent testing from September, and the second from the beginning of December 1928. The engine satisfactorily passed the State tests, which were carried out from 10 December 1930 to 15 January 1931. Flight testing was performed in 1932 on the TSh-2 aeroplane. Refinement work was cancelled in 1934, and the engine was not built in series. Twenty-one M-27s were built.

The following versions of the M-27 are known:

M-27 The initial version without reduction gear and supercharger.

M-27R A version with reduction gear that was being developed in 1931 at the IAM. Maximum power 830hp.

M-27RN A proposed version with reduction gear and supercharger. Development was not proceeded with.

M-27, coupled version. A version intended for installation in the G-1 aeroplane. The prototype powerplant was tested in March-April 1933.

GM-27 A power-boat version with reverse gear that was being developed at the IAM in 1931.

The M-27 was installed in the prototype of the TSh-2 ground-attack aircraft. The engine was planned to be used as replacement for the Italian ASSO engine on the civil version of the MBR-4 (MP-4) flying-boat, which was under development at that time, as well as for installation in R-8 and R-12 aeroplanes.

Characteristics

18-cylinder in-line W-shaped, block-type (blocks positioned at 40° to each other), four-stroke, watercooled, direct-drive engine

Power rating	700/900hp (according to the specification)
	700/850hp according to factory figures (in fact, 707/828hp)
Bore/stroke	135/160mm (5.31/6.30in)
Volume	41.1 litres (2,508cu in)
Compression ratio	6.4:1
Weight	633kg (1,395lb) (without exhaust pipes)

CHAPTER SEVEN

The High-powered Aero-engines Developed at the NAMI

In January 1921 the Scientific-Automobile Laboratory in Moscow became the Scientific Auto-Motor Institute (NAMI), which was headed by Professor N.R. Brilling, an experienced specialist in engine construction. The institute was charged with examining and testing imported and indigenous engines, including aircraft powerplants. From the outset of the institute's establishment, the Department of Light Engines was assigned to work on aero-engines. Many well-known engine designers, such as A.A. Mikulin, V.Ya. Klimov and A.D. Charomskiy, initially worked there. The NAMI soon began to create original engine projects, a design bureau being established in 1923 to carry out this work. Two years later a specialized Department of Aero Engines was set up there.

The NAMI specialists worked on improving the design of the M-5 Liberty engine, and on the creation of new Liberty-based versions. Later the institute entered into competition with the Motor factory to create a 100hp engine for training aeroplanes, to the order of the UVVS. A further step was participation in the contest for a new high-powered water-cooled engine for the air force. The UVVS Scientific Committee approved a specification for such an engine in May 1925.

As early as October 1925 a preliminary project for the M-600 engine was developed at the NAMI. As the basis for the new type, NAMI used the design of the Wright T3 Tornado vee engine, but the M-600 was not a mere copy. Although it was similar to the T3, the Soviet engine had four aluminium blocks, with three cylinders in each. The block was the same as that of the Tornado, but its dimensions were slightly increased. The M-600 had a cylinder diameter of 150mm (5.91in) and a stroke of 170mm (6.69in), while the American engine had cylinders of 146mm (5.75in) diameter and a stroke of 162mm (6.38in). The crankshaft and conrods were supported on roller bearings. The gas-distribution mechanism incorporated ideas from Packard and Curtiss engines, while the carburettor was copied from that of the British Rolls-Royce Condor engine.

At a meeting of the UVVS Scientific Committee on 12-14 October 1925 the M-600 project was pronounced the contest winner, as it was technologically simpler. Moreover, according to estimates, the engine would cost half as much as the one developed by the Ikar factory, and was five times cheaper than the engine designed by the engineer Kireev.

It was decided to arrange series production of the M-600, and the UVVS allocated the designation M-13 to the new engine. The NAMI proceeded to refine the project, which was approved by the Scientific Committee in April 1926.

At that time the NAMI did not have its own prototype production facilities. Therefore, in July 1926, Aviatrest issued orders to different enterprises for the manufacture of components for the new engine. The blocks were to be cast at Factory No. 9 in Zaporozhye, forgings were ordered from the Bolshevik factory in Leningrad, and other parts were to be made at the Ikar factory in Moscow. Two prototypes were built simultaneously.

The most serious difficulties arose with the casting of the sophisticated blocks, which included cylinder heads. The appearance of small cracks was the biggest problem. In course of manufacture at Zaporozhye, seventy-five castings were rejected as defective. All forgings were delivered to Moscow in April 1927, and the blocks in November, the month that the Ikar factory began assembling the first engine.

The prototype was ready at the end of February 1928, about three months behind the scheduled completion date. On 27 February the engine was presented to a Commission consisting of representatives of the UVVS and Aviatrest and the Commission revealed a number of problems. These were eliminated, and on 6 March the M-13 was presented to the Commission for a second time. Further refinement followed, and on 10 April cold running of the engine was carried out.

After that the engine was test run, and the initial tests were going rather well until worn-out connecting-rod sleeves had to be replaced. Testing resumed on 8 May. Bench testing of the first M-13 prototype lasted (with some intervals) until 15 October 1928, when the crankcase cracked. The work continued with the second prototype, and the M-13 tests were completed at the beginning of 1930.

As early as June 1926 plans were made to start M-13 production at the GAZ No. 6 factory in Rybinsk. Specialists from Rybinsk were engaged to refine series production technology and to adapt the engine's design to meet production requirements. On 2 October 1927 a special commission accepted the work done as satisfactory. In July 1928 Mikulin designed a new block for the M-13 that was easier to cast.

In parallel with the aicraft version of the M-13, it was planned to build a marine version, designated GM-13. This differed in having a lower compression ratio, an imported Stromberg carburettor, and reversal reduction gearing (in variants with both right- and left-hand rotation). It is recorded that the GM-13 was to have 'cooling by sea-water', but it is doubtful that it was intended to run salt water through the cylinder-block casings; it seems more likely that installation of a water radiator was stipulated. Work on the marine engine was started about the summer 1926.

The NAMI Board approved the first version of the GM-13 project on 1 August

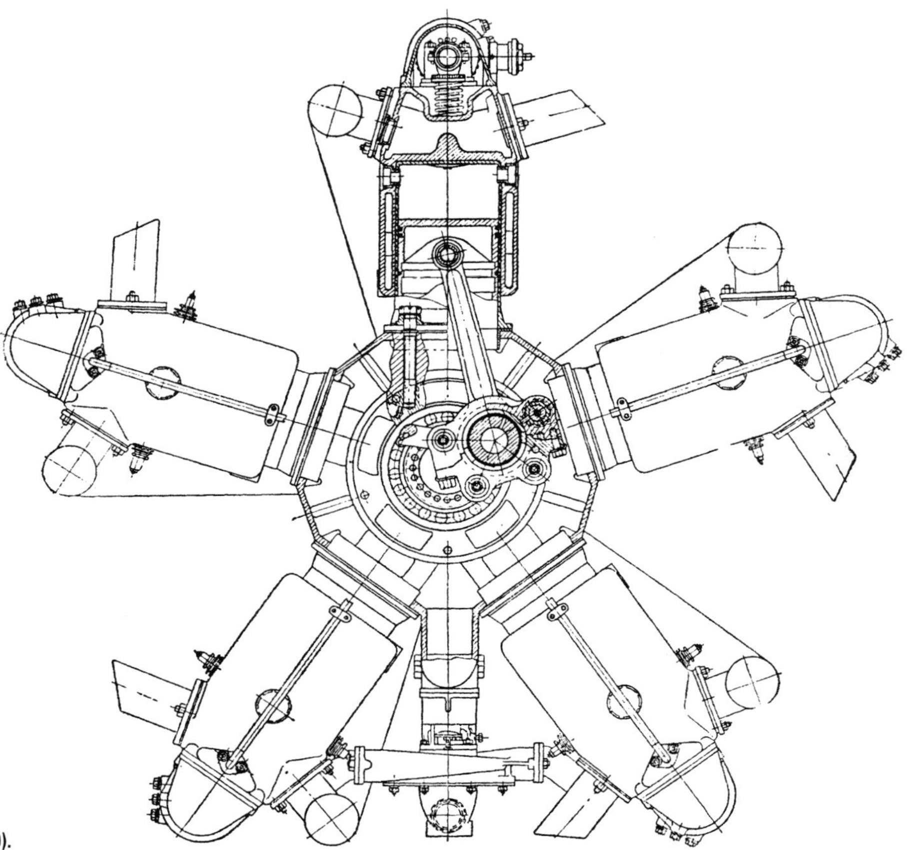

A drawing of the M-20 (AM-20).

1927. Later, the second project was prepared, the 2GM-13 with GCS, a starter, and an electric generator. It was planned to boost maximum power to 1,000hp. There was no intention to build a prototype; the work was to be carried out on the first series-production unit. It was planned to introduce the GM-13 into series production at the Rybinsk factory from the second half of 1930.

There was one more variant of the basic design. Designated M-13M, it employed many components from the Wright T4 Typhoon. The project for this engine was completed at the NAMI during January 1927-February 1928.

However, by the end of 1928 the M-13 was considered an outdated design. Having almost the same power rating as German BMW VI, which was being introduced into series production in the USSR as the M-17, the M-13 was heavier and larger. As the result, arrangements for M-17 series production were initiated in Rybinsk. The M-13 was not submitted for State testing.

In the second half of the 1920s the NAMI created another high-powered aero-engine, the NAMI-500 (the designations M-20 and AM-20 were also used). A.A. Mikulin played a leading role in its development, hence the designation AM-20. (Though this was informal, and can be found only in NAMI documents. This was the first aero-engine to have an 'AM' designation, using the designer's initials.) The engine had an unusual configuration of 'radial blocks', combining the block layout and air cooling. The NAMI-500 was being developed during September 1927-August 1928, and a prototype was ordered from Factory No. 29 in Zaporozhye (the former GAZ No. 9). This engine was built quickly, in June-August 1928, and bench testing started in September, but the engine did not reach the estimated power rating and suffered from a range of problems.

For 1929 the NAMI planned the development of an 800hp M-20A version, but it did not come to fruition, probably because of the unsuccessful M-20 tests.

The famous M-34 engine, created under the leadership of A.A. Mikulin, can be considered to represent the peak of design efforts by the NAMI's Department of Aero Engines, where its development started. Following the establishment of the Aviation Motor-Building Institute (IAM), most of the specialists from the NAMI, the Propeller-Engine Department of TsAGI and from some other factories were moved there. Development work on a considerable proportion of Soviet aero-engines, including the M-34, was also transferred to this institute. As this engine formed the basis of a large family, it is covered in a separate chapter.

M-13 (M-600)

Created at the NAMI under the leadership of N.R. Brilling and A.A. Mikulin, this engine used some components from the Wright T3 Tornado. Development was started in May 1925, and in October of the same year it was pronounced the winner of the contest for a high-powered engine. The project was completed in February 1926, and in April it was approved by the UVVS Scientific Committee. Prototypes were under construction from July 1926 at the Ikar factory in Moscow, the first being completed in February 1928. Testing began in April of the same year. In March 1929 the second prototype was built, and at the end of the year it began tests that continued until the beginning of 1930.

It was planned to set up series production at GAZ No. 6 factory in Rybinsk, but the arrangements were not even started. Two engine prototypes were built.

Characteristics

12-cylinder in-line vee, four-stroke, watercooled engine

Bore/stroke	150/170mm (5.91/6.69in)
Volume	36.0 litres (2,197cu in)

Power rating, compression ratio, and weight dependant on version

The following versions of the engine are known:

M-13 The first version of the engine; two prototypes were built and tested. Direct-drive engine without supercharging. Power rating, according to the project, 600/750hp (in fact up to 790hp).

Characteristics

Compression ratio	6.5:1
Weight	612kg (1,349lb) (after refinement, 615kg (1,356lb))

Later, engine power was boosted to 820/880hp, accompanied by a weight increase to 800kg (1,800lb).

M-13M A projected modified version using components from the Wright T4 Typhoon.

GM-13 A marine version. Geared (in variants with right and left rotation), watercooled engine with reverse clutch, without supercharging.

Characteristics

Power rating	720/800hp (according to the project)
Compression ratio	5.1:1-5.3:1
Weight	1,000kg (2,200lb)

2GM-13 An improved version of the projected marine engine, with GCS application. Power rating up to 1,000hp.

The engine was planned for installation in the R-5, MRT-1 and I-3 aeroplanes, and motor torpedo-boats.

M-20 (AM-20, NAMI-500)

This engine was developed at the NAMI during September 1927-May 1928 under the leadership of A.A. Mikulin and V.A. Dobrynin. A single prototype was built in June-August 1928 at Factory No. 29 in Zaporozhye, and tested from September 1928 until February 1929.

Characteristics

Four-stroke air-cooled engine with five cylinder blocks positioned in radial layout, with four cylinders in each block. Power rating depended on version.

The following versions of the engine are known:

M-20 A 500hp engine of which a single prototype was built and tested.

M-20A A project for an improved version with a power rating of 800hp.

CHAPTER EIGHT

MK: *Motor Kireeva* (Kireev's Engine)

The third entrant in the contest for a high-powered watercooled engine under the order of 1925 was the MK-14 (or merely MK or M-K), designed by engineer V.V. Kireev. Before the October Revolution this designer worked at the RBVZ factory, first in Riga and then in Petrograd. There he created the rather successful RBVZ-6, which was introduced into series production and installed on *Ilya Muromets* heavy bombers.

At the beginning of 1923 Kireev turned to the vee layout, and forwarded a project to the UVVF. On 31 March, the Head of the UVVF signed an agreement with the designer for the development of a new engine.

At the end of 1925 a preliminary project for the engine was shown to the Scientific Committee. The MK-14 had separate cylinders, its crankshaft and conrods were mounted on roller bearings, and the pistons and valves were oil-cooled. The oil was fed to a spiral channel in the steel piston from the conrod, returned to the conrod, and was then directed to the crankshaft.

Two versions were developed with different compression ratios (achieved by placing different washers under the cylinder heads). An unusual feature of this vee engine was that the exhaust nozzles were directed to the inner side of the cylinder rows. The project stipulated the use of a planetary reduction gear and a carburettor of original design. The MK-14 had to be started using a cartridge starter (self-starter).

Though it did not quite satisfy the requirements of the 1925 contest, Kireev's engine was also reviewed at the meeting that considered the results of the contest. The MK-14 was deemed too sophisticated, as it had about 750 parts, while the M-600 proposed by the NAMI had only 215. According to estimates, the MK-14 would cost from five to seven times as much as the M-600.

Nevertheless, those at the meeting noted the engine's original and the novelty of many of Kireev's solutions. It was therefore decided to build his engine as an experiment.

Kireev continued refining the project. In August 1926 the UVVS signed an agreement with the Bolshevik factory in Leningrad for the manufacture of three prototypes of the MK-14, for which 250,000 roubles were allocated. The deadline for completion of the the first prototype was 1 June 1928.

The Bolshevik factory belonged to Ordnance-Armoury Trust, but produced series M-5 aero-engines. It took ten months for the factory to prepare and equip an engine prototype production shop, and manufacture of the engine's components started in September 1927. Kireev repeatedly introduced changes into the drawings, and demanded that parts be manufactured in several versions at the same time. There was a lack of special steel, tools and fixtures. A number of parts had to be adapted to suit the available materials, equipment and technology of the factory. Rollers for the roller bearings were ordered from Britain and Sweden. On top of everything else, finance for the work was considerably reduced from the second half of 1927, and the allocated funds were insufficient.

In the summer of 1928 a commission appointed by the UVVS Scientific Committee and headed by professor Martens examined the state of the work, and recommended cancellation. In March 1929 the Ordnance-Armoury Trust Board issued an order for work to cease, but on 5 April the Revvoensovet revoked this order.

During this period Kireev's project had changed considerably. The diameter of the cylinders was increased, as well as the piston stroke. Supercharging using a GCS was introduced, and subsequently a turbo-supercharger. Eventually Kireev planned to turn to five-valve cylinder heads. According to estimates the engine was to reach 950hp even without turbo-supercharging.

By March 1929 the first prototype was almost half-complete. Expenditure was double the planned amount.

On 3 April 1930 a new commission, headed by Mezheninov, Head of the Air Force Staff, visited the Bolshevik factory. Seven years had passed, but the experimental engine was still not complete. In the spirit of the time, there had to be a guilty party, and the finger was pointed at Kireev, who was labelled a 'saboteur'. The commission recommended that the work be cancelled and Kireev arrested, and that is what happened, all work having ceased as early as 5 April.

With its designer already imprisoned, on 29 June the MK-14 was withdrawn from the factory plan by order of the Head of the Ordnance-Armoury Trust. The engine parts were packed and sent to the IAM in Moscow, but their ultimate fate is unknown, as is the lot of Kireev himself.

MK (MK-14)

A project, created under the leadership of V.V. Kireev in Leningrad, for the contest of 1925. The engine was under development from 1923, and the prototype was being built in 1927-30 at the Bolshevik factory in Leningrad as an experimental unit, but was not completed.

Characteristics

12-cylinder in-line vee, four-stroke, watercooled, geared engine with GCS (in final version).

Initial power rating	600hp (later 800hp and 950hp)
Bore/stroke	132/180mm (5.20/7.09in) (later 166.5/230mm (6.56/9.06in))
Compression ratio	5.7:1 (alternative value 6.2:1)

CHAPTER NINE

The Engines Built at the Bolshevik Factory in Leningrad

Two engine factories under the Bolshevik name are known. In the 1920s GAZ No. 9 factory in Zaporozhye was using this name, and at the same time the name was given to the former Obukhovskiy factory in Leningrad. The Leningrad-based enterprise belonged to the Ordnance-Armoury Trust but, nevertheless, in the middle of the 1920s it was tasked with arranging series production of Liberty engines.

Having established an aero-engine production capability, the factory then began to to develop its own engine designs. The first such engine was developed during October 1925-May 1926 by engineer L.Ya. Palmen. Called the AMB-20 (*Aviatsionniy Motor Bolshevika*, 20hp – the Bolshevik's 20 hp aero-engine), it was a four-stroke, 2-cylinder, horizontally-opposed engine. The prototype was built during June 1926-February 1927, and underwent testing in May-June 1927. No customers were found for it, and it did not enter series production.

Later the Bolshevik factory designers proceeded to develop a family of high-powered aero-engines on their own initiative. To date, few records of this work have been traced. Judging by the report prepared in February 1929 for P.I. Baranov, head of the UVVS, the family included two engine types. The first, the 600-700hp *Bolshevik I*, was for some time even included in the State plan for experimental work, under the designation M-24. The project was presented to the UVVS for review three times. By January 1929 it was only half-complete, and the funding was then withdrawn. The second engine, the 450-500hp *Bolshevik II*, was developed in April-June 1928, but prototype manufacture was not started.

According to other records, three engines were under development; the AMB-500, AMB-600 and AMB-700, with respective power ratings of 500hp, 600hp and 700hp. However, only the last of these was reported to be under construction. Allegedly, both water- and air-cooling was under consideration.

Lastly, there is a record indicating that, in November 1926, the Bolshevik factory started developing a high-powered air-cooled engine.

AMB-20 (*BOLSHEVIK*)

This engine was developed during October 1925-May 1926 by engineer L.Ya. Palmen at the Bolshevik factory in Leningrad, and a single prototype was built there in February 1927. The prototype underwent testing in May-June 1927, but was not introduced into series production. In 1928 this prototype was mounted on an LAKM-1 light aeroplane, and remained in use until 1931.

The prototype engine was installed in an LAKM-1 light aeroplane.

Characteristics

2-cylinder, four-stroke, horizontally-opposed, air-cooled engine

Power rating	20/25hp
Bore/stroke	80/96mm (3.15/3.78in)
Compression ratio	5.0:1
Weight	32kg (71lb)

M-24 (*BOLSHEVIK I*, AMB-700)

This projected 700hp engine was developed during November 1926-October 1927 at the Bolshevik factory. One prototype was being built in October 1927-February 1928, but it was not completed.

BOLSHEVIK II (AMB-500)

A project for a 500hp engine, developed in April-June 1928 at the Bolshevik factory. The prototype was not built.

CHAPTER TEN

The Contest for Aero-engines for Training Aircraft, and Further Evolution of the M-11

In the early 1920s the 120hp M-2 was the primary engine used in Soviet Union training aircraft. However, this French-designed rotary became outdated, and suffered from low efficiency and poor reliability. At the end of 1923 the UVVF announced a contest for a 100hp engine for use in training aircraft. The required characteristics were specified in very basic terms: air-cooling, a low compression ratio (for operating on low-quality fuels), and the minimal use of imported materials and components. The engine layout was not specified, though it was required that it should be stationary (i.e., not rotary).

At that time there were only a few design groups in the Soviet Union capable of creating a new aero-engine. As a result, Aviatrest depended on the NAMI and charged it with the work. In the manner of the era, no specific individuals were made responsible for the work, and the project, designated NAMI-100, did not have a leading designer. General supervision of the engine's development was carried out by N.R. Brilling, and the process of its creation involved the participation of such well-known specialists as A.A. Mikulin and A.D. Charomskiy.

The designers chose a classic 5-cylinder radial configuration for the project, which had been completed by 1 February 1925. The NAMI did not have its own workshops, so a suitable factory had to be found to build the prototype engines. Not until June did the institute manage to agree to have the engine built by the GAZ No. 9 factory in Zaporozhye, which began construction of the prototypes on 1 July 1925.

The design department of the GAZ No. 4 Motor factory also entered the contest, but on its own initiative and much later than its competitor. In the middle of 1924 the factory's designers prepared their first figures for the engine, which was called M-100. On 27 September the factory received an official order from the NK UVVS, and on the same date the factory provided Aviatrest with its estimate of costs for developing the engine and building prototypes. As at the NAMI, the factory did not appoint an official leader for the project. The design department also lacked a head, and worked under direct leadership of A.D. Shvetsov, the factory's chief engineer. Some sources state that N.A. Okromeshko was the informal leader of the design group.

The Motor factory's designers considered several layouts for the new powerplant, including unusual configurations such as a parallel coupled installation of four cylinders with gear transmission to a common shaft, and the crosswise positioning of four cylinders. In the end they settled for the same configuration as the NAMI; a 5-cylinder radial. In the course of development the designers rejected the idea of a conical combustion chamber and non-parallel valve positioning, and introduced a progressive screwed-on cylinder head. In December 1924 they decided to change from a cam to individual distribution shafts for each cylinder. The M-100 project was completed only a month later

The M-11 (M-100) prototype on the test bench at the Motor Factory.

than the NAMI-100. By this time both engines had received new designations from the UVVS, the NAMI-100 becoming the M-12, and the M-100 the M-11.

Shvetsov, Okromeshko and their team had the suport of the most powerful aero-engine factory in the country at the time, and this allowed them not only to make up for the delay, but also to leave their competitor behind when the stage of prototype manufacture was reached. On 4 November 1925 bench testing of the first M-11 prototype began. However, its crankshaft soon broke. By that time five more engine had been built at the Motor factory, all of them differing slightly.

The first M-12 prototype was assembled in March 1926, and its first start-up on the bench took place on 17 March. The testing revealed numerous problems, and on 17 May the first M-12 was sent to the NAMI in Moscow, which also tested the engine for some time. The engine then underwent refinement. In particular, a variant was created in which the main ball bearings were replaced by split-shell bearings.

The M-11 passed its official factory tests at the GAZ No. 4 factory in August 1926. The M-12 was being refined at the NAMI until September, and it then went through one more testing cycle and was transferred to the NII VVS. The M-12 was bench tested there from 15 December 1926, but the tests were not completed because the engine broke down.

For further testing it was decided to build a number of M-11 and M-12 engines at the GAZ No. 9 factory. In March 1927 modified drawings of the M-12 were sent to the factory, and M-11 drawings followed in July. The NAMI engine was evidently favoured, both by the UVVS and Aviatrest, as thirty M-12s were ordered, whereas only two M-11s were to be built, the order for the latter being received only on 6 September.

Both design groups continued to refine their engines. This caused a delay in manufacturing at Zaporozhye, as new drawings and revisions kept arriving from Moscow. On 10 October a new set of documentation for the M-12 was received, and in November the revised drawings for the M-11 arrived.

The M-12 was still in favour, and in 1928 Aviatrest planned to manufacture eighty units. However, multiple failures of the engine during testing forced the UVVS to secure a reserve, and it ordered the manufacture of thirty M-12s and ten M-11s at the GAZ No. 9 factory.

The M-12 engine during tests.

As it was intended that the factory would undertake series production of the NAMI engine, attention was mainly directed to this type. Large quantities of special fixtures and tools were prepared for M-12 manufacture. On the other hand, the M-11 was being built as a purely experimental engine. The technology for its series production was not under development, and the expenditures for production equipment were minimal. Strangely, the result was quite the opposite. The quality of the M-11s appeared to be better, and there were fewer defective parts.

By 1 April 1928 two improved M-12s had been completed, and their testing started on 12 May. Assembly of the first M-11 began on 1 June and was finished by 3 July, and on 12 August it was transferred to bench testing.

The M-12 was still suffering from numerous defects, and the designers continued to introduce considerable changes. A divided crankshaft (with a Morse cone joint), combined with a divided master rod, was proposed as another modification.

By 4 September six more M-12s and two M-11s were being assembled. Both engine types were being tested in parallel. By December three M-12s and two M-11s were undergoing comparative testing. Ultimately, the Motor factory's engine proved more reliable and won the contest, the NAMI powerplant having suffered various failures. For example, on 1 December the crankshaft of one of the engines broke.

It should be noted that the changes proposed by the Zaporozhye factory's designers significantly influenced the refinement of the M-11. So much so, in fact, that the engine may be considered to be the result of a joint effort.

Already, in September, specialists at the Zaporozhye factory had realized that the Motor-designed engine had better prospects, and preparations for M-11 series production began. In December the Testing Commission reported to Moscow that work on the M-12 was gradually being run down.

On 10 December 1929 the final revision of the M-12 drawings was approved. Although the required changes were introduced into the design of two prototypes, this did not considerably improve the engine's reliability. The Aviatrest administration ordered cancellation of

NAMI staff with an M-23.

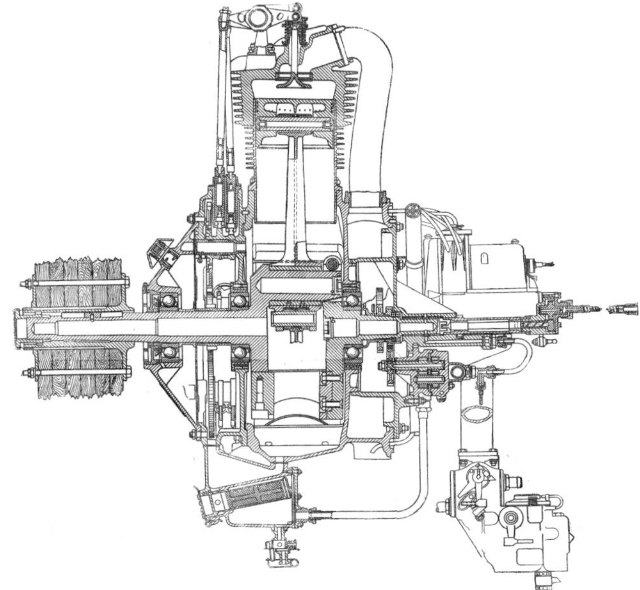

A cross-section through the M-11A.

work on the M-12, while those already built were to be used on snowmobiles, with their output limited to 80hp.

Meanwhile, the NAMI was developing another engine, related to the M-12. This was NAMI-65, later designated M-23. On 7 March 1927 a project for a '3-cylinder engine of NAMI-100 type' was officially approved, and construction of a prototype was proposed. The NAMI-65 was similar in design to its 'big brother' and used a number of its parts. The same factory in Zaporozhye was tasked with manufacturing the M-23 prototype. The first components were built in July 1928, but the manufacturing process was protracted and the first prototype was not completed until 1 July 1929.

As with the M-12, the M-23 underwent a lengthy and painstaking process of refinement. The factory tests took place in March-April 1930, and lasted quite a long time. The M-23 used the cylinders from the M-12. Initially, however, slightly different cylinders had been developed, but they broke continuously during preliminary testing. The new tests also revealed a number of defects: a valve plate broke, and an exhaust pipe burnt through. There was high engine vibration at low revolutions.

A further period of refinement followed, and at the end of the year State testing of the M-23 took place, which the engine passed at last. The prototype was installed in a AIR-3 aircraft, which carried out several flights thus powered.

The manufacture of a prototype batch of thirty M-23s was planned for 1932, but the engine was already facing strong opposition. Specialists in the UVVS adhered to the position that a 65hp engine was unnecessary, and that the 100hp engine would suffice. In addition, the basic M-12 type was definitively rejected. Consequently the M-23 was not put into series production.

On the other hand, the M-11 was successfully put into production, and it became the first series-built Soviet-designed aero-engine. Factory No. 29 (the renamed GAZ No. 9) delivered its first batch of ten engines for military acceptance in August-September 1929. In October these were followed by the second batch, also of ten engines, and in January 1930 by the third, of ten more M-11s. Series production engines were designated M-11a or M-11/A. All of these batches were partly experimental. For instance, three types of suction-pipe attachment and two types of main bearings were used in the engines of the second batch.

The former Motor factory, which by that time had become a part of Factory No. 24, was not involved in the further improvement of the M-11, all such work being carried out by the designers at Factory No. 29. In January 1930 they developed a new cylinder head with a stiffening ring in the lower part of the cylinder, a cylinder fastening flange similar to the one used in the Jupiter engine, and a master rod in plain instead of roller bearings.

In March 1930 a number of M-11s were installed in U-2 trainers, and Service testing of the engine began at the flying school in Borisoglebsk.

The M-11 production rate increased steadily, 103 being assembled in 1930, 326 in 1931 and 883 in 1932. The engine was continuously improved. In April 1931 a crankshaft installation on plain bearings was introduced, freeing the manufacturers from the need to acquire high-quality ball bearings from abroad.

As early as 1931 the designers at Factory No. 29 prepared plans for a whole family of engines based on the M-11, including the 3-cylinder M-50, 5-cylinder M-51, 7-cylinder M-48 and 9-cylinder M-49. The development work was carried out by the factory's Experimental Design Department under the leadership of A.S. Nazarov. In fact, work on the low-powered engines was carried out by a group headed by M.A. Kossov.

The group started with the M-51, which had a different gas-distribution mechanism from the M-11 and higher rpm. The M-51 prototype was built in February 1932, its cold running started in March, and this was followed by full-scale testing. In May-June the M-51 had already been transferred to State testing (it was fitted

The M-50 (3M-11) engine.

An M-23 engine in the Russian Air Force Museum at Monino.

with M-11 cylinders), and in October it passed State testing fitted with its own cylinders. In June 1933 the engine was flight tested in a U-2 aircraft.

At the end of 1932 a prototype of the M-48 was built, and in April the M-50 (designated 3M-11) also passed State tests. The most powerful engine of the family, the M-49, underwent factory testing only. In 1933 plans to replace the M-11 with the M-51 in series production were already under consideration.

However, in 1934, owing to arrangements to produce new engine types (under Gnome-Rhône licence) at Factory No. 29, it was decided to transfer M-11 production to the new Factory No. 16, in Voronezh. All work on the new engine family had ceased in Zaporozhye by early April 1934. M.A. Kossov and some of his colleagues left the factory and continued their work at the NII GVF, where they created the MG-11, MG-21 and MG-31 engines, further developments of the M-51, M-48 and M-49 respectively. However, these powerplants had little in common with the M-11 apart from the basic dimensions of their cylinders.

The process of refining the M-11 continued at Voronezh under the leadership of A.S. Nazarov, who took up the post of chief designer. Several versions of the basic engine were developed at Factory No. 16, including the M-11E, which was boosted in rpm and compression ratio to produce 160hp. The M-11E prototype underwent State testing in October 1937, but it was insufficiently reliable and only a small number was built.

Before the Great Patriotic War (Second World War), owing to arrangements for series production of the M-105 engine at Factory No. 16, manufacture of the M-11 was transferred to Factory No. 154, also in Voronezh. Here, M-11 production continued until the factory was evacuated to Andizhan in October 1941. After the German defeat the factory was returned to Voronezh. The development of new M-11 versions at factory No. 154 was headed by M.A. Kossov, and later by E.V Urmin. The latter became the head of the OKB-41 design bureau in Moscow, where several more versions were designed. The M-11's evolution was concluded under the leadership of I.A. Muzhylov, when OKB-41 created the last versions.

The M-11 was in mass production for more than 20 years. To retain a logical order, this chapter includes data for all versions of the M-11 up to the time it was phased out of series production. Information about engines of the MG family and other subsequent types based on the M-11 appears in a succeeding chapter.

M-12 (NAMI-100)

The NAMI-100 was developed at the NAMI in 1924-25 under the leadership of N.R. Brilling, to the same 1923 requirement for a 100hp engine as the M-11. The first M-12 prototype was built at the GAZ No. 9 factory in Zaporozhye in March 1926. In December 1926 it was tested at the NII GVF and attained 101/124hp, but the breakage of a counterweight damaged the crankcase and a cylinder. The M-12 underwent testing and refinement during 1926-28, but in December 1928 the M-12 lost the contest with the M-11 during comparative tests. All work on the M-12 was cancelled at the beginning of 1929, thirty-five engines having been built.

One of the projects for the U-2 trainer was designed for this engine.

An engine designed by M.A. Kossov and based on the M-11 is sometimes designated M-12.

Characteristics

5-cylinder radial, four-stroke, air-cooled, direct-drive engine.

Power rating	100/120hp
Bore/stroke	125/140mm (4.92/5.51in)
Volume	8.6 litres (525cu in)
Compression ratio	5.0:1
Weight	163kg (359lb)

M-23 (NAMI-65)

Developed at the NAMI under the leadership of V.A. Dollezhal and I.Sh. Neiman, this engine used parts and units of the M-12. The M-23 was intended for light aeroplanes (a so-called 'sporting' engine). Development was carried out from 1926, and the prototype was built at Factory No. 9 in Zaporozhye in July 1929. The engine underwent State testing in March-April 1930, and was flight tested in an AIR-3 in January 1930. A small batch of M-23s was built, but the engine was not installed on series aircraft as it suffered from serious vibration.

The M-23 was installed in the AIR-2, AIR-8, Omega, G-10, G-20 and G-22 aircraft prototypes and in the A-15 light autogyro, and was specified in the Sh-1 amphibian project.

Being one of the most-produced Soviet piston aero-engines, the M-23 was the first series engine totally of Soviet design.

Characteristics

3-cylinder radial, four-stroke, air-cooled, direct-drive engine.

Power rating	65/74hp
Bore/stroke	125/140mm (4.92/5.51in)
Volume	5.16 litres (315cu in)
Compression ratio	5.1:1
Weight	109.9kg (242lb) (with M-12 cylinders)

An AIR-3 aeroplane powered by an M-23 engine.

The Yak-Sh experimental helicopter from the Yakovlev Design Bureau was fitted with a M-11FR-1 engine (1948).

M-11

The M-11 (initially designated M-100) was developed in 1924-25 under the leadership of A.D. Shvetsov and N.V. Okromeshko, in accordance with the requirements of the 1923 contest for a 100hp engine. The design embodied a number of original and advanced engineering solutions, such as screwed-on cylinder heads and a gas-distribution mechanism driven not by a cam but by individual shafts. The engine was considerably simpler and cheaper to produce than the outdated M-2.

The first engine prototypes were built at the GAZ No. 4 Motor factory in October 1925. The powerplant was refined in Moscow, and then in Zaporozhye in 1926-28. In December 1928 the M-11 won the contest after comparative testing with the M-12. Series production was arranged at Factory No. 29 in Zaporozhye. Later the engine was repeatedly modernized under the leadership of A.S. Nazarov, S.D. Kolosov, M.A. Kossov, E.V. Urmin, A.I. Ivchenko and S.S. Samsonov. In 1935 production was transferred to Factory No. 16 in Voronezh, and then to Factory No. 154, also in Voronezh. Production of the M-11 totalled 74,734 units. The engine was undemanding with regard to fuel and oil quality, reliable and rather efficient. The M-11 was phased out of series production in 1959.

Characteristics

5-cylinder radial, four-stroke, air-cooled, direct-drive engine.

Bore/stroke	125/140mm (4.92/5.51in).
Volume	8.6 litres (525cu in)
Compression ratio	5.0:1

Weight and power rating dependant on version

The following versions of the M-11 are known:

M11-100 (M-100) A version built at the GAZ No. 4 factory. Power rating 100/110hp, weight 152kg (335lb). Eight prototypes built.

M-11A (M-11a or M-11/A) A version built at Factory No. 29. Power rating, 100/110hp, weight 160kg (353lb). The later series had Claudel carburettor (which replaced the Zenith carburettor), a sump and a different composition. In total, 250 were built.

M-11B A version with new pistons. Power rating, 100/110hp. In total, 125 were built.

M-11V This 1932 version had sliding bearings on a crankpin (instead of roller bearings), a Soviet-built K-11-4 carburettor, and a crankshaft, cylinders and conrods of modified design. Power rating, 100/110hp. In total, 505 were built.

M-11G A 1933 version with a modified set of piston rings, a lightened master conrod, and the possibility of fitting synchronizing gear. Power rating, 100/110hp. This version was in mass production until 1940, and more than 15,000 were built. The M-11G was modernized in 1937-39. Changes were made to the design of crankcase front section and crankshaft nose part, pneumatic starting was introduced, the control rods were placed under cowlings, and valve cases were installed.

M-11G modified for operation in horizontal position. Several of these were built in 1935 for the L-1 air-cushion boat.

M-11D A version boosted to higher rpm. The M-11D prototype was built in 1939, and series production started in 1940. Power rating, 115/125hp, weight, 158kg (348lb). Equipped with K-11A or K-11B carburettors, the M-11D was built in large numbers up to 1947. To reduce manufacturing costs and increase production rate, the engine underwent considerable simplification in 1943. The design of the cylinder heads and crankshaft were changed, the engine's composition was modified, and the pneumatic starter was removed.

M-11E A version developed at Factory No. 16. A small batch was built in 1936-38. In October 1937 the engine underwent

RIGHT: **An M-11G in an example of the famous U-2 (Po-2) biplane in the Monino museum collection.**

BELOW: **An M-11 mounted horizontally in the L-1 air-cushion boat.**

A UT-2 trainer, powered by an M-11D, in 1945.

ABOVE: **The Shche-2 light transport aeroplane, powered by two M-11Ds.**

BELOW: **Factory No. 135 manufactured five Yak-8 light transport aeroplanes, powered by two M-11Ds.**

State testing but was rejected. Flight testing was carried out in a UT-1 aircraft.

Characteristics

Power rating	150/160hp
Compression ratio	6.0:1
Weight	154kg (339lb)

M-11I A version created in 1938. A prototype was built, but series production was not arranged. The type had a new cylinder-piston group, a cam-driven gas-distribution mechanism, pneumatic starting and a crankshaft designed for a variable-pitch propeller. Power rating, 170/200hp, compression ratio 5.5:1.

M-11K This version was a further development of the M-11D, with modified crankshaft, crank case front cover and cylinders. It was in series production from the beginning of 1948. Pneumatic starting was introduced from the third series. Power rating, 115/125hp.

M-11L A version based on the third-series M-11K, this was in series production from September 1949. It had shielded ignition, an electric generator, increased ribbing on the cylinder heads and an additional compression ring. Power rating, 115/125hp.

M-11FR-1 A prototype of this version was built in 1946, and the type was in series production from the middle of 1947. It had a crankshaft for a variable-pitch propeller, a compressor, a shielded ignition system, a vacuum pump, an electric generator and pneumatic starting.

Characteristics

Power rating	140/160hp
Compression ratio	5.5:1
Weight	180kg (397lb)

M-11FR The last modification of the M-11, this was a version of the M-11FR-1 with an improved oil system, a K-11BP floatless carburettor, an R-2 rpm governor and forged (instead of cast) pistons. It was in series production from late 1948 until 1952. Weight 180kg (397lb) (without compressor, vacuum pump and electric generator).

Many other engine types were created using the M-11 as a basis. These are described in other chapters.

The M-11 and its versions were installed on the following production aeroplanes: U-2 (Po-2), Sh-2, AIR-6 (Ya-6), UT-1, UT-2, Yak-6, Yak-18, SAM-5bis, Shche-2 (TS-1), and LK-1. Prototypes powered by the M-11 were the BOK-2 (RK), BOK-5, AIR-6, AIR-9, AIR-9bis, AIR-10, AIR-12, SAM-5, SAM-5-2bis, SAM-25, NV-1, NV-2, NV-4, U-4, U-5, G-15, G-20, G-23bis, G-27, G-30 (powered glider), LIG-7, MP (powered glider), MiG-8 *Utka* (duck), *Pegas*, Yak-5, Yak-8, Yak-10, Yak-13, Ts-25M (powered glider), MU-3, IT-9, K-10, Gyup-1, *Kukaracha*, SPL, VVA-1, Anito-1, AT-1, MB-1, LEM-2, LEM-3, KAI-1 (UPB), KhAI-4, KhAI-8 (not completed), SK-7 (not completed), Aviavnito-3, LK-4, BICh-14 and E-3, Yak-Sh (helicopter) and the A-6, A-8, A-13 and A-14 autogyro prototypes.

M-48

Developed by the design bureau of Factory No. 29 in Zaporozhye in 1933-34 under the leadership of A.S. Nazarov, this engine used some components and subassemblies of the M-11 and was in the same family as

ABOVE: **The postwar M-11FR engine.**

ABOVE RIGHT: **A reproduction of an AIR-3 biplane, powered by an M-11FR.**

The Yak-10 liaison aeroplane of 1946, powered by the M-11FR, did not remain in series production for long, being quite quickly replaced by the Yak-12.

An M-11FR mounted in an amateur-built amphibious aircraft, 2002.

The M-48 engine.

An M-48 in a U-3 aeroplane.

The M-51 engine.

the M-49 and M-51. Prototype M-48s were built and tested, and in 1935 the engine was flight-tested in a U-3. The M-48 did not enter series production, but served as the basis for development of the MG-21.

Use of the M-48 was planned for the projected TsKB-9 light liaison aeroplane.

Characteristics

7-cylinder radial, four-stroke, air-cooled direct-drive engine with GCS.

Power rating	200hp (195hp in some sources)
Bore/stroke	125/140mm (4.92/5.51in)
Volume	12.0 litres (732cu in)
Compression ratio	5.0:1
Weight	194kg (428lb)

M-49

Developed at the design bureau of Factory No. 29 in Zaporozhye in 1933-34, under the leadership of A.S. Nazarov. This engine used some components and subassemblies of the M-11 and was in the same family of engines as the M-48 and M-51. The M-49 prototypes were built and tested, but the engine was not put into series production. All work on the engine was cancelled in April 1934. The M-49 served as the basis for development of the MG-31.

Characteristics

9-cylinder radial, four-stroke, air-cooled direct-drive engine with GCS.

Power rating	270/310hp
Bore/stroke	125/140mm (4.92/5.51in)
Compression ratio	5.0:1
Weight	248kg (547lb)

M-51

Developed in 1931 at the design bureau of Factory No. 29 in Zaporozhye, under the leadership of A.S. Nazarov, this was a further evolution of the famous M-11. The M-51 differed mainly in having a GCS and in using one cam ring instead of five camshafts. The engine incorporated some M-11 components and subassemblies, and was in the same family of engines as the M-48 and M-49. Compared with the M-11, the process of engine assembly and the installation of components was simplified. The crankshaft was mounted on roller bearings, and the crankshaft nose was splined. The prototypes were built and tested, and bench-running tests were conducted from March 1932. In May-June that year the engine, fitted with M-11 cylinders, underwent State testing, and in October it successfully passed State testing with its own cylinders. The M-51 was planned to enter series production in 1933, but this was not arranged. Later the M-51 became the prototype for the MG-11.

Characteristics

5-cylinder radial, four-stroke, air-cooled direct-drive engine with GCS.

Power rating	125/145hp
Bore/stroke	125/140mm (4.92/5.51in)
Volume	8.6 litres (525cu in)
Compression ratio	5.0:1
Weight	150kg (331lb) (later 155kg (342lb))

M-50 (3M-11)

Developed in 1931 at the design bureau of Factory No. 29 in Zaporozhye, under the leadership of A.S. Nazarov, this engine used M-11 components and subassemblies. The M-50 prototypes were built and successfully passed testing. The engine was being refined until 1934 at the Department of Light Engines of the NII GVF, under the leadership of M.A. Kossov. The M-50 was not introduced into series production owing to the absence of orders.

Characteristics

3-cylinder radial, four-stroke, air-cooled, direct-drive engine.

Power rating	60hp
Bore/stroke	125/140mm (4.92/5.51in)
Compression ratio	5.0:1
Weight	125kg (276lb)

CHAPTER ELEVEN

The History of the M-17

In the early 1920s Soviet Russia purchased various versions of the BMW III and BMW IV aero-engines from the German manufacturer. As early as late 1923 BMW representatives approached the Soviet Government with a proposal to produce the company's engines in the Soviet Union. Documents of the VSNKh dated February 1924 state that '… the proposal of the BMW company … is highly interesting and timely'. However, the engine types offered were not sufficiently powerful. In January 1925 test data concerning the new 12-cylinder BMW VI vee engine were transmitted from Munich to Moscow. At that time this was the most powerful aero-engine in Germany, and the documents raised considerable interest among Soviet experts. That same year two BMW VIs were ordered from the German company, and they subsequently passed bench testing at the NAMI.

As a result it was proposed that the engine be built in the USSR. On 26 August 1926, having considered six foreign watercooled engines, the NK UVVS decided that the BMW VI was the most desirable for production in the Soviet Union. This decision was supported by the leadership of Aviatrest, who stated: 'the BMW VI engine meets the requirements of the UVVS both in power rating and operational characteristics. This engine will cause fewer difficulties in production than any other type.'

At first, the discussions were based on the idea of lending the vacant Russkiy Reno factory in Rybinsk (later State Automobile Factory No. 3) to the Germans as a concession, but it was then decided to obtain a manufacturing licence and secure German assistance in setting up production of the engine.

In February 1927 a delegation headed by I.K. Mikhailov, a member of the Aviatrest board, left for Germany, where they toured the BMW factory in Munich. Negotiations were carried out in Germany for more than six months, and a number of prominent Soviet specialists participated in them, including V.Ya. Klimov, later to become famous. A contract with BMW was concluded in October 1927. It was signed on behalf of the Soviets by the chairman of the Aviatrest board, M.G. Urivaev, and for the Germans by directors F.-I. Popp and R. Feught. The contract granted Aviatrest the rights to produce the BMW VIaE6.0 and BMW VIaE7.3 versions of the engine. The German company undertook to inform the other party about all changes introduced into series engines for five years after signature the contract.

In return Aviatrest paid $50,000, and after acceptance of the first fifty engines was to pay 7.5 per cent from the price of each engine produced, but no less than $50,000 per year. The contract came into effect on 10 October 1927.

Engineering drawings, technical manuals, parts lists and drawings of fixtures and special tooling were sent to Russia by BMW. Additional production equipment was ordered, also with the help of the German partners. The contract stipulated that Soviet specialists be trained in Germany, and that German engineers would be provided to help set up production in the USSR. In addition, the Soviets hired a number of highly-skilled German workers, mainly from among those who sympathised with communist ideology. About 100 German engineers and workers went to Russia.

To start production, sets of the most complex parts were ordered from BMW, and engine components, including all of the electrical equipment, were purchased from subcontractors. One problem was that the blank forgings for some parts were not manufactured by the Munich-based company, but were purchased from other companies. Crankshaft forgings were supplied by Krupp, for instance. However, with the help of BMW the matter of arranging the supply of blanks for the initial production period was also settled.

It was decided to set up BMW VI production (under the designation M-17) at GAZ No. 6 factory in Rybinsk (from 1928, Factory No. 26). This factory had previously repaired automobiles, but in May 1924 had been transferred to Aviatrest. It had been inactive for a long time, and required considerable restora-

The chief designer of Factory No. 26, V.Ya. Klimov, explains the M-17 design during a course for foremen.

tion and modernization. This caused considerable delay in starting series production of the engines, and the first M-17s were not manufactured until the spring of 1930. However, these engines were not completely assembled from German parts, but used only the imported crankshafts. Meanwhile, the information on engine improvements had been promptly forwarded from Germany. This also included drawings for the BMW VIb version. Some of the German modifications had been introduced into the M-17. In fact the early-series M-17 was closer to the BMW VIb than to the BMW VIa, but its cylinders were the same as those of the latter. Faults in manufacturing processes, poor-quality materials and strengthening of the weakest parts meant that the Soviet-built engines were heavier than the German original, weighing 31kg (68lb) more on average, and had a lower power rating.

On 15 August 1930, after the successful testing of an engine from the first batch (series 'A') produced at Factory No. 26, the M-17 was officially introduced into operation by Service units of the VVS RKKA.

The production rate was considerably behind schedule. By the end of 1930 the Rybinsk factory had built 165 engines, and, by April 1931, 334. The M-17 was in great demand by aircraft factories, as it was used for the mass-produced R-5, R-6, TB-1, and TB-3 aeroplanes. The UVVS therefore ordered that engines should be transported singly in carriages attached to passenger trains, regardless of the carriage load.

To compensate for the shortfall in M-17 production, the STO issued a decree in January 1930 ordering that production of the new engine be arranged at Factory No. 24 in Moscow. A set of drawings was forwarded from Rybinsk, production in Moscow started in April, and by June the first three engines had been assembled and set up for factory bench testing.

However, the quality of the engines produced by Factory No. 24 turned out to be very poor. Moreover, the factory introduced a range of unapproved changes to the engine's design and the production technology, mainly aimed at simplifying manufacture. For instance, the camshaft cams were given a simplified profile, and this upset the phases of gas distribution. Valve shapes were changed, and the cylinders did not correspond to those of the BMW VIa or the BMW VIb. All of the pistons were different, and they were adjusted 'on the spot'. The engines' compression ratio did not exceed 6.15:1, though 6.3:1 was specified.

These changes considerably reduced the engine's ouput, which was 615-630hp instead of the specified 680hp. As a result, all M-17s built at Factory No. 24 were recognised as being of poor quality. Under an order issued by the head of the VVS on 27 November 1930, they were accepted as training engines at a reduced price. Although the Moscow factory built thirty engines, only seventeen left the warehouse. Following the successful demonstration of the M-15-powered I-5 fighter before K.E. Voroshilov, the People's Commissar of Military and Naval Affairs, in the summer of 1930, the director of Factory No. 24 was given permission to cancel production of the M-17 and start series production of the M-15 and the related M-26. The UVVS objected in vain to this decision, which later proved to be a mistake.

Meanwhile, the Rybinsk factory continued delivering growing numbers of M-17s. During 1931, 679 engines were assembled, meeting the demands of aircraft factories and providing stock to replace worn-out engines in VVS units. From February 1931 some engines were fitted with crankshafts forged at the Artillery Factory in Motovilikha. At the same time, other changes pertaining to the BMW VIb were introduced (new valve seats, a crankshaft with a modified end, corrugated cylinder liners, etc.), which led to the appearance of the M-17B. By 10 June seven of these engines had passed military acceptance.

The M-17B began to receive the Soviet-built carburettors and fuel pumps,

FAR LEFT: **An R-5 reconnaissance aeroplane has its M-17 engine started by an automobile-based starter, known in the English-speaking world as a Hucks Starter, after its inventor.**

LEFT: **The M-17 engine.**

BELOW: **The TB-1 was powered by two M-17s.**

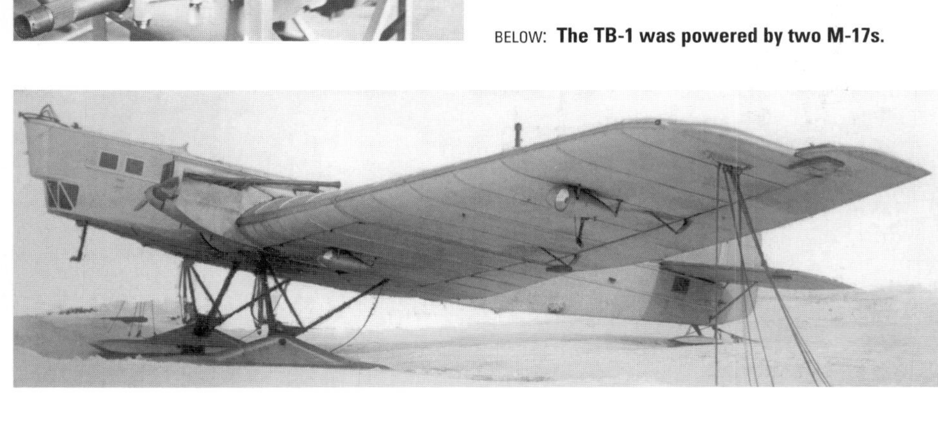

The first series-production version of the TB-3 heavy bomber was powered by M-17s.

replacing those imported from France. The Soviet K-17 carburettor, developed at Factory No. 24, was tested on the M-17 for the first time in April 1931.

In 1930 the series-built M-17s had a compression ratio of 6.0:1. The first high-altitude versions, with a compression ratio of 7.3:1, were built in November 1930. Subsequent batches were made up of engines having both compression ratios, in different proportions. The first such batch, series 'Z', manufactured in February 1931, included twenty engines of the high-altitude M-17E7.3 type. Later, a number of complete batches of high-altitude engines were built. For instance, all engines of the 'L' series had a compression ratio of 7.3:1.

Almost from the beginning of M-17 production, plans were being made for the engine's further modernization. Soviet designers not only followed in the footseps of the Germans, but also tried to introduce their own innovations. In particular, a scheme for experimental work, approved by the Revvoensovet on 1 October 1930, included 'the M-17 with a four-valve head'. This engine was planned to undergo State testing by 1 June 1931, but no information about this work has been traced. During 1933-34 engine modernization under the leadership of engineer Rogov resulted in an M-17 boosted to 800hp, which passed its tests in April 1934. No fewer than three prototypes were built, and one was installed in the personal R-5 of Ya.I. Alksnis, head of the VVS. However, this work had no influence on series production.

The lack of interest in the modernized M-17 was related to the appearance of the indigenous M-34, created under the leadership of A.A. Mikulin. This engine was developed as an intended replacement for the M-17, and had the same overall dimensions and attachment points. The M-34 definitely had better development prospects than the obsolescent BMW engine, with its separate cylinder liners. Introduction of the M-34 into series production in 1933 decreased interest in the development of new versions of the German engine. It was planned that Mikulin's engine would replace the M-17 on the assembly lines.

Indeed, M-17 production was growing until 1934, when it reached a peak of 5,662 engines per year. At that time Factory No. 26 was building about half of the total number of aero-engines produced in the country. Then the recession began.

In 1935 the Rybinsk factory began to set up production of the French Hispano-Suiza 12Ybrs engine (built as the M-100 in the USSR), and this gradually became the factory's main product. However, the aviation versions of the M-17 were being manufactured until the end of 1939. The last was the M-17F, a low-altitude version intended mainly for light bombers and attack aeroplanes. This engine featured a number of modifications that facilitated maintenance and allowed longer periods

Maintenance of a TB-3's M-17 in the Crimea, 1942.

An M-17 in the R-6 'cruiser' (escort aeroplane).

Left **An R-5 reconnaissance aeroplane and light bomber on display in the Russian Air Force Museum at Monino.**

Below left **The PS-9 airliner, powered by two M-17s, was the twin-engine version of the ANT-9 tri-motor.**

Right **The MBR-2 flying-boat, powered by an M-17 driving a pusher propeller, serving with the Baltic Fleet in the mid-1930s.**

between scheduled maintenance (up to 400hr). By then the M-17 was a completely Soviet version of the engine, which had no German counterpart. The reason for keeping the M-17 in production for so long lay in the high number of aeroplanes in service with the air force and Civil Air Fleet that were powered by it. For instance, it was installed on more than a half of the available TB-3 bombers, which also needed spare engines.

From 1936 another application was found for the M-17. The engine was adapted for installation in tanks, and designated M-17T. These engines powered the mass-produced BT-7 and T-28 tanks. In 1936 the Rybinsk factory was already producing three tank engines for every aero-engine. In 1940 the M-17T was replaced in production by the improved M-17L, which powered the T-35 heavy multi-turret tank. It remained in production until the beginning of 1941, when the last five engines were delivered for military acceptance.

In 1941, by order of the Chief Armoured Forces Directorate of the RKKA, an attempt was made to arrange production of M-17 tank engines at the Gorkovskiy Automobile Factory in Gorkiy, but this did not come about owing to the severe conditions in the first year of the Great Patriotic War.

Almost throughout the war, different workshops assembled aviation and tank versions of the M-17 from sets of parts. No information has been found about the total number of engines assembled in this manner. However, more than 27,000 factory-built M-17s were produced, 19,000 of which were aero-engines.

The German-designed M-17 had a considerable influence on the Soviet aviation industry, mainly because it was produced in far greater quantities in the USSR than in its country of origin.

M-17

This engine, widely used in Soviet aviation during the first half of 1930s, was a copy of the German BMW VI, an agreement for the licensed production of which, including technical assistance in setting up production, was signed with the BMW company in October 1927.

The M-17 was in series production at Factory No. 26 in Rybinsk from 1930 to 1941, and at Factory No. 24 in Moscow in 1930. The first engines were assembled in Rybinsk in the spring of 1930, using a number of parts imported from Germany and fuel pumps and carburettors supplied from France. Mass-production of the M-17 was set up in 1931. Gradually the Soviet manufacturers mastered production of the complete engine, though electrical equipment (magnetos and spark plugs) was imported for a long time. The mass-production of different aviation versions of the M-17 was carried until 1939, and tank versions were built until 1942, when Factory No. 466 attempted to resume production of the engine and built the last ten M-17s. In total 27,534 engines were built, almost all of them in Rybinsk.

The engine was officially introduced into service with VVS RKKA units on 15 August 1930.

Characteristics

12-cylinder in-line vee, direct-drive, four-stroke, water-cooled engine, with provision for synchronization.

Power rating	dependant on the version
Bore/stroke	160/190mm (6.30/7.48in) (199mm (7.83in) in cylinders with articulated connecting rods)
Compression ratio	6.0:1 or 7.3:1
Weight	540-553kg (1,190-1,219lb)

The following versions of the M-17 are known:

M-17 The first series version of the engine, this had an imported ignition system and a Zenith 60DCJ or 60DCL carburettor. It was produced in two variants: with a compression ratio of 6.0:1 under the designation M-17 or M-17E6.0, with flat-head pistons, power rating 505/680hp; or with a compression ratio of 7.3:1 under the designation M-17-7.3 or M-17E7.3, with dished piston heads; power rating, 500/730hp. The engine weighed 540kg (1,190lb). Engines of 'type

The SSS (3S) attack aircraft, powered by an M-17F. These aircraft were used by the Republicans in the Spanish Civil War, and by the Soviet forces during the conflict with the Japanese near Lake Khasan in 1938.

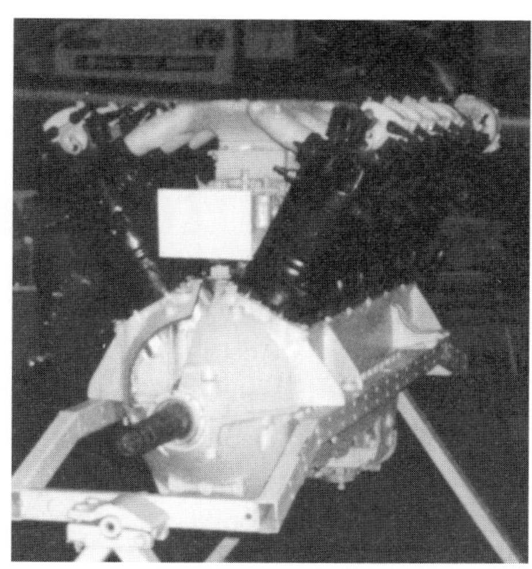

An M-17F on display in the Monino museum.

A' designation ('of lower standard') were assembled from parts having dimensions beyond the limits of fixed tolerances but still serviceable. Such engines were heavier (up to 570kg (1,257lb)), and had a lower maximum power rating (645hp for a compression ratio of 6.0:1, and 705hp for compression ratio of 7.3:1). These engines were accepted at a 20 per cent discount.

M-17B An improved version of the M-17 similar to the German BMW VIb, with some parts strengthened (in particular the crankshaft nose), a modified crankshaft end, new valve seats and smaller exhaust valves. This engine was in production from June 1931 in the following variants: M-17B (compression ratio 6.0:1 and power rating 505/680hp); M-17B-7.3 (compression ratio 7.3:1 and power rating 505/730hp). Later, some of these engines were converted into the M-17F by replacing some parts and units.

Boosted M-17 An experimental, rpm-boosted version which had maximum power rating of up to 800hp. This engine was created in Rybinsk in 1933-34 under the leadership of engineer Rogov. Three prototypes were built, and the engine underwent bench testing in April 1934 and was test flown in an R-5. It was not introduced into series production.

M-17, coupled version An experimental coupled version; the powerplant for the G-1 (*Gigant*, giant) aeroplane. Two M-17s were installed nose-to-nose, driving a common angle gear. Bench testing of the powerplant took place at Zhukovskiy Academy in April 1934.

M-17F An improved series-built version of the M-17, this had sliding bearings under the pins of articulated connecting rods, valves of the type used on the M-5 engine, a K-17a carburettor, Soviet electrical equipment, and was equipped with an electric generator (from 1935).

Characteristics

Power rating	500/715hp
Compression ratio	6.0:1 (only this variant was built)
Weight	550kg (1,212lb)

M-17T A tank version developed in 1935 and in series production in 1936-39; 7,951 were built. Compared with the original aero-engine it was derated in rpm, had a K-17a carburettor, a strengthened cooling system and an oil coil. The pneumatic starter was replaced by an electric starter. Power rating 500hp, compression ratio 6.0:1. This powerplant was installed on Soviet series-built tanks of the following types: BT-7, BT-7A, OT-7, T-28, T-28E, T-35; and on PT-1 and T-29 experimental tanks.

M-17L A version of the M-17 intended for installation in the T-35 heavy tank. In series production in 1940-41, 530 being built. This had a strengthened front part of the crankcase, the lower cover of the crankcase was removed, an air supply was arranged from the inner spaces, and it was provided with a pneumatic starter. Power rating, 650hp, compression ratio 6.0:1.

Different versions of the M-17 powered the following types of series production aircraft: I-3, I-7, TB-1, TB-3, R-5, R-6, MBR-2, K-5, PS-9, PS-89 (ZiG-89). It was also installed in the following aircraft prototypes: TSh-1, TSh-2, G-37, MI-3, MI-3D; and was planned for the use in the MR and G-1 (*Gigant*) aeroplane projects.

A pair of T-28 tanks, powered by M-17Ts, parade through Red Square, Moscow, on 7 November 1939.

The T-35 five-turret heavy tank was powered by the M-17L.

CHAPTER TWELVE

Jupiter Engines from Zaporozhye

The Jupiter air-cooled radial engine, created at the Bristol Aeroplane Company in Britain under the leadership of Roy Fedden (later Sir Roy), was very successful. It was built in large numbers in Britain, and licensed production was arranged in France, Germany and, later, Poland.

The issue of arranging Jupiter production in the Soviet Union was first raised in 1927. On 1 November 1927 the matter was considered at a meeting in the office of P.I. Baranov, head of the UVVS. Two possibilities were proposed; acquiring a license or agreeing to grant the British company an engine-building factory on a concession basis. However, at that time, direct contact with the Bristol company was not considered. Two reasons apparently existed for this situation: relations with Great Britain had deteriorated (in 1927, after 'the Arcos case', diplomatic relations were broken off), and British engines were built using the Imperial system of measurement. At the meeting it was therefore decided to approach the French Gnome-Rhône company to arrange production of Jupiter engines on a concession basis at Factory No. 29 in Zaporozhye.

Opinions soon changed, however, and it was decided to obtain a licence. The negotiations were carried out in parallel in France (with Gnome-Rhône) and Germany (with Siemens). These companies produced metric versions of the Jupiter that differed only slightly but were not interchangeable owing to the different systems of tolerances and fits used in their respective countries. Gnome-Rhône was obviously favoured, and the negotiations with the German competitor were conducted only as a means of gaining the most favourable conditions from the French.

In Paris the negotiations were led by Petrov, the representative of the Soviet military department. Under the decree of the STO, 500,000 roubles in gold had been assigned for obtaining the licence. Initially, Gnome-Rhône requested payment for each engine produced (from 10 to 12 per cent of its cost), with an annual production rate of no fewer than 150 engines. As the Soviets planned to undertake mass production of Jupiters, this seemed very disadvantageous. Eventually the French company agreed to a fixed price of $250,000, without any payments related to the number of engines produced. By 30 March 1928 the parties had basically reached an agreement.

However, a decree issued by the STO on 18 May limited the payment to $100,000 dollars. After another month of negotiations the Sovnarkom accepted the Gnome-Rhône company's terms, and on 22 June ordered that the agreement be signed. The approved text travelled between Moscow and Paris for two more months before it was signed by representatives of both parties, M.G. Urivaev, chairman of the Aviatrest Board, and P. Weiler, representing the French company. on 23 August 1928.

Under the agreement Gnome-Rhône was to grant Aviatrest the right to produce the Jupiter VI (Gnome-Rhône 9A) in all its forms, including geared versions and those equipped superchargers. The French company provided drawings of the engine, manuals, parts lists, calculations, assembly instructions, drawings of tools and fixtures, and technical charts. Company specialists also prepared the drawings for reorganization of the Zaporozhye factory to build the new engine. It was assumed at the time that the factory would be supplied with production tooling ordered with the help of Gnome-Rhône in France and Germany, and Bristol in Britain.

For an additional fee the French company offered to supply dies, templates, moulds, measuring cramps and gauges. The matter of providing sample Jupiter engines was not discussed, as there were several in the USSR by then. In addition, the Soviets purchased a batch of 250 completed Jupiters of different versions.

The agreement allowed Soviet-built engines to be exported only to Afghanistan. Later this condition was violated when, during the Spanish Civil War, the USSR sold the Republicans I-15 fighters powered by M-22 engines (the designation bestowed upon the Jupiter in the Soviet Union). An interesting feature of the agreement with Gnome-Rhône was a clause not only requiring the French to inform the Soviets of all changes in the design of series engines, but also requiring Aviatrest to advise Gnome-Rhône of all changes introduced in Soviet production. All other licence agreements, with BMW and, later, Hispano-Suiza and Curtiss-Wright, only stipulated the transfer of information from the licensee.

According to the schedule, all documentation was to be received from France by May 1929, and in September 1930 the factory was to test the first series batch of ten engines. In reality, all the drawings had arrived at Zaporozhye by 1 June 1929, their acceptance being carried out in Paris by S.N. Osipov, an engineer from Factory No. 29. At the factory the documentation was processed by the technical department under the leadership of engineer Pivovarov. This department had been established in September 1928, specially for carrying out work on the Jupiter. By January 1930 the staff of the department consisted of 39 specialists.

By 15 December the French drawings had been copied and converted to Soviet standards. In parallel, from September 1929, the factory had begun the development of production rigs and fixtures. About a quarter of the drawings for these had been received from France, but the remainder had to be prepared by the factory specialists. In total, Zaporozhye engineers designed 367 fixtures. By 1 January 1930 the development of the 'process sheets' (technical charts) had been completed.

Other Soviet enterprises also assisted in arranging Jupiter production. Some tooling was manufactured at Factory No. 26 in Rybinsk, and the fixtures were built at

Factory No. 24 in Moscow. It was planned to obtain some tooling from abroad, but it was left too late to place the orders, and the necessary tools were manufactured in the USSR.

For the first Soviet-built engines the spark plugs, carburettors, fuel pumps, magnetos and parts of gas-distribution mechanism were purchased in France. These components were delivered through Gnome-Rhône, which received a 5 per cent commission for this service. For the first ten engines the Soviets also purchased forgings and castings. Delay in arranging their production in the USSR resulted in the order of one more batch of forgings, which was sent by sea from Havre to Revel (now Tallinn) in Estonia on 8 March 1930.

The Soviet-built engine, designated M-22, was initially to correspond to the French 420hp 9Ad version, but with a strengthened crankshaft. However, in the course of production preparations the design was brought closer to the 480hp 9Aq. As the Soviet system of tolerances and fits differed from that used by the French, it transpired that Zaporozhye-built engines were not interchangeable with either the French or German Jupiters.

In December 1930, three months later than scheduled, the factory started testing the first ten M-22s (series 'A'). During testing, the maximum power rating attained was 567hp. During 1930 the factory built twenty-five engines, which had a considerable percentage of imported parts.

The second batch (series 'B'), also of ten engines, was delivered in April 1931, and all the castings were Soviet-made. Unfortunately, the indigenous castings were inferior to the imported ones, as a different alloy was used in Zaporozhye and the wrong techniques were employed. Initially, many castings were rejected because of cracks.

The series 'B' engines had crankshaft end caps of steel, and the materials for some parts were changed. Series 'A' and 'B' engines had an increased compression ratio (6.55:1 to 6.58:1), and the period between scheduled maintenance was defined as 50hr.

From the third series (series 'V'), which consisted of forty engines, the period between scheduled maintenance reached 100hr. Fixed bushings for the master rods were also introduced on this batch, instead of floating bushings. By this time the engines were entirely Soviet-made, but some powerplant units were still imported. Production of the series 'V' was completed in August 1931, and the engines were accepted in September. In fact, it took the whole of 1931 to refine the design and arrange its production. During this year only sixty-eight M-22s were built, obliging the Soviets to continue importing French Jupiters.

A considerable increase in the delivery of Zaporozhye-built engines began in 1932, when, according to air force records, 357 engines were produced (Aviatrest records put the total at 400). After that the M-22 was built almost without modification until the beginning of 1936.

In 1933-34 it was also planned to arrange production of the M-22s at the new Factory No. 19 in Perm. In fact, not a single engine of this type was assembled there, because the factory was redirected to the production of the M-25 (the Soviet copy of the American Wright Cyclone).

In total, more than 2,717 Jupiters were built in the USSR. This engine was the primary type used in fighter units of the VVS RKKA in the first half of 1930s.

As early as July 1928 it had been planned to follow manufacture of the 9Aq type, which corresponded to the British Jupiter VI, with production of the high-altitude 9As version (Jupiter VII), and also to build a counterpart of the Jupiter VIII. The drawings for the 9As were accepted in France in November 1929 and delivered to the Soviet Union at the beginning of 1930.

Then priorities changed. According to the plan for experimental work approved by Revvoensovet, two main directions for M-22 modernization were indicated. The engine was to be fitted with gearing and with the supercharger, these versions being designated M-22R and M-22N respectively. Considerable attention was paid to the geared version, as it was intended for bombers and passenger aircraft. Drawings of the Farman-type gear from the 9Akx engine were received from France, and development of this version was carried out according to the plans of both the air force and Civil Air Fleet. State testing of the M-22R and M-22N was planned for October-November 1931.

RIGHT: **The I-5 fighter, powered by the M-22.**

BELOW: **The M-22 engine.**

The I-Zet fighter, powered by the M-22. The aircraft seen here is fitted with a device to enable it to hook on to a trapeze slung beneath a TB-3 carrier aeroplane in flight.

The Civil Air Fleet tried to arrange development of a special 'arctic' M-22 for operation in the northern regions of the country, but the factory refused to carry out the work on this modification.

Development of the new M-22 versions was performed by the technical design department of Factory No. 29, headed by A.S. Nazarov. As early as 19 August 1931 the project for M-22R development, financed by the Civil Air Fleet, had been completed. However, no information on the manufacture of the prototype has yet been found. Development of the M-22N was carried out, but this version, too, was not manufactured.

This situation could be explained by the fact that Nazarov was performing unplanned work on a more extensive modernization of the M-22 that was financed by the factory. The M-22U project, initiated in April-May 1932, combined the installation of a GCS of the M-22N type with new cylinder heads (similar to those to the Pratt & Whitney Hornet), a greater area of cylinder ribbing, and a splined-end crankshaft (to take a variable-pitch propeller). Nazarov also introduced a range of other changes to the design. The new engine was intended primarily for fighters. The project was submitted to the UVVS and introduced into the plan for 1933 under the designation M-58.

Several M-58 prototypes were built, and passed bench testing. During the engine's refinement its power rating was increased to 800hp, but the Achilles' heel was its supercharger, which had poor reliability. Consequently an interim version was created, the M-58MN, which was less highly supercharged. This engine satisfactorily passed factory tests, and State testing followed in September 1934. From November 1935 to May 1936 the M-58MN was test flown in a UTI-3 aeroplane (the two-seat trainer version of the I-16 fighter) at the NII VVS.

The long period of refinement considerably reduced the value of the M-58. While at low altitudes the M-58's power rating exceeded that of the M-25 (Wright SR-1820-F3) and M-75 (Gnome-Rhône 9K), both of these engines had better performance at altitudes greater than 3,000m (10,000ft). Thus, introduction of the M-58MN into series production would conflict with the officially declared course of development for high-altitude engines for fighters. In addition, by the time testing had been completed, production of the basic version of the M-22 had ceased. The Zaporozhye factory was preparing for series production of the M-85 (Gnome-Rhône 14Krsd) and M-75 engines, which were of considerably different design to the M-22.

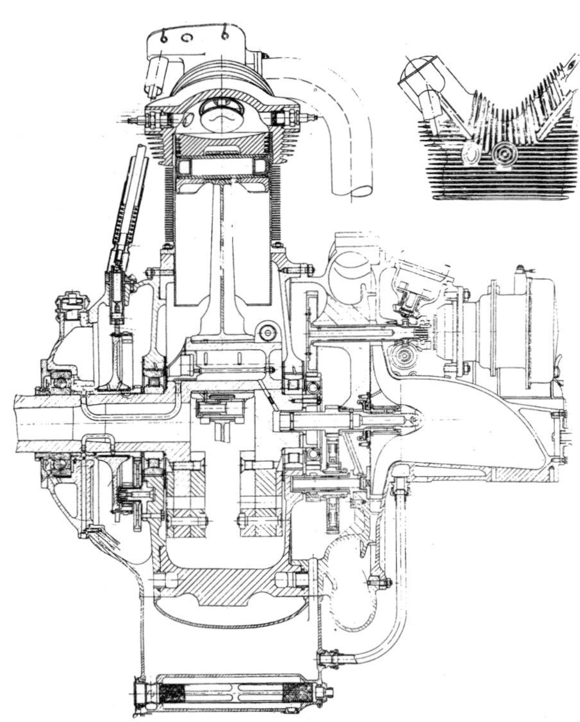

A drawing of the M-58 (M-22U) engine.

The M-58MN engine.

The last straw for the M-58 programme was a comment written by the head of the VVS, Ya.I. Alksnis, on the the NII VVS assessment of the M-58MN test report, which read: 'Considering the availability of the M-25, this type is not of any interest'. After that, all further work on the M-58 was cancelled.

Thus ends the story of the Soviet-built Jupiters. Factory No. 29 replaced the type on its production lines with engines based on other Gnome-Rhône powerplants, the Mistral and Mistral Major.

ABOVE: **An M-22 fitted with the AP-11bis experimental integrated exhaust muffler, during tests in July 1937.**

RIGHT: **An M-22 in the Russian Air Force Museum at Monino.**

M-22

Widely used in the Soviet Union in 1930s, this was a copy of the French Gnome-Rhône 9A engine, which in turn was a licence-built reproduction of the British Bristol Jupiter VI. Agreement on licence production and technical assistance was signed with Gnome-Rhône company in August 1928, and series production was arranged at Factory No. 29 (Zaporozhye). The first series batch was accepted in December 1930. It was planned that, after arranging series production of the M-15, this would replace the M-22 in Soviet military aviation, but the M-22 demonstrated greater reliability. Production of the M-22 continued until the end of 1935, 2,717 engines being built.

Characteristics

9-cylinder radial, direct-drive, four-stroke, air-cooled engine, with the option of synchronizing gear.

Power rating	480/570hp
Bore/stroke	146/190mm (5.75/7.48in)
Volume	28.64 litres (1,748cu in)
Compression ratio	6.5:1
Weight	378kg (833lb)

The following versions of the engine are known:

M-22 The main series version. Steel end-caps to the crankshaft were introduced at the beginning of 1931.

M-22R A geared version, this had planetary gear with conic satellite gears (of the Farman type), similar to that used on the Gnome-Rhône 9Akx. It was planned to build five engine prototypes by 1 October 1931 and carry out State testing from 1 November. Engineering drawings for the M-22R had been prepared by 19 August 1931, but no information on the manufacture of a prototype has been found. Power rating, 480/585hp, weight, 408kg (899lb) (according to project data).

M-22N A version with a lower compression ratio and a GCS. It was planned to build one prototype by 1 June 1931 and carry out State testing from 1 October of that year, but no information on the engine's manufacture has been found. Power rating, 585/585hp, weight (according to the specification) 385kg (849lb).

M-22 'Arctic' A version intended for operation in the northern regions of the

The I-15 biplane fighter was powered by the M-22.

An A-7 autogyro, powered by an M-22.

LEFT: **The M-58N engine.**

RIGHT: **The M-58MN during tests in a UTI-3 fighter-trainer, the two-seat version of the I-16.**

USSR. A specification for this version was issued by the Chief Department of the GVF in 1931, but the project did not come to fruition.

The M-22 was installed in the following series-built aircraft: I-5, I-15, I-16 (early types), K-5, Stal-3, KhAI-1, I-Zet. It also powered the following prototypes: TB-5, Sh-5, AIR-7, K-12, ASK, BICh-17 (not flown); and was specified for the Stal-4 project. The engine powered the series A-7-3a autogyro and the A-7/A-7bis autogyro prototypes, and was installed on the I-4 and KR-1 aeroplanes as a replacement for imported Jupiters.

M-58 (M-22U)

A further development of the M-22 engine (Gnome-Rhône 9A Jupiter), initially designated M-22U. The development was undertaken during April-May 1932 in the technical design department of Factory No. 29 (Zaporozhye), under the leadership of A.S. Nazarov, with the aim of replacing the M-22. It was an unplanned version, being created on the factory's initiative. It differed from the standard M-22 in having Hornet-type cylinder heads, hollow air-cooled exhaust valves, cylinders with closer ribbing, new flanges, roller bearings for the crankshaft (except for the front bearing), a new conrod lubrication system, a splined crankshaft end, installation of a GCS, and the use of titanium alloys. Manufacture of the first three prototypes, designated M-58, started in April 1932. These had imported magnetos and carburettors. The first prototype underwent testing from October of the same year, and considerable wear of the cam rings, excessive oil consumption and cracks in the crankcase were noted. The second prototype was assembled in February 1933, shortly followed by the third, lightweight, engine.

From April 1933 the M-58 was included in the State plan for experimental work. The later prototypes had a rear-facing exhaust instead of the original side-facing type, the cylinder heads were strengthened, the spark plug seatings were distanced, air-cooling of the exhaust valves was replaced by sodium-cooling, and the conrod and crankshaft counterbalance fasteners were strengthened. Due to unreliable operation of the GCS, the supercharging level was reduced by decreasing the rpm and diameter of the impeller. At the same time the front sliding bearing was replaced by a roller bearing. In this form the M-58MN underwent bench testing from April 1934. In April-May it was tested without supercharging, and in July-August the GCS-equipped engine passed 50hr factory testing. In September that year the M-58MN passed State testing, during which it suffered breakages in the GCS drive, piston rings and valve springs, broken-off valves and cracks in the crankcase. It was planned to build a small batch of fifteen to twenty M-58MNs in 1934.

In October 1935 an M-58MN was installed in a UTI-3 at Factory No. 22 in Gorkiy. This aircraft underwent flight testing at the NII VVS from 30 November 1935 to 25 May 1936.

The Zaporozhye factory was also preparing the fully-supercharged M-58N. Although a prototype of this engine was assembled, no information regarding its testing has been found. Work on the M-58N ceased in June 1936.

Characteristics

9-cylinder radial, direct-drive, four-stroke, air-cooled engine with single-stage single-speed GCS.

Power rating	630/800hp according to the project, actually 630/785hp
Bore/stroke	160/190mm (6.30/7.48in)
Volume	34.4 litres (2,099cu in)
Compression ratio	5.5:1
Weight	dependant on version

The following versions of the engine are known:

M-58 The first three engine prototypes with full-scale supercharging. Power rating, 630/680hp, weight 445-450kg (981-992lb).

M-58MN Two (probably three) further prototypes with decreased supercharging. Power rating, 630/785hp, weight 465-476kg (1,025-1,049lb).

M-58N This version differed from the M-58MN in its GCS drive, impeller and diffuser.

In total, six (or, according to other sources, eight) M-58s were built.

It was planned to install the M-58 in the I-14, I-15, DI-6 and I-16 fighters.

CHAPTER THIRTEEN

A Family of Air-cooled Engines Developed at Factory No. 24

Development of the first engine in this family, the M-15, was started as early as October 1926 at the GAZ No. 2 Ikar factory in Moscow, under the leadership of A.A. Bessonov and A.P. Ostrovskiy. According to the requirement, the 9-cylinder air-cooled radial engine was to be a Soviet counterpart of the Pratt & Whitney Hornet, intended as a mass-produced high-altitude engine for fighters. An acceptable high-altitude performance was to be achieved by means of a GCS.

The M-15 was not a direct copy of the Hornet, but embodied quite a number of original engineering solutions. In particular, all articulated connecting rods were of the same length, with master rod lugs of the same radii. The same piston stroke in all cylinders was achieved by varying the height of the cylinder flange installation relatively to the crankcase. Principally, all that remained of the original Hornet was the design of the cylinder and its head.

In spite of several reorganizations at the factory (the creation of the OMO TsKB, and the merging of the GAZ No. 4 and GAZ No. 2 factories in March 1927 to create Factory No. 24), development work on the engine proceeded. In August 1927 the initial version of the project was completed, and the manufacture of two prototypes started in September.

By this time the designers had prepared the second version of the project, designated 2M-15. In this version the engine was lightened, its cylinder heads strengthened, and design of the valves changed. On 14 September 1927 the NK UVVS approved the project, and the factory started issuing engineering drawings of the engine.

Testing of the first M-15 prototype began in July 1928, but the results did not satisfy the designers. The estimated power rating was not reached, and the engine's weight exceeded the figure in the specification. Thus the third prototype was built according to the drawings for the 2M-15. It was completed in August 1929 and put to bench testing in the same month.

It was proposed that a unified family of engines of different power rating, based on the 2M-15, be created. This family was to include, in addition to the 2M-15, the 7-cylinder 300hp M-26 and 14-cylinder 750hp M-29. It is possible that the M-29 was being developed as a coupled M-26. The projects for the M-26 and M-29 had been completed by February 1929, but only the M-26 reached the stage of prototype manufacture. Development work on the M-29 was cancelled at the preliminary documentation stage.

Even before completion of the factory's testing programme, a 2M-15 was installed in the second prototype I-5 fighter. After the aircraft had demonstrated the engine's capabilities in flights from the Moscow Central Airfield, People's Commissar Voroshilov agreed that the engine should be put into series production, even though it had not yet passed State tests. Some documents indicate that Voroshilov signed the draft of this order directly at the airfield. However, at that time such procedures were more relaxed, and it quite often happened that a series production engine

RIGHT: **An M-15 in the Russian Air Force Museum at Monino.**

BELOW: **The second I-5 fighter prototype, powered by an M-15.**

(even one from a later series) was submitted for State testing.

On 1 April 1930 a decree was issued, cancelling the order for M-17 production at Factory No. 24 and replacing it with a order for a batch of 2M-15s and M-26s. On 1 June the 2M-15 was officially introduced into service under the M-15 designation.

Thus, series production of the engine started before it had undergone State testing. The M-15 and M-26 became the first Soviet series-built engines equipped with GCS. However, it transpired that the air force had no need for the M-26, and the M-15 had no considerable advantages over the more reliable M-22. The UVVS refused to take the engines ordered, and passed the order to the Chief Directorate of the GVF. At that time civil aviation received the 'crumbs from the table' of the military, so the authority gladly agreed to take the engines.

Later, the M-15 underwent State testing three times, and on every occasion it was rejected owing to different failures. The M-26 managed to pass State tests successfully in March 1931, and was subsequently accepted for Service testing.

In fact, delivery of series-production M-15s started in January 1931. At first they passed through the military acceptance procedure, similar to engines intended for air force use, but from November 1931 the GVF representatives began to carry out the acceptance procedure.

Fifteen of the first-series M-26s had been assembled by 27 March 1931. However, production of the M-15 and M-26 did not last long. On 5 August 1931 a decree of the USSR Revvoensovet was issued concerning the reduction of the number of aero-engine types in series production. Only the M-11, M-17, M-22 and M-28 were kept in production. The high failure rate of ANT-9 and K-5 aeroplanes, powered by the M-26 and M-15 respectively, had an additional adverse impact on the engines' reputation. They were phased out of production, and taken out of operation shortly thereafter.

At the beginning of 1931 it was planned to create an improved engine version, designated M-15a, that was boosted up to 500hp. At first it was planned to give this task to Factory No. 24, and then to the IAM, but both organizations persistently rejected the work. As a result, even the project for this version was not developed.

M-15

The M-15 used components of the Pratt & Whitney Hornet, and was one of the first Soviet engines equipped with GCS. It was intended for installation in fighters. The M-15 was being developed at the Ikar factory from October 1926, under the leadership of A.A. Bessonov and N.P. Ostrovskiy. Two prototypes were being built at that factory from September 1927, and It was planned to proceed to testing from April 1928, but in fact the tests started in July of that year.

An improved version of the engine, designated 2M-15, was tested from August 1929. From 1 June 1930 the 2M-15 was taken into service with the VVS RKKA as the M-15. It was in series production at Factory No. 24 in Moscow from the beginning of 1931, and the engine's acceptance procedure began in June of the same year. The type was submitted for State testing four times, on 21 July 1930, 20 December 1930, 17 January 1931 and 21 September 1931. On every occasion the testing was stopped owing to failures of the GCS drive and supercharger impeller.

In total, 406 engines of this type were built. However, the M-15 was superseded by the M-22 in the military, mainly because of its low reliability. In January 1932 the M-15 lost to the M-22 after comparative tests at the NII VVS. All M-15 engines were passed on for civil aviation use.

Characteristics

9-cylinder radial, four-stroke, air-cooled, direct-drive engine with GCS and synchronization.

Bore/stroke	150/170mm (5.91/6.69in)
Volume	27.02 litres (1,649cu in)
Compression ratio	5.4:1 (actually 5.5:1-5.7:1)

Power rating and weight dependant on version and series

The following versions of the engine are known:

M-15 An original version, two prototypes of which were built. Power rating according to the project, 500/600hp, weight 420kg (926lb).

LEFT: **An M-15 engine during assembly.**

BELOW: **The K-5 airliner was M-15 powered.**

2M-15 The second version, with strengthened cylinder heads and new valves. This engine was in series production as the M-15. Power rating, 450/550hp (500/650hp according to the project data), weight of an 'A' series engine 419.5kg (925lb), and of a 'G' series unit, 450kg (992lb). Engines of the 'B' series had a shortened crankshaft, strengthened cylinder head attachment and strengthened gears for the GCS drive. The 'V' series engines had new valve springs, strengthened nuts for cylinders attachment, and one-piece rods for the valve levers.
M-15a A project for an improved 500hp version. Weight 400kg (880lb).

The engine was installed on K-5 and I-5 (prototype) aeroplanes, and was proposed for installation in the I-4 fighter.

This accident to a K-5 was caused by the failure of its M-15 engine.

M-26 (KIM)

This engine was developed under the leadership of A.A. Bessonov at Factory No. 24 with the aim of replacing imported Wright J6 engines, and used M-15 parts and subassemblies. The M-26 was under development from September 1928 to February 1929. Originally it was named 'transitional from M15', but later it was given the designation KIM (*Kommunisticheskiy Internatsional Molodyozhi*, or Communist International of Youth). The prototypes underwent testing in 1930. The M-26 was transferred to State testing twice, in June 1930 and February 1931, and on the second occasion passed its tests successfully. The engine was in series production during 1931-33 at Factory No. 24 in Moscow, and 446 were built. Used only in civil aviation, the M-26 was phased out of production and service due to its low reliability.

The M-26 was installed in the ANT-9 and Stal-2 series-built aeroplanes and the A-4 autogyro (a small series). It was also proposed for the projected MFS aircraft.

Characteristics

7-cylinder radial, four-stroke, air-cooled, direct-drive engine with GCS.

Power rating	270/300hp (according to project data, 300/350hp)
Bore/stroke	150/170mm (5.91/6.69in)
Compression ratio	5.4:1
Weight	300kg (660lb) (according to project data); actually 315kg (694lb) without propeller hub

M-29

The M-29 was a projected 14-cylinder engine based on a coupled version of the M-26. It was under development from September 1928 to February 1929 at Factory No. 24. In 1930 the task of creating the engine was transferred to the IAM, but no work was carried out on it there. The prototype was not built.

Characteristics

14-cylinder two-row radial, four-stroke, air-cooled, direct-drive engine with GCS. In 1930 it was planned to create a geared version of the engine.

Power rating	750/1,000hp
Bore/stroke	150/170mm (5.91/6.69in)
Weight	500kg (1,100lb) (according to project data)

LEFT: **An M-26 engine stored at Monino.**

BELOW: **The series ANT-9 airliner was powered by three M-26s.**

CHAPTER FOURTEEN

The FED Engines

In March 1928 the UVVS issued a specification for a 1,500hp watercooled engine, designated M-28. The development order was to be given to Factory No. 24, but Aviatrest jibbed, refusing to include the M-28 in its plan. However, the Economic Directorate of the OGPU, which organized employment of the imprisoned, took the initiative. Hitherto, only menial physical labour had been given to prisoners, but now it was decided to exploit their mental capabilities as well.

Following the so-called 'Industrial Party' case, a considerable number of highly skilled engineers and technicians with pre-revolutionary technical experience were arrested. Such people now formed the staff of prison design bureaux, and they were stimulated by promises of shorter sentences or even release if their work was successful. One such bureau, that for engine construction, was a part of Factory No. 24.

Having received the M-28 specification in 1929, the bureau started development of an X-shaped engine that received an FED designation. However, this engine was of considerably lower power than requested in the M-28 specification; only 900hp. The change to higher power might have been officially approved, but no document verifying this has been found. The engine was being developed by A.A. Bessonov, L.B. Edelshtein, M.G. Bortnikov and S.S. Balandin.

Several versions were under development simultaneously, a geared version, a supercharged version and even a diesel. The history of FED-8 diesel appears in a separate chapter concerning Soviet diesel engines.

After establishment of the IAM, further work on the FED family was transferred to this institute. In October 1931 the OKB of the OGPU delivered two sets of engine drawings, one to the VAO (which replaced Aviatrest) and another to the IAM. By this time Factory No. 24 already had already manufactured several prototypes of the FED engines, and more were approaching completion. In total, ten prototypes were assembled.

Apparently, judging by surviving documentation on the FED-1, FED-3, FED-8 and FED-10, all or almost all of the ten prototypes were different. Testing of the FED-1 started as early as autumn 1930, and the crankcase and con-rods of the engine were strengthened as a result.

The most refined engine was FED-3, which had a single-speed GCS. After two series of factory tests, during which a master rod on one of the prototypes failed, the type was put to State testing in April 1931. The tests were performed on the bench of Department No. 6 of the NII VVS. Though the maximum power rating proved to be higher than calculated, the nominal power rating fell short of the specified level almost by 100hp. After 25hr of testing it became necessary to replace all of the con-rod bushings. The engine was deemed unsatisfactory.

After transferring work on the FED to the IAM, the institute could not find a specialist to undertake the work of refining the engine. In fact, no serious attention was paid to it any more, interest soon died and it was excluded from the official plans.

The FED-3 X-shaped engine.

FED-1

The first engine of the FED family, which was being developed from 1929 at the OKB of the OGPU, where imprisoned engineers were employed. A prototype, manufactured at Factory No. 24, underwent testing from autumn 1930.

Characteristics

24-cylinder in-line, X-shaped, four-stroke, watercooled, direct-drive engine without supercharging.

Power rating	900hp (according to project data)
Bore/stroke	135/160mm (5.31/6.30in)
Volume	55.0 litres (3,356cu in)

FED-3 (M-28)

The most refined engine of the FED family, this differed from the FED-1 in having a GCS. Two prototypes were built at Factory No. 24, and underwent testing during 1931-32. In April-June 1931 the engine passed its tests at the NII VVS.

The type was not installed in any aircraft, but its use was stipulated in specifications for the TB-4 and TB-7 (not Pe-8) heavy bombers and I-13 fighter.

Characteristics

24-cylinder in-line, X-shaped, four-stroke, watercooled, direct-drive engine with single-speed GCS.

Power rating	900/1,050hp according to the project; actually 813/1,170hp
Bore/stroke	135/160mm (5.31/6.30in)
Volume	55.0 litres (3,356cu in)
Compression ratio	6.8:1
Weight	851kg (1,876lb); (according to project data 830kg (1,830lb)) (with propeller hub)

The FED-3 displayed in the Salyut Factory museum.

FED-10

The last engine of the FED family, this was boosted in rpm comparing to the FED-3.

Characteristics

24-cylinder in-line, X-shaped, four-stroke, watercooled, direct-drive engine.

Power rating	1,000hp
Bore/stroke	135/160mm (5.31/6.30in)
Volume	55.0 litres (3,356cu in)

CHAPTER FIFTEEN

The First Engines of the IAM

The Aviation Motor-Building Institute (IAM) was established in December 1930, and the specialists from the NAMI, VMO TsAGI, NII VVS and the factories were gathered into it. A.A. Mikulin, V.Ya. Klimov, A.A. Bessonov, V.A. Dollezhal, S.K. Tumanskiy and other designers moved there, and the institute became not only a scientific, but a design and development organization.

Along with the specialists, the IAM took over development of the engines on which they had been working, including the M-15a, M-19a, M-27N/NR, M-29, M-32, M-34, M-38 and M-44, and the FED family.

Later, the M-34 became the progenitor of a large engine family designed by Mikulin, so this type is covered separately, together with the other engines created on its basis both at the IAM (from 1932 the TsIAM) and at other design organizations. The fate of the M-15a, M-19a, M-27 and FED engines have been described in previous chapters.

Work on the watercooled 600hp M-32, intended for installation in fighters, was initially given to Factory No. 24, where the first versions of the engine's layout were created. Three preliminary projects existed, developed by V.M. Yakovlev, P.I. Orlov and A.P. Ro respectively. After the variants had been considered, the unusual 16-cylinder vee engine designed by Yakovlev was selected. According to the system then prevailing, a chief designer for the engine was not appointed. The work was carried on under the 'team method', one department making calculations on the engine's systems, another doing the strength calculations, and a third being engaged in engineering development, and so on. The organization as whole (a factory in this case) was responsible for the engine type. This system led to a complete absence of personal responsibility and delayed the work considerably. It was repeatedly suggested that it be changed. For instance, in May 1930 it was proposed to charge A.D. Shvetsov with leadership on M-32 development.

Transfer of the M-32 programme to the IAM slowed down the engine's creation (it was almost stopped for several months).

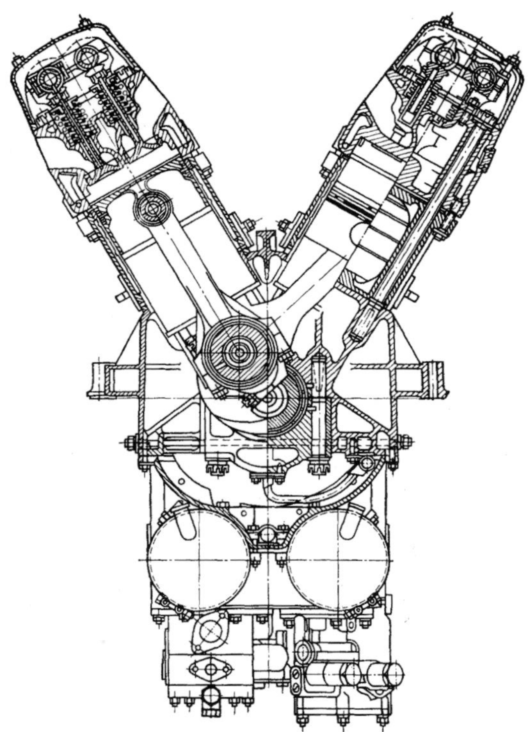

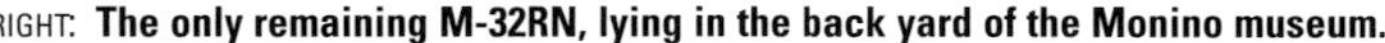

ABOVE: **A cross-section of the M-32.**

RIGHT: **The only remaining M-32RN, lying in the back yard of the Monino museum.**

Not until in February 1931 were the engine drawings and calculations received from the factory. Apparently the preliminary design was at an advanced stage of readiness, as on 1 April it was approved by the IAM's technical council.

By 1 January 1932 all of the engineering drawings had been issued, three-quarters of the casting moulds had been manufactured, and casting had begun. On 20 October that year the first M-32 prototype was started up on the bench. During further refinement work the cylinder-block jackets were strengthened, then cracking of the main bearings and block heads was found.

In 1934 a new specification for the M-32RN version was issued, stipulating the use of a GCS to boost the power to 650hp. It was planned eventually to adopt ethylene-glycol or even steam cooling.

The M-34RN was built and bench-tested. In total, five M-32 prototypes were manufactured, and refinement work continued until 1935. By then the engine was outdated, and the required level of the GCS reliability had still not been reached. Consequently work on the engine was cancelled.

Almost the same path was followed by the M-38. Its development was also started at Factory No. 24 in 1930, under the leadership of N.A. Ostrovskiy. As with the M-32, in February 1931 the engine's documentation was received by the IAM. In May the project was completed, and by January next year about a third of the parts had been built. The prototype engine was ready in October 1932, but first tests revealed insufficient strength of the cam, cylinder heads and pistons. In January 1933 the cast pistons were replaced by forged ones, and the gas-distribution mechanism was improved, using the mechanism of the Bristol Mercury as a pattern. However, the specified power rating of 600hp was not reached. After it had been decided to introduce the Wright Cyclone into series production in the USSR, the value of the unrefined M-38 fell immediately, and work on it was cancelled at the end of 1933.

The third project, the M-44, was taken over by the IAM from VMO TsAGI, where in 1929-30 an experimental single-cylinder M-170 was being developed (also known as the M-170/44). It was planned to use this to examine the possibility of developing an aero-engine with cylinders of increased diameter (222mm (8.74in)), while the designers wanted to get 170hp from a single cylinder.

The M-32RN engine.

The M-170 programme was transferred to the IAM, where development of the 12-cylinder M-44 was started in February 1931, using the cylinder-piston group of the M-170 as a basis. The M-44 was intended for heavy bombers of the TB-6 and TB-7 type, which were included in the plan for the VVS RKKA's expansion.

The engine was basically ready by May 1931. However, it was included in the plan of experimental work for 1932 as a type of secondary importance, as it was expected that refinement of the M-170/44 would be completed. As development of the M-44 continued, the engine's specification underwent some changes, the acceptable weight limit increasing from 1,500 to 1,800kg (3,300 to 4,000lb).

The manufacture of prototypes (two were being built in parallel) did not start until the beginning of 1933. That year the factory testing of the first prototype began, and the second followed in 1934. Some parts for a third prototype were manufactured, but its assembly was not completed. At the same time development of a GM-44 marine version of the engine, with a reverse clutch, started.

The M-44 did not justify its designers' hopes. Its power rating proved to be considerably lower than the specified 2,200hp. At the end of 1934 work on it was cancelled. Although the marine version was built, and tested until the beginning of 1936, it was not put into production.

For quite some time the TsIAM was engaged in work on the M-200 engine. As the prototype was built the end of 1930s, its story appears in a later chapter.

M-32

This engine, intended for Soviet fighters, was being developed from 1929 at the Ikar factory, and the programme was then transferred to the IAM, where development continued from February 1931 under the leadership of V.M. Yakovlev. The work was completed in March 1931, and on 1 April the project was approved by the IAM's technical council. In 1931-32 five (or, according to some sources, six) prototypes were built. Bench testing started in October 1932, and revealed cracking of cylinder-block heads and spalling of the bearings. Refinement work continued until the beginning of 1935, but the main defects were not eliminated and the engine was not put into production.

Characteristics

16-cylinder in-line vee, four-stroke, direct-drive, water-cooled engine.

Power rating	600/750hp (according to the specification 650/700hp)
Bore/stroke	120/120mm (4.72/4.72in)
Volume	21.7 litres (1,324cu in)
Compression ratio	6.0:1.
Weight (M-32RN)	460kg (1,014lb)

The following versions are known:

M-32 The original direct-drive version without GCS, one prototype of which was built. Weight 430kg (948lb) (according to the specification 400kg (900lb))

M-32RN A geared version with a single-speed GCS. It was planned to use ethylene-glycol or steam cooling at a later stage.

The type was proposed for installation in the I-9, I-13 and DI-6 fighters.

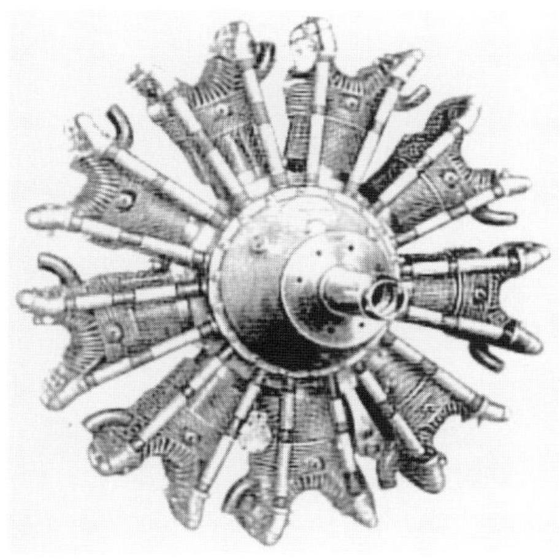

Above **The M-38 engine.**

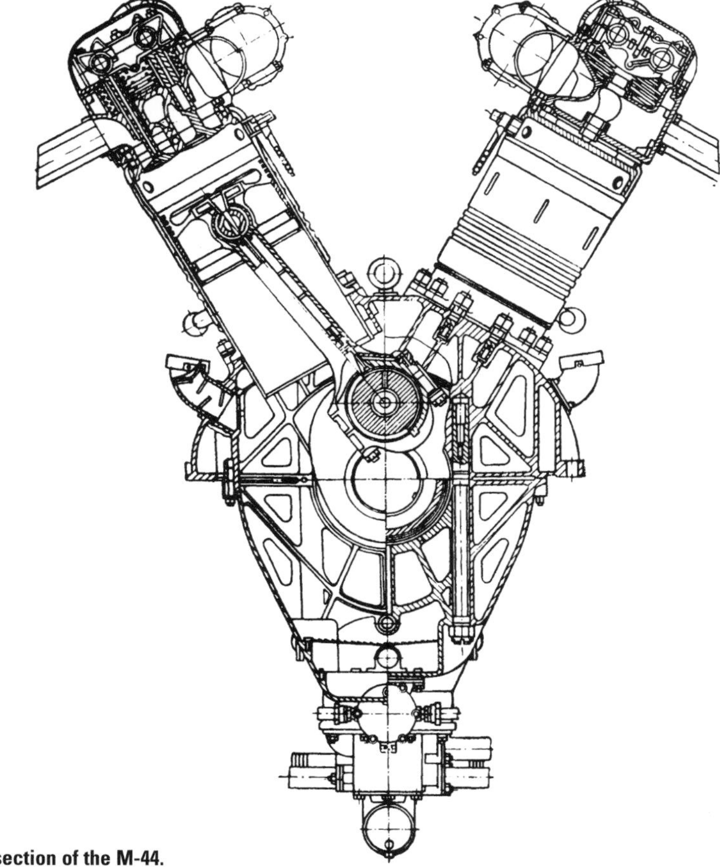

A cross-section of the M-44.

M-38

This engine, intended for fighters, was being developed under the leadership of F.V. Kontsevich from 1930 at Factory No. 24, and from February 1931 at the IAM. Its layout was completed in May 1931, and the engineering drawings were ready in January 1932. In 1932 the IAM's experimental factory built two prototypes, and they underwent bench testing from the autumn of 1932, cracked pistons and an unreliable gas-distribution system requiring modification. Work continued until the autumn 1933, but further development was cancelled as the measured power did not reach the level required in the specification, and weight exceeded the prescribed limit of 400kg (900lb).

The type was proposed for installation in the I-5, I-9, I-14 and I-15 fighters, and the KR-2 shipborne reconnaissance aeroplane.

Characteristics

9-cylinder radial, four-stroke, air-cooled, direct-drive engine.

Power rating	570/600hp (projected) (575hp actual)
Bore/stroke	135/160mm (5.31/6.30in)
Volume	30.7 litres (1,873cu in)
Compression ratio	6.0:1
Weight	460kg (1,014lb) (in the specification 450kg (992lb))

M-44

Intended for heavy bombers, this Soviet aero-engine had the highest power rating of the first half of the 1930s. The M-44 was under development at the IAM from February 1931, under the leadership of N.P. Serdyukov, using as a basis the M-170 (M-170/44) experimental single-cylinder engine created in 1929-30 at the VMO TsAGI. Three prototypes were built in 1933-35, including one GM-44 marine version. Work on the type was cancelled in mid-1936.

Characteristics

12-cylinder in-line vee, four-stroke, watercooled, geared engine.

Bore/stroke	222/286mm (8.74/11.26in)
Volume	132.8 litres (8,104cu in)
Compression ratio	6.0:1 (according to other sources 5.0:1)
Power rating	dependant on version
Weight	dependant on version

The following versions of the engine are known:

M-44 An aero-engine, of which two prototypes were built. Power rating 1,700/2,000hp, weight 1,700kg (3,700lb) (according to other sources 1,800kg (4,000lb)).

GM-44 A marine version with a reverse clutch. In 1935 one prototype was built, which underwent testing in 1935-36. Power rating 1,870hp.

The type was proposed for installation in the TB-6 and TB-7 (not Pe-8) bombers.

CHAPTER SIXTEEN

Engines of Unusual Layout Developed During 1923–32

The engines created in Soviet Russia in the 1920s and at the beginning of the 1930s included a number of quite original designs.

One of the first engines developed by order of the State was the creation of L.I. Starostin. This had eight cylinders in parallel, in a layout similar to that of cartridges in revolver barrel, rotation being transmitted to the output shaft via a swashplate. Starostin proposed and realized this layout much earlier than in Poland and Great Britain.

The first version of this project, rated at 240hp, was reviewed and approved by the GUVP's Technical Committee, and the ensuing work was supervised by the Aviation Department of the GUVP. The engine was designated M-9, and on 8 February 1923 the GUVP Board decided that a prototype would be built. The M-9 was merely an experimental engine, and on 15 March the Ikar factory was given an order to manufacturing the prototype.

To develop the engineering drawings, the factory signed an agreement with Starostin, this agreement also stipulating the payments for the work of the draughtsmen. As the educational level of the project's originator, an ordinary manager at the factory, was insufficient for complete development of the engine, specialists from the NAMI were brought in to make the performance calculations. During refinement of the project the estimated power was increased to 400hp.

Manufacture of the M-9 prototype took quite a long time. On 25 August 1925 cold running was started, and the engine failed almost immediately, the load on the bearings being considerably higher than estimated. New bearings were ordered from Sweden, but did not arrive until the middle of 1926.

Real testing of the M-9 started in January 1927 and continued until June. The engine produced less power than estimated, and its reliability proved to be very poor. Such a layout was never again adopted in the Soviet Union.

Another original project was the 'double compression' engine, which was being developed at the NAMI from 1920. This was a two-stroke engine with double compression and subsequent expansion, the cycle being run in sequence in three cylinders. The work was carried out under the leadership of N.R. Brilling, and saw the participation of V.N. Fomin and A.A. Mikulin. The engine was designated NRB, and in some documents was described as the M-7 (the same designation as that given to Bessonov's low-powered engine).

Preliminary design of the NRB was completed in October 1923, and the NK UVVS considered and approved it. Project refinement continued until July 1924. The Motor factory in Moscow was given an order for a prototype, and its manufacture started at the beginning of 1925. By August about a third of the engine parts had been built. The NRB was completed in August 1927, and underwent testing from September 1927 to February 1929.

In March-April 1928 engineer Agapov prepared a preliminary project for a two-stroke engine with opposed pistons. The designer promised power rating of 1,400hp, which was very high for the time, plus low engine weight, calculated at 0.4kg/hp (0.88lb/hp). Agapov's engine had three cylinders placed on the sides of a triangle, three crankshafts and six pistons. On 5 February 1929 the Aviatrest

The M-9 engine, designed by Starostin, on displayed in the Monino museum.

Technical Council reviewed the project, but, although it was thought to be interesting, a prototype was not built. Later, many design solutions from Agapov's project were used in the M-200 engine.

Several ideas for engines having a rotary pump layout appeared in Soviet Union. In the middle of the 1920s the UVVS received a proposal for Prokhorov's rotary engine project. In January 1931 the IAM carried out the development work on such a layout devised by M.S. Kurnevich. However, in both cases the work did not progress beyond calculations and drawings.

In August 1931 engineer Gantman of the BNK factory proposed his own layout for a four-stroke light-fuel engine. It included two inverted 6-cylinder engines positioned in parallel, each having its own GCS, and driving a common gear. A cannon was fixed between the engines, with its barrel passing through a hollow output shaft of the gear. Gantman's project was reviewed, but no advantages were found as compared with more conventional vee engines.

M-9

This engine had cylinders positioned in parallel, the rotation being transmitted via a swashplate. The type was under development from 1922 at the Ikar factory, under the leadership of L.I. Starostin, NAMI specialists also being involved. A single prototype was built as experimental unit in August 1925 at the Ikar factory. During its initial tests the engine failed, and it was being refined until January 1927. Tests were completed in June of that year.

Characteristics

8-cylinder direct-drive engine with parallel positioning of cylinders, port-slot gas-distribution, and without supercharging.

Power rating	400hp (according to the project)
Bore/stroke	140/180mm (5.51/7.10in)
Compression ratio	3.1:1

NRB (NRB-100, M-7)

This 100hp 'double compression' two-stroke engine was being developed from 1920 at the NAMI, under the leadership of N.R. Brilling. A single prototype was built in 1925-27 at the Motor factory, and underwent testing from September 1928 until February 1929.

Gantman's Engine

A project designed by engineer Gantman at the BNK factory in 1931.

Characteristics

12-cylinder, two-row, inverted, geared engine with two crankshafts and two GCSs, with the possibility of a cannon installation.

Power rating	360hp
Volume	14,25 litres (870cu in)
Weight	340kg (750lb)

CHAPTER SEVENTEEN

Unfulfilled Orders

At the end of the 1920s the leaders of the VVS RKKA enthusiastically began setting the industry new tasks. In spite of the weaknesses of engineering and production resources, the UVVS devised ever newer specialized aircraft and engines. During the preparation of a document entitled 'Weapon Systems for the VVS RKKA', more than twenty new specifications were issued for different types of aero engines.

However, the leaders of the VAO and, later, the GUAP NKTP, simply rejected the idea of working on the designs, which were not supported by by appropriate financing, materials or components. Moreover, it was clear that, if several tens of engine types were developed simultaneously, it would be necessary to break up such few design teams as then existed.

As a result, most of the UVVS orders of the period remained unfulfilled. As no work was done on these projects, few records of them remain. Even the principal characteristics of many of them cannot be found. For example, the only thing known about the M-31 is that it had to be a water-cooled 500-600hp engine with GCS, with a weight not exceeding 420kg (926lb). Judging by some documents, it may be concluded that this designation was intended for one of the foreign engines to be introduced into series production in the USSR, most likely the Curtiss V-1550 Conqueror.

Practically no information has been found about the M-36, M-37, M-39, M-40 and M-41 air-cooled engines of different power ratings.

The task of developing the M-43 was given to the IAM. According to the specification it was to be a watercooled 700-1,000hp engine weighing 820kg (1,808lb). However, nothing was done on it, and on 8 September 1930 it was excluded from the institute's plan. At the same time, the M-46 'high-powered air-cooled engine' was also removed from the plan.

No information about the M-45 and M-47 engines has so far been found.

The futility of making ambitious plans that were not supported by any serious arrangements to bring them to fruition soon became clear to everyone. On 5 August 1931 the Revvoensovet issued a decree about reducing the number of types of aircraft and engines. According to this, only the most promising and well-developed projects were to be retained in the plans for factories and institutes.

CHAPTER EIGHTEEN

Amateur Designs of the 1920s and 1930s

Besides the designers at the factories and institutes, aero-engine development was carried out by small groups of amateur designers and even by individual enthusiasts. They mainly worked on the creation of small engines intended for light aeroplanes, no such powerplants being in series production in the Soviet Union. Quite often these amateur-designed engine used components and parts from imported and Soviet-built aero, automobile and motorcycle engines.

As no records of such designs were kept, information about these engines can be found only in unofficial documents and in media publications, and only a few have so far been discovered.

Tuzhkut

This engine was created in 1927 by a group of students at the Siberian Polytechnic Institute in Tomsk, under the leadership of Professor A.V. Kvasnikov (the engine's name was an abbreviation of the surnames of students who participated in the project). The engine used components from an M-2-120 rotary engine.

Characteristics

2-cylinder horizontally-opposed, four-stroke, air-cooled, direct-drive engine.

Power rating 20/24hp

Kivi's engine during tests.

AB-55

This engine was developed in 1930 by A.G. Bedunkovich, using components from a 1910 Anzani engine. Power rating, 55hp.

Stulov's Engine

E.E. Stulov modified a marine engine into a 2-cylinder horizontally-opposed aero-engine.

Kivi's Engine

P.I. Kivi developed and built a two-stroke, 10hp rotary engine.

Liliput (Lilliputian)

In 1932 technician Shirev, who served at the Aircraft Mechanics School of the VVS in Leningrad, built a 7hp engine in the school workshops.

Morgulin's Engine

In 1936 engineer Morgulin, working in the AVIAVNITO (*Aviatsionnoe Vsesoyuznoe Nauchnoe Inzhenerno-Tekhnicheskoe Obshchestvo*, or Aviation All-Union Scientific Engineering-Technical Society) section of the UNIADI, developed a low-powered air-cooled radial engine. The project was submitted for a contest of homebuilt engines, and its author was awarded a diploma, but a prototype was not built.

CHAPTER NINETEEN

The M-56 and MGM Engines

In 1933 E.V. Urmin at the TsIAM started development of a new 14-cylinder air-cooled engine. This engine was included in the UVVS plan and designated M-56, and on 28 August 1934 an official specification was issued for it. The main feature of the M-56 was its small overall diameter.

By October 1934 the project had been completed, and manufacture of the first prototype had started. Two more prototypes were built by 1 December 1935. During factory testing the crankshaft failed twice.

In 1936 three more M-56 prototypes were assembled, including one with improved cylinder heads similar to those used in the M-87. Refinement work on the M-56 lasted until December 1937, but by this time the engine was considered outdated. It was still not reliable enough, as the cylinders overheated. Finally, the engine was excluded from the TsIAM's plan for 1938.

However, Urmin managed to arrange the introduction of the MGM engine into the plan, and this was an improved version of the M-56. The project work was completed in December 1937. The engine was boosted in rpm and supercharged from 700hp to 850hp. The aluminium crankcase was replaced by a steel one, the crank mechanism was strengthened, and a joint was introduced to the crankshaft (the M-56 had a split master rod). The cylinder-piston group from the M-56 was combined with the gear, crankcase nose section and, partly, with the GCS of the M-25.

Testing of the first MGM started in November 1938, but the prototype suffered a breakdown with the accompanying destruction of five pistons. The engine's performance was not recorded.

Two more MGM prototypes were built, these having a compression ratio of 7.0:1 (compared with 6.5:1 for the first prototype). Later, it was planned to incorporate a considerable number of M-62 and M-63 components and units in the MGM design, including the two-speed GCS of the M-62.

However, the MGM did not promise considerable advantages over the M-85, which was already in series production, or over the much better M-62. Further work on the MGM was cancelled, and Urmin was sent to Zaporozhye, where he replaced S.K. Tumanskiy as chief designer at Factory No. 29. In Zaporozhye Urmin became involved in refining the M-88 and participated in development of the M-89.

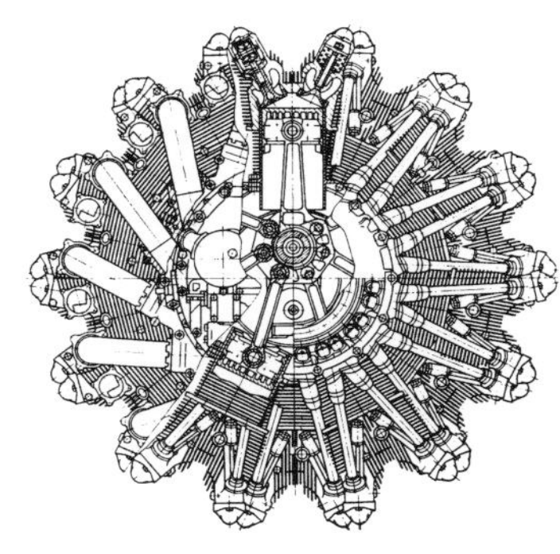

A drawing of the M-56.

M-56

This engine was being developed from 1933 at the TsIAM, under the leadership of E.V. Urmin. Six prototypes were built and tested from December 1935, and the type was being refined until December 1936. The engine was not introduced into series production. Later, some features of the design were used in the MGM engine.

Characteristics

14-cylinder two-row radial, four-stroke, air-cooled, geared engine with single-speed GCS.

Power rating	700/700hp
Bore/stroke	130/135mm (5.12/5.31in)
Volume	25.1 litres (1,532cu in)
Compression ratio	6.3:1

MGM

This engine, a further evolution of the M-56, was being developed at the TsIAM in 1937, under the leadership of E.V. Urmin. Three prototypes were built and tested from December 1937, and refinement continued until 1941. The type was not introduced into series production.

Characteristics

14-cylinder two-row, radial, four-stroke, air-cooled geared engine with single-speed GCS.

Power rating	700/850hp
Bore/stroke	130/135mm (5.12/5.31in)
Volume	25.1 litres (1,532cu in)
Compression ratio	7.0:1 (first prototype 6.5:1)

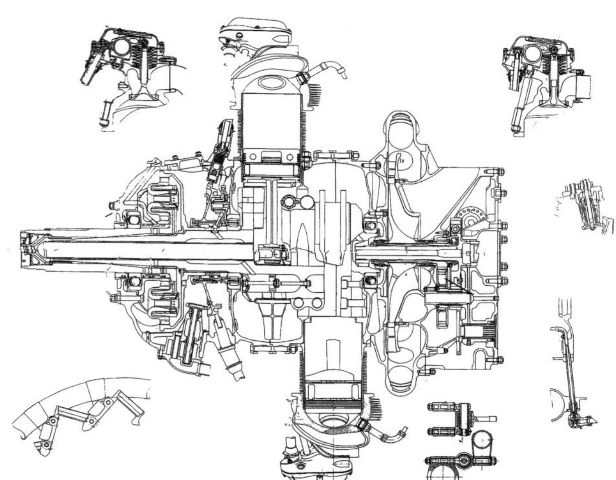

A drawing of the MGM.

CHAPTER TWENTY

The Low-powered TsIAM Engines

The TsIAM was not only involved in the development of high- or medium-powered engines. Some of the institute's designers worked on low-powered air-cooled engines intended for sport and training aeroplanes.

From 1935, within the bounds of a plan for engine development work, a group of engineers led by A.A. Bessonov developed an MM-1 engine that was to become the Soviet counterpart of the de Havilland Gipsy Six. However, the Soviet engine differed from the British type both in dimensions and design. Manufacture of a prototype was started in January 1936, and it underwent bench testing from March 1936. These tests were successfully completed in December 1936, when a service life of 100hr had been reached. In total, four MM-1s were built.

In 1937 the engine underwent State testing, and in 1938 it was also flight tested on the Moskalev SAM-10 and SAM-11 aeroplanes.

The development plan also included an MM-2 , an inverted-vee type to be based on MM-1 subassemblies. Project development was planned to start only after completion of MM-1 refinement.

However, after a manufacturing licence for Renault engines was acquired and arrangements made for their production in Voronezh, the interest in both Soviet types disappeared and all work on them ceased.

A group of young specialists headed by V.A. Dollezhal and working under their own initiative developed two related engines to power light aeroplanes. Designated VAD-2 and VAD-3, they had an unusually high number (for their power rating) of small-diameter cylinders. Engineering drawings were completed in February 1936, and the development work was supported by a committee that assisted in the creation of the 'Sky Flea' aeroplane. However, the finance for building the prototype engines could not be found.

MM-1

6-cylinder in-line inverted, air-cooled, four-stroke, direct-drive engine without GCS.

This engine was installed in the SAM-10 and SAM-11 aeroplanes.

Characteristics

Power rating	250/300hp
Bore/stroke	125/140mm (4.92/5.51in)
Volume	10.03 litres (612cu in)
Compression ratio	5.3:1
Weight	235kg (518lb)

MM-2

12-cylinder in-line inverted vee, air-cooled, four-stroke, direct-drive engine without GCS.

The prototype was not built.

Characteristics

Power rating	450hp

VAD-2

4-cylinder in-line inverted, air-cooled, four-stroke, geared engine without GCS.

The prototype was not built.

Characteristics

Power rating	30hp.
Bore/stroke	62/64mm (2.44/2.52in)
Volume	0.775 litres (47cu in)
Compression ratio	5.8-6.5:1
Weight (estimated)	33-36kg (73-79lb)

VAD-3

6-cylinder in-line inverted, air-cooled, four-stroke, geared engine without GCS.

The prototype was not built.

Characteristics

Power rating	45hp
Bore/stroke	62/64mm (2.44/2.52in)
Volume	1.16 litres (71cu in)
Compression ratio	5.8-6.5:1
Weight (estimated)	45-50kg (99-110lb)

LEFT: **The MM-1 engine.**

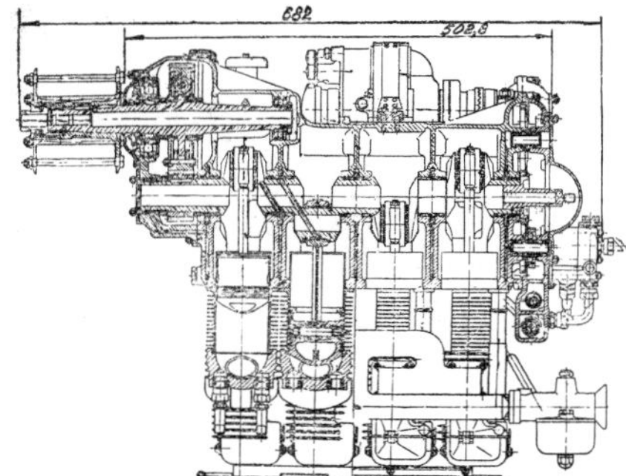

RIGHT: **A cross-section of the VAD-2 engine project.**

CHAPTER TWENTY-ONE

Automobile Engines Modified for Use in Aircraft

The idea of using automobile engines, which were cheaper than aero-engines, to power primary training aircraft was quite popular in 1930s. In April 1936 the VVS RKKA issued specifications for a light training aircraft, and for a modified automobile engine to power it.

Work on adapting automobile engines for aviation use was carried out by designers at the Gorkiy Automobile Factory (GAZ), under the leadership of E.A. Agitov. The first such modification was done in 1936, when a 46.5hp GAZ engine was adapted for installation on the home-built KSM-1 aeroplane. When the aircraft was tested by the NII VVS in 1936 its engine was found to be unsatisfactory. In mid-1936 a specially modified GAZ-Avia-60 (or MGAZ-60) was created, using a 52hp engine from an M-1 automobile as the basis for modification. The powerplant had its compression ratio increased and was considerably lightened by replacing the cast-iron block with an aluminium one, drilling out the crankshaft journals and other changes. The engine was given a new driveshaft nose with a thrust bearing and had an improved lubrication system, as well as two-spark ignition in accordance with aviation regulations. At the beginning of 1937 the MGAZ-60 was test flown in the G-23 Komsomolets-2 aeroplane.

In 1939 the GAZ-11 engine was developed using the engine from a 'model 24' car (a copy of American Dodge). The GAZ-11 was uprated to 85hp and equipped with reduction gearing. It was also slightly lighter than the automobile engine. However, single-spark battery-type ignition was retained. In August 1939 the engine was flown in a KSM-1 aeroplane, and in March 1940 this aircraft was tested at the NII VVS but its engine was found unsatisfactory. The KSM-1 crashed in November 1939 in Gorkiy and was not restored.

Further work on modifying automobile engines for aviation use was cancelled, this activity being resumed to higher standards by the designers of home-built aircraft in the postwar period.

MGAZ-60

A modification of a 4-cylinder automobile engine into an aero-engine.

The prototype engines were installed in a G-23 aeroplane and on the aircraft built by A.I. Pleskov.

Characteristics

4-cylinder in-line, watercooled, four-stroke, direct-drive engine without GCS.

Power rating	62.5hp
Bore/stroke	98.5/108mm (3.88/4.25in)
Volume	3.28 litres (200cu in)
Compression ratio	5.6:1
Weight	120kg (265lb)

GAZ-11

A modification of a 6-cylinder automobile engine into an aero-engine.

The prototype engines were installed in the KSM-1, G-25bis and U-2 aeroplanes.

Characteristics

6-cylinder in-line, watercooled, four-stroke, geared engine without GCS.

Power rating	83/85hp
Bore/stroke	82/110mm (3.23/4.33in)
Volume	3.48 litres (212cu in)
Compression ratio	6.5:1
Weight	183kg (403lb)

The MGAZ-60 installed in the G-23 aeroplane.

The GAZ-11 engine.

CHAPTER TWENTY-TWO

The Engines of A.A. Mikulin

Aleksander Aleksandrovich Mikulin (1895-1985) was one of the most renowned Russian aero-engine designers. While studying at technical school he began to devise original engines, and there was even an attempt to build one in the school workshop. In 1908, as a schoolboy, he took a great interest in model aircraft, and in 1909 he took second place in the model contest in Kiev. Igor Sikorskiy, future creator of the *Ilya Muromets*, was the winner. When Mikulin was 15 his talent for designing helped him to earn his first money. Having seen one of the first Russian aviators, Sergey Utochkin, make a forced-landing owing to magneto failure, Mikulin suggested that he install a second magneto, and his scheme was adopted. Thenceforth Utochkin sent the teenager ten roubles (a considerable amount for those times) from every town where he performed demonstration flights.

In 1912 Mikulin entered the Kiev Polytechnic Institute. During his studies there he designed and built an original marine engine that attracted the attention of well-known engine specialist Professor N.R. Brilling. In 1913, when Mikulin was undergoing work experience at one of the factories in Riga, he performed balance calculations for a prototype automobile engine intended for series production, and thus eliminated dangerous vibrations. The gifted student was immediately offered the post of chief designer, but decided to continue his studies.

In 1914, at the invitation of his uncle, N.E. Zhukovskiy, the famous aerodynamicist, Mikulin moved to the Moscow Emperor's High Technical School. He became an active member of an aeronautics group that included such students as Tupolev, Vetchinkin, Stechkin and Yuryev. After the start of the First World War Mikulin ceased his studies and began work as a designer at the military inventions laboratory. He would receive his engineer's diploma as a gift for his 60th birthday, many years later, by which time he was already an academician. (The Head of the Air Force Academy, which issued the diploma, was reprimanded for violating the rules, as Mikulin had never studied at the Academy!)

Working at the laboratory, the young designer won a contest conducted by a Military Ministry for the best project for an airborne incendiary bomb, and he also participated in the creation of a bomb sight and a huge wheeled tank named the Netopyr (bat). In 1915, working with his friend B.S. Stechkin, Mikulin designed an original 300hp two-stroke engine for the tank. The engine, called the AMBS-1, was built in a shed near the college. In 1916 it was tested, but ran for only three minutes and broke down due to bending of its con-rods.

After the October Revolution Mikulin worked at the TsAGI, where he developed snowmobiles, and then at the NAMI, where the first Soviet automobile, aero and tank engines were being developed, under the leadership of Brilling. In 1924 he was tasked with developing an engine for a tankette (small tank), of which a small batch was later built. In two years, having started as a draughtsman, Mikulin became the NAMI's chief aero-engine designer, and participated in creation of the M-12 and M-13 engines.

From 1928 development work began on the powerful 12-cylinder M-34 vee engine. From 1930 this work was transferred to the recently established IAM (later renamed the TsIAM), and Mikulin moved there too. The first M-34 engine

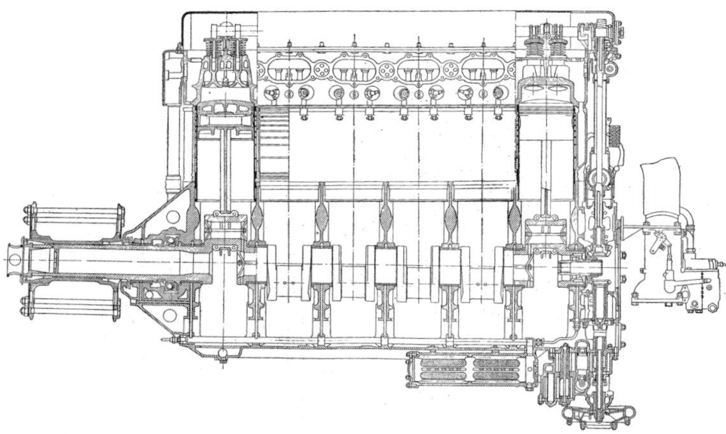

ABOVE: **A drawing of the M-34.**

RIGHT: **The M-34 engine.**

ABOVE: **The TB-3 heavy bomber, powered by four M-34s.**

RIGHT: **The M-34N supercharged engine.**

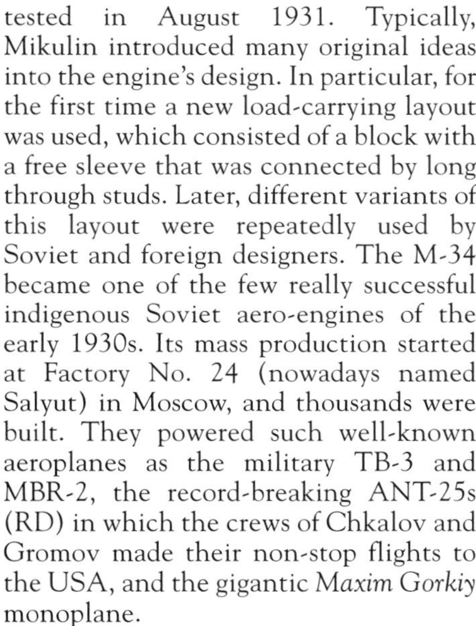

tested in August 1931. Typically, Mikulin introduced many original ideas into the engine's design. In particular, for the first time a new load-carrying layout was used, which consisted of a block with a free sleeve that was connected by long through studs. Later, different variants of this layout were repeatedly used by Soviet and foreign designers. The M-34 became one of the few really successful indigenous Soviet aero-engines of the early 1930s. Its mass production started at Factory No. 24 (nowadays named Salyut) in Moscow, and thousands were built. They powered such well-known aeroplanes as the military TB-3 and MBR-2, the record-breaking ANT-25s (RD) in which the crews of Chkalov and Gromov made their non-stop flights to the USA, and the gigantic *Maxim Gorkiy* monoplane.

The succesful M-34 formed the basis for a whole family of aero-engines of different powers and layouts. In-line, double-shaft and inverted engines using M-34 components were proposed. Experiments were carried out using ethylene-glycol and combined (air-glycol) cooling. Designers also worked on the installation of a cannon in the cylinder vee, and on a tandem powerplant comprising two M-34s driving contrarotating propellers through coaxial shafts.

All of these designs remained only projects or prototypes. On the other hand, the M-34 itself was repeatedly modified. Versions appeared with gearing and supercharging, with direct fuel injection and turbo-supercharging. There were also versions for tanks, self-propelled guns, motor torpedo boats and armoured river boats. V.M. Yakovlev worked with Mikulin on these engine versions (he developed a reversing clutch for the GAM-34 marine engine), as did V.A. Dobrynin, who from December 1934 was the chief designer at Factory No. 24, where all the Mikulin-designed engines were built.

For the M-34N Mikulin developed, for the first time in Russia, a two-speed geared supercharger, but the engine was put into series production with a simpler and more reliable single-speed GCS designed by Danilevskiy.

To mark Mikulin's contribution, on 9 August 1936 the USSR Defence Committee redesignated the engine AM-34, incorporating the designer's initials. Mikulin was appointed chief designer at Factory No. 24.

He continued to refine the successful engine by increasing its supercharging and revolutions. However, prolonged development of the AM-34FRN version caused discontent among the leaders of the aviation industry and Mikulin was dismissed from the post of chief designer, only the development work on the AM-34 being left to him. During the years of the Stalin repressions his failures could have cost him quite dearly (he was not a member of Communist party), but he seems to have escaped the fate of being denounced as a 'people's enemy'. This was probably due to the sensational flights to America made by AM-34-powered aircraft. The RD aeroplane and its M-34RD engine were triumphantly exhibited outside the USSR.

Then came new successes. They were related to the AM-35 engine, a development of the AM-34FRNV, and more than 4,000 of the AM-35A version were built. The AM-35A powered the MiG-1 and MiG-3 fighters used at the beginning of the Great Patriotic War. It also powered the TB-7 (Pe-8) heavy bomber and was installed in the TsKB-55 (BSh-2) attack aeroplane prototype. However, this aircraft, produced in large quantities as the Il-2, was introduced into mass production with a special low-altitude AM-38 engine developed from the AM-35A. Mikulin's deputy, M.R. Flisskiy, played an important role in the development of both the AM-35 and AM-38. For Mikulin, 1940 was a year of success. Factory No. 24 was increasing production of his engines, and he was awarded the title of Hero of Socialist Labour.

After that, Mikulin's engines, which followed an unbroken numerical sequence from the M-34, evolved along two main lines. These were closely interconnected, and the successful solutions implemented in one line were frequently adopted for the other. Besides, many units and subassemblies were common to all the engines of the family.

The first line comprised engines for attack aeroplanes. These were optimized for low altitudes, and were undemanding of oil and fuel quality. The line started with the AM-38, from which were

The record-breaking RD (ANT-25) aeroplane, powered by the M-34RD. Aircraft of this type were flown by crews led by V.P. Chkalov and M.M. Gromov from Moscow to the western coast of the USA via the North Pole.

The MiG-1 fighter powered by the AM-35A.

The famous Il-2 armoured attack aircraft, powered by the AM-38.

The AM-42 engine.

developed the AM-38F (in series production from October 1943) and AM-42 (which passed State testing in April 1944). These were built in large numbers by Factory No. 24, which during the war was evacuated to Kuibyshev and remained there, and also by Factory No. 45, which was established in 1942 in the old workshops of the former enterprise in Moscow. The Il-2 'flying tanks' powered by the AM-38 and AM-38F served on all fronts. By the end of the war they had been joined by the more up-to-date Il-10, powered by the AM-42. Later the Il-10 took part in the Korean War, and remained in Soviet Air Force service until the second half of the 1950s.

Attack-aircraft engines were developed at the design bureau of Factory No. 24 in Kuibyshev. For some time Mikulin was chief designer for three factories simultameously; Factory No. 24 in Kuibyshev, No. 45 in Moscow and the new experimental Factory No. 300, also in Moscow. Then the duties were divided: while Mikulin continued to head the two teams in Moscow, Flisskiy was appointed chief designer in Kuibyshev. Thus the subsequent engines for attack aircraft were created without the direct participation of Mikulin, and in documents they were designated without the 'AM' prefix. In some cases the letters 'MF' (Mikhail Flisskiy) were used. Nevertheless, there was a continuous exchange of documentation and sample power units between Moscow and Kuibyshev.

The further developments of the AM-42 were the M-43, M-44, M-45, M-46 and M-47. The last of these, rated at 3,000hp, was tested on the prototype Il-20 attack aeroplane in 1948. After that the factory was converted to turbojet production, and development work on piston engines ceased. However, in 1951 AM-42 production was resumed, but no serious design development was undertaken.

The second line of M-34 evolution comprised powerful high-altitude engines for fighters and high-speed bombers. These engines originated from the AM-35A. From 1939 Mikulin was developing an improved version with an intercooler, designated AM-37. In April 1941 this engine successfully passed its State tests and entered series production. However, many of the AM-37's teething troubles remained unsolved, and in the autumn of 1941, after a small batch had been built, it was phased out. Mikulin did not give up, but went on to create the AM-39 with a two-speed GCS, which he brought up to 2,130hp during 1944-45. Development work was carried out at experimental Factory No. 300, in the Luzhniki district of Moscow, which had been specially assigned to the A.A. Mikulin Design Bureau. Originally the AM-39 shared many parts with the AM-38F, and then with the AM-42, and consequently series-production Factories Nos 24 and 45 became involved in the manufacture of units for engine prototypes. The new powerplant underwent bench and flight testing. Its turbo-supercharged versions were tested on Mikoyan's MiG-7 (I-224) interceptor prototypes, and the versions optimised for low-altitude use were tested on Tupolev bomber prototypes, including a small batch of Tu-10 ('68') aeroplanes.

In April 1944 the AM-39 passed its State tests, but it was not put into series production. Further development continued until 1946. On the whole, this line of M-34 descendants was less successful, as none of them was mass-produced in as large numbers as the attack-aircraft engines.

The Mikulin piston engines formed an unbroken chain of development using the same basic construction, retaining a common general layout and load-distribution scheme, as well as the principal cylinder dimensions. At the same time, with unchanged engine volume, the maximum power rating from the early M-34 to the M-47 increased more than threefold. It is noteworthy that, while many Soviet aero-engine designers initially based their developments on foreign engines or on components of indigenous engines, Mikulin went his own original way, only occasionally adopting well-proven features of other designs. However, such originality quite often caused long periods of design refinement, during which the engine began to lag behind its competitors.

Conversely, other designers did not hesitate to use Mikulin's ideas in their projects, and even complete units from his engines. For example, a number of A.P. Ro's and E.V. Urmin's engine projects used M-34 cylinder blocks. Superchargers from the AM-38 were installed on the diesel engines designed by A.D. Charomskiy.

For his achievements in the development of indigenous aero-engines during the war, Mikulin was awarded the Stalin Prize four times (in 1941, 1942, 1943 and 1946). In 1943 he was elected a Full Member of Academy of Sciences, though officially he had not completed his higher education.

From April 1946 the A.A. Mikulin Design Bureau tasked with developing turbojet engines, and this work forced the immediate cessation of work on piston aero-engines. For about one more year Flisskiy continued developing engines for attack aircraft in Kuibyshev, but then the turbojets forced out the piston engines there, too.

Mikulin's turbojets were as original as his piston engines. He took neither German nor British designs as a basis for his developments. The first jet engine of Mikulin's design, the TKRD-1 (AM-TKRD-01), had a considerable nominal thrust for the time of 3,000kg (6,600lb), and a maximum thrust of 3,500kg (7,700lb) (later increased to 3,780kg (8,333lb)). Its testing started in 1947, and a year later it passed the State testing programme. From September 1948 to May 1949 these engines were used in a '140' bomber prototype, but the powerplant did not go into series production. The AM-TRD-02 (385/4,180kg (849/9,215lb) thrust) also remained as a prototype, which underwent State testing in 1949 and was being refined until 1951.

The powerful AMRD-03, under development from June 1949, became the first successful Mikulin turbojet. Its first prototype was bench-tested in 1951, and it was subsequently introduced into series production as the AM-3 (8,700kg (19,000lb) thrust), powering such well-known aircraft as the Tu-16 and Tu-104. Later, in the course of series production, its thrust was increased to 11,500kg (25,400lb) in the RD-3M version.

In the mid-1950s, due to an unhappy relationship with the Minister of the Aviation Industry, Mikulin had to leave his design bureau. His former deputy, S.K. Tumanskiy, replaced him, and successfully completed several projects that had been started under Mikulin. The latter moved to the Academy of Sciences, where he worked on diverse projects unconnected with aviation. He subsequently took a great interest in the problem of longevity, suggesting a number of ideas, such as air

LEFT: **The AM-37 powerplant of aeroplane '63', which became the Tu-2 prototype.**

BELOW: **An AM-39 during State tests, February 1944.**

'ozonization' and periodical earthing of the human body. He was never again involved in the design of aero engines.

M-34 (AM-34)

This was one of the most mass-produced Soviet aero-engines of the second half of the 1930s. It was under development from 1928, initially at the NAMI and then at the IAM (TsIAM), under A.A. Mikulin's leadership. Intended as a replacement for the M-17 (BMW VI), it had the same overall dimensions and attachment points but its design was fundamentally different. It was a block-type engine (for the first time the cylinder block was joined together with very long internal studs) with centrally-coupled connecting rods. Development was completed in March 1931, and in April its engineering drawings were transferred to Factory No. 24 for the prototypes to be manufactured. On 21 September 1931 the first engine was delivered to the TsIAM for testing. For the bench testing, imported carburettors and magnetos were used. After the engine had been run for 38hr the State tests began in November 1931. In November 1932 the M-34 was repeatedly State tested with Soviet-designed 92KD-3 carburettors (designated K-34 in production), and several defects were revealed. For a third time State bench tests were carried out, in January 1933, and again the engine broke down and failed. In October that year the M-34 underwent State flight-testing in a TB-3 bomber.

Despite the problems, series production of the new engine started in 1932 at Factory No. 24 in Moscow, and by the end of the year the VVS had received 64 M-34s. In 1933 790 were built. In 1934 the M-34 was exhibited in Paris as one of the significant achievements of Soviet aviation. It was in series production at Factory No. 24 until 1943, in a variety of versions. Production ceased in 1940, only tank and marine versions being manufactured thereafter. Right up to 1946 repeated attempts were made to resume M-34 production for motor torpedo boats, but the factories were fully occupied with VVS orders. In total, 10,538 M-34s were built. At a later stage different workshops assembled M-34s using spares and overhauled components. To mark Mikulin's achievements, from August 1936 the type was redesignated AM-34, though in practice both the old and new designations were used.

Special versions of the M-34 powered tanks, self-propelled guns, motor torpedo boats and armoured river boats.

Characteristics

12-cylinder in-line vee, four-stroke, watercooled engine.

Power rating and weight	dependant on version
Bore/stroke	160/190mm (6.30/7.48in) (FRN version, and later versions with cylinders having articulated connecting rods: 196.7mm (7.74in))
Volume	early versions had a volume of 45.82 litres (2,796cu in). Starting from the FRN version the volume was increased to 46.66 litres (2,847cu in)
Compression ratio	6.0:1 (all mass-produced versions)

Some M-34s prepared for transportation beneath a TB-3.

The following versions of the engine are known:

M-34 The first version introduced into series production. Direct-drive, 750/800hp engine. Weight 680kg (1,499lb). The first batches were completed with imported Zenith 90R carburettors, later series having Soviet K-34s. This version was in production up to the end of 1939.

Coupled M-34 A project consisting of two engines driving a single propeller. This version was planned for installation in the projected K-7 aeroplane.

M-34F A small batch of this version was built in 1933. Power rating, 750/830hp.

M-34R A geared version, 750/800hp. Weight 670kg (1,477lb). A small batch of nine engines was manufactured in July 1932. State testing, originally planned for November 1932, lasted from March to May 1933. The type was in series production from the end of that year, being produced in large quantities up to the end of 1939. On 23 May 1934, during repeated State testing, a service life of 500hr was reached.

M-34RD Under a special State order, ten M-34R engines were built in 1934 for installation in the ANT-25 (RD). This version differed in having a higher quality of manufacture (using different technology), smaller tolerances, more thorough adjustment and K-34RD carburettors. Slight boosting of rpm increased maximum power to 830hp. Later, about fifty M-34Rs were built for TB-3 bombers converted as VIP transports to fly Soviet Government officials to European capitals.

M-34N A 750/820hp direct-drive engine with GCS, this was under development from 1931. Originally it was planned that the engine would pass State testing by 15 June 1932, but the first two-speed supercharger, designed by P.I. Orlov, A.A. Mikulin and A.N. Danilevskiy proved quite unreliable. The second (at this time single-speed) was created by Danilevskiy at the TsIAM. Two M-34N prototypes underwent State testing in November 1933, and series production started in September 1934. The engine's supercharger was built as a separate removable unit, and could also be installed on other versions of the engine. The K-34B carbu-

The M-34R geared engine.

The huge MK-1 twin-hull flying-boat had six M-34Rs.

ABOVE: **Eight M-34Rs powered the ANT-20 *Maksim Gorkiy*, the largest Soviet aircraft of the 1930s.**

ABOVE RIGHT: **Used for a number of flights to European capitals, TB-3s were also powered by the M-34RD, sometimes also designated M-34RSP.**

An M-34RD in an ANT-25.

An M-34RN in a TB-3 bomber, May 1935.

An outboard M-34RN of a DB-A aeroplane. In the winter of 1935-36, S.A. Levanevskiy's crew attempted to fly one of these aircraft to the USA via the North Pole.

The M-34RNA engine.

An M-34RNA displayed at Monino.

The M-34RNA engine displayed in the Central House of Aviation and Space in Moscow.

The M-34NB engine.

The R-Zet reconnaissance aeroplane and light bomber, powered by the M-34NB.

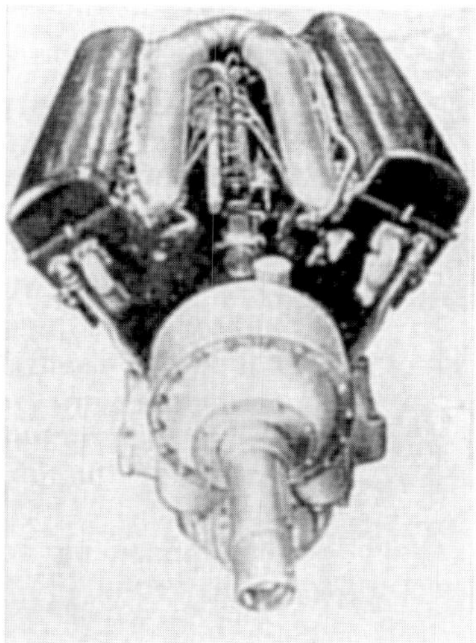

The M-34NV prototype with direct fuel injection.

rettor was fitted, and was later installed on all versions of the engine with GCS. A lightweight (560kg (1,235lb)) version of the M-34N, with a magnesium alloy crankcase, was being designed, and it was also planned to make a GCS that could be switched off. In 1934 negotiations regarding the development of a new GCS for the M-34N were conducted with Hispano-Suiza and Farman in France.

M-34N with PTK steam-turbine supercharger. The PTK was developed at the KhAI in 1938, and further refinement was carried out from 1939 at the Central Boiler-Turbine Institute. In 1940 the engine was being bench- and flight-tested, but it was not introduced into series production.

M-34RN A geared version with GCS, rated at 750/820hp. The type was built in a small series. Although the prototype was required to be submitted for State testing by 1 December 1932, factory tests of the first M-34RN did not start until 1 May 1934. Its improved version was transferred for State testing in September, but it failed because the pistons burnt through. The supercharger was identical to that of the M-34N.

M-34NA An improved version of the M-34N. Minor changes of some components were introduced to increase the engine's service life. Power rating 750/820hp.

M-34RA An improved version of the M-34R, with changes similar to those in the M-34NA. Power rating 750/820hp.

M-34RNA A geared version with GCS, this incorporated all the minor changes introduced on the NA and RA types. Power rating 750/820hp, weight 748kg (1,649lb).

It was flight tested on a TB-3 bomber in May 1935, and series production started at the end of 1935. The M-34RNAs of early batches had oil-cooled valves.

M-34NB An improved version of the NA with a strengthened crankcase, a lightened crankshaft with a modified nose, and refined GCS. Power rating 750/820hp, weight – 638kg (1,406lb). The prototype was built with a TK-1 turbo-supercharger and tested in an R-Z aeroplane in 1936.

M-34RNB A geared version similar to the NB, with lightened reduction gear compared with the RNA type. Power rating 750/820hp, weight 725kg (1,598lb). There was also a prototype built with two TK-1 turbo-superchargers developed by V.I. Danilevskiy. The M-34RNB was in series production from October 1935 until the end of 1939. Another prototype of this engine, boosted to 900/1,000hp, was tested in November 1939.

M-34P A version of the M-34RN with a cannon mounted in the cylinder vee, firing through a hollow gear shaft. The specification for this engine was issued in August 1934. No information on the manufacture of a prototype has yet been found.

A powerplant comprising two M-34s, one driving a propeller and the other driving a powerful supercharger, was being developed at the Air Force Academy in March 1934. It was intended for use in a stratospheric aeroplane.

M-34 running on fuel with the addition of gaseous hydrogen. Such an engine was tested at the TsIAM in the second half of the 1930s.

M-34RSO A project of 1938 with mixed cooling, having air-cooled sleeves and ethylene-glycol-cooled cylinder heads. Power rating 1,050/1,200hp.

M-34NV A prototype engine with direct fuel injection. Power rating 985hp. The injection system was developed by S.A. Kosberg and N.P. Serdyukov at the TsIAM in 1934. The engine passed its 60hr bench tests in 1935 and was flight-tested in R-Z and TB-3 aircraft in 1937. It was not introduced into series production.

M-34RNV A prototype engine similar to the M-34NV but equipped with a reduction gear.

M-34RNV-TK (also designated M-34NRV-TK) This prototype engine, built in late 1938, differed from the M-34RNV in having a TK-1 turbo-supercharger. Power rating 700/850hp, estimated weight 810kg (1,786lb).

M-34NF A prototype which had a GCS and TK-1 turbo-supercharger. It was flight-tested in a TB-3 bomber. Compression ratio 6.6:1, power rating 787/985hp.

M-34 A version intended to drive an ATsN-1 centralized supercharging unit developed under the leadership of

ABOVE: **The RSh prototype aeroplane, modified from a series-production R-Zet, powered by an M-34TK engine with a turbo-supercharger, summer 1938.**

RIGHT: **The M-34FRN engine, demonstrated at the Paris Air Show.**

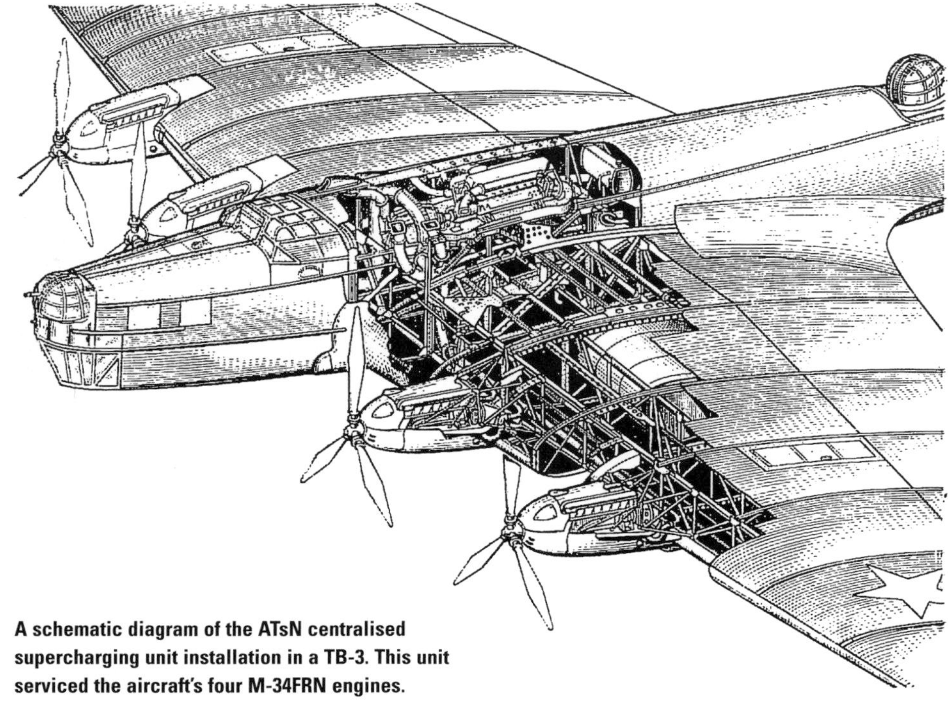

A schematic diagram of the ATsN centralised supercharging unit installation in a TB-3. This unit serviced the aircraft's four M-34FRN engines.

S.A. Treskin in 1935. It was flight tested in a TB-3 bomber.

M-34N2B A version with GCS, two turbo-superchargers and four K-4 carburettors. Power rating 789/1,033hp. A single prototype was built.

M-34FRN (also designated M-34RFN or M-34RNF) A boosted version of the M-34RN. The prototype was submitted for State testing in January 1935, but withdrawn owing to defects. A small batch was built in 1935, but the type was still being refined up to the spring of 1938.

Characteristics

Estimated power rating	1,050/1,200hp
Actual power	900/1,200hp
Volume	46.66 litres (2,847cu in)
Weight	735kg (1,620lb).

The crankshaft, gearing, crank case and the side joint of the connecting rods were strengthened, the lubrication system was changed, the improved GCS was installed, and a new gas-distribution mechanism was fitted. The carburettors were installed behind the GCS (earlier, there was one carburettor installed in front of the GCS). In 1937 the M-34FRN prototype was exhibited at the Paris Air Show. In 1938 a small batch of M-34FRNs fitted with two TK-1 turbo-superchargers was built (designated M-34RNFT). Power rating 1,017/1,200hp (some sources, 750/1,200hp), estimated weight 690kg (1,521lb) (some sources, 810kg (1,786lb)). Engines of this type were flight tested in a DB-A bomber.

M-34FRNA A mass-produced version based on the FRN, equipped with four carburettors.

M-34FRNB Another mass-produced version based on the FRN, but equipped with six carburettors. In February 1937 the M-34FRNB (RFNB) version with the K-85 carburettor, strengthened crankcase and lightened gearing was transferred to State testing. Power rating 1,000/1,050hp. A small batch of these was built, with provision for the installation of the ATsN-2 centralized supercharging unit created at the TsIAM under the leadership of K.V. Minkner. Driven by an additional M-100 engine, the ATsN-2 provided simultaneous supercharging for four M-34FRNBs. The powerplant system comprising four M-34FRNBs and an ATsN-2 was tested in a TB-7 bomber prototype in the winter and spring of 1938/39.

M-34FRN with vapour cooling. This was being developed from early 1935 by R.I. Bartosh at the TsIAM. In 1936 a small batch was built, the engines being intended for the I-21 fighter prototype. The M-34FRN had a step-up gear and non-standard lower crankcase with sealed opening to allow the wing spar to pass through. At the beginning of 1937 several flights of the I-21 prototype were carried out.

M-34FRNV A further evolution of the M-34FRNB. Power rating 1,050/1,200hp. This version was developed with three variants of gearing and with two types of GCS. It was first submitted for State testing in December 1937 (weight 749kg (1,651lb)), but broke down under test. Compared with the M-34FRNB, the engine had a modified crankcase and bronze bushings for the main supports using hyperbolic boring. The valve casings were made of magnesium alloy. The engine was composed of different units and had a longer gear-shaft nose, a strengthened crankcase with a modified lubrication system, and four K-4 carburettors. In April 1938 it was repeatedly submitted for State testing, after having a number of components strengthened (the weight increased to 763.5kg (1,683lb), compared to the projected weight of 740kg (1,631lb)). The engine satisfactorily operated for 100hr and, as a result, a small initial batch of fifty was built. The M-34FRNV was in series production during 1939-40. In May-June 1938 a version with direct fuel injection (power rating 1,050/1,200hp, weight 810kg (1,786lb)) was tested. The M-34FRNV was the last mass-produced version of the M-34.

M-34FRNV-TK A version of the M-34FRNV with two TK-1 turbo-superchargers. Project weight (with turbo-superchargers) 850kg (1,874lb), power rating 950/1,200hp. The engine was tested in September 1939.

M-34FRGN No information on this version has so far been found.

M-34RB This version was created by removing the GCS from the M-34RNB. Such modifications were carried out in 1938-39.

GM-34 A version intended for motor torpedo boats, this had a reversing gear, a free-wheel sleeve and modified cooling and exhaust systems. It was being developed by V.M. Yakovlev from 1932. It was planned to transfer the engine for State testing by October 1932, but it did not pass its State tests until December 1934, being introduced into series production the same year. Power rating 675/800hp, weight 864kg (1,905lb).

GM-34F An improved version of the GM-34, it had bronze main bushings, and the crankshaft, block heads and some

The M-34FRNV engine.

The M-34R engine with a turbo-supercharger, tested in a TB-3.

ABOVE: **The M-34RB engine.**

RIGHT: **The GM-34 (GAM-34) marine engine.**

BELOW: **A G-5 torpedo boat powered by two GM-34s.**

RIGHT: **A brace of GM-34s in the engine-room of a G-5 torpedo boat.**

components were taken from the M-34FRNV. The engine, which entered series production, used a benzine-alcohol fuel mixture.

Characteristics

Power rating	800/1,000hp
Compression ratio	7.3:1
Weight	1,080kg (2,381lb)

GM-34FN A version of the GM-34F with an FN-25 GCS and one K-4 carburettor. The oil system was taken from the GAM-34BS, and the engine used a benzine-alcohol fuel mixture. It was in series production from August 1939.

Characteristics

Power rating	1,200hp
Compression ratio	6.0:1
Weight	1,110kg (2,447lb)

GM-34BP A version for armoured river boats, fitted with a reversing gear. The engine was built in series. Power rating 800hp.
GM-34BS An improved version of the GM-34BP, in series production until 1943. The engine used a benzine-alcohol fuel mixture. Power rating 850hp, weight 1,045kg (2,304lb).
GM-34BT A version for tanks, developed from the marine engine and having a modified cooling system using a fan, and new gearing. The engine had an electric starter instead of the pneumatic one. Power rating 850hp. A small batch of this type was built in 1939.

The engines of the M-34 (AM-34) family powered the following series production aeroplanes: TB-3, KR-6, R-Z, ANT-25 (RD, DB-1), MBR-2, MTB-1, TB-7, (Pe-8, first small batch), DB-A; and the following prototypes: LR, TSh-3, MI-3D, T-1 (ANT-41), TB-4, K-7, MG (ANT-20), PS-124, I-21 (TsKB-32, with steam cooling), PI (not completed), K-13, MK-1, Stal-MAI and MI-3. The engine was also specified for the following aircraft projects: TB-6, Stal-5, ANT-15, TSh-B (ANT-17 and ANT-18), VIT-2, ANT-51 (S3), the Samsonov and Danilevskiy armoured attack aircraft with caterpillar undercarriage (based on the TSh-2), and Kamov's helicopter-tank.

Engines of GM-34 (GAM-34) type powered the following motor torpedo-boats: G-5 (in series production until 1943), G-6, G-8 and SM-4 (only one prototype of each was built). They were also specified in the projects for the G-9 and G-10 boats. The armoured river boats of Projects 1124 and 1125 (in mass production until 1944) were powered by this engine.

The GM-34BT (GAM-34BT) powered prototypes of the T-100 and SMK tanks, which underwent service testing at the front during the war against Finland in the winter of 1940. This engine was also installed in the prototype SU-100y (*Igrek*) self-propelled gun, used in the battle of Moscow during the winter of 1941.

M-33

Simultaneously with the M-34 development, the NAMI, and later the IAM, developed an in-line engine unified with the M-34. It is quite possible that this project was later partly used in the development of the M-52.

Characteristics

6-cylinder in-line, four-stroke, watercooled engine.

Power rating	400hp
Bore/stroke	160/190mm (6.30/7.48in)

M-35

This engine, which was being developed from 1930 under the leadership of A.A. Mikulin, was intended for heavy aircraft. It was a coupled M-34 with two shafts driving a common gear. It was planned that factory testing would start from 1 April 1933. In 1932 the project was deemed unsuccessful and the work on it was stopped. No information about completion of the prototype engine has been found.

It was planned to use the engine in the TB-4 and ANT-20 aeroplanes.

Characteristics

24-cylinder, four-stroke, watercooled, geared engine.

Power rating	1,580hp (according to the specification 1,500-1,800hp)
Bore/stroke	160/190mm (6.30/7.48in)
Weight	1,300kg (2,900lb)

M-52

This was an engine of medium power rating that used one M-34 cylinder block. It was under development in 1931-32 at the IAM, State testing being scheduled for October 1932. No information about the manufacture and testing of the M-52 prototypes has been found.

It was planned to introduce the M-52

The TB-4 six-engined bomber prototype was powered by M-34s.

into series production and use it for the planned artillery-spotter aircraft, the VS-2 'chemical attack aeroplane' and the P-3 conversion trainer.

Characteristics

6-cylinder in-line, four-stroke, watercooled engine.

Power rating	350/450hp
Bore/stroke	160/190mm (6.30/7.48in)
Compression ratio	6.0:1
Weight	300kg (660lb) (according to project data)

Project for a 12-cylinder in-line engine

At the end of 1934 A.A. Mikulin proposed a geared 12-cylinder 500hp in-line engine with horizontal cylinders. Its weight was estimated at 360kg (793lb), and it was intended for a light fighter. It was planned to have air-cooled cylinders and ethylene-cooled cylinder heads. The project was subject to severe criticism, as the concept of the light fighter was considered a mistake. Detailed development of the engine was not carried out, and a prototype was not built.

M-55

This was an inverted version of the M-34. The engine's factory tests were planned for August-October 1933, but the work was cancelled in 1932 as it was considered that the M-55 would not offer any considerable advantages over the basic M-34.

Characteristics

12-cylinder inverted vee, four-stroke, watercooled engine.

Power rating	750hp
Bore-stroke	160/190mm (6.30/7.48in)
Compression ratio	6.0:1
Weight	600kg (1,300lb) (according to project data)

M-35 (AM-35)

This engine, a further development of the AM-34FRNV, should not be confused with the earlier M-35 designed by Mikulin. It was being developed at Factory No. 24 from the end of 1938, with M.R. Flisskiy as chief designer. Compared with the AM-34FRNV, the M-35 had an improved cylinder block, and a new single-speed GCS was introduced that had variable-incidence guide vanes ('Polikovskiy's blades') in the inlet. The crankcase was strengthened, and the suction inlets changed. In March 1939 the engine successfully passed its factory tests, and in April it passed its State tests. However, the VVS was not satisfied, as its maximum power rating was 1,300hp, instead of 1,500hp stated in the specification, and the specified weight was exceeded by 10kg (22lb). In addition, instead of the prescribed two-speed GCS, the engine had a single-speed unit. Therefore, one of the AM-35 prototypes passed 100hr tests with increased supercharging. Based on the results of this experiment, a version with boosted supercharging, the AM-35A, was created, and was built in large quantities at Factory No. 24. There were also plans to introduce this engine into series production at Factories Nos 19 and 452.

Formally, AM-35A production ceased at the end of 1941, but in fact it was being manufactured in small quantities in 1942-43, after Factory No. 24 had been evacuated to Kuibyshev. The last batches of AM-35As were built using components from the AM-38F. In total, 4,659 AM-35s and AM-35As were produced.

Characteristics

12-cylinder in-line vee, four-stroke, watercooled, geared engine with single-speed GCS. Engine starting by compressed air. There was provision for the installation of a synchronisation mechanism.

Bore/stroke	160/190mm (6.30/7.48in) (in cylinders with articulated connecting rods, 196.7mm (7.74in))
Volume	46.66 litres (2,847cu in)
Compression ratio	7.0:1
Power rating	dependant on version
Weight	dependant on version

The following versions of the engine are known:

AM-35 The first version. A small batch was built from August 1939. Power rating 1,200/1,350hp, weight 780kg (1,720lb). A variant with aluminium main bearing inserts (instead of bronze), was tested. More than fifty engines were built during 1939-40.

AM-35NV A project for an AM-35 with direct fuel injection, developed in October 1939. Later it was partly used in the AM-35ANV.

AM-35G ('glycol') A project for an AM-35 cooled by pure ethylene-glycol. Power rating 1,200/1,350hp, weight (according to project data) 770kg (1,698lb).

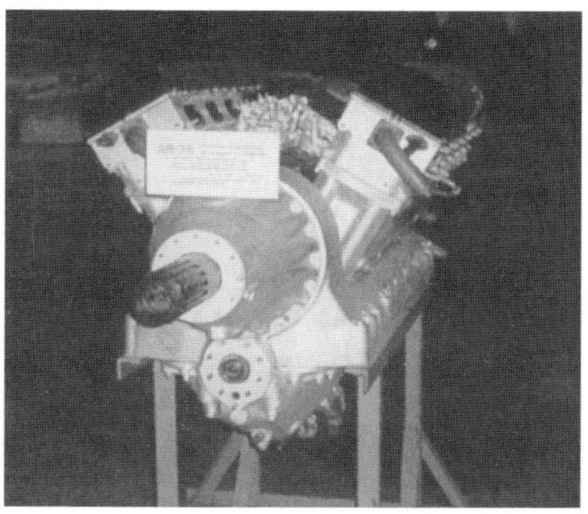

The AM-35A engine.

AM-35TK A 1939 project using turbo-supercharging. Two variants were evaluated, with the TK-2 and TK-35 turbo-superchargers respectively. Weight (according to project data) 780kg (1,720lb). No information regarding completion of the prototype has been found.

AM-35A An improved version with increased supercharging. Power rating 1,200/1,350hp, weight 830kg (1,830lb). Nominal altitude was increased from 4,500m (14,800ft) to 6,000m (20,000ft). This engine was being tested from October 1939. The first prototypes had poor acceleration and operated unevenly at low speed. In May 1940 the engine underwent joint tests, and in July went for State testing, which was successfully completed in September. From the end of 1940 it was in large-scale production. At the beginning of 1941 a strengthened GCS impeller was introduced, and from spring of the same year it was fitted with mechanical (instead of electro-mechanical) drive for the variable-incidence blades at the GCS inlet. Three variants of gearing, with different reduction ratios, were developed for the AM-35A. The first batches were built with a gear ratio of 0.9, and from the fifth batch the ratio was 0.732. The third variant of the gearing was not used in series-production engines. In January 1941 three prototypes with floatless carburettors were built and tested. Although this variant was planned for production, it did not reach this stage. About 4,500 AM-35As were built up to the end of 1943, 4,034 being manufactured in 1941.

AM-35ANV A version of the AM-35A

The GAM-35 marine engine prototype.

The AM-36 (M-36) prototype.

with direct fuel injection. Power rating 1,200/1,350hp, weight 870kg (1,918lb). The prototype was built in the summer of 1941, but was not tested owing to evacuation of the factory. Work on this version was officially cancelled at the beginning of 1942.

AM-35A-TR A project of 1940 for a version equipped with Efremov's turboreactors. Power rating 1,200/1,650hp.

GAM-35FN A project of 1943, this was a marine engine with a reversing clutch. Power rating 1,150hp. No information on completion of the prototypes has been found.

Engines of the AM-35 family powered the following series production aeroplanes: MiG-1, MiG-3, MiG-3U, TB-7 (Pe-8); and the following prototypes: Er-2 (Er-4), PS-124 (MGbis, ANT-124bis) and BSh-2 (TsKB-55). It was planned to use AM-35ATKs for a projected high-altitude version of the DB-3 bomber.

M-36 (AM-36)

This three-block in-line Y-shaped engine was designed using three M-34 blocks, one of which was inverted. It was under development from May 1939 in two versions; with carburation and with direct fuel injection. Engineering drawings were issued in August of that year, and a batch of five prototypes was laid down. The first M-36 prototype was completed on 18 December 1939, and running trials started on 30 December, followed by testing. The engine was being refined until the beginning of 1942, when all work was cancelled because it was considered that it had no prospects.

It was planned to use this engine in Tairov's projected fighter.

Characteristics

18-cylinder in-line Y-shaped, four-stroke, watercooled, geared engine with GCS.

Power rating	1,600/2,000hp (other sources, 2,000/2,250hp)
Bore/stroke	160/190mm (6.30/7.48in) (in cylinders with articulated connecting rods, 196.7mm (7.74in))
Volume	68.73 litres (4,194cu in)
Compression ratio	6.0:1
Weight	1,160kg (2,557lb) (according to project data 1,050kg (2,314lb); with direct injection, 1,090kg (2,403lb))

M-37 (AM-37)

The designation M-37 was originally allocated to an engine in the 1932-33 plan, but its development did not take place. For its second use the designation was given to a further development of the AM-35A, with boosted supercharging and an intermediate water-air radiator (intercooler) positioned behind the GCS. Development was in process from December 1939, at first at the factory's initiative, but the engine was then included into the plan of 1940-41. In 1940 a batch of ten prototypes was completed, and testing started on 5 January 1941. The engine was a long time in refinement. In April 1941 the AM-37 passed State tests and was introduced into series production, but it did not attain the required level of reliability. Moreover, aircraft designers could not cope with the cooling problems of this rather temperature-stressed engine. In 1941 Factory No. 24 in Moscow built twenty-nine AM-37s, but production ceased in October. Production of the AM-37 was not resumed after the factory's evacuation.

The engine was flight-tested in October 1940 in a DB-240, and in January 1941 in the '103' bomber prototype. The M-37 was also tested in MiG-1 and MiG-3 fighters.

Characteristics

12-cylinder in-line vee, four-stroke, watercooled, geared engine with single-speed GCS and intercooler. Engine starting by compressed air. There was provision for synchronizing gear.

Power rating	1,200/1,500hp (1,500/1,600hp in the specification)
Bore/stroke	160/190mm (6.30/7.48in) (in cylinders with articulated connecting rods, 196.7mm (7.74in))
Volume	46.66 litres (2,847cu in)
Compression ratio	7.0:1
Weight	885kg (1,951lb) (800kg (1,800lb) in the specification)

The following versions of the engine are known:

AM-37 A series production version. Power rating 1,200/1,500hp, weight 885kg (1,951lb).

AM-37A A planned improved version with a nominal power rating of 1,600hp and a weight of 850kg (1,874lb). It was to be factory tested in February 1940. No information on its completion and testing has been found.

AM-37TK A turbo-supercharged AM-

37. No further information has been found.

AM-37P A 1940 project for an AM-37 with a cannon installed in the cylinder vee, firing through the hollow reduction-gear shaft. No information on its completion and testing has been found.

AM-37u/v (AM-37UV) (*udlinyonniy val*, or lengthened shaft) An AM-37 with a lengthened shaft and remotely-mounted gearing, intended for Gu-1 fighter, which had a layout similar to that of the Bell P-39 Airacobra. The order for the engine's development was issued in October 1940, and work started in 1941, but it was not built. The data resulting from this project was later used for the AM-41.

The AM-37 powered the following prototypes: DB-4 (TsKB-54), FB ('103'), TIS-A, Er-2 (Er-4), IDS (Gr-1, not flown), I-200, MiG-7, and MiG-5 (DIS-200, not completed).

The engine was specified for the following projected aircraft: IOP, IT, SPB, E-2, OKO-7, SK-3, ODB (P), I-63, TSh, OKO-8, DB-LK ('380'), Gu-1, BOK-17 and Il-2.

M-38

This designation was first allocated to F.V. Kontsevich's radial engine, which was developed and tested in 1929-32 but not put into series production. In 1939 the design bureau of Factory No. 24 was tasked with developing an engine under the same designation but having completely different characteristics: power rating 3,000/3,500hp, volume 77 litres (4,699cu in), weight 1,450kg (3,197lb). Although it was planned to have the engine ready for factory testing in the first quarter of 1941, development does not appear to have gone ahead.

M-38 (AM-38)

The third type to have this designation was a low-altitude engine based on the AM-35A and specially created for the BSh-2 (Il-2) attack aircraft. Compared with the AM-35A it had a strengthened crankshaft and gear shaft nose, a new specially developed GCS drive, and modified oil and cooling systems. Tests of the first prototypes started in October 1939, and in November of that year the AM-38 passed its factory testing programme. During the course of development in 1940 the engine's compression ratio was reduced from 7.0:1 to 6.8:1, and its oil and cooling systems were improved.

The AM-38 was in series production from the beginning of 1941, though officially it did not pass its State tests until six months later, in July 1941. The engine was built at Factory No. 24 in Moscow and, after its evacuation, in Kuibyshev. From June 1942 the AM-38 was also produced at Factory No. 45, which had been established in the old workshops of the Moscow factory. The AM-38 was the most-produced Mikulin-designed engine, 43,191 being built. It was in series production until 1946.

Characteristics

12-cylinder in-line vee, four-stroke, watercooled, geared engine with single-speed GCS. Engine starting by compressed air.

Bore/stroke	160/190mm (6.30/7.48in) (in cylinders with articulated connecting rods, 196.7mm (7.74in))
Volume	46.66 litres (2,847cu in)

Compression ratio, power rating and weight dependant on version

The following engine versions are known:

AM-38 A series version, in production from 1941 to 1943.

Characteristics

Power rating	1,500/1,600hp
Compression ratio	6.8:1
Weight	860kg (1,896lb)

AM-38F A version with boosted rpm for take-off, this engine had an oil centrifuge, its camshafts and inlet valves were strengthened, and the cylinder-block

The '63' high-speed bomber prototype under construction.

An AM-38 being installed in an Il-2.

An AM-38F in the Salyut Factory museum.

heads were made of a different alloy. The diameter of the GCS impeller was reduced, and its compression ratio was reduced to allow the use of low-quality fuel. The AM-38F was in series production at Factory No. 24 from October 1942, and at Factory No. 45 from 1943. The engine did not pass its official State tests until May 1943. In June 1944 experiments with water injection under boosted conditions were conducted.

Characteristics

Power rating	1,500/1,700hp
Compression ratio	6.0:1
Weight	880kg (1,940lb)

GAM-38F A projected marine version of the AM-38F, created in the spring of 1944. It had a modified crankcase, crankshaft and GCS, and a reversing clutch and an additional water pump were introduced. The prototype was not built.

The AM-38 and AM-38F engines powered series-production Il-2 attack aircraft, as well as prototypes of the TIS-MA and MiG-3 fighters. There were plans to use the AM-38 in the projected ODB(P) aeroplane.

AM-38Fs were exported to Poland, Czechoslovakia and Yugoslavia.

M-39 (AM-39)

This was a further development of the AM-37, based the AM-38F with two-speed GCS and intercooler. Work was started in 1942 at the design bureau of Factory No. 300 (OKB-300), while some components for the prototype engines were manufactured at Factories Nos 24 and 45. The refinement testing of the first AM-39 prototype with four carburettors was carried out in January 1943. During 1943-46 several more versions of the engine were developed. In March 1944 the AM-39 passed State tests, but it was not introduced into large-scale production.

In April 1944 ten AM-39s were built at Factory No. 45, and in May-June of that year twenty-two engines were converted from AM-38Fs using components manufactured at Factory No. 45. The last four engines were built in 1945.

Characteristics

12-cylinder in-line vee, four-stroke, watercooled, geared engine with two-speed GCS and intercooler. Engine starting by compressed air. Synchronization could be provided.

Bore/stroke	160/190mm (6.30/7.48in) (in cylinders with articulated connecting rods, 196,8mm (7.74in))
Volume	46.66 litres (2,847cu in)
Power rating	dependant on version
Weight	dependant on version

The following versions of the engine are known:

AM-39 Based on the AM-38, with carburettor installation. Power rating 1,500/1,800hp.

AM-39A Based on the AM-38F, with carburettor installation. Power rating 1,500/1,800hp (according to the specification, 1,700/1,800hp). The prototype underwent testing in March 1944.

AM-39A-TK A version with TK-B turbo-superchargers. The prototype was tested in an I-224 fighter in February 1944. There was also a projected version with two TK-300B turbo-superchargers.

AM-39B A version with an air-to-air intercooler (instead of a water-air type).

AM-39B-TK An AM-39B variant with turbo-supercharging. Power rating 1,580/1,890hp. The engine was tested in I-224 in June 1944.

AM-39FK A version with pre-combustion ignition. Power rating 1,600/1,850hp. Two prototypes were built at the beginning of 1946, and their factory tests were started. In 1947 seven more engines were produced. The AM-39FK was not transferred to State testing.

AM-39FN (FNV) A boosted version with direct injection, based on the AM-38F. This was being developed at OKB-300 from the beginning of 1944. It had improved hydraulics for the GCS, an increased-diameter GCS impeller, increased-diameter valves, and suction inlets similar to those used on the Allison V-1710. The engine's initial power rating of 1,600/1,850hp was further increased to 1,730/2,130hp. Weight 970kg (2,138lb). Testing were carried out from August 1944, and official factory tests were performed in January 1945. In the summer of that year the engines were tested in the Tu-2 bomber. All development work was cancelled in September 1945 under the order of Mikulin, because the AM-39FN2 appeared to be more successful.

AM-39FN2 A version similar to the AM-39FN, but based on the AM-42. Power rating 1,600/1,850hp, weight 1,080kg (2,380lb). Five prototypes were built in the first quarter of 1946, and were used for State testing.

Engines of the AM-39 family powered a small batch of Tu-10 bombers, and they were also used on the following prototypes: '68' (Tu-4), I-231 (2D, MiG-3DD), ITP (M-2), VP(K), TIS-MA and I-224 (MiG-7). It was planned to use the AM-39 in the projected SPS aeroplane.

AM-40

This was a modified version of the AM-39FN2. In 1946-48 thirty-four such engines were built at Factory No. 24. In 1947 the AM-40 was flight-tested in a Tu-4 (the first with this designation, a version of the '68' aeroplane).

AM-41 (AM-39UV)

This engine was based on the AM-39, with a lengthened shaft and remotely-mounted gearing. The order for AM-37UV (or AM-37u/v) development was issued on 31 October 1940, and State testing was planned to be completed by 1 November 1941. The engine was intended for installation in the Gu-1 fighter, which was similar in layout to the Bell P-39 Airacobra.

In fact, the engine's development did not started until 1942, and the AM-37 was soon replaced by the AM-39. Only three prototypes were built. Refinement of the AM-41 prototype was completed in the summer 1943. The engine was tested on the Gu-1 prototype, but during flight testing the aircraft was lost in an accident. All development work on the AM-41 was

The AM-38F restored to running condition, before its first start, 2002.

The same AM-38F at the *Aviadvigatel 2002* show in Moscow. The author is standing nearby.

ABOVE: **An AM-39 with an AMTK turbo-supercharger.**

RIGHT: **The AM-39FN2 (AM-40).**

The Tu-4 prototype (the first with this designation, also known as aeroplane '68'), powered by AM-40s, during testing at the NII VVS in September 1946.

The AM-41 removed from the crashed Gu-1 aeroplane.

then cancelled. This engine was not submitted for State testing.

The engine powered the Gu-1 fighter prototype.

Characteristics

12-cylinder in-line vee, four-stroke, watercooled engine with lengthened shaft and remotely-mounted gear, two-speed GCS and intercooler. Engine starting by compressed air. Synchronization could be provided.

Power rating	1,400/1,600hp
Bore/stroke	160/190mm (6.30/7.48in) (in cylinders with articulated connecting rods, 196,8mm (7.74in))
Volume	46.66 litres (2,847cu in)
Weight	980kg (2,160lb)

M-42 (AM-42)

This low-altitude engine for attack aircraft, a further evolution of the AM-38F, was developed at the design bureau of Factory No. 24. Compared with the AM-38F it had a reduced compression ratio, increased supercharging, and strengthened crankshaft, conrods and pistons. Crankshaft counterweights were introduced and changes were made to the oil system. The engine rpms were increased.

The first five prototypes were built in November 1942. Later, small batches were produced (three to five engines per month) for refinement and testing. The AM-42 passed its 50hr factory test in January 1943. In March-May that year it was flight-tested in a specially modified Il-2 (Il-AM-42). It was planned to conduct State tests of the AM-42 in March 1943, but refinement of the engine had not been completed by then. In May of that year Mikulin was discharged from his post as chief designer at Factory No. 24, and further work on the engine was carried out by Flisskiy. On 23 September 1943 the AM-42 was transferred for State tests for the first time, but they were not completed because of the burnt-through pistons. In the course of refining the prototype the K-42BPA floatless carburettor was modified, the cylinder block load-carrying studs and piston skirts were strengthened, the cylinder sleeves thickened and the gearing strengthened. The AM-42 passed State tests in April-May 1944.

The AM-42 had already been introduced into series production at Factory No. 24 early in 1944, and it was built in large quantities up to 1948. In early 1951 production of an improved version, with a service life of 400hr, was resumed. The type was phased out of production in the USSR in 1954, after 10,232 had been built.

Starting from the spring of 1952 the AM-42 was built under licence in Czechoslovakia (as the M-42) at the Dimitrov factory.

The engine was exported to Poland, Hungary, Rumania, Czechoslovakia, China and North Korea.

Characteristics

12-cylinder in-line vee, four-stroke, watercooled, geared engine with single-speed GCS. Engine starting by compressed air.

Bore/stroke	160/190mm (6.30/7.48in) (in cylinders with articulated connecting rods, 196.7mm (7.74in))
Volume	46.66 litres (2,847cu in)
Compression ratio	5.5:1
Power rating	dependant on version
Weight	dependant on version

The following versions of the engine are known:

AM-42 A version introduced into mass production. Power rating 1,750/2,000hp, weight 980kg (2,160lb) (later series 996kg (2,196lb)).

AM-42TK A version with TK-300B turbo-superchargers. The prototype was built in March 1943 and tested in Mikoyan's '5A' fighter prototype.

AM-42 A version with pre-combustion ignition and a compression ratio of 7.0:1. The prototype was bench tested in 1944.

AM-42FNV A version with direct fuel injection. Power rating 1,650/2,000hp, weight 1,000kg (2,200lb). Bench testing

The Il-10 attack aircraft, powered by AM-42. These aircraft participated in the last operations of Second World War, and later saw action in Korea.

The '65' high-altitude reconnaissance bomber prototype, powered by AM-44TKs.

of the prototype were completed on 22 August 1945.

AM-42B-TK A version with two TK-300B turbo-superchargers. Power rating 1,750/2,000hp. The engine was tested in a '4A' fighter prototype.

AM-42FB-TK A version with two TK-1A turbo-superchargers.

The AM-42 powered the Il-10 and Il-10M production attack aeroplanes. Czechoslovakian M-42s were installed in the B-33 attack aircraft (the Czech version of the Il-10). The AM-42 also powered the following prototypes: Il-8, Il-16, I-225 ('5A') and Su-6. It was planned to use the AM-42 in the projected Tu-8B.

M-43 (AM-43)

A further evolution of the M-42, this was initially included in the plan of 1943 as the AM-43TR equipped with Efremov's turbo-reactor and a two-speed GCS. Later, documentation for the AM-42 served to provide the basis for the AM-43's development, the turbo-reactor and two-speed GCS being rejected. The AM-43 had a single-speed GCS and was boosted in rpm compared with the AM-42. Development work was carried out at the design bureau of Factory No. 24 in Kuibyshev, under the leadership of M.R. Flisskiy. The first prototype AM-43 was built in September 1944, and was equipped with the K-42BP floatless carburettor from the AM-42. Later, during refinement, it was modified for direct fuel injection, the gas-distribution mechanism was changed, valve diameter was increased, and new suction inlets and an intercooler were introduced. Some of the engine's components were taken from the AM-39.

In August 1945 the AM-43 was tested at Factory No. 24. Officially it was excluded from the plan for the NKAP's experimental work in June 1945, but refinement continued for another year. The engine was flight tested in the '63P' (Tu-1) aeroplane, but was not introduced into series production.

Characteristics

12-cylinder in-line vee, four-stroke, watercooled, geared engine with single-speed GCS. Engine starting by compressed air.

Power rating	2,000/2,150hp (later increased to 2,150/2,300hp)
Bore-stroke	160/190mm (6.30/7.48in) (in cylinders with articulated connecting rods, 196.7mm (7.74in))
Volume	46.66 litres (2,847cu in)
Weight	1,090kg (2,403lb)

The following versions of the engine are known:

AM-43TR According to a requirement of 1943, this was to be an engine with a two-speed GCS and Efremov's turbo-reactor. Power rating 2,000/2,150hp, weight 1,100kg (2,400lb) (including turbo-reactor).

AM-43 The first version, equipped with carburettor, and built as a prototype. Power rating 2,000/2,150hp.

AM-43NV A version with direct fuel injection. Power rating 2,150/2,300hp, weight 1,090kg (2,403lb)

AM-43TK – a version with TK-300B turbo-superchargers.

The AM-43 powered the '63P' (Tu-1) heavy fighter prototype. It was planned to use the engine in the projected Tupolev's '64'.

M-44 (AM-44)

Initially designated AM-42V, this engine was being developed in 1944-45 at the design bureau of Factory No. 24. In 1944 several prototypes were built. In July 1944 the engine was flight-tested in a Tu-2 bomber.

Characteristics

12-cylinder in-line vee, four-stroke, watercooled, geared engine with GCS. Engine starting by compressed air.

Bore/stroke	160/190mm (6.30/7.48in) (in cylinders with articulated connecting rods, 196.7mm (7.74in))
Volume	46.66 litres (2,847cu in)

ABOVE: **The AM-45 engine.**

LEFT: **An AM-44TK in the '67' bomber prototype.**

The following versions are known:
AM-44 The first version, built as a prototype.
AM-44B-TK A version with TK-1B (TK-300B) turbo-superchargers. Power rating 1,650/1,950hp.

M-45 (AM-45, MF-45)

This was a further evolution of the AM-44, with a two-stage GCS. The engine was being developed from January 1945 at the design bureau of Factory No. 24, under the leadership of M.R. Flisskiy. A two-stage, four-speed supercharger was specially developed by the TsIAM for installation on this engine, and was bench tested at the institute in March-April 1945.

In June 1945 the first bench tests of the AM-45 prototypes were carried out, but they revealed that the GCS was insufficiently reliable. Development of three new versions of the GCS was completed in April of the following year. Sixteen AM-45s of different versions were built.

Characteristics

12-cylinder in-line vee, four-stroke, watercooled, geared engine with GCS. Engine starting by compressed air.

Bore/stroke	160/190mm (6.30/7.48in) (in cylinders with articulated connecting rods, 196.7mm (7.74in))
Volume	46.66 litres (2,847cu in)
Power rating	dependant on version
Weight	dependant on version

The following versions are known:
AM-45 A version with a two-speed, two-stage GCS. Power rating 1,750/2,450hp (according to the specification 2,200/2,500hp), weight 1,200kg (2,600lb). The engine was factory tested in the spring of 1946. In September 1947 it satisfactorily passed joint tests.
AM-45D A version with a power rating of 1,750/2,700hp. Its development was completed in the first quarter of 1946. Three prototypes were built, but no record of their tests has been found.
AM-45Sh A version with a power rating of 2,400/3,000hp. In 1948 two prototypes were built and underwent factory tests.

M-46 (AM-46)

A further evolution of the AM-45, this was developed at the design bureau of Factory No. 24, under the leadership of M.R. Flisskiy. Two prototypes were built in the first quarter of 1946, and underwent bench testing. The engine was not introduced into series production.

Characteristics

12-cylinder in-line vee, four-stroke, watercooled, geared engine with GCS. Engine starting by compressed air.

Bore/stroke	160/190mm (6.30/7.48in) (in cylinders with articulated connecting rods, 196.7mm (7.74in)).
Volume	46.66 litres (2,847cu in)

Two versions of the engine are known:
AM-46 A version of 1,040/2,550hp. Two prototypes were built and bench tested.
AM-46TK A version with TK-300B turbo-superchargers. Maximum power rating 2,300hp.

No information about AM-46 installations in aircraft has been found.

AM-47 (AM-47)

The last piston engine of the AM family, this was being developed in 1946-48 under the leadership of M.R. Flisskiy at the design bureau of Factory No. 24 in Kuibyshev. Prototypes were built, and bench and flight tests (on the prototype Il-20 attack aircraft) were carried out. Further work on the engine was cancelled in 1948, owing to the factory converting to jet engine production.

Characteristics

12-cylinder in-line vee, four-stroke, watercooled, geared engine with GCS. Engine starting by compressed air.

Maximum power rating	3,000hp
Bore/stroke	160/190mm (6.30/7.48in) (in cylinders with articulated connecting rods, 196.7mm (7.74in))
Volume	46.66 litres (2,847cu in)

CHAPTER TWENTY-THREE

The Engines of A.D. Shvetsov

Arkadiy Dmitrievich Shvetsov was born in Perm in 1892. After finishing school he entered the Moscow Emperor's High Technical School, but he had to interrupt his studies owing to lack of money. It was not until 1921 that he got his Diploma in Engineering.

After graduation Shvetsov started working at the GAZ No. 4 Motor factory (later Factory No. 24). In 1923 a contest for a 100hp engine for training aircraft was announced, for which Shvetsov with N.V. Okromeshko proposed an engine that later became known as the M-11. The type was adopted by the VVS RKKA and introduced into mass production. It was repeatedly modified by other designers, namely Uvarov, Kossov and Muzhilov, and was manufactured at different factories in the Soviet Union, as well as in Poland and China, right up to 1952. By the end of the 1920s Shvetsov had already become chief engineer of Factory No. 24.

As stated in previous chapters, at the beginning of the 1930s it became evident that Soviet aero-engine development lagged behind that of Western countries. This inhibited the creation of new aircraft types, primarily fighters, so suitable foreign engines were selected and negotiations for their production in the USSR were begun. The 9-cylinder Wright Cyclone R-1820 radial was one engine selected for series production in Soviet factories, and in the autumn of 1932 a delegation headed by I.I. Poberezhskiy left for the USA to negotiate with the Wright company. The group also included A.D. Shvetsov and N.P. Basilev. The delegation arrived in New York on 5 December, and negotiations started on 7 December and ended on 22 April 1932. The American company agreed to prepare all documentation in metric units, and to build and test the pattern engines built to the metric system.

In May 1932 this agreement was ratified by a special decree of the Soviet Government. Later, the USSR Defence Committee and the STO issued several more decrees, specifying the quantity of engines built to British Imperial and metric systems, as well as the engine spares and essential components to be purchased in the USA. In particular, an STO decree issued on 28 November 1933 covered the purchase of about 150 complete engines, 100 engines as parts, and the acquisition of the most complex components for another 100 engines, at a total cost of 4,350,000 roubles. At the end of December 1933 the first Cyclone engine was shipped to the USSR.

At about the same time the Wright company prepared the metric engineering drawings and built a prototype, and in January 1934 put it to bench testing. The 100hr bench test was completed in the USA by April 1934.

In the USSR the new Factory No. 19 in Perm was chosen for production of the American engine. According to an STO decree of 15 December 1933, the first fifty engines were to be assembled by the end of 1934, using the parts purchased from Wright. By this time, however, the Cyclone R-1820 was outdated. Realizing this, in March 1934 the STO ordered that a design department be established at the factory to improve the American engine as regards its power rating, critical altitude and reliability, and to decrease its fuel and oil consumption. Shvetsov was appointed chief designer of Factory No. 19.

On 1 June 1934 the first engine assembled in Perm from American parts was put on the test bench. Given the Soviet designation M-25, this type became the first in a long line of air-cooled engines developed by Shvetsov, all of which retained some features of the Cyclone to a certain extent.

Shvetsov began improvement of the M-25, and during July-August 1935 it successfully passed its State tests. By the end of the year the designers had succeeded in replacing most of the imported parts with indigenous equivalents. In 1935 an improved version, the M-25A, was created, followed a year later

RIGHT: **The M-25 engine.**

BELOW: **The R-10 reconnaissance aeroplane, powered by the M-25V, 1938.**

by the M-25B, which was introduced into series production in 1937.

In 1937 the M-62, the first considerably modified version of the M-25, was submitted for State testing. This became the most well-known engine designed by Shvetsov, even surpassing the M-11 in production longevity and numbers built. Its series manufacture started in 1938, and was in also built in Poland as the K-9. The M-62 powered the I-16 and I-153 fighters and the Li-2 (PS-84) passenger aircraft, and was used in the An-2 biplane after the Second World War.

In 1938 the M-63 was created, and in 1939 it was followed by the M-64 (which did not go into series production). These engines also could be considered improved versions of the Cyclone.

At the same time Shvetsov, using, to a certain extent, the engineering decisions introduced by the Wright company, moved increasingly further away from the basic design of Cyclone. The proposals contained in the plan of experimental work for 1938-39 included 14-cylinder and 18-cylinder engines based on the M-25. At the time the plan was being prepared, Shvetsov had already started work on these. The M-70 became the first of a family of 18-cylinder engines, and the M-80 introduced a family of 14-cylinder engines. The M-70 was followed by the M-71 and M-72, and the M-80 by the M-81 and M-82.

The last-named type, which was under development from 1939, had almost nothing in common with the Cyclone. In May 1941 the M-82 was introduced into series production. During the war it became one of the primary engine types in the Soviet VVS, powering the famous La-5 and La-7 fighters and the Su-2, Tu-2, and Pe-8 bombers.

On 1 April 1944 the M-82 was renamed the ASh-82, while the M-62 became the ASh-62. By that time production of the M-25 and M-63 had ended, so they retained their former designations. All subsequent Shvetsov engines were given the 'ASh' prefix, an abbreviation of his initials.

The ASh-82 remained in production after the war. It underwent several modifications (in particular, the ASh-82T for civil aircraft and the ASh-82V for helicopters), and it is still in use on Il-14s. The engine was also built in China and Czechoslovakia. Further versions of the ASh-82 were the ASh-83 and ASh-84. A small series of the former was built, but the latter existed only in the prototype form.

Of the 18-cylinder engine family, the most well known was the ASh-73, developed in 1945. It was in series production from 1948 until 1957 at two factories, in Rybinsk and Perm. The turbo-supercharged version, designated ASh-73TK, was installed in the Tu-4 heavy bomber, a copy of the American Boeing B-29. While the TK-19 turbo-supercharger was copied from the American example installed in the B-29, the bomber's engine was not copied, Shvetsov's powerplant being used instead. A low-altitude ASh-73 with a GCS powered the Be-6 flying-boat.

It is worth noting that the post-war ASh-21, which powered the Yak-11 and UTB, was actually one half of an ASh-82.

Shvetsov's most powerful engine was the ASh-2, which effectively combined two ASh-82s to produce a four-row, 28-cylinder radial. This engine was created as part of a post-war programme to develop high-powered engines for heavy bombers. The last version, the ASh-2K, was tested in 1951, and its maximum power rating was brought up to 4,700hp. The engine's output was taken from seven impulse turbines and transferred to the shaft through gearing. Refinement of this engine ended in 1952, when it became clear that piston engines could not compete with turbojets and turboprops.

For his work, Shvetsov was honoured with the title of Hero of Socialist Labour, and he was a Stalin Prize Laureate on four occasions. He died on 19 March 1953. Engines developed by him are still flying, having far outlasted their creator.

It is logical to start the descriptions of Shvetsov's engines with the M-25, as it formed the basis for all subsequent types of Shvetsov design. As the M-65, ASh-21 and M-3, developed by other designers, were based on units and components of the 'ASh' family, their descriptions are also included into this chapter.

The M-62 engine.

The ASh-62IR displayed at the Salyut Factory museum, Moscow.

M-25

The M-25, a copy of the Wright R-1820-F3, was one of the most extensively produced Soviet aero-engines of the second half of the 1930s. The agreement with the American company for licensed production and technical assistance was signed on 22 April 1933, and M-25 production was set up at Factory No. 19 in Perm. On 1 June 1934 the first engine, assembled from American parts, underwent factory testing. The M-25 was a metric-dimensioned version of the R-1820-F3 with modifications corresponding to 1934-type Cyclone and a K-25 carburettor (a copy of the Solex). The first attempt to pass the 100hr State test was a failure, as a cylinder head broke off, but the second attempt, on 2 August 1935, proved successful. The first series engines had parts and units imported from the USA (valve springs, piston rings

An ASh-62IR with a VISh-21-D-22 propeller, which had wooden blades, was tested on an Li-2 in 1942.

An ASh-82FN on display in the Monino museum.

and bearings), but these gave way to Soviet-made components from the beginning of 1936. From March 1937 Factory No. 19 introduced a conveyer system for engine assembly.

Different versions of the M-25 were manufactured by Factory No. 19 until the beginning of 1942, and in total 13,888 were built. During 1938-39 Factory No. 27 in Kazan assembled M-25s from units manufactured in Perm.

Characteristics

9-cylinder radial, air-cooled, geared engine with single-stage single-speed GCS.

Bore/stroke	155.5/174.5mm (6.12/6.87in)
Volume	29.87 litres (1,822cu in)
Compression ratio	6.4:1
Power rating	dependant on version
Weight	dependant on version

There was provision for synchronization and the installation of an electro-inertial or pneumatic starter.

The following versions of the engine are known:

M-25 A direct-drive engine, the first series production version, assembled using a large number of imported parts. Power rating 635/700hp. State tests were completed successfully in July-August 1935. The first engines had Stromberg carburettors and weighed 434kg (957lb), the later series had K-25 carburettors and weighed 435kg (959lb).

M-25A A direct-drive engine with increased rpm. Power rating 715/730hp, weight 439kg (968lb).

M-25R (R for *Reduktorniy*, or geared) A geared version. Several prototypes were built and fitted with imported reduction gears.

M-25V A direct-drive engine with increased rpm compared with the M-25A. Power rating 750/755hp, weight 453kg (999lb). This version passed State tests in August 1936 and was introduced into series production in 1937. From 1938 it was equipped with an electro-inertial starter, and from January 1939 with a pneumatic self-starter. From 1941 an improved 750/790hp version, having commonality with the M-62 and M-63, was being manufactured. This had two roller bearings on the crankshaft, and a master con-rod bushing with side seals.

The M-25V engine.

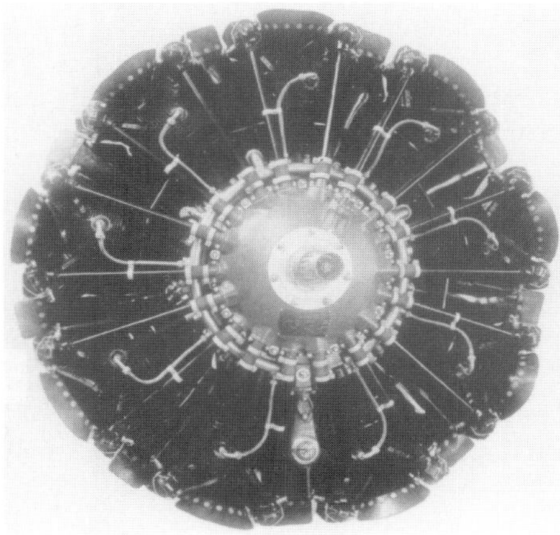

M-25V-TK A version of the M-25V having two TK-1 turbo-superchargers. The engine was flight tested in 1938.

M-25 for air-cushion boats, developed at the TsKB-1. This version was modified for vertical installation, the oil drainage system being suitably adapted. A small series was built by Factory No. 19.

The M-25 was exported to China and Spain.

M-25s and their variants powered the following series-production aircraft: I-14, I-15bis, I-16 (most of those built), R-10, DI-6, I-153 (small series), KOR-1 (Be-2) and IP-1; and the following prototypes: ARK-3, MDR-6, IP-4, RV-23, G-31 (powered glider) and OKO-1. It was planned to use the engine in the projected TA aeroplane. The Germans installed captured M-25Vs in the light Go 244 military transport.

M-62 (ASh-62)

The most famous and extensively used of Shvetsov's engines, the M-62 was in series production for more than sixty years. The plan of experimental work for 1937 stipulated that the M-25 was to be fitted with a two-speed GCS, and this resulted in the creation of the M-62. It differed from the M-25 in having a two-speed GCS based on the American unit used with the SR-1820-G103, a greater ribbed area on the cylinder heads, a one-piece cam (without

An M-62 in an I-16 fighter under restoration in 2000.

ABOVE: **The I-153, the last Soviet series-production biplane fighter, seen here in August 1939, was powered by the M-62.**

RIGHT: **An M-62IR in a BSh-1 attack aircraft, January 1939. Aeroplanes of this type, produced under the licence from the Vultee company, did not enter service with the VVS RKKA but were used as mail carriers in Soviet civil aviation, designated PS-43.**

an aluminium hub), strengthened pistons with lengthened skirts, a modified master conrod, a crankshaft on two roller bearings, and a modified crankcase and gas-distribution mechanism.

In January 1938 the M-62 was underwent State tests, but during these the GCS drive and one cylinderhead broke down. The second State tests were successfully completed. Mass production started in March 1939, and at different times it was built at Factories Nos 19 (1937-47, Molotov), 24 (1938-41, Moscow), 478 (1949-53, Zaporozhye), 36 (1944-50, Rybinsk) and 154 (from 1952, Voronezh). It was also manufactured at a factory in Chuzhou, China, from 1956, and at the PZL factory in Kalisz, Poland, from 1960. In total, 40,361 engines of M-62/ASh-62 type were built in the USSR.

Characteristics

9-cylinder radial, air-cooled engine with GCS.

Bore/stroke	155.5/174.5mm (6.12/6.87in)
Volume	29.87 litres (1,822cu in)
Compression ratio	6.4:1
Power rating	dependant on version
Weight	dependant on version

There was provision for synchronization and the installation of an electro-inertial or pneumatic starter.

The following versions of the engine are known:

M-62 A direct-drive engine with a single-stage two-speed GCS. Power rating 800/1,000hp, weight 520kg (1,146lb). The engine was intended for fighters. At first a small series of twenty-five engines was built in Perm in 1937. From 1939 the M-62 was in mass production at Factories Nos 19 and 24. Owing to numerous defects, manufacture was interrupted twice, in October and December 1939. Up to November 1939 the M-62 was built with imported bearings. From July 1940 the master conrod bushing with side seals (an American-type design) was introduced. In the second half of 1941 manufacturing of this version ceased at both factories, 6,884 M-62s having been built.

M-62R A geared version with a two-speed GCS and pneumatic starting. Power rating 850/975hp, weight 573kg (1,263lb). The engine had a cam of modified design and a different rpm governor drive. It was in series production at Factories Nos 19 (1938-39) and 24 (1939-40). Initially the gearing was assembled from American parts. Only 99 M-62Rs were built.

M-62IR (ASh-62IR) A geared version with a single-speed GCS and an electro-inertial starter. Power rating 820/1,000hp (later – 840/1,000hp), weight 560kg (1,235lb). The first tests were held in May 1938, and State testing was successfully completed on 11 May 1939. The most-produced version of the M-62 (more than 3,500 were made), the M-62IR (ASh-62IR) was built by Factories Nos 19 (1940-43), 24 (1938-40), 36 (1944-50), 478 (1949-53) and 154 (from 1952). From 1942 only this version was being built, and it was repeatedly improved.

The first series had imported gearing, but from December 1939 Soviet-made gears were used. In 1941 a crankshaft with two pendulum counterweights, on both crank cheeks, was introduced. From the end of 1942 the installation of synchronization was not stipulated. From the summer of 1943 graphitized pistons were used, and from August of that year changes to the ignition system were introduced. Starting from the sixth series a deformation taper of the sleeve was introduced, and from the 12th series a suspension-type exhaust valve seat (succeeded by a floating-type seat from the 15th series onwards). The 15th series (weight 567kg (1,250lb)), built from 1964, became the most-produced. Engines from the last batches in this series had 600hr service lives. The attaching rings for the piston pins were replaced by blanks, the master conrod and gear lubrication system were

An ASh-62IR engine in the Russian Air Force Museum at Monino.

The Li-2 (PS-84), powered by two M-62Irs and built under licence from the Douglas company, was a copy of the famous DC-3. This is the Li-2NB night bomber version, January 1944.

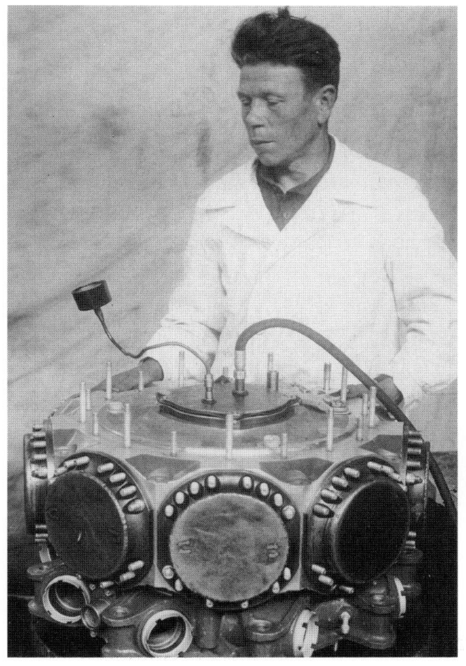

An ASh-62IR being assembled at Factory No. 36 in Rybinsk.

The KOR-2 (Be-4) shipborne reconnaissance flying-boat, powered by an M-62IR, 1944.

An ASh-62IR in an An-2 biplane.

The search-and-rescue version of the An-2 in service with the Soviet Air Force, June 1957.

modified, bronze sleeves for the pins of the crankshaft counterweights were introduced (as in the ASh-82T), and an oil centrifuge and a AKM-62IRA carburettor were fitted. From 1956 the ASh-62IR was licence-built in China as the HS5, and from 1960 in Poland as the ASz-62.

M-62TK An M-62 with two TK-1 turbo-superchargers. In August 1939 it underwent factory testing in an I-16 fighter, and in 1940 service tests were carried out. A small series was built.

M-62 with TK-2 turbo-superchargers and a 'turbo-reactor' designed by N.I. Efremov (an additional ramjet engine developed at TsAGI, operating on exhaust gases and radiator heating). This version underwent testing in 1939 and in August 1940. Weight of the turbo-reactor, 25kg (55lb).

M-62 for air-cushion boats developed at the TsKB-1. A version adapted for operation in the vertical position, this had a more powerful oil-suction pump and a K-85 carburettor. Sixteen were built at Factory No. 24 in 1940.

M-62V This designation was intended for the series production version of the M-65 prototype (see below).

ASh-62IR with TK-19 turbo-supercharger. A small series was built in 1953-54.

ASh-62M A version of the 15th series ASh-62IR intended for agricultural aeroplanes, this had a KPM gearbox and a VG-7500 generator. The ASh-62M could be easily transformed into the ASh-62IR if necessary.

ASh-62N A version with direct fuel injection, based on the 15th-series ASh-62IR. It had a fuel pump of increased capacity. Weight 590kg (1,301lb). A small batch was built, and the engine underwent service testing in an An-2.

ASz-62IR-M18 A Polish version with modified hydraulics, intended for the M-18 Dromader agricultural aeroplane.

ASz-61IR-M18/DHC3 A version of the ASz-62IR-M18 intended for the DHC-3 aeroplane.

K9 A 1,170hp version of the ASz-62IR with increased rpm. It was built in three variants: the K9-AA, K9-VV and K9-VS.

Engines of the M-62 (ASh-62) family were installed on the following Soviet production aircraft: I-153, I-16, PS-35 (ANT-35), PS-84 (Li-2), KOR-2 (Be-4), GST (MP-7) and An-2. Polish-built engines were used on the M-18, M-24, *Kruk*, DHC-3 and DC-3. The M-62 also powered the following prototypes: KhAI-52, Polikarpov's *Ivanov*, ANT-51 and I-207.

ASh-62IRs were exported to China, Vietnam, Korea, Bulgaria, Yugoslavia, Romania, Hungary, Czechoslovakia, Poland, the GDR, Cambodia, Nicaragua, Afghanistan and Cuba.

M-63

This was a further development of the M-62, with boosted rpm and supercharging. It had lengthened pistons with strengthened heads, an enlarged front counterweight on the crankshaft, a strengthened master con-rod, a new carburettor and needle bearings in the exhaust valve lever. The first three prototypes were designed and manufactured in 1938, refinement taking the whole year. In December 1938 the M-63 was transferred for State tests, which were successfully completed in January 1939. By then, a small series of twenty engines had already been built. From 1939 the M-63 was in series production at Factory No. 19 in Molotov.

The decision to cease production was taken at the beginning of 1941, but manufacture was not stopped until the middle of the year, 3,087 M-63s having been built.

Characteristics

9-cylinder radial, air-cooled engine with single-stage GCS.

Bore/stroke	155.5/174.5mm (6.12/6.87in)
Volume	29.87 litres (1,822cu in)
Compression ratio	7.2:1
Power rating	dependant on version
Weight	dependant on version

There was provision for synchronization and the installation of a pneumatic starter.

Aero clubs still use An-2s for dropping parachutists.

An ASh-62IR engine in an I-15bis fighter reproduction at the MAKS 2002 Air Show, Zhukovsky.

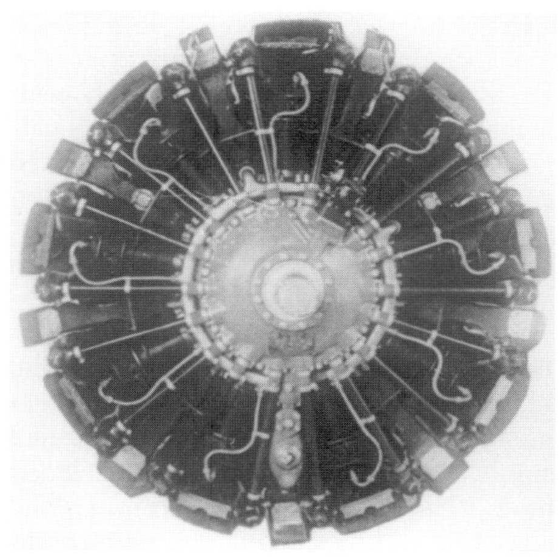

The M-63 engine.

The last version of the I-16 fighter (type 29) was powered by the M-63.

The following versions of the engine are known:

M-63 A direct-drive version that went into series production. Power rating 900/1,000hp, weight 515kg (1,135lb). In July 1940 a modified master conrod bushing with side seals was introduced.

M-63R A geared version of 1938. Several prototypes were built. In 1938 it underwent bench testing, and in March 1940 it was flight-tested on the Ivanov aeroplane designed by N.N. Polikarpov.

M-63TK A version of the M-63 with two TK-1 turbo-superchargers, power rating 800/1,000hp. Several prototypes were built.

The M-63 powered the following series-production aeroplanes: I-16, Che-2 (MDR-6) and KhAI-5 (small batch); and the following prototypes: Ivanov, I-207/9, I-153V and IS-1.

M-64

This type was a further development of the M-63, with boosted rpm. In March 1939 the first M-64 prototype began its factory tests. It was planned to achieve 1,200-1,300hp, but the designers failed to reach the estimated figures. In August the engine passed its 50hr joint tests, and then came a change of the GCS drive. During the second joint tests, in November, only 850/1,050hp was registered. After modifying the cam at the beginning of 1940, the prototype achieved 900/1,100hp but this was no advance on the M-63. The M-64 was not introduced into series production.

Characteristics

9-cylinder radial, air-cooled engine with single-stage two-speed GCS.

Bore/stroke	155.5/174.5mm (6.12/6.87in)
Volume	29.87 litres (1,822cu in)

Two versions of the engine were being prepared:

M-64 A direct-drive engine. Power rating 900/1,100hp, weight 600kg (1,300lb).

M-64R A geared version similar to the M-63R but with lengthened reduction-gear nose. Estimated weight 600kg (1,300lb).

There were plans to install the M-64 in the KOR-3 ship-based catapult-launched reconnaissance aeroplane.

The M-64R engine.

M-65

The M-65 was not designed under Shvetsov's leadership, but was a descendant of his M-62, and is therefore included into this chapter. It was developed at the design bureau of Factory No. 24 in 1939. Bazarov was chief designer of the M-65, and Bogomolov was the factory's chief designer. The new engine differed from the M-62 in having increased-diameter suction valves, a modified gas-distribution mechanism and a different, more reliable GCS.

In September 1939 the factory tests were conducted, followed at the end of January 1940 by the 50hr joint tests. In February-March 1940 the M-65 was flight-tested in an I-153 fighter. In May of that year refinement work on the engine was cancelled by the air force requirement. Only five prototypes were built.

There were plans to install the M-65 in a version of the I-207 fighter.

Characteristics

9-cylinder radial, air-cooled engine with single-stage two-speed GCS.

Power rating	840/1,100hp
Bore/stroke	155.5/174.5mm (6.12/6.87in)
Volume	29.87 litres (1,822cu in)
Compression ratio	6.4:1
Weight	530kg (1,168lb)

M-80

The plan of experimental work for 1938-39 included a '14-cylinder engine based on the M-25', later designated M-25D14 and eventually redesignated M-80). The first M-80 prototype was assembled in August 1938, and on 18 August factory bench testing started. At the beginning of 1939 the engine was transferred for State tests. However, only a limited number of prototypes was built, as the M-81, which had better characteristics, had already been developed.

Characteristics

14-cylinder, two-row radial, air-cooled, geared engine with single-stage GCS.

Power rating	1,200/1,400hp (according to the project, 1,200/1,500hp).
Bore/stroke	155.5/174.5mm (6.12/6.87in).

Two versions of the type are known:
M-80 – an engine with single-speed GCS.
M-80R2 – a version with two-speed GCS.

The M-81 engine.

M-81 (M-81R)

A further development of the M-80R2, the M-81 introduced some assemblies and parts from the M-63 and a two-speed GCS. The M-83 was being developed from 1938. In March 1939 four M-81s were delivered to aircraft factories. In August 1939 the M-81 passed its 50hr joint tests. A small batch of ten engines was ordered, which had to be manufactured at Factory No. 19 by 1 January 1940. At the beginning of January an M-81 from this batch satisfactorily passed its 100hr factory tests, and in the summer passed its State tests. On 30 March a DB-3F with two M-81s made its first flight, and during the same month the engine was tested in an I-185 fighter. Work on the M-81 was cancelled at the end of 1940, priority being given to the M-82.

Characteristics

14-cylinder two-row radial, air-cooled, geared engine with single-stage two-speed GCS.

Power rating	1,300/1,600hp (according to project data 1,280/1,500hp)
Bore/stroke	155.5/174.5mm (6.12/6.87in)
Weight	890kg (1,962lb)

Variants of the M-81 with a lengthened reduction gear nose, and with cams and GCS drive, as used on the M-64, were being developed.

The M-81 was installed in the DB-3F and I-185 prototypes.

M-82 (ASh-82)

A further evolution of the M-81, the M-82 had reduced piston stroke, a steel impeller for the GCS and a lengthened crankcase nose. It was being developed from 1939 under the leadership of A.D. Shvetsov and I.P. Evich. The project was completed by the beginning of 1940. Many design features of the M-62 and M-63 were incorporated in the new engine. The first State tests were held in the spring of 1940, and Factory No. 19 built a batch of prototypes.

The second State tests were successfully passed on 22 May 1941. Before completion of the tests, on 13 May, the NKAP had issued a decree initiating series production of the engine.

The M-82 (designated ASh-82 from 1 April 1944) was built by Factory No. 19 in Molotov from 1941, and by Factory No. 29 in Omsk from 1942. During the war 24,000 engines of this family were manufactured. The ASh-82 became one of the most widely used engines in the VVS RKKA during the Great Patriotic War, powering the La-5 and La-7 fighters and the Tu-2 and Pe-8 bombers.

The ASh-82 was repeatedly modified. After the war, versions were created for transport aircraft and helicopters. Series production of the ASh-82 ceased in the USSR in 1962, after 57,898 had been built. During 1962-1980 two versions of the ASh-82 were manufactured under licence in Dongan, China. From 1954 it was also built in Czechoslovakia.

The ASh-82T was in production at Factory No. 19 until 1955, and production of the ASh-82VM helicopter version was still being built even later.

Engines of the ASh-82 family were exported to Poland, Czechoslovakia, the GDR, Hungary, Romania, China, North Korea, Vietnam, Austria, Egypt, Afghanistan, India, Iraq, Spain and Finland.

Later, ASh-82 assemblies and units were used in the creation of the ASh-21, M-3 and ASh-2 engines.

ABOVE: **The M-82F engine.**

RIGHT: **An Il-4 bomber was used to test M-82Fs at Komsomolsk-on-Amur in February 1942.**

Characteristics

14-cylinder two-row radial, air-cooled, geared engine with single-stage two-speed GCS.

Bore/stroke	155.5/155mm (6.12/6.10in)
Volume	41.2 litres (2,514cu in)
Compression ratio	7.0:1 (except ASh-82T and ASh-82V)
Power rating	dependant on version
Weight	dependant on version

There was provision for synchronization and the installation of an electro-inertial or pneumatic starter.

According to the project data, two versions of reduction gearing (giving compression ratios of 6.4:1 or 7.0:1), and a single-speed (variant I) or two-speed GCS were planned.

The following versions of the engine are known:

M-82-111 The first series-production version, with different reduction gearing and a floatless AK-82BP carburettor. This version was manufactured at Factory No. 19 starting in 1941. Power rating 1,400/1,700hp, weight 850kg (1,874lb) (with deflectors). In 1942 the guide vane of the GCS was changed.

M-82A-111 An improved version developed in 1942, with increased service life. Power rating 1,400/1,700hp, weight 870kg (1,918lb).

M-82F This had an improved GCS drive and modifications to the oil system. The engine did not have limitations on boost time. Power rating 1,400/1,700hp, weight 870kg (1,918lb). The type was manufactured in Molotov starting from December 1942, in M-82F-111 and M-82F-212 variants with different reduction gears and methods of starting.

ABOVE: **Lavochkin La-5 fighters, powered by M-82FNs, were widely employed on the Eastern Front from the middle of the Second World War.**

M-82FN (originally designated M-82FNV, redesignated ASh-82FN from 1 April 1944) A version with direct injection. Its supercharging was increased, the ribbing on the cylinder heads was improved, the valves were changed, the pistons strengthened and the GCS drive modified. The prototypes were tested at the end of 1942, and starting from January 1943 it entered series production at Factories No. 19 (ASh-82FN-111 and ASh-82FN-212 variants) and No. 29 (ASh-82-312 variant with the third type of reduction gear). On the engines of the fourth series (early 1945) the crankshaft

BELOW: **An La-5 fighter with its engine cowling removed, 1943.**

The Tu-2 bomber, powered by AS-82FN engines.

The Il-12 military transport, powered by two ASh-82FNs, July 1947.

The ASh-82FN was not only installed in Soviet-designed aeroplanes. Seen here is the nacelle of an American PBN-1 flying-boat, modified to accommodate an ASh-82FN. More than a dozen similarly-engined flying-boats, designated KM-2, served with Soviet Polar Aviation.

The FTK fighter prototype, powered by the M-82FN-TK, 1944.

ABOVE: **The Il-14, powered by ASh-82T engines.**

RIGHT: **An ASh-82T in an Il-14 airliner, 2002.**

was strengthened similarly to the ASh-83, and on the engines of the fifth series (spring 1945) liners with a parabolic profile and strengthened flanges were introduced. Series production ceased in 1950.

M-82NV (ASh-82NV) A version with two TK-3 turbo-superchargers, this was flight tested in July-August 1944 in an La-7 fighter. The engine was not introduced into series production.

ASh-82M An experimental 1,630/2,100hp engine based on the ASh-82FN, this was being factory tested from the spring of 1946, and twenty-six prototypes were built. Refinement work was carried out until early 1948, but the engine was not put into series production.

ASh-82MF A further development of the ASh-82M. Power rating 1,750/2,250hp. Several prototypes were built in the first quarter of 1946, but the engine was not put into series production.

ASh-82T A version for transport aeroplanes, based on units of the ASh-82FN and ASh-83. The reduction gear was modified, and floating valve seats were introduced. The engine had the electro-inertial starter.

Characteristics

Power rating	1,530/1,900hp (later series, 1,530/1,950hp)
Compression ratio	6.9:1
Weight	1,020kg (2,249lb)

An ASh-82T dismantled for study in a classroom at the Samara Aerospace University, 2001.

Development of the ASh-82T was carried out from 1951. In 1953 it passed State tests, and it was in series production during 1953-55 in Perm.

ASh-82V A helicopter version, with a master clutch in the crankcase nose and a fan for forced air cooling.

Characteristics

Power rating	1,350/1,700hp
Compression ratio	6.9:1.
Weight	1,100kg (2,400lb)

This engine was developed in 1951, and series production started at the factory in Perm from 1952.

M-82T Czechoslovakian version of the ASh-82T manufactured at the Dimitrov Factory from 1954.

HS7 Chinese version of the ASh-82V.

HS8 Chinese version of the ASh-82T. Power rating 1,850hp. This type was in series production from 1962 to 1980.

Engines of the M-82/ASh-82 family were installed in the following series production aeroplanes: La-5, La-7, La-9, La-11, Tu-2, KM-2 (a version of PBN-1 Nomad), Pe-8 (on some aeroplanes of the later series), Su-2, Pe-2 (aeroplanes manufactured in 1944), Pe-4, Il-12 and Il-14; and in the Mi-4 and Yak-24 production helicopters. They also powered the following aircraft prototypes: NB(T), I-185, Yak-3, I-

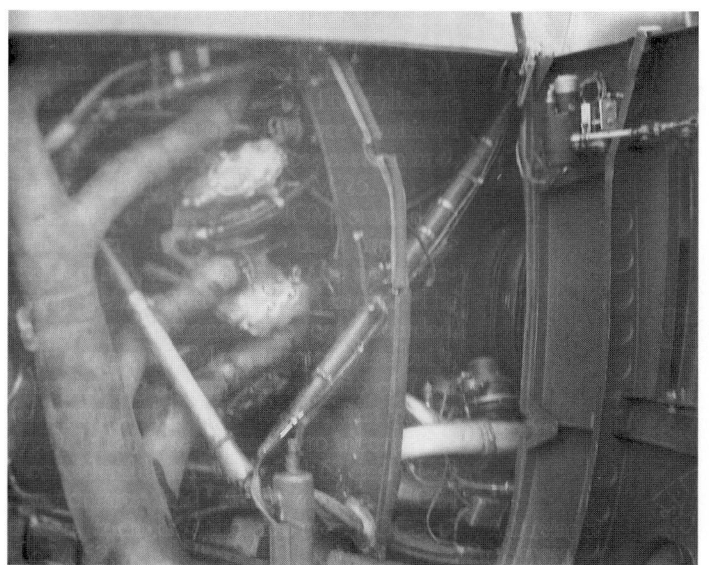
An ASh-82V in an Mi-4 helicopter (port side, cowling opened).

The Mi-4 helicopter, powered by the ASh-82V.

An Mi-4 (V-12) helicopter, powered by an ASh-82V, lifts a cargo off the ground with the help of a boom and a winch.

The Yak-24 helicopter was powered by a pair of ASh-82Vs.

211(E), Il-2, Su-7 and Su-12. Engines of this family were also planned to be used in the PTS-51, R-9 (LBSh), T-107, '71' (Tu-14, the first one with this designation) and OPB-41 projects.

ASh-83 (ASh-83FN)

The ASh-83 was a further development of the ASh-82FN, with boosted supercharging and rpm. The engine crankcase nose was changed, the crankshaft was strengthened, the diameter of the GCS impeller was increased, and cut-outs in the impeller were eliminated. A liner of parabolic profile (later with the technological taper) and with a strengthened flange was introduced, along with minor changes in the gas-distribution mechanism and oil system, and a new direct-injection unit. From the end of 1944 until September 1945 the ASh-83 was being flight-tested in a La-7 fighter. The engine was manufactured in small series from April 1945 at Factory No. 19 in Molotov, ninety-three having been built by the end of 1946.

Characteristics

14-cylinder two-row radial, air-cooled, geared engine with single-stage two-speed GCS.

Bore/stroke	155.5/155mm (6.12/6.10in)
Volume	41.2 litres (2,514cu in)
Compression ratio	6.9:1
Power rating	1,500/1,900hp according to project data, but actually increased to 1,585/1,900hp
Weight	915kg (2,017lb) (according to other sources 921kg (2,030lb))

The ASh-83 before State testing, October 1944.

The ASh-83 during flight testing in a Tu-2 bomber.

The ASh-83 was installed in the Tu-2 and La-7 (La-120) prototypes. It was also specified for the projected '64' (Tu-10) and I-211.

ASh-84 (ASh-84TK)

This was a high-altitude version of the ASh-83, with a GCS, turbo-supercharging, and a two-speed fan for forced cooling. The engine was intended for a long-range high-altitude reconnaissance aeroplane. In 1947 three prototypes were built, and underwent bench testing from 1947. The engine was not introduced into series production.

The ASh-84TK to be used in the projected '74' (Tu-22).

Characteristics

14-cylinder two-row radial, air-cooled, geared engine with a single-stage, two-speed GCS, a turbo-supercharger, and a two-speed fan for forced cooling.

Power rating	1,700/1,800hp (according to other sources 1,700/2,000hp)
Bore/stroke	155.5/155mm (6.12/6.10in)
Volume	41.2 litres (2,514cu in)

M-70

The M-70 was introduced into the plan of experimental work for 1938 under the designation M-25D18, and it was to be developed as a 18-cylinder engine based on the M-25. In fact it was being developed from 1937. At the end of that year the first prototype underwent refinement testing, and in January 1938 it underwent the official factory tests. Refinement was being carried out during the whole of 1938. The engine suffered from cracks in the master con-rod and the GCS impeller, and the exhaust valves burnt through. In the end, the engine's performance did not meet air force requirements.

Characteristics

18-cylinder two-row radial, air-cooled, geared engine with GCS.

Power rating	1,400/1,500hp
Bore/stroke	155.5/174.5mm (6.12/6.87in)
Volume	59,59 litres (3,636cu in)
Compression ratio	6.4:1

M-71

A further evolution of the M-70, using M-63 components, the M-71 was being developed from the beginning of 1939, and four prototypes were built that year. The engine underwent bench testing in August 1939. Starting from the fifth prototype (January 1940) a crankshaft with two pendulums was introduced. The process of M-71 refinement took a long time; it passed State tests in the autumn of 1942, but was not introduced into series production.

Characteristics

18-cylinder two-row radial, air-cooled, geared engine with GCS.

Bore/stroke	155.5/174.5mm (6.12/6.87in)
Volume	59.7 litres (3,643cu in)
Power rating	dependant on version
Weight	dependant on version

The following versions of the engine are known:

M-71 A version with a power rating of 1,700/2,000hp (according to project data, 1,800/2,000hp), and a weight of 970kg (2,138lb) (according to project data, 900kg (2,000lb)). The engine was factory tested in 1940, and in March-April 1942 it was tested in an I-185 fighter prototype.

M-71TK A projected version of the M-71 with TK-M turbo-superchargers, evaluated in 1939. Power rating 1,500/ 2,000hp.

M-71F A version boosted in rpm, with a power rating of 1,850/2,200hp. This engine was built in a small series.

M-71F-TK A version of the M-71F with TK-3 turbo-superchargers. In the summer of 1943 this engine was flight-tested in a DVB-102 bomber.

The M-71 powered the I-185, Su-6, Su-8 and La-7 prototypes. The following aircraft projects specified use of the engine: PB-IS, PB-1, SPB, DB-LK, R-9 (LBSh), I-187, D, NB (T), '64' (Tu-10) and OPB.

RIGHT: **An M-71 in the DVB-102 long-range, high-altitude bomber prototype.**

The M-71 engine.

BELOW: **The I-185 fighter prototype was powered by the M-71.**

M-72

This was a boosted version of the M-71, with a single-stage two-speed GCS. Series production was planned to begin in the third quarter of 1945 at Factory No. 19, but an improved M-73 (ASh-73) was introduced into production instead.

The M-72 powered the LL-143 flying-boat prototype (Be-6 prototype), and it was specified for the DVB-202 and DVB-302 projects (in its M-72TK form with TK-M turbo-superchargers).

Characteristics

18-cylinder two-row radial, air-cooled, geared engine with single-stage, two-speed GCS.

Bore/stroke	155.5/174.5mm (6.12/6.87in)
Volume	59.58 litres (3,635cu in)

ASh-73

A further evolution of the ASh-72, with decreased piston stroke, this was the first engine of this family to go into series production. The engine was being developed from 1944, and at the end of 1945 three prototypes were built, followed by five more. The prototypes used some American-built components. As with the R-3350, new magnetos and main bearings were introduced. Bench testing was undertaken at Factory No. 19 from the beginning of 1946, and in August that year the State tests were started. The ASh-73 engine finally passed these in 1948.

From the beginning of 1946 Factory No. 19 was being prepared for ASh-73 production, and series production started in 1947. The engine was built at Factory No. 19 until 1953, and at Factory No. 36 in Rybinsk until 1957. In total, 14,310 engines were built.

ABOVE: **The ASh-73TK engine.**

Characteristics

18-cylinder two-row radial, air-cooled, geared engine with single-stage single-speed GCS.

Bore/stroke	155.5/170mm (6.12/6.69in)
Volume	58.1 litres (3,545cu in)
Compression ratio	6.9:1
Power rating	dependant on version
Weight	dependant on version

The following versions of the engine are known:

ASh-73 A version without turbo-supercharging, built in series. Power rating 2,000/2,400hp, weight 1,330kg (2,932lb).

ASh-73TK A version with two TK-19 turbo-superchargers (copied from the American type) and an intercooler. This was the main series-production version. Power rating 2,000/2,400hp, weight 1,355kg (2,987lb). In the course of series production the engine was repeatedly modified. On the fourth series the crankcase nose was changed, strengthened articulated connecting rods were introduced, and the accessory drive was changed. On the fifth series the middle part of the crankcase and the pistons were strengthened, and the ignition was improved. On the sixth series the master con-rod and crankshaft cheeks were strengthened, lightweight shortened pistons were introduced, and some changes were made to parts. On the seventh series exhaust valves with floating seats were introduced, the composition of parts was changed, and the reduction gear was improved.

ASh-73TKF A version with boosted rpm. Power rating 2,360/2,720hp. Prototypes were built and bench tested, but the type was not introduced into series production.

ASh-73TKFN (ASh-73FNTK, or ASh-73TKNV) A version with direct fuel injection. Power rating 2,400/2,800hp. Development was being carried out from 1949, and prototypes were built and bench tested.

ASh-73 'compound' A project of 1949 with an impulse turbine installed on the ASh-73TK. No information regarding prototype manufacture has been found.

ABOVE: **An ASh-73TK on display in the Central House of Aviation and Space in Moscow.**

BELOW: **The Be-6 flying-boat, powered by ASh-73s, at Taganrog in March 1951.**

The ASh-73 powered the Tu-4 and Be-6 production aircraft, and the following prototypes: Tu-75, Tu-80 and S-82 (not completed). This engine was also specified for the following projects: Il-18 airliner (first version), '76' (Tu-24) and DVB-102DM bombers, and T-117 transport aeroplane.

The ASh-73 and ASh-73TK were exported to China.

ASh-21

This was half an ASh-82. Development was carried out in 1945 at OKB-29 in Omsk, under the leadership of V.S. Nitchenko. Many parts from the ASh-62IR and ASh-82FN were used. The

The Soviet Tu-4 heavy bomber differed from the Boeing B-29 in only two respects: it was fitted with Soviet cannons instead of American machine-guns, and powered by ASh-73TKs.

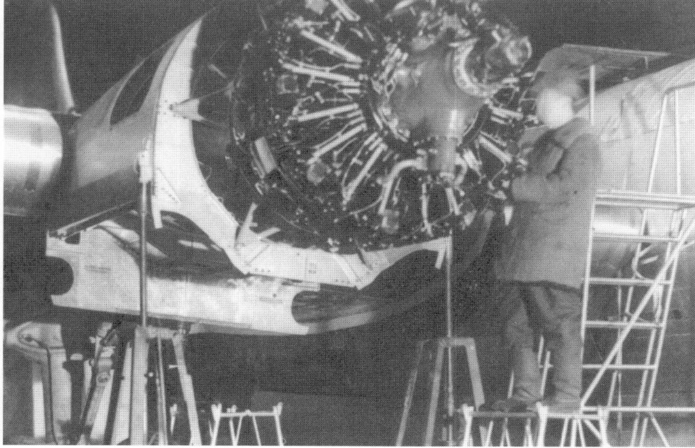

An ASh-73TK engine being installed in one of the first Tu-4s, Kazan, 1946.

prototypes were built at the beginning of 1946 and underwent factory testing in the same year. The type was in series production at Factory No. 29 from 1947 until 1955, 7,636 engines being built.

Characteristics

7-cylinder radial, air-cooled, geared engine with single-stage single-speed GCS and direct injection.

Power rating	570/700hp (according to project data, 600/700hp)
Bore/stroke	155.5/155mm (6.12/6.10in)
Volume	20.6 litres (1,257cu in)
Compression ratio	6.4:1
Weight	487kg (1,074lb)

The engine was exported to Czechoslovakia, Austria, Albania, Algiers, Bulgaria, Vietnam, Guinea, the GDR, Egypt, Iraq, Yemen, Poland, Romania and Syria.

From 1952 the ASh-21 was manufactured under licence in Czechoslovakia at the Dimitrov Factory as the M-21 (weight 495kg (1,091lb)).

The ASh-21 powered the series-built Yak-11 and UTB and the TA (TA-1), TAF and Yak-16 prototypes. It was specified for An-2 projects and for Chetverikov's projected amphibian reconnaissance aircraft. Components and units of the ASh-21 were used in the development of the M-26 (AI-26).

An ASh-21 engine of the 1947 production output.

An ASh-21 on display at Monino.

The UTB bomber trainer, seen in October 1946, was basically a Tu-2 powered by less-powerful ASh-21s instead of ASh-82FNs.

M-3

The M-3 was a 'sesquialteral' version of the ASh-82FN. Development work was

The Yak-200 bomber trainer prototype, powered by ASh-21s, summer 1953.

carried out at OKB-29 in Omsk, under the leadership of V.S. Nitchenko during 1945-46. At the beginning of 1946 the general layout of the engine was completed, and in the spring the designers started to issue engineering drawings. Two prototypes were built in February 1948, and factory bench-testing started in March. The engine was not introduced into series production.

This engine was not installed in any aircraft, but in 1947-48 the S.A. Lavochkin Design Bureau was developing a fighter powered by the M-3, and the A.N. Tupolev Design Bureau was planning to use it in the projected '75' (Tu-26) and '76' (Tu-28) bombers.

Maintenance work on an ASh-21 in the Be-8 flying-boat prototype, summer 1948.

Characteristics

21-cylinder three-row radial, air-cooled, geared engine with a single-stage single-speed GCS and two turbo-superchargers.

Power rating	2,400/3,200hp (according to the specification 2,800/3,200hp, later 2,500/3,200hp)
Weight	1,500kg (3,300lb)

ASh-2

A 'doubled' version of the ASh-82FN with forced cooling, intended for the Soviet heavy bombers. This engine was being developed at OKB-19 in Molotov from 1946, and was built in a small series at Factory No. 19.

Characteristics

28-cylinder four-row radial, air-cooled with forced cooling, geared engine with a single-stage single-speed GCS.

Bore/stroke	155.5/155mm (6.12/6.10in)
Volume	82.4 litres (5,028cu in)
Compression ratio	7.0:1
Power rating	dependant on version
Weight	dependant on version

The following versions of the engine are known:

ASh-2 A version rated at 2,500/3,500hp. Weight 1,850kg (4,078lb). Two prototypes were built in the first quarter of 1946 and underwent factory testing.

ASh-2TK A version with turbo-supercharging (two TK-19F turbo-superchargers were installed). Power rating 3,070/4,000hp, weight 2,080kg (4,586lb). Several prototypes were built. Factory and State tests were carried out in 1948.

ASh-2K A version with a two-speed GCS, two TK-2 turbo-superchargers and seven impulse turbines. Power rating 3,700/4,700hp, weight 2,550kg (5,622lb). This engine was being developed from September 1949, and at the end of that year it was transferred to bench testing, which lasted until March 1950. During the second half of 1950 the engine was tested in a Tu-4LL engine test-bed aircraft. Refinement work had been completed by November 1951, but the type was not introduced into series production because it was inferior to the VD-4K.

The ASh-2 was specified for the '72' (Tu-24) and '487' projects.

ASh-3TK

The 5,500/6,000hp ASh-3TK was being developed in 1947-48. No information regarding prototype manufacture has been found.

ASh-93

No information on this type has been found.

CHAPTER TWENTY-FOUR

The Engines of V.Ya. Klimov

Vladimir Yakovlevich Klimov (1892-1962) is one of Russia's most famous aero-engine designers. The son of a builder, in 1916 he graduated from the Moscow Emperor's Technical High School, having been awarded his diploma for an aero-engine project that studied of the formation of the fuel/air mixture in a carburettor. The Technical School Council applied for a special grant for Klimov, to be used for his scientific studies and the preparation of a thesis.

After the revolution Klimov combined the scientific and teaching professions. He worked in an automobile engine laboratory, and then in the NAMI and IAM (TsIAM). In the latter, in the early 1930s, Klimov headed the Department of Light Fuel Engines. At the same time he was lecturing at the Bauman Moscow Technical High School (*Moskovskoe Visshee Tekhnicheckoe Uchilishche*, MVTU) and the Zhukovskiy Air Force Academy, and for a time he held the Aero-Engine Design Chair in the Moscow Aviation Institute (*Moskovskiy Aviatsionniy Institut*, MAI).

At the beginning of 1933 it became clear that a large programme aimed at creating completely indigenous aero-engines had practically failed. Only four engines out of ten types planned for 1931, and five out of fourteen planned for 1932, had reached the prototype stage. Only A.A. Mikulin's M-34 entered series production, and even this lagged behind Western engines in its specific power rating and altitude characteristics (owing to the lack of a supercharger). This situation inhibited the development of aircraft construction in the Soviet Union.

It therefore became necessary to acquire suitable engines from abroad, the fundamental decision to do so being made in May 1933. The French 12-cylinder vee, watercooled Hispano-Suiza 12Y was among the engines selected by the Soviet experts. This was quite modern for its time, being powerful and light-weight, and having a gearbox and a centrifugal supercharger. Its nominal power rating was 750hp, maximum was 850hp, and it had a dry weight of 438kg (966lb). The engine was produced in a number of versions, including the special fighter model 12Ycrs, which had provision for mounting a cannon in the vee between the cylinder blocks and firing through the hollow gearbox shaft.

The preference for the French company was determined both by political and technical reasons (during this period USSR-French relations improved significantly). It was assumed that the production technology of French engines was closer to the Soviet industry's capabilities in terms of methods and materials than, for example, British technology. Moreover, it obviated the need to convert dimensions from British Imperial to metric. The Soviets had also gained previous experience in the production arrangements from licence-production of the Gnome-Rhône 9A air-cooled engine (designated M-22 in the USSR).

On 13 August 1933 the USSR Defence Committee adopted a resolution to acquire from France twenty to thirty Hispano-Suiza engines, with spares and tooling, and to negotiate for a manufacturing licence and the French company's technical assistance in setting up series production in the USSR. On 28 November the STO ordered thirty completed engines, fifty more as complete sets of parts and assemblies, and also the hardest-to-produce parts for another fifty engines. The amount allocated for this purpose was 1,650,000 roubles. On 15 December the STO called for the negotiations to be speeded up, referring to the urgent need for modern powerplants, especially for fighters.

A commission headed by Klimov departed to France, where its members examined the engine and demanded that the company verify the declared performance by a 100hr running test. Hispano-Suiza was reluctant to do so, but finally agreed. A 12Ybrs was selected from a twenty-engine batch manufactured for the French Air Force. The tests started in January 1934, but in the eleventh hour of testing the engine's crankshaft broke along the crank journal, and then cracks appeared in the cylinder block jacket.

The French company hastily began to modify the engine. Balance weights were introduced at the crankshaft webs; the con-rod ends, cylinder blocks and crankcase were reinforced; and the diameter of the gearbox shaft was increased. Some of these improvements had been evaluated earlier, and had been introduced on sample engines delivered in connection with licensed manufacture in Czechoslovakia. With these modifications, engine weight increased to 475kg (1,047lb), and it was again put on the test bench. This time the tests were more successful, though long running at maximum power inevitably resulted in malfunctions. The tests were completed in March 1934.

The Soviet authorities were pushing for the licence. The head of the UVVS, Ya.I. Alksnis, called for the contract to be signed before the tests were completed. The first order for eight standard engines (without the recent modifications) was completed on January 1934. Two were shipped from France on 28 January, followed by the remaining six on 27 February. Six were of the 12Ybrs type, and two were 12Ycrs engines with provision for the installation of 20mm Hispano S9 cannon.

Military Engineer Levin, a member of the Soviet commission, proposed acceptance of the engine in its original version, without modifications, but with its power rating limited to 750hp. Even with this limitation the engine surpassed all Soviet-made types in specific power rating and altitude characteristics. Repeated testing demonstrated that, in this case, the Hispano-Suiza's service life was long enough. At last, on 14 June 1934, a contract was signed with the French company for support in arranging series production in the USSR. It stipulated that the company should supply documentation and engine samples, and familiarize Soviet specialist with the production technology. The contract expired on 26 March 1938, and up to that time the French company agreed to keep the Soviets informed of all changes introduced on series production engines.

Production of the French engine, designated M-100 in the USSR, was initially planned to start at Factory No. 24 in Moscow, but was transferred to Factory No. 26 in Rybinsk, which had hitherto been producing M-17s under licence from the German BMW company. According to the original plans, Factory No. 26 was to convert to manufacturing V-1800 Conqueror engines under licence from the Curtiss-Wright Corporation. The American company had prepared metricated documentation and engine samples, but although the engine's manufacturing processes and techniques had been adapted to suit the equipment available in Rybinsk, the factory was ordered not to start Conqueror production.

According to a an STO decree, fifteen Hispano-Suizas were to be assembled there from the French parts by the end of 1934, and no fewer than 600 were to be manufactured next year. The same decree called for organization of a design department to be involved in improving of the Hispano-Suiza by increasing its power rating, improving its high-altitude characteristics and reliability, and reducing fuel and oil consumption. In July 1934 a design department was set up at Factory No. 26, and Klimov was appointed chief designer. Arrival of the documentation from France was delayed, in contravention of the contract, and this in turn delayed the start of production. As a result the Soviet Trade Representative Office in France exacted a 2,600,000-franc penalty from Hispano-Suiza.

Under Klimov's supervision the documentation was adapted to Soviet standards, and Soviet equivalents of the materials used by the French company were selected. In February 1935 the sets of engine parts and units arrived from France. In March 1935 the first M-100s, which were similar to the French 12Ybrs version, left the Rybinsk workshops. The M-100 differed from the French original only in minor details, such as lubrication holes and piston-pin fits. The early-series engines incorporated many French-built parts.

The M-100 powered the famous SB bomber, created by the A.N. Tupolev Design Bureau. It was produced in large quantities, and was exported to China and Spain. The first Soviet M-100s were heavier than the French original and had a lower power rating, but the engine still had potential for further modernization.

As a result, the M-100 became the forefather of the large family of Soviet piston aero-engines designed under Klimov's leadership, all of which retained the characteristic dimensions and certain design features of the Hispano-Suiza. Initially Klimov made only moderate improvements to the French original, creating the M-100A and M-100AU. Then the design was changed more substantially. The evolution of Hispano-Suiza versions did not follow a single path. It included dead ends as well, and certain types did not attain series production. The first successful engine developed by Klimov on the basis of the Hispano-Suiza was the M-103, with a power increase of more than 100hp. A further development of the M-103 was the M-104. The numeric designations for all engines of this family were in '100' series.

At the beginning of the Second World War Klimov's design bureau was developing two prospective engines, the M-105 and M-106. The latter was under refinement for a long time, being produced only in a small numbers five years after the design work had been started. Unlike the M-106, the M-105 became the most-produced engine for the Soviet VVS during the war. It was manufactured at four factories until 1947, and was repeatedly improved. The power rating of the ultimate version, the M-105PF-2, reached 1,290hp. Klimov's engines powered the most ubiquitous wartime Yakovlev fighters (Yak-1, Yak-3, Yak-7 and Yak-9), the LaGG-3 fighter and the Pe-2 dive-bomber. The M-105 was exported to Albania, Bulgaria, Poland, Czechoslovakia, Yugoslavia, China and North Korea.

To mark Klimov's contribution, in March 1944 he was granted the right to designate his creations using his personal initials, 'VK'. Thus the M-105 became the VK-105, and all of Klimov's subsequent engines received similar designations. The earlier designs (the M-103 and M-104), which had been in service in military and civil aviation up to that time, retained their original designations.

Klimov's later piston aero-engines, the VK-107, VK-108 and VK-109, were not produced in such great numbers, though the M-107 was manufactured in large numbers and powered Yak-3 and Yak-9 fighters. The aeroplanes powered by these

The M-100 in a classroom at the Moscow Aviation Institute.

The M-100A during State testing, January 1936.

The SB high-speed bomber, powered by M-100As with VISh-2 variable-pitch propellers.

engines were in service at the end of the Second World War, and remained in use until the beginning of the 1950s. They were also exported, as well as being used in the Korean War.

For Klimov, the VK-107VRDK (VK-107R-E3020), built in 1945, marked the transitional stage from piston engines to jets. This engine included a special gear to drive a moto-compressor jet engine. The VK-107R was installed on a Mikoyan series I-250 ('N') fighter that was in service with Soviet naval aviation. Sukhoi's I-107 (Su-5) prototype also had this engine.

During the war the USSR lagged seriously behind both enemies and allies in jet development. After Germany's defeat, documentation relating to the German BMW 003 and Jumo 004 turbojets, and examples of both, were taken to the USSR, and the engines were put into production as the RD-10 and RD-20 respectively. However, they were already inferior to the West's latest jet engines.

In the spring of 1946 a number of Soviet designers, including Klimov, were tasked

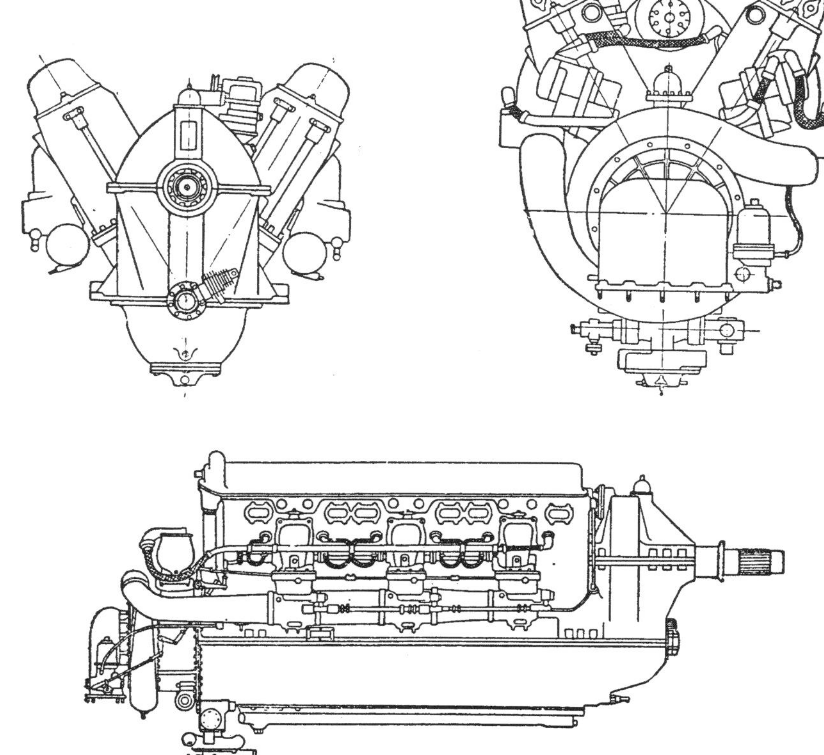

ABOVE: **Drawings of the M-105.**

LEFT: **Captain S.I. Makovskiy, Hero of the Soviet Union, near his Yak-9K fighter. This was powered by an M-105PF engine, which had an NS-45 cannon mounted in the cylinder vee.**

RIGHT: **A VK-107A restored by enthusiasts, 1999.**

The M-100A engine being tested with the VISh-2 variable-pitch propeller, summer 1937.

with developing indigenous high-thrust turbojets. However, fulfilment of the task required considerable time. In December 1946 Klimov, as a member of a Soviet delegation, was sent to Great Britain to negotiate the purchase of batches of Rolls-Royce Nene 1 and Derwent 5 turbojets. On returning to Moscow he was instructed to copy the Nene for production in the USSR. For this purpose the OKB-45 design bureau had been established at Factory No. 45 in Moscow, and it was headed by Klimov. By the end of 1947 the first RD-45 (the Soviet version of the Nene 1) had been built in this factory.

Because of his preoccupation with jet engines, Klimov curtailed his piston-engine activities. Improvement of the 1,900hp VK-109 and further modification of VK-108 ceased at the beginning of 1947. Development of the more powerful 2,100hp VK-110 and 3,700hp VK-150 was cancelled in the early stages, and Klimov no longer worked on piston engines. Different factories had manufactured a total of more than 100,000 piston engines of his design.

Simultaneously with copying the Nene, OKB-45 was creating its own first turbojet, the VK-1. This retained the layout and main design features of the British engine, but had greater thrust owing to various improvements. The VK-1 was mass-produced from 1949. While fewer than 10,000 RD-45s were built, more than 85,000 VK-1s were produced in the USSR alone. It was also manufactured in Poland and China. Versions of the VK-1 engine family (VK-1, VK-1A, VK-1F) powered the MiG-15bis and MiG-17 fighters and the Il-28 and Tu-14 bombers.

These first jet engines were followed by number of turbojet and turboprop types designed under the leadership of Klimov, the VK-2, VK-3, VK-5, VK-7, but none of them was manufactured in such large numbers as the VK-1.

Klimov's achievements were recognised at the highest levels in the Soviet Union. He was twice awarded the Golden Star of Hero of Socialist Labour (in 1940 and 1957), and received the Stalin Prize four times (in 1940, 1943, 1946 and 1949). From 1953 Klimov, as a prominent scientist, was a full member of the USSR Academy of Sciences.

During his last years Klimov headed OKB-117 in Leningrad, now part of the V.Ya. Klimov Factory enterprise. In the early 1960s S.P. Izotov replaced him as head of OKB-117, and today this design bureau is well-known for its helicopter turboshaft engines.

M-100 (Hispano-Suiza 12Ybrs)

This was a licensed copy of French Hispano-Suiza 12Ybrs, manufactured under a contract of 14 June 1934. The M-100 in different versions was in mass production from 1935 to 1940 at Factory No. 26 in Rybinsk, 6,061 engines being produced.

M-100s, M-100As and M-100AUs were exported to Spain and China. In 1939 negotiations were conducted for supplying M-100s to France.

Characteristics

12-cylinder in-line vee, carburetted, watercooled, geared engine with single-stage single-speed GCS.

Bore/stroke	150/170mm (5.91/6.69in)
Volume	36.03 litres (2,198cu in)

Power rating, compression ratio, and weight dependant on version

The following versions of the engine are known:

M-100 The first series-production version. Power rating 655/750hp, compression ratio 6.0:1, weight 470kg (1,036lb).

M-100A An improved version with flexible gear-wheel, strengthened blocks, modified valves and increased GCS pressure. The M-100A prototypes were tested from May 1935, and the version had passed State tests by 15 January 1936. It was introduced into series production in March 1936. Power rating 775/860hp, compression ratio 5.8:1 (prototype 5.87:1), weight 477kg (1,052lb).

M-100, coupled version. A 1936 project comprising two M-100s installed in tandem and driving co-axial contrarotating propellers through a special shaft. A prototype was built, and underwent bench testing at the end of 1936.

M-100, cannon version. Similar to the Hispano-Suiza 12Ycrs. As early as April 1934 the design bureau of B.G. Shpitalniy was tasked with modifying the M-100 for the installation of the Soviet 20mm ShVAK cannon, and then for the planned 37mm cannon. As a pattern, Shpitalniy was given a French-built 12Ycrs. Negotiations about modifying the engine for the Soviet 37mm cannon were also carried with the French company, but agreement was not reached. As a result of Shpitalniy's work, the ShVAK cannon was installed in the cylinder vee of the M-100 so that it could fire through the hollow shaft of the reduction gear. Several prototypes were built and bench tested, and at the end of 1936 one was installed in the I-17bis fighter prototype. Flight testing continued until 1938. Later, elements of the M-100 cannon version were used in the design of the M-105P.

M-100A, part of the ATsN-2 centralized supercharging unit designed by K.V. Minkner. The ATsN-2 was to operate as the first supercharging stage for four AM-34FRN engines on the TB-7 bomber. The ATsN-2 and the M-100A that powered it were mounted in the aircraft's fuselage. The unit successfully passed bench testing and was flight tested on the TB-7 prototype in the winter and spring of 1938/39.

M-100AU An improved version with increased service life, in production in 1938-40.

M-100SO A 1938 project with combined cooling (air-cooled cylinders and glycol-cooled cylinder heads) and cannon. Engine power rating 950/1,000hp. Later a variant with a two-speed GCS and cannon was planned.

An M-103 engine in the S-22 high-speed reconnaissance aeroplane prototype. This aircraft was launched into series production as the BB-22 or Yak-2.

The M-103A during State testing, still with a K-100 carburettor, October 1937.

M-100s powered the SB bombers and the I-17bis and Stal-7 prototypes. The engine was specified for the SPS-89 and DI-7 projects.

M-103

The M-103 was a further evolution of the M-100A, with increased compression ratio, a changed driving ratio in the GCS gear (rpm increased), and boosted rpm and supercharging. The cylinder blocks were strengthened, and the engine had new gas seals, a crankshaft with caps, and new pistons with flat bottoms. Development was carried out in 1936, and the engine went for State testing in October 1936. Two of the prototypes tested suffered cracked cylinder blocks. New State tests were performed in 1937, and M-103 production started in May 1938 at Factory No. 26 in Rybinsk and continued until 1942. In total, 11,681 engines were built.

M-103s were exported to Spain and China.

Characteristics

12-cylinder in-line vee, carburetted, watercooled, geared engine with single-stage single-speed GCS.
Compression ratio 6.6:1
Power rating, bore/stroke, volume, and weight dependant on version.

The following versions of the engine are known:

M-103 The first series-production version.

Characteristics

Power rating	850/1,000hp
Bore/stroke	150/170mm (5.91/6.69in)
Volume	36.03 litres (2,198cu in)
Weight	495kg (1,091lb)

M-103A A version having cylinders of decreased diameter, and a strengthened crankshaft, crankcase, cylinder block and liner. Some engine accessories were modified. Series production of the M-103A started in 1939.

Characteristics

Power rating	850/1,000hp
Bore/stroke	148/170mm (5.83/6.69)
Volume	35 litres (2,135cu in)
Weight	510kg (1,124lb) (495kg (1,091lb) according to project data)

M-103P, cannon version. An M-103A with provision for a 20mm ShVAK cannon installation in the engine vee, a project of 1938. Power rating 950/1,000hp, weight 510kg (1,124lb). It was planned to carry out engine tests in the fourth quarter of 1938. No information on manufacture of the prototype has been found.

M-103SP, coupled version. A version comprising two tandem-mounted M-103Ps driving co-axial contrarotating propellers via special shaft. In May 1939 two prototypes were manufactured, and underwent bench testing. In 1939-40 the coupled version was flight tested in the prototype of V.F. Bolkhovitinov's short-range 'S' bomber.

M-103G A variant with glycol cooling (instead of water); a 1938 project. It was planned to start bench testing in October 1938. Several prototypes were built in the first half of 1939 and bench tested. Power rating 900/930hp, weight 500kg (1,100lb).

M-103A-TK An M-103A with a TK-2 turbo-supercharger (created by the TsIAM). The engine's development was carried out from early 1938. Power rating 820/1,000hp, weight 570kg (1,257lb). It was planned to start bench testing in the first quarter of 1939, and to flight-test two engines in an SB bomber from 1 August 1939.

A restored M-103A with fittings for the SB nacelle cowling.

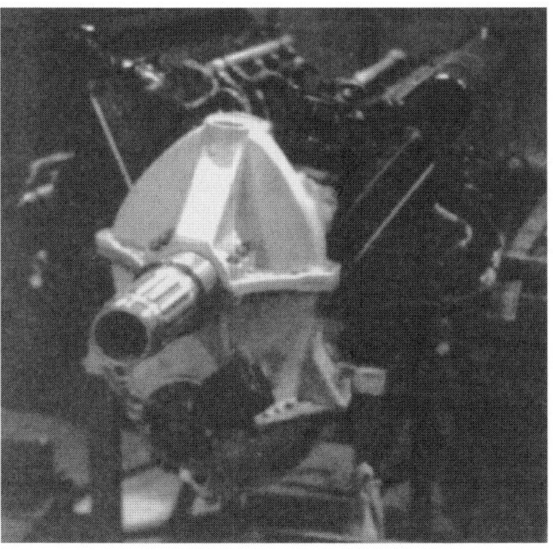

The SB bomber, powered by M-104s, August 1939.

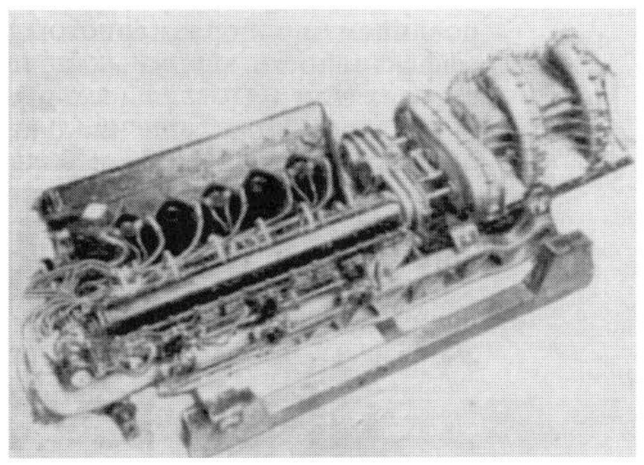

An M-103 as part of the ATsN-2 centralized supercharging unit of the TB-7 heavy bomber.

M-103A driving an ATsN-2 centralized supercharging unit. A batch of this version was manufactured in 1940.

M-103U An M-103A with minor changes aimed at increasing the engine's service life. In series production from the end of 1939.

M-103 engines of various versions powered the SB, Yak-2 (BB-22) and TB-7 (first series, as part of the ATsN-2) series production aircraft, and the 'S', VIT-1, VIT-2, MBR-2 and MBR-7 (MS-8) prototypes. It was also planned to use this engine in the projected KOR-2 and 'I' aircraft.

M-104

Originally, the M-104 was being developed as a version of the M-103 with a two-speed single-stage GCS. Engine characteristics according to the specification: power rating 1,050/1,100hp, weight 550kg (1,213lb). The E-23 GCS (the first two-speed GCS in the USSR) was created by G.E. Blokhin at the TsIAM. Basically the M-104 was an M-103A with decreased supercharging. In 1939 the M-104 prototypes underwent bench and flight testing, and series production of the type started at Factory No. 26 in Rybinsk that same year, 232 being built before it was phased out of production at the end of 1939.

The M-104 was installed in series-production SB bombers.

Characteristics

12-cylinder in-line vee, carburetted, watercooled, geared engine with single-stage two-speed GCS.

Bore/stroke	148/170mm (5.83/6.69in)
Volume	35.08 litres (2,140cu in)
Compression ratio	6.6:1

M-105 (VK-105)

This was a further development of the M-103A, with a strengthened crankshaft, crankcase, cylinder blocks and con-rods. A two-valve (instead of three-valve) gas-distribution mechanism and a two-speed single-stage GCS were introduced, compression ratio was increased, and the engine was boosted in rpm.

A project, designated M-105S, was being developed from 1937. According to the specification the power rating was to reach 1,050/1,100hp, and the engine was to weigh of 510kg (1,124lb). The M-105S was to be transferred for State testing by November 1938, but as early as July 1938 the M-105 prototypes were being flight-tested on a VIT-2 aeroplane. Engine refinement was protracted, and not until July 1939 was it introduced into series production. According to the plan, series production of the M-105 was to start at Factory No. 26 in October 1939. In the course of refinement early in 1940, crankshaft counterbalances were introduced, the AK-105 carburettor (later designated K-105) replaced the AK-103, and many minor changes were made. By October 1940 the first series batch (fifty engines) with K-100 carburettors had been built. Before the spring of 1940 the reliability of the M-105 was quite poor. Cracks appeared in the valve box and main crankshaft journals, and the exhaust valves burnt through. After modification the estimated weight was exceeded, reaching 570kg (1,257lb) instead of planned 550kg (1,213lb).

Series production of the M-105 was undertaken at Factory No. 26 in Rybinsk. In course of production the engine was repeatedly modified. Later, Factories No. 16 in Voronezh (from December 1940)

The DB-240 (Er-2) bomber, powered by M-105s, October 1940.

and No. 27 in Kazan (from beginning 1941) also built the engine, and in addition it was planned to set up production at Factories Nos 234, 384 and 451, and the GAZ automobile factory. During the German offensive in September-October 1941, Factory No. 16 was evacuated to Ufa, and Factory No. 26 to Kazan, where it merged with Factory No. 27. Manufacture of the M-105 almost ceased until February 1942, when the production rate began to increase. In July 1942 Factory No. 16 reached its pre-war level of production, and Factory No. 26 did the same in August of that year. During the war Factory No. 466 in Gorkiy was also involved in M-105 production. At the end of 1945 this factory was transferred to Leningrad, to the site of Factory No. 274, where arrangements were made for production of the M-107A.

The M-105 (redesignated VK-105 from 8 March 1944) was produced in greater numbers than any other Soviet engine of the Second World War, and powered both fighters and bombers. In total, 75,250 were built. Factory No. 24 alone manufactured 1,424 M-105s, 5,821 M-105P/PAs, 10,605 M-105R/RAs and 57,360 M-105PF/PF-2s. Production of all versions except the M-105PF (VK-105PF) ceased in 1943, in order to increase the production rate by limiting the number of versions built. The last version, the VK-105PF-2 was in production until 1947.

Engines of the M-105 family were exported to Albania, Poland, Czechoslovakia, China, Bulgaria, Yugoslavia and North Korea.

The M-105PD prototype.

Characteristics

12-cylinder in-line vee, carburetted, watercooled (glycol or glycerine anti-freeze was used in winter), geared engine with a two-stage, two-speed GCS.

Bore/stroke	148/170mm (5.83/6.69in)
Volume	35.08 litres (2,140cu in)
Compression ratio	7.1:1
Power rating	dependant on version
Weight	dependant on version

The following versions of the M-105 (VK-105) are known:

M-105 The first series-production version. Power rating 1,020/1,100hp, weight 570kg (1,257lb).

M-105R A version for bombers and reconnaissance aeroplanes, having a different ratio of reduction gearing. Power rating 1,050/1,100hp, weight 580kg (1,279lb).

M-105P A version of the M-105 for fighters, having a different reduction gear ratio and increased distance between the axes of the crankshaft and reduction gear. As with the M-100P and M-103P, it was planned to mount a cannon in the engine vee, but unlike those two types the new engine had two synchronization mechanisms controlling two machine-guns each. The first prototypes of the M-105P were built in March 1939, and by the end of 1939 a small batch had been produced. In January 1940 the engine was flight-tested

An engine nacelle of a 277th series SB with M-105 engines.

An M-105P in the second prototype I-26 (Yak-1) fighter, June 1940.

in the I-26-1 fighter (Yak-1 prototype). Officially, the M-105P was introduced into service and series production on 23 May 1940. Power rating 1,050/1,100hp, weight 600kg (1,323lb). Alternatively, ShVAK (20mm), VYa-23 (23mm), and N-37 (37mm) cannon could be mounted on the engine.

M-105PA An development of the M-105P, in series production from 1941. The PA differed in having a strengthened crankcase, stiffened con-rods, a K-15BP (K-105) floatless carburettor and an R-7 (instead of R-2) rpm governor. On the later series, hyperbolic boring of main-bearing brasses was introduced. Power rating 1,050/110hp, weight 600kg (1,323lb). Alternatively, ShVAK (20mm), VYa-23 (23mm), and MPSh-37 (37mm) cannon could be mounted on the engine.

M-105RA A counterpart of the PA version with different reduction gear (from the M-105R). Power rating 1,050/1,100hp, weight 580kg (1,279lb). From July 1941 the M-105RA was installed on production Pe-2 bombers. There was a version of the M-105RA with a mechanism to divert power to drive the pump of an RU-1 liquid-propellant rocket engine. The engine prototypes were manufactured at Factory No. 16, and flight testing was carried out in a Pe-2 from September 1943 to January 1945.

M-105TK A version of the M-105 with two TK-3 turbo-superchargers and modified reduction gear. The first prototypes were manufactured in April-May 1939. From December 1939 until April 1940 they were flight tested on a prototype of the high-altitude '100' (VI-100) fighter.

M-105P-TK A project of 1939, this was a version of the M-105P with two TK-2 turbo-superchargers.

M-105F with two TK-F turbo-superchargers. Prototypes of this version were manufactured in April-May 1941 and bench tested until the end of 1941. In March-April 1942 they were flight-tested in a Pe-2.

M-105PD (VK-105PD) A high-altitude

Front-line maintenance of an M-105RA in a Pe-2 bomber.

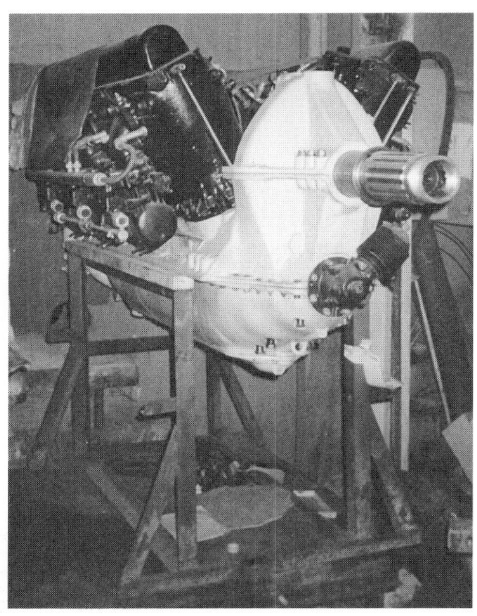

A restored M-105RA, 2000.

The M-105TK engine in the '100' high-altitude fighter prototype, the prototype of the Pe-2 bomber.

The Yak-9 fighter, powered by the an M-105PF fitted with a 37-mm cannon, February 1943.

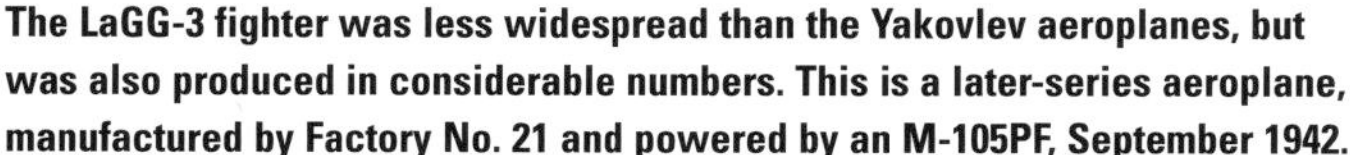

The LaGG-3 fighter was less widespread than the Yakovlev aeroplanes, but was also produced in considerable numbers. This is a later-series aeroplane, manufactured by Factory No. 21 and powered by an M-105PF, September 1942.

An M-105PF2, mounted in a Yak-3 fighter, used as a teaching aid at the MAI.

version based on the M-105PA and equipped with a two-stage E-100 GCS designed by V.A. Dollezhal. Initially this version was designated M-105DT. The first stage of the supercharger had a drive with an hydraulic clutch. Power rating 1,160hp, weight 645kg (1,422lb). This engine was being developed from 1940. In December of that year a prototype was flight tested on an I-28 (Yak-5). In February-March 1941 official bench testing was carried out. It was planned to introduce the M-105PD into series production from June 1941, but the first batch was not produced until 1942. In September 1942 the M-105PD was repeatedly flight tested on a Yak-7PD fighter, and then on a Yak-9PD in April-June 1943. The 1943-series engines had an increased gear ratio in the GCS drive. The engine did not have an intercooler, and overheated as a consequence. The VK-105PD was being refined until 1945. There were plans to mount the ShVAK (20mm) cannon on the engine.

M-105PF (VK-105PF) An M-105PA with boosted supercharging. This modification was made in May 1942 under the initiative of OKB-115 and the NII VVS. The engine's power rating increased at low altitudes, but its high-altitude characteristics worsened. When the M-105PF was being refined, the piston pins and GCS were strengthened, the crankshaft modified, the diameter of the reduction gear's elastic coupling was increased, and the K-105F carburettor replaced the K-105BP. On the later series the crankshaft was additionally strengthened. Power rating 1,180/1,260hp, weight 600kg (1,323lb). The ShVAK (20mm), 11P-37 (37mm) or NS-37 (37mm) cannon could be mounted on the engine. The M-105PF was the most-produced version of the M-105. The M-105PAs of the 1942 series were field-modified into M-105PFs. In 1943 experiments on water injection into the M-105PF suction inlets were carried out, flight tests being performed using a Pe-2 bomber. The M-105PFs (as well as M-105PF-2s in the later stages) were sometimes modified by the workshops of training units and flying schools to have shorter pistons, thus reducing compression ratio and power but increasing service life.

M-105RF A version similar to the M-105PF, with M-105RA reduction gear and without provision for cannon installation. Power rating 1,180/1.260hp, weight 580kg (1,279lb). Prototypes were built.

M-105REN A version of the M-105R driving a compressor to inflate an air cushion. Prototypes were built in 1941, and in

Pe-2 bombers, powered by M-105PF engines, in flight over Germany.

that year the engine was tested on an experimental Pe-2 with an air-cushion undercarriage.

M-105PF-2 (VK-105PF-2) A version of the M-105PF (VK-105PF) with increased supercharging pressure. The prototypes were being tested from the summer of 1943, and the engine was in mass production from September 1944. Power rating 1,240/1,290hp. The ShVAK (20mm), B-20M (20mm), ShA-20M (20mm), NS-23 (23mm), N-37 (37mm) or NS-37 (37mm) cannon could be mounted on this engine.

M-105PV A further development of the M-105PD (VK-105PD) with an E-100 supercharger, based on M-105PF. Power rating 1,250hp. In August-September 1944 this engine was flight-tested in a Yak-3PD fighter. The NS-23 (23mm) cannon was mounted on the engine.

M-105, coupled version. A powerplant comprising two M-105s mounted in tandem and driving contrarotating co-axial propellers. It was a 1941 project, and variants for tractor and pusher propellers were designed.

The engines of the M-105 family were used on the following series production aircraft: Ar-2 (SB-RK), SB, Yak-4 (BB-22), SPB (D) (small series, not introduced into service), Pe-2 (PB-100), Pe-3, Pe-3bis, Yak-1, Yak-3, Yak-7, Yak-9 and Er-2. They were also fitted to the following prototypes: MMN, VIT-2, EI (not completed), Su-1, BB-MAI, IP-21, SK-1, SK-2, MDR-6B and Pe-2VI. Various engines of the M-105 family were planned for the projected 'I', 'D', and RK-I projects.

In Finland, captured M-105PFs were used to convert French Morane-Sauliner MS.406 fighters into an indigenous version named the *Morko Moraani* (Moran-Werewolf). On some of the aircraft the engines were fitted with captured Soviet 12mm UB machine-guns in place of the cannon.

M-106

The M-106 was an attempt to boost the M-105 by supercharging. It was supposed that it would become a primary engine for fighters and, to some extent, bombers. Development was carried out from 1938.

Compared with the M-105, the engine had pistons and cylinder blocks of modified design, strengthened crankshaft and reduction-gear pinions, and a decreased compression ratio. The overall dimensions and the attachment points were the same as for the M-105. Initially, the M-106 was being developed with a two-speed GCS, but later a single-speed unit was chosen for the M-106-1sk variant. In March 1939 two prototypes with two-speed GCSs were built.

Refinement of the M-106 was lengthy. It suffered from uneven running during transient modes, oil leaks, pinking, and carbon build-up.

In January 1943 the prototypes were flight-tested in Yak-1 fighters, and during November 1942-January 1943 on Yak-9s. Factory No. 26 in Ufa built more than 150 M-106s, the type being phased out of production in May 1943.

Characteristics

12-cylinder in-line vee, carburetted, watercooled (glycol or glycerine anti-freeze was used in winter), geared engine with single-stage single-speed GCS.

Bore/stroke	148/170mm (5.83/6.69in)
Volume	35.08 litres (2,140cu in)
Compression ratio	6.0:1 (according to some sources, 6.5:1).
Power rating	dependant on the version
Weight	dependant on the version

The following versions of the M-106 engine are known:

M-106 (M-106-1sk) This version, sometimes called the M-106P, was in series production during 1942-43. It allowed the possibility of mounting a ShVAK 20mm cannon in the engine vee. Power rating 1,250/1,350hp, weight 600kg (1,323lb). M-106 for bombers. Similar to the M-106-1sk, but without the provision for mounting a cannon, and intended for installation in bombers. It was being developed in 1939.

M-106PV (PV – *Povishennoy Visotnosti*, or increased altitude) A high-altitude version with a two-stage E-100 GCS with an hydraulic clutch, similar to the M-105PD. It was tested on a Yak-9PD fighter in October 1943. In 1944 the supercharger rpm was increased, water/alcohol injection was introduced and a new ignition system was installed. The modernized M-106PV was flight-tested on a Yak-9PD in April 1944. More than fifty modernized M-106PVs were built. The ShA-20M (20mm) lightened cannon was mounted with this engine.

M-106 with Efremov's turbo-reactor. A 1940 project of with a turbo-reactor (tunnel radiator) designed by Efremov which created jet thrust. No information about construction of the prototype has been found.

M-106TK A 1940 project of with two TK-1 turbo-superchargers.

The M-106 engines (M-106-1sk) were installed on production Yak-1 fighters, but these were not introduced into service and their engines were removed. The M-106PVs powered series-production Yak-9PD fighters built at Factory No. 301. Application of various versions of the M-106 was also planned for the projected DB-240 (Er-2), SB, I-26 (Yak-1) and I-301 (LaGG-1) aeroplanes.

M-107 (VK-107)

The M-107 was a further development of the M-105 with boosted rpm. It was being developed as the M-107P (cannon) version from March 1940. The engine had a modified air/fuel supply system compared with that of the M-105. Some of the

The Yak-9U fighter, powered by the VK-107A and armed with three cannons, in March 1945.

compressed air was supplied from the GCS, round the carburettor and directly into the cylinders, while the carburettor supplied the enriched fuel mixture. The M-107 had cylinder blocks of slightly modified design. A four-valve (instead of three-valve) gas-distribution mechanism with strengthened drive was introduced, and the reduction gear was improved.

According to the plans, the engine's servicing interval was to be increased to 100hr by 1 May 1941. Series production was to be started, and 2,000 M-107s were to be completed by the end of the year. However, bench testing revealed vibration, oil leaks which caused a decrease in oil pressure, failures of spark plugs, breakdown of the crankshaft main bearings, and leaking of the gas seals. Overheating was also a problem. After some refinements the M-107 successfully passed its 50hr test. During 1941 twenty-nine engines were manufactured, these being used for various tests. Series production started in 1942. Certain versions were manufactured until 1948 at Factory No. 26 in Ufa. On 8 March 1944 the engine was redesignated VK-107. Owing to some drawbacks in the design, manufacture was halted several times (in September-December 1945 and April-October 1946). In total, 7,902 M-107/VK-107s of different versions were built.

The VK-107A was exported to Albania, Hungary, China, Poland and Yugoslavia.

Characteristics

12-cylinder in-line vee, carburetted, watercooled (glycol and glycerine anti-freeze was used in winter), geared engine with single-stage two-speed GCS.

Bore/stroke	148/170mm (5.83/6.69in)
Volume	35.08 litres (2,140cu in)
Compression ratio	6.75:1
Power rating	dependant on version
Weight	dependant on version

The following versions of the engine are known:

M-107 (M-107P) The first series-production version of 1941. Power rating 1,300/1.400hp, weight 765kg (1,687lb). This version suffered from failures of con-rods, pistons and crankcases. During 1941-42 686 M-107s were manufactured. Installation of a ShVAK (20mm) cannon was planned for this version.

M-107, coupled version. A project of 1940-41 for a powerplant comprising two M-107s driving two contrarotating co-axial propellers via a special shaft.

The Pe-2I bomber prototype, powered by VK-107A engines.

A VK-107A in a Yak-3 fighter at the NII VVS in May 1944.

A VK-107R (VK-107VRDK) in the I-320 ('N') fighter.

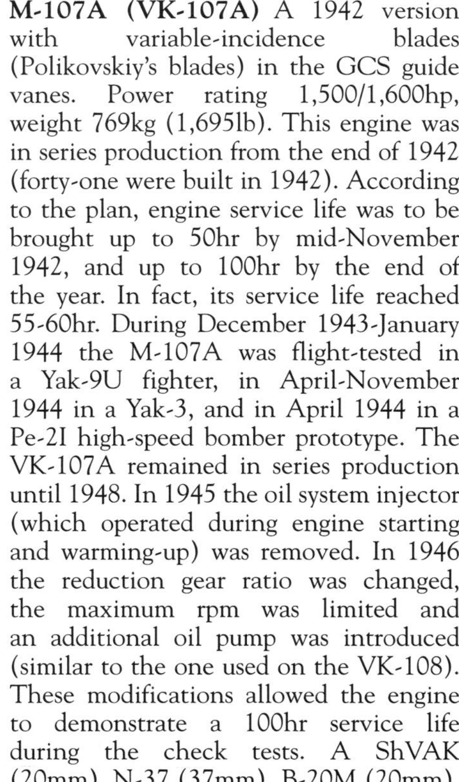

M-107A (VK-107A) A 1942 version with variable-incidence blades (Polikovskiy's blades) in the GCS guide vanes. Power rating 1,500/1,600hp, weight 769kg (1,695lb). This engine was in series production from the end of 1942 (forty-one were built in 1942). According to the plan, engine service life was to be brought up to 50hr by mid-November 1942, and up to 100hr by the end of the year. In fact, its service life reached 55-60hr. During December 1943-January 1944 the M-107A was flight-tested in a Yak-9U fighter, in April-November 1944 in a Yak-3, and in April 1944 in a Pe-2I high-speed bomber prototype. The VK-107A remained in series production until 1948. In 1945 the oil system injector (which operated during engine starting and warming-up) was removed. In 1946 the reduction gear ratio was changed, the maximum rpm was limited and an additional oil pump was introduced (similar to the one used on the VK-108). These modifications allowed the engine to demonstrate a 100hr service life during the check tests. A ShVAK (20mm), N-37 (37mm), B-20M (20mm), NS-23 (23mm) or N-45 (45mm) cannon could be mounted on the M-107A (VK-107A).

VK-107R (originally designated VK-107-E3020) A version of the VK-107A driving a moto-compressor jet engine designed by Fadeev and Kholshchevnikov in 1943-45. The jet-engine drive was a power take-off system via a long shaft. Power rating without the jet engine 1,450/1,650hp; and 2,800 equivalent hp with the jet running (3,000ehp according to other sources). Factory bench tests were carried out from March 1945, and in July 1946 the engine demonstrated a service life of 35hr. Already, in March-May 1945, the VK-107R had flown in the I-250 ('N'), and in April-July of that year in the I-107 (Su-5). From the second half of 1945 the engine was in series production at Factory No. 466 (VK-107A engines were supplied, as a component of the VK-107R, by Factory No. 26) and powered the I-250 fighters.

The M-107 (VK-107) engines were installed in the following series-production aircraft: Yak-3, Yak-9, I-250 ('N') and

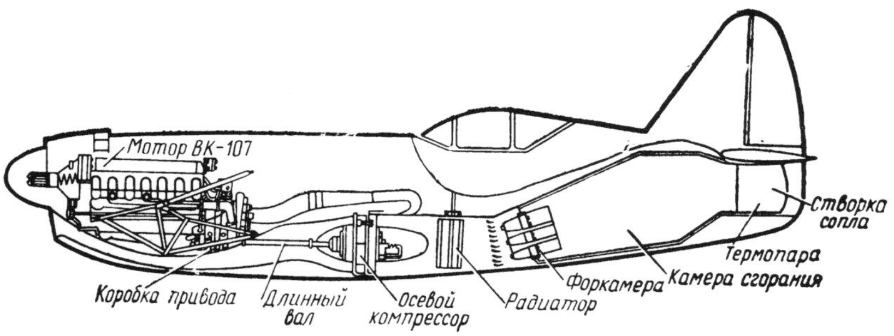

A schematic diagram depicting the installation of the piston engine and moto-compressor jet in the I-320 fighter prototype.

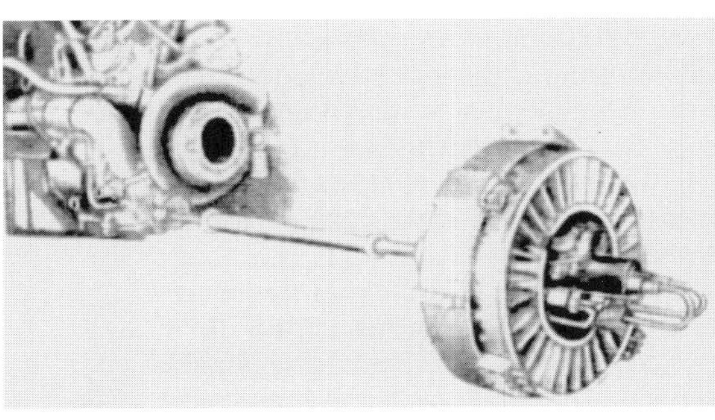

A sketch of the compressor drive of the moto-compressor jet.

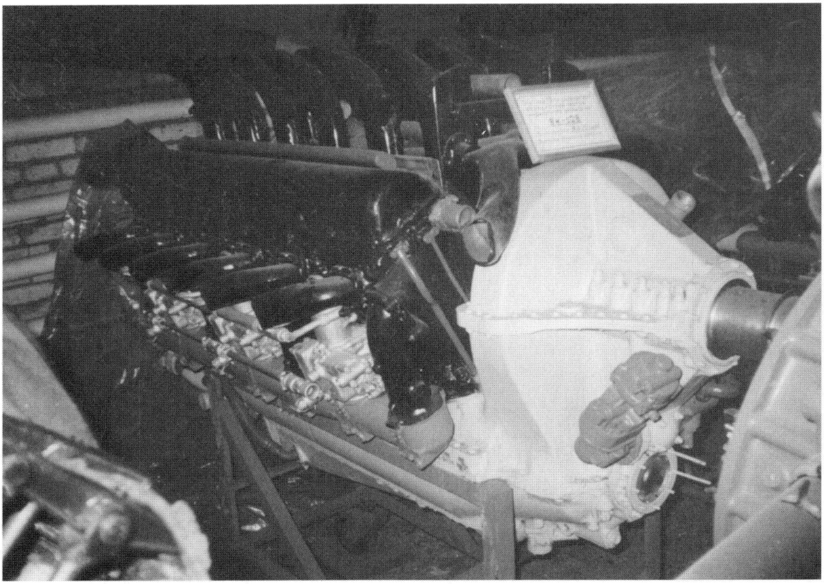

A surviving VK-108 in the Monino museum.

ABOVE: **A VK-108 before State testing, July 1945.**

LEFT: **The VB-109 high-altitude bomber prototype, powered by VK-108s.**

Pe-2I (small series); as well as in the following prototypes: DIS (VM-14), Pe-2M, ITP (M-1), '110', MDR-6B, LaGG-3, I-107 (Su-5),and I-1 (not completed). It was planned to use this engine for the projected B-10, B-10M, '104', PPI (Che-1), BB-22, EI and I.

VK-108

This was a further development of the M-107A (VK-107A) with increased supercharging. The prototypes were built in 1943-44. The VK-108 had a two-speed GCS with improved hydraulics and increased rpm (due to the introduction of a new GCS drive). Modifications were introduced to the cylinder-block seals, the crankshaft was strengthened, a new design of cylinder liner was used, the crankshaft's flexible coupling was modified, the pistons were strengthened and the gas-distribution mechanism improved. The GCS was given vaned diffusion, and its impeller was strengthened. An additional oil-pump was provided, and a new magneto installed. In 1944-46 Factory No. 26 in Ufa built forty-nine prototypes. Refinement of the VK-108 ceased in 1947 because the design bureau was overloaded with jet engine development work.

Characteristics

12-cylinder in-line vee, carburetted, watercooled (glycol or glycerine anti-freeze was used in winter), geared engine with single-stage two-speed GCS. Provision was made for a cannon installation in the engine vee.

Bore/stroke	148/170mm (5.83/6.69in)
Volume	35.08 litres (2,140cu in)
Compression ratio	6.65:1
Power rating	dependant on the version
Weight	dependant on the version

Two versions of the engine are known:

VK-108 A 1944 version with a power rating of 1,550/1,850hp. The engine was flight-tested in a Yak-3 fighter from December 1944 to March 1945. The tests were halted because of the engine's unsatisfactory operation (jolting, smudging and frequent failures). In December 1945 the VK-108 was flight-tested in a VB-109 bomber prototype.

VK-108F A boosted version. Several prototypes were built in the first quarter of 1946. Power rating 1,550/2,000hp. Factory bench tests were carried out in September 1946. Further refinement ceased in 1947.

The VK-108 was installed in prototypes of the Yak-3 and VB-109. An experimental variant of the Yak-3 powered by the VK-108 became the fastest Soviet piston-engined fighter, attaining a speed of 745km/h (463mph) in the course of testing.

VK-109

The VK-109 was a further development of the VK-108. It was developed during 1945-46, and the prototypes were built from 1945. Factory bench teste took place in 1946. It was planned to complete refinement by August 1946, but work on the engine ceased at the beginning of 1947 because of the transition to jets.

There were plans to use this engine on the VB-109 bomber.

Characteristics

12-cylinder in-line vee, carburetted, watercooled (glycol or glycerine anti-freeze was used in winter), geared engine with single-stage two-speed GCS.

Power rating	1,650/1,800hp (according to some sources 1,800/2,075hp)
Bore/stroke	148/170mm (5.83/6.69in)
Volume	35.08 litres (2,140cu in)

M-110

A projected inverted-vee engine with combined cooling, the cylinder heads being cooled with glycol, and the cylinders being air-cooled. The project was completed in 1939, but no information about the building of the prototypes has been found. According to the specification it was to have a power rating of 900/950hp and a weight of 490kg (1,080lb). At a later stage the engine was designated M-110A, with an estimated power rating of 900/960hp and a weight of 510kg (1,124lb).

VK-110

This projected engine of 1946, with a 2,000hp power rating, was cancelled in 1947 because of the transition to jet engines.

M-120

This engine comprised three M-103A cylinder blocks arranged radially at 120-degree angles to each other; one block upwards and the other two downwards in an inverted-Y arrangement. The M-120 was being developed from 1938, and it was planned to start bench testing from 1 November 1939. In fact the engineering documentation was completed by 1 June 1939, and manufacture of the first prototypes (a batch of five) was started in the second half of 1939. The first prototype was assembled on 30 October. Bench tests were conducte in 1940, and in November of that year two M-120TKs were flown in a DB-4 bomber. In August 1941 the engine underwent State tests, but these were not completed because the main connecting rod and the supercharger broke down. The type was not introduced

The M-120 engine.

The DVB-102 long-range, high-altitude bomber prototype, powered by M-120TKs, January 1942.

The powerplant of the DVB-102 bomber prototype, with the cowlings closed and open.

into series production, and refinement work ceased in 1942.

Characteristics

18-cylinder in-line three-block radial, watercooled, geared engine with a single-stage two-speed GCS.

Bore/stroke	148/170mm (5.83/6.69in)
Volume	54 litres (3,295cu in)
Compression ratio	6.6:1
Power rating	dependant on version
Weight	dependant on version

The following versions of the engine are known:

M-120 Power rating 1,500/1,600hp, weight 895kg (1,973lb) (according to project data 850kg (1,874lb)).

M-120TK with turbo-supercharging. A version with a power rating of 1,400/1,600hp. Weight 950kg (2,094lb).

M-120UV ('long shaft') A version with a remote reduction gear connected to the engine via a long shaft. Power rating 1,600/1,800hp.

M-120UV-TK A variant of the M-120UV with turbo-supercharging; a project of 1940.

The M-120TK was installed in the long-range DB-4 bomber prototype. The following projects planned to use various versions of the M-120: PB ('57'), FB ('58'), ODB (P), DVB-102, IVS and OI-2.

VK-150

A project for a 24-cylinder 3,700hp engine, evaluated in 1946. Work on the VK-150 ceased in 1947 owing to the design bureau's transition to jet engine development. No prototypes were built.

CHAPTER TWENTY-FIVE

Gnome-Rhône – the Last Attempt

Various piston aero-engines developed by the Gnome-Rhône company were introduced into series production in Russia at different times. Before the October Revolution the French company had a factory in Moscow that was later nationalized. The M-2 (Le Rhône J) rotary engine was in series production in the USSR until the beginning of the 1930s, and was built in fairly large quantities. In September 1930 Factory No. 29 in Zaporozhye submitted the first batch of M-22 engines for military acceptance. This engine, a licensed copy of French version of the Bristol Jupiter radial, remained in production in the Soviet Union until late 1935. At that time the factory in Zaporozhye was already arranging production of new types, the M-85 and M-75, under licence from Gnome-Rhône.

A story of their appearance in the Soviet Union started with a note of 12 August 1933, sent by Ya.I. Alksnis, head of the VVS, to Zilbert, Commissar of the NII VVS. In his note Alksnis suggested that the Soviet delegation that was preparing to visit France to carry out negotiations with Hispano-Suiza should review the Gnome-Rhône two-row radial at the same time. He supposed that the design similarity of the engines (which in fact did not exist) would allow Factory No. 29 to arrange production of the new engine production relatively easily. The head of the air force suggested that two or three samples be purchased for testing, plus another twenty or thirty for installation in aircraft prototypes.

In September 1933 the delegation, comprising representatives of Soviet engine manufacturers, departed for France. It was headed by V.Ya. Klimov, and the air force was represented by M.A. Levin. At that time the extensive programme of high-powered engine development that had been carried out in the USSR at the end of 1920s and the beginning of 1930s had yielded only one practical result; the M-34 (later AM-34) designed by A.A. Mikulin, which had been introduced into series production. However, by the time mass production of this engine had begun, its specific weight and fuel efficiency were already inferior to those of modern Western types. This delay in engine-building had a negative effect on the creation of new aircraft types, and especially military aeroplanes. It was decided to purchase manufacturing licences for foreign-designed engines, and to send a delegation to France with this purpose. The delegation's main task was to obtain a licence for production of the Hispano-Suiza 12Y.

The Gnome-Rhône engines also attracted the keen interest of Soviet specialists; not only the two-row 14K noted initially by Alksnis, but also the less-powerful related 9K. It was initially planned to install these engines in new Soviet bombers. On 7 June 1934 the Defence Committee issued a special decree ordering Klimov, Levin and the Director of Factory No. 29, Aleksandrov, to finalize negotiations with Gnome-Rhône in the shortest possible time and secure a production licence for both types, and acquire the necessary documentation and engine samples.

As a result, an agreement was signed with Gnome-Rhône on technical support in arranging series production of two engines of the 'K' family: the 9K Mistral and 14K Mistral Major. The former received the Soviet designation M-75, and the latter was designated M-85 (for a short time it was redesignated M-70, but the designation then reverted to M-85). The agreement stipulated that the French company would supply components and

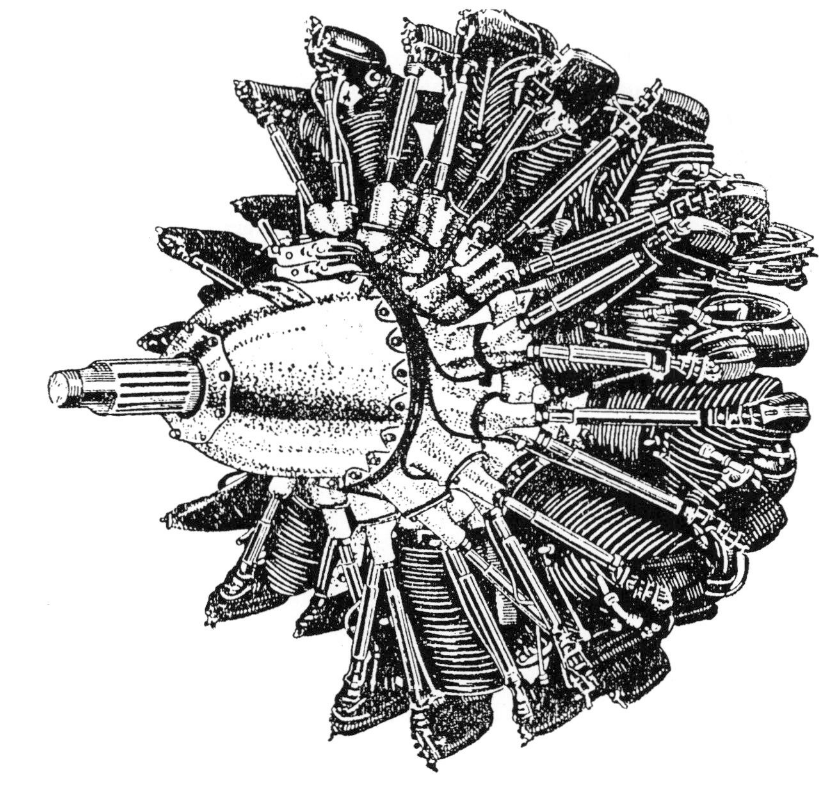

The M-85 as depicted in the engine manual.

parts for the first engine batches to be manufactured in the USSR, and train fifteen Soviet engineers at the Gnome-Rhône factory.

In October 1933, while negotiations were still under way, the GUAP NKTP decided to start the development of new aeroplanes to be powered by the French engines. The procedure of accepting technical documentation and engine samples was started in France in 1934, with A.V. Kashirin heading the process. In March a 14Kdrs was delivered to Moscow, and in April it passed its 100hr bench tests at the TsIAM.

Factory No. 29 in Zaporozhye was tasked with setting up series production of the Gnome-Rhône engines. Initially, M-75 and M-85 production were set up in parallel, but very soon the latter type was given priority. This was because the M-75 competed with the M-25 (a copy of American Wright Cyclone). The engines had approximately the same power rating, but the M-25 had the advantage at an altitude, while the M-75 outperformed it at ground level. Arrangements for Cyclone production in the USSR had been started earlier than those for the M-75. Initially it was planned that M-75 production would help overcome the shortage of M-25s during the start of mass production. The M-75 was planned to power some series of I-16 fighters. However, the Cyclone production rate in Perm was increasing, and it was no longer necessary to use effort and resources to launch mass production of the M-75.

By 1 September 1935 the first M-75 had been assembled from imported parts in Zaporozhye, and was put to 100hr factory testing. However, as early as October a proposal to phase the type out of production was received. Series production of the M-75 was scheduled for 1936, and 150 engines were planned to be built. In fact only five engine samples were manufactured. On 5 October the GUAP suggested that the planned production be reduced to fifty engines, but these, too, were not built. At the end of the year all efforts were concentrated on increasing production of the M-85, while work on the M-75 was cancelled.

Initially, it was planned to modernize the M-75 by creating an rpm-boosted version (designated M-76) with a supercharger that could be turned off in flight. A specification was prepared for this engine, but it is doubtful whether its development went beyond rough estimations.

In the first half of 1935 the assembly of M-85s (which corresponded to the 14Kdrs) started. The early-series engines had a number of imported French parts, including exhaust manifolds and collectors, fuel pumps, compressors and all electrical equipment. Acceptance of the first series was started in July. In August two engines underwent extended testing, and by 1 November 1935 fifty-seven had passed military acceptance. There was a shortage in imported magnetos, and the Soviet-built VM-14 magneto, which was to replace the French one, had not been brought to serviceable status by the end of the year. In October 1935 the M-85 was submitted for 100hr State bench testing at the NII VVS for the first time. However, the testing were marred by two consecutive failures. On 8 December 1935 two new engines underwent State tests and passed them 'satisfactorily'. The Soviet copy of the 14Kdrs matched the French original in power rating and fuel consumption, but differed in having increased oil consumption and a considerably shorter period between scheduled overhauls. The GUAP demanded that the factory reach the 150hr maintenance period, but the factory officially declared the figure of 100hr. In fact, early-series M-85s operated only for 50 to 60hr in air force units.

Although the M-85 was a modern engine in 1933, by the end of 1935 it had become somewhat obsolete. A programme for design modernization was started, and this led to the creation of a large engine family based on the M-85. This process was characterized by the fact that different leaders headed the work at different stages, and they were often persons who had never been involved with the M-85 and its 'descendants'. While M-25 improvement was led by A.D. Shvetsov from the very beginning until the end, and similar work on the M-100 was under the leadership of V.Ya. Klimov, about ten chief designers

LEFT: **The M-75 engine.**

BELOW: **Most M-85s powered DB-3 long-range bombers. This is one of the first-series aeroplanes, in the autumn of 1937.**

followed in succession at Zaporozhye during this period.

On 1 January 1935 the OKB-29 design bureau was established, with the purpose of further improving the M-85. The bureau was headed by A.S. Nazarov, who was well-known for his work on modifying the M-11 and arranging M-22 production. He had also developed a number of original engine designs which, however, did not enter series production. In 1936 the engineers of OKB-29 developed a more powerful M-85F version by modifying the M-85's supercharger drive and thereby boosting its supercharging. In April 1936 engineering drawings of the engine were transferred for prototype manufacturing, and the type was introduced into series production as the M-86 that same year.

More substantial modernization of the M-85 was started at the design bureau still led by Nazarov. The M-85V project aimed for increased compression ratio and the introduction of a new GCS with a central inlet (earlier GCS types took in air via the helix).

In the middle of 1936 Nazarov came into serious contention with subordinates, and he was transferred to the post of chief designer at the new Factory No. 16 in Voronezh. This factory was building M-11s, and was preparing for series production of French Renault in-line engines in 1936. In the autumn of 1937 Nazarov was arrested under accusation of sabotage, and continued to work at the OTB of the NKVD at Factory No. 82 in Tushino, which was involved in diesel engine development.

Engineer Vladimirov succeeded Nazarov at Factory No. 29. He proceeded to complete development of the M-85V, which by that time had been redesignated M-87. During Vladimirov's leadership work was started on the development of a version with a two-speed GCS (this programme was headed by G.P. Vodolazhskiy). Initially, this version was described in the plan as an 'M-85 with a two-speed supercharger', and no changes other than the new GCS were stipulated. Vladimirov did remain chief designer for long. At the end of 1937 engineer Filin was appointed acting chief designer.

By that time three M-87 prototypes had been completed and transferred to factory testing, while a small batch of the engines was being manufactured in parallel. Thus the factory simultaneously produced three engine types: the M-85, M-86 and M-87; at that the M-85 was being produced in large quantities. Later-series M-85s used some components of the succeeding types and were partly unified with them. However, Filin did not live to see this happen. During the period of mass repression he was listed as a saboteur and was arrested by the NKVD. No information about his fate has been found.

An M-87A in the I-180 fighter prototype.

In 1938 OKB-29 was headed by S.K. Tumanskiy, who faced the task of completing refinement and arranging series production of the M-87, as well as developing an engine with a two-speed GCS, designated M-88. The factory encountered considerable difficulties in refining the M-87. The engine's GCS drive failed, the pinions of the reduction gear became chipped, piston pins broke and piston heads burnt through. The leaders of the NKAP concluded that the factory was incapable of refining the M-87 on its its own, and a group of specialists led by V.Ya. Klimov was transferred to Zaporozhye from Factory No. 26. The result of their work was the M-87A, which was built in large quantities from the autumn of 1938. In October 1938 the first seventy M-87As passed military acceptance. By the end of the year 711 engines had been accepted, and production of the outdated M-85 and M-86 had ceased.

In April 1939 it was proposed that another Gnome-Rhône engine be built in the USSR, the small 14-cylinder 14M type. This time the Soviets wanted to avoid acquiring a licence by simply purchasing an engine and copying it. However, NII VVS specialists managed to prove that this process would take no less than two years, after which the engine would become obsolete. The idea of copying the Gnome-Rhône 14M was therefore rejected.

The quantities of engines built at Factory No. 29 did not satisfy the demands of aircraft manufacturers, and from time to time the industry asked for engines stored in VVS depots to be released. In the end it was decided to get Factory No. 24 in Moscow to participate in M-87 production. At that time the factory was building engines designed by A.A. Mikulin, and series production of the M-87 was ordered to be arranged there in 1939. The factory management fought tooth and nail against 'alien' engines, reasonably thinking that they ought not ruin an established production line. The result was unnecessary expenses on preparing the drawings and making production fixtures that were never used. The Moscow-based factory assembled only nine engines from components manufactured by Factory No. 29.

The M-87A lagged behind contemporary Western engines not only in having a short service life. New Gnome-Rhône designs already had surpassed it in power rating and efficiency. The French had developed the 14N50, which outclassed

ABOVE: **The DB-3F long-range bomber, powered by M-88s.**

LEFT: **An M-87A engine is loaded into a PS-84K transport aeroplane, 1940.**

the M-87A in all respects. Soviet industry leaders estimated this time lag at one-and-a-half to two years. This forced designers to accelerate the process of new type development, and all of the design bureau's efforts were concentrated on the M-88. One suggested potential improvement was the adoption of a new two-speed supercharger that had been tested in January 1938 on the experimental M-87-2N engine. In parallel, at the end of 1937 an 'M-88, 1938 pattern' was built. This featured the old supercharger type from the M-87 but had a considerable number of minor changes.

Factory testing of the fully-fledged M-88 started on 17 December 1938. This engine combined the new GCS with innovations from the 'pattern of 1938'. On 22 December the engine was presented for State testing for the first time, but it had numerous defects and was not accepted. It suffered from breakdowns of piston pins and connecting rods, and piston burn-through. During refinement the pistons and their pins, the crankshaft, connecting rods and crankcase were strengthened. The pistons were given side ribbing similar to those of Pratt & Whitney engines. The M-88 did not pass joint testing until April 1939, and on 26 April the Soviet Government issued a decree on the type's introduction into series production.

However, the reliability of the new engine still remained poor; it did not pass 100hr State tests until in November 1939. By this time the prototypes had already been installed in a TsKB-30F (DB-3F) long-range bomber, which was being flight tested from May 1939, but the results of the first flights forced the aircraft's developers to reinstall M-87As. In December 1939 they again tried to use M-88s on a DB-3F prototype, but the tests ended after three flights. The plan to start M-88 series production in 1938 was completely disrupted. This paralysed the process of setting up mass production of many new aircraft types, in particular the DB-3F bomber.

The plan for M-88 production for 1939 was less than half-fulfilled. By 1 September only twenty-seven engines (of different versions) had been assembled. Deliveries of M-88s in the first quarter of 1940 supported only 50-60 per cent of the bomber's production, and engine quality was still poor. A considerable number of engines that had passed acceptance at Factory No. 29 were rejected by incoming quality control at the aircraft factories. In the first quarter of 1940 about 100 engines had to be removed after flight testing at aircraft factories.

Development of an improved version of the engine, the M-88A, started in July 1939, and a prototype underwent joint testing from 1 February 1940. Series production of the M-88 continued, but gave rise to numerous complaints from the air force. A range of defects (first of all in the supercharger) and the short service life forced the air force to stop accepting the engines. Series production was resumed only at the end of 1940, after the main shortcomings had been eliminated.

All of these troubles cost Tumanskiy dear. He was frequently scolded by higher authorities, and was finally removed from his post. Later on he worked at A.A. Mikulin's Design Bureau, became one of his deputies, and then replaced Mikulin as chief designer at Factory No. 300 in Moscow.

From autumn 1940 M-88 refinement was headed by the new chief designer of OKB-29, E.V. Urmin, who had earlier worked at the TsIAM. Under his leadership a number of new engine versions (the M-88B and M-88F) were created.

The M-88 formed the basis of an original project for a 'block-type engine' completed at the end of 1939 by G.P. Vodolazhskiy. The project comprised two M-88 engines placed side-by-side and driving a common shaft. A cannon barrel could be positioned inside the hollow shaft.

Urmin led the development of the M-89, the last direct descendant of the Gnome-Rhône 14Kdrs. Its main distinctive feature was a three-speed supercharger designed by Vodolazhskiy in the second half of 1939, originally for use with the M-88A. In March next year the official specification was prepared for the M-89, and on 15 June 1940 the Defence Committee issued a decree ordering that the engine be submitted for State testing by 1 March 1941.

The first five M-89 prototypes were assembled as early as the first quarter of 1941. During refinement its designers managed to increase power considerably by increasing the compression ratio. While the maximum power rating of the M-88A was 1,000hp, the improved M-89 provided 1,500hp. In June 1941 the improved M-89 passed its 50hr factory tests. By that time the factory had already started manufacturing the first batches of the engine. In spite of the factory's evacuation due to the approach of German forces in August 1941, M-89 production continued at a new site in Omsk, and 107 had been assembled by the end of the year. However, the M-89 was insufficiently refined, and it was decided to cease its production in favour of increasing the output of M-88Bs, the main type built at the factory.

The M-89 was the last version the Gnome-Rhône 14K engine created in the Soviet Union. A slightly longer history was enjoyed by the offshoot line, which had no direct French ancestor. This was the range of 18-cylinder engines based on the cylinder-piston group of the M-88. The first estimates for an 18-cylinder engine based on the M-85 had been made as early as April 1936, under the leadership of Nazarov. Later, the proposal for such engine was included in the plan of development work for 1938 as an '18-cylinder engine of Gnome-Rhône 18L type'. In fact, no development was done, possibly because negotiations on acquiring a licence for production of a contemporary 18R engine were being conducted in France from the spring of 1938. Although the negotiations lasted for more than a year, they were unsuccessful. The French company was tardy, and then it was discovered that the engine had not passed official certification testing.

In 1939 the design bureau in Zaporozhye started development of an 18-cylinder M-90 engine to have a maximum output of 1,950hp. The project, which included components from both the M-75 and M-88, was completed in August, and in November the first prototype was put on the test bench. In 1939 five engines were built, and five more were assembled in the following year. Refinement work on the M-90 continued during the war, and about twenty more engines were built. In December 1943 the engine was at last submitted for State testing, but its declared performance was not confirmed. Reliability was quite poor, and work on the M-90 was finally cancelled.

The M-92, included into the plan of development work for 1943, was to be a further development of the M-90. Almost no information about the work on this engine has been found. Another member of the 18-cylinder engine family was the BKM engine (BKM being an abbreviation of *besklapanniy motor*, or valveless engine). This powerplant was to employ sleeve-valve-type gas-distribution similar to that of Bristol engines. The first specification under this designation was prepared as early as May 1935. However, that BKM engine, having a working volume of 10 litres (610cu in), was to have a single-speed GCS and a power rating of 650/700hp. It was most probably to be an M-22 modification. However, the later BKM type, according to a specification of 8 March 1940, had to have a power rating of 1,700/2,000hp, and to be equipped with a two-speed GCS and direct fuel injection. It is not known whether Soviet engineers even to tried to solve such a complex problem as sleeve-type gas-distribution.

In January 1939 a specification for the 27-cylinder M-95 radial engine was prepared. Its development was seriously delayed, and general layout of the engine was finalized only in 1942.

Factory No. 29 was evacuated to Omsk in August 1941, where engine production continued. The first M-88B was assembled there on 7 November 1941, using the parts brought from Zaporozhye. This engine was manufactured in large numbers until the end of the Second World War, and powered the Il-4 (DB-3F) bomber.

From 1943 Factory No. 29, in parallel with the M-88B production, started manufacturing the M-82 (ASh-82) engines designed by A.D. Shvetsov. About a year later the production rate of the latter type surpassed that of the M-88, to which less attention was being paid. In fact, no considerable improvements were introduced into the M-88 design until the end of the war. In May 1944 Urmin was transferred to Moscow as chief designer of OKB-41, which was developing low-powered engines. Urmin was replaced at OKB-29 by V.S. Nitchenko, who dealt only with the ASh-82 and versions based upon it.

The M-89 engine.

Factory No. 29 was not returned to Zaporozhye after the war, but stayed in Omsk together with its design bureau. During German occupation the old factory site was used as aircraft repair shops. When retreating, the Germans removed the equipment and blew up some buildings. After the liberation of the Ukraine, a new Factory No. 478 was set up in Zaporozhye, tasked with restoring M-88B production there, in addition to the engine's production in Omsk. During the first half-year of 1945 Factory No. 478 assembled seventy-two engines from parts brought from Omsk. After the war the factory manufactured motorcycle engines, and arrangements for helicopter-engine production were started in 1946.

Production of the M-88B was ceased at Factory No. 29 in 1946.

M-75

This was a licensed copy of the French Gnome-Rhône 9K Mistral. Two M-75 prototypes were built in 1935. In August that year the engine passed 100hr factory testing. Mass production of the M-75 was planned for 1936, but it was not started.

The M-75 was proposed for installation in an I-16 fighter, but was not used in any aircraft.

Characteristics

9-cylinder radial, four-stroke, air-cooled, geared engine with a single-speed GCS.

Power rating	650/700hp
Bore/stroke	146/165mm (5.75/6.50in)

M-76

This was the boosted version of the M-75, equipped with a supercharger that could be turned off in flight. The engine's development was cancelled at an early stage.

Characteristics

9-cylinder radial, four-stroke, air-cooled, geared engine with a single-speed GCS.

Power rating	700/800hp
Weight	440kg (970lb) (according to the specification)

The M-85 engine.

M-85

A licensed copy of the French Gnome-Rhône 14Kdrs, the M-85 was in production at Factory No. 29 in Zaporozhye from the beginning of 1935. The first engines were built there in June 1935, the first series incorporating some imported components and electric equipment (magneto, carburettor, valves, GCS bearings, exhaust pipes, fuel pump, compressor and plugs). Two prototypes underwent lengthy factory testing in July-August 1935. The engine was submitted for State bench tests on 27 October at the NII VVS, and passed them successfully (at the second attempt) in January 1936. During the tests a power rating of 761/812hp was registered.

Later-series M-85s were partly unified with the M-86; in particular, the strengthened crank mechanism was taken from the latter type. The engine was phased out of production in 1937. In total, 468 engines were built.

The M-85 powered production DB-3 bombers and was used for the following prototypes: I-207, DG-58 (PB, not completed), DG-58R (R-9, not completed), R-9 (LBSh), PS-35 and DI-8. It was planned to use this engine in the projected SB bomber version.

Characteristics

14-cylinder two-row radial, four-stroke, air-cooled, geared engine with a single-speed GCS.

Power rating	720/800hp (with fixed-pitch propeller, 765hp)
Bore/stroke	146/165mm (5.75/6.50in)
Volume	38.68 litres (2,360cu in)
Compression ratio	5.5:1
Weight	600kg (1,323lb)

M-86

A further evolution of the M-85, the M-86 was developed in 1936 at OKB-29 under the leadership of A.S. Nazarov, and differed from the M-85 in having a strengthened crank mechanism, increased ribbing of the cylinder lining, and a strengthened GCS. The M-86 was in series production at Factory No. 29 in 1937-39, 548 being built.

The engine was installed on production DB-3s and prototypes of the ANT-37bis (DB-2B) and R-9 (LBSh).

Characteristics

14-cylinder two-row radial, four-stroke, air-cooled, geared engine with a single-speed GCS.

Power rating	800/950hp
Bore/stroke	146/165mm (5.75/6.50in)
Volume	38.68 litres (2,360cu in)
Compression ratio	5.5:1
Weight	610kg (1,345lb)

M-87

Developed in 1937-38 at OKB-29, this engine was based on the M-86 but differed in having increased ribbing on the cylinder linings, reduced-radius cylinder head inner surfaces (owing to increased compression ratio), pistons with internal ribbing at the bottom, an increased number of piston rings, and a fuel mixture supply to the GCS in the centre inlet (not through the helix). Several versions were in series production at Factory No. 29 in Zaporozhye from 1938 until 1941. The M-87 was also assembled at Factory No. 24 in Moscow. In total, 5,464 M-87s were built. The type was phased out of production in the beginning of 1941.

Characteristics

14-cylinder two-row radial, four-stroke, air-cooled, geared engine with a single-speed GCS.

Power rating	800/950hp
Bore/stroke	146/165mm (5.75/6.50in)
Volume	38.65 litres (2,359cu in)
Compression ratio	6.1:1
Weight	640kg (1,411lb)

The following versions of the engine are known:

M-87 The first series version, developed in 1936-37. In series production from the end of 1937 until April 1938. Power rating 950/950hp, weight 640kg (1,411lb).

M-87A An improved version that was under development from 1937 with the participation of a group of designers from Factory No. 26, under the leadership of V.Ya. Klimov. In series production from October 1938.

M-87B A series version of 1940 with a strengthened crankcase, nitrated cylinder liners, ribs on piston skirts and a new

The PS-35 (ANT-35) airliner prototype, powered by M-85s. Series aircraft of this type had M-62IRs.

An M-87A in a DB-3B bomber, 1939.

An M-87A in the I-28 fighter prototype, 1939.

ABOVE: **Although there was only one prototype of the MTB-2A amphibian, powered by the M-87As, it participated in combat operations conducted by the Black Sea Fleet Air Force during the Second World War.**

RIGHT: **The record-breaking *Rodina* aeroplane, powered by M-86s, was a modification of the DB-2A long-range bomber prototype. Designer P.O. Sukhoi is seen near the aeroplane. The *Rodina*, flown by the female crew of P. Osipenko, V. Grizodubova and M. Raskova, made a non-stop flight from Moscow to the Soviet Far East.**

carburettor. About 1,000 M-87Bs had been manufactured by 1 October 1940.

M-87D A 750hp diesel engine developed at the TsIAM in 1937 under the leadership of P.P. Konyukhov. The prototype was built in 1938 and bench tested. The history of this version is given in the chapter describing diesel engines.

The M-87 engine and its versions powered the following series-production aeroplanes: DB-3, DB-3F (Il-4), BB-1 and GST. These engines were also used in the following aircraft: IS (I-220), DB-LK, R-9 (LBSh), Sh-Tandem (MAI-3), I-180, I-28, MTB-2 (ANT-44bis) and MDR-5 (MS-5).

M-88

A further evolution of the M-87, with a two-speed GCS, the M-88 was being developed from 1937 at OKB-29 as the M-85V. It differed from the M-87 in having a strengthened crankcase, crankshaft and connecting rods, waffle ribbing of the piston bottom, and the installation of an AK-88 carburettor and some other units. The M-88 prototypes were built in 1938 and bench tested. The first direct-drive version was flight-tested in an I-180 fighter prototype starting from 1 December 1938. On 26 April 1939 the M-88 was officially introduced into series production. In November that year the engine passed its State tests. From the end of 1939 the type was in series production at Factory No. 29 in Zaporozhye, but its manufacture was ceased because of numerous defects. In total 204 M-88s were built up to 1 January 1940. In January 1940 the engine was officially adopted into service, and its production resumed, however it did not pass the service testing until October 1940. The engine refinement was headed by E.V. Urmin. The task of arranging M-88 production was also given to Moscow-based Factory No. 24, but no engines of this type were built there.

In August 1941 Factory No. 29 was evacuated to Omsk, where M-88 production had resumed by autumn 1941. During the first half of 1945 Factory No. 478 in Zaporozhye was assembling M-88Bs from

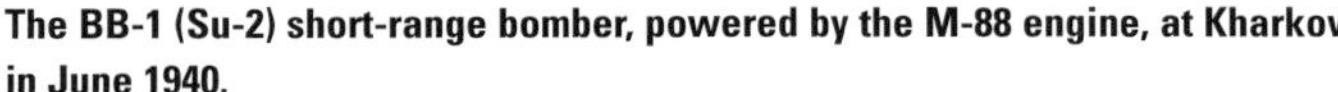

The BB-1 (Su-2) short-range bomber, powered by the M-88 engine, at Kharkov in June 1940.

The M-88s of the first series had poor reliability. This BB-1 was damaged while landing at Podolsk airfield in November 1940 following an engine failure.

the parts brought from the Omsk factory. The type was in production until 1946, 16,087 being built.

Characteristics

14-cylinder two-row radial, four-stroke, air-cooled, geared engine, with a two-speed GCS.

Power rating	1,025/1,225hp (according to the 1938 specification) Actual power rating and weight dependant on version
Bore/stroke	146/165mm (5.75/6.50in)
Volume	38.65 litres (2,359cu in)
Compression ratio	6.1:1

The following versions of the engine are known:

M-88b/r (or **M-88BR**) A direct-drive, right-hand or left-hand rotation 1,000/1,090hp engine (according to the specification 1,000/1,100hp). Weight 660kg (1,455lb) (according to the specification 618kg (1,362lb)). The first prototypes were built in March 1939 and flight-tested in an OKO-6 fighter in December 1939.

M-88 (or **M-88R**) A geared 1,000/1,100hp engine, this version was flight-tested in an OKO-6bis fighter, and series production started in the autumn of 1939. The M-88 passed State tests in November-December 1939. Weight 684kg (1,508lb).

M-88NV A project for an M-88 with direct fuel injection. The engine was being developed at the TsIAM in 1940. Power rating (according to the specification) 1,050/1,150hp.

M-88A A geared 1,100/1,100hp engine (according to the specification 1,000/1,250hp; according to the project 1,100/1,300hp). Weight 650kg (1,433lb) (first prototypes 640kg (1,411lb)). This version was being developed from the summer of 1939, and differed in having a changed GCS gear ratio, increased ribbing area, and a number of strengthened components. It featured a new rear cover for the crankcase, lengthened cylinder sleeves, and strengthened gears. The prototypes underwent bench testing from January 1940. From August 1949 the type was equipped with the AK-88 carburettor. The M-88A was introduced into series production. In 1940 some of the prototypes were boosted by supercharging to 1,200hp, their weight reaching 670kg (1,477lb).

M-88B This version was in production from the second half of 1940, and differed from the M-88A in having increased ribbing of the cylinder heads and sleeves, strengthened connecting rods and pistons, modified drives to the units, an AK-88B carburettor with an economizer, and oil injectors in the crankshaft. Power rating 950/1,100hp, weight 684kg (1,508lb). The engine had improved altitude performance. The M-88B was the most mass-produced version of the M-88; during the war period alone 10,585 were manufactured in Zaporozhye and Omsk.

M-88B-NV A prototype of an M-88B with direct fuel injection, which underwent testing in April 1944.

M-88TK (M-88B with a TK-3 turbo-supercharger) This version was being developed from 1939, and was initially to have a TK-1 turbo-supercharger, later

Maintenance work on BB-1s of the 135th Short-Range Bomber Air Regiment in Kharkov. An uncowled M-88 is clearly visible in the foreground.

replaced by the more advanced TK-3. The prototypes were tested in an Il-4TK aeroplane in March 1943. Power rating (according to the specification) 900/1,100hp.

M-88B with TK-M turbo-supercharger. A projected version.

M-88V A high-altitude version based on the M-88B with a GCS taken from the M-89. Power rating 1,000hp at 7,300m (24,000ft) altitude. To provide crew cabin pressurization an air bleed was arranged from the GCS.

M-88F A 1,250hp version of which a small batch of about twenty engines was manufactured in 1943.

M-88F-NV A version with direct fuel injection. The prototype was tested in January 1944.

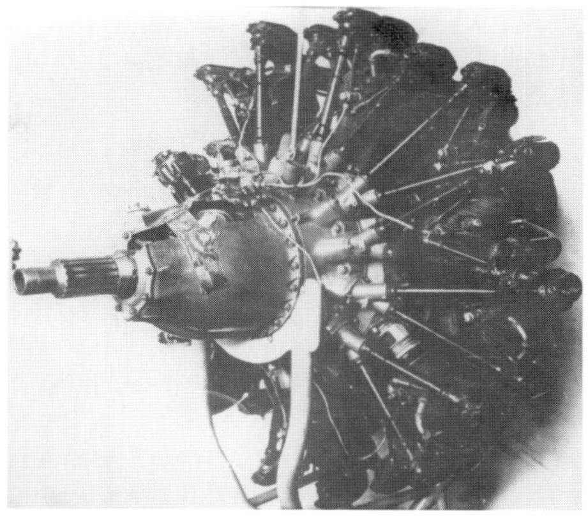

ABOVE: **The M-88B engine.**

RIGHT: **An M-88B in the Monino museum, rear view.**

The M-88 engine and its versions powered the following series-production aeroplanes: Il-4 (DB-3F), Su-2, I-28 and GST. These engines were also used in the following prototypes: Ta-1 (OKO-6), Ta-3 (OKO-6bis), OKO-4 (not completed), I-190, I-180, IS, IS-2 and MDR-7. It was planned to use the M-88 for the projected Il-12, BSB and DB-LK ('150') aircraft.

'Block-type engine' designed by Vodolazhskiy

This engine, designed by G.P. Vodolazhskiy at the end of 1939, consisted of two M-88s installed side-by-side and driving the output shaft through a common gear. A hollow shaft allowed installation of a cannon barrel inside it. The prototype was not built.

Characteristics

28-cylinder (consisting of two two-row radial engines), four-stroke, air-cooled, geared engine with a two-speed GCS.

Power rating	2,000/2,500hp
Bore/stroke	146/165mm (5.75/6.50in)
Volume	77.3 litres (4,717cu in)
Compression ratio	6.1:1
Weight	about 1,200kg (2,650lb)

M-89

The last type in this family engines, this was a further development of the M-88. The M-89 was being developed at OKB-29 in 1939-40, under the leadership of S.K. Tumanskiy, who was later replaced by E.V. Urmin. Compared with the M-88, the M-89 had increased compression ratio and supercharging, and its cylinder heads were modified. According to the engine's development schedule, prototype testing was to start in the first quarter of 1939, but the first bench tests did not start until March 1941. After these tests the engine was subjected to considerable improvements: its compression ratio was further increased, the diameter of supercharger impeller reduced, and the gas-distribution phases changed. At the same time the engines built before the modernization underwent flight testing (from March in a DB-3F bomber, and from May in a Ta-3

An M-88B engine being installed in an Il-4 bomber.

The Il-4TK high-altitude bomber prototype, powered by M-88B engines with turbo-superchargers.

The M-90 engine.

fighter prototype). The engine suffered from cylinder-head overheating, vibration and presence of swarf in the oil.

In the summer of 1941 the M-89 was introduced into series production, but this ceased at the beginning of 1942 due to the engine's low reliability, 107 having been built.

Characteristics

14-cylinder two-row radial, air-cooled, geared engine with a three-speed GCS.

Power rating	1,150/1,400hp (according to the specification)
Bore/stroke	146/165mm (5.75/6.50in)
Volume	35.7 litres (2,179cu in)
Weight	750kg (1,653lb) (according to the specification)

The following versions of the engine are known:

M-89 The first version, built in a small series for testing purposes. Power rating, 1,250/1,300hp, compression ratio 6.4:1, weight 800kg (1,765lb).

M-89 An improved version with a power rating of 1,380/1,550hp, a compression ratio of 7.0:1, and a weight of 815kg (1,797lb).

M-89NV A projected version with direct fuel injection, developed in 1941. The prototype was not built. The project was removed from the plan for 1942, having lost the competition with the M-82NV. Power rating (according to the project) 1,150/1,300hp, weight 760kg (1,676lb).

M-90

This engine was being developed at OKB-29 from the the spring of 1939 under the leadership of S.K. Tumanskiy, who was later replaced by E.V. Urmin. Initially it was a coupled version of the M-75. Later the project used the M-88's cylinder-piston group, but the cylinder ribbing area was increased. Engine layout had been completed by 15 August 1939, and a set of engineering drawings was ready by 15 October. The first M-90 prototype was put on the test bench on 29 November 1939. During that year four more prototypes were built, followed by five more in the next year. The required power rating was not reached, and the engine suffered from breakages of the crankshaft and the pinions of the gas-distribution mechanism, and cracking of a rear cover of the crankcase. Although it was planned to introduce the M-90 into series production in 1941, this was not done. Refinement and the manufacture of new prototypes continued in 1941-43. The M-90 underwent State tests in December 1943, but did not meet the required performance. All work on the type was cancelled at the beginning of 1944. In total more than twenty M-90s were built.

Characteristics

18-cylinder two-row radial, four-stroke, air-cooled, geared engine with a two-speed GCS.

Power rating	1,500/1,950hp (according to the specification), actual 1,550/1,750hp)
Bore/stroke	146/165mm (5.75/6.50in)

M-92

A project of 1943, this was a further evolution of the M-90. The engine was to pass joint tests from December 1943, but a prototype was not built.

Characteristics

18-cylinder two-row radial, four-stroke, air-cooled, geared engine with a two-speed GCS.

Power rating	1,850/2,150hp (according to the specification)
Bore/stroke	146/165mm (5.75/6.50in)

BKM (valveless engine)

A project for an engine featuring a sleeve system for gas-distribution and intended for 'land-based and naval bombers'. It was planned to submit the prototype to State testing in 1942.

Characteristics

18-cylinder two-row radial, four-stroke, air-cooled, geared engine with a two-speed GCS.

Power rating	1,850/2,150hp (1,500/1,650hp according to an earlier specification of July 1940)
Bore/stroke	146/165mm (5.75/6.50in)
Weight	900kg (1,985lb)

M-95

The M-95 was a project of 1942, developed under the specification of January 1939. The cylinder-piston group from the M-88A/B was used.

Characteristics

27-cylinder three-row radial, four-stroke, air-cooled (with forced blowing), geared engine with a single-speed GCS.

Power rating	2,000/3,000hp
Bore/stroke	146/165mm (5.75/6.50in)
Volume	38.65 litres (2,359cu in)
Compression ratio	6.1:1
Weight	1,400kg (3,090lb)

CHAPTER TWENTY-SIX

The Engines of M.A. Kossov, and Other Attempts to Create a Low-powered Engine Based on the M-11

Mass-production of the successful 100hp M-11 gave rise to the idea of creating a unified family of aero-engines based upon it. The first attempt to realize this idea was made at the design bureau of Factory No. 29 in Zaporozhye, where a range of engines was developed in 1930-32 under the leadership of A.S. Nazarov. They were the 3M-11 (3-cylinder), M-51 (5-cylinder), M-48 (7-cylinder), and M-49 (9-cylinder) engines. All of them used parts and units from the production M-11. A young engineer named M.A. Kossov participated in the work on these engines.

Mikhail Aleksandrovich Kossov (1908-92) graduated from Kiev Polytechnic Institute in 1930 and soon proved to be a gifted designer. In 1932-33 a group of specialists working on the development of low-powered engines was transferred from Zaporozhye to Moscow, to the Department of Light Fuel Engines of the NII AD GVF. The department was accommodated in the quarters of the Airship-Building Training Centre in Tushino, Moscow region (now within the precincts of the city), and Kossov was appointed its head. All documentation on the M-48, M-49 and M-51 was transferred to the NII AD GVF.

Using these powerplants as a basis, the department developed a series of engines that retained many parts and units of the M-11, but differed in having supercharging and a more advanced drive for the gas-distribution system. The engine designations were also changed. The M-51 became MG-11, the M-48 turned into the MG-21, and the M-49 was redesignated MG-31. In the course of these engines' development, the engineers increased the level of their commonality, these three types having up to 90 per cent of their parts in common. The gas-distribution mechanisms were changed, certain parts were strengthened, and indigenous carburettors replaced the imported units. The engines now operated using mineral oil, not castor oil as before. The 'MG' prefix in the designation denoted 'civil engine' (*Motor Grazhdanskiy*), and all of the engines developed at the NII AD GVF had this prefix in their designations.

The MG-11, MG-21 and MG-31 were built and underwent ground- and flight-testing. In course of refinement their design was gradually changed, thus moving away from the original M-11. The MG-31 proved to be the most successful, and entered series production. In 1936-38 it was built by Factory No. 82 in Tushino, which from 1936 was considered to be the experimental factory belonging to the department. During that same year the Department of Light Fuel Engines was transferred to the site of Factory No. 82, which also built prototypes of other engines developed at the NII AD GVF. The MG-31 was successfully used on aeroplanes and helicopters into the early post-war years.

In 1933 a project for an MG-50 was

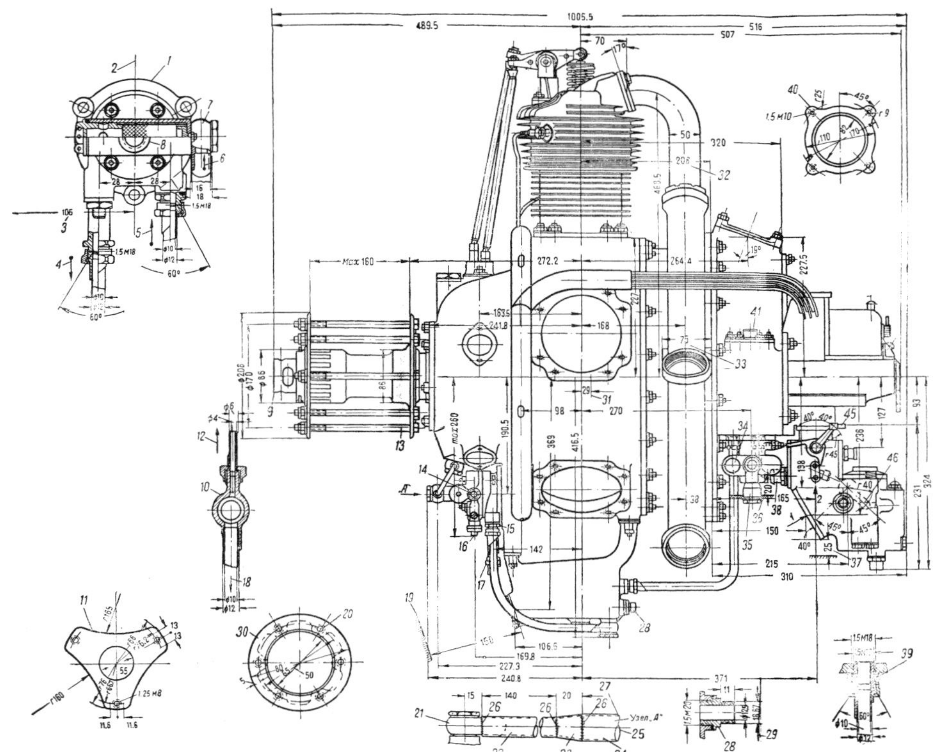

A drawing of the MG-11 engine.

A Stal-2 passenger aeroplane powered by an MG-31.

The M-13 before State testing, 1948.

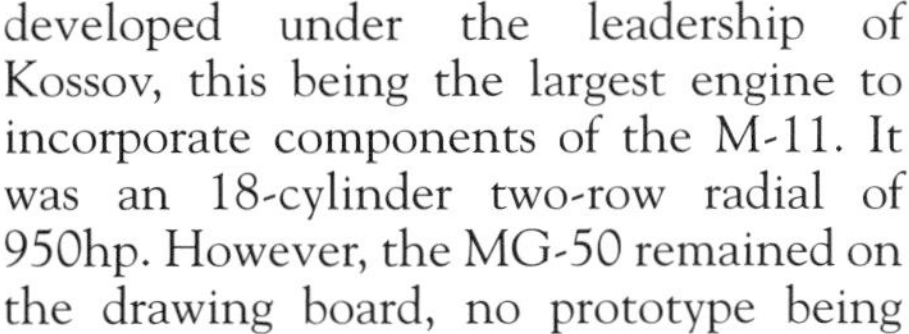

developed under the leadership of Kossov, this being the largest engine to incorporate components of the M-11. It was an 18-cylinder two-row radial of 950hp. However, the MG-50 remained on the drawing board, no prototype being built.

Kossov did not confine himself to radial-engine development. From 1933 his department was carrying out development work on a 4-cylinder in-line, inverted engine designated MG-40. It was to be the Soviet counterpart of the de Havilland Gipsy Minor engine, which had been chosen as a pattern. A sample of the British engine was purchased, transported to the USSR and underwent extensive examination. The MG-40 retained the main design features of the Gipsy Minor, but was not a direct copy. The cylinders of the Soviet engine were of completely different design and were fitted with twisted heads, which are rarely used on in-line engines.

Work on the MG engine family continued until the second half of 1938, when Factory No. 82 was placed under NKVD supervision. A design bureau was set up at the factory, its staff consisting of imprisoned engineers. After such a transition the GVF retained only its repair capabilities, the factories that had been manufacturing aircraft and engines for the Civil Air Fleet being transferred to the NKOP. Kossov, together with a group of designers, moved to Factory No. 16 at Voronezh, which had been tasked with introducing the MG-31 into series production. In Voronezh Kossov not only worked on refining the MG-31, but also participated in adapting the Renault engines for series production in the USSR.

However, in 1940 Factory No. 16 was switched to production of the M-105, and M-11 manufacture was transferred to a new Factory No. 154 in the same town. Kossov worked there, and in October 1941 Factory No. 154 was evacuated to Andizhan, Central Asia, where it was accommodated in former cotton warehouses. In 1942 Kossov developed the 5-cylinder M-12 engine, a further evolution of the MG-11, and in 1943 he created the M-13, a combination of components from the M-11D, M-11FM and MG-31F. Prototypes of both engines were built and underwent factory testing. In 1943 the M-12 was flight-tested in a U-2 biplane.

In May 1944 most of the design staff was moved from Factory No. 154 to Factory No. 41 in Moscow, where E.V. Urmin was appointed chief designer of the OKB-41 design bureau. At the end of 1944 and beginning of 1945 Urmin, who did not agree with Kossov's concept of the engine's development, created his own variants of the M-12 and M-13. Compared with Kossov's designs, Urmin's engines used more components from the series M-11D. Later, some units of Kossov's M-12 were used in the M-11FR engine. Urmin's M-12 was being refined until the middle of 1946, when it was cancelled. His M-13 suffered the same fate.

In 1947 another M-13 of lower power rating (250hp) was developed at Factory No. 41. At that time OKB-41 was headed by I.A. Muzhilov. This M-13, created by designer Aksyutin, passed its State tests in June 1948. However, it is not known whether M-11 parts and units were used in this engine. By that time the M-11 had been repeatedly modified and had become obsolete (it was created as early as 1928), though it was still in series production. Development of a new engine based on the M-11 seemed inexpedient, and a new unified family of low- and medium-powered engines was being prepared that had nothing in common with the M-11.

Already, in 1945, Kossov had moved to OKB-300, headed by A.A. Mikulin, where he participated in the creation of the first Soviet turbojet engines. In 1949 he headed a division at the NAMI that was working on the development of gas turbine engines for automobiles. The NAMI-053 and NAMI-053A became the first Soviet automobile gas turbine engines, and were tested on a ZIL-127G bus and KrAZ-214G truck. Kossov continued his association with these engines, gave lectures at the Air Force Academy and the Moscow Automobile and Road Institute (*Moskovskiy Avtomobilno-Dorozhniy Institut*, MADI), and then worked at the Institute of Theoretical Engineering of the USSR Academy of Sciences.

MG-11

This was a low-powered engine based on the M-51 and equipped with a GCS. The MG-11 was created at the Department of Light Fuel Engines of the NII AD GVF, under the leadership of M.A. Kossov. It differed from the M-11 in the drive of its gas-distribution system, the design of its valves and cylinder heads, and in having a single-speed GCS. On some engines the standard K-11 carburettor was replaced by an imported Zenith DCL42. Several MG-11 prototypes were built and underwent bench testing. In course of refinement the new engine retained progressively fewer original M-11 parts. In 1935 the MG-11 was tested in a U-2 aeroplane. A version of the MG-11 fitted with a Rut-type supercharger was being developed at the UNIADI. In total, Factory No. 82 manufactured thirteen MG-11s.

Characteristics

5-cylinder radial, air-cooled, four-stroke, direct-drive engine with a single-stage single-speed GCS.

Power rating	150/180hp
Bore/stroke	125/140mm (4.92/5.51in)
Volume	8.6 litres (525cu in)
Compression ratio	5.0:1
Weight	175kg (386lb) (excluding pneumatic self-starter, fuel pump and propeller hub)

The following versions of the engine are known:

MG-11 A basic version developed in 1934-35.

MG-11A An improved version developed in 1936. The characteristics of this version have not been found.

MG-11N A version of 1936 with direct fuel injection.

MG-11F A boosted version developed in 1937, nominal power rating 165hp. There was a variant of this version with a special carburettor for inverted flight.

MG-11FN A version of the MG-11F with direct fuel injection.

MG-11 engines powered the following prototypes: U-2, U-5bis (small batch), NV-2bis, NV-6 (UTI-6) and MU-4.

MG-21

This type was unified with the 7-cylinder MG-11. It was being developed from 1933, under the leadership of M.A. Kossov, at the Department of Light Fuel Engines of the NII AD GVF, and was a further evolution of the M-48. Compared with the M-48 the MG-11 had a higher level of commonality with other types in this family, its gas-distribution mechanism was modified, and a strengthened crankshaft was introduced (similar to the one fitted to the M-49). The transmissions to the GCS and pistons were also strengthened, and the cup-type seal on the crankshaft nose was improved. The engine was provided with a K-17 carburettor from the M-17, and had a supercharger similar to that used on the MG-11 but with boosted rpm (owing to change in the drive-gear ratio). The first MG-21 prototypes were built in 1934 and underwent bench testing and refinement in 1934-35. The MG-21 successfully passed its State tests in August 1935. Flight-tests of the engine were performed in the KAI-2 aeroplane in 1937. In the following year a SAM-5-2bis powered by the MG-21 established an altitude record.

The MG-21 was not put into series production. Three prototypes were built at Factory No. 82.

Two versions of the engine are known:

MG-21 A version developed in 1934.

MG-21A A version developed in 1936. Power rating 210/250hp.

The MG-21s powered prototypes of the KAI-2 and SAM-5-2bis aeroplanes.

Characteristics

7-cylinder radial, air-cooled, four-stroke, direct-drive engine with a single-stage single-speed GCS.

Power rating	200/220hp
Bore/stroke	125/140mm (4.92/5.51in)
Volume	12.05 litres (735cu in)
Compression ratio	5.0:1
Weight	214kg (472lb) (excluding pneumatic self-starter, fuel pump and propeller hub)

MG-31

The most powerful of all the engines of the MG family that were built, the MG-31 was unified with the MG-11 and MG-21. It was being developed from 1933, under the leadership of M.A. Kossov, at the Department of Light Fuel Engines of the NII AD GVF, and was a further evolution of the M-49. Compared with that engine, the MG-31 had greater commonality with other types in this family. It had a strengthened front part of the crankcase, a new gas-distribution mechanism, and deflectors. The pistons and the transmission to the GCS were also strengthened. The engine had a K-17 carburettor with a bored-out diffuser, and the early-series engines were also fitted with the imported Zenith 60DCL carburettor.

The first prototypes were built in 1934, factory testing being carried out in the

The U-5 training airplane, powered by the MG-11F.

An MG-21 during testing at the NII GVF.

ABOVE: **The MG-31 engine.**

RIGHT: **The MG-31F engine.**

same year. In December 1934 the MG-31 was submitted for State testing for the first time, but failed owing to cracks in the crankcase, unscrewing of cylinder heads and breakage of a pinion in the gas-distribution drive. From February 1935 more than seventy changes were introduced into the design. Various components were modified, including the crankcase, gas-distribution system, the accessory drive unit, and the pistons and cylinders. These changes were followed by two stages of factory testing; 130hr and 150hr. In February 1935 State tests were again carried out, but the engine's cylinder heads began to unscrew. Not until 1936 did the MG-31 successfully pass its State tests. In January-February 1937 the engine was test flown in a Stal-2 aeroplane.

An MG-31 in the Stal-2.

From 1936 the MG-31 was in series production at Factory No. 82, and from the end of 1937 it was replaced by the improved MG-31F version. In total, 129 engines of this type were built. Production ceased due to the enterprise coming under NKVD supervision. According to a decree of July 1939, Factory No. 16 in Voronezh was to introduce the MG-31 into series production. It was planned to build the first batch of ten engines by the end of the year, but not one MG-31 was assembled in Voronezh. After the war's end it was planned to resume MG-31 manufacture at one of the factories, but the idea was abandoned. The MG-31F remained in service until the end of 1946.

Characteristics

9-cylinder radial, air-cooled, four-stroke, direct-drive engine with a single-stage single-speed GCS.

Bore/stroke	125/140mm (4.92/5.51in)
Volume	15.5 litres (946cu in)
Compression ratio	5.0:1
Power rating	dependant on version
Weight	dependant on version

The following versions of the engine are known:

MG-31 The basic version, in series production from 1936. Power rating 270/320hp (according to test results, 270/310hp), weight 247kg (544lb).

MG-31A A prototype of an improved engine developed in 1936.

MG-31N A prototype engine with direct injection.

MG-31F A boosted version. It passed factory testing in 1937, and in the same year was introduced into series production. The engine had strengthened pistons and connecting rods, an improved oil system, and was equipped with synchronization. Power rating 270/335hp, weight 250kg (551lb) (according to some sources 255kg (562lb)).

MG-31FN A prototype engine with direct fuel injection, developed in 1937 and based on the MG-31F.

MG-31F2 A prototype that underwent factory testing. No further details of this version have been found.

The MG-31s powered series-production Stal-2 aeroplanes, and were installed in the following prototypes: UTI-5 (NV-2bis), U-5 (LSh), MA-1, Sh-7, LIG-8, DKL, RAF-11, RAF-11bis, P-3 (LIG-5), SKh-1 (LIG-10) and SAM-16 (not completed); and the *Omega-II* (2MG)

ABOVE: **A side view of an MG-31 in a helicopter prototype.**

RIGHT: **An MG-31 in a helicopter prototype, front view.**

helicopter. Use of this engine was also planned for the projected MBR-6 and UT-3 aeroplanes.

MG-40

The only non-radial engine of the MG family, this was being developed from 1933 under the leadership of M.A. Kossov at the Department of Light Fuel Engines of the NII AD GVF. The MG-40 was to be a Soviet counterpart of de Havilland Gipsy Minor. Soviet designers used the general layout and connecting-rod and piston design of the British engine, but the cylinders and cylinder heads, crankcase, and engine accessory positioning and drives were different. In 1936 several prototypes were built and underwent bench and flight testing. In 1937 the MG-40 was tested in an NV-5 aeroplane. The engine was not introduced into series production.

The MG-40 powered a prototype of the NV-5. It was also to power the projected G-26 aeroplane.

Characteristics

4-cylinder in-line, inverted, air-cooled, four-stroke, direct-drive unsupercharged engine.

Power rating	145hp
Bore/stroke	120/140mm (4.72/5.51in)
Volume	6.33 litres (386cu in)
Compression ratio	6.35:1
	(first prototype 5.2:1)
Weight	155kg (342lb)

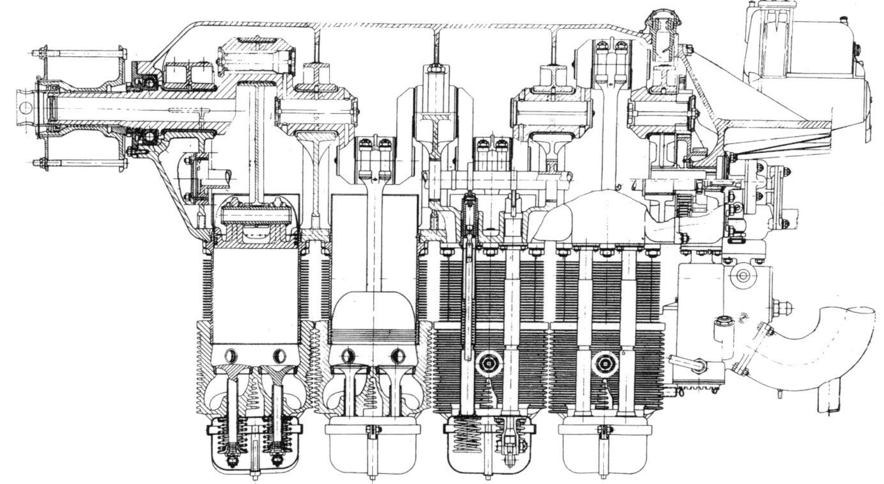

A drawing of the MG-40.

MG-50

The MG-50 was being developed from February 1933 under the leadership of M.A. Kossov at the Department of Light Fuel Engines of the NII AD GVF. It was to have the highest power rating of all engines of the MG family, but it did not reach the stage of prototype manufacture.

This engine was to be used in an ANT-14 aeroplane.

Characteristics

18-cylinder two-row, radial, air-cooled, four-stroke, geared engine.

Power rating	800/950hp
Bore/stroke	125/140mm (4.92/5.51in)
Volume	31.0 litres (1,891cu in)

M-12

The engine was being developed as a project in 1942, under the leadership of M.A. Kossov at the design bureau of Factory No. 154 in Andizhan. The M-12 included some components and units of series-production M-11Ds and MG-11s. Compared with the M-11, the new engine was considerably boosted in rpm and compression ratio. In 1942 two prototypes were built: one had cylinder heads of the M-11 type, and the other had cylinder heads resembling those of the American Wright Cyclone. Both prototypes underwent factory testing from September 1942. At the beginning of 1943 it was planned to put the M-12 through a 100hr joint test, but this did not take place. Refinement continued throughout 1943, and during that year the M-12 was tested in a U-2 biplane. In March 1944 the engine underwent State testing on the bench, but these were stopped after 30hr of operation when the engine failed.

In total, six or seven prototypes were built, including two engines assembled in July 1944 at Factory No. 41 in Moscow. The parts and components for these were brought from Andizhan. The work on Kossov's M-12 continued until the autumn of 1944. Later, the units of this engine were combined with a cylinder group from the M-11D to create the M-11FR.

The M-12 powered several U-2 and UT-1 aeroplanes.

Characteristics

5-cylinder radial, air-cooled, four-stroke, direct-drive unsupercharged engine.

Power rating	190/200hp
Bore/stroke	125/140mm (4.92/5.51in)
Volume	8.6 litres (525cu in)
Compression ratio	6.2:1
Weight	215kg (474lb) (with M-11 cylinder heads)
Weight	165-170kg (364-375lb) (according to the specification)

M-12 (M-11Ya)

The M-11Ya project was created under the leadership of E.V. Urmin in 1945 at the design bureau of Factory No. 41 in Moscow. Later, the engine was redesignated M-12. The prototype was assembled at the end of 1945 and underwent testing from January 1946, but the results were unsatisfactory: the pistons stuck, oil leaked, bearings broke and the cylinder heads overheated due to insufficient ribbing.

Characteristics

5-cylinder radial, air-cooled, four-stroke, direct-drive unsupercharged engine.

Bore/stroke	125/140mm (4.92/5.51in)
Volume	8.6 litres (525cu in)

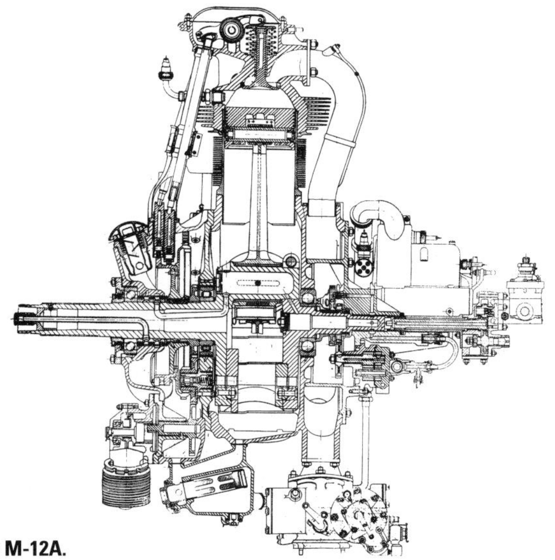

A cross-section of the M-12A.

M-13 (M-13K)

In September 1944 M.A. Kossov proposed a project for an M-13K, to be assembled from parts of the M-11D (pistons), M-11FM (cylinders) and MG-31F (master connecting rod and cam). The crankshaft was redesigned. The M-13K had a GCS similar to the MG-31F type.

No information about completion of the prototype has been found.

Characteristics

9-cylinder radial, air-cooled, four-stroke, direct-drive engine with a single-stage single-speed GCS.

Power rating	300hp
Bore/stroke	125/140mm (4.92/5.51in)

M-13

This engine was created under the leadership of E.V. Urmin at the end of 1944 in the design bureau of Factory No. 41, in parallel with Kossov's M-13K and to the same specification. It mated the cylinders from the M-11D with a new crankcase, master connecting rod and crankshaft, and was equipped with a GCS.

No information regarding completion of the M-13 prototype has been found.

Characteristics

9-cylinder radial, air-cooled, four-stroke, direct-drive engine with a single-stage single-speed GCS.

Power rating	300hp
Bore/stroke	125/140mm (4.92/5.51in)

M-13

This engine was created under the leadership of I.A. Muzhilov at OKB-41 in 1946, and the leading designer on the engine's development was Aksyutin. In June 1947, five months ahead of schedule, the M-13 successfully passed its joint tests, and in June 1948 it passed its State tests, but it was not put into series production.

No information regarding flight testing of the M-13 has been found.

Characteristics

7-cylinder radial, air-cooled, four-stroke, direct-drive unsupercharged engine.

Power rating	210/250hp

CHAPTER TWENTY-SEVEN

Voronezh-built Renault Engines

On 11 January 1936 I.V. Stalin and People's Commissar of Defence K.E. Voroshilov instructed the head of the UVVS, Ya.I. Alksnis, and the head of the NKOP First Chief Directorate, M.M. Kaganovich, to prepare a draft of an STO decree on acquiring a licence and technical support for arranging series production of a family of in-line air-cooled aero-engines. This draft had been provided by 17 January. The possibility of purchasing de Havilland (Gipsy series), Renault or Walter engines was considered. Each of these families included 4-cylinder, 6-cylinder and 12-cylinder engines. A sum of 500,000 roubles in hard currency was allocated for the purchase of specimen engines, licences, technical documentation and sets of the most complex parts and units.

A commission headed by I.E. Maryamov, the director of Factory No. 24, visited Great Britain, France and Czechoslovakia, and as a result, the French engine family was chosen. On 16 October 1936 the Soviet representatives signed an agreement with the Renault company and with its affiliate, the Caudron aircraft company. According to the agreement the Soviet Union was licensed to produce six aircraft types and the three aero-engine types that powered them. The document also stipulated a transfer of engineering drawings, parts lists, technical descriptions, specimens of aeroplanes and engines, and the supply of sets of the most complex engine parts and units. Soviet engineers were to be trained at Renault factories.

Initially, production of Renault engines was planned to be set up at Factory No. 24 in Moscow, but then Factory No. 16 in Voronezh was chosen instead. At that time the factory was producing M-11s. On 14 February 1937 the first group of Soviet engineers, headed by Engineer Miroshnikov, left Voronezh for Paris to carry out acceptance of the documentation. The factory was to set up production of the 4-cylinder Renault 4Pei, 6-cylinder Renault 6Q03 and 12-cylinder Renault 12O01. These were in-line, air-cooled engines having considerable commonality. The agreement stipulated the provision of technical assistance by the French side up to 1939.

At that time the chief designer at Factory No. 16 was A.S. Nazarov, who had been transferred from Zaporozhye. Under his leadership the factory's engineering department started to work on the documentation that had been brought from France. However, in the second half of 1937 a wave of repressions fell on the management of the factory. Almost all of the factory's leaders, including its director and chief designer, were denounced as saboteurs and arrested. One of the preferred charges was frustration of the planned schedule for introducing the Renault engines into series production. The repressions, which considerably reduced the number of highly-qualified specialists at the factory, greatly worsened the situation. S.D. Kolosov was appointed new leader of the factory's engineering department.

The work of the engineering department included adapting the French engineering documentation to Soviet standards, recalculating the strengths of parts and units in accordance with Soviet standards, and also developing production methods applicable to the available factory equipment, materials and tooling. In addition, some changes were introduced into the engine designs to achieve a higher level of commonality. The Renault 4P was designated MV-4 in the USSR, the 6Q became the MV-6 and the 12O the MV-12. There are two possible interpretations of the 'MV' prefix: *Motor Vozdushniy* (air-cooled engine) or *Motor Voronezhskiy* (Voronezh-built engine). It is difficult to say which is correct, and it could even be that both are wrong.

Engineering documentation, specimen engines and purchased parts and units gradually arrived during the course of 1937-38. Introduction of the MV-6 was

The MV-4 engine.

An MV-6 in the *Omega* helicopter prototype.

The MV-4 was experimentally mounted in a UT-2, replacing its standard M-11G.

proceeding apace, but work on the MV-4 slowed down, and the designers almost reached deadlock with the MV-12. Initially, its prototype was the 450hp Renault 12O01, and the Voronezh factory had prepared drawings of this type by October 1938. However, by that time Renault had ceased production of the 12O01, which had been replaced by the 500hp 12R01. The Soviets therefore decided to purchase a specimen of the more up-to-date variant. However, while the order was being arranged the Renault 12R01 also was phased out of production and replaced by a modified 12R03 version.

In the second half of 1939 the French sold the USSR a sample of the Renault 12R03, which was to become the prototype of the more-powerful MV-12F.

In fact, only the MV-4 and MV-6 entered series production at Voronezh. The first Soviet-assembled engines were completed in the autumn of 1938. They included a large percentage of French-built parts and units, such as all crankcase casting, suction inlets, fuel pumps and compressors. Magnetos and spark plugs were also supplied from France.

According to the plan, the factory was to manufacture a hundred MV-6s, forty-five MV-4s and ten MV-12s in 1938, but there was a year's delay. By March 1939 Factory No. 16 was ready for mass-production of the MV-4 and MV-6, and by the end of the year about 200 MV-4s and a smaller number of MV-6s had been built. They were virtually entirely Soviet-built, the only exception being the French magnetos of the MV-6. Deliveries of the MV-4 were impeded by the lack of carburettors, the supply of which was delayed by the manufacturer.

It was planned to carry out an extensive modernization programme at a later stage, to equip the engines with a two-speed GCS, a turbo-supercharger and gearing. Special attention was paid to the MV-12, which was intended to be installed in light fighters, and to be fitted with synchronization and cannon. It was also suggested that a 24-cylinder engine based on coupled MV-12s might be created.

In fact the MV-12 was not introduced into production in the USSR, and it is even doubtful that any such engine was assembled from French-built parts. Two improved versions of the engine were under development; the MV-12R (later redesignated M-12R) and the MV-12F. No information about completion of the engine prototypes has been found.

The MV-4 was just slightly improved in the USSR in course of its production, and an MV-6A version of the MV-6 was developed and introduced into series production.

The MV-4 was not widely used in Soviet aviation, and the MV-6 was installed in only one production aircraft, the Yakovlev UT-3 trainer. The French engines proved to be troublesome in service. In particular, serious problems were encountered with engine starting, not only in freezing cold but also in relatively warm weather (by Russian standards) at about five degrees above zero. During service testing in hot summer in the Volga region the MV-6 overheated repeatedly.

At the end of 1939 Factory No. 16 was tasked with building the M-105. Manufacture of the MV-4 and MV-6 effectively ceased, though assembly of both types continued in small quantities, using the available stock of parts. The last MV-4s were manufactured in 1940, and the last MV-6s in 1941.

In the autumn of 1941 the stock of unused MV-4s was evacuated to Kazan together with Factory No. 16. The fate of these engines is unknown; they were probably scrapped.

MV-4

This was a licensed copy of the French Renault 4Pei Bengali. Compared with the French prototype, the Voronezh-built MV-4 had a crankshaft with shortened crank pins (similar to that of the MV-6), and the connecting rods and cowling attachment brackets were also taken from the MV-6. The French carburettor was replaced by a Soviet KV-4 type. Engineering drawings were issued by May 1938, followed by the start of engine component manufacture. In July five engines were on the assembly line, as permitted by temporary production technology. The first two MV-4s were completed by Factory No. 16 in September 1938, using a large proportion of imported parts and units. In October one engine began to go through the factory test programme. State testing of the MV-4 took place in November-December 1938; the engine with a French-built crankcase, magnetos and spark-plugs being used. The MV-4 was test flown in a UT-2 aeroplane during May-June and August-October 1939. During flight-testing heavy vibration was observed throughout a wide range of the flight envelope, and difficulties were experienced in starting the engine in low ambient temperatures.

The MV-4 was introduced into series production in March 1939. By September 160 had been built, and by the middle of December more than 180. However, due to the lack of KV-4 carburettors the assembled engines were held in storage at the factory. From November 1939 to July 1940 the MV-4 was tested on a SAM-14 aeroplane.

Production of the MV-4 ceased at the end of 1939. At the beginning of the following year the last six engines of this type were assembled.

In 1939 work on equipping the MV-4 with a GS-16 cartridge starter was carried out. Use of the GS-16 (instead of the pneumatic self-starter) lightened the engine by 12kg (26lb) and simplified starting at low ambient temperatures.

The MV-4 was installed the SAM-14 and UT-2 prototypes.

Characteristics

4-cylinder in-line inverted, four-stroke, air-cooled, direct-drive unsupercharged engine.

Power rating	140/152hp
Bore/stroke	120/140mm (4.72/5.51in)
Volume	6.33 litres (386cu in)
Compression ratio	5.75:1
Weight	147kg (324lb) (without generator)

MV-6

This was a licensed copy of the Renault 6Q03. The preliminary review of the engineering drawings received from the French company was completed in Voronezh in October 1937, and the final review had been done by February 1938. In March the factory issued the drawings of the engine subassemblies. By January 1939 the production technology of most engine parts had been refined, the drawings of all tooling issued, and even about three-quarters of the necessary production fixtures had been manufactured. This work was followed by the manufacturing of engine parts. In general the MV-6 was similar to the French sample, but had a modified fuel mixture supply to cylinders and different exhaust valves. The individual conductor screening was replaced by collective

ABOVE LEFT: **The MV-4 in the Russian Air Force Museum at Monino is incorrectly positioned, with its valves facing upwards.**

ABOVE RIGHT: **An MV-6 in the Monino museum.**

RIGHT: **The *Omega* helicopter, powered by two MV-6 engines.**

screening, and a breather similar to the one used on the MV-4 was installed. Testing of the French engine, with some original parts replaced by Soviet-built units, started in May-June 1938. By the middle of October three engines had been assembled. The MV-6 underwent factory testing five times between September 1938 and February 1939, but failed every time; valves and pistons burnt though, and the piston pins broke. In February-March 1939 the engine passed the 100hr threshold for the first time while running on the factory test bench, and in March-April the MV-6 passed its State tests. On 27 April 1939 the engine was officially approved for introduction into air force service.

The MV-6 was in series production at Factory No. 16 in Voronezh from 1939. The first-series batches used a large proportion of imported parts, later replaced by indigenous ones. However, all MV-6s had French magnetos. In September-October 1940 the engine was flight tested in a SAM-11bis aeroplane.

Series production of the MV-6 ceased at the end of 1939, but a number were subsequently assembled using the available reserve of components. Nine were built in 1940, and eight in 1941.

Characteristics

6-cylinder in-line inverted, four-stroke, air-cooled, direct-drive unsupercharged engine.

Power rating	250/270hp
Bore/stroke	120/140mm (4.72/5.51in)
Volume	9.5 litres (579cu in)
Compression ratio	6.2:1
Weight	235kg (518lb) (according to some sources 250kg (551lb))

The following versions of the engine are known:

MV-6 The first series version, in production from the beginning of 1939.

MV-6A A version with increased area of cylinder-head ribbing and a GS-16 cartridge starter. In series production from the second half of 1939.

MV-6 with a two-speed GCS. A project of 1938-39. Power rating 225/275hp. The prototype was not built.

MV-6 with a two-speed GCS and a turbo-supercharger. A project of 1938-39. Power rating 230/300hp. The prototype was not built.

The MV-6 and MV-6A powered a small batch of UT-3 aeroplanes, and prototypes of the following aircraft: SAM-10bis, Ya-19, SAM-11bis, G-28 *Krechet* (Merlin), BICh-21 (SG-1), UK-1B (not completed), OKA-38 (Soviet copy of the German Fieseler Fi 156 *Storch*), plus the *Omega* (2MG) helicopter.

These engines were also specified for the following projected aircraft: the MU-5, SAM-12 and Sh-7 aeroplanes, Gotselyuk's aeroplane, Belyaev's variable-wing aeroplane, the Soviet copy of the Caudron C.690 that was being created at the Dubrovin Design Bureau, and the AKS autogyro.

MV-12

The MV-12 was a licensed copy of the Renault 12O01. Preparation for series production was begun at Factory No. 16 in Voronezh, but it was not started.

Characteristics

12-cylinder inverted-V-shaped, in-line inverted, four-stroke, air-cooled, direct-drive engine with a single-speed GCS.

Power rating	390/450hp
Bore/stroke	114/122mm (4.49/4.80in)
Volume	14.93 litres (911cu in)
Compression ratio	6.2:1 (according to some sources 6.4:1)
Weight	350kg (772lb) (according to some sources 419kg (924lb))

The following versions of the engine are known:

MV-12 A Soviet copy of the Renault 12O01.

MV-12F A project of 1939-40, based on the Renault 12R01 or 12R03 without a GCS, with synchronization and a pneumatic self-starter. Power rating 440/500hp, estimated weight 405-420kg (893-926lb).

MV-12R (M-12R) A project for a geared engine, 1939-40. Testing was planned for the fourth quarter of 1940, but the prototype was not built.

Characteristics

Power rating	700/750hp
Bore/stroke	120/140mm (4.72/5.51in)
Volume	19 litres (1,159cu in)
Weight	460kg (1,014lb) (according to the specification)

MV-12 geared, with a two-speed GCS and a cannon installation. An unrealized project of 1938-39. Power rating 500/600hp.

MV-12 geared, with a two-speed GCS, turbo-supercharger and cannon installation. An unrealized project of 1938-39. Power rating 500/650hp.

The MV-12 was intended for the Soviet copy of the Caudron C.713 fighter-trainer that was being developed by the Dubrovin Design Bureau.

An MV-6A installed in the UT-3M bomber trainer prototype.

CHAPTER TWENTY-EIGHT

The Last Piston Engines Developed at the TsIAM

In the second half of the 1930s, after a range of strong design bureaux had been established at the engine factories, the role of the TsIAM in the practical development of new aero-engines was considerably weakened. The institute focused its efforts on scientific research, prospective analysis and the development of important engine components such as superchargers. However, until the beginning of the Second World War several TsIAM divisions continued working on new aero-engines. Engineers at the institute created a family of AN-1 diesel engines that were then refined and prepared for series production by other enterprises, copied the German Junkers Jumo 205 diesel engine using specimens captured in Spain, and worked on refinement and further development of the M-56 radial engine (the MGM engine).

During the pre-war years the TsIAM was involved in three noteworthy projects. The first was an SM engine designed by E.V. Urmin, which was actually an inverted AN-1R diesel. This remained on the drawing board. However, two other types were built and underwent bench testing.

Using the experimental MF-1 powerplant as a basis, the TsAGI created the M-200 two-stroke, which at 700hp had a rather high power rating for such an engine. The M-200 had opposed pistons (two pistons in each cylinder) and two crankshafts driving common gearing. Although this layout was borrowed from the Germans, in contrast to the Junkers designs it was not a diesel engine.

The M-300, which was being developed under the leadership of A.A. Bessonov, who moved to the TsIAM in 1934, was of similar layout to the M-250 engine of G.S. Skubachevskiy and V.A. Dobrynin, being a radial having cylinder blocks. However, the M-300 was larger than the M-250, with thirty-six cylinders instead of twenty-four, and therefore had a considerably higher power rating of up to 3,500hp.

By the beginning of the war the M-200 and M-300 prototypes had been built and testing had begun. In October 1941, as German troops approached Moscow, the TsIAM was evacuated to Ufa. The institute's workshops, which remained in Moscow, were converted to repair engines brought from the Front. Development work on the M-200 and M-300 was not continued at Ufa, and at the beginning of 1942 they were officially excluded from the plan of experimental work. This was the last time that the TsIAM was involved in the development of aero-engines, and subsequently it carried out only scientific research.

SM

In August 1939 the NKAP received for consideration the SM engine project developed at the TsIAM OKB-5 design bureau, under the leadership of E.V. Urmin. This was an inverted version of the AN-1R diesel, converted to use light fuel and featuring the installation of a cannon in the cylinder vee, firing through a hollow shaft of the engine gearing. The SM prototype was not built.

Characteristics

12-cylinder in-line inverted-vee, four-stroke, watercooled, geared engine with a single-stage, single-speed GCS.

Power rating	1,750/2,000hp
Bore/stroke	180/200mm (7.08/7.87in) (209.95mm (8.27in) in cylinders with articulated connecting rods)
Volume	62.0 litres (3,783cu in)
Weight	950kg (2,094lb) (estimated)

Two versions of the engine are known

SM The standard version.

SM, coupled version. A tandem installation of two SMs, with the shaft of the rear engine running though the hollow shaft of the front engine. The engines drove contrarotating propellers through these

The M-300 with wooden mock-up gearing.

coaxial shafts. Total power rating of the powerplant was estimated at 3,500/4,000hp.

M-200

At first, this engine was introduced into the plan of 1931 merely as 'Fomin's engine', as the concept was developed by V.N. Fomin. It was a two-stroke engine with opposed pistons and gas-distribution of a port-slot type. The engine's layout was similar to that of Junkers diesels, but the M-200 ran on light fuel (with direct injection) and had spark-plug ignition.

Development of the engine remained in the theoretical calculation stage for quite a long time. By the end of 1935 an MF-1 single-cylinder unit had been built, and was used to refine the cylinder-piston group of the future engine. In addition to Fomin, L.B. Edelshtein, S.K. Tumanskiy and S.A. Kosberg participated in the work on the M-200. Design development was not completed until 1937, the prototype being built the following year. During bench testing the pistons broke.

The engine drawings were completed in the first half of 1937, and manufacture of two prototypes was started in the autumn. Assembly of the first began in November 1936, and of the second in December. One prototype was bench tested in 1940-41. During testing the pistons failed. Refinement of the M-200 was halted in the autumn of 1941, and in January 1942 the type was officially excluded from the plan.

It was planned to develop an 18-cylinder powerplant comprising three M-200 blocks joined in a triangular configuration and having three crankshafts.

Characteristics

6-cylinder in-line, two-stroke, liquid-cooled engine with opposed pistons and direct injection.

Nominal power rating	650-700hp
Bore/stroke	100/100mm (3.94/3.94in)
Volume	9.42 litres (574cu in)
Weight	370kg (816lb)

M-300

The last TsIAM engine, the M-300 was developed under the leadership of A.A. Bessonov in 1939-40. It a radial layout of cylinder blocks (six blocks with six cylinders in each) and direct fuel injection. Engineering and assembly drawings were completed in February 1940, and a month later the technology for prototype manufacture was defined. At the same time a full-scale engine mock-up was built. The most complex parts for the prototypes were ordered from Factories Nos 24 (Moscow), 26 (Rybinsk), 28 (Moscow), and 29 (Zaporozhye). At the end of 1940 the TsIAM workshops began assembling two prototypes. One was completed at the end of that year and started bench testing in 1941, during which a connecting rod failed. The second was not completed. Development work on the M-300 ceased after the TsIAM's evacuation to Ufa. At the beginning of 1942 the engine was officially excluded from the working plan for the TsIAM.

Characteristics

36-cylinder radial block-type (six blocks of six cylinders each), four-stroke, liquid-cooled engine with direct fuel injection and reduction gearing (with reduction gear variants for coaxial and reversible-pitch propellers).

Power rating	3,000/3,500hp
Bore/stroke	140/160mm (5.51/6.30in)
Volume	88.5 litres (5,400cu in)
Weight	1,600kg (3,530lb) (1,626kg (3,585lb) according to some sources)

CHAPTER TWENTY-NINE

Diesel Aero-engines

The idea of using diesel engines in aviation had already gained popularity towards the end of the 1920s. Although the diesel is heavier and more sophisticated to produce, and thus more costly, it runs on cheaper fuel that is unsuitable for carburettor-type engines. In addition, the diesel is more efficient, its fuel consumption being considerably lower than that of light-fuel engines. With regard to its application to aircraft, it offers a lower total weight of engine (or engines) plus fuel. The diesel was expected to provide significant advantages for long-range bombers and reconnaissance aeroplanes, large seaplanes and record-breaking aircraft.

The first attempts to create aviation diesels in Russia date back to the mid-1920s. During May to December 1924 V.Ya. Klimov, destined to become a famous aero-engine designer, developed a project for a 500hp VYaK engine, but this did not come to fruition. Several small diesels were later designed by A.A. Mikulin.

Initially, the leaders of the Soviet aviation industry planned to use foreign diesel types. In 1930 several examples of a radial air-cooled aviation diesel were purchased from Packard in the USA. Although it was planned to introduce this engine into series production in the USSR starting in 1932, the idea was later abandoned.

The early 1930s saw the rise of Soviet aviation diesel development. In the autumn of 1930 an experimental 200hp EN-1 diesel and a 500hp M-42 diesel intended for combat aircraft were included in the plan of work for the VMO TsAGI. However, the latter type was soon removed from the plan.

The real evolution of diesels started a year later, when a national programme for their development was formulated. Several scientific institutions became involved in work on diesels: the IAM (later TsIAM) in Moscow; the Central Scientific-Research Diesel Institute (*Tsentralniy Nauchno-Issledovatelskiy Dizelniy Institut*, TsNIDI, later VNIDI) in Leningrad; the Ukrainian Institute of Internal Combustion Engines (*Ukrainskiy Institut Dvigateley Vnutrennego Sgoraniya*, UIDVS, later UNIADI) in Kharkov; the Institute of Industrial Power Engineering (*Institut Promishlennoy Energetiki*, IPE), also in Kharkov; and the OTB of the NKVD in Moscow.

As the Soviet Government paid special attention to the development of aviation diesels, the VVS and RKKA Command leaders actively supported the programme. Army Commander (later Marshal) M.N. Tukhachevskiy, who was supervising the development of new equipment for the Red Army, wrote in January 1932: 'The creation of the aviation diesel is one of the most important problems in aeronautical development.'

Six diesel types were included in the plan of experimental work on aero-engine development for 1932-33. They were designated N-1 to N-6, the letter 'N' denoting *Neftyanoy* (of crude oil type), though almost all of them were to run on petroleum-oil. The programme included requirements for the development of liquid- and air-cooled, four- and two-stroke diesels of different power rating (from 500hp to 2,000hp). According to the specification, the estimated engine weight was to be defined as 1.3-1.5 kg (2.87-3.31lb) per horsepower.

The N-1 (AN-1) diesel engine.

The TsNIDI had been involved in the development of different kinds of diesel engines, for ships, tractors, tanks and automobiles. Specialists at the institute had gained experience in the creation of high-speed (high-revolution) diesels potentially suitable for powering an aircraft. A group headed by Professor L.I. Martens began the development of a powerful four-stroke diesel aero-engine. A vee layout withj two cylinder blocks was chosen, with six cylinders in each block. Later this engine was refined at the TsIAM and at Factory No. 24 in Moscow, but it was not a success.

The UIDVS originated from a small laboratory for internal combustion engines, which in July 1931 was tasked with developing the N-3 aviation diesel. The institute was headed by Ya.M. Mayer, and the department under the leadership of G.I. Aptekman was directly involved in the engine's creation. In January 1932 a preliminary project for the diesel, designated AD-1, was presented to the UVVS. The AD-1 was also a 12-cylinder air-cooled vee engine, and its prototype was built at the end of 1934. It was bench tested, but lagged behind the competing N-1 (AN-1), developed at the TsIAM. From 1935 the UIDVS was also involved in the creation of a diesel engine for an airship.

In 1937 the UNIADI (the renamed UIDVS) was redirected to the development of tank diesels. The engines designed there included the very successful BD-2 (designated V-2 in series production), which powered the famous T-34, KV and IS tanks, self-propelled guns, and also the *Voroshilovets* artillery tractors. In May 1935 an aviation version of the BD-2 was developed, the BD-2A diesel, fitted with the GCS from the AM-34RN. This diesel was bench tested, and from January 1936 it was flight tested in an R-5 biplane. The plan of UNIADI work for 1937 included a programme of AD-3 diesel aero-engine development.

The M-40 diesel engine.

A specification for development of the N-4 two-stroke air-cooled 500-600hp engine was given to the IPE in Kharkov. Some time later this programme was transferred to the Kharkov Aviation Institute (*Kharkovskiy Aviatsionniy Institut*, KhAI). No information on the manufacturing and testing of this engine has been found.

The OTB of the NKVD was a *sharaga* manned by imprisoned engineers, most of whom were proclaimed to have been to be 'saboteurs' on the 'Promparty case'. These highly-skilled specialists of the pre-revolutionary school were blamed for failures of the first five-year plans of the Soviet industry. Formally, this Special Technical Bureau was headed by one Goryainov (an NKVD officer). The OTB of the NKVD was developing two diesel engines, the N-5 (also designated FED-8) and N-6 (MSK). Development of the N-5 saw participation of such well-known engine designers as N.R. Brilling, B.S. Stechkin and A.A. Bessonov, while Stechkin and Kurchevskiy were involved in the work on the N-6. The OTB of the NKVD was based at Factory No. 24 in Moscow.

By March 1933 three diesel types, the N-1, N-2 and N-3. had been chosen out of the six engines at different stages of development. The selected engines were considered to have the best prospects, and it was ordered that work on them was to be accelerated, while the remainder would gradually be abandoned.

A leader soon appeared among the three preferred designs; the N-1 (AN-1) created at the IAM. This engine had been developed by the IAM's Department of Crude Oil Engines (*Otdel Neftyanikh Dvigateley*, OND), under the leadership of A.D. Charomskiy. Earlier, most of the OND staff had the worked at the NAMI's Group for Crude Oil Engines, where such well-known designers as A.A. Mikulin and V.Ya. Klimov had been involved in the development of high-speed diesels. At the end of 1931 the OND presented to the VVS administration a project for the AN-1 four-stroke 12-cylinder-vee diesel engine.

A large family of aviation diesels was based on the AN-1. The first prototype, built in 1933, was followed by a range of its versions: the AN-1A, AN-1R (geared) and AN-1RTK (with gear and supercharger). The last was built in a small batch for extended testing.

The AN-1 was being refined for a long time, mainly because of shortcomings in its fuel system. As a result the nozzles, governors and high-pressure pumps were imported from the Bosch company in Germany, and the production of such units in the USSR was arranged only shortly before the beginning of the Second World War. Soviet-built equipment employed the layout and basic solutions of German units, but were not exact copies. Moreover, the indigenous nozzles and pumps were considerably inferior to their German counterparts in reliability and service life.

The long period of AN-1 refinement again gave rise to the idea of copying aviation diesels developed in the West. At that time the German types, which featured two opposed pistons in each cylinder, were under consideration. Initially, and for quite a long time, the Jumo 4 diesel was evaluated, and then the TsIAM was instructed to copy the more advanced Jumo 205, which had been captured in Spain. Ultimately, however, the indigenous aviation diesels were introduced into series production.

It was the AN-1RTK that formed the basis for two series-production diesels, the M-30 and M-40, that were introduced into air force service. The M-30 was developed at the OTB of the NKVD. In spite of the enterprise's old name it was now a new organization, though the principles of its work had not changed. The engines were still being developed by imprisoned engineers, but at that time they were called not 'saboteurs', but 'people's enemies' or 'foreign spies'. Among them were A.D. Charomskiy, B.S. Stechkin, A.S. Nazarov, V.P. Glushko and U. Keller. The last-named was a Swiss engineer from the Zultzer company who had been collecting information on use of his company's engines in Russia and had been accused of espionage.

In the second half of 1938 Factory No. 82 in Tushino (now the Chernyshov Factory), which earlier had been manufacturing radial carburettor-type engines of low and medium power to meet the needs of the Civil Air Fleet, was transferred to the OTB of the NKVD. At that time the OTB's chief designer was F.Ya. Tulupov (not imprisoned). Using the AN-1RTK as a basis, the OTB developed the M-30 diesel, which was built by Factory No. 82 in small batches until October 1941.

In parallel with M-30 development, another version of the AN-1RTK, the M-40, was being created at the TsIAM under the leadership of V.M. Yakovlev. These two diesels had many parts in common, differing mainly in the design of their supercharging systems. The M-40 was introduced into series production at the Kirov Factory in Leningrad.

The TsIAM was also developing other aviation diesel types. In 1933 the institute was told to create the N-9 radial air-cooled diesel engine. Apparently, development of this engine did not even reached the prototype stage. On the other hand, a lot of effort was applied to the development of the M-87D, a 14-cylinder diesel based on the M-87 light-fuel engine. It was being refined in co-operation with Zaporozhye-based Factory No. 29 until 1940, but with no results.

Shortly before the Second World War the TsIAM was working on the high-powered (2,200hp) M-20 48-cylinder diesel. This had an unusual rhombic layout with two opposing pistons in each cylinder. In 1940 a 4-cylinder section of this engine was tested. Then the TsIAM worked for some time on an AN-20, 'half' an M-20 with 24 cylinders, rated at 1700hp.

An M-50 engine designed by V.M. Yakovlev, and also evolved from the AN-1, was being developed from 1940 as an aero-engine. However, in 1942 its marine version, the M-50R, was brought to the fore and introduced into series production, being built for more than thirty years.

Another organization involved in prewar aviation diesel development was the NII GVF. From the very beginning the NII GVF's structure included an engine development department, which was later detached as a scientific research institute (the NII AD GVF) and then again merged with the NII GVF. The NII AD GVF had a Department of Heavy Oil Fuel Engines headed by T.M. Melkumov, and it worked on a small D-11 air-cooled diesel that incorporated components and units of the widely used M-11 radial engine. This diesel was bench tested and then test flown in a U-2 biplane. Factory No. 82 even started production of a batch of 100 D-11s, but after the factory was transferred to come under NKVD supervision the NII GVF's designers were moved to Voronezh-based Factory No. 156. Melkumov stayed in Moscow and continued giving lectures at the Air Force Academy. In 1939-1940 the Academy was refining the D-11, which was assembled from the parts manufactured at Factory No. 82. In the meantime, Factory No. 156 was tasked with creating a 130hp M-10 diesel using the D-11 as a basis. This project remained in the plans until the end of 1943, but the engine was not built.

The M-30 and M-40, which had been installed in the TB-7 (Pe-8) heavy bomber, evinced poor characteristics in service. It was difficult to adjust the fuel supply, and the engines stopped unexpectedly and could not be restarted at high altitudes, especially in the cold. They were already being removed from aircraft by August 1941, and their production ceased at the end of the year.

In April 1942 a new Factory No. 500 was established in the workshops of the evacuated Factory No. 82. It resumed, though in small numbers, production of the M-30. From June 1942 Charomskiy, by then released, became chief designer of this factory, and in July a new design bureau, OKB-500, was established, specializing in the development of aviation diesels. It continued to refine the M-30, which was now fitted with the GCS from the AM-38 and designated M-30B. This diesel was introduced into series production under the designation ACh-30B, being built by Factories No. 500 and No. 45 in Moscow. The ACh-30B powered series-production Er-2 bombers.

However, the ACh-30B's reliability was still poor, and this led to the final ceasing of its production in September 1945. The diesel-powered Er-2 was phased out of air force service, and the redundant diesel engines were modified into marine and tank versions or used for local power stations. Charomskiy was relieved of his post as chief designer at OKB-500, being replaced by V.M. Yakovlev. Work on ACh-31 and ACh-32 diesels, further developments of the ACh-30B, was completed under Yakovlev's leadership, but neither of these was introduced into series production.

After the war the Yakovlev-led OKB-500 developed several high-powered diesel engines for heavy bombers. The first was the 2,400hp M-52, the development of which had been started at the design bureau of Factory No. 45. It was followed by the 4,400hp M-224, a copy of the German 'square' Jumo 224 diesel. Originally in Germany, and later at Factory No. 500, a group of German engineers led by Herrlach had worked on this engine's development under the general supervision of Soviet specialists. All work on the M-224 was cancelled in November 1947, as Yakovlev had managed to demonstrate the advantages of his new project, the huge 42-cylinder 6,000hp M-501 intended for installation in Tupolev's strategic bomber, a long-range carrier of nuclear weapons. Work on this diesel continued until 1953, but in the end only its marine version, the M-501M, saw series production. From 1947 OKB-500 became involved in the development of turbojets,

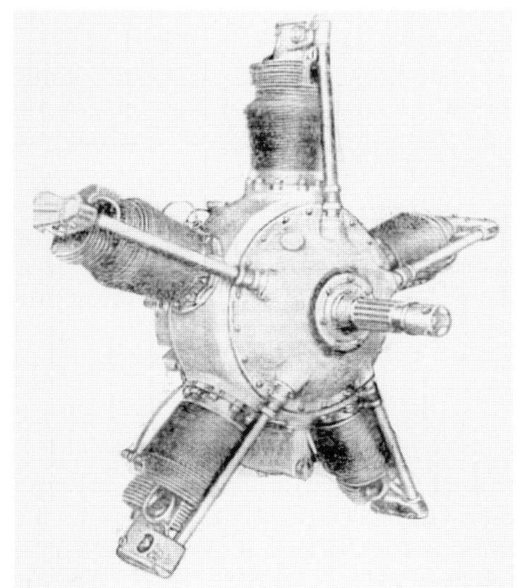

LEFT: **The D-11 diesel engine.**

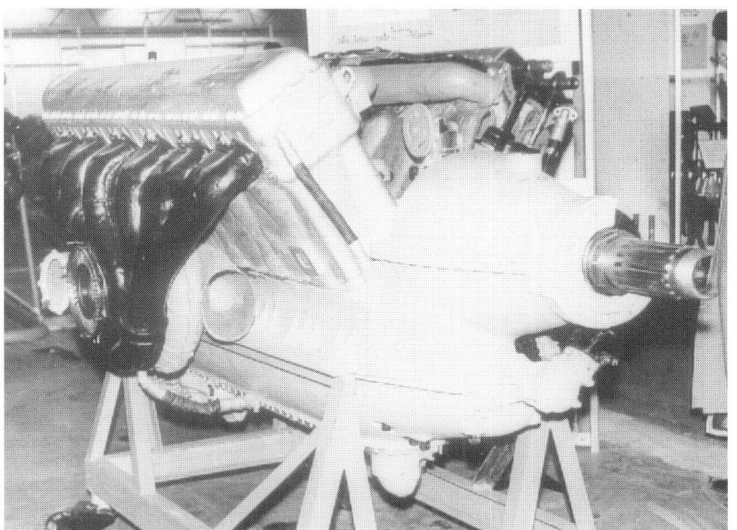

RIGHT: **The ACh-30B diesel engine.**

and as its first task in this sphere the bureau successfully copied the British Rolls-Royce Derwent, which was introduced into series production in the USSR as the RD-500.

In the mid-1950s all development work on piston engines, including diesels, was cancelled. Some designers began developing turbojets and turboprops, while others turned to engines for armoured vehicles. In 1946-47 Charomskiy, having been relieved from the post of chief designer, moved to the TsIAM, where he created his last diesel aviation engine, the M-25. Unlike all of his previous designs, it was a two-stroke engine with two opposed pistons in each horizontally positioned cylinder. Tank developers became interested in this engine, and it formed the basis for a whole family of tank engines. Many M-25 components were used in the 5TDF engine that powered the well-known T-64 tank.

Interest in diesel aviation engines was rekindled in Russia in the early 1990s, when projects for small and comparatively inexpensive business aircraft having very long flight duration began to appear. In Rybinsk, under the leadership of A.S. Novikov, the 3-cylinder DN-200 engine with opposed pistons was developed. Testing and refinement of its cylinder-piston assembly was started on the single-cylinder test bench in 1991. A number of other noteworthy engine projects have appeared in the last decade, but at present no diesel aero-engines are being produced in Russia.

There follows a description of all indigenous diesel aero-engines, shown in order of evolution. The fate of imported diesels is described in the chapter covering the history of foreign piston aero-engines in the Soviet Union.

N-2

Development of this engine was started under the leadership of Professor L.K. Martens at the TsNIDI (later VNIDI) in Leningrad. Its main feature was supercharging provided by a 6-cylinder piston compressor. The engine's gas distribution was of two-valve type. Later, this engine's development was transferred to the TsIAM in Moscow. The N-2 prototype was built in 1932 at Factory No. 24 in Moscow, and was bench tested there. Refinement work continued until late 1933, but then the AN-1, which offered better prospects in the same power range, came to the fore.

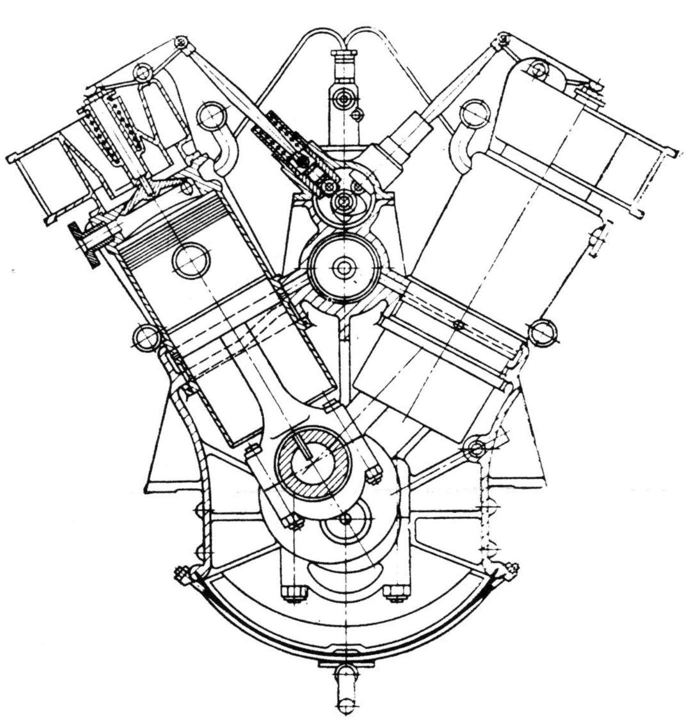

A cross-section of the N-2 diesel designed by Martens.

Characteristics

12-cylinder in-line vee, watercooled, four-stroke diesel with 6-cylinder piston supercharger.

Power rating	1,500hp (according to the specification 1,000hp)
Weight	1,300kg (2,870lb) (according to the specification)

AD-1 (N-3)

In July 1931 the Laboratory of Internal Combustion Engines (later UIDVS and UNIADI) in Kharkov was instructed to develop the N-3 diesel aero-engine. The work was carried out under the leadership of Ya.M. Mayer and G.I. Aptekman. Characteristic features of the N-3 were a vee of 45 degrees and the casting of load-carrying studs into the aluminium crankcase. The prototype was completed in the autumn of 1934 and underwent testing from December 1934 to June 1935. The recorded power rating of the N-3 was lower than specified, and preference was given to the AN-1 diesel developed at the TsIAM. Three prototypes of the N-3 were built.

Characteristics

12-cylinder in-line vee, four-stroke, watercooled diesel.

Power rating	500hp (according to the specification, but actually 437hp)
Bore/stroke	150/165mm (5.91/6.50in)
Weight	650kg (1,433lb) (according to the specification)

N-4

This diesel was being developed in 1931-32, initially at the IPE and then at the KhAI in Kharkov. No information on prototype manufacture and testing has been found.

Characteristics

Two-stroke watercooled diesel.

Power rating	500-600hp (according to the specification)
Weight	500-600kg (1,100-1,320lb)

N-5 (FED-8)

This engine was being developed at the OTB of the NKVD, at Factory No. 24 in Moscow. B.S. Stechkin, N.R. Brilling and A.A. Bessonov participated in the development work. The FED-8 was completed in 1932 and had a mixed valve-slot gas distribution. The prototype was built and bench tested. After liquidation of the design bureau, refinement work on the FED-8 continued at the TsIAM until 1934, but without any significant results.

The engine was planned to be installed on a TB-5 bomber.

Characteristics

24-cylinder in-line X-shaped, two-stroke, watercooled diesel.

Power rating	2,000/2,400hp (according to the specification)
Weight	3,000kg (6,600lb) (according to the specification)

The FED-8 X-shaped engine.

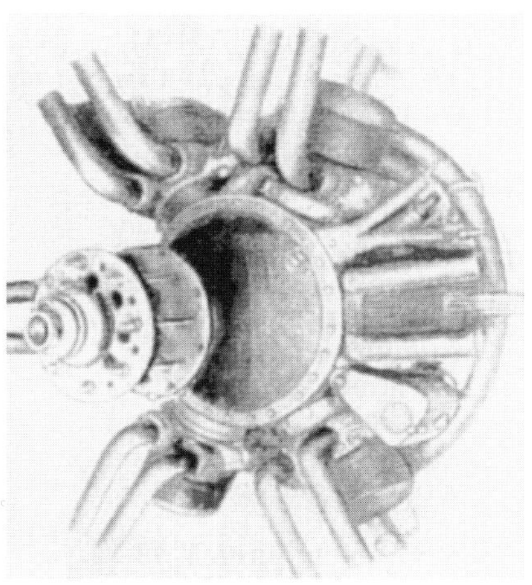

The MSK (N-6) diesel.

N-6 (MSK)

This engine was being developed by Stechkin and Kurchevskiy at the OTB of the NKVD, at Factory No. 24 in Moscow (hence the 'MSK' abbreviation, from *Motor Stechkina-Kurchevskogo*, or the engine of Stechkin and Kurchevskiy). The diesel had an unusual layout for a radial engine, having an even number of cylinders (six). Each engine cylinder drove one of the cylinders of a 6-cylinder piston compressor (supercharger). In 1932 a prototype of the MSK was built in the workshops of the TsIAM, and underwent bench testing.

Characteristics

6-cylinder radial, two-stroke, air-cooled diesel with a piston supercharger.

Power rating	500hp (according to the specification)
Weight	380kg (838lb) (according to the specification)

A BD-2A diesel on a test bench.

A BD-2A mounted in an R-5 reconnaissance biplane in place of the standard M-17.

BD-2A

An aviation version of the BD-2 tank diesel, with a power rating of 400/420hp, the BD-2A was created in 1933 at the UNIADI in Kharkov. Its development started in May 1935 under the leadership of G.I. Aptekman. Compared with the tank version, the aviation diesel was lightened and provided with a supercharger from the M-34RN engine. In December 1935 two prototypes were built. From July to December 1936 the BD-2A was tested in an R-5 aeroplane, but tests showed that

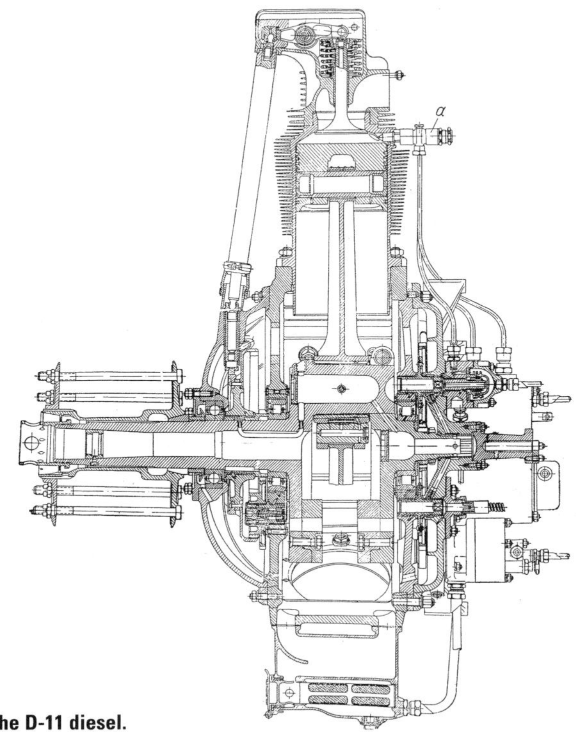

A cross-section of the D-11 diesel.

the engine had no advantages over the series M-34RNB.

Characteristics

12-cylinder in-line vee, four-stroke, watercooled diesel with a GCS.

Power rating 600hp

N-9

The task of creating the N-9 diesel engine was given to the TsIAM at the end of 1933. No information on the engine's development and prototype manufacture has been found. It was planned to start its factory tests on 1 June 1935.

Characteristics

9-cylinder radial, air-cooled diesel.

Nominal power rating 500hp

Weight 600kg (1,320lb) (according to the specification)

M-87D

This diesel was based on the M-87 carburetted two-row radial. The M-87D was developed jointly by an engineering team at the TsIAM, led by P.P. Konyukhov, and the design bureau of Factory No. 29 in Zaporozhye. The work started in 1937, and the engine retained the single-speed GCS from the M-87, but its crankshaft was strengthened and fitted with a pendular counterweight. The M-87D prototype was built in Zaporozhye at the end of 1938, and in February 1939 bench testing began, but soon stopped owing to crankshaft failure. The M-87D was being refined until 1940, when all the work on it was cancelled.

Characteristics

18-cylinder two-row radial, four-stroke, air-cooled, geared diesel engine with a single-speed GCS.

Power rating 750/800hp

Bore/stroke 146/165mm (5.75/6.50in)

Weight 750kg (1,653lb)

M-20

This high-powered diesel was intended for heavy bombers. The M-20 was being developed in 1940-41, and had an unusual rhombic layout with four crankshafts, and two opposed pistons in each of its 48 cylinders.

In the autumn of 1940 a 4-cylinder section of the M-20 was built at Factory No. 82 in Moscow. It was bench tested from December of that year, and the registered power rating exceeded estimates. (The projected maximum power of the M-20 was 2,200hp, but the test results showed a potential of 3,000hp.) The prototype was to be completed by the middle of 1941, but the plans came to naught. Refinement of the 4-cylinder engine section continued until early 1943.

It was planned to use the M-20 in the projected DVB-102DM bomber.

Characteristics

48-cylinder, rhombic, two-stroke, watercooled, geared diesel with opposed pistons.

Power rating 3,000hp (estimated)

AN-5

This project, comprising 'half' of an M-20 diesel with 24 cylinders, was being developed at the TsIAM in 1941-43. The prototype was not built.

Characteristics

24-cylinder, rhombic, two-stroke, watercooled, geared diesel with opposed pistons.

Power rating 1,500/1,750hp (estimated; according to some sources 1,500/1,700hp)

Weight 800-850kg (1,764-1,874lb)

D-11 (M-11D, M-10)

This low-powered diesel incorporated parts and components of the series M-11G carburettor-type engine. The D-11 was under development from 1936 at the Department of Heavy Oil Fuel Engines of the NII GVF (NII AD GVF), under the leadership of T.M. Melkumov.

The first prototype was built in 1937, and Factory No. 82 started production of a 100-engine batch in 1938. However, D-11 production ceased after the factory came under NKVD supervision in the middle of the year. The manufactured parts and units of the engines were transferred to the workshops of the Air Force Academy, where six were assembled in 1939-40.

In 1940 the D-11 underwent bench testing and was test flown in a U-2 aeroplane. It was noted that the D-11 operated poorly at low rpm and vibrated considerably. In February 1940 a D-11 was transferred to joint testing, but it broke down after running only 4hr. In April another was tested, but this also failed.

In March 1943 this diesel, designated M-10, was included in the work plan for the design bureau of Factory No. 154 in

Andizhan, but no information on any work carried out there has been found.

Characteristics

5-cylinder radial, four-stroke, air-cooled, direct-drive diesel.

Power rating	100/120hp (according to the specification 110/130hp)
Bore/stroke	125/140mm (4.92/5.51in)
Volume	8.6 litres (524cu in)
Compression ratio	15.0:1
Weight	180kg (397lb) (according to some sources 200kg (440lb))

AN-1 (N-1)

This engine was under development from 1931 at the Department of Crude Oil Engines of the IAM (TsIAM), under the leadership of A.D. Charomskiy and in accordance with the specification for the N-1 diesel. At the end of that year a preliminary project for the AN-1 was presented to the Air Force Directorate for consideration. The engine's general layout and load-carrying scheme were similar to those of the M-34. The gas distribution was of four-valve type.

The first AN-1 prototype was built in the summer of 1933 in the TsIAM workshops. It was bench tested in 1933-34, when it was noted that the engine ran unsteadily at low rpm and suffered from poor starting at low temperatures. In October-November 1935 the AN-1 passed its State tests, and as a result it was suggested that a batch of thirty-five to forty engines be built. At the end of 1936 the AN-1 was flight-tested (50hr test) in the ANT-36 (RDD), which was the ANT-25 (RD) record-breaking aircraft modified to take the diesel engine.

Later, the engine was repeatedly modified, including work on non-aviation versions. The AN-1 was not introduced into series production, but different versions were built in small batches. In total, about 100 were built.

Characteristics

12-cylinder, in-line vee, four-stroke, watercooled diesel.

Bore/stroke	180/200mm (7.09/7.87in) (in cylinders with articulated connecting rods, 209.95mm (8.27in))
Volume	61.04 litres (3,724cu in)
Compression ratio	13.5:1
Power rating	dependant on version
Weight	dependant on version

The following versions of the engine are known:

AN-1 The first prototype version, built in the summer of 1933. Initially it had no GCS, then it was tested with a single-speed GCS designed by P.I. Orlov. According to the plan factory tests were to start on 1 November 1933, but the AN-1 was tested and refined during 1933-34. Power rating 750/800hp (814hp was recorded during the tests), weight (according to the specification) 950kg (2,094lb); later increased to 975 kg (2,149lb). The engine actually weighed 1,003kg (2,211lb), and, after refinement and some local strengthening, 1,021kg (2,251lb). In October-November 1936 the AN-1 passed its State tests, and at the end of 1936 it was test-flown in an ANT-36. The AN-1 was inferior to contemporary German engines, having a higher specific weight and greater frontal area.

AN-1A This modified version of 1936, equipped with a single-speed GCS, was being developed and refined under the leadership of Charomskiy and, after his arrest, by F.Ya. Tulupov. The AN-1A was boosted in rpm. Power rating 850/900hp, weight 1,040kg (2,293lb). The engine was transferred to State testing in 1936, but failed. In January 1937 it passed its 100hr State tests, demonstrating a power rating of 900/913hp. A small batch of this version was built at the TsIAM workshops. In the beginning of 1937 it was tested in a TB-3D aeroplane, the tests ended in a crash.

AN-1R This geared version of the AN-1A was being developed in parallel with the AN-1A during 1936. Power rating 850/900hp, weight (according to the specification) 1,000kg (2,200lb). The engine passed State bench testing at the beginning of 1938, and underwent flight testing that same year. In January 1939 the AN-1R was transferred to the TsIAM for refinement. Series production was planned to be set up at Factory No. 82, but it was then decided to build a later version, the AN-1RTK.

AN-1RTK An improved version with turbo-supercharging, this engine was under development from 1936, initially under the leadership of Charomskiy and then by V.M. Yakovlev. In January 1938 the AN-1RTK was transferred to State testing. It had two turbo-superchargers designed by V.I. Dmitrievskiy and I.E.

An AN-1 diesel in the ANT-36 (RDD) prototype.

An AN-1A diesel in a TB-3D.

Sklyar, and an E-88 GCS. Power rating 1,000/1,200hp. In 1939 the engine passed high-altitude bench testing in Pamirs. In 1940 a version with a modified supercharging system was built, which had four turbo-superchargers designed by M.A. Kuzmin and I.E. Sklyar, but it did not have a GCS. This diesel had power rating of 1,000/1250hp and weighed 1,100kg (2,430lb). In 1940 a special version equipped with a cabin pressurization drive was being prepared for the planned round-the-world flight of M.M. Gromov.

AN-1M A marine version of the AN-1A with a reverse clutch and without supercharging. Power rating 850/950hp, weight 1,350kg (2,976lb). The engine was being developed from 1937 at the design bureau of Factory No. 24, under the leadership of V.M. Yakovlev. In 1939 the AN-1M passed factory tests. At the end of 1939 all work ceased because the People's Commissariat of the Navy changed the engine specification.

MN-1 A marine version of the AN-1 with a reverse clutch and without supercharging. This engine was being developed at the TsIAM under the leadership of V.M. Yakovlev. In 1939 it was transferred to State testing four times, but did not pass. Power rating 1,000/1,000hp, weight 1,500kg (3,300lb). The MN-1 was being refined until the middle of 1940, but was not introduced into series production.

The AN-1RTK formed the basis for the development of the M-30, M-40 and M-50 diesels. The results of the AN-1R and MN-1 development were used in creation of the M-50R marine engine, which entered series production. Many AN-1 components were used in the series-built V-2 tank diesel.

The AN-1 was test flown in the ANT-36 (RDD) and TB-3D aeroplanes.

M-30 (AD-5, ACh-30)

This diesel, based on the AN-1RTK, was being developed from 1939 at the OTB of the NKVD, at Factory No. 82 in Tushino, under the leadership of F.Ya. Tulupov. Charomskiy also participated in its development, but at that time as an imprisoned engineer. Initially the type was designated AD-5.

At the end of 1939 manufacture of the first five prototypes was started. In the spring of 1940 the initial engine version, with four turbo-superchargers and without GCS and intercoolers (weight 1,100kg (2,430lb)), passed its tests. From May 1940 the AD-5 began to be introduced into series production at Factory No. 82 as the M-30. The factory started production in 1941. There were plans to transfer M-30 production from Tushino to the Kharkov Tractor Factory (*Kharkovskiy Traktorniy Zavod*, KhTZ), and the KhTZ was preparing for the engine's production, but no M-30s were built there.

The M-30 was the first diesel aero-engine introduced into series production in the USSR, and also the first to go into service with the VVS RKKA. It powered series-production bombers and was used in combat. However the M-30 had poor reliability. It did not deliver full rpms, it suffered oil blowouts and failures of the oil pumps, it stopped unexpectedly and restarting was problematic in cold conditions and at high altitudes. As a result, M-30 production was halted after the evacuation of Factory No. 82. The last four diesels were assembled in Kazan from components delivered from Moscow. Even earlier, in August 1941, these engines were removed from TB-7s and replaced by AM-35As.

However, from June 1942 M-30 production was resumed at Factory No. 500, in the workshops of the evacuated Factory No. 82. That same year the engine was modified (a GCS and intercoolers being introduced) at OKB-500 under the leadership of Charomskiy (now released). Production of the improved version started at the end of 1942 under the designation M-30B, and it was later redesignated ACh-30B. In 1944-45 the ACh-30B was also manufactured at Factory No. 45 in Moscow. In September 1945 the engine was removed from the production lines of both factories. In total, 1,526 (according to some sources 1,423) M-30s, M-30Bs and ACh-30Bs were built.

The ACh-30B formed basis for a number of series-produced tank and marine diesels. In 1946-47 the redundant ACh-30Bs were disassembled and their components and parts used in M-50R marine diesels. Some ACh-30Bs, after

An AN-1R diesel with reduction gear.

An ACh-30B diesel engine in the Monino museum.

The Er-2 long-range bomber, powered by ACh-30Bs, during tests at Irkutsk in February 1944.

minor modification, were used in small DKE power stations providing electricity for villages.

Characteristics

12-cylinder in-line vee, four-stroke, watercooled diesel.

Bore/stroke	180/200mm (7.09/7.87in) (in cylinders with articulated connecting rods, 209.95mm (8.27in))
Volume	61.04 litres (3,724cu in)
Compression ratio	13.5:1
Power rating	dependant on version
Weight	dependant on version

The following versions of the engine are known:

M-30 The first series-production version, with four turbo-superchargers but without a GCS and intercoolers. Power rating 1,250/1,500hp, weight 1,200kg (2,645lb) (according to some sources 1,150kg (2,535lb)). The engine was in series production at Factory No. 82 (forty-four built in 1941) and at Factory No. 500 (thirty-two built in 1942). Production ceased at the end of 1942. In 1942 some M-30s were modified into M-30Bs.

M-30F A prototype of 1942. Power rating 1,500/1,750hp.

M-30B (ACh-30B) A modified version equipped with a GCS. Two variants of this engine were under development by OKB-500. They differed in the type of GCS fitted; one being taken from the AM-38 and the other from the M-105. In July 1942 the former variant passed its 100hr tests. The latter was less successful, though it was the type that had initially been planned for series production. In the end, the version with the AM-38 GCS (which had a reduced-diameter impeller) and two T1-82 turbo-superchargers and intercoolers was introduced into series production. From August 1942 Factory No. 500 started modifying incomplete M-30s into M-30Bs, thirty-five engines being so updated, and then began M-30B production, building thirty-four in 1942. During January-April 1943 the M-30B was tested on an Er-2 bomber, and in August on an Il-6 long-range-bomber prototype. Service testing of M-30Bs in Pe-8 bombers of long-range aviation was carried out in February 1943. Officially, the ACh-30B was accepted for series production on 19 June 1943. From spring of that year Factory No. 45 started preparing for ACh-30B manufacture. In fact, series production of these diesels began at both factories in the fourth quarter of 1943. The ACh-30B underwent just a few changes in the course of production. In particular, additional fuel filters were introduced from April 1945. Production ceased at both factories in September 1945. Power rating 1,250/1,500hp, weight of the prototypes 1,280kg (2,822lb), weight of the series production engine 1,290kg (2,844lb) (later series 1,310kg (2,888lb)). In total, 1,450 were built.

M-30D This boosted version for an attack aircraft was rated at 1,750/2,000hp. In March 1943 Factory No. 500 was tasked with developing this version. No information about its development and manufacture have been found.

ACh-30BF A boosted version of the ACh-30B with additional fuel injection into the engine air after it had passed through the turbo-superchargers. The engine was being developed from 1943, and prototypes were tested from the spring of 1944. From August 1944 the ACh-30BF was tested in an Il-6 bomber prototype, and the 100hr factory tests were success-

The Pe-8, powered by four ACh-30B diesels.

The '67' bomber prototype with ACh-30B diesels.

An ACh-30B on a test bench at the MAI, 1948.

fully completed in March 1945. State tests were started that same month, but the engine was rejected owing to poor acceleration and complicated starting procedures. After some refinement the ACh-30BF was tested in a Tu-2 bomber. Refinement work continued until 1947. Power rating 1,250/1,900hp, weight 1,280kg (2,822lb). In total, seventeen engines were completed by modifying ACh-30Bs.

ACh-30B with moto-compressor jet engine. This version was being developed at the TsIAM from early 1944, under the leadership of Tolstov. It was based on the ACh-30B series-production engine but had a redesigned supercharging system. The jet engine compressor was driven by the turbines of turbo-superchargers. The engine was undergoing factory bench testing from June 1944 through May 1945. It was not introduced into series production and was not installed in an aircraft. Thrust of the jet engine, 873kg (1,925lb). Total power with the jet engine running, 4,500 equivalent hp. Total weight of the powerplant 1,700kg (3,750lb).

TD-30B A tank diesel engine developed using the ACh-30B as a basis. Development was carried out from 1945, and it originated from experiments with long-duration running of the ACh-30B at low rpm. The TD-30B was developed under the leadership of A.Ya. Nosach at the design bureau of the KhTZ in 1946-47. It was in series production at the KhTZ from 1948, and was the basis for the creation of the successful TD11B tank diesel.

Diesel engines of the M-30/ACh-30B family powered the Er-2 and TB-7 (Pe-8) series-production bombers, and a prototype of aeroplane '67', a modified Tu-2 bomber. It was planned to use these diesels in the projected 'MN', Il-6, Tu-8S and PS-84 (bomber version).

The Er-2 bomber, powered by ACh-30BF diesels.

M-40

Another branch of AN-1RTK development, this engine was being created at the TsIAM under the leadership of V.M. Yakovlev, with the participation of M.A. Kuzmin and A.Ya. Nosach. The M-40 was closer to the original AN-1RTK than the M-30. It differed from the latter mainly in the design of its supercharging system, but retained the same basic approach. It had four E-88 turbo-superchargers without a GCS but with two water intercoolers.

The M-40 prototype was submitted for State testing in May 1940, but failed. In June it was test flown in the BOK-15 aeroplane that was being prepared for a round-the-world flight by M.M. Gromov. This version of the M-40 had a special drive for cabin pressurization.

From the spring of 1940 the M-40 was being introduced into series production at

The TB-7 (Pe-8) heavy bomber, powered by M-40 diesels, 1941.

the Kirov factory in Leningrad. During the first half of 1941 this factory built fifty-eight engines. From the spring of 1941 the M-40 was installed in series-production TB-7 bombers.

Production of these diesels ceased in the autumn of 1941, 120 having been built. Even earlier, in August 1941, the M-40s were removed from all aeroplanes and preserved. In 1942 the M-40 underwent testing in an Er-2 bomber. In 1944 Factory No. 500 was disassembling M-40s and using their components in ACh-30Bs.

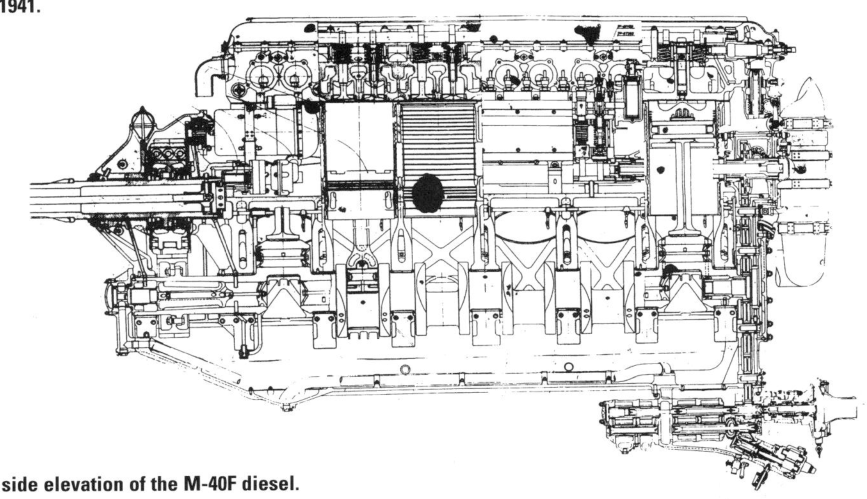

A side elevation of the M-40F diesel.

Characteristics

12-cylinder in-line vee, four-stroke, watercooled diesel.

Bore/stroke	180/200mm (7.09/7.87in) (in cylinders with articulated connecting rods, 209.95mm (8.27in))
Volume	61.04 litres (3,724cu in)
Compression ratio	13.5:1
Power rating	dependant on version
Weight	dependant on version

The following versions of the engine are known:

M-40 A series-production version. Power rating 1,000/1,250hp, weight 1,150kg (2,535lb).

M-40F A prototype with boosted rpm. Power rating 1,250/1,500hp, weight 1,200kg (2,645lb). This version underwent State testing in the summer of 1940, and in November that year it was recommended for series production (a small batch was built in 1941). In the summer of 1941 the M-40F was tested in an Er-2 aeroplane.

The M-40 diesels powered series-production TB-7 (Pe-8) bombers, and the BOK-15 and Er-2 prototypes.

M-31 (ACh-31)

In 1942 OKB-500 was instructed to develop the M-31 diesel, which was to have a power rating of 1,500/1,900hp and weigh 1,260kg (2,778lb). It was planned to carry out tests from December 1943, and to introduce the engine into series production in 1944. A preliminary project for the M-31 was developed in 1943, under the leadership of A.D. Charomskiy. A further evolution of the ACh-30BF, with similar two-phase carburation (the benzine injected first, followed by kerosene), the engine had two turbo-superchargers and a GCS.

The first ACh-31 prototypes were built and bench tested in 1944. In 1945 the diesel was being refined with aim of achieving a 50hr service life, and a small batch of ACh-31s were built by Factory No. 500. The engine was test-flown in an Il-12 in August 1945. Further refinements were carried out in 1946, the power rating reached 1,500/2,000hp. However, the diesel again demonstrated poor reliability and complexity in operation. In total, sixty-four such engines (or fifty-eight according to other data) were built in 1945-46.

In April 1946 the ACh-31 underwent 100hr factory testing, but failed. It was not until July 1947 that two engines managed to pass the 100hr test programme. However, at the request of the factory's leaders the ACh-31 was removed from the plan of experimental work in 1947.

The ACh-31 powered prototypes of the Il-12 and Er-2.

Characteristics

12-cylinder in-line vee, four-stroke, watercooled diesel.

Power rating	1,500/1,900hp (from 1946, 1,500/2,000hp)
Bore/stroke	180/200mm (7.09/7.87in) (in cylinders with articulated connecting rods, 209.95mm (8.27in))
Volume	61.04 litres (3,724cu in)
Compression ratio	13.5:1
Weight	1,387kg (3,058lb)

The following versions of the engine are known:

ACh-31 A version built in a small batch in 1945-46.

ACh-31A A project of 1944. No details have been found.

ACh-32

This engine, a further development of the ACh-31, was developed at OKB-500, the project work being completed in November 1944. The first prototype was built at the end of 1945. During bench running in early 1946 the bearings failed. After repair the engine underwent bench testing, and was being refined in 1946-47. The ACh-32 was not introduced into series production.

The ACh-32 was to be installed in an Er-2.

Characteristics

12-cylinder in-line vee, four-stroke, watercooled diesel.

Power rating	1,500/2,300hp (according to some sources, 1,600/2,400hp)
Bore/stroke	180/200mm (7.09/7.87in) (in cylinders with articulated connecting rods, 209.95mm (8.27in))
Volume	61.04 litres (3,724cu in)
Compression ratio	13.5:1
Weight	1,350kg (2,976lb)

M-35

A projected high-powered diesel for heavy bombers, the M-35 was being developed at the TsIAM in 1946-47, under the leadership of A.D. Charomskiy. No further details have been found.

M-52

Initially, the task of developing this diesel was given to Factory No. 45, and V.M. Yakovlev was appointed chief designer. When Yakovlev left to head OKB-500, the work on the M-52 also transferred there. According to the specification, the engine's power rating was 2,400hp. No information on the manufacture and testing of the prototype has been found.

M-501

A project for a diesel intended for heavy bombers, the M-501 was being developed during 1946-47 at OKB-500, under the leadership of V.M. Yakovlev. The engine had seven blocks of six cylinders each, and was equipped with a turbo-supercharger (with two-sided air supply) and a GCS. The exhaust from the turbo-supercharger was used to create jet thrust. During prototype tests in 1952, 6,000hp was reached. The engine was being refined up to 1953. Although the aviation version of the M-501 was not introduced into series production, an M-501M marine version was built in series.

It was planned to use the M-501 in a projected Tupolev heavy bomber.

Characteristics

42-cylinder four-stroke, liquid-cooled diesel with a radial arrangement of seven blocks, equipped with a turbo-supercharger and a GCS.

Power rating	4,750/6,205 equivalent hp (including 116/205kg (256/452lb) exhaust jet thrust).
Bore/stroke	160/170mm (6.30/6.69in)
Volume	143.55 litres (8,760cu in)
Weight	2,950kg (6,503lb) (with turbo-supercharger, 3,400kg (7,500lb))

The following versions of the engine are known:

M-501 An aviation engine. Not introduced into series production.

M-501M The marine version, with reverse clutch. In series production.

DN-200

This diesel was created by the design bureau of the Rybinsk Motor Factory, under the leadership of A.S. Novikov. The DN-200 had opposed pistons in horizontal cylinders. A single-cylinder experimental section of the engine was tested in 1991.

Characteristics

3-cylinder two-stroke diesel with horizontal cylinders.

Power rating	160/200hp
Volume	1.758 litres (107cu in)
Weight	165kg (364lb)

A mock-up of the DN-200 diesel engine.

CHAPTER THIRTY

Projects for H-shaped Engines by A.P. Ro

In 1931 engineer A.P. Ro, who was working at the TsIAM, proposed a project for an H-shaped 24-cylinder engine with two crankshafts driving common gearing. It was the first project for aero-engine of H configuration in the Soviet Union, and probably in the world. In this respect Ro was ahead of the Napier company in England, which later developed the successful Dagger engine that was mass-produced and powered the Hawker Hector and Handley Page Hereford. Ro's engine used four cylinder blocks of the latest engine of that time, the M-34 created by A.A. Mikulin.

However, this project was soon removed from the plan of TsIAM work, probably to concentrate effort on the creation of a high-powered M-35 engine that was being developed in W, X and Vee configurations, the use of M-34 cylinder blocks also being stipulated for the first two versions of this. Later, on his own initiative, Ro produced several more projects for H-shaped aero-engines. The projects of 1932, 1934 and 1936 were based on blocks from the M-34, and the project of 1937 used blocks from the M-100 (Hispano-Suiza 12 Ybrs). All of these projects were developed personally by the designer, and no prototypes were built.

In December 1939 A.P. Ro and E.V. Urmin proposed that an H-shaped engine be built at the TsIAM, based the 'improved blocks from the M-34' (probably from the M-34FRNV), with supercharging and direct fuel injection. The engine's dry weight was estimated at 1,400kg (3,086lb), and its designers promised a maximum power rating of 3,000hp. However, the project was not introduced in the plan of TsIAM work.

At the beginning of 1940 A.P. Ro, using his 1937 project as a basis, created a project for a new engine using four blocks from the M-103A. Later it was redesigned to use M-105 blocks. This project was considered promising, and was included into the State plan for aero-engine development work under the designation M-130. In March 1940 the M-130 specification was approved by the head of the VVS. In accordance with a Government decree, a design bureau was established at Factory No. 27 in Kazan to complete M-130 development. It was also planned to build the prototypes there, and later to introduce the engine into series production at this factory.

However, the work on the M-130 did not last long. Under pressure from the NKVD leaders and of L.P. Beriya, head of the NKVD, in person, the M-130 was displaced from the plan by the competing X-shaped MB-100 being created at the NKVD OTB by imprisoned engineers under the leadership of A.M. Dobrotvorskiy. The MB-100 was based on blocks from the M-103A (and, later, from the M-105), but it had a slightly inferior estimated performance. Work on the M-130 was cancelled by a Government decree of 26 September 1940, and the staff of the design bureau, which had been enlarged with imprisoned engineers transferred from Moscow, was tasked with MB-100 project development.

After the war A.P. Ro was lecturing in the Aero-Engine Design Chair of the MAI.

M-130

The initial version of the M-130 was developed by A.P. Ro at the TsIAM in 1939-40, and used some components from his project of 1937. It was an H-shaped two-shaft engine with four blocks from the M-105. In 1940 a design bureau was established at Factory No. 27 in Kazan, where the final variant of the M-130 was being created under the Ro's leadership. Completion of type development was planned for September 1940, and factory testing was to start in January 1941. However, under a Government decree of 26 September 1940, work on the M-130 was cancelled.

Characteristics

24-cylinder in-line H-shaped, four-stroke, watercooled, geared engine with a two-speed GCS.

Power rating	2,300/2,400hp (according to some sources 2,300/2,500hp)
Bore/stroke	148/170mm (5.83/6.69in)
Volume	70.0 litres (4,272cu in)
Compression ratio	6.6:1
Weight	1,000kg (2,200lb) (according to the project), 1,150kg (2,535lb) (according to the specification)

CHAPTER THIRTY-ONE

The Engines of A.M. Dobrotvorskiy

In the 1930s A.M. Dobrotvorskiy was working in the design bureau of Factory No. 24, where he participated in the creation of versions of the M-34. In particular, he designed several carburettors for this engine. During Stalin's repressions he was arrested and ended up in the OTB of the NKVD, in Butyrskaya prison in Moscow. In 1939-40 a project for the X-shaped MB-100 was created under Dobrotvorskiy's leadership. It was actually a combination of two M-103As, later on replaced by two M-105s.

In June 1940 the NKVD offered the MB-100 project for consideration by the NKAP. Regardless of the fact that the MB-100's characteristics were inferior to those of the M-130, which was being developed in Kazan, it was given priority. It is probable that a personal appeal to the Government by the head of the NKVD, L.P. Beriya, played a role. In accordance with a Government decree of 26 September 1940, the design bureau of Factory No. 27 in Kazan was instructed to refine the MB-100 project, and a group of imprisoned engineers was transferred to Kazan from Moscow to bolster the staff.

According to the plan, the first two prototypes were to have been assembled by 1 December 1941, and State tests were to start in September 1942. However, the war against Germany ruined all plans, the factories receiving increased orders for series-production engines. The priority in experimental work was given to the modification of engines already in production. In the autumn of 1941 Factory No. 16 was evacuated from Voronezh to Kazan, and it absorbed Factory No. 27. Nevertheless, in December 1941 Factory No. 16 was told to start preparing for series production of the MB-100.

Several prototypes were built, and underwent bench testing in Kazan, and later they were flight-tested in an Er-2 bomber. Work on this engine continued until 1945. A further development of the MB-100 was the MB-102, but this was not built.

MB-100

The preliminary project for the MB-100 was prepared in 1939-40 at the OTB of the NKVD in Moscow, under the leadership of A.M. Dobrotvorskiy. Later it was being refined at the design bureau of Factory No. 27 in Kazan, and at the design bureau of Factory No. 16 after the merger of these two factories.

The MB-100 prototypes were manufactured, and underwent bench and flight testing, the latter being carried out in March-June 1944, using an Er-2 bomber. Fitting cowlings round this very large engine proved difficult.

The MB-100 was installed in a modified series Er-2 bomber. It was also intended for one of the fighters being developed by the A.S. Yakovlev Design Bureau.

Characteristics

24-cylinder in-line X-shaped, four-stroke, watercooled, geared engine with a single-stage, single-speed GCS.

Power rating	2,100/2,200hp
Bore/stroke	148/170mm (5.83/6.69in)
Volume	70.0 litres (4,272cu in)
Compression ratio	6.6:1
Weight	1,325kg (2.921lb) (according to the project 1,300kg (2,870lb), according to the specification 1,250kg (2,756lb)).

MB-102

MB-102 was a boosted version of the MB-100, with a two-speed GCS. It was under development in 1942-43 at the design bureau of Factory No. 16 in Kazan.

No information about prototype manufacture or testing has been found.

Characteristics

24-cylinder in-line X-shaped, four-stroke, watercooled, geared engine with a single-stage, two-speed GCS.

Power rating	2,370/2,450hp (according to the 1942 specification); (2,450/2,550hp according to the 1943 specification)
Bore/stroke	148/170mm (5.83/6.69in)
Volume	70.0 litres (4,272cu in)
Compression ratio	6.6:1
Weight	1,400kg (3,090lb) (according to the specification)

CHAPTER THIRTY-TWO

The Engines of S.D. Kolosov

S.D. Kolosov became chief designer at Factory No. 16 in Voronezh at the end of 1937, after A.S. Nazarov was denounced as a 'people's enemy' and arrested. As chief designer, Kolosov oversaw the preparation of engineering documentation for all the engine types being manufactured or introduced into production by the factory: the M-11, the Renault family (MV-4, MV-6 and MV-12), the MG-31F and the M-105. He developed several versions of these engines, the MV-12R (M-12R), MV-12F and MV-6A, the last being introduced into series production. In addition, Kolosov participated in the refinement of drawings for the M-250, prototypes of which were being manufactured in Voronezh, and it was planned to introduce this engine into series production there.

Before the war the M-16 was introduced into the plan for experimental work, and this project was developed at the factory's design bureau. A low-powered engine intended for mass use by aero clubs, it had a horizontally-opposed layout and air cooling. The M-16 was a fully original design created by Kolosov. Unfortunately, the specified power rating of the engine was not reached, and all work on it was cancelled.

During the war, when Factory No. 16 was evacuated to Kazan and tasked with series production of the M-105P and, later, the M-105PF, a modified version of the M-105PF, designated M-116P and later M-1, was created there under Kolosov's leadership. The prototype was built and underwent bench and flight testing, but the engine did not go into series production because preference was given to the M-107A (VK-107A).

From 1946 the design bureau of Factory No. 16 was redirected to jet engine development. Kolosov was given the job of copying the German BMW 003 turbojet, which was later introduced into series production at the factory as the RD-20.

M-16

A low-powered horizontally-opposed engine intended for light aircraft, the M-16 was developed at the design bureau of Factory No. 16 in Voronezh under the leadership of S.D. Kolosov. It had some imported components, including French magnetos. The prototype was built in the autumn of 1939 and underwent factory tests. On 22 December 1939 it was subjected to a 50hr joint test, but the maximum power attained did not exceed 65hp, while the specification required 70hp. Moreover, the engine's weight exceeded the limit prescribed by the specification.

All work on the M-16 was cancelled in 1941, owing to the factory being overloaded with the manufacture of M-105s for military aircraft (it had previously specialized in the production of low- and medium-powered engines).

Characteristics

4-cylinder horizontally-opposed, four-stroke, air-cooled, direct-drive unsupercharged engine.

Power rating	60/65hp (according to the specification 70hp)
Bore/stroke	100/100mm (3.94/3.94in)
Volume	3.14 litres (192cu in)
Compression ratio	5.5:1
Weight	80kg (176lb) (according to the specification 75kg (165b))

M-1 (M-116P)

Development of M-116P was undertaken at the design bureau of Factory No. 16 in

LEFT: **The M-16 engine.**

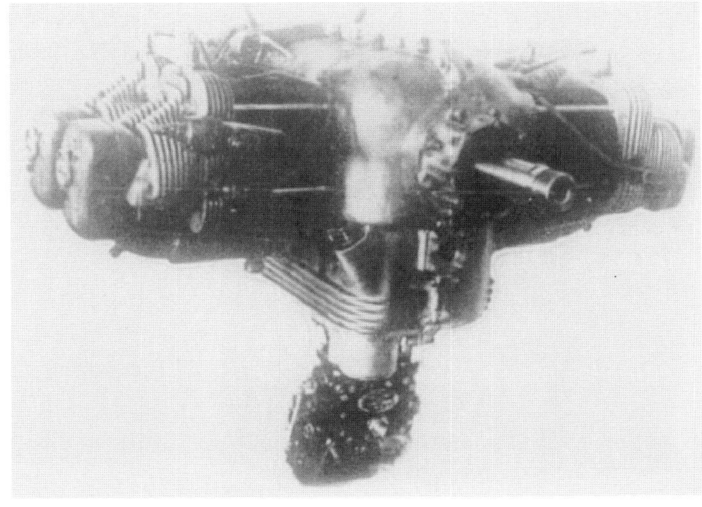

RIGHT: **The M-1 engine from the front.**

A side view of the M-1.

Kazan from 1942. The engine was a modernization of the series M-105P (later M-105PF) engine. The cylinder diameter was changed back to 150mm (5.90in), as on the M-103, and new cylinder liners were introduced, as well as a four-valve gas-distribution mechanism with improved hydraulics, and strengthened crankshaft and gearing. The cooling of the upper part of the engine block was improved, lubrication of the main bearing was changed, and a number of minor changes introduced. The engine was boosted in rpm compared with the M-105PF.

By 20 January 1943 all engineering drawings for the engine, already redesignated M-1, had been transferred to the prototype manufacturing workshop. The first prototypes were built in February-March, and factory tests started on 27 March. During June-August the 70hr factory bench tests took place, and in November of the same year two prototypes were installed in a Pe-2 bomber. Its first flight with M-1s took place on 16 November 1943, and flight testing lasted until February 1944.

The M-1 was not introduced into series production, as it was considered to have less commonality with the M-105PF than the M-107A (VK-107A).

The M-1 was installed in a modified series Pe-2 bomber. It was also intended for installation in one of A.S. Yakovlev's fighters.

Characteristics

12-cylinder in-line vee, four-stroke, liquid-cooled, geared engine with a single-stage, two-speed GCS.

Power rating	1,300/1,500hp
Bore/stroke	150/170mm (5.90/6.69in)
Volume	36.0 litres (2,197cu in)
Compression ratio	6.6:1
Weight	660kg (1,455lb)

CHAPTER THIRTY-THREE

The Conrod-free Engines of S.S. Balandin

In 1935 engineer S.S. Balandin proposed a new mechanism for converting reciprocating motion into rotary motion. Having rejected the traditional crank mechanism, he replaced it with an original device using straight rods and an interim shaft, which required the cylinders to be positioned in opposed pairs. This innovation allowed the designer to produce a more compact engine, and to increase its output and service life owing to decreased friction.

Balandin initially proposed this layout for steam engines, but from 1937 he started to work on internal combustion aero-engines. That year Balandin developed his first aero-engine, designated OMB, which used the cylinders, piston heads and pistons from the popular M-11A. A four-cylinder OMB was built and underwent factory and joint testing. Comparative trials between the OMB and a series M-11G of conventional radial layout showed that Balandin's engine had certain advantages regaring calorific intensity, service life and fuel consumption. The OMB was being tested until 1941.

Using the experience gained from his work on the OMB, Balandin created a unified family of MB engines ('MB' stood for *Motor Besshatunniy*, or conrod-free engine). The family consisted of the 4-cylinder MB-4 (an improved version of the OMB) and an 8-cylinder MB-8 (comprising two MB-4s driving a single shaft). These were followed by similar designs that differed mainly by cylinder diameter, the MB-4b and MB-8b. Prototypes of all of these engines were built and bench-tested.

After the war Balandin was tasked with creating a new, extra-high-powered M-127 engine (9,000hp). An OKB-500-II design bureau was established for this purpose at Factory No. 500 in Tushino (the factory also accommodated the OKB-500-I design bureau of V.M. Yakovlev, which was working on aviation diesels). In the beginning the OKB-500-II developed a project for a 12-cylinder, 2,100hp OM-127o engine, and then proceeded to work on the OM-127, an 8-cylinder block from

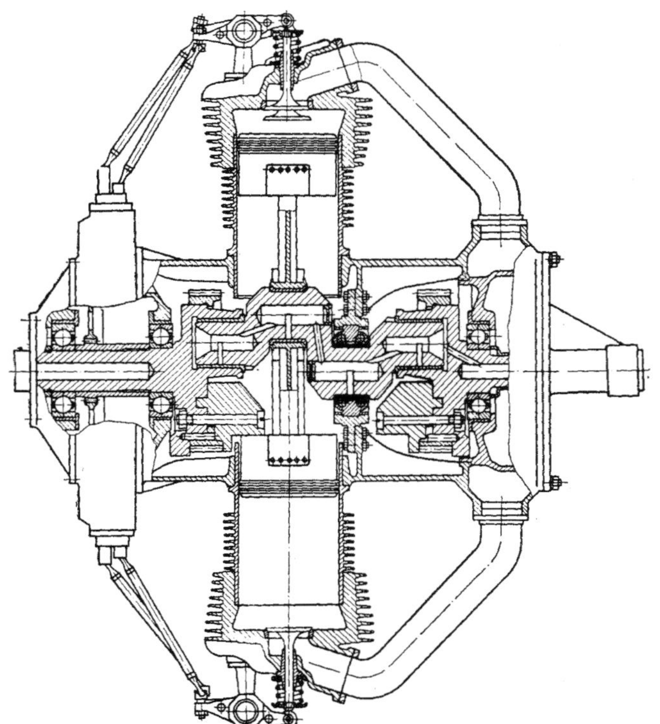
A drawing of the OMB engine.

An early-series OM-127RN engine.

the 24-cylinder M-127. The latter was to be assembled using three OM-127 blocks installed one behind another. A specific feature of this engine was double action, i.e. ignition took place on both sides of each piston.

Later, the OM-127 was modified into a separate OM-127RN engine with its own gear and impulse turbines. Several OM-127s and OM-127RNs were built and underwent factory testing. Using the experience gained during OM-127RN refinement, the M-127 project was transformed into the 10,000hp M-127K, equipped with impulse turbines and new gearing, and having increased compression ratio. Factory No. 500 started manufacturing the components and units of this engine, which was intended for heavy bombers.

In 1948, under Balandin's leadership, engineering drawings were prepared for an even higher-powered engine. This was a two-stroke diesel that, according to estimates, could reach 14,000hp.

However, by that time the aviation industry had started the transition to jet engines. Turboprops and turbojets, which had been under development in the Soviet Union, already held sway at these power ratings. The design bureau of V.M. Yakovlev, also at Factory No. 500, was ordered to copy the Rolls-Royce Derwent V turbojet and, to concentrate all efforts on this important and urgent work, OKB-500-II was disbanded and most of its staff merged into Yakovlev's OKB-500-I.

After liquidation of his design bureau, Balandin continued the development of conrod-free engines intended for automobiles. However, none his designs reached series production.

Interest in the layout proposed by Balandin did not die, however. Several types of conrod-free engines using Balandin's mechanism or versions of it, and rated from 200hp to 750hp, are presently being developed in Russia.

OMB

The first conrod-free aero-engine designed by S.S. Balandin, this was being developed from 1937. The OMB was considered merely an experimental type, intended to validate the proposed mechanism. The engine used many components and units from the series M-11A; the cylinders, cylinder heads, pistons and piston pins. New components in the OMB were the crankcase and the conrod-free mechanism for converting reciprocating motion into rotary motion. The rods were modified from the conrods of the M-11A. This extensive borrowing later allowed designers to perform a fair comparison of the OMB and M-11A (which had a traditional radial layout).

The prototype was built at the Air Force Academy at the end of 1937, and its tests started the following year. The second prototype was completed in 1938, and in 1939-41 it underwent official factory testing and 50hr joint testing. Compared with the M-11A, the OMB had lower fuel consumption, lower calorific intensity, and could use lower-quality fuel. However, it was heavier and had lower power rating.

The OMB was the basis for the creation of a family of conrod-free MB engines.

Characteristics

4-cylinder X-shaped (cylinder pairs were placed perpendicular to each other in different planes), air-cooled, four-stroke, direct-drive unsupercharged engine.

Power rating	83/90hp (according to the project 82hp)
Bore/stroke	125/140mm (4.92/5.51in)
Volume	6.88 litres (420cu in)
Compression ratio	5.0:1
Weight	195kg (430lb)

The OMB engine.

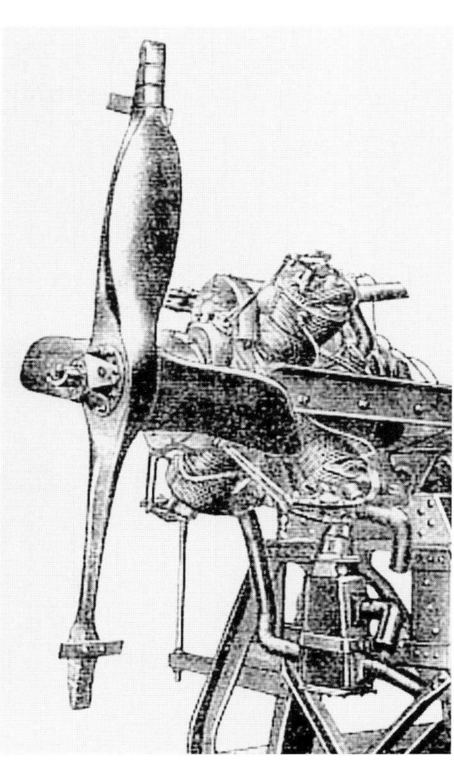

The OMB during bench tests.

MB-4

A further development of the OMB, this engine was created under the leadership of S.S. Balandin and was the first of a unified family of conrod-free engines. The MB-4 was a real aero-engine, equipped with all the necessary components for that time: a compressor, an electric generator, a pneumatic self-starter and an hydraulically controlled variable-pitch propeller. Compared with the OMB, compression ratio was increased, and the engine was boosted in rpm. Its cylinders, gas-distribution mechanism and fuel mixture injection system were improved. New pistons were introduced, simplifying the engine's manufacture. The conrods featured an articulated design for more convenient assembly.

A prototype of the MB-4 was built and underwent bench testing. Its specific power rating was too low for the time, but it should be borne in mind that the unified crankcase allowed the possibility of

The MB-4 engine.

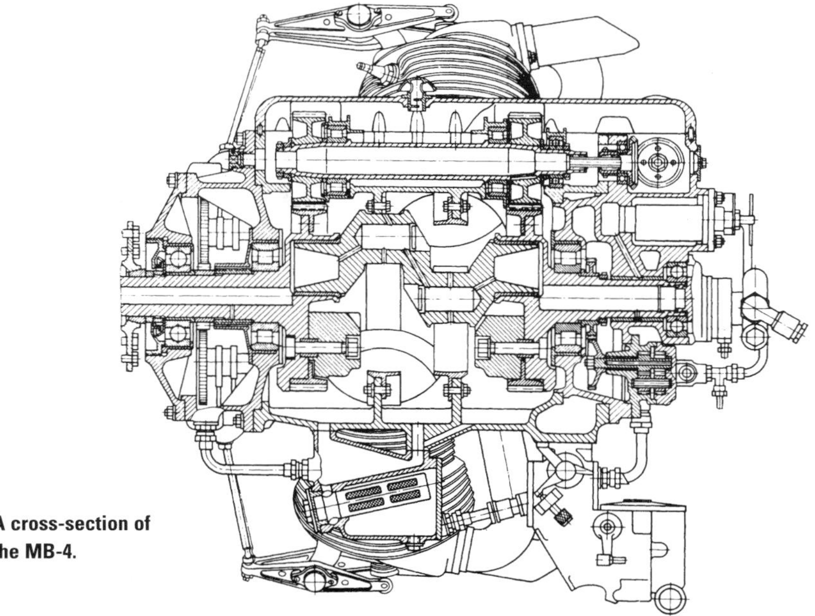

A cross-section of the MB-4.

installing cylinders of larger diameter (as was done later in the MB-4b), and the conrod-free mechanism was designed for transmission of up to 500hp. Thus the engine's strength was excessive, providing designers with possibilities for further improvement.

Characteristics

4-cylinder X-shaped (cylinder pairs were placed perpendicular to each other in different planes), air-cooled, four-stroke, direct-drive unsupercharged engine.

Power rating	140hp
Bore/stroke	125/140mm (4.92/5.51in)
Volume	6.86 litres (419cu in)
Compression ratio	5.8:1
Weight	156kg (344lb)

MB-8

This 8-cylinder engine was unified with the MB-4. In fact, it consisted of two MB-4s placed in tandem. The two engine types were being developed simultaneously, and the MB-8 had the same subassemblies as the MB-4.

A prototype of the MB-8 was built and underwent bench testing.

Characteristics

8-cylinder X-shaped (cylinder pairs were placed perpendicular to each other in different planes), air-cooled, four-stroke, direct-drive unsupercharged engine.

Power rating	280hp
Bore/stroke	125/140mm (4.92/5.51in)
Volume	13.73 litres (838cu in)
Compression ratio	5.8:1
Weight	248kg (545lb)

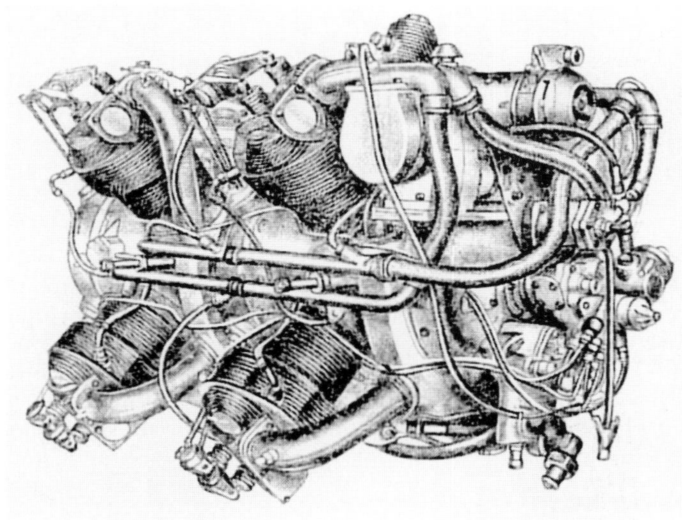

RIGHT: **The MB-8 engine.**

BELOW RIGHT: **The MB-4b engine.**

MB-4b

An rpm-boosted version of the MB-4 with cylinders of larger diameter.

A prototype of the MB-4b was built and underwent bench testing.

Characteristics

4-cylinder X-shaped (cylinder pairs were placed perpendicular to each other in different planes), air-cooled, four-stroke, direct-drive unsupercharged engine.

Power rating	200hp
Bore/stroke	146/140mm (5.75/5.51in)
Volume	9.37 litres (572cu in)
Compression ratio	5.8:1
Weight	210kg (463lb)

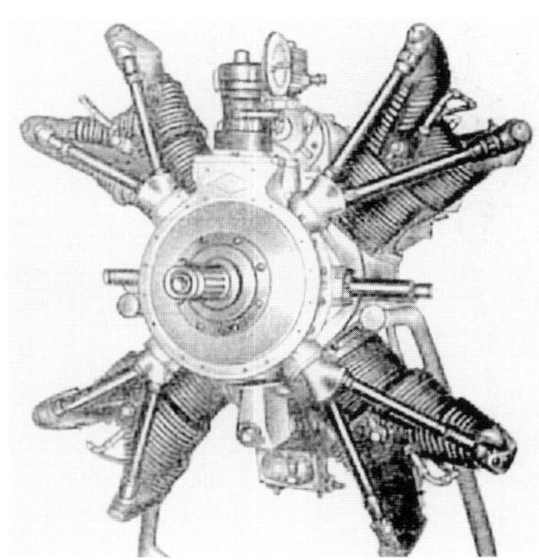

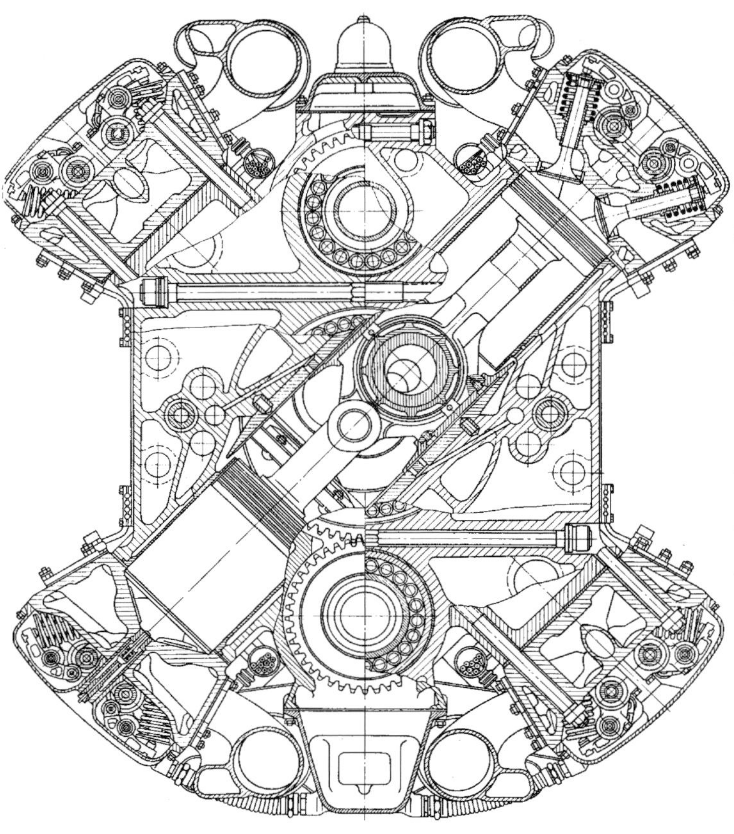

A drawing of the OM-127o.

MB-8b

An rpm-boosted version of the 8-cylinder MB-8 (made in the same way as the MB-4b), with cylinders of larger diameter.

A prototype of the MB-8b was built and underwent bench testing.

Characteristics

8-cylinder X-shaped (cylinder pairs were placed perpendicular to each other in different planes), air-cooled, four-stroke, direct-drive unsupercharged engine.

Power rating	400hp
Bore/stroke	146/140mm (5.75/5.51in)
Volume	18.74 litres (1,144cu in)
Compression ratio	5.8:1
Weight	354kg (761lb)

OM-127o

Within the bounds of the M-127 project, the design of this engine's primary section was carried out during the initial stage. Development was being performed at OKB-500-II in Tushino from 1945. The engine's construction was fundamentally different from that of the MB family of engines; it had water cooling and a block structure. The lower-case 'o' in the designation denoted 'single action' (from the Russian *odinarnogo deystviya*), i.e. the combustion chamber was located on one side of the piston. The engine was being developed in two variants, with and without turbo-supercharging. A prototype was not built, as the designer turned to a more efficient double-action scheme.

Characteristics

12-cylinder X-shaped (four blocks were set in pairs perpendicular to each other in different planes), geared engine with a GCS (in its second variant, also with turbo-supercharging).

Power rating	1,750/2,100hp (with turbo-supercharger 2,150/2,800hp)
Bore/stroke	160/170mm (6.30/6.69in)
Volume	41.0 litres (2,502cu in)
Compression ratio	7.2:1
Weight	950kg (2,094lb) (with turbo-supercharger 1,200kg (2,645lb)).

OM-127RN

This engine, designated OM-127, was also being developed initially as a section (one third) of the M-127. A number of design features of the OM-127o were used, but the new engine had double-action cylinders (with combustion chambers on both sides of the piston), articulated rods (for convenient assembly), oil cooling of rods and pistons, and a direct fuel injection system. The cylinders were continuous, going from one block into the opposite one, and the heads of the lower and upper cylinder blocks differed.

Later, the OM-127 was modified into a separate OM-127RN engine with its own gearing, and a prototype was built and underwent factory bench testing in 1947-48. During refinement the engine's compression ratio was increased from 5.5:1 to 7.0:1, and later up to 7.5:1. Two impulse turbines were installed, which also drove the propeller (for testing the components of the M-127K project).

Characteristics

8-cylinder X-shaped (four blocks were set in pairs perpendicular to each other in different planes), geared engine with a GCS.

Power rating	3,200hp (with impulse turbines, 3,500hp)
Bore/stroke	155/146mm (6.10/5.75in)
Volume	22.0 litres (1,342cu in)
Compression ratio	7.5:1 (initially – 5.5:1)
Weight	2,030kg (4,475lb) (with impulse turbines, 2,150kg (4,740lb))

M-127

An extra-high-powered engine intended for heavy bombers, the M-127 consisted of three OM-127s in tandem, with their conrod-free mechanisms positioned at 120 degrees relative to each other. Each of the three sections had four blocks in X-shaped configuration. The engine was under development from 1945 at OKB-500-II, under the leadership of S.S. Balandin.

In the course its development, using experience gained during work on the OM-127RN, the M-127 was modified into the higher-powered M-127K, equipped with impulse turbines. A prototype of this version was built and underwent factory bench testing.

Refinement work on the M-127K ceased

in 1948, owing to the closure of OKB-500-II.

Characteristics

24-cylinder X-shaped (four blocks were set in pairs, perpendicular to each other in different planes), geared engine with a GCS.

Bore/stroke	160/170mm (6.30/6.69in)
Volume	82.0 litres (5,004cu in)
Compression ratio	6.9:1 (later 7.1:1)
Power rating	dependant on version
Weight	dependant on version

The following versions of the engine are known:

M-127 The original version of the engine, with a power rating of 8,000/9,000hp. A prototype was not built.

M-127K A version of the M-127 with modified cylinder heads and equipped with impulse turbines. Power rating 8,000/10,000hp, weight 3,450kg (7,606lb). The engine had two types of gearing: for a single propeller and for a pair of coaxial contrarotating propellers. Several prototypes were built and underwent factory bench testing.

A project existed for an M-127K variant with a new gas-distribution mechanism that reduced the engine's overall dimensions.

RIGHT: **An OM-127RN of the later series.**

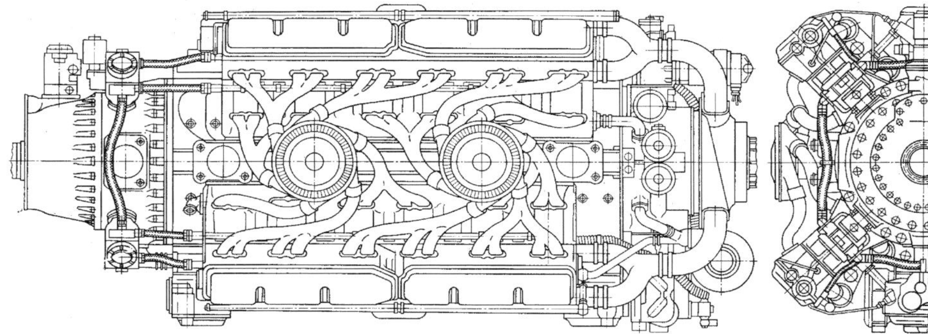

BELOW: **A drawing of the M-127K.**

CHAPTER THIRTY-FOUR

Lesser-known Projects of 1939–1947

In the pre-war years, during the Second World War and for several postwar years some piston aero-engines were under development in the USSR for which information is very scarce. Details of their design, characteristics, and sometimes even the basic engine layout, remain unknown. Even so, some of these engines were notable for their original design features. Some had non-standard designations, indicating that they were not included in the State plan for aero-engine development, and that the work on them was being carried out under the initiative of certain authorities or enterprises.

The Pavlyuchuk-Burov Engine (PB)

In July 1935 P.N. Pavlyuchuk and I.F. Burov, working at the NII VVS, proposed a design for a two-shaft vee engine with coupled cylinders. In September of that year it was decided to manufacture one section of such an engine, using M-11, M-17 and M-22 components, to test the viability of the concept. This section was built in the NII VVS workshops at the end of 1936, and bench tests started in April 1937. The proposed layout provided designers with the possibility of creating a compact engine, but the design was more sophisticated.

Characteristics

24-cylinder coupled vee, two-shaft, four-stroke, liquid-cooled, geared engine.

Power rating	600hp
Bore/stroke	90/100mm (3.54/3.94in)
Volume	15.45 litres (943cu in)
Compression ratio	7.2:1
Weight	290kg (639lb)

In 1938 an improved version was developed, having an estimated power rating of 850/900hp and a weight of 420kg (926lb).

M-32

This designation was first used for a 16-cylinder engine created under the leadership of V.M. Yakovlev. In 1939 it was again allocated, this time to a medium-powered engine being developed at the design bureau of Factory No. 154 in Voronezh. The project was completed in 1939-40. In 1941 manufacture of the main components and units of a prototype was started, but the process was interrupted by the war and further evacuation to Andizhan. After evacuation, the work on the M-32 was not resumed. At the beginning of 1942 the engine was officially excluded from the plan of development work.

Characteristics

9-cylinder radial, four-stroke, air-cooled, direct-drive unsupercharged engine.

Power rating	400/400hp
Weight	330kg (727lb)

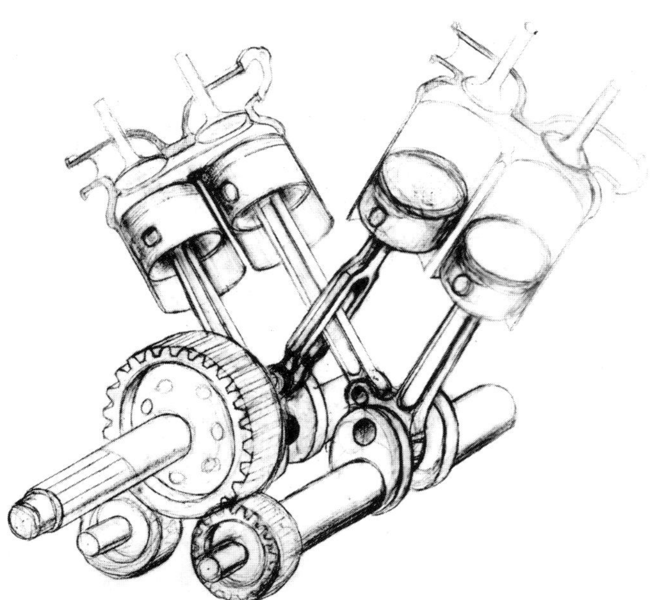

The crank mechanism of Pavlyuchuk-Burov's engine; a sketch drawn by one of the designers.

A part of the PB engine at the NII VVS in 1938.

I.A. Uvarov's Circular Engine

In 1938 I.A. Uvarov proposed an original project for an engine having one circular cylinder divided into six chambers. Twelve pistons performed an oscillatory motion in accordance with the four-stroke cycle, transmitting the motion to the engine's shaft through complex gearing. Uvarov's engine was to have very high specific power rating.

In 1939 a prototype was built, which underwent bench testing during 1939-41. Plans to build a prototype batch were not implemented owing to the outbreak of war.

Characteristics

Circular, six-chamber geared engine without a GCS.

Power rating	1,600hp (maximum, according to the project)
Bore/stroke	127/127mm (5.00/5.00in)
Compression ratio	8.0:1
Weight	300kg (660lb)

M-Sh

This engine of unconventional layout was intended for ground-attack aircraft ('M-Sh' being an abbreviation of *Motor Shturmovika*, or engine for attack aeroplane). Preliminary development of the M-Sh was undertaken in 1943 at the design bureau of Factory No. 19 in Molotov. Specific features of the engine were the inclined positioning of cylinders and crank-less gearing. No information on further work on this project has been found.

The possibility of cannon installation, with the barrel passing through a hollow output shaft, was to be provided for.

Characteristics

12-cylinder radial engine with inclined cylinders and crank-less gearing.

Power rating	1,450/1,850hp
Weight	800kg (1,760lb) (according to the specification)

Uvarov's engine in the Monino museum.

M-111TK

In 1947 development of the high-powered M-111TK aero-engine started at the design bureau of Factory No. 26 in Ufa, under the leadership of N.D. Kuznetsov. From the end of 1947 OKB-26 became increasingly involved in the work on jet engines. After completing the copying of the German Jumo 004 turbojet, which was introduced into series production in the USSR as the RD-10, the design bureau proceeded to develop and manufacture the RD-12 and RD-14. Because of this overload, all work on the M-111TK was cancelled in 1948. Kuznetsov was transferred to Kuibyshev, where he headed a design bureau of German engineers working on turboprop engine development.

Characteristics

36-cylinder, liquid-cooled engine with turbo-supercharging.

Power rating	4,700/5,500hp (according to the project)

CHAPTER THIRTY-FIVE

The Engines of G.S. Skubachevskiy and I.V. Dobrynin

Before the beginning of the Second World War the Soviet Union lagged considerably behind both its enemies and allies in aero-engine development. In particular, the country had no engines of 2,000hp and higher. To fill this gap, development work on the M-120, M-36 (AM-36), M-130, M-300 and MB-100 engines was accelerated. Another step in this direction was the establishment of the KB-2 design bureau at the MAI, which was tasked with creating the M-250 engine.

At the beginning of 1939 the People's Commissar of the Aviation Industry, M.M. Kaganovich, in a discussion with G.S. Skubachevskiy, holder of of the Aero-Engine Design Chair at the MAI, defined the main characteristics for a new aero-engine. Using this specification, Skubachevskiy, in co-operation with a team of teaching staff and students, developed a preliminary project for the power plant. The new engine had a radial layout of cylinder blocks (such a layout had been proposed for the first time in the M-20 project, developed by A.A. Mikulin and V.A. Dobrynin back in the mid-1920s).

In July 1939 the Soviet Government issued a decree establishing the KB-2 design bureau at the MAI, and ordered it to develop a new 2,200/2,500hp engine. G.S. Skubachevskiy was appointed head of the bureau, and V.A. Dobrynin (1895-1978) became his deputy, as he had vast practical experience in engine design. Dobrynin had worked at the TsIAM, and had then been chief designer at Factory No. 24 for several years. In the latter post he had made an important contribution to the setting-up of M-34 (AM-34) series production, and had participated in the development of M-34 versions, particularly the M-34FRN. The KB-2 staff consisted mainly of MAI teachers, postgraduates and undergraduates (in their last years of study).

Development of the M-250 started in September 1939 and was completed by March 1940. Two versions were being developed: one with a carburettor and the other with direct fuel injection. Initially it was planned that the prototypes would be built in the workshops of the TsIAM but, later, Factory No. 16 in Voronezh was given the task.

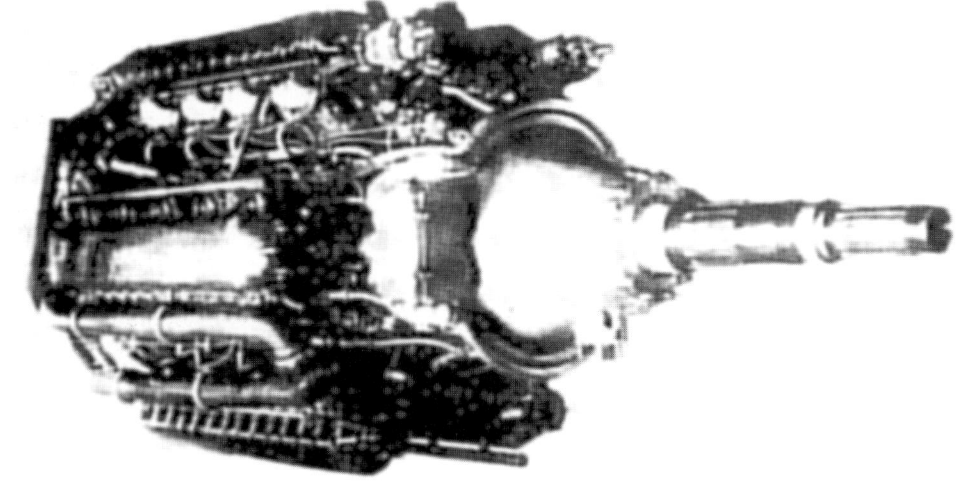

The M-250 engine.

Most of the KB-2 staff were transferred to Voronezh in 1941, where they joined the factory design bureau headed by S.D. Kolosov, Dobrynin becoming his deputy. Skubachevskiy remained at the MAI, where he led a special team established under the Aero-Engine Design Chair, which also worked on the M-250.

Factory No. 16 started manufacturing five M-250 prototypes, the first of which was bench tested on 22 June 1941, just after the radio announcement of Germany's aggression against the Soviet Union. With German troops advancing towards Voronezh, the factory was evacuated to Kazan in October 1941. The staff of the former KB-2 was not evacuated with the factory, but separately, to Ufa, where they formed the nucleus of the new OKB-250 design bureau headed by Dobrynin. However, the detached design bureau lost its manufacturing base. It was planned that series-production Factory No. 26, which had been evacuated to Ufa from Rybinsk, would support the design bureau, but it was overloaded with the increased production of Klimov engines and was not keen to take on extra work. As a result, the parts and units for the M-250 prototypes were manufactured slowly at different enterprises, and quite often the quality was poor. All of these setbacks delayed the engine's creation.

In October 1943 OKB-250 was transferred to Factory No. 36 in Rybinsk, which had been established in the workshops of the evacuated Factory No. 26, and the design bureau was renamed OKB-1 of Factory No. 36. However, during the war years this factory was also overburdened, and plans to put the M-250 into series production were not realized.

In June 1946 development work on the M-250 ceased, but by that time OKB-1, now renamed OKB-36, had begun to develop an improved M-251TK version that used the main components of its predecessor. The engine's chief designer was A.L. Dynkin. In 1947 this engine passed factory and joint tests, followed by State tests in 1948. It was manufactured in a small series as the VD-3TK, and in 1950 was tested in a Tu-4 bomber.

In 1949 OKB-36 started the development of the M-253K compound engine, with impulse turbines driving a propeller through gearing. Its maximum rating was to be 4,300hp. The first M-253K prototype underwent testing in January 1950, and a year later the new engine passed its State tests. The M-253K was built in a small series as the VD-4K. In 1950-51 it was test-flown in Tu-4 and Tu-85 bombers.

However, the advent of jet engines quickly devalued OKB-36's achievements in creating powerful piston aero-engines. The Tu-85 heavy bomber, which was to be powered by the VD-4K, did not enter series production. Under Dobrynin's leadership OKB-36 switched to the development of turbojets. It developed the VD-5 prototype, followed by the more successful VD-7, which was introduced into series production. The VD-7 powered the 3M and Tu-22 bombers.

In the autumn of 1941 Skubachevskiy was evacuated to Alma-Ata together with the MAI, and his participation in M-250 development temporarily ceased. After the institute was returned to Moscow, in 1944-46 he fulfilled the combined post of Dobrynin's deputy and lecturer at the MAI. Thenceforth he no longer participated in engine development work, and for many years held the Aero-Engine Design Chair at the MAI.

The VD-4K engine.

M-250

This high-powered piston aero-engine featured a new layout of radial cylinder blocks. The preliminary project for the M-250 was prepared at the Aero-Engine Design Chair of the MAI in July 1939. Engineering development was completed at KB-2 of the MAI during September 1939 – March 1940, under the leadership of G.S. Skubachevskiy and V.A. Dobrynin. The M-250 was designed in two versions: one with a carburettor, and the other with direct fuel injection.

A batch of five prototypes was manufactured at Factory No. 16 in Voronezh, and it was planned that this factory would carry out series production of the engine. The first prototype began bench testing on 22 June 1941. Refinement work was carried out at Voronezh until September 1941, then at OKB-250 in Ufa, and from October 1943 at OKB-1 (OKB-36) in Rybinsk. In 1943 it was planned to set up series production at Factory No. 26 in Ufa. In accordance with a decree of the USSR Council of Ministers issued on 25 June 1946, all development work on the M-250 was cancelled.

Ten M-250s were built. The planned batch of forty to be built at Factory No. 36 was not completed. Some of the assembled engines were later used in the programme for the improved M-251TK.

It was planned to install the M-250 in an Il-2 attack aeroplane, in a Yakovlev fighter and, later, in an I-218 heavy fighter and attack aeroplane (with a pusher propeller).

Characteristics

24-cylinder radial block-type (six blocks of four cylinders each), liquid-cooled, geared engine with a single-stage, three-speed GCS.

Power rating	2,200/2,500hp
Bore/stroke	140/138mm (5.51/5.43in)
Volume	51.0 litres (3,112cu in)
Compression ratio	6.2:1
Weight	1,280kg (2,822lb)

M-251TK (VD-3TK)

A further development of the M-250, this engine was created at OKB-36 in Rybinsk, under the leadership of V.A. Dobrynin. Compared with the M-250, its crankcase and crankshaft were of modified design, and it had strengthened connecting rods, increased-diameter cylinders (the positioning of the cylinder axes was retained), and longer-stroke pistons. Two TK-19 turbo-superchargers (copied from the American ones) were introduced, but the GCS was retained. The GCS had an impeller of increased diameter and single-speed drive. Two versions of gearing were developed; for a standard propeller and for coaxial contrarotating propellers.

The engineering drawings for the M-251TK were transferred for prototype manufacture in October-December 1946. The engine underwent factory testing from August 1947. In December of that year the type passed its 50hr joint tests, in June 1948 is passed 100hr factory tests, and in July-October 1948 it passed its State tests.

In January 1949 a decision was made to manufacture a batch of twenty engines at Factory No. 36, under the designation VD-3TK. In total, thirty-four were built.

In January-July 1950 VD-3TK engines were test-flown in Tu-4 bombers.

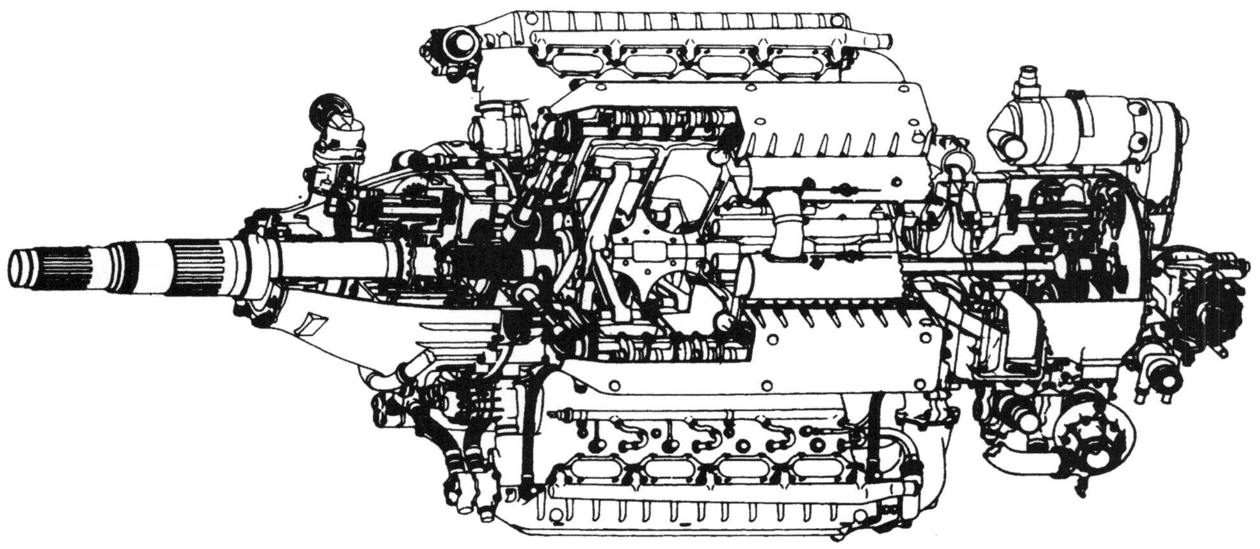

A schematic diagram of the VD-3TK.

The VD-3TK engine.

A VD-4K engine on display in the Rybinsk factory's museum.

The Tu-85 heavy bomber prototype, powered by four VD-4Ks.

A VD-4K engine in the Tu-85

A VD-4K in the Tu-85.

The VD-3TK powered a prototype of the Tu-4 bomber.

Characteristics

24-cylinder radial block-type (six blocks of four cylinders each), liquid-cooled, geared engine with a single-stage, single-speed GCS and two turbo-superchargers.

Power rating	2,500/3,500hp
Bore/stroke	148/144mm (5.83/5.67in)
Volume	59.43 litres (3,626cu in)
Compression ratio	6.6:1
Weight	1,520kg (3,351lb) (according to some sources 1,620kg (3,572lb))

M-253K (VD-4K)

A compound engine based on the VD-3TK, the M-253K was developed at OKB-36 in Rybinsk under the leadership of V.A. Dobrynin, with P.A. Kolesov as chief designer. Three impulse turbines were positioned between cylinder blocks at the point of exhaust nozzle attachment. Two TK-19 turbo-superchargers were replaced by one original turbo-supercharger fitted with a jet nozzle. The gear ratio of the GCS drive was reduced, and some changes were made to the design of the engine gearing.

The M-253K was under development from January 1949. In September of that year the engineering development was completed and prototype manufacture was started. The first M-253K was completed by January 1950. In June the engine underwent its 100hr factory tests, and in November-December it underwent joint testing. Its State tests were successfully passed in January-February 1951.

It was planned to build a small batch of M-253Ks (under the VD-4K designation) in 1951, to be used for military testing. In total, twenty-three were built.

In 1950 the VD-4K was test-flown in a Tu-4 bomber, and during July-August 1951 in a Tu-85 bomber prototype. In the course of refinement of the Tu-85 powerplant a forced-cooling fan was installed.

The VD-4K engines were installed in the prototypes of the Tu-4 and Tu-85 bombers.

Characteristics

24-cylinder radial block-type (six blocks of four cylinders each), liquid-cooled, geared engine with a single-stage, single-speed GCS, turbo-supercharging and a forced-cooling fan.

Power rating	3,250/4,300hp
Bore/stroke	148/144mm (5.83/5.67in)
Volume	59.43 litres (3,626cu in)
Compression ratio	7.0:1
Weight	2,065kg (4,552lb) without turbo-supercharger (without a fan, generator and some other units, 1,900kg (4,190lb)) Weight of the turbo-supercharger without automatic control equipment, 220kg (485lb).

CHAPTER THIRTY-SIX

The Engines of A.G. Ivchenko and their Evolution

When German troops approached the Zaporozhye region, Factory No. 29 was evacuated to the Russian East. The abandoned factory workshops were used by the Germans for repairing aero-engines brought from the Front. When the Soviet troops liberated Zaporozhye it was decided not to move Factory No. 29 back, as was done with other factories evacuated to Siberia and the Urals, but to establish a new factory there. Thus Factory No. 478 was created. In the beginning it repaired M-88 engines, and later an ASh-82FN assembly line was set up.

On 5 May 1945 the OKB-478 design bureau, headed by A.G. Ivchenko (1903-68), was established at the factory, and from 1 July 1946 the design bureau received independent status.

In 1945 OKB-478 started developing a family of helicopter engines, the first specialized helicopter engines in the Soviet Union. Earlier, modified MG-31Fs and MV-6s, as well as American R-975-AN-1s, had been used to power the first Soviet helicopters. The new engine family was to consist of three unified single-row air-cooled radial engines of different power ratings. For these engines, cylinder dimensions and a piston stroke similar to those of the ASh-82FN were chosen, and many other design features were also borrowed from this successful engine. This approach reduced production costs and simplified manufacture, which used available production jigs. However, unlike the ASh-82FN, the helicopter engines did not have a direct fuel injection system, but carburettors. Different power ratings were achieved by having different numbers of cylinders; the M-27 had five, the M-26 seven, and the M-29 nine. All of the designations assigned to the new engines had previously been allocated to other types, but these had not been widely used and no longer existed in the mid-1940s.

The first engine to be created was the M-26, and work started in 1945. This engine had seven cylinders in a single row, like the ASh-82FN. In July 1945 bench tests were started, and on 15 July one engine was test-flown in a modified Junkers-Ju 52/3m. The first M-26s did not have specific components peculiar to a helicopter powerplant, such as forced cooling and a clutch. In fact the M-26 was a counterpart of the ASh-21, which at that time was being created at OKB-29 as 'half' of an ASh-82FN, and was also equipped with a carburettor. The M-26 was slightly heavier than prescribed by the specification, and suffered from oil leaks. It underwent State tests twice, and they were finally passed in November 1946.

Development of the M-26GR helicopter engine was completed at the beginning of 1946, and by September it had passed its factory tests. That same year Factory No. 478 started introducing the M-26GR into series production, and by the end of the year it had manufactured ten. From 1947 this engine was built in large quantities, and was used on various Soviet helicopters, including the popular Mi-1. In 1948 the engine was redesignated AI-26V. Repeatedly modified, it remained in mass production for a long time.

An AI-26V engine stored in the Monino museum.

Two other engines of this family, the M-27GR and M-29GR, appear to have been less successful, all development work on them being cancelled at the beginning of 1948.

Also in 1948, OKB-478 started development of the M-4 engine for light helicopters. It was built and tested, and flight-tested in Ka-10 helicopters, but was not put into series production.

In 1947 OKB-478, under the leadership of Ivchenko, started to develop an engine family for light aircraft. These engines were of completely original design, though they retained certain similarities with the AI-26V. The family comprised three radial air-cooled engines: the 5-cylinder M-10, 7-cylinder M-12 and 9-cylinder M-14. All of these designations, too, had been used before. The new engines all had the same-diameter cylinders, but differed in piston stroke and compression ratio. The smallest, the M-10, had neither gearing nor supercharger. The M-12 and M-14 had a supercharger, but still no gearing; gearing appeared on the M-14 only in the course of further improvement. The M-10 and M-12 passed their bench and flight tests in 1947-48, but were not introduced into series production, though their application was specified in specifications for several light aeroplanes.

On the other hand, mass production of the M-14 started in 1948 and continued to the present. Various versions have been developed for aeroplanes and helicopters. In addition, locally-designed versions were built in Poland, Czechoslovakia and China. In the Soviet Union the engine was designated M-14, but was soon

An AI-14R in the Monino museum.

The Yak-18T trainer, powered by the M-14P.

redesignated AI-14. In other countries corresponding national designations were used.

Initially, the AI-14 was manufactured in Zaporozhye, and then production was transferred to Voronezh-based Factory No. 154. There, in 1960, a design bureau was established on the basis of the factory's design department, headed by I.M. Vedeneev. In 1962 this team was given the status of a branch of the Ivchenko Design Bureau. Under the leadership of Vedeneev this bureau created the AI-14RF and AI-14VF versions of the engine.

Work on turboprop development began in Zaporozhye from 1953. In 1955 Ivchenko started creating the AI-20 turboprop, which appeared to be a success, and in 1958 it was introduced into series production. This engine powered such well-known aircraft as the Il-18, An-10, An-12, An-32, Il-38 and Be-12. No other piston engine was created at Zaporozhye, the design bureau working only on improvement of the AI-26V.

In 1948 A.G. Ivchenko was awarded the Stalin Prize for his achievements as a designer of piston engines. In the 1960s he became an Academician, a Lenin Prize Laureate and a Hero of Socialist Labour.

From 1966 the design bureau at Voronezh (now called the Machine-Building Design Bureau, as it works not only on piston engines, but also on gears for helicopters) became an independent design bureau and continued modernization of the AI-14, again redesignated M-14. A mass-produced M-14P version was developed, as well as a range of further versions, the 'PA', 'PM', 'PS', 'PT', 'PR' and 'SKh'. This work was performed under the leadership of A.G. Bakanov, who took Vedeneev's place in 1973. The design bureau developed helicopter versions as well; the M-14V26, M-14V1 and M-14V2.

Different versions of the M-14 were in production not only in Russia, but also in Poland, Czechoslovakia, Romania and China, and the engine was exported to many countries. From the mid-1970s the M-14 was the only piston engine being built in the Soviet Union.

With the growth of light aviation in the country, there arose a demand for an engine with a lower power rating than the M-14P. An attempt was therefore made to create such an engine, again using the M-14P as a basis. In the mid-1990s the M-3 was developed, which had three cylinders and many components borrowed from the M-14P. The use of M-14P components was intended to simplify manufacture and maintenance of the new engine, and reduce its cost. Although the M-3 was introduced into series production, it was not widely adopted. Among its drawbacks were a high level of vibration and poor starting, especially in winter. In fact only one aeroplane, the SL-90, of which a small batch was manufactured, was powered by the M-3. The engine was also used in a number of home-built aircraft, but they remained in use for a relatively short time. By the year 2000 the M-3 had been removed from service. The remaining M-3s were dismantled and their parts used as spares for the M-14.

The recently produced 9-cylinder M-9 could be considered a further evolution of the M-14, as it retains many components of this engine.

M-26 (AI-26)

This designation had been used earlier for the series-production KIM engine, built in the 1930s and unified with the M-15.

From 1945 OKB-478, under the leadership of A.G. Ivchenko, developed the first Soviet helicopter engine. Bench testing of the M-26 prototype (without a fan, special gearing and a starting clutch) started on 26 July 1945, and was followed that same month by flight testing in a modified Ju 52/3m.

In April 1946 the M-26 underwent State tests for the first time. Its weight exceeded that given in the specification, and the prototype suffered from oil

An AI-26V in Samara Aerospace University.

leaks. In October-November 1946 the M-26 successfully passed its State tests.

Development of the M-26GR ('GR' for *Gelikopter*, helicopter) helicopter engine was completed at the beginning of 1946. It underwent factory testing until 26 November, six prototypes having been built for this purpose. In October 1947 factory testing of a G-4 helicopter powered by a pair of M-26GRs started.

From the end of 1946 Factory No. 478 in Zaporozhye began to prepare for M-26GR series production. In total, ten series had been manufactured by the end of the year. Mass-production was launched in 1947, and up to the beginning of 1970s more than 1,300 M-26GRs of different versions had been built at Zaporozhye. In 1947-49, during engine refinement, several rpm-boosted variants of the engine were created. The period between scheduled maintenance for the M-26 gradually increased, and by the end of production it had reached 700hr. In 1948 the engine was redesignated AI-26V.

From 1963 to 1968 this engine was in production in Poland at the factory in Rzeszow as the LiT-3, and later as the PZL-3S.

The Mi-1 helicopter, powered by the AI-26V.

Characteristics

7-cylinder radial, four-stroke, air-cooled, geared engine with forced air-cooling, a starting clutch and a single-stage, single-speed GCS.

Bore/stroke	155.5/155mm (6.12/6.10in)
Volume	20.6 litres (1,257cu in)
Compression ratio	6.4:1
Power rating	dependant on version
Weight	dependant on version

The following versions of the engine are known:

M-26 The original version of the engine, without forced air-cooling fan and starting clutch, but with conventional planetary gearing. Several prototypes were built. The engine underwent factory bench testing in July-August 1945, and flight testing in July of the same year. It was twice submitted for State tests, in April and October 1946. Weight 395kg (871lb) (according to the specification, 375kg (827lb)).

M-26GR A helicopter version, its development was completed at the beginning of 1946. The engine had a forced air-cooling fan, a starting clutch and modified gearing with a shaft set perpendicular to the engine's axis. The engine was built in two variants for the G-4 helicopter: the M-26GRP (M-26GRPr) right-hand and M-26GRL left-hand. Factory testing lasted until October 1946, and joint testing was carried out in September 1947. Flight testing on a G-4 helicopter began in October that year. Power rating 400/500hp; later variant 420/500hp.

M-26GR (f) A transitional 'half-boosted' version (boosted on rpm). Power rating 420/550hp.

M-26GRF A version with high rpm boosting. Power rating 420/575hp. A small batch was produced.

AI-26V A series version based on the M-26GRF. Power rating 460/574hp, weight 450kg (992lb).

LiT-3 (PZL-3S) A Polish version of the AI-26V with a maximum power rating of 600hp. This engine was manufactured at Rzeszow during 1963-67.

The AI-26V was exported to Poland, Bulgaria, Hungary, Romania, Czechoslovakia, East Germany and China.

The M-26GR and AI-26V powered G-4 (small batch) and Mi-1 (including the Polish SM-1 and SM-2 versions) production helicopters, as well as the B-5, B-9, B-10, B-11 and Yak-100 helicopter prototypes.

M-27

The M-27 designation was used earlier for a W-shaped engine prototype built in 1931. According to the plan of development work for 1945, the designation was given to a 350hp helicopter engine unified with the M-26. It was planned to test the prototype in September 1946.

In the first quarter of 1946 OKB-478 issued engineering drawings for the M-27, but no information on its manufacture and testing has been found.

Characteristics

5-cylinder radial, four-stroke, air-cooled geared engine with forced air-cooling, a starting clutch and a single-stage, single-speed GCS.

Power rating	300/350hp
Bore/stroke	155.5/155mm (6.12/6.10in)
Compression ratio	6.4:1
Weight	300kg (660lb) (according to the specification)

M-29

The M-29 designation had been used earlier for a of two-row radial engine project; A.A. Bessonov's coupled M-26.

In 1945 a specification for the development of a 9-cylinder helicopter engine, unified with A.G. Ivchenko's new M-26GR, was issued. The project was completed in 1946. One year later three prototypes had been built, and factory testing started. In August 1947 a maximum power of 615hp was reached, but the specification required 750hp. In 1948 all work on the M-29 was cancelled by order of the ministry.

Characteristics

9-cylinder radial, four-stroke, air-cooled geared engine with forced air-cooling, a starting clutch and a single-stage, single-speed GCS.

Power rating	625/750hp (according to the specification) (recorded power rating 615hp)
Bore/stroke	155.5/155mm (6.12/6.10in)
Compression ratio	6.4:1

M-4GR (AI-4V)

This light-helicopter engine was created especially for the Kamov Design Bureau. A specification for development of the M-4GR was issued in 1946, and in November 1948 the prototype was underwent joint testing. The engine was of unconventional layout, the axis of the air-cooling fan being perpendicular to the plane of the cylinders and crankshaft axis. Several prototypes were built. In 1948 the engine was redesignated AI-4V. Starting from September 1949 the AI-4V underwent flight testing in a Ka-10 light helicopter. The engine was not put into series production.

The AI-4V powered a Ka-10 helicopter.

Characteristics

4-cylinder horizontally-opposed, four-stroke, air-cooled geared (with two gears) engine with forced air-cooling, and with starting and free-running clutch.

Power rating	50/55hp

M-10 (AI-10)

This designation had previously been used twice. It was initially allocated to the modified version of the Liberty engine (M-5) that was being tested in 1926. On the second occasion it was allocated to a small diesel engine that the design bureau of Factory No. 154 was ordered to develop in 1941. The engine was not built.

In 1946 OKB-478 was tasked with developing an 80hp engine for light aeroplanes. In October 1947 three prototypes were built and used for factory bench testing. In May 1948 the M-10 passed State tests and was redesignated AI-10. From October 1945 to January 1950 the M-10 was tested in an Yak-20 aeroplane.

The engine was not introduced into series production.

The M-4G (AI-4V) engine.

Characteristics

5-cylinder radial, four-stroke, air-cooled direct-drive unsupercharged engine.

Power rating	80/90hp (according to the specification 80 hp)
Bore/stroke	105/105mm (4.13/4.13in)
Volume	4.627 litres (282cu in)
Compression ratio	5.5:1
Weight	105kg (231lb) (without generator, vacuum pump, compressor and governor for variable-pitch propeller)

M-12

The M-12 designation had previously been used for several engine types. It was first allocated to an engine created at the NAMI that was a competitor to the well-known M-11. Later, during the Second World War, the designation was applied to two engine types at the same time, Kossov's and Urmin's engines, which were developed at the design bureau of Factory No. 154.

In 1947 OKB-478 started development of a 7-cylinder engine unified with the M-10. In 1948-49 the M-12 prototypes passed bench testing, but the type was not introduced into series production.

Application of the M-12 was planned for an amphibious aircraft to be used by the Civil Air Fleet.

Characteristics

7-cylinder radial, four-stroke, air-cooled, direct-drive engine with a single-stage, single-speed GCS.

Power rating	155/180hp
Bore/stroke	105.5/115mm (6.12/4.53in)
Compression ratio	6.0:1
Weight	145kg (319lb) (without generator, vacuum pump and compressor).

AI-226

A projected helicopter engine based on the ASh-62IR. The prototype was not built, and no details of the design have been found.

M-14 (AI-14)

The M-14 designation had previously been given to a W-shaped engine developed at the NAMI.

In 1946 OKB-478 started development of a 9-cylinder engine, unified with the M-10 and M-12. In May 1948 the M-14 passed State tests.

Series production of the engine as the AI-14 was arranged at Factory No. 478 in Zaporozhye (now named Motor Sich) and at Factory No. 154 in Voronezh from 1956. Factory No. 154 built the engine under the designation M-14. Production of different versions of this engine was also arranged in

An AI-14R with a two-blade propeller in the Aerospace University in Samara.

A sectioned AI-14R in Samara.

The M-14VF engine.

LEFT: **A Ka-26 helicopter, powered by two AI-14VF engines in nacelles flanking the fuselage.**

BELOW: **A UKa-15 helicopter, the training version of the Ka-15 shipborne helicopter, powered by an AI-14V engine, at Kirovskoe airfield, Crimea, in August 1956.**

Poland, Czechoslovakia, Romania and China. The M-14 is still being manufactured and remains in service.

Engines of the M-14/AI-14 family and their foreign-built copies were exported to Bulgaria, Romania, Poland, Czechoslovakia, East Germany, Japan, France, Great Britain, the USA, Hungary, Mongolia, North Korea, Sweden, Yugoslavia and Zambia.

Characteristics

9-cylinder radial, four-stroke, air-cooled engine with a single-stage, single-speed GCS.

Bore/stroke	105/130mm (4.13/5.12in)
Volume	10.16 litres (620cu in)

Power rating, compression ratio, and weight – dependant on version

The following versions of the engine are known:

M-14R (AI-14R) The first series version, it was equipped with gearing. Maximum power rating 260hp.

AI-14RA A version of the M-14R with a modified accessory drive and minor improvements.

Characteristics

Power rating	217/256hp
Compression ratio	5.9:1
Weight	200kg (441lb)

AI-14V A helicopter version of 1951, with a forced air-cooling fan and a starting clutch.

AI-14RF An rpm-boosted version of the AI-14RA. Maximum power rating 300hp.

AI-14RFP A version of the AI-14RF intended for aerobatics, it had a modified oil system.

AI-14VF A helicopter version of 1956, with modifications similar to the AI-14RF. Power rating 235/280hp, weight 238kg (525lb).

AI-14RS A snowmobile version.

M-14P A further development of the AI-14RFP with additional rpm-boosting. Maximum power rating 360hp, weight 214kg (472lb).

M-14PM A direct-drive engine for a pusher propeller. Cylinder heads had increased ribbing. Maximum power rating 315hp, weight 208kg (459lb).

M-14PM1 A geared version of the M-14PM. Maximum power rating 360hp.

M-14PT A geared engine for a pusher propeller, with a more powerful generator and an air-cooling fan drive. The gear shaft end had a smooth flange. Maximum power rating 360hp, weight 216kg (476lb).

M-14PF A version of the M-14P with an improved GCS. Maximum power rating 400hp, weight 214kg (472lb).

M-14PA A version for a reversible-pitch propeller, equipped with an electric heating system. Maximum power rating 360hp.

M-14PR A version of the M-14P with a different type of electric generator. Maximum power rating 360hp, weight 214kg (472lb).

M-14N A version of the M-14P with direct fuel injection, a new magneto and an electric starter. Maximum power rating 360hp.

M-14Kh A version of the M-14P with a gear shaft end having a smooth flange and a system of condensation drainage. Maximum power rating 360hp, weight 214kg (472lb).

M-14PS A version with a modified generator drive. The gear shaft end had a smooth flange. Maximum power rating 360hp, weight 214kg (472lb).

RIGHT: **A front view of the starboard AI-14VF engine in a Ka-26.**

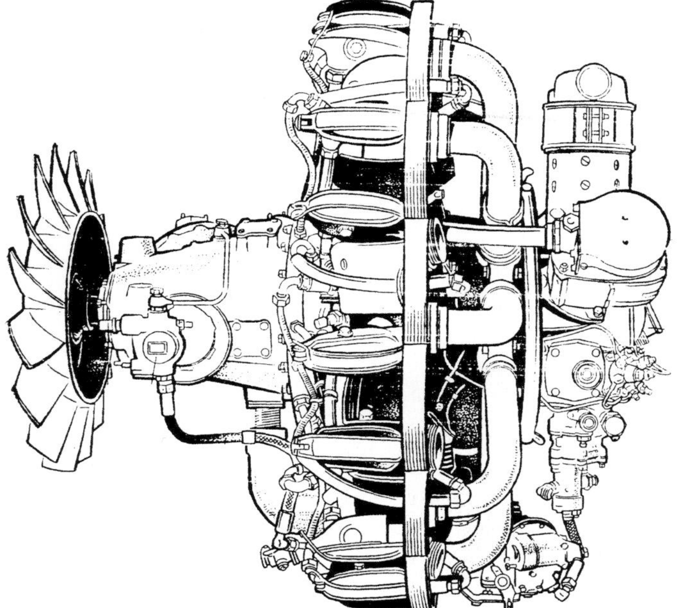

A side view of the AI-14VF from the engine's technical manual.

BELOW: **The starboard AI-14VF of a Ka-26 helicopter.**

LEFT: **An illustration of the M-14P from the engine's technical manual.**

An M-14P engine at the MAI.

ABOVE: **A Yak-50 sports aeroplane, powered by the M-14PF.**

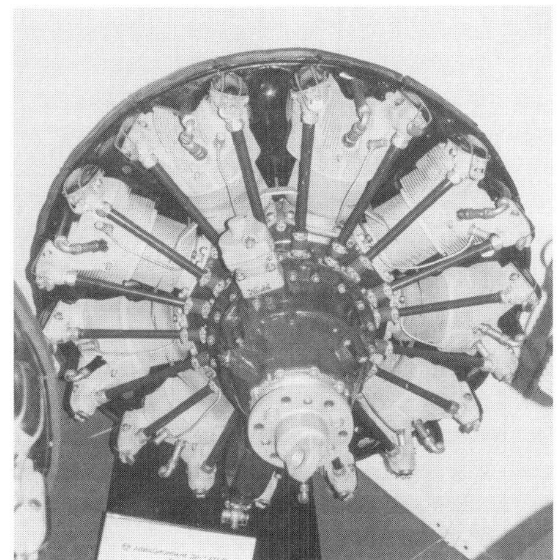

ABOVE: **The M-14PF engine.**

BELOW: **A Yak-52 trainer powered by an M-14PF.**

M-14SKh A version for agricultural aeroplanes, equipped with an additional generator and electric starter. Maximum power rating 360hp, weight 221kg (487lb).
M-14V26 A version for the Ka-26 helicopter, with the gear output shaft perpendicular to the crankshaft axis. Power rating 275/325hp, weight 252kg (556lb) (without generator, compressor and exhaust manifold).
M-14V26V1 A 1966 high-altitude boosted version of the M-14V26. Maximum power rating 370hp, weight 255kg (562lb).
M-14V1 A version of the M-14V26V1. Power rating 360hp, weight 254kg (560lb).
M-14V2 A further development of the M-14V1. Power rating 400hp, weight 254kg (560lb).
AI-14RA A Polish-built version of the AI-14RA. This engine was in production at the WSK factory at Kalish from 1963.
AI-14RDP An improved version of the AI-14RA, equipped with a pneumatic starter.
AI-14RD An improved version of the AI-14RDP, equipped with an electric starter. Maximum power rating 276hp.
M-362RF A Czechoslovakian version of the AI-14VF, created at the beginning of 1965. The engine was adapted for operation in an inclined position. Power rating 280/305hp. weight 265kg (584lb). Several prototypes were built, and the engine underwent flight testing in an HS-3A helicopter.
M-462 A Czech copy of the AI14RF, in series production.
M-462RF A Czechoslovakian modernization of the AI-14RF, built in 1965. The engine had new gearing, a GCS and a strengthened crankshaft. Power rating 280/315hp (according to some sources 280/325hp), weight 227kg (500lb). The type was in production at the Avia factory during 1966-80. About 1,500 were built.
HS6 A Chinese copy of the AI-14R, in production from 1963.
HS6A A Chinese copy of the AI-14RF, in production from 1965. More than 5,000 were built.

Engines of the AI-14/M-14 family powered the following aeroplanes: Yak-12 (later versions), Yak-18, An-14 *Pchelka* (Bee), PZL-101 *Gawron*, PZL-104, Wilga 35, PZL-130 *Orlik*, Yak-50, Yak-52, Yak-53, Yak-54, Yak-55, Su-26, Su-29, Su-31, Z37 *Cmelak*, L60S (mass-conversion of the L60), CJ-6, CJ-6A and Yu-11 series. These engines also powered the Ka-15, Ka-18, Ka-26 and Mi-34 (small batch) production helicopters.

They also powered the following prototypes: *Kvant*, *Akrobat* (MAI-Aviatika-900), *Aushra*, Tu-24, VSKhS (Tu-VSKhS, Tu-54), M-500, T-419 *Strekoza* (Dragonfly), SM-92 *Finist*, SM-94, Yak-58, *Molniya-1* (Lightning), T-401, T-411 *Aist* (Stork), T-435 *Pelican*, Su-38, *Peking*, and the prototype HS-3A helicopter.

Use of these engines was planned for the projected AE, A-6, SKV and *Pchela* (Bee) aeroplanes.

The Su-31M aerobatic aircraft, powered by the M-14PF.

The prototype of the Yak-54 light passenger aircraft, with an M-14PF engine in pusher configuration, 2000.

M-3

This engine used many M-14P components and units, including the complete subassembly of cylinder and cylinder head. The M-3 was developed at the Machine-Building Design Bureau in Voronezh in 1993, under the leadership of A.G. Bakanov. It was in series production, but did not see wide application.

The M-3 powered a small batch of SL-90 aeroplanes and some home-built aircraft.

Characteristics

3-cylinder radial, four-stroke, air-cooled engine.

Power rating	105hp
Bore/stroke	105/130mm (4.13/5.12in)

CHAPTER THIRTY-SEVEN

The Engines of the Voronezh Engine-building Design Bureau

During the 1990s, in parallel with improvement work on the M-14 and the creation of a 3-cylinder M-3 engine based upon it, a range of original piston aero-engines was developed and built at the Machine-building Design Bureau in Voronezh, under the leadership of A.G. Bakanov. These powerplants, of differing layouts and purpose, have power ratings ranging from 40hp to 450hp. They are still in the development stage.

Especially noteworthy are the M-29 (work on its refinement has been transferred to the Kazan Engine-Building Production Enterprise (*Kazanskoe Motorostroitelnoe Proizvodsvennoe Ob'edinenie*, KMPO)), and new family of radial engines. The latter is being developed in co-operation with the Voronezh Mechanical Factory design bureau, which will arrange series production. The family includes the 9-cylinder M9 engine (the factory documentation gives the designation without the traditional hyphen), the 7-cylinder M7 and the 5-cylinder M5, which range in power from 170hp to 420hp. All engines of this family have a common cylinder-piston group, as well as a considerable number of common parts in the gas-distribution mechanism and common accessories. Development began with the M9, which is a further evolution of the M-14P design. However, the M9 is not a direct modification, because more than two thirds of its parts have been developed anew. Compared with the M-14P, the primary components of the M9 have been strengthened, and the powerplant is boosted in rpm. It is planned that the period between major overhauls for the new family of engines will be twice as long as that for the M-14P, reaching 1,000hr. The M9 and M7 were shown to the public for the first time during the Aero-Engine 2002 exhibition in Moscow. At present the M9F is being built in small series, the M7 prototype is undergoing bench testing and the first prototype of the M5 is under construction.

M-16

The designation M-16 was previously used in the 1920s, for the in-line (single-block) variant of the M-5 Liberty, and for a low-powered engine by S.D. Kolosov.

Development of an X-shaped M-16 was started at the end of the 1990s. No information on the prototype's completion and testing has been released.

The engine is intended for the Yak-56 and Yak-57 aeroplanes.

Characteristics

8-cylinder four-stroke, air-cooled X-shaped engine with direct injection.

Power rating	300hp
Weight	150kg (331lb)

The M-18-02 engine.

M-17

This designation had been used previously for the Soviet version of the German BMW VI.

The M-17 horizontally-opposed 4-cylinder engine was built and tested at the end of the 1990s.

Characteristics

4-cylinder horizontally-opposed, four-stroke, air-cooled engine with direct injection and an electric starter.
Power rating and weight; dependant on version.

The following versions of the engine are known:

M-17 The basic version. Power rating 175hp (it is planned to boost it up to 200hp), weight 118kg (260lb).

M-17F An rpm-boosted version. Power rating 250hp, weight 163kg (359lb).

It is planned to install the M-17 in the Be-103, Il-103, Yak-112 and Tu-34 aeroplanes, and in the RT-6 wing-in-ground-effect aircraft.

M-18

This designation was used in 1925-26 for the experimental W-shaped engine.

The M-18 was originally developed for pilotless aircraft. The characteristics given in its specification were similar to those for the P-032, which was being developed at the design bureau of the Scientific-Production Enterprise 'Trud' in Kuibyshev. Development of the M-18 started at the end of 1982, and the prototype was built and passed bench tests. However, similar engines created in Kuibyshev (by then renamed Samara) proved better, and were introduced into series production. The Voronezh designers therefore had to seek other applications for the M-18; they included powered hang-gliders and ultralight aircraft. For this purpose, the M-18-02 version was created. However, again it was not a great success, and the M-18 did not enter series production.

Characteristics

2-cylinder horizontally-opposed, two-stroke, air-cooled engine.

The following versions of the engine are known:
M-18-01 A basic version. Power rating 40hp, weight 13.7kg (30lb).
M-18-02 A version with an electric starter. Power rating 55hp.

M-25

The M-25 designation was previously used in the second half of the 1930s for the Soviet-built version of the Wright Cyclone.

The M-25 was intended to replace the M-14, of which it was a further development.

Characteristics

9-cylinder radial, four-stroke, geared, air-cooled engine with a single-stage, single-speed GCS and direct injection.
Power rating and weight dependant on version.

The following versions of the engine are known:
M-25 The basic version. Power rating 450hp, weight 215kg (474lb).
M-25-01 A version with turbo-supercharger.

The M-25 was planned to be installed in the Yak-18T, Yak-54, Yak-55M, Yak-58, Su-26, SM-92 *Finist*, T-401, M-500 and *Molniya-1* (Lightning) aeroplanes.

M-29

The designation M-29 was first used in the early 1930s for a two-row radial engine that was being developed at Factory No. 24 but was never built.

The M-29 is intended for ultralight aircraft and powered hang-gliders. Several prototypes were built, passed factory bench tests and were flight-tested in an Aviatika-890 aeroplane.

At the end of the 1990s the M-29 documentation and prototypes were transferred to the KMPO, where the type underwent a major redesign. The enterprise created a family of two unified engines, the P-800 and P-1000, based on the M-29.

The M-29 engine.

Characteristics

4-cylinder horizontally-opposed, two-stroke, geared, air-cooled engine with forced air-blowing and an electric starter.

Power rating	75hp
Weight	53kg (119lb)

The M9 at the Aviadvigatel 2002 show.

M9F

The M-9 designation has been used twice previously: for Gorokhov's projected engine and for Starostin's revolver engine.

The M9F is a further development of the M-14P and M-25. Initially, publications referred to this engine as the M-9X, but at present the design bureau brochures and the factory call it the M9F. This is the basic

A cross-section of the M9F.

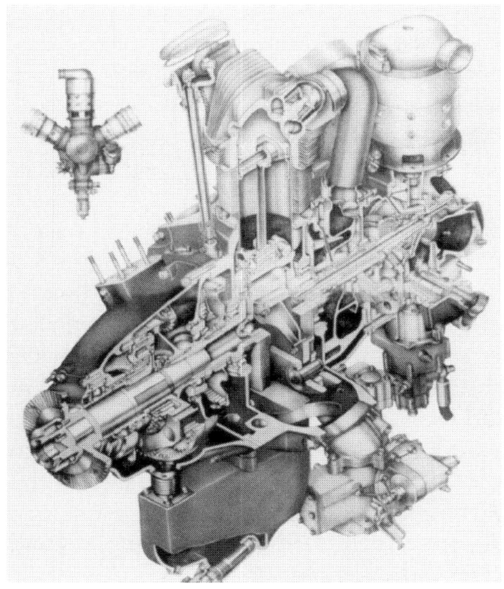

The M9FS series engine.

A modification of the M-14P to M9 standard, proposed by one of the repair factories of the Russian Defence Ministry.

engine of the unified family. Compared with the M-14P it has strengthened crankshaft and conrods, uses different technology in the manufacture of its pistons, and has a number of other minor changes. Development was carried out in co-operation with the Voronezh OKBM and the Voronezh Mechanical Factory. The M9F prototype was built in 2001, and the engine is currently being manufactured in small series. The existing prototypes have carburettors, but there are plans to create a variant with fuel injection into suction inlets.

The engine is intended for installation in the Su-26, Su-29, Su-31, Su-31M and Su-49 aeroplanes.

Characteristics

9-cylinder radial, four-stroke, air-cooled engine with a single-speed, single-stage GCS.

Power rating	420hp
Bore/stroke	105/130mm (4.13/5.11in)
Volume	10.16 litres (620cu in)
Weight	220kg (485lb)

M7

The designation M-7 was used at the end of the 1920s for the prototype of the NRB engine being developed under the leadership of B.S. Stechkin.

The M7 is a 7-cylinder engine unified with the M9F. The prototype was completed at the beginning of 2002, and it is now under test.

This engine is intended for general-aviation and light aircraft.

Characteristics

7-cylinder radial, four-stroke, air-cooled engine with a single-speed, single-stage GCS.

Power rating	270hp
Bore/stroke	105/130mm (4.13/5.11in)
Weight	170kg (375lb)

M5

The designation M-5 was used in the 1920s and 1930s for the Soviet copy of the Ford Liberty engine.

The M5, now under construction, is a 5-cylinder engine unified with the M9F and M7.

The engine is intended for general-aviation and light aircraft.

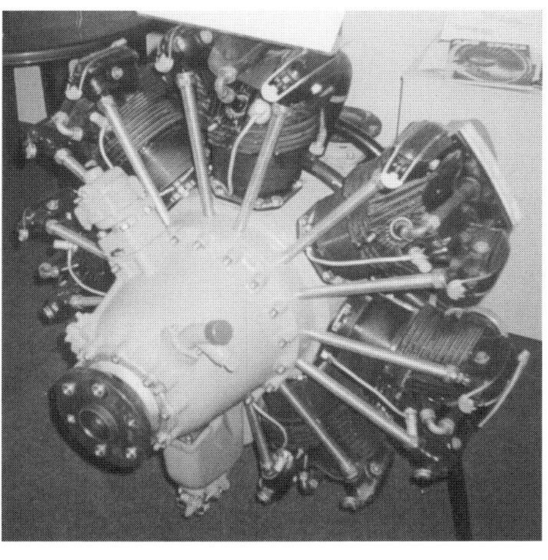
The M7 engine.

Characteristics

5-cylinder, radial, four-stroke, air-cooled engine with a single-speed, single-stage GCS.

Power rating	170hp
Bore/stroke	105/130mm (4.13/5.11in)
Weight	135kg (298lb)

M-6

The M-6 designation was used in the 1920s for the Soviet copy of the Hispano-Suiza engine, built in Zaporozhye.

The project for the horizontally-opposed M-6 has been under development since 2000 at the OKBM, in co-operation with the TsIAM. A specific feature of this engine is the extensive application of automobile engine production technology. It is planned that the M-6 will be an adaptation of a horizontally-opposed automobile engine for aircraft use, similar to the work carried out by the GAZ design bureau in 1930s. As possible prototypes, Porsche and Subaru engines (which have aviation-versions) have been evaluated.

The engine is planned for installation in the Il-103 aeroplane.

Characteristics

6-cylinder horizontally-opposed, four-stroke, liquid-cooled engine.

Power rating	340hp
Bore/stroke	105/82mm (4.13/3.22in)
Volume	4.3 litres (262cu in)
Compression ratio	9.0:1
Weight	270kg (595lb)

CHAPTER THIRTY-EIGHT

Wankel-type Engines

Work on Wankel-type engines started in the Soviet Union in 1961. The NAMI, NATI and the All-Union Scientific-Research Institute of Engine Industry (*Vsesoyuzniy Naucho-Issledovatelskiy Institut Motornoy Promishlennosti*, VNIImotoprom) began developing engines for automobiles and motorcycles, while the Scientific-Research Institute of Engine-Building (*Naucho-Issledovatelskiy Institut Dvigatelestroeniya*, NIID) worked on engines for armoured vehicles. In 1974 the SKB RPD VAZ was established in Tolyatti. Taking a Japanese Mazda engine as a basis, the Tolyatti designers started developing a family of Wankel-type engines for vehicle applications. In 1976 the SKB RPD VAZ created the 65hp VAZ-311 engine.

In the second half of the 1980s the Tolyatti designers began to evaluate the possibility of using Wankel-type engines in aviation. As a first step the VAZ-413, which had undergone minor changes, was tested in a SL-90 *Leshiy* (Wood-goblin) aeroplane, and then in a *Volga-2* air-cushion boat. The tests showed the advantages of the Wankel-type engine, lightness and compactness, but its reliability was insufficient for aviation applications and its oil consumption was high.

In 1990, at the request of the M.L. Mil Design Bureau, the SKB RPD VAZ started development of its first aero-engine, the VAZ-430, intended for helicopters. Two such engines were to power the Mi-34VAZ light helicopter. The work was led by V.A. Shnyakin. The VAZ-430 was developed under the airworthiness regulations for aero-engines, and its parts were ordered from enterprises within the aviation industry. However, it was not a success.

Using one of the VAZ-430 versions (the VAZ-4305), fitted with automobile engine pars, the design bureau of the Aviadvigatel association in Perm developed the D-200 aero-engine, equipped with reduction gearing. The D-200 was built and bench tested, but at the end of the 1990s the work was cancelled.

However, the development of aero-engines at Tolyatti continued. In 1991, at the request of the LM-Aero company, a single-section VAZ-1187 engine was created for use on hang gliders. A further development was the higher-powered VAZ-1188, but this work was also cancelled.

In 1995 the Tolyatti designers began developing a family of Wankel-type aero-engines, including the two-section VAZ-416 and three-section VAZ-426, both with reduction gearing. Later there appeared the direct-drive VAZ-4265 (a version of the VAZ-426) and the four-section VAZ-526. Prototypes of these engines were built and passed bench testing, but none was introduced into series production.

VAZ-430

This engine was being developed at the SKB RPD from 1990. The VAZ-430 prototype was built and underwent 150hr bench testing, but its development was cancelled owing to the loss of finance. One VAZ-430 version served as the basis for the D-200 engine.

The engine was planned for installation in the Mi-34VAZ helicopter.

Characteristics

Wankel-type two-section, liquid-cooled engine for helicopters.

VAZ-1187

This engine was developed by the SKB RPD VAZ from 1991, and passed bench and service testing. It was installed in hang gliders, and one such hang-glider won the Russian National Championships in 1994. A prototype batch of fifteen engines was manufactured at the VAZ factory in Tolyatti.

Characteristics

Wankel-type single-section, liquid-cooled engine for hang gliders.

Power rating	40hp (several engines were boosted to 55hp)
Volume	0.365 litres (22cu in)

The prototype of the L-6m amphibian, powered by two VAZ engines.

The VAZ-1187 engine.

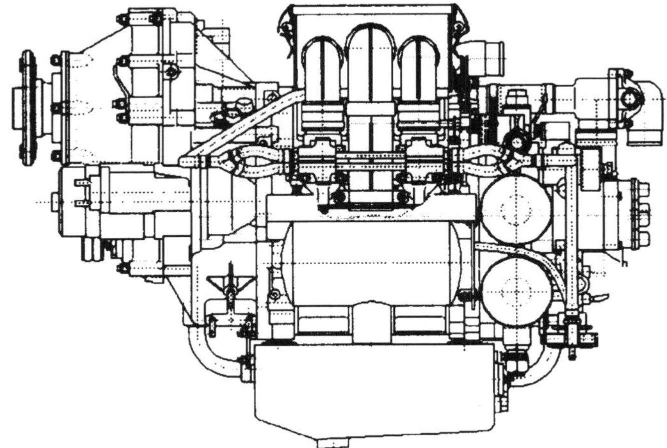

A drawing of the VAZ-416.

VAZ-1188

This was a development of the VAZ-1187, boosted in rpm up to 60hp. Work on this engine was cancelled in 1999.

Characteristics

Wankel-type single-section, liquid-cooled engine.

Power rating	60hp
Volume	0.365 litres (22cu in)

VAZ-416

This engine for light aircraft was being developed at the SKB RPD VAZ. Several prototypes were built and underwent bench testing. The engines were flight-tested on the prototype of the L-6M amphibious aircraft developed by Aero Volga in Samara. This aircraft was exhibited at the Hydro-Aviation Airshow in Gelendzhik in September 2002.

Characteristics

Wankel-type two-section, geared engine for light aeroplanes.

Volume	1.308 litres (80cu in)
Power rating	dependant on version
Weight	dependant on version

The following versions of the engine are known:

VAZ-416 without turbo-supercharging. Power rating 180/200hp, weight 110kg (242lb)

VAZ-416 with turbo-supercharging. Power rating 240hp, weight 125kg (275lb)

VAZ-426

This light-aircraft engine was unified with the VAZ-416. Prototypes were built and underwent 240hr testing. Considerable drawbacks of the design were its high oil consumption and low service life. Type certification was planned for 2000, but it is not yet completed.

Characteristics

Wankel-type three-section engine.

Volume	1.962 litres (120cu in)
Power rating	dependant on version
Weight	dependant on version

The following versions of the engine are known:

Geared VAZ-426 without turbo-super-

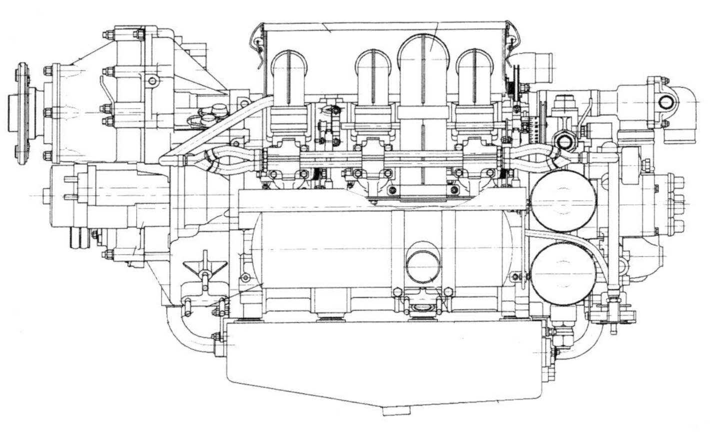

A drawing of the geared VAZ-426.

The VAZ-426.

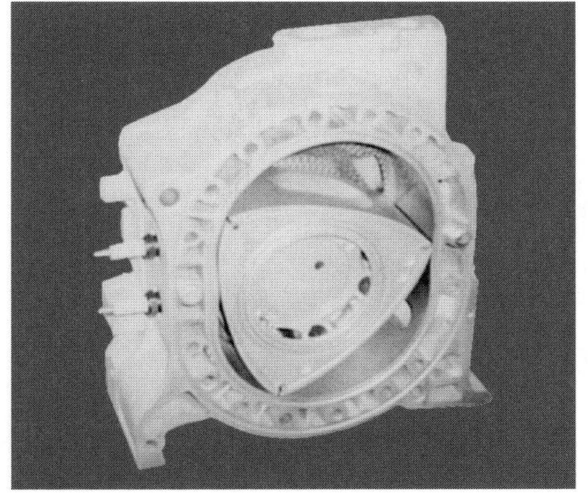

A section of the VAZ-426.

A drawing of the direct-drive VAZ-4265.

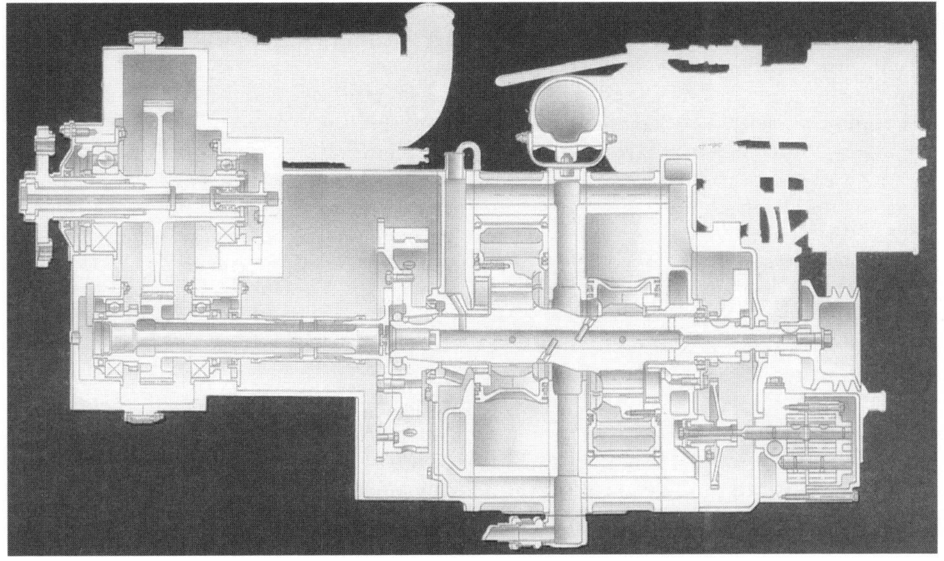

A cross-section of the D-200.

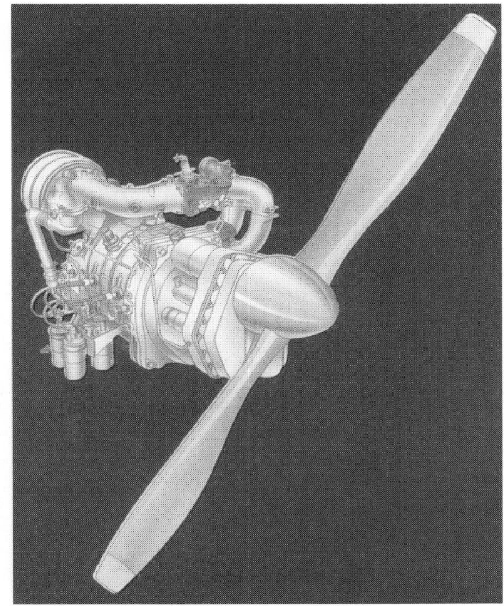

A view of the D-200 engine.

charging. Power rating 240/300hp, weight 130kg (287lb).
Geared VAZ-426 with turbo-supercharging. Power rating 400hp, weight 150kg (331lb).
Direct-drive VAZ-4265 without turbo-supercharging. Power rating 270hp, weight 130kg (287lb).

It is planned to install the engine in an *Aksai* helicopter.

VAZ-526

An engine for light aircraft, unified with the VAZ-416 and VAZ-426. No information about the prototypes' tests has been released.

Characteristics

Wankel-type four-section, direct-drive engine.

Power rating	400hp
Volume	2.616 litres (160cu in)
Weight	175kg (386lb)

D-200

Created by the design bureau of the Aviadvigatel association in Perm, this light-aircraft engine was based on the VAZ-4305. The D-200's gearing differed considerably from that of VAZ engines. Several prototypes were built and underwent bench testing, but work on the engine ceased at the end of the 1990s.

Characteristics

Wankel-type two-section, geared engine.

Power rating	220hp
Weight	145kg (320lb)

CHAPTER THIRTY-NINE

The Engines of the Samara Machine-Building Design Bureau

At the beginning of the 1980s the development of small pilotless reconnaissance aircraft (unmanned air vehicles, or UAVs) started in the Soviet Union and, consequently, suitable engines were required for them. In July 1982 a decree of the USSR Council of Ministers on the development of indigenous pilotless aircraft and their engines was issued. The Experimental Design Bureau of the 'Trud' Scientific-Production Enterprise (*Opitno-Konstruktorskoe Byuro Nauchno-Proizvodstvennogo Ob'edineniya 'Trud'*, or OKB NPO 'Trud') in Kuibyshev was given the task of creating such powerplants, and the development work was headed by A.A. Ermakov. It was necessary to develop a range of small two-stroke engines with comparatively short service lives, suitable for UAVs. As engines had never previously been built in the Soviet Union, a range of suitable Western engines (British, German and Austrian) were purchased, thoroughly examined, and some of their engineering solutions copied.

The first Soviet UAV engine, designated P-020, was built by January 1983. It passed factory, State and, later, Service tests. A small batch of pilotless reconnaissance aeroplanes, designated '60' and powered by the P-020, was built. However the engine did not find widespread use. On the other hand, the more powerful P-032, created in 1985, was introduced into series production. It powered the *Pchela-1T* (Bee) UAV, which constituted part of the *Stroy-P* system. Intended for use by regiments of airborne troops, the system was mounted on a BMD armoured-vehicle chassis. It was being supplied to the Russian Armed Forces from 1991, and was used in combat in Chechnya in 1995.

The P-032 formed the basis for a family of engines. The type itself was repeatedly improved, boosted in power rating and fitted with different gearing. Owing to the reduction of military orders in the 1990s, versions for civil applications were prepared, the P-032MR and B-32 being intended for hang gliders. However, they were not widely used owing to their short service life, a consequence of their original purpose.

On the basis of the P-032 the more-powerful P-065 was created; a pair of coupled P-032s driving common gearing.

At the end of the 1980s the SB-039 engine for pilotless helicopters was built. It passed bench and flight testing, but was not introduced into series production.

P-020

This engine was under development from July 1982 under the leadership of A.A. Ermakov. A range of engineering solutions introduced into its design were taken from a Limbach engine. Because of the short

The P-032 engine.

The *Pchela-1T* unmanned aerial vehicle.

A sectioned P-020 at Samara Aerospace University.

A P-032 at the MAI.

service life required by the specification, the engine had linerless cylinders made of aluminium alloy. The P-020 prototype was built in January 1983, and started factory bench tests in March. From June of that year the P-020 was flight tested on a prototype of pilotless aircraft '60'. In November 1984 the engine passed its State tests, and in April 1988 it underwent Service testing.

The P-020 was in series production at the NPO 'Trud' factory in Kuibyshev, seventy-three engines being built.

The engine was installed in the pilotless reconnaissance aircraft '60' (small batch).

Characteristics

2-cylinder horizontally-opposed, two-stroke, direct-drive, air-cooled engine.

Power rating	20hp
Bore	66mm (2.60in)
Volume	0.274 litres (17cu in)
Compression ratio	7.3:1
Weight	9.9kg (22lb) (according to some sources 9.76kg (21lb))

P-032

Development of the P-032 started in 1984 to the order of the A.S. Yakovlev Design Bureau, to power the new pilotless aircraft '61'. The engine differed considerably from the P-020, though the designers retained the concept of linerless cylinders.

The first factory bench tests of the prototype were conducted in February 1985. In January 1988 the engine passed State tests, and in 1989 it was introduced into series production at the NPO 'Trud' (now Motorostroitel) factory in Samara. More than 150 engines were built.

The P-032 powered the *Pchela-1T* UAV that formed part of the *Stroy-P* reconnaissance system supplied to the Russian Armed Forces from 1991. In May 1995 it was used for the first time in combat actions in Chechnya.

Characteristics

2-cylinder horizontally-opposed, two-stroke, air-cooled engine.

Bore	72mm (2.83in)
Volume	0.44 litres (27cu in)
Compression ratio	7.0:1
Power rating	dependant on version
Weight	dependant on version

The following versions of the engine are known:

P-032 The basic series version. Direct-drive 32hp engine. Weight 13.1kg (29lb) (according to some sources 12.5kg (28lb)).

P-032MR A boosted, geared version of the P-032 with forced air blowing. Power rating 38hp. A small batch of this version was built.

P-032-71 A project for a boosted geared version using design features of the P-032MR. The engine had a disconnecting clutch, which allowed it to be started with the propeller stationary. This version was being developed in October-November 1992 for installation in the *Bekas* (Snipe) ('71') UAV. Power rating 23/33hp, weight 25kg (55lb).

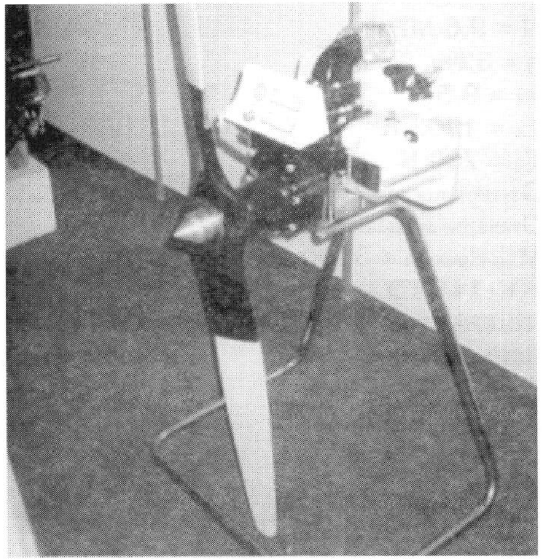

The P-032MR engine.

A P-032 mounted in the *Pchela-1T* unmanned aerial vehicle.

The P-032 engine powered the production *Pchela-1T* UAV, and prototypes of the *Moskit* (Mosquito) and *Shmel* (Bumblebee) pilotless aircraft. It was planned to install this engine the the projected *Bekas* UAV.

P-033

An improved version of the P-032, boosted in rpm and with minor changes in the gas distribution system. The prototype was built and underwent bench testing.

Characteristics

2-cylinder horizontally-opposed, two-stroke, air-cooled engine.

Power rating	38hp
Bore	72mm (2.83in)
Volume	0.44 litres (27cu in)
Compression ratio	7.0:1

P-065

The P-065 comprised a pair of vertically mounted P-032s driving the large cog wheel of a common gearing. Prototypes were built and underwent factory bench testing, which revealed some problems (the gearing broke down). Further work on the P-065 was cancelled.

The engine was intended for UAVs.

Characteristics

4-cylinder two-row, horizontally-opposed, two-stroke, air-cooled engine.

Bore	72mm (2.83in)
Volume	0.88 litres (54cu in)
Compression ratio	7.0:1

The P-065 engine.

SB-039

This engine for a pilotless helicopter was developed at the end of the 1980s. Prototypes were built and underwent bench and flight testing on a Kamov helicopter. The type was not introduced into series production.

Characteristics

2-cylinder horizontally-opposed, two-stroke, air-cooled engine.

Power rating	67hp
Weight	75kg (165lb)

B-32

A further development of the P-032, with increased service life. Prototypes were built and tested.

Characteristics

2-cylinder horizontally-opposed, two-stroke, air-cooled engine.

Power rating	32hp
Bore	72mm (2.83in)
Volume	0.44 litres (27cu in)

The SB-039 engine.

CHAPTER FORTY

The Engines of the Kazan Engine-Building Production Enterprise (KMPO)

The P-1000 two-stroke aero-engine, created by the design bureau of the Kazan Engine-Building Production Enterprise, was demonstrated for the first time during the MAKS-2001 airshow in Zhukovskiy. This engine, a result of modernizing the M-29, has been developed and built at the Voronezh Machine-Building Design Bureau. The improved powerplant features a range of changes. In particular the Kazan designers, not satisfied with the linerless cylinders characteristic of the M-29, introduced steel thin-shelled cylinder liners. The carburettors were also changed. In fact a unified family based on the M-29 was created, consisting of two engines of different displacement volumes, designated P-800 and P-1000. These underwent factory bench testing. The P-1000 was test-flown on the prototype of a light twin-engine amphibious hydroplane. These engines have not yet been introduced into series production, though it was planned to start in 2001. Neither have they undergone certification testing.

P-800

This engine was developed earlier than the P-1000, and was used for refinement of the major design solutions. The P-800 has an original gearing, with power taken from the middle of the crankshaft. From 2002 the factory's brochures ceased to mention the P-800; it was probably decided to concentrate efforts on refinement of just one engine type, the P-1000.

Characteristics

4-cylinder horizontally-opposed, two-stroke, geared, air-cooled engine.

Power rating	65hp
Bore/stroke	62/66mm (2.44/2.60in)
Volume	0.8 litres (49cu in)
Compression ratio	9.5:1
Weight	48kg (106lb)

P-1000

This engine differs from the P-800 in having greater displacement volume (due to increased bore), the installation of two electric generators instead of one, and increased gear ratio. The P-1000 can have forced air-blowing.

Characteristics

4-cylinder horizontally-opposed, two-stroke, geared, air-cooled engine.

Power rating	80hp
Bore/stroke	72/66mm (2.83/2.60in)
Volume	1.075 litres (66cu in)
Compression ratio	9.5:1
Weight	55kg (121lb)

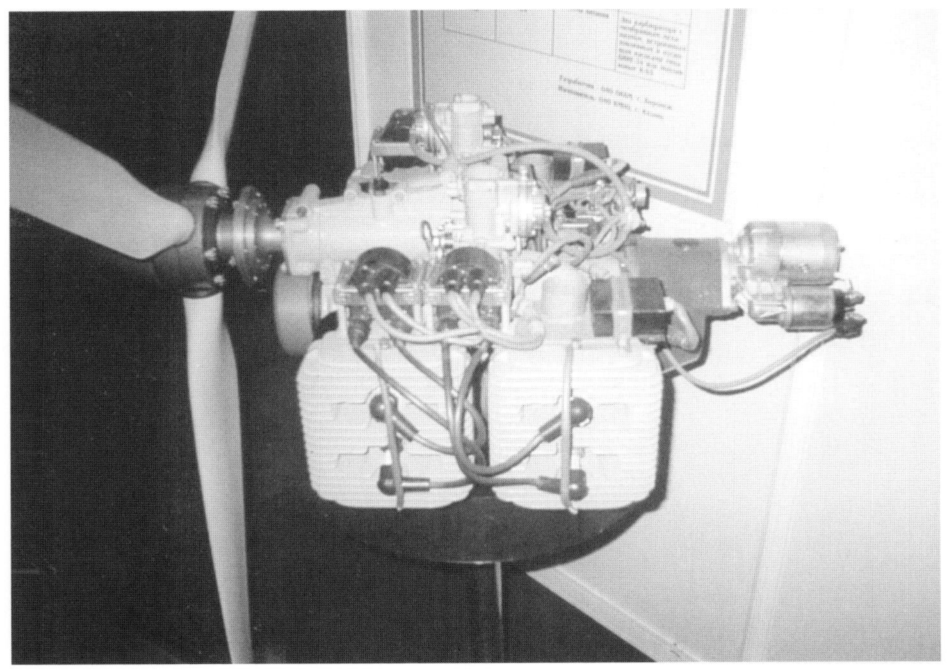

The P-800 engine.

CHAPTER FORTY-ONE

The Engines Developed at the Rybinskie Motory Enterprise During the 1980s–1990s

In the mid-1990s, using the RMZ-640 two-stroke engine created at the beginning of 1980s for the *Buran* (Blizzard) snowmobile as a basis, the design bureau of the Rybinskie Motory enterprise, under the leadership of S.M. Tikhomirov, developed a family of *Buran-Avia* low-powered aero-engines. The family included the single-cylinder RMZ-320MR and the RMZ-640MR and RMZ-640MR-2 2-cylinder engines. They differed from the basic RMZ-640 in having reduction gearing and slight boosting. All three engines underwent factory bench testing, and were test-flown on hang gliders and ultralight aircraft.

The engines of the *Buran-Avia* family are manufactured in small quantities by the diesel factory in Rybinsk, which is the part of the Rybinskie Motory enterprise (now named Lyulka-Saturn). These engines are widely used on series ultralight aircraft, as well as on home-built aeroplanes. Compared with imported engines of the same power, the Rybinsk-built types are cheaper but have a shorter time between overhauls.

RMZ-320MR

This engine is one half of a basic RMZ-640, with a new crank case and reduction gearing. It is in small-series production.

The engine is intended for powered hang gliders.

Characteristics

Single-cylinder two-stroke, geared, air-cooled engine with forced air-blowing.

Power rating	20hp
Volume	0.3175 litres (19cu in)
Compression ratio	8.0:1
Weight	30kg (66lb)

RMZ-640MR

The boosted version of the RMZ-640, equipped with gearing.

Characteristics

2-cylinder in-line, two-stroke, geared, air-cooled engine.

Power rating	38hp
Volume	0.635 litres (39cu in)
Compression ratio	8.0:1
Weight	dependant on version

Two versions of the engine are known:

RMZ-640MR A version with forced air-blowing. Weight 45kg (99lb).

RMZ-640MR-2 A version with cooling without forced air blowing, and equipped with an electric generator. Weight 49kg (108lb).

The RMZ-640MR engines are used in a number of production hang gliders, for example the R-16 *Ural*.

LEFT: **An RMZ-640 modified for installation in a home-built aeroplane.**

BELOW: **The RMZ-320MR engine.**

The RMZ-640MR.

CHAPTER FORTY-TWO

Engines for Ultralight Aircraft, Based on Motorcycle Engines

As there are no special engines for light aircraft (ultralights, hang gliders and paraplanes) in production in Russia, small local companies are repeatedly trying to create such powerplants using components from available motorcycle and automobile engines.

The Arei company of Krasnoyarsk achieved some success in this field. Since 1996 it has manufactured the A-170, which uses one cylinder, piston and conrod, and half of a crankshaft from the *Izh-Yupiter-5* motorcycle engine. The crankcase and gearing have been developed and built anew.

In 1993 in Izhevsk specialists at the Aviator company, under the leadership of M. Shalagin, developed the DSh-2, which used the cylinder-piston group from the motorcycle produced by the Izhevsk factory. The engine was modified for liquid cooling, and provided with the possibility for gearing. Several prototypes were built and underwent testing, and the DSh-2 was introduced into small-series production from 1998. Later the DSh-700 was developed and built, in which the cylinders from an *Izh-Planeta-Sport* motorcycle engine (modified for liquid cooling) were mounted on the crankcase of the Rybinsk-built RMZ-640. The DSh-700 underwent bench and flight testing, but was not introduced into series production.

A similar approach was shown by the Motiv design group, working at the TsIAM. Their *Izh-Motiv-700* liquid-cooled engine also used sleeves, pistons and conrods from the *Izh-Planeta-Sport* motorcycle engine. Another engine created by this group was the DD-700/45R, which had a horizontally-opposed layout and air-cooling, but also included the cylinder-piston group from the same motorcycle engine. Both the *Izh-Motiv-700* and DD-700/45R were built as prototypes only.

A-170

This engine, intended for paraplanes, was developed in the first half of the 1990s and has been in small-series production since 1995 by the Arei company in Krasnoyarsk.

The A-170 engine.

A paraglider cart with an A-170 engine.

Characteristics

Single-cylinder two-stroke, geared, air-cooled engine.

Power rating	14/16hp
Bore/stroke	62/57.2mm (2.44/2.25in)
Volume	0.1733 litres (11cu in)
Compression ratio	10.5:1
Weight	12.2kg (27lb)

DSh-2

The DSh-2 was developed by M. Shalygin at the Aviator company in Izhevsk in 1993. It underwent bench and flight testing, and was in small-series production from 1998.

Characteristics

2-cylinder in-line, two-stroke, geared, liquid-cooled engine. (A direct-drive version is also available.)

Power rating	60hp
Bore/stroke	76/75mm (2.99/2.95in)
Volume	0.68 litres (41cu in)
Weight	51kg (112lb) with radiator and exhaust system (engine weight without these, 30.5kg (67lb))

The DSh-2 engine.

DSh-700

Several prototypes of the DSh-700 were built by the Aviator company in Izhevsk.

Characteristics

2-cylinder in-line, two-stroke, liquid-cooled, geared engine.

Power rating	60hp

IZh-MOTIV-700

This engine was developed by the Motiv design group at the TsIAM. Several prototypes were built and underwent bench testing at the TsIAM.

Characteristics

2-cylinder in-line, two-stroke, liquid-cooled geared engine.

Power rating	60hp.
Bore/stroke	76/76mm (2.99/2.99in)
Volume	0.68 litres (41cu in)
Compression ratio	9.0:1
Weight	45kg (99lb) (according to some sources 50kg (110lb))

The *IZh-Motiv-700* engine.

The DD-700/45R engine.

DD-700/45R

This engine was developed by the Motiv design group at the TsIAM. A prototype was built and bench-tested at the TsIAM.

Characteristics

2-cylinder horizontally-opposed, two-stroke, air-cooled, geared engine.

Power rating	45hp
Bore/stroke	72/86mm (2.83/3.39in)
Volume	0.7 litres (43cu in)
Compression ratio	9.0:1
Weight	50kg (110lb)

CHAPTER FORTY-THREE

Postwar Homebuilt Engines

The lack of indigenous series-built low-powered engines, and the relatively high cost of imported powerplants, resulted in a considerable proportion of Russian home-built aircraft being fitted with converted forms of engines not originally intended for aviation use.

At present, the most widespread of these are conversions of the RMZ-640 engine from the *Buran* snowmobile. Each amateur designer modifies this engine in his own way, though, as a rule, all of them install a V-belt gear with three or five belts. A series of modifications allows the engine to be boosted up to 45hp. For instance, additional scavenge ports are introduced, duration of the gas-distribution phases is changed, petalled valves are installed at the inlet, the carburettor is changed, and the forced air-blowing scheme is modified. In some cases liquid cooling, duplicated ignition and gearing are used. A modified *Buran* engine costs from six to seven times less than the specialized *Buran-Avia* engine.

Motorcycle engines from the Irbit, Kovrov and Izhevsk factories are also the subject of modification, as well as Czech-built *Java-350* engines. Most often they are the boosted engines from sporting motorcycles intended for cross-country racing, moto-ball, and so on. Amateur designers also adapt engines from small motorcycles, as well as *Vikhr* and *Neptune* marine engines and two-stroke compressor engines from Skoda 368 refrigerators. Examples are also known of modified low-powered two-stroke engines from *Druzhba* (Friendship) power saws.

A special place in the world of home-built aero-engines is held by modified automobile engines. In recent years it has become especially popular to convert the horizontally-opposed air-cooled engines of the Japanese Subaru company, usually the EA71, EA81 and EA82. These engines receive homebuilt reduction gears, and several small companies manufacture such gears in small batches. The Virazh Club in Omsk arranged for the conversion of the Subaru EA71 into the geared *Subaru R* aero-engine with duplicated ignition. In some cases such conversions are carried out on Volkswagen and Trabant automobile engines.

Sometimes an amateur designer creates an almost new engine, retaining only the most complex components of an automobile engine. For example, in 1994-99 at the Mirazh Club, several prototypes of a 3-cylinder liquid-cooled aero-engine with cylinders and pistons from a German Wartburg automobile were built.

More rarely, a low-powered engine is assembled from aero-engine components. In particular, several cases are known where two- and three-cylinder engines were built using the cylinders and pistons from engines of the AI-14/M-14 family. For instance, the designers of the Virazh Club in Omsk attempted to build a 2-cylinder aero-engine using components from an AI-14.

Most homebuilt engines have a standard layout and use traditional design solutions. However, there have been some original ideas. In 1996 N.N. Dyachenko of Pyatigorsk proposed a project for an 'orbital' conrod-free TND-1 engine, and was granted a patent for his conrod-free mechanism. The prototype of his 4-cylinder TND-1 engine used the sleeves and pistons from a motorcycle engine.

The variety of Russian homebuilt aero-engines is so large that it is impossible to list all the types here.

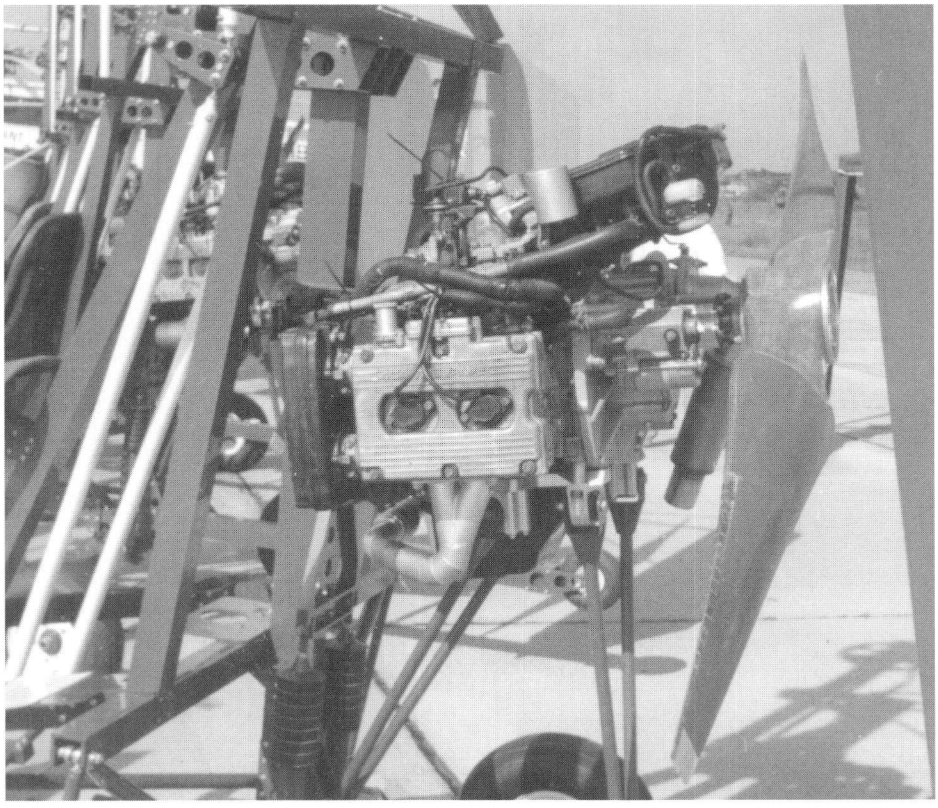

A modified Subaru engine in a home-built hang glider.

CHAPTER FORTY-FOUR

Foreign Piston Aero-engines in Russia

Historically, aviation came to Russia from the West. The first aircraft, as well as their engines, were acquired in France. Later, aeroplanes and engines were purchased in Germany, Great Britain and the USA, but the country's own aviation industry was soon established and growing.

In 1911 Russia's first indigenous aero-engine, of rather original configuration, was developed and built; Ufimtsev's bi-rotary engine. Then several other types appeared, but these were only experimental. The military, which was almost the only major consumer of the aviation industry's products at that time, directed its attention towards foreign equipment.

The assembly of aero-engines from imported parts began in Russia in 1913, and from 1916 full-scale production was carried out. However, most factories were subsidiaries of foreign companies such as Gnome, Salmson and Renault. The factories, which were owned by Russians, manufactured the engines under licence.

Later, indigenous engines suitable for series production appeared. But, as a rule, all of them were only versions or somewhat modified copies of foreign types. For example, engineer Kalep's engine was a modernized version of the French Gnome rotary, and the RBVZ-6 was an improved German Mercedes. Of nine makes of aero-engine in service with the Russian Army in 1916, only the RBVZ-6 could be considered a Russian-designed version of a Western type. The others were simply copies.

A rapid increase in aircraft manufacture took place during the First World War. The Military Ministry demanded more and more combat aircraft, but the growth of production capacity in the engine companies fell considerably behind the needs of the aviation industry. In 1917 1,099 aeroplanes were manufactured in Russia, compared with only 374 aero-engines. Thus indigenous engine production could not even meet the needs of Russian aircraft manufacturers, let alone the demand for spare engines for front-line army units, which operated a considerably greater number of foreign aeroplane types than Russian ones. The aircraft were mainly imported from France.

The Russian aero-engine industry could provide only 5 per cent of the army's annual requirement. The bulk comprised imported engines from France, Great Britain and Italy. During the First World War Russia imported more than 4,000 aero-engines, mainly during 1916-17.

As a result, the famous Ilya Muromets bombers were powered not only by Russian-built RBVZ-6s, but also by Sunbeams, Renaults and Salmsons. Being short of aircraft, Russian military aviation units also used captured German and Austrian aeroplanes, as well as engines removed from enemy aeroplanes and airships that had been shot down.

On the whole, the aviation forces of the Tsarist Government (and then of the Provisional Government) had at their disposal a rather mixed stock of aero-engines, mainly of foreign origin.

When, in October 1917, the Bolsheviks came to power, they did not at first pay proper attention to aviation. Owing to their low level of education, or to idealistic ideas of the brotherhood of the working people and a world without wars, some of them considered aircraft merely as toys for the rich. However, the outbreak of the Civil War made it evident that the Red Army desperately needed combat aircraft.

By that time the production of aircraft and engines in Russia had decreased

LEFT: **A 14-cylinder Salmson engine in an *Ilya Muromets*.**

BELOW: **A Sunbeam engine imported from Britain.**

sharply. This decline was related to the discontinuation of component supply by the country's former allies, general economic dislocation in the country and irregular operation of the national transportation system. It was also a direct consequence of fratricidal war in remote areas of Russia, where regimes were constantly changing. For instance, the large engine factory in Aleksandrovsk passed through the hands of four different belligerents, and the retreating forces attempted to evacuate it each time. As a result, most of the factory's equipment was pilfered.

A Fokker C.IV of the aerial photographic service, powered by a Liberty engine.

The RKKVF had no choice but to rely on scant deliveries from the Moscow factories, the resources accumulated in Tsarist army depots, cargoes not yet shipped from Arkhangelsk and captured equipment. The Whites had no serious engine-building resources at all, acquiring all their aero-engines from abroad.

Some of the aircraft supplied to the Whites, as well as single machines belonging to interventionist units, were captured by the Reds. These aircraft provided the RKKVF with new aero-engine types such as the British Rolls-Royce Eagle, Bentley B.R.2 and Royal Aircraft Factory products, and the American Sturtevant. Of most interest was the 400hp Ford Liberty 12A that powered the Airco D.H.4 and D.H.9A aircraft captured from the Whites. The D.H.9A was tested at the NOA in 1920, and the Liberty engine was later copied and introduced into mass production at two factories as the M-5.

By the end of the Civil War the Reds had used every aircraft that could stagger into the air, and by 12 May 1922 the Air Fleet of Soviet Russia had on its strength forty-one types of aero-engine manufactured by thirty-one different companies.

It took a long time for the Russian aero-engine factories to recover from the consequences of the Civil War and economic dislocation. Not until 1928 did they manage to attain the production levels of 1916. After the Civil War the aircraft and engines in service with the RKKVF were in a terrible state. Not only were they obsolete, but they were also completely worn out.

Consequently, in the 1920s Soviet Russia actively proceeded to purchase foreign aircraft and aero-engines. The ending of the First World War left the European nations and the USA with huge quantities of surplus military equipment, including aero-engines. Most of the outstanding military orders were cancelled, and the equipment already produced remained in warehouses. This allowed the Soviets to buy aero-engines comparatively cheaply.

The first purchases were made in Sweden. The NAB company sold Russia the German 260hp Mercedes D.IVa engines that had been secretly transported from Germany to Sweden to prevent their capture by the victorious nations. A contract for the delivery of forty-eight engines was signed on 22 December 1921. These engines were later used to power the D.H.4s acquired from Great Britain.

A number of different engine types were brought to Russia together with aeroplanes. In 1921 the Soviet Republic purchased a number of German aircraft in Denmark, in particular LVGs and Halberstadts, both powered by the 220hp Benz. In Britain, Liberty-powered D.H.9 bomber/reconnaissance aeroplanes were acquired, as well as about 100 Martinsyde F.4 fighters with 300hp Hispano-Suiza 8Fb engines. This engine also powered about twenty Martinsyde F.6 reconnaissance aeroplanes and two Bristol F.2B Fighters obtained in Britain. Two Handley Page H.P.19 Hanley torpedo-bombers, purchased in 1923 for evaluation, had 450hp Napier Lions, and this engine also powered the passenger-carrying de Havilland D.H.34 and Vickers Vernon aircraft (as well as the Vickers Viking amphibian) bought by the USSR.

During 1922-24 the Soviets imported from the Netherlands a range of Fokker aircraft: D.VII fighters powered by the 180hp BMW IIIa, D.XI fighters with Hispano-Suiza 8Fbs and Liberty powered C.IV reconnaissance aeroplanes. In addition, two D.XIIIs with Lions were purchased for evaluation. This engine also powered two C.V reconnaissance aircraft that were acquired. A small number of C.Is with BMW IIIa engines and C.IIIs powered by 185hp Mercedes were also delivered to Russia. Twenty Fokker F.III passenger aeroplanes, purchased in 1923 for the GVF, had 360hp Rolls-Royce Eagles.

In Italy, Ansaldo Balilla A.1 fighters with 220hp SPA engines, SVA.10 reconnaissance aeroplanes powered by the same engines, and an Ansaldo A 300/3 with a 300hp Fiat A 12bis engine were acquired. The latter engine type was also installed in the Savoia S.16bis flying-boats imported to Russia in 1923-24.

In 1925 four Farman Goliath bombers with 450hp Lorraine-Dietrich LD 12Eb engines were delivered from France.

Meanwhile, the indigenous aircraft industry was growing gradually, but there was still a constant shortage of aero-engines. In 1923 it was planned to build 334 aeroplanes, while 123 engines were stored in depots and a maximum of eighty were to be supplied from Soviet factories. Taking into account the spare powerplants required by air force units, a minimum of 160 engines had to be purchased abroad. In 1924 the Soviet Government signed contracts for the delivery of engines from the USA, Great Britain, Germany and France, and, later, from Italy. In the summer of 1924 the People's Commissariat of Foreign Trade (*Narodniy Komissariat Vneshney Torgovli*, NKVT) was instructed to import 250 Liberties, and about 100 had been delivered to Soviet depots by 12 September. Initially, an order for 106 such engines was placed, and then 400 more were ordered in the USA in January 1925. In 1925 the US contractors were delivering about twenty engines a

Maintenance work on a Lorraine-Dietrich engine in a Farman Goliath bomber.

A Bristol Lucifer mounted in the ANT-3 passenger aeroplane.

month. American Liberties were apparently supplied from old reserves. They were not tested before shipment, so on arrival in Russia they had to be overhauled before being installed in aircraft. The overhauls were carried out not in an engine factory, but at the Aviarabotnik aircraft factory, where a special department had been established for this purpose. Engine acquisition in the USA continued for more than six years. In addition to new engines, used American powerplants were acquired and delivered at the beginning of the 1930s. These engines were overhauled at the Bolshevik factory in Leningrad and modified into tank engines, equipped with forced-cooling fans. In addition, in 1928-29 the Packard and Atlas companies were supplying the components for Soviet-built M-5 engines (particularly crankshafts). This resulted in the emergence of an engine series having mixed metric/Imperial sets of components. Parts for the Liberty engines were also purchased through the Dutch Fokker company.

From 1924 British suppliers were delivering the Liberty, and from July 1925 the Soviets began to receive Siddeley Puma engines, having ordered 150. An order was placed in France for 100 Lorraine-Dietrich LD 12Eds to be shipped in July-December 1925. An agreement was also concluded in Germany with BMW, which from the beginning of 1925 supplied the BMW IIIa and, from May of that year, the BMW IVa. By the beginning of July 1925 the Soviets had received eighty-nine BMW IIIas, sixteen BMW IVas and thirty-one Pumas. At the end of 1925 fifteen engines of unknown type were ordered from Fiat in Italy.

On-site engine acceptance at foreign factories was carried out by Soviet commissions. In the USA such a commission was headed by Miroshnikov, in Britain by Vladimirov, in Germany by Klimov and in France by Dyakov. There was no such commission in Italy; representatives from the Soviet commission in France visited the factories there when necessary.

The delivered engines were used on different aircraft built in Soviet factories. Thus Pumas powered about 130 R-2 training/reconnaissance aeroplanes, and American and British Liberties were installed in the R-1, the Soviet copy of the D.H.9A, as well as in some prototypes. For example, a Liberty was mounted in the R3-M5 prototype. The Lorraine-Dietrich powered the R3-LD reconnaissance aeroplanes, a special version with a longer crankshaft end (to allow for the installation of a nose radiator) being supplied from France. The German engines were mainly delivered to the Junkers concession factory in Fili, near Moscow, or used as spares. The BMW IVs were installed in the Kalinin K-1, K-2 and K-3 prototype aircraft.

The Soviet aircraft industry was growing faster than the engine industry, and the demand for imported engines was increasing. In May 1926 Groza, the acting head of VVS Staff, wrote to the People's Commissar of Military and Naval Affairs: 'As for the engines, we have to continue the extensive purchases from abroad ...'.

Aero-engines were not acquired solely for aeroplanes. Their use in tanks has already been mentioned, and a batch of Wright T4 Typhoons was purchased for use in navy boats.

Undoubtedly it was absolutely impractical to rely only on foreign purchases. Indigenous aero-engine production needed to be established, but the Soviet Government's financial and material resources were rather limited. An alternative was tried, in the form of concessions. The idea of establishing concession enterprises became rather popular in the mid-1920s. The Soviets considered it a means of mastering modern technologies comparatively easily and quickly, as the concessionaire bore all of the factory reconstruction and modernization costs. The Germans became the leaders in this undertaking. In 1922 the Soviets entered into negotiations with Junkers and Daimler on establishing aero-engine production in Russia. The choice was made in favour of Junkers company, which was backed and secretly financed by the German war ministry. On 26 November 1922 an agreement was signed with the company, granting concessions on the production of aircraft and aero-engines. The Germans wanted to use the former RBVZ factory in Petrograd, but finally settled for the incomplete automobile factory in Fili, near Moscow, which had also belonged to RBVZ. According to the agreement, Junkers was to arrange the production of up to 450 engines annually. The Soviets suggested production of the Napier Lion or Ford Liberty, but Junkers preferred its own types; the 310hp L-4 and 500hp L-5 in particular. In total, the company was to build 1,125 engines during the term of agreement, but, in reality, engine production in Fili was never established before liquidation of the concession in 1927.

From April 1925 similar negotiations were conducted with BMW. It was intended to allocate the former Russkiy Reno factory in Rybinsk to the company, for production of the BMW IIIa and BMW IV. In September 1925 a group of Soviet engine-building specialists headed by V.Ya. Klimov visited Munich to negotiate with BMW. Finally, in December, the idea of concession with the company was abandoned, and discussions on acquiring a licence were started.

In April 1924 the Vickers concern in England made an offer to the Soviet Government, proposing, together with Rolls-Royce, to set up aircraft and aero-engine production in Russia. Soviet representatives were to choose the types of aircraft and powerplants in England. Three possible variants of the enterprise were proposed: a joint stock company (with two-thirds British capital), a concession, or the sale of licences to Soviet factories. In its report to the Revvoensovet, the UVVS noted: 'The offer is to be considered as being of great importance and carrying weight ...'. Correspondence with Vickers continued until November 1924, but the project was never realized, possibly owing to political friction between Great Britain and the USSR.

Italian engine manufacturers became interested in concessions in Russia later than other companies. In September 1927 the Isotta-Fraschini company sent a letter via the Soviet Trade Mission in Rome, in which it proposed arranging the production of Asso aero-engines of two types, 200hp and 500hp, or assembly from Italian-built parts. A second proposal followed in January 1928, but Aviatrest rejected it. The last attempt was made by the Italians in the spring of 1929, when it was suggested that a trilateral agreement be set up between aircraft manufacturer SIAI, engine builder Isotta-Fraschini and Aviatrest. The building of an industrial complex combining aircraft and engine manufacture, using the former Matias factory on the coast of the Azov Sea as a basis, was proposed. The complex was to produce forty flying-boats and a hundred engines annually. Negotiations continued until December 1930, but the terms and conditions offered by the Soviets did not suit the Italians.

In September 1927 the UVVS considered the possibility of offering a factory in Zaporozhye as a concession to the French Gnome-Rhône company for the production of its Jupiter engines.

The last instance of a concession being considered occurred in December 1929, when Kharlamov, chairman of the NTK UVVS, suggested that a concession be offered to the Curtiss company for production of its V-1650 Conqueror engine. To accelerate the process of setting up production, the air force was prepared to accept the engine in its original Imperial-dimensioned version. Negotiations with Curtiss were carried out in 1930, but the concession was never agreed.

In the second half of the 1920s the Soviet leaders began to give priority to the development of indigenous engine factories. However, many of the engines produced by the country's enterprises were obsolete. For example, in 1921 production of the 80hp Le Rhône rotary had to be halted. As indigenous engines of satisfactory quality and reliability were not yet available, the Soviets began to look for suitable foreign designs. Initially, a production licence for the French Hispano-Suiza 8Ab was activated. This had been obtained by Tsarist Russia but had not been used at that time. Using the 8Ab as a basis, the Soviet M-4 was built. Some time later Soviet engineers copied a captured Liberty (the copy was designated M-5) and an Hispano-Suiza 8Fb (M-6). However, these had been developed during the First World War, and Western manufacturers already had higher-powered and more advanced designs. In order to choose the best of them, it was decided to purchase specimen engines in different countries. On 22 December 1924 the NTK UVVS recommended that the following types be acquired: Packard, Wright T3, Bristol Jupiter, Rolls-Royce Condor, Farman, Bristol Cherub, Salmson and a Beardmore diesel. Most of these engines were actually purchased, and underwent testing and thorough examination (two Condors were delivered in 1925, for example). In addition to the above types, in 1925 Aviatrest received from the USA two Curtiss D.12s and one Wright T4. That same year five Bristol Lucifer IIIs were imported from England, followed later by another fifteen (five Lucifer IIIs and ten Lucifer IVs).

In 1928 specimens of the Siemens Sh 20 (the German version of the Jupiter), the American Pratt & Whitney Hornet, and the 700hp Farman engine were purchased.

All of these engines were thoroughly examined and tested. Thus, in August-October 1924, the aero-engine department of the NAMI bench-tested the LD 12Ed, with V.Ya. Klimov in charge. The same engine type was run on the manufacturer's test-bench in France in the presence of a Soviet commission headed by B.E. Stechkin. During 1925-26 the Liberty, Condor IV, Junkers L-5 and Wright T3 were tested on the benches at the NAMI. The Curtiss D.12 and another example of the T3 passed tests at the Ikar factory in Moscow. In July 1927 the French Hispano-Suiza 12H51 was tested at the same factory. In August-November 1928 NAMI specialists carried out examinations of Packard's 600hp 2A-1500 and 800hp 3A-2500.

Some engines were delivered to the USSR in aircraft. Thus, Avia BH-33 fighters and Breguet 19 and Potez 25

Lorraine-Dietrich powered R-3LD reconnaissance aeroplanes were used in operations against rebels in Central Asia in the early 1930s. This one crashed in the Turkmenistan mountains.

Foreign-built engines at the MAI in the early 1930s. A Packard is in the foreground, with a Lion visible behind it.

A Packard 2A-1500 during tests at the NAMI.

ABOVE: **The R-3 reconnaissance airplane prototype, powered by a Napier Lion.**

LEFT: **A Fiat A.20 engine in an Italian CR.20 fighter tested at the NII VVS.**

LEFT: **The first TB-1 bomber prototype was powered by Napier Lions.**

BELOW: **The German Junkers K.30 (JuG-1), powered by L-5 engines.**

reconnaissance aeroplanes were powered by Jupiter engines of different versions, and Fiat CR.20 fighters had 415hp Fiat A.20s. The aircraft were tested and evaluated at the NII VVS.

Such tests were aimed both at studying foreign engine-building expertise, and at selecting engine types to be purchased abroad or introduced into production in the Soviet Union. As to engineering expertise, many early Soviet engines used components from foreign designs. The M-13, created at the NAMI, used the cylinder blocks of the Wright T3, its carburettor was copied from the Condor, and the gas-distribution mechanism and its components were taken from the Packard. The Soviet M-14, built at the Ikar factory and later redesignated W18, had Curtiss D.12-type cylinder blocks.

In October 1924 the Soviet authorities were considering the Napier Lion and Lorraine-Dietrich 12Eb as possible candidates for unlicensed copying. The Lion was described by UVVS specialists as: 'one of the best European engines'. The first R-3 reconnaissance aeroplane prototype and the 2I-N1 (DI-1) fighter prototype were powered by this engine. The TB-1 bomber was originally designed to be powered by Lions, too.

However, these plans were not realized, as a new favourite appeared in the form of the American Wright T3, which was considered very promising. The first specification for the famous TB-3 bomber (initially designated T1-4RT3) counted upon the use of this very engine. In June 1925 aircraft designer Kalinin prepared a project for a shipborne fighter which also used the T3, and the same engine was to be installed in the three-engine Ju G-1 (K.30) bombers being purchased from Junkers through its Swedish subsidiary. However, certain difficulties arose regarding this deal. The Wright company wanted to know the buyer's nationality and the intended role of the aircraft. As a result it refused to sell the T3s to Germany, and the Ju G-1s were powered by German L-5 engines. In March 1925 P.I. Baranov, head of the UVVS, requested clarification of the possibility of acquiring a licence for the T3. In June of that year it was suggested that a copy of the T3 be made, using the available specimen as a pattern, and introduced into unlicensed series production at the Ikar factory. No other information about these events has been found.

The E-1 experimental aircraft, powered by a 175 hp Salmson.

In October 1925 Factory No. 9 in Zaporozhye was tasked with copying the 450hp Hispano-Suiza. A small design bureau was established for this purpose, but the order was soon cancelled and the design bureau was closed down.

Many foreign companies offered the Soviet Union production licences for their aero-engines. On 18 October 1924, for example, such a letter was received from the French Salmson company, in which five types of low- and medium-powered engines were listed. In June 1926 licensed production of the American Typhoon engine, for speedboat use, was discussed. This was urged by the commanders of the navy, who suggested that the Typhoon be put into production instead of the planned indigenous GM-13. In September 1928 the Curtiss-Wright Corporation offered to sell all documentation and production jigs for the Typhoon, as it was being phased out of production in the USA, but the Soviets elected to create marine versions of indigenous aero-engines.

Those responsible for the Civil Air Fleet were interested in the air-cooled Curtiss-Wrights. A Soviet delegation led by G.I. Silin, deputy chief inspector of the GVF, visited the USA in 1930 and attempted to reach agreement on the production of the 350-400hp and 600-700hp Curtiss-Wright engines in the USSR.

The head of the UVVS, P.I. Baranov, was hatching more extensive plans. During his visit to the USA in January 1930 he negotiated for the establishment of a combined aircraft- and engine-building stock company for arranging the production of Curtiss-Wright equipment. The key subject of the discussions was production of the V-1650 Conqueror. In November 1929 this engine was recommended by the NTK UVVS, which compared it with the Hispano-Suiza 12Hb, Napier Lion VIIB and Rolls-Royce Kestrel F.XIIB engines. B.S. Stechkin also examined the Conqueror during his visit to the USA, and reported favourably on it. The Soviet Union purchased twelve Conquerors in the USA, and they were used on the first TB-3 prototype, the I-8 (ANT-13) and DI-4 fighter prototypes, and on the experimental Stal-6 aeroplane. In 1934 one of the Conquerors was modified at the TsAGI's Factory of Experimental Designs (*Zavod Opitnikh Konstruktsiy*, ZOK) A drive for the cooling fan was introduced and the reduction gearing was changed. The engine was installed on the 11-EA experimental helicopter, which was being tested and refined until the spring of 1941.

However, plans for Conqueror production in the USSR were not realized. President Hoover's government pursued a policy of reducing trade with Bolsheviks, raising new barriers for commerce and putting pressure on companies that co-operated with Amtorg, an organization registered in the USA as an American corporation with Soviet capital, and acting as a trade mission at a time when there were no diplomatic relations between two countries. This resulted in a decision by the Sovnarkom on 7 September 1931 not to place orders in the USA.

Quite an epic took place regarding the attempt to arrange Packard radial diesel production in the USSR. At the end of 1930 a specimen of this 225hp engine was purchased in the USA, delivered to the IAM and disassembled for examination. In 1931 the VAO purchased four more Packards, and it was planned to test the diesel engine in an ANT-9 aeroplane. The development of aviation diesel engine construction was considered to be of great importance in the USSR. Soviet representatives asked the Packard company to sell a them a licence and provide technical

ABOVE AND LEFT: **The TB-3 prototype was initially powered by Curtiss Conquerors. Later they were replaced by German BMW VIs, which were also installed in some early series production bombers of this type.**

assistance in setting up series production of the engine, but this was refused.

Then it was decided to take a different approach. The Soviet intelligence service was given the task of obtaining the necessary material. At the end of June 1931 the foreign department of the OGPU presented the VAO with a full set of documentation for the latest version of the 230hp Packard diesel engine, dated November 1930. Specifications, technical documentation and about 1,500 drawings were delivered to Moscow.

On 25 July 1931 the STO issued a decision to start series production of this diesel engine in 1932. The VAO was ordered to assemble the first batch of five units by the end of 1932, while the TsIAM was to adapt American documentation to Soviet standards. However in January 1932 the GUAP asked the government to cancel this task, as the engine's design was not a success and the type had been phased out of production in the USA. This request was complied with.

At the same time, two licences were successfully obtained in Germany and France. In January 1925 material concerning the testing of the new 12-cylinder BMW VI was delivered from Munich to Moscow. These reports aroused interest among Soviet specialists, and two specimens of the new engine were ordered in Germany that same year, and had been assembled and bench-tested by July. At a meeting on 26 October 1926 the NTK UVVS stated that it preferred the BMW to the Italian Asso and French Hispano-Suiza engines. Negotiations with the Germans were successfully concluded, and the licence agreement came into force from 14 October 1927. Factory No. 26 in Rybinsk built several versions of the BMW VI under the designation M-17 until 1941.

The Jupiter engine, developed by the Bristol Engine Company's designers in England, was in series production in four European countries at the end of the 1920s; Great Britain, France, Poland and Germany. Relations between the USSR and Great Britain were rather tense, and negotiations for the purchase of a production licence were simultaneously carried out with French Gnome-Rhône and German Siemens companies. The terms offered by the French seemed the most favourable, so in 1928 a licence agreement was concluded with Gnome-Rhône for the production of the French version of the Jupiter VI, the 480hp Gnome-Rhône 9Aq. Its series production, as the M-22, was set up in 1930 at Factory No. 29 in Zaporozhye.

In both cases, in order to examine the engines and to carry out advance preparation of aircraft prototypes, batches of original German and French Jupiters were purchased. At the same time, Jupiter versions that were not to be introduced into production in the USSR were also imported. For instance, the Gnome-Rhône 9Ad (420hp), 9As (a high-altitude version, counterpart of the Jupiter VII) and 9Akx (geared) engines were delivered. These passed tests at the NAMI, IAM and NII VVS. In particular, the NII VVS tested the Gnome-Rhône 9As in April 1930. The imported BMW VI engines were installed on the following aircraft prototypes: TB-1 and TB-3 bombers, R-5, R-6, and R-7 reconnaissance aeroplanes, LSh, TSh-1, TSh-2 and ShON ground-attack aircraft, I-3, DI-3 and D-2 (DI-2) fighters, and MBR-2 and MDR-2 flying-boats. A number of projects depending on the use of these engine types were prepared (such as the MT-1, designed as early as 1926). The Jupiters powered prototypes of the I-4, I-5, I-6 and I-Z fighters, of the TB-5 heavy bomber (which had four 9Akx engines) and of the ANT-14 and K-6 airliners.

As the arrangements for Jupiter production in Soviet factories were behind schedule, foreign-made engines were purchased for the first batches of new aircraft. Thus, imported BMW VIs were installed on almost all TB-1s and most of the early R-6s and TB-3s. The German-built engines, which were lighter and slightly higher-powered, were usually installed in commanders' aircraft. It is noteworthy that the TB-3 was permitted to be powered by the BMW VI and M-17 at the same time, provided the engines had the same compression ratio. The German engines also powered the first batches of R-5 reconnaissance aeroplanes. In addition, a batch of ten R-5s exported to Iran in 1931 also had this powerplant. German engines were imported to the USSR together with Dornier Wal flying-boats purchased in Italy. However, the first two Wals were fitted with Lorraine-Dietrich engines.

The Gnome-Rhône 9Ads imported from France were installed in the I-4 fighter. In fact, production of the M-22 was started as production of the fighter was coming to an end. The 9Aq engines upon which the M-22 was based were installed in the first batches I-5 fighters manufactured at Factory No. 39. The Jupiters were being delivered from France until 1933.

Similar engines were arriving from Germany as well. From Heinkel the Soviet Union purchased KR-1 catapult-launched shipborne reconnaissance aeroplanes powered by the Siemens Sh.20, the German version of the Jupiter VI. The components of the French and German versions of the Jupiter were not interchangeable.

In the late 1920s/early 1930s the USSR purchased foreign low- and medium-powered engines that had no Soviet counterparts. In 1928 a small batch of 5-cylinder Titan radial engines were acquired in France for the prototype ANT-9 airliner. It was also planned that the series-production aircraft would be powered by these engines, but the UVVS insisted on the higher-powered American Wright J6 Whirlwind. On 28 December 1929 the order already placed with the French company was cancelled and a forfeit was paid.

The first batch of Whirlwinds was purchased in the USA by Baranov in January 1930, and the second batch in the summer of the same year, by Silin. These engines were installed in all ANT-9s of the first series, and also in some of succeeding series. As well as being in VVS RKKA service, the Whirlwind-powered aircraft were also operated by different departments of civil aviation and by Soviet-German airline Deruluft. One of the American engines was installed in the prototype Stal-2 passenger aeroplane, which underwent testing in August 1935. A J6 also formed part of the powerplant of the 'Helicogyro' of Italian designer V. Isacco, who worked at the NII GVF in 1932-35. The engine, driving a tractor propeller, was placed in the nose of the aircraft, which was tested in 1935. A lower-powered J4a was used in the AIR-4 light aeroplane designed by A.S. Yakovlev.

In the middle of the 1920s a batch of 100hp Bristol Lucifer engines was purchased in Britain. They were mounted in several aircraft prototypes: A.N. Tupolev's ANT-2, an aeroplane built by A.N. Pavlov and B.I. Cheranovskiy's BICh-7. When Soviet-built M-11s appeared, Lucifers were no longer required.

Soviet factories built almost no engines below 100hp. Therefore, to enable light aircraft to be created in the 1920s and the early 1930s, such engines were purchased abroad, though only in small quantities, to save valuable hard currency. The importing of fifteen Bristol Cherubs has been noted earlier. These were used in home-built light aircraft such as the C-5 *Burevestnik* (Petrel), *Tri Drouga* (Three Friends) and some other designs. In the same year, 1925, even the lower-powered 18hp Blackburne Tomtit engine was purchased. Such engines were mounted in the OSO-1 and RAF-1 light aeroplanes. The Soviet Union also imported small quantities of 60hp Cirrus and 85hp Siemens engines. The latter powered the AIR-2 aeroplane.

Czechoslovakian Walter radial engines were very popular in the USSR at the end of the 1920s and beginning of the 1930s. Two types of these engines were imported, the 60hp NZ-60 and 85hp NZ-85. The former powered many light-aircraft prototypes: the Igrado 3B/M, AIR-2, AIR-3, AIR-8, *Omega*, K-9 and G-10. The latter was installed in V.B. Shavrov's Sh-1 amphibian.

In February 1930 P.I. Baranov attempted to purchase a batch of five 100hp Kinner K-5s in the USA. However, the deal probably did not take place.

In 1929 an S.62bis flying-boat powered by an Asso 750, together with a spare engine, was purchased from the SIAI company in Italy. An engine alone cost 480,000 lire. The aircraft passed its tests in Sevastopol, and the spare engine was bench-tested at the TsIAM. The results confirmed that the aircraft was suitable for operations in the USSR.

Within the framework of the contract for acquiring a batch of flying-boats in Italy and obtaining a licence for the aircraft's production, 125 Asso 750s were ordered from Isotta-Fraschini in September 1930. Fifty of these engines were intended for installation in the aircraft being assembled at Sesto Calende for the Soviet Union, and seventy-five were delivered as spares, as well as for the MBR-4s (the Soviet designation for the S.62bis) that were to be built in Taganrog. The same engines powered five large S.55 flying-boats that had been purchased for the Far Eastern Department of the Civil Air Fleet. Later, several small batches of Asso 750s were acquired to replace worn-out engines. This engine proved to be unreliable when operating in the Soviet Union's cold climate.

In 1929 the American Allison company made a special proposal to develop an air-cooled 1,000hp diesel aero-engine for the USSR. The work was to be headed by designer Gilmer. After considering the proposal, the Soviet representatives rejected Allison's offer.

At the beginning of the 1930s the Soviet leadership, having overestimated the engineering design capabilities of the

All I-4 fighters were powered by imported French Jupiters. Here, an engine undergoes maintenance in one of the naval aviation squadrons.

The KR-1 (Heinkel HD.55) shipborne reconnaissance aeroplane was powered by the German version of the Jupiter, manufactured by Siemens.

The S-62B flying-boat, powered by an ASSO 750.

A Bristol Mercury engine in the first I-14 fighter prototype.

A Jumo 4 diesel on display in the Russian Air Force Museum at Monino.

The R-5 converted into a flying test-bed for the German Jumo 4 diesel.

country's industry, took action to compel aircraft manufacturers to use Soviet-developed engines exclusively. An extensive programme for the construction of experimental engines was carried out. In this connection, in August 1931 the Revvoensovet decided to stop purchasing foreign engines for prototype aircraft. All new Soviet aircraft had to be designed to use indigenous engines.

However, this did not stop the process of importing foreign aero-engines for evaluation. Under the STO decree for the construction of experimental aircraft and engines, the plan for 1929-33 permitted the purchase of ten engines annually, 725,000 roubles in gold being allocated for this purpose. Thus, in 1931, negotiations were carried out with BMW for the purchase of ten new BMW IX engines and twenty sets of reduction gears for BMW VIs. One BMW IX had been ordered as early as on 10 September 1930. By February 1931 it had been built and bench-tested in Germany, but it had broken down during the tests. No information on the fate of this order has been found.

In the autumn of 1932 a team from the Fairey company delivered to Moscow, along with a Firefly fighter, a Rolls-Royce Kestrel engine that attracted considerable interest from the Soviet specialists. Soviet engineers even made drawings based on this specimen engine.

Several Jumo 4 diesels with opposed pistons were purchased from Junkers and bench-tested at the TsIAM and in a special ED-1 'flying laboratory', a converted R-5 reconnaissance aeroplane. The tests were completed in 1935. It was planned to install a Jumo 4 in the record-breaking ANT-25 (RD), but successful development of the indigenous AN-1 diesel led to its use in the ANT-36 (RDD), a further development of the ANT-25.

By April 1932 it was evident that the Soviet engine manufacturers' plans had failed. The weakness of the design organizations, the lack of qualified personnel, outdated production technology and the general backwardness of related sectors (primarily the electrical and metallurgical industries), meant that only one engine of indigenous design, A.A. Mikulin's M-34, had reached the stage of practical application in 1930-31. This situation delayed the development of Soviet aircraft manufacture. In particular, the country had no modern indigenous high-altitude engine for fighter aircraft. A commission headed by M.N. Tukhachevskiy (later Marshal), recommended that licences be obtained for engine types in production in the USA. The Wright R-1820 Cyclone and Curtiss V-1800 Conqueror were chosen for manufacture in the USSR.

The Soviets blackmailed Curtiss-Wright to a certain extent by simultaneously approaching Pratt & Whitney, but in the end the licences were purchased from the former company. The Soviet Air Force leadership hovered between the Cyclone SR-1820-F3 and its F5 high-altitude version, finally opting for the more refined F3.

Cyclone production was to be set up at Factory No. 19 in Perm, the engine being designated M-25, and the Conqueror was to be built at Factory No. 26 in Rybinsk. In the summer of 1933 the Soviets contracted Curtiss-Wright to adapt the Conqueror production process to suit the machinery available in Rybinsk. By 24 February 1934 the engine drawings had been converted to the metric system and, according to the schedule, the factory was to deliver the first batch of ten engines at the end of the year.

However, work on the Conqueror production arrangements was unexpectedly stopped. A contract with Hispano-Suiza for licence production of its new 12Ybrs engine was signed in France. The original plan was to build the engine at Factory No. 24 in Moscow, but this plant was overloaded with M-34 production. Then 12Ybrs production was allotted to the Rybinsk factory. As a result, all the V-1800 parts that had been produced by the factory were written off and scrapped.

When the Soviet delegation was preparing to visit Paris in 1933 for negotiations with Hispano-Suiza, Ya.I. Alksnis, head of the UVVS, suggested that they review Gnome-Rhône's two-row radial at the same time. This resulted in licences being obtained for two Gnome-Rhône radials, the two-row 14K Mistral Major and the single-row 9K Mistral. Preparation for series production of these engines began at Factory No. 29 in Zaporozhye.

The 14Krsd version was series-built in the USSR as the M-85. Just a few 9Ks were manufactured as the M-75, the type soon being phased out of production.

Those three engines, the Wright Cyclone, Hispano-Suiza 12Ybrs and Gnome-Rhône 14Krsd, formed the basis for the creation of three Soviet aero-engine families. Development of the Hispano-Suiza line was continued by V.Ya. Klimov, improvements to the Cyclone were carried out by A.D. Shvetsov, and evolution of the Gnome-Rhônes was continued at OKB-29 under the leadership of A.S. Nazarov, S.K. Tumanskiy, E.V. Urmin and other designers.

As previously, original American and French engines were purchased to power new prototype aircraft. It was expected that, by the time series production of an engine had been arranged, the aeroplanes that were to have these engines would be ready.

Under an STO decree of 28 November 1933, 150 complete Cyclones, as well as 150 sets of parts for assembly in the USSR, were to be ordered in the USA. On 15 December the government decided to increase the number of completed engines to 200, comprising fifteen built to Imperial dimensions and 185 built to metric dimensions. However, it took the Americans rather long time to prepare the metric version, and by 11 February 1934 only thirty Imperial-system engines had actually been ordered. Each one cost 16,000 roubles in gold. The first Cyclone was shipped from the USA at the end of December 1933. In February 1934 the GUAP received a new directive requiring it to purchase 145 Imperial-system versions (including the thirty ordered earlier) and only twenty of the metric version.

The Cyclone SR-1820-F3, designated RTsF-3 in the USSR, powered prototypes of the I-15, IP-1, DI-6 and I-16 (second prototype) fighters. The I-14 fighter, at first powered by the Bristol Mercury VS2, was also fitted with the Cyclone in 1933 (in the I-14bis, the second prototype). Two RTsF-3s powered N.N. Polikarpov's SPB bomber prototype, and the same powerplant was installed in the first prototype of the famous SB (ANT-40RTs) bomber and in the prototype of the MBR-5 flying-boat.

As the aircraft manufacturers slightly outpaced the engine manufacturers, in some cases imported engines were also installed in series-production fighters. Some I-16s and all I-14s were powered by the original American-built engines.

The Hispano-Suiza engines were purchased in smaller quantities than the Cyclones. The same STO decree of 28 November 1933 stipulated that thirty

A French Hispano-Suiza 12Ydrs engine in the second prototype of the SB high-speed bomber (ANT-40IS).

assembled engines be ordered from the French company. On 24 November 1934 the Soviet trade mission in Paris placed the first order, which included six 750hp 12Ybrs engines and two 12Ycrs, which had provision for cannon installation. The first two units were shipped from the factory on 21 January 1935, and the remaining six (including both 12Ycrs) on 27 February. Later batches included the 12Ydrs version and the improved 860hp 12Ybrs.

The 12Ydrs and 12Ybrs were installed in the second prototype of the SB bomber (ANT-40IS). Series-production SBs were powered only by Soviet license-built M-100 and M-100A engines. A 12Ybrs also powered an I-17 fighter prototype, while the second prototype, the I-17-2, was planned to have the 12Ycrs. The DAR flying-boat had two 12Ydrs engines. The uncompleted IP-2 (DG-52) aircraft was to be powered by the Hispano-Suiza 12Xbrs, and the projected LK-3 (DG-56) was to have a pair of the same. The unusual MP torpedo-bomber, which was to be delivered to the target by a carrier aircraft, had the 12Ybrs. The original French engines did not power any Soviet series-production aircraft.

The Gnome-Rhône 14Krsd engines delivered to the USSR were also used only on prototypes. S.V. Ilyushin's TsKB-26 and TsKB-30 (DB-3) bombers, P.O. Sukhoy's DB-2 and A.N. Tupolev's MTB-2 (ANT-

44) flying-boat were powered by these engines. The third prototype of the SB bomber, powered by Gnome-Rhônes, was modified into the DI-8 heavy fighter. The twin-engine LK-2 (G-38) 'cruiser' was to be powered by 14Krsd engines, but was not completed. Gnome-Rhônes were also specified for the projected TsKB-43 fighter and ANT-43 passenger aeroplane.

The USSR's last aero-engine production licence was acquired from Renault. In January 1936 the STO decided to obtain a licence and technical support for a family of in-line inverted air-cooled engines. Three such families were under consideration: the British de Havilland Gipsy, the Czechoslovakian Walter and the French Renault. A delegation was sent to Europe, where it visited the relevant factories and examined the engines. Specimens of a number of engine types had been purchased beforehand for evaluation.

Several Walter Micron and Junior engines were delivered to the USSR. The former was not only bench tested, but was also installed in a G-22 light aircraft. In 1935 a small batch of 120hp Gipsy IIIs was purchased. Four powered the aforementioned Isacco 'Helicogyro', being mounted at the tips of its rotor blades. In 1936 a Gipsy engine underwent extensive bench testing at the NII GVF. Later, a 130hp Gipsy Major was delivered together with a Miles Hawk Trainer aircraft, and the engine passed its tests at the NII GVF. However, in the end the French engines were chosen.

An agreement with Renault was signed on 16 October 1936. In 1938-39 Factory No. 16 in Voronezh produced small quantities of the 4-cylinder and 6-cylinder Renault engines, designated MV-4 and MV-6 respectively.

To power new prototype aircraft, small batches of Renault 4Pei and 6Q engines were purchased in France. The former powered prototypes of A.S. Yakovlev's UT-1 and Ya-21 training aircraft, and the latter was used in the prototype of the twin-engine S-17 (UT-3).

By the middle of the 1930s Soviet military and civil aviation had been fully supplied with indigenous engines, but many of them were versions of foreign-designed types. The M-17, M-25, M-100 and M-85, along with the M-11 and M-34, which had been developed in the USSR, were the primary types in service with the air force and Civil Air Fleet.

From then right up to the Second World War there were no large acquisitions of foreign aero-engines, and no large-scale production under foreign licences was undertaken in the Soviet Union. This does not mean that foreign-built engines did not come in to the country. During that period they reached the USSR as individual examples for assessment, installed in purchased aircraft, or as captured trophies of war.

During the second half of the 1930s the Soviet Union continued purchasing

ABOVE: A Gnome-Rhône 14Kdrs mounted in the DB-3 bomber prototype is turned over by means of a starter truck.

RIGHT: A Gipsy Major engine in a Miles Hawk Trainer. On completing its tests the aircraft was transferred to the personal flight of the Chief of the Air Force.

BELOW: The S-17 prototype, powered by Renault 6Q engines, during tests. The aircraft later went into series production as the UT-3.

BELOW: This Avro C.30A Autogyro, powered by an Armstrong-Siddley Genet Major engine, was tested in the USSR in 1935.

sample aircraft in various countries. For example, in 1935 an Avro (Cierva) C.30A Autogyro with a 140hp Genet Major radial engine was acquired in Britain.

At the beginning of 1936 a batch of ten Avia Ba.122 specialized aerobatic aircraft were ordered in Czechoslovakia. Half of these were powered by Walter Castor engines, while the remainder had Walter Pollux engines (both were radials). The complete batch of aircraft was delivered to the Soviet acceptance commission in 1936. In the Soviet Union the aircraft and their engines underwent a thorough examination at the NII VVS and OELID TsAGI, because both engine types were specially designed to allow lengthy operation in inverted flight.

In 1937 a Fairey Fantôme fighter powered by an Hispano-Suiza 12Ycrs was delivered from Belgium. A year earlier a Dewoitine D.510R with the same engine had been purchased in France. The 12Ycrs was well known in the USSR, but Soviet specialists were interested in the powerplant installation, including its cooling system, and the operation of the cannon mounted in the cylinder vee.

A number of American aircraft were purchased, both for examination and with licensed manufacture in mind. For instance, a batch of Douglas DC-3s powered by Cyclone G2s was imported for use by the VVS RKKA and the GVF. In fact, most aircraft were ordered with different versions of Cyclone. The Northrop 2E attack aircraft and Martin 139WR bomber used the Cyclone F53, the Vultee V-1A floatplane and Vultee V-11GB attack aircraft had the F52, and the Douglas DF and Martin 156 flying-boats were powered by the G2. Seversky fighters were also Cyclone powered, the 2PA-A having a G-2 and the 2PA-L a G-7. The Consolidated 28-2 flying-boats purchased in the USA as sets of subassemblies had R-1820-G3s.

However, two Consolidated 17AF Fleetsters purchased in 1934 for the operation to rescue the crew of the sunken steamship *Chelyuskin* had 575hp Pratt & Whitney Hornets. Another engine by this manufacturer, the 750hp Wasp S3H1, powered the Sikorksy S-43A Baby Clipper amphibian that arrived in the USSR in the spring of 1937. A pair of R-1340-S3H1 Wasps powered the Lockheed L-10E purchased in the autumn of 1937 especially to find and rescue S.A. Levanevskiy's crew, lost during an attempted long-range record flight from Russia to the USA. In August 1937 a Consolidated 28-1 flying-boat powered by Pratt & Whitney R-1830-64s was purchased for the same purpose.

ABOVE: **A Walter Castor II in an Avia B.122 aerobatic biplane. These aircraft were purchased for use by fighter-pilot schools.**

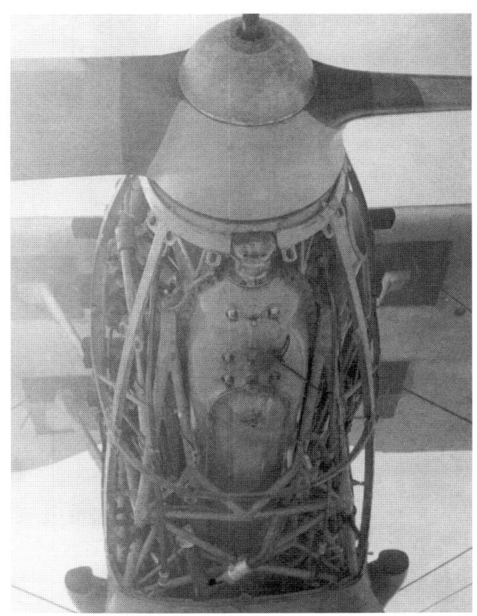

RIGHT: **The powerplant of the Fairey Fantome fighter evaluated at the NII VVS.**

A Wright GR-1820-G2 in the sample Vultee V-11G attack aircraft delivered to the USSR.

The Wright R-1820-G7 in the Seversky 2PA fighter, during tests at the NII VVS.

Some engine types were brought to the Soviet Union as trophies, captured during different military conflicts. Samples of German and Italian aircraft used by the Nationalists during the Spanish Civil War were shipped from Spain. A Junkers-Ju 52/3m bomber, complete with its three BMW 132s, was transported to the Soviet Union. Another type was a Heinkel He 51 fighter, powered by a slightly improved version of the BMW VI well known to Soviet specialists. Considerable interest was shown in the Daimler-Benz DB 600CG engines that arrived together with a Heinkel He 111B bomber. Once flight-testing of the aircraft was completed at the end of May 1939, its engines were transferred to the TsIAM. A Messerschmitt Bf 109B-1 fighter tested at the NII VVS was powered by a Jumo 210. During July 1938-January 1939, before the aircraft was flight-tested, its engine was overhauled and bench tested.

An Italian 600hp Fiat A.30RAbis engine was brought to the USSR from Spain in April 1937, together with fragments of a Fiat CR.32 biplane fighter. Some time later another example of this fighter was captured, this time in serviceable condition, and it underwent flight testing at the NII VVS. The Italian engine was considered outdated, and was transferred to the museum of the Air Force Academy.

This Lockheed L-10E, powered by R1340-S3H1s, was purchased from the USA especially to search for S. Levanevskiy and his crew, who disappeared during an attempted flight to the USA over the Arctic.

A Ju 86 bomber with Jumo 205 diesels, captured in Spain, had a most significant influence on Soviet aero-engine manufacture. In fact what was delivered was not a bomber, but its remains. Under the confusing designation DB-30 or 'aeroplane 30', the parts were thoroughly examined in Moscow, and the Soviet intelligence service concluded that the Germans had established series production of diesel aero-engines, and that the Luftwaffe had thousands of such aircraft in service. This overestimation resulted, firstly, in an urging forward of indigenous diesel programmes, and, secondly, in a decision to copy the Jumo 205, which surpassed the Soviet designs in some respects. The TsIAM was instructed to examine and copy the German engine. A serviceable engine was assembled from two damaged units, and underwent bench testing. Under a decree from Sovnarkom, Factory No. 26 was tasked with producing the first series of fifty such engines by 1 June 1938. However, successful refinement of the Soviet AN-1 diesel allowed this work to be cancelled.

At the end of 1930s several captured Japanese fighters were brought from China, where Soviet volunteers had also been involved in the military conflict. The Japanese Kawasaki Ki-10 (Army Type 95 Fighter) was powered by a rather outdated German BMW IX manufactured under licence in Japan. More up to date was a 610hp Kotobuki engine used in a Mitsubishi A5M (Navy Type 96 Carrier-borne fighter). An example of the Kotobuki engine was assembled at the NII VVS from the remains of three captured aircraft. The last Japanese engine brought to Moscow was a 780hp Ha-1 Otsu, which was transported together with a Nakajima Ki-27 (Army Type 97 Fighter). The aircraft also underwent flight-testing. Soviet documents mention plans to restore a 14-cylinder Japanese engine at Factory No. 29 in Zaporozhye, but no further information has been found.

During the conflicts at Khasan and Khalkhin-Gol not a single aircraft was captured by the Soviets. Later, in February 1940, one more Japanese aero-engine was seized in the Far East, but in very poor condition. This was acquired when a Mitsubishi Ki-15-I (Army Type 97 Reconnaissance Aeroplane), powered by a Nakajima Ha-8 engine, forced-landed in the region of Blagoveshchensk.

On the other hand, many different engine types were collected in September 1939 during the advance of the Red Army in the territory of the Western Ukraine and Western Byelorussia, which earlier had belonged to Poland. Several hundred Polish aircraft of different types fell into Soviet hands. In addition to the engines installed in the aircraft, many more were found on airfields and in warehouses, repair shops and railway stations. These engines mainly comprised Jupiter VIIF, Mercury IVS2, VS2, Pegasus IIM, VIII, XX and Walter Junior, all of which had been produced in Polish factories. A small quantity of British-built Pegasus XIIs was also found.

The NII VVS tested two captured Polish aircraft, a PZL-37Abis *Los* (Elk) bomber with two Pegasus XIIBs, and an RWD-8 trainer with a Walter Junior. The latter was captured in large numbers, and there were plans to pass them to air force flying training schools in the Southern regions of the country, but this did not happen. Plans to use Pegasus engines in Soviet civil aircraft were also not realized.

A Special-Purpose Squadron of the Civil Air Fleet received two Lockheed L-10A Electra passenger aeroplanes with Wasp Junior SB engines from the fleet of captured Polish aircraft. They remained in service until the end of 1941.

When the Baltic Republics were annexed by the Soviet Union, the aircraft of their air forces were taken over by the VVS RKKA. Most of them were outdated types that were immediately written off, but a few remained in Soviet service: Lithuanian ANBO IVs with Pegasus IIL and IIM engines, ANBO 41s with Pegasus XIs and ANBO 51s with Armstrong-Siddeley Genet Major IVs; and Latvian Henschel Hs 126Bs with Bramo-Fafnir 323As. The Red Army also captured a single Avro Anson with Armstrong Siddeley Cheetah IXs and a Gloster Gladiator with a Mercury VIII. The Baltic Department of Civil Air Fleet received two examples each of the de Havilland D.H.89 and Percival Q.6, all with Gipsy Six engines. In Lithuania an interned Polish Lockheed L-14H passenger aeroplane with Pratt & Whitney R-1690-S1EG Hornets was found. The BMW 132s that powered the Estonian and Latvian Ju 52/3ms were not new to the Soviet specialists.

At the end of the 1930s, considering the approaching war and realizing that the indigenous aero-engine industry was lagging behind its foreign counterparts, the Soviet leadership took new steps to broaden contacts with Western companies. Attempts were made to purchase examples of modern engines and technical documentation for examination, and in some cases to obtain licences.

As early as the autumn of 1937 the Soviet trade mission in London had started negotiations to purchase specimens of two engines, the Mercury and Pegasus, from the Bristol Engine Company. However, Bristol refused, demanding a contract for a batch of no fewer than fifty units and declining to sell a licence. In December 1938 in Moscow an offer was received from Napier-Halford company, proposing sales of Dagger engines, and some time later a proposal was made regarding the Alvis Leonides. It is not known whether these engines were bought. In March-August 1939 the Soviets carried out negotiations in London for the purchase of a Fairey P.4/34 aeroplane, but its Merlin engine was of greater interest. At the same time, in June, the Soviet representatives investigated the possibility buying a Mercury engined Bristol Blenheim IV bomber. On 3 July the Sovnarkom made a special decision concerning negotiations with Bristol regarding the purchase of examples of the Taurus, Pegasus and Hercules engines. In August the negotiations with Bristol reached the point where a draft of a five-year licence agreement covering these three engines was prepared. Apparently everything went wrong either after the start of the Second World War or after the start of the Soviet-Finnish War, which strained relations between the USSR and Great Britain.

In an effort to overcome the slow progress on improving the Cyclone, compared with the faster pace of progress at the Wright company, in January 1939 a new $900,000 agreement on technical assistance was prepared. Under its terms the American company was to provide documentation for the G100 and G200-series engines, as well as for the R-2600 two-row radial. Representatives of the company suggested that the new high-powered R-3350 engine be added to the agreement, but this was vetoed by the US War Department. The agreement was signed and came into force on 29 March 1939. A group of Soviet engineers left for the USA to accept the technical documentation. In addition, in December the Soviets wanted to purchase four G205As, six G205Bs and ten R-2600-A5Ds (later the order was reduced to four units), but not one engine was received. The work was delayed by the introduction of a 'moral embargo' during the Soviet-Finnish War. From 26 December the Soviet specialists were not allowed into the Wright factory workshops. However, as early as 8 February 1940 the first batch of drawings was shipped to the USSR on board the steamship *Mayakovskiy*. By 3 August all documentation for the G100 had been accepted. Later, this documentation was used in improvement work on the M-62 and M-63. The agreement with the Wright company remained in force until May 1941, when the Americans suspended it for a year. Up to that time the Soviets had paid the company $169,000. In 1942 the agreement was extended, but this was only a formality, and it remained in a suspended state until the war's end.

Attempts were made to purchase engines in other countries. In May 1939 the Italian Isotta-Fraschini company was approached by Soviet representatives about the possibility of purchasing from five to eight examples of its Delta RC.35JCD engine. The Italians quoted a price of 63,000 roubles per engine. At the time Renault was selling its 12R03, of almost the same layout and power, for 45,000 roubles per unit, so the Soviets rejected any idea of buying the Delta. A year later, in July 1940, an attempt was made within the bounds of the Soviet-Italian trade agreement to order four examples each of the Piaggio P.XII RC.35 and Isotta-Fraschini 180RT.CC.45. However, it transpired that the agreement stipulated that batches of at least 100 engines had to be bought.

From the summer of 1938 negotiations were held in Paris on obtaining a licence for the Gnome-Rhône 18P. The discussions lasted for more than a year, but did not result in an agreement. In a similar manner to the Wright negotiations, an attempt was made to reach a second agreement with Hispano-Suiza, but the French refused because the first agreement had ended in them paying a considerable forfeit for their delay in providing the drawings, and they were not prepared to risk incurring another penalty.

Information about foreign engines also came to the Soviet Union through unofficial channels. For instance, in 1940 the Soviet intelligence service brought to Moscow the drawings for the American R-2600, V-3420 and V-1710 aero-engines. These were copied and passed to different design bureaux.

From the autumn of 1939 there was a short period of co-operation between the Soviet Union and Hitler's Germany. Both parties demonstrated ostentatious friendliness, and delegation after delegation visited both countries. In the spring of 1940 the aircraft purchased by Soviet aviation industry delegation in Germany were delivered to Moscow. They comprised Messerschmitt Bf 109E and Bf 110C fighters, Dornier Do 215B and Junkers Ju 88A bombers, Bucker Bu 131D and Bu 133 and Focke-Wulf FW 58b and FW 58C trainers, and Fieseler Fi 156 liaison aircraft. In addition, a high-speed Messerschmitt Bf 108 liaison aircraft was delivered at the end of the year. The aircraft and their engines were thoroughly examined at the NII VVS and LII NKAP. During this period the Soviet specialists were able to study the Daimler-Benz DB 601A, Junkers Jumo 211J, Argus As 10C and Hirth HM 60R engines. The Soviet delegations that visited Germany were also shown captured British and American aircraft, and the list of equipment requested by the USSR from Germany included captured British aero-engines (in particular the Bristol Hercules).

In 1940-41 the DB 601A was bench tested at the TsIAM. The design of the

The Fiat A.30RAbis engine of the CR.32 fighter captured in Spain and studied at the NII VVS.

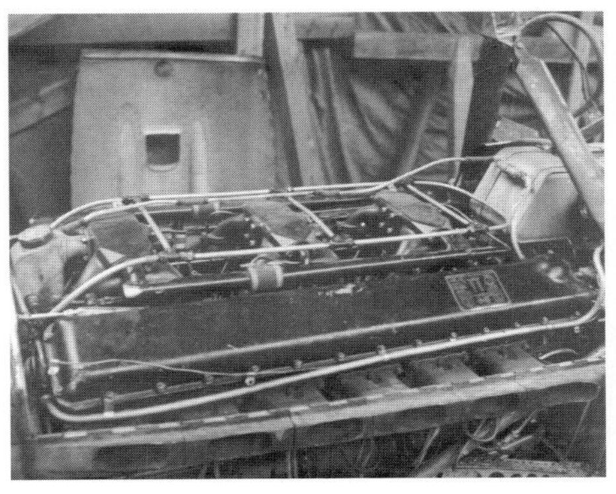

A Polish-assembled Pegasus engine in one of the PZL-37 *Los* bombers captured in September 1939.

hydraulic clutch of this engine's GCS drive was copied, and later used on some Soviet types. In 1941 a proposal to purchase a manufacturing licence for the DB 601A, and the possibility of establishing its production at a Soviet factory, were under consideration.

On the whole, by the time of Germany's aggression against the Soviet Union, both the Soviet Air Force and the Civil Air Fleet were fully equipped with indigenous engines. Foreign-built engines constituted only a portion of a per cent of the total number in service. By that time the Soviet engine types that were based on licensed designs were so far removed from their prototypes that in many respects they could be considered original engines.

However, the beginning of the Great Patriotic War again brought a need for the mass importation of foreign engines. During the first months of combat the Soviet Air Force lost thousands of aircraft and their engines. Germany's offensive forced the evacuation of the engine factories to regions deep inside Russia. Engine production decreased considerably, as did that of aircraft.

Some compensation for these losses came in the form of aid from the Allies. As early as September 1941 the aircraft carrier *Argus* delivered some Hurricane fighters to Murmansk. This delivery was followed by the first convoys, which brought aircraft and aero-engines, among other important cargoes, to the northern ports of Russia. From the beginning of 1942 military equipment was also delivered through the southern route, via Iraq and Iran, and, from September of that year, by air over the Bering Strait. This route was called ALSIB in the USA, while in the USSR it was named the Krasnoyarsk air route, Krasnoyarsk being the final destination.

In total, during the war the Soviet Union received from Britain and the USA 18,700 aircraft and about 5,700 spare engines for them. The engines delivered in the greatest quantities were the Allison V-1710 (about 10,000), Wright R-2600 (about 7,500), Pratt & Whitney R-1830 (more than 2,000) and Rolls-Royce Merlin (about 5,000). The USSR received smaller numbers of the Pratt & Whitney R-2800 (about 250), Pratt & Whitney R-1340 (about 100), Bristol Pegasus (more than 60) and Bristol Hercules (more than 50).

The Allison engines arrived with Bell P-39 and P-63, Curtiss P-40 and North American P-51 fighters. The R-2600s were delivered with North American B-25 and Douglas A-20 bombers. The Pratt & Whitney R-1830s powered Douglas C-47 transports and Consolidated PBN-1 flying-boats and PBY-6A amphibians. The Merlins powered Hawker Hurricane and Supermarine Spitfire fighters, the Pegasus engines were used on Handley Page Hampden TB.I torpedo-bombers and on the sole Short Stirling bomber received by the Soviets. The Hercules engines were installed in Armstrong Whitworth Albemarle transport aeroplanes. The R-2800s arrived with Republic P-47 fighters, and the R-1340s with North American AT-6 trainers.

The imported engines differed favourably from the Soviet products in being of higher-quality manufacture and in having lower fuel and oil consumption. Many of them had exceptional high-altitude performance. These powerplants operated well on thin mixtures, providing highly efficient fuel consumption in the cruise. On the other hand, the British and American engines were more demanding of fuel and oil quality, and required appropriately trained ground personnel and adherence to maintenance instructions.

For example, from the second half of 1942 the V-1710 had bearings of so-called 'white alloy' (an alloy of lead, silver and some cadmium). These bearings operated better at high revolutions and under heavy loads, but were very sensitive to quality of oil and the ingress of dust. They also required thorough adjustment at the installation stage. Besides that, the Allison had a range of short-period boost modes that had to be skilfully used, otherwise, the oil overheated, bearings melted and jammed and the conrods broke. Consequently there were frequent incidents.

At first the V-1710s operated for only 35 to 40 per cent of their normal service life. The situation was complicated by the lack of spares. In August 1944 technical specialists from one of the front-line regiments reported: 'The engine does not operate for the specified 250hr service life ... During two years of service no engine operated for more than 60 to 70 per cent of the specified service life'.

The same situation prevailed with other

One of the DB 601A engines in the Messerschmitt Bf 110C fighter obtained from Germany and tested at the NII VVS, June 1940.

The Soviet delegation to the USA studies the powerplant of a Douglas A-20 bomber.

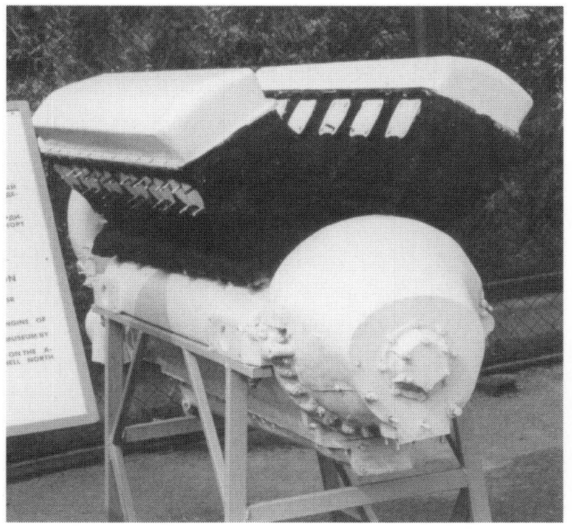

An Allison engine in the Victory Museum on Poklonnaya Hill in Moscow. Missing parts are covered by hoods.

Maintenance of a Bell P-63 fighter's Allison V-1710 engine.

The R-1830 displayed in the museum on Poklonnaya Hill.

Maintenance of an R-2600 in an A-20 of the 51st Mine and Torpedo-Bombing Air Regiment, 1944.

A spare R-2600 is transported to an A-20, 1944.

types of foreign-built engines, and by the end of the war they were being used only with imported oils and high-quality fuel. In some cases, for example with the Hercules, special additives for the Soviet motor oil were delivered, without which the oil eroded the surface of the main bearings.

By the middle of the war the Soviet factories had arranged production of some spares for imported engines. For instance, Factory No. 36 in Rybinsk was building main and conrod inserts for Merlins and Allisons.

The Lend-Lease deliveries considerably affected the manufacture of Soviet engines. As early as September 1941 the Specialloid company in Britain was given an order for the production of pistons, piston rings and valves for the M-105. The necessary drawings were brought from Moscow to London.

Large quantities of aluminium were supplied to the USSR from the USA, Great Britain and Canada, partly compensating for the loss of the aluminium factories in the German-occupied territories. Throughout the war the USA supplied ignition cables, hoses, rolled non-ferrous metal, carburettor seals, brass gauze, pipes, special lacquers and paints. Production of machine tools in the USSR decreased considerably during the war, as the specialized factories were overloaded with the production of weapons. Machine tools were imported from the USA and Great Britain. In addition, the Allies delivered a range of special machine tools that were not manufactured in the USSR at that time. The importation of cutting and measuring tools, abrasives, carbons, thermal and foundry equipment and bridge cranes also played an important part. In general, the influence of these imports on the Soviet aero-engine industry during the war is separate subject that cannot be covered here.

Unlike Britain, where the engines supplied from the USA under the Lend-Lease programme were often installed in indigenous aircraft, all aeroplanes produced in the USSR were powered only by indigenous engines. However, plans for the installation of Western engines existed. In May 1943 almost all of the country's aircraft design bureaux were instructed to prepare preliminary projects

A Merlin 46 in a Spitfire delivered to the USSR during the war.

A Handley Page Hampden torpedo-bomber, powered by Pegasus engines, serving with the 24th Mine and Torpedo-Bombing Air Regiment of the Northern Fleet Air Force.

for versions their aircraft powered by imported engines. It was planned to modify the Yak-1, Yak-7, Yak-9, LaGG-3 and Pe-2 to take Merlins and V-1710s, and to fit the La-5 with the R-2600 and R-2800, the Il-4 with the R-2600 and R-1830-33, and the Li-2 with the R-1820-71. However, preliminary calculations showed that none of the suggested variants offered sufficient improvement to justify reorganization of series production. As a rule, while benefiting in one respect they lost in another. Thus, according to calculations, the Yak-1 with the Merlin V would have been capable of 665km/h (413mph) at 6,000m (19,700ft), and its range would have increased by 70km (43miles). On the other hand, its speed at ground level fell by 15km/h (9.32mph), and its take-off run increased by as much as 40 per cent. Installation of the V-1710 provided a small increase in maximum speed (by 15km/h (9.32mph)) and range (by 130km (81miles)), but at the same time worsened all of the fighter's other performance parameters. If used on the Pe-2 the Merlin would have improved almost all of its performance except for the take-off run, but the Allison was completely unacceptable for installation in the aircraft.

The longest effort to introduce American engines centred on the Li-2 transport aeroplane. The idea seemed logical, as the Li-2 was the Soviet copy of the DC-3. On 15 June 1942 the State Defence Committee (*Gosudarstvenniy Komitet Oboroni*, GKO) issued a decree for the purchase 2,000 R-1820-G2 engines in the USA for installation in these aircraft. The G2 version was similar to the Soviet-built M-62IR, which it was to replace. The R-1820-G2 powered the batches of DC-3s purchased by the USSR before the war.

The Soviet mission in the USA inquired about the supply of 2,000 R-1820-G2s, but received a refusal. This was not because the Americans had other plans for their use, but because the version had been phased out of production at the beginning of 1942. Only 120 were found in the Wright company depots, and these were offered to the Soviet representatives. Fifty-two were selected and shipped to the USSR. On the way to the Soviet Union one ship was sunk and ten engines went down with it. The delivered G2s were apparently used as spares for the DC-3s still in service.

Then the possibility of installing G100-series engines in the Li-2 was considered, but production of this version had ceased at the beginning of 1943. The Americans proposed the improved G202 series, but its installation would have required too many modifications to the aeroplane. As a result, on 7 October 1943 the already-approved order was cancelled. Instead, representatives of the US Army Air Force offered 2,000 R-1830-92s, which powered the C-47. However, this engine was not only 100kg (220lb) heavier, but also required considerable strengthening of the wing, fuselage and undercarriage. Thus the Li-2 remained powered by the same Soviet-built M-62IR (ASh-62IR) engines. The offer of the R-1830-92s was at first rejected, but after several days the Soviets suddenly realized that there was a need for spare engines for the C-47s in service, and asked for 300. Now the Americans refused, as the engines had already been reassigned elsewhere. Finally, an order for 120 engines was agreed and they were shipped to the USSR.

In 1944 the NKAP was actively urging the purchase of 1,500 R-985-16 engines in the USA (half of them equipped with synchronization mechanism), for new Soviet trainers. This plan was supported by A.S. Yakovlev, who was not only a designer but also the Deputy of the People's Commissar. The official request was made on 18 September 1944, and after extensive correspondence twenty R-985-AN1s were purchased. Although it was planned to install them in Shche-2 aircraft, only one instance of their use is known, on the G-3 helicopter. For this purpose the engines were fitted with forced-cooling fans and angled reduction gearing.

Throughout the war the Soviet Union sought to obtain examples of the latest aero-engines from its allies for examination. In January 1943 a request was made to the USA for examples of the R-2800, R-3350, V-3420 and V-1650, but was denied. Later, the R-2800 was delivered with P-47 Thunderbolt fighters, and the engine was thoroughly examined in the USSR. However, it was its supercharger that created the real interest, as it endowed the engine with exceptional high-altitude performance. In 1944 the A.I. Mikoyan Design Bureau prepared a project for converting a MiG-3 fighter to take the R-2800-63 engine and C-23 turbo-supercharger from P-47D-RE, using aeroplane 'E' (the I-211, or MiG-3 with ASh-82FN engine) as a basis. On 8 April 1944 the project was submitted to the NII VVS for consideration, but it did not go beyond that.

Of special interest was the high-powered R-1830-92, which the Soviets had wanted to obtain as early as 1940. On 31 July 1943 an official request was made directly to Gen Henry 'Hap' Arnold, commanding the US Army Air Force. On 6 August he replied: 'The situation is under study'. On 15 August the decision was temporarily postponed, and on 2 September an official refusal was sent. At the same time negotiations were being carried out with the Wright company, which was prepared to grant a licence, but only with the approval of the military.

Eventually an R-3350 was received, though unofficially. From July to November 1944 four Boeing B-29 bombers powered by this engine forced-landed in the Vladivostok region. As the Soviet Union was at war with Japan at that time, the aircraft were interned, and it was decided not to return them. The American bomber was copied by the A.N. Tupolev Design Bureau and introduced into series production as the Tu-4, which was powered not by the R-3350 but by the indigenous ASh-73TK. However, the Wright engine considerably influenced the design of the Soviet powerplant. Examination of the R-3350 allowed some of the successful solutions it embodied to be copied, in particular the bearing units. The TK-19 turbo-supercharger was completely copied from the American one by specialists at the TsIAM. Moreover, the first prototypes of the ASh-73TK were bench tested with American components (spark plugs, generators, starters, magnetos and bearings).

To accelerate the preparations for ASh-73TK series production, it was suggested that a large number of components be purchased in the USA, and negotiations were started with American suppliers. The Soviets were searching for a company ready to establish the manufacture of modern spark plugs in the USSR (not only American, but also British companies were being considered). On 24 November 1945 the Jack and Geintz company provided a proposal for the supply of starters and electric generators, but the VVS command insisted on its engines having only Soviet-built components.

Considerable interest was also shown in British engines. On 27 January 1943 an inquiry was sent to Great Britain about the possibility of purchasing examples of the Rolls-Royce Merlin 61 and Vulture, Bristol Centaurus and Napier Dagger and Sabre engines. The Merlin 61 and Sabre appeared in the Soviet Union at the end of the war together with Spitfire IX and Hawker Typhoon aircraft. In 1943 licence production of Merlins in the USSR was discussed. This was first suggested by Pashinin and Bogomolov, representatives of the Soviet Trade Mission, who wrote: 'We consider it extremely important to raise the question of obtaining licences for manufacturing the latest versions of British Rolls-Royce engines in our country ...'. Shakhurin, the People's Commissar of the Aviation Industry, considered obtaining a licence to be premature, and suggested purchasing ten to fifteen engines for examination. This matter was even discussed at a session of the GKO. Finally, doubts about the possibility of assembling and adjusting such a sophisticated engine (the US Packard company had already failed in such an attempt) led to a refusal to negotiate.

Evaluation of the high-powered and reliable Bristol Hercules, used in the USSR on the Albemarle, led to an intention to review its bigger brother, the Centaurus. On 17 November 1943 a letter from Bartlett, the Commercial Director of Bristol Engines, was received in Moscow. The letter contained the consent to sell the engines, and in January 1944 the company offered a production licence for the Centaurus. When discussing this offer in February, Shakhurin again suggested that five to ten engines of different types, including Centaurus, should first be purchased and evaluated in the USSR.

On 6 January 1945 several Centaurus VIIs were delivered to Murmansk, and in the same month the TsIAM started to set up the test bench. On 3 March the engines were delivered to Moscow, and testing started at the end of March and finished on 21 May. On 13 September the British again offered a licence. However, as refinement of the ASh-73TK progressed, interest in the Centaurus waned and finally faded away. Another engine sent by Bristol was a Hercules 100 (Soviet specialists had evaluated the XI and XIV versions earlier). It was examined but considered even less interesting.

The examination of captured German equipment also had a considerable influ-

The *Omega* helicopter prototype, powered by Pratt & Whitney engines, 1946.

An exhibition of foreign-built engines at the MAI in 1948.

A captured Messerschmitt Bf 109 fighter with its engine cowlings open at the NII VVS.

ence on Soviet engine construction. During the war practically all engine types introduced into service in Germany were captured by the Soviets. They were studied in the aircraft they powered, as well as separately. Among them were engines hitherto unknown in the USSR, such as the BMW 801 (which was shown to the Soviets in 1940 but not sold), DB 603, DB 605, DB 606, Jumo 207 and Jumo 213. The NII VVS, LII NKAP, NII GVF, TsIAM and MAI were involved in the examination of captured engines, and some of these underwent extensive bench testing. In 1942, for example, the TsIAM tested the DB 601Aa, and in 1942-43 the Jumo 207A diesel. The MAI tested the Jumo 211 in 1944.

Many engines were captured by Soviet troops after they entered Germany. Several engine factories, design offices and scientific research institutes were found in the occupied territory. The Special Chief Directorate of the NKAP was charged with arranging the removal of the most interesting examples and documentation. Thus five coupled Daimler-Benz engines (apparently of DB 606 type) were taken to the USSR for examination. German prototype engines that had not been introduced into series production were also found. One of these that aroused great interest was the six-block liquid-cooled 2,900hp Jumo 222 radial, which had been created under the leadership of F. Brandner in 1939-43 and produced in a small quantity. In July 1945 two such engines were brought to Moscow, and five were found in total.

The Jumo 224 diesel developed by the same designer attracted even more attention. Work on this engine had started in Germany in 1943. It had 24 cylinders with two pistons in each, its take-off power rating was 4,800hp, and it had very compact dimensions for such a powerful engine. Conversely, its installation was very complicated, and the synchronizing reduction gear was very heavy. By the time Soviet troops approach Dessau, in April 1945, the Germans had managed to manufacture about 80 per cent of the engine's components, but the documentation was burnt and the assembled units destroyed.

Under a decree issued by the Council of Ministers on 17 April 1946, a special team of twenty engineers, headed by V.M. Yakovlev, was to be sent to Germany to collect all available material on the Jumo 224, and to arranging reconstruction of a full set of engineering drawings. German designers gathered at the OKB-1 design bureau in Dessau were to work on these drawings. This German team, which included 275 specialists, was headed by M. Gerlach. Reconstruction of the drawings was completed in September 1946, and at the start of 1947 the German Kleibach and Metallgus factories started manufacturing the casts for the crankcase parts of the Jumo 224 prototypes (the engine was redesignated M-224). Negotiations were also held with the Czechoslovakian Poldi company for manufacture of the crankshafts and other forged parts.

In October 1946 a group of German engineers working on this diesel was taken to the Soviet Union. The group was accommodated at Factory No. 500 in Tushino, where V.M. Yakovlev was chief designer, and was supplemented by specialists found in Soviet prisoner-of-war camps.

The Jumo 222 (redesignated M-222) and M-224 were considered quite promising engines for the new generation of Soviet long-range bombers. Several preliminary projects using these engines were prepared by the A.N. Tupolev Design Bureau.

German specialists carried out refinement of the M-224 design until November 1947, and certain design solutions were tested on captured Jumo 205 and Jumo 207 diesels, some components from these engines having been used in the M-224. Then V.M. Yakovlev slowed down the work, and proved that his projected M-501 engine had better prospects. All work on

Foreign-built engines in the backyard of the Monino museum. Left to right: Jumo 211, Renault 12R03, Siddley Puma, BMW IV and Hispano-Suiza 8Fb.

the M-224 was finally stopped by a decree of the Minister of the Aviation Industry issued on 17 June 1948. For some time the German group was out of work, and in 1950 they were transferred to another programme.

Soviet troops did not only search for German aircraft and engines in occupied Germany and other European countries; any captured British or American aircraft were examined as well. For instance, a Hawker Tempest fighter was found in the German test centre at Rechlin (the British had refused to provide the USSR with one of these).

Two Soviet regiments were equipped with restored Boeing B-17 and Consolidated B-24 heavy bombers. They did not participate in combat, but remained in air force service for about four years after the war.

Combat operations in the Far East added several hundred captured Japanese aeroplanes and considerable number of engines. Most of them were scrapped. Only certain aircraft types underwent extensive testing, such as the Mitsubishi Ki.46-II reconnaissance aeroplane and Nakajima Ki.84 fighter. A Mitsubishi MC-20 commercial transport with 1,080hp Ha.102 engines served with Soviet Pacific Fleet aviation for some time, and was then transferred to perform aerial reconnaissance for fishing.

The captured German aircraft were widely used during the postwar period by Soviet Air Force, frontier troops, the Civil Air Fleet and departmental aviation. The air force mainly used the transport and liaison aeroplanes, and the coastguard employed Arado Ar 196 reconnaissance floatplanes. From 1943 the captured Ju 52/3ms with BMW 132 engines were transferred to civil aviation (many of these aircraft were captured at Stalingrad). After the war this fleet was supplemented by twin-engine Siebel Si 204s powered by As 411TA-1s. Before they were ferried to the USSR these aeroplanes were overhauled in the factories in Czechoslovakia where they had been built. There were also several Junkers W 34 and Fieseler Fi 156 aeroplanes in Soviet service. The departmental aviation had a rather mixed fleet, consisting of several aircraft of each of a variety of types. The exception was Polar Aviation of the Main Northern Sea Route, which had about ten Si 204s in service.

All of these aeroplanes were in service until the beginning of the 1950s. When the last Ju 52/3ms were written off, there remained a large stock of spare engines for them (334 captured BMW 132s had been brought to the USSR).

This Japanese Nakajima Ha.115 engine is displayed on Poklonnaya Hill together with the wreckage of a Ki.43 fighter.

The M-10 auxiliary powerplant of the Tu-4 bomber was an exact copy of the unit in the Boeing B-29.

The German piston starter for a turbojet engine. Its Soviet copies were fitted on RD-10 and RD-20 turbojets, which were also copied from German jet engines.

The last Lend-Lease aircraft remained in use until about the same time. Owing to the lack of spares (for engines initially), their serviceability worsened considerably during the two or three years immediately after the war. For example, the repair of R-

Captured German transport aeroplanes were operated by Soviet civil aviation after the war. This is a Siebel Si 204D in the Pamirs.

1830s for the GVF's C-47s had practically ceased by July 1948. The air force had better reserves of new engines, and its Lend-Lease aircraft therefore served considerably longer.

The last P-39s, P-63s, B-25s and A-20s were written off in the first half of the 1950s. However, the situation was not always defined by the worn-out state of the engines. In January 1947 the Fighter Aviation command of the Air Defence Force searched in vain for a possible user for fifty R-2800s from P-47 fighters. These engines had accumulated only 2-5hr each, and it seemed a pity to scrap them. However, no-one wanted them, even free of charge.

After the war the Soviet engine factories manufactured only indigenous piston aero-engines. However, two types could be considered exceptions, both being auxiliary powerplants. When unlicensed production of the B-29 bomber was being arranged in the USSR, its auxiliary powerplant was also copied. A small 2-cylinder four-stroke vee engine which rotated the shaft of the electric generator, it was produced in the USSR as the M-10.

The second type was a small two-stroke engine with two horizontally-opposed cylinder, used as a starter for German turbojets. Such starters were manufactured in the USSR for the RD-10 and RD-20 turbojets, copies of the German Jumo 004 and BMW 003 engines.

The administration of the Soviet Civil Air Fleet was making extensive plans for the postwar years in co-operation with American and British companies. The plans for 1946-47 stipulated the purchase of large quantities of aircraft and engines, mainly in the USA. Negotiations with some companies (Pratt & Whitney in particular) were already in progress, but the shortage of hard currency, and then the beginning of the Cold War, negated all these plans.

Almost immediately after the end of the Second World War the Soviet Air Force started the transition to jet-powered aircraft, and the range of applications for piston aero-engines narrowed. In the middle of the 1950s they were used in passenger, cargo, auxiliary, agriculture, training and sports aircraft, and also in helicopters.

Gradually concentrating on the production of more-sophisticated jet engines, the Soviet engine manufacturers transferred production of piston types to the countries of the Warsaw Treaty. This was stipulated in the international work-sharing programmes of the Council for Mutual Economic Assistance (CMEA), which integrated the countries of the Soviet Bloc.

As a result of these programmes, from the late 1950s the USSR again began importing piston aero-engines, though in small quantities. The engines were delivered both with light aeroplanes and as spares. Czechoslovakia manufactured indigenous piston engines, so the main quantities of foreign-built powerplants came from there. The first were Zlin Z-226T Trener trainers powered by 160hp Walter Minor 6-IIIs. These aeroplanes were imported from 1957, and were later supplemented by the Z-326 Trener Master, with the same engine. Along with the aeroplanes, about 500 spare Minor engines were acquired. At about the same time Czechoslovakia supplied the USSR with twin-engine Aero Ae-45s with lower-powered 108hp Minor 4-IIIs. At the beginning of the 1960s a new aircraft type of the same class was delivered, the L-200 Morava with the 210hp M-337 engine. More than 400 M-337s were imported into the USSR. All Czechoslovakian engines were in-line, inverted and air-cooled. In addition, some 4-cylinder M-332s were imported for various Soviet prototype aircraft.

Czechoslovakian engines were often used in home-built designs. The Minor powered the MAI-58 light aeroplane, and the M-332 was fitted in the KhAI-18, KhAI-20 and RIIGA-3 aeroplanes and the KhAI-24 autogyro. An M-337 powered the KhAI convertiplane. In 1996 the *Yegorych* aeroplane was converted to take an overhauled Minor. Some of the engines imported in 1960s-1970s are still being used in Russia.

In the middle of the 1980s samples of

This flying reproduction of an *Ilya Muromets* bomber is powered by Czech M-332s disguised as earlier Argus engines. The upper cylinders are fakes, but the lower ones are real.

The Il-103 is powered by a Teledyne IO-360ES.

Teledyne IO-360ES4s in the Be-103 amphibian.

low-power two-stroke piston engines were purchased in different Western countries. Among them were engines by Hirth, Limbach, Rotax, Weslake and some other companies. They were transferred to the TsIAM in Moscow, and to design bureaus in Kuibyshev and Voronezh. The engines were examined and partly copied during the creation of Soviet counterparts intended to power UAVs.

President Gorbachev's insufficiently considered reforms and destructive privatization struck the aircraft and engine industries heavily. For some time both industries were practically paralysed, and when in due course the market for piston engines (initially for light aircraft) began to revive, foreign companies were the first to exploit it.

Austrian manufacturer Bombardier-Rotax is undoubtedly the leader in this market. At present six types of two-stroke and two types of four-stroke engine, with power ratings from 40hp to 115hp, are being offered on the Russian market by this company. They are being used on Russian prototype and series-production aircraft. The Rotax engines are installed on light aircraft, hang gliders and even on airships. Among them are the Aviatika MAI-890 and *Ptenets-2* (Nestling) light aeroplanes, the Che-15 hydroplane, the *Express 07*, *Express MR* and MD-50 hang gliders and the *Aerostatika-02* airship. The Rotax 582 is used on the *Shmel* (Bumblebee) hang glider, and the Rotax 912 on the *Dubna-2* light aircraft. Several thousand Rotax engines have been imported into Russia.

The German Hirth engines have entered Russia in considerably smaller numbers. Importation of these started in 1994, and by the beginning of 2002 more than 200 had been sold in Russia, mainly of the Hirth 2703 type. They power the *Poisk-06* and *Kruiz* hang gliders, the MPD-2 paraplane and the *Sigma* light aeroplane. The FO-2 AGRO hang glider is powered by the 80hp Hirth XM 500UL.

As for the higher-powered piston aero-engines, the products of the Czech LOM and American Teledyne Continental companies are available on the Russian market. The latter are considered very expensive by Russian standards, and only fifty of them have been imported. Teledyne Continental IO-360ES engines were used for a small batch of Il-103s, and similar engines powered three prototypes of the Be-103 amphibian.

The M-332 and M-337, manufactured by LOM in Prague, are becoming increasingly popular in Russia. They are the only piston aero-engines certificated in this country capable of operating reliably on local types of fuel and oil. The M-332 powers the *Delfin 3*, *Alfa* M and MAI 219SKh prototype aircraft, and a pair of M-332s are planned for Mi-60 MAI helicopter. The M-337 powers the Su-38L and SL-39VM-1 aeroplanes. Czech engines are planned for projected new versions of the Il-103, Be-103, *Accord* and *Aerolada* aircraft.

Along with Z-37 agricultural aeroplanes imported into Russia from the Czech Republic, some spare M-436s (a version of the AI-14R) were acquired.

Given the absence of series production of piston aero-engines of certain power ratings in Russia, the country will continue to depend on imported engines for several more years at least.

APPENDIX I

Engine Characteristics

Table 1
Part 2, Chapter 2 Tsarist Heritage

Engine type		Number of cylinders	Layout	Type of cooling	Gear	Super-charging	Power rating, hp	Bore	Stroke	Volume	Comp-ression ratio	Weight
M-1 (RBVZ-6)		6	I	Liquid	No	No	150	130mm (5.12in)	180mm (7.09in)	8.61litres (525cu in)	–	292kg (644lb)
M-2 (Le Rhône J)	M2-110	9	Radial	Liquid	No	No	110	112mm (4.41in)	170mm (6.69in)	15.07litres (920cu in)	4.5:1	–
	M2-120						120					145kg (320lb)
M-3 (Renault WC)		12	V	Liquid	No	No	220/225	125mm (4.92in)	150mm (5.91in)	–	–	367kg (809lb)

Table 2
Part 2, Chapter 3 Eight-cylinder Hispano-Suiza Engines

Engine type		Number of cylinders	Layout	Type of cooling	Gear	Super-charging	Power rating, hp	Bore	Stroke	Volume	Comp-ression ratio	Weight
M-4		8	V	Liquid	Yes	No	200/300	120mm (4.72in)	130mm (5.12in)	11.76litres (718cu in)	5.3:1	240kg (529lb)
M-6	M-6	8	V	Liquid	No	No	300/340	140mm (5.51in)	150mm (5.91in)	18.48litres (1,128cu in)	5.35:1-5.45:1	275kg (606lb)
	M-6T12				Yes		–				4.75:1	–
M-6A		8	V	Liquid	–	–	450	–	–	–	–	–
Ispano I		4	I	Liquid	No	–	150/170	140mm (5.51in)	150mm (5.91in)	9.24litres (564cu in)	5.35:1	–
Ispano W		12	W	Liquid	No	–	450/510	140mm (5.51in)	150mm (5.91in)	27.72litres (1,692cu in)	5.35:1	–
M-21		8	V	Air	No	–	–	140mm (5.51in)	150mm (5.91in)	18.48litres (1,128cu in)	–	–

Table 3
Part 2, Chapter 4 RAM – the first Soviet high-powered aero-engine

Engine type	Number of cylinders	Layout	Type of cooling	Gear	Super-charging	Power rating, hp	Bore	Stroke	Volume	Comp-ression ratio	Weight
RAM (M-8)	12	V	Liquid	No	No	750	165mm (6.50in)	200mm (7.87in)	51.0litres (3,112cu in)	5.4:1	760kg (1,675lb)

Table 4
Part 2, Chapter 5 Soviet-built Liberty engines

Engine type	Number of cylinders	Layout	Type of cooling	Gear	Super-charging	Power rating, hp	Bore	Stroke	Volume	Comp-ression ratio	Weight
M-5	12	V	Liquid	No	No	400/440	127mm (5.0in)	178mm (7.01in)	27.01litres (1,648cu in)	5.4:1[1]	410-420kg (904-926lb)
M-9 (*Liberty X*)	24	X	Liquid	No	No	500/530	127mm (5.0in)	178mm (7.01in)	–	5.4:1	–
M-10	12	V	Liquid	No	No	400/440	127mm (5.0in)	178mm (7.01in)	27.01litres (1,648cu in)	5.4:1	–
M-14	12	V	Liquid	No	No	450/480[2]	130mm (5.12in)	170mm[3] (6.69in)	27.1litres[4] (1,654cu in)	6.0:1[5]	415kg (915lb)[6]
M-14P	12	Inverted V	Liquid	No	No	450/500	130mm (5.12in)	170mm (6.69in)	27.1litres (1,654cu in)	6.0:1	–
M-16 (*Liberty I*)	6	I	Liquid	No	No	200/250	130mm (5.12in)	170mm (6.69in)	–	6.0:1	250kg (551lb)
M-5 equipped with magneto	12	V	Liquid	No	No	400/440	127mm (5.0in)	178mm (7.01in)	27.01litres (1,648cu in)	5.4:1	420kg (926lb)
Project of Brilling and Aleksandrov	12	V	Liquid	No	No	450	127mm (5.0in)	178mm (7.01in)	27.01litres (1,648cu in)	5.4:1	–
Liberty W18 (V18-I)	8	W	Liquid	No	No	600/700	127mm (5.0in)	178mm (7.01in)	–	5.4:1	–

[1] early series – 5.25:1 to 5.35:1
[2] according to the project, 450/500hp
[3] according to the project, 178mm (7.01in)
[4] according to the project, 28.2litres (1,721cu in)
[5] initially 5.4:1, and 6.25:1 for the second prototype
[6] later improved to 407kg (897lb)

Table 5
Part 2, Chapter 6 The engines of the GAZ No. 2 Ikar factory and their evolution

Engine type		Number of cylinders	Layout	Type of cooling	Gear	Super-charging	Power rating, hp	Bore	Stroke	Volume	Comp-ression ratio	Weight
M-7 (AB-20)		2	0	–	No	No	15	–	–	–	–	–
V12 (*KERTIS V*)		12	V	Liquid	No	1-speed	450/610	125mm (4.92in)	160mm (6.3in)	23.55litres (1,437cu in)	5.5:1	510kg (1,124lb)
W18 (*KERTIS W*)		18	W	Liquid	No	No	670/800[1]	125mm (4.92in)	160mm (6.3in)	35.0litres (2,160cu in)	6.35:1[2]	575kg (1,268lb)[3]
KERTIS I		6	I	Liquid	No	No	250	125mm (4.92in)	160mm (6.3in)	–	5.5:1	–
M-19	M-19	12	V	Liquid	No	1-speed	500/600[4]	135mm (5.31in)	160mm (6.3in)	27.47litres (1,493cu in)	6.4:1	475kg (1,047lb)
	M-19a					No	600/650					–
M-27	M-27	18	W	Liquid	No	No	700/850[5]	135mm (5.31in)	160mm (6.3in)	41.1litres (2,508cu in)	6.4:1	633kg (1,395lb)
	M-27R				Yes	No	700/830					–
	M-27RN				Yes	1-speed	–					–
	GM-27				Yes	No	–					–

[1] during testing a power rating of 601/735hp was reached
[2] the first prototype, 5.5:1
[3] the first prototype, 560kg (1,235lb)
[4] during testing a power rating of 525/600hp was reached
[5] 700/900hp according to the specification, and a power rating of 707/828hp was reached during testing

Table 6
Part 2, Chapter 7 The high-powered aero-engines developed at NAMI

Engine type		Number of cylinders	Layout	Type of cooling	Gear	Super-charging	Power rating, hp	Bore	Stroke	Volume	Comp-ression ratio	Weight
M-13 (M-600)	M-13	12	V	Liquid	No	No	600/750[1]	150mm (5.91in)	170mm (6.69in)	36.0litres (2,197cu in)	6.5:1	612kg (1,349lb)[2]
	M-13M				No	No	–				–	–
	GM-13				Yes	No	720/800				5.1:1-5.3:1	1,000kg (2,200lb)
	2GM-13				Yes	1-speed	1,000				–	–
M-20	M-20	20	Five blocks in radial	Air	–	–	500	–	–	–	–	–
	M-20A				–	–	800	–	–	–	–	–

[1] a power rating of 650/790hp was reached during testing, and later on the engine was boosted up to 820/880hp
[2] the weight after refinement was 615kg (1,356lb), and later it increased to 800kg (1,800lb)

Table 7
Part 2, Chapter 8 MK – *Motor Kireeva* (Kireev's engine)

Engine type	Number of cylinders	Layout	Type of cooling	Gear	Super-charging	Power rating, hp	Bore	Stroke	Volume	Comp-ression ratio	Weight
MK (MK-14)	12	V	Liquid	Yes	No[1]	600[2]	132mm (5.2in)[3]	180mm (7.09in)[4]	–	5.7:1[5]	–

[1] the final version of the engine allowed the possibility of GCS installation
[2] later versions, 800hp and 950hp
[3] later 166.5mm (6.56in)
[4] later 230mm (9.06in)
[5] later 6.2:1

Table 8
Part 2, Chapter 9 MK – The engines built at the Bolshevik factory in Leningrad

Engine type	Number of cylinders	Layout	Type of cooling	Gear	Super-charging	Power rating, hp	Bore	Stroke	Volume	Comp-ression ratio	Weight
AMB-20	2	O	Air	–	No	20/25.6	80mm (3.15in)	96mm (3.78in)	–	5.0:1	32kg (71lb)
M-24 (AMB-700)	–	–	–	–	–	700	–	–	–	–	–
AMB-500	–	–	–	–	–	500	–	–	–	–	–

Table 9
Part 2, Chapter 10 The Contest for aero-engines for training aircraft, and further evolution of the M-11

Engine type		Number of cylinders	Layout	Type of cooling	Gear	Super-charging	Power rating, hp	Bore	Stroke	Volume	Comp-ression ratio	Weight
M-12		5	Radial	Air	No	No	100/120	125mm (4.92in)	140mm (5.51in)	8.6litres (525cu in)	5.0:1	163kg (359lb)
M-23 (NAMI-65)		3	Radial	Air	No	No	65/74	125mm (4.92in)	140mm (5.51in)	5.16litres (315cu in)	5.1:1	109.9kg (242lb)
M-11	M-11-100	5	Radial	Air	No	No	100/110	125mm (4.92in)	140mm (5.51in)	8.6litres (525cu in)	5.0:1	152kg (335lb)
	M-11A						100/110					163kg (353lb)
	M-11B						100/110					–
	M-11V						100/110					–
	M-11G						100/110					–
	M-11D						115/125					158kg (348lb)
	M-11E						150/160				6.0:1	154kg (339lb)
	M-11I						170/200				5.5:1	–
	M-11K						115/125				5.0:1	–
	M-11L						115/125					–
	M-11FR-1						140/160				5.5:1	180kg (397lb)
	M-11FR						140/160				5.5:1	180kg (397lb)
M-48		7	Radial	Air	No	1-speed	200[1]	125mm (4.92in)	140mm (5.51in)	12.0litres (732cu in)	5.0:1	194kg (428lb)
M-49		9	Radial	Air	No	1-speed	270/310	125mm (4.92in)	140mm (5.51in)	–	5.0:1	248kg (547lb)
M-51		5	Radial	Air	No	1-speed	125/145	125mm (4.92in)	140mm (5.51in)	8.6litres (525cu in)	5.0:1	150kg (331lb)[2]
M-50 (3M-11)		3	Radial	Air	No	No	60	125mm (4.92in)	140mm (5.51in)	–	5.0:1	125kg (276lb)

[1] according to some sources 195hp
[2] later 155kg (342lb)

Table 10
Part 2, Chapter 11 The history of the M-17

<table>
<tr><th colspan="2">Engine type</th><th>Number of cylinders</th><th>Layout</th><th>Type of cooling</th><th>Gear</th><th>Super-charging</th><th>Power rating, hp</th><th>Bore</th><th>Stroke</th><th>Volume</th><th>Comp-ression ratio</th><th>Weight</th></tr>
<tr><td rowspan="7">M-17</td><td>M-17E6.0</td><td rowspan="7">12</td><td rowspan="7">V</td><td rowspan="7">Liquid</td><td rowspan="7">No</td><td rowspan="7">No</td><td>505/680</td><td rowspan="7">160mm (6.3in)</td><td rowspan="7">190mm (7.48in)[1]</td><td rowspan="7">–</td><td>6.0:1</td><td>540kg (1,190lb)</td></tr>
<tr><td>M-17E7.3</td><td>500/730</td><td>7.3:1</td><td>540kg (1,190lb)</td></tr>
<tr><td>M-17B</td><td>505/680</td><td>6.0:1</td><td>–</td></tr>
<tr><td>M-17B-7.3</td><td>500/730</td><td>7.3:1</td><td>–</td></tr>
<tr><td>M-17F</td><td>500/715</td><td>6.0:1</td><td>550kg (1,212lb)</td></tr>
<tr><td>M-17T</td><td>500</td><td>6.0:1</td><td>–</td></tr>
<tr><td>M-17L</td><td>650</td><td>6.0:1</td><td>–</td></tr>
</table>

[1] in cylinders with articulated connecting rods, 199mm (7.83in)

Table 11
Part 2, Chapter 12 Jupiter engines from Zaporozhye

<table>
<tr><th colspan="2">Engine type</th><th>Number of cylinders</th><th>Layout</th><th>Type of cooling</th><th>Gear</th><th>Super-charging</th><th>Power rating, hp</th><th>Bore</th><th>Stroke</th><th>Volume</th><th>Comp-ression ratio</th><th>Weight</th></tr>
<tr><td rowspan="3">M-22</td><td>M-22</td><td rowspan="3">9</td><td rowspan="3">Radial</td><td rowspan="3">Air</td><td>No</td><td>No</td><td>480/570</td><td rowspan="3">146mm (5.75in)</td><td rowspan="3">190mm (7.48in)</td><td rowspan="3">28.64litres (1,748cu in)</td><td rowspan="3">6.5:1</td><td>378kg (833lb)</td></tr>
<tr><td>M-22R</td><td>Yes</td><td>No</td><td>480/585</td><td>408kg (899lb)</td></tr>
<tr><td>M-22N</td><td>No</td><td>1-speed</td><td>585</td><td>385kg (849lb)</td></tr>
<tr><td rowspan="3">M-58</td><td>M-58</td><td rowspan="3">9</td><td rowspan="3">Radial</td><td rowspan="3">Air</td><td>No</td><td>1-speed</td><td>630/680</td><td rowspan="3">160mm (6.3in)</td><td rowspan="3">190mm (7.48in)</td><td rowspan="3">34.4litres (2,099cu in)</td><td rowspan="3">5.5:1</td><td>445-450kg (981-992lb)</td></tr>
<tr><td>M-58MN</td><td>No</td><td>1-speed</td><td>630/785</td><td>465-476kg (1,025-1,049lb)</td></tr>
<tr><td>M-58N</td><td>No</td><td>1-speed</td><td>–</td><td>–</td></tr>
</table>

Table 12
Part 2, Chapter 13 A family of air-cooled engines developed at Factory No. 24

Engine type		Number of cylinders	Layout	Type of cooling	Gear	Super-charging	Power rating, hp	Bore	Stroke	Volume	Comp-ression ratio	Weight
M-15	M-15						500/600[1]					420kg (926lb)[1]
	2M-15	9	Radial	Air	No	1-speed	450/550	150mm (5.91in)	170mm (6.69in)	27.02litres (1,649cu in)	5.4:1[2]	419.5kg (925lb)[3]
	M-15a						500					400kg (880lb)[1]
M-26 (KIM)		7	Radial	Air	No	1-speed	270/300[4]	150mm (5.91in)	170mm (6.69in)	–	5.4:1	315kg (694lb)
M-29		14	Two-row radial	Air	No[5]	1-speed	750/1,000	150mm (5.91in)	170mm (6.69in)	–	–	500kg (1,100lb)

[1] according to the project
[2] actually 5.5:1 – 5.7:1 (for series engines)
[3] engine of 'A' series; for 'B' series engines, 450kg (992lb)
[4] according to the project, 300/350hp
[5] a geared version of the engine was planned

Table 13
Part 2, Chapter 14 The FED engines

Engine type	Number of cylinders	Layout	Type of cooling	Gear	Super-charging	Power rating, hp	Bore	Stroke	Volume	Comp-ression ratio	Weight
FED-1				No	No	900[1]				–	–
FED-3 (M-28)	24	X	Liquid	No	1-speed	813/1,170[2]	135mm (5.31in)	160mm (6.3in)	55.0litres (3,356cu in)	6.8:1	851kg (1,876lb)[3]
FED-10				No	–	1,000				–	–

[1] according to the project
[2] according to the project, 900/1,050hp
[3] according to the project, 830kg (1,830lb)

Table 14
Part 2, Chapter 15 The first engines of the IAM

Engine type		Number of cylinders	Layout	Type of cooling	Gear	Super-charging	Power rating, hp	Bore	Stroke	Volume	Comp-ression ratio	Weight
M-32	M-32	16	V	Liquid	No	No	–	120mm (4.72in)	120mm (4.72in)	21.7litres (1,324cu in)	6.0:1	430kg (948lb)[1]
	M-32RN				Yes	1-speed	600/750				6.0:1	460kg (1,014lb)
M-38		9	Radial	Air	No	No	570/600[2]	135mm (5.31in)	160mm (6.3in)	30.7litres (1,873cu in)	6.0:1	460kg (1,014lb)
M-44	M-44	12	V	Liquid	Yes	No	1,700/2,000	222mm (8.74in)	286mm (11.26in)	132.8litres (8,104cu in)	6.0:1[3]	1,700kg (3,700lb)[4]
	GM-44				Yes	No	1,870				6.0:1	

[1] according to the project, 400kg (900lb)
[2] 575hp actually recorded
[3] according to some sources, 5.0:1
[4] according to some sources, 1,800kg (4,000lb)

Table 15
Part 2, Chapter 16 Engines of unusual layout developed during 1923-32

Engine type	Number of cylinders	Layout	Type of cooling	Gear	Super-charging	Power rating, hp	Bore	Stroke	Volume	Comp-ression ratio	Weight
M-9	8	*	Liquid	No	No	400	140mm (5.51in)	180mm (7.1in)	–	3.1:1	–
M-7 (NRB)	–	–	–	–	–	100	–	–	–	–	–
Gantman's engine	12	Inverted I, two-row	Liquid	Yes	1-speed	360	–	–	14.25litres (870cu in)	–	340kg (750lb)

* cylinders positioned in parallel, with rotation transition via a swashplate

Table 16
Part 2, Chapter 19 The M-56 and MGM engines

Engine type	Number of cylinders	Layout	Type of cooling	Gear	Super-charging	Power rating, hp	Bore	Stroke	Volume	Comp-ression ratio	Weight
M-56	14	Two-row radial	Air	Yes	1-speed	700	130mm (5.12in)	135mm (5.31in)	25.1litres (1,532cu in)	6.3:1	–
MGM	14	Two-row radial	Air	Yes	1-speed	700/850	130mm (5.12in)	135mm (5.31in)	25.1litres (1,532cu in)	7.0:1*	–

* first prototype, 6.5:1

Table 17
Part 2, Chapter 20 The low-powered TsIAM engines

Engine type	Number of cylinders	Layout	Type of cooling	Gear	Super-charging	Power rating, hp	Bore	Stroke	Volume	Comp-ression ratio	Weight
MM-1	6	Inverted I	Air	No	No	250/300	125mm (4.92in)	140mm (5.51in)	10.03litres (612cu in)	5.3:1	235kg (518lb)
MM-2	12	Inverted V	Air	No	No	450	125mm (4.92in)	140mm (5.51in)	–	–	–
VAD-2	4	Inverted I	Air	Yes	No	30	62mm (2.44in)	64mm (2.52in)	0.775litres (47cu in)	5.8:1-6.5:1	33-36kg (73-79lb)
VAD-3	6	Inverted I	Air	Yes	No	45	62mm (2.44in)	64mm (2.52in)	1.16litres (71cu in)	5.8:1-6.5:1	45-50kg (99-110lb)

Table 18
Part 2, Chapter 21 Automobile engines modified for use in aircraft

Engine type	Number of cylinders	Layout	Type of cooling	Gear	Super-charging	Power rating, hp	Bore	Stroke	Volume	Comp-ression ratio	Weight
MGAZ-60	4	I	Liquid	No	No	62.5	98.5mm (3.88in)	108mm (4.25in)	3.28litres (200cu in)	5.6:1	120kg (265lb)
GAZ-11	6	I	Liquid	Yes	No	83/85	82mm (3.23in)	110mm (4.33in)	3.48litres (212cu in)	6.5:1	183kg (403lb)

Table 19
Part 2, Chapter 22 The engines of A.A. Mikulin

<table>
<tr><th colspan="2">Engine type</th><th>Number of cylinders</th><th>Layout</th><th>Type of cooling</th><th>Gear</th><th>Super-charging</th><th>Power rating, hp</th><th>Bore</th><th>Stroke</th><th>Volume</th><th>Comp-ression ratio</th><th>Weight</th></tr>
<tr><td rowspan="22">M-34</td><td>M-34</td><td rowspan="22">12</td><td rowspan="22">V</td><td rowspan="11">Liquid</td><td>No</td><td>No</td><td>750/800</td><td rowspan="16">160mm (6.30in)</td><td rowspan="16">190mm (7.48in)</td><td rowspan="16">45.82litres (2,796cu in)</td><td rowspan="14">6.0:1</td><td>680kg (1,499lb)</td></tr>
<tr><td>M-34F</td><td>No</td><td>No</td><td>750/830</td><td>–</td></tr>
<tr><td>M-34R</td><td>Yes</td><td>No</td><td>750/800</td><td>670kg (1,477lb)</td></tr>
<tr><td>M-34RD</td><td>Yes</td><td>No</td><td>750/830</td><td>–</td></tr>
<tr><td>M-34N</td><td>No</td><td>1-speed</td><td>750/820</td><td>–</td></tr>
<tr><td>M-34RN</td><td>Yes</td><td>1-speed</td><td>750/820</td><td>–</td></tr>
<tr><td>M-34NA</td><td>No</td><td>1-speed</td><td>750/820</td><td>–</td></tr>
<tr><td>M-34RA</td><td>Yes</td><td>No</td><td>750/820</td><td>–</td></tr>
<tr><td>M-34RNA</td><td>Yes</td><td>1-speed</td><td>750/820</td><td>748kg (1,649lb)</td></tr>
<tr><td>M-34NB</td><td>No</td><td>1-speed</td><td>750/82^{0}</td><td>638kg (1,406lb)</td></tr>
<tr><td>M-34RNB</td><td>Yes</td><td>1-speed</td><td>750/820</td><td>725kg (1,598lb)</td></tr>
<tr><td>M-34RSO</td><td>Mixed</td><td>Yes</td><td>No</td><td>1,050/1,200</td><td>–</td></tr>
<tr><td>M-34NV</td><td rowspan="10">Liquid</td><td>No</td><td>1-speed</td><td>985</td><td>–</td></tr>
<tr><td>M-34RNV-TK</td><td>Yes</td><td>1-speed + turbo-super-charger</td><td>700/850</td><td>810kg (1,786lb)</td></tr>
<tr><td>M-34NF</td><td>No</td><td>1-speed + turbo-super-charger</td><td>787/985</td><td>6.6:1</td><td>–</td></tr>
<tr><td>M-34N2B</td><td>No</td><td>1-speed + turbo-super-charger</td><td>789/1,033</td><td rowspan="7">6.0:1</td><td>–</td></tr>
<tr><td>M-34FRN</td><td>Yes</td><td>1-speed</td><td>900/1,200</td><td rowspan="6">160mm (6.30in)</td><td rowspan="6">190mm (7.48in)[1]</td><td rowspan="6">46.66litres (2,847cu in)</td><td>735kg (1,620lb)</td></tr>
<tr><td>M-34FRNB</td><td>Yes</td><td>1-speed</td><td>1,000/1,050</td><td>–</td></tr>
<tr><td>M-34RNFT</td><td>Yes</td><td>1-speed + turbo-super-charger</td><td>1,017/1,200</td><td>810kg (1,786lb)[2]</td></tr>
<tr><td>M-34FRNV</td><td>Yes</td><td>1-speed</td><td>1,050/1,200</td><td>749kg (1,651lb)[3]</td></tr>
<tr><td>M-34FRNV[4]</td><td>Yes</td><td>1-speed</td><td>1,050/1,200</td><td>810kg (1,786lb)</td></tr>
<tr><td>M-34FRNV-TK</td><td>Yes</td><td>1-speed + turbo-super-charger</td><td>950/1,200</td><td>850kg (1,874lb)</td></tr>
</table>

[1] in cylinders with articulated connecting rods, 196.7mm (7.74in)
[2] weight without turbo-superchargers 690kg (1,521lb)
[3] weight of series production engine 763.5kg (1,683lb)
[4] with direct fuel injection

Table 19 *continued*

Engine type		Number of cylinders	Layout	Type of cooling	Gear	Super-charging	Power rating, hp	Bore	Stroke	Volume	Comp-ression ratio	Weight
M-34	GM-34	12	V	Liquid	Yes	No	675/800	160mm (6.30in)	190mm (7.48in)	45.82litres (2,796cu in)	6.0:1	864kg (1,905lb)
	GM-34F				Yes	No	800/1,000	160mm (6.30in)	190mm (7.48in)[1]	46.66litres (2,847cu in)	7.3:1	1,080kg (2,381lb)
	GM-34FN				Yes	1-speed	1,200				6.0:1	1,110kg (2,447lb)
	GM-34BP				Yes	No	800	–	–	–	–	–
	GM-34BS				Yes	No	850	160mm (6.30in)	190mm (7.48in)[1]	46.66litres (2,847cu in)	–	1,045kg (2,304lb)
	GM-34BT				Yes	No	850				–	–
M-33		6	I	Liquid	No	No	400	160mm (6.30in)	190mm (7.48in)	–	–	–
M-35		24	X	Liquid	Yes	No	1,580	160mm (6.30in)	190mm (7.48in)	–	–	1,300kg (2,900lb)
M-52		6	I	Liquid	No	No	350/450	160mm (6.30in)	190mm (7.48in)	–	6.0:1	300kg (660lb)
Project for 12-cylinder in-line engine		12	I horizontal	Mixed	–	–	500	–	–	–	–	360kg (793lb)
M-55		12	Inverted V	Liquid	No	No	750	160mm (6.30in)	190mm (7.48in)	45.82litres (2,796cu in)	6.0:1	600kg (1,300lb)
AM-35	AM-35	12	V	Liquid	Yes	1-speed	1,200/1,350	160mm (6.30in)	190mm (7.48in)[1]	46.66litres (2,847cu in)	7.0:1	780kg (1,720lb)
	AM-35T				Yes	1-speed	1,200/1,350					770kg (1,698lb)
	AM-35TK				Yes	1-speed + turbo-supercharger	–					780kg (1,720lb)
	AM-35A				Yes	1-speed	1,200/1,350					830kg (1,830lb)
	AM-35ANV				Yes	1-speed	1,200/1,350					870kg (1,918lb)
	AM-35A-TR				Yes	1-speed	1,200/1,650					–
	GAM-35FN				Yes	1-speed	1,150					–
AM-36		18	Y	Liquid	Yes	1-speed	1,600/2,000[5]	160mm (6.30in)	190mm (7.48in)[1]	68.73litres (4,194cu in)	6.0:1	1,160kg (2,557lb)
AM-37	AM-37	12	V	Liquid	Yes	1-speed	1,200/1,500	160mm (6.30in)	190mm (7.48in)[1]	46.66litres (2,847cu in)	7.0:1	885kg (1,951lb)
	AM-37A						1,600					850kg (1,874lb)
M-38		–	–	–	–	–	3,000/3,500	–	–	77litres (4,699cu in)	–	1,450kg (3,197lb)
AM-38	AM-38	12	V	Liquid	Yes	1-speed	1,500/1,500	160mm (6.30in)	190mm (7.48in)[1]	46.66litres (2,847cu in)	6.8:1	860kg (1,896lb)

[1] in cylinders with articulated connecting rods, 196.7mm (7.74in)
[5] according to some sources, 2,000/2,250hp

Table 19 *continued*

Engine type		Number of cylinders	Layout	Type of cooling	Gear	Super-charging	Power rating, hp	Bore	Stroke	Volume	Comp-ression ratio	Weight
AM-38	AM-38F	12	V	Liquid	Yes	1-speed	1,500/1,700	160mm (6.30in)	190mm (7.48in)[1]	46.66litres (2,847cu in)	6.0:1	880kg (1,940lb)
AM-39	AM-39	12	V	Liquid	Yes	1-speed	1,500/1,800	160mm (6.30in)	190mm (7.48in)[1]	46.66litres (2,847cu in)	6.8:1	–
	AM-39A					1-speed	1,500/1,800				6.0:1	–
	AM-39B-TK					1-speed + turbo-super-charger	1,580/1,890				–	–
	AM-39FK					1-speed	1,600/1,850				–	–
	AM-39FN					1-speed	1,730/2,130[6]				–	970kg (2,138lb)
	AM-39FN2					1-speed	1,600/1,850				–	1,080kg (2,380lb)
AM-41		12	V	Liquid	Yes	2-speed	1,400/1,600	160mm (6.30in)	190mm (7.48in)[1]	46.66litres (2,847cu in)	–	980kg (2,160lb)
AM-42	AM-42	12	V	Liquid	Yes	1-speed	1,750/2,000	160mm (6.30in)	190mm (7.48in)[1]	46.66litres (2,847cu in)	5.5:1	980kg (2,160lb)[7]
	AM-42FNV					1-speed	1,650/2,000					1,000kg (2,200lb)
	AM-42B-TK					1-speed + turbo-super-charger	1,750/2,000					–
AM-43	AM-43	12	V	Liquid	Yes	1-speed	2,000/2,150	160mm (6.30in)	190mm (7.48in)[1]	46.66litres (2,847cu in)	–	1,090kg (2,403lb)
	AM-43TR					2-speed	2,000/2,150				–	1,100kg (2,400lb)
	AM-43NV					1-speed	2,150/2,300				–	1,090kg (2,403lb)
AM-44	AM-44	12	V	Liquid	Yes	1-speed	–	160mm (6.30in)	190mm (7.48in)[1]	46.66litres (2,847cu in)	–	–
	AM-44B-TK					1-speed + turbo-super-charger	1,650/1,950				–	–
AM-45	AM-45	12	V	Liquid	Yes	2-stage, 2-speed	1,750/2,450	160mm (6.30in)	190mm (7.48in)[1]	46.66litres (2,847cu in)	–	1,200kg (2,600lb)
	AM-45D					–	1,750/2,700				–	–
	AM-45Sh					–	2,400/3,000				–	–
AM-46	AM-46	12	V	Liquid	Yes	Yes	1,040/2,550	160mm (6.30in)	190mm (7.48in)[1]	46.66litres (2,847cu in)	–	–
	AM-46TK					Yes + turbo-supercharger	2,300				–	–
AM-47		12	V	Liquid	Yes	Yes	3,000	160mm (6.30in)	190mm (7.48in)[1]	46.66litres (2,847cu in)	–	–

[1] in cylinders with articulated connecting rods, 196.7mm (7.74in)
[6] power rating of the first prototypes, 1,600/1,850hp
[7] weight of later series engines 996kg (2,196lb)

Table 20
Part 2, Chapter 23 The engines of A.D. Shvetsov

Engine type		Number of cylinders	Layout	Type of cooling	Gear	Super-charging	Power rating, hp	Bore	Stroke	Volume	Comp-ression ratio	Weight
M-25	M-25	9	Radial	Air	No	1-speed	635/700	155.5mm (6.12in)	174.5mm (6.87in)	29.87litres (1,822cu in)	6.4:1 (968lb)	434kg (957lb)[1]
	M-25A						715/730					439kg
	M-25V						750/755[2]					453kg (999lb)
M-62 (ASh-62)	M-62	9	Radial	Air	No	2-speed	800/1,000	155.5mm (6.12in)	174.5mm (6.87in)	29.87litres (1,822cu in)	6.4:1	520kg (1,146lb)
	M-62R				Yes	2-speed	850/975					573kg (1,263lb)
	ASh-62IR				Yes	1-speed	820/1,000[3]					560kg (1,235lb)[4]
	ASh-62N				Yes	1-speed	840/1,000					590kg (1,301lb)
M-63	M-63	9	Radial	Air	No	2-speed	900/1,000	155.5mm (6.12in)	174.5mm (6.87in)	29.87litres (1,822cu in)	7.2:1	515kg (1,135lb)
	M-63TK					2-speed + turbo-super-charger	800/1,000					–
M-64	M-64	9	Radial	Air	No	2-speed	900/1,000	155.5mm (6.12in)	174.5mm (6.87in)	29.87litres (1,822cu in)	–	600kg (1,300lb)
	M-64R				Yes	2-speed	–					600kg (1,300lb)
M-65		9	Radial	Air	No	2-speed	840/1,100	155.5mm (6.12in)	174.5mm (6.87in)	29.87litres (1,822cu in)	6.4:1	530kg (1,168lb)
M-80		14	Two-row radial	Air	Yes	1-speed	1,200/1,400	155.5mm (6.12in)	174.5mm (6.87in)	–	–	–
M-81		14	Two-row radial	Air	Yes	2-speed	1,300/1,600	155.5mm (6.12in)	174.5mm (6.87in)	–	–	890kg (1,962lb)
M-82 (ASh-82)	M-82	14	Two-row radial	Air	Yes	2-speed	1,400/1,700	155.5mm (6.12in)	155mm (6.10in)	41.2litres (2,514cu in)	7.0:1	850kg (1,874lb)
	M-82A						1,400/1,700					870kg (1,918lb)
	M-82F						1,400/1,700					870kg (1,918lb)
	M-82FN						–					910kg (2,006lb)
	M-82M						1,630/2,100					–
	M-82MF						1,750/2,250					–
	ASh-82T						1,530/1,900[5]				6.9:1	1,020kg (2,249lb)
	ASh-82V						1,350/1,700					1,100kg (2,400lb)

[1] weight of later series engines 435kg (959lb)
[2] an improved version, in production from 1941, 750/790hp
[3] later series, 840/1,000hp
[4] weight of the 15th series engines, 567kg (1,250lb)
[5] later series, 1,530/1,950hp

Table 20 *continued*

<table>
<tr><th colspan="2">Engine type</th><th>Number of cylinders</th><th>Layout</th><th>Type of cooling</th><th>Gear</th><th>Super-charging</th><th>Power rating, hp</th><th>Bore</th><th>Stroke</th><th>Volume</th><th>Comp-ression ratio</th><th>Weight</th></tr>
<tr><td colspan="2">ASh-83</td><td>14</td><td>Two-row radial</td><td>Air</td><td>Yes</td><td>2-speed</td><td>1,585/1,900</td><td>155.5mm (6.12in)</td><td>155mm (6.10in)</td><td>41.2litres (2,514cu in)</td><td>6.9:1 (2,017lb)[6]</td><td>915kg</td></tr>
<tr><td colspan="2">ASh-84</td><td>14</td><td>Two-row radial</td><td>Air</td><td>Yes</td><td>2-speed + turbo-super-charger</td><td>1,700/1,800[7]</td><td>155.5mm (6.12in)</td><td>155mm (6.10in)</td><td>41.2litres (2,514cu in)</td><td>–</td><td>–</td></tr>
<tr><td colspan="2">M-70</td><td>18</td><td>Two-row radial</td><td>Air</td><td>Yes</td><td>Yes</td><td>1,400/1,500</td><td>155.5mm (6.12in)</td><td>174.5mm (6.87in)</td><td>59.59litres (3,636cu in)</td><td>6.4:1</td><td>–</td></tr>
<tr><td rowspan="4">M-71</td><td>M-71</td><td rowspan="3">18</td><td rowspan="3">Two-row radial</td><td rowspan="3">Air</td><td rowspan="3">Yes</td><td>1-speed</td><td>1,700/2,000</td><td rowspan="3">155.5mm (6.12in)</td><td rowspan="3">174.5mm (6.87in)</td><td rowspan="3">59.7litres (3,643cu in)</td><td rowspan="3">–</td><td>970kg (2,138lb)</td></tr>
<tr><td>M-71TK</td><td>1-speed + turbo-super-charger</td><td>1,500/2,000</td><td>–</td></tr>
<tr><td>M-71F</td><td>1-speed</td><td>1,850/2,200</td><td>–</td></tr>
<tr><td>M-72</td><td>18</td><td>Two-row radial</td><td>Air</td><td>Yes</td><td>2-speed</td><td>–</td><td>155.5mm (6.12in)</td><td>174.5mm (6.87in)</td><td>59.58litres (3,635cu in)</td><td>–</td><td>–</td></tr>
<tr><td rowspan="4">ASh-73</td><td>ASh-73</td><td rowspan="4">18</td><td rowspan="4">Two-row radial</td><td rowspan="4">Air</td><td rowspan="4">Yes</td><td>1-speed</td><td>2,000/2,400</td><td rowspan="4">155.5mm (6.12in)</td><td rowspan="4">170mm (6.69in)</td><td rowspan="4">58.1litres (3,545cu in)</td><td rowspan="4">6.9:1</td><td>1,330kg (2,932lb)</td></tr>
<tr><td>ASh-73TK</td><td>1-speed + turbo-super-charger</td><td>2,000/2,400</td><td>1,355kg (2,987lb)</td></tr>
<tr><td>ASh-73TKF</td><td>1-speed + turbo-super-charger</td><td>2,360/2,720</td><td>–</td></tr>
<tr><td>ASh-73TKFN</td><td>1-speed + turbo-super-charger</td><td>2,400/2,800</td><td>–</td></tr>
<tr><td colspan="2">ASh-21</td><td>7</td><td>Radial</td><td>Air</td><td>Yes</td><td>1-speed</td><td>570/700</td><td>155.5mm (6.12in)</td><td>155mm (6.10in)</td><td>20.6litres (1,257cu in)</td><td>6.4:1</td><td>487kg (1,074lb)</td></tr>
<tr><td colspan="2">M-3</td><td>21</td><td>Three-row radial</td><td>Air</td><td>Yes</td><td>1-speed + turbo-super-charger</td><td>2,400/3,200</td><td>155.5mm (6.12in)</td><td>155mm (6.10in)</td><td>–</td><td>–</td><td>1,500kg (3,300lb)</td></tr>
<tr><td rowspan="3">ASh-2</td><td>ASh-2</td><td rowspan="3">28</td><td rowspan="3">Four-row radial</td><td rowspan="3">Air</td><td rowspan="3">Yes</td><td>1-speed</td><td>2,500/3,500</td><td rowspan="3">155.5mm (6.12in)</td><td rowspan="3">155mm (6.10in)</td><td rowspan="3">82.4litres (5,028cu in)</td><td rowspan="3">7.0:1</td><td>1,850kg (4,078lb)</td></tr>
<tr><td>ASh-2TK</td><td>1-speed + turbo-super-charger</td><td>3,070/4,000</td><td>2,080kg (4,586lb)</td></tr>
<tr><td>ASh-2K</td><td>2-speed + turbo-super-charger</td><td>3,700/4,700</td><td>2,550kg (5,622lb)</td></tr>
<tr><td colspan="2">ASh-3TK</td><td>–</td><td>–</td><td>–</td><td>–</td><td>–</td><td>5,500/6,000</td><td>–</td><td>–</td><td>–</td><td>–</td><td>–</td></tr>
</table>

[6] according to some sources 921kg (2,030lb)
[7] according to some sources 1,700/2,000hp

Table 21
Part 2, Chapter 24 The engines of V.Ya. Klimov

<table>
<tr><th colspan="2">Engine type</th><th>Number of cylinders</th><th>Layout</th><th>Type of cooling</th><th>Gear</th><th>Super-charging</th><th>Power rating, hp</th><th>Bore</th><th>Stroke</th><th>Volume</th><th>Comp-ression ratio</th><th>Weight</th></tr>
<tr><td rowspan="3">M-100</td><td>M-100</td><td rowspan="3">12</td><td rowspan="3">V</td><td rowspan="2">Liquid</td><td rowspan="3">Yes</td><td rowspan="3">1-speed</td><td>655/750</td><td rowspan="3">150mm (5.91in)</td><td rowspan="3">170mm (6.69in)</td><td rowspan="3">36.03litres (2,198cu in)</td><td>6.0:1</td><td>470kg (1,036lb)</td></tr>
<tr><td>M-100A</td><td>775/860</td><td>5.8:1[1]</td><td>477kg (1,052lb)</td></tr>
<tr><td>M-100SO</td><td>Combined</td><td>950/1,000</td><td>–</td><td>–</td></tr>
<tr><td rowspan="5">M-103</td><td>M-103</td><td rowspan="5">12</td><td rowspan="5">V</td><td rowspan="5">Liquid</td><td rowspan="5">Yes</td><td rowspan="4">1-speed</td><td>850/1,000</td><td>150mm (5.91in)</td><td rowspan="5">170mm (6.69in)</td><td>36.03litres (2,198cu in)</td><td rowspan="5">6.6:1</td><td>495kg (1,091lb)</td></tr>
<tr><td>M-103A</td><td>850/1,000</td><td rowspan="4">148mm (5.83in)</td><td rowspan="4">35.0litres (2,135cu in)</td><td>510kg (1,124lb)</td></tr>
<tr><td>M-103P</td><td>950/1,000</td><td>510kg (1,124lb)</td></tr>
<tr><td>M-103G</td><td>900/930</td><td>500kg (1,000lb)</td></tr>
<tr><td>M-103A-TK</td><td>1-speed + turbo-super-charger</td><td>820/1,000</td><td>570kg (1,257lb)</td></tr>
<tr><td colspan="2">M-104</td><td>12</td><td>V</td><td>Liquid</td><td>Yes</td><td>2-speed</td><td>1,050/1,100</td><td>148mm (5.83in)</td><td>170mm (6.69in)</td><td>35.0litres (2,135cu in)</td><td>6.6:1</td><td>550kg (1,213lb)</td></tr>
<tr><td rowspan="10">M-105 (VK-105)</td><td>M-105</td><td rowspan="10">12</td><td rowspan="10">V</td><td rowspan="10">Liquid</td><td rowspan="10">Yes</td><td rowspan="5">2-speed</td><td>1,020/1,100</td><td rowspan="10">148mm (5.83in)</td><td rowspan="10">170mm (6.69in)</td><td rowspan="10">35.0litres (2,135cu in)</td><td rowspan="5">7.1:1</td><td>570kg (1,257lb)</td></tr>
<tr><td>M-105R</td><td>1,050/1,100</td><td>580kg (1,279lb)</td></tr>
<tr><td>M-105P</td><td>1,050/1,100</td><td>600kg (1,323lb)</td></tr>
<tr><td>M-105RA</td><td>1,050/1,100</td><td>580kg (1,279lb)</td></tr>
<tr><td>M-105PA</td><td>1,050/1,100</td><td>600kg (1,323lb)</td></tr>
<tr><td>M-105PD</td><td>2-stage</td><td>1,170/1,200</td><td>7.0:1</td><td>645kg (1,422lb)</td></tr>
<tr><td>M-105PF</td><td rowspan="4">2-speed</td><td>1,180/1,260</td><td rowspan="4">7.1:1</td><td>600kg (1,323lb)</td></tr>
<tr><td>M-105RF</td><td>1,180/1,260</td><td>580kg (1,279lb)</td></tr>
<tr><td>M-105PF2</td><td>1,240/1,290</td><td>–</td></tr>
<tr><td>M-105PV</td><td>1,250</td><td>–</td></tr>
</table>

[1] compression ratio of the prototype engine, 5.87:1

Table 21 *continued*

<table>
<tr><th colspan="2">Engine type</th><th>Number of cylinders</th><th>Layout</th><th>Type of cooling</th><th>Gear</th><th>Super-charging</th><th>Power rating, hp</th><th>Bore</th><th>Stroke</th><th>Volume</th><th>Comp-ression ratio</th><th>Weight</th></tr>
<tr><td colspan="2">M-106</td><td>12</td><td>V</td><td>Liquid</td><td>Yes</td><td>1-speed</td><td>1,250/1,350</td><td>148mm (5.83in)</td><td>170mm (6.69in)</td><td>35.0litres (2,135cu in)</td><td>6.0:1[2]</td><td>600kg (1,323lb)</td></tr>
<tr><td rowspan="3">M-107 (VK-107)</td><td>M-107</td><td rowspan="3">12</td><td rowspan="3">V</td><td rowspan="3">Liquid</td><td rowspan="3">Yes</td><td rowspan="3">2-speed</td><td>1,300/1,400</td><td rowspan="3">148mm (5.83in)</td><td rowspan="3">170mm (6.69in)</td><td rowspan="3">35.0litres (2,135cu in)</td><td rowspan="3">6.75:1</td><td>765kg (1,687lb)</td></tr>
<tr><td>M-107A</td><td>1,500/1,600</td><td>769kg (1,695lb)</td></tr>
<tr><td>M-107R</td><td>1,450/1,650[3]</td><td>–</td></tr>
<tr><td colspan="2">VK-108</td><td>12</td><td>V</td><td>Liquid</td><td>Yes</td><td>2-speed</td><td>1,550/1,850</td><td>148mm (5.83in)</td><td>170mm (6.69in)</td><td>35.0litres (2,135cu in)</td><td>6.65:1</td><td>–</td></tr>
<tr><td colspan="2">VK-109</td><td>12</td><td>V</td><td>Liquid</td><td>Yes</td><td>2-speed</td><td>1,650/1,800[4]</td><td>148mm (5.83in)</td><td>170mm (6.69in)</td><td>35.0litres (2,135cu in)</td><td>–</td><td>–</td></tr>
<tr><td rowspan="2">M-110</td><td>M-110</td><td rowspan="2">12</td><td rowspan="2">Inverted V</td><td rowspan="2">Combined</td><td rowspan="2">Yes</td><td rowspan="2">1-speed</td><td>900/950</td><td rowspan="2">148mm (5.83in)</td><td rowspan="2">170mm (6.69in)</td><td rowspan="2">–</td><td rowspan="2">–</td><td>490kg (1,080lb)</td></tr>
<tr><td>M-110A</td><td>900/960</td><td>510kg (1,124lb)</td></tr>
<tr><td colspan="2">VK-110</td><td>–</td><td>–</td><td>–</td><td>–</td><td>–</td><td>2,000</td><td>–</td><td>–</td><td>–</td><td>–</td><td>–</td></tr>
<tr><td rowspan="3">M-120</td><td>M-120</td><td rowspan="3">18</td><td rowspan="3">Inverted Y</td><td rowspan="3">Liquid</td><td rowspan="3">Yes</td><td>2-speed</td><td>1,500/1,600</td><td rowspan="3">148mm (5.83in)</td><td rowspan="3">170mm (6.69in)</td><td rowspan="3">54.0litres (3,295cu in)</td><td rowspan="3">6.6:1</td><td>895kg (1,973lb)</td></tr>
<tr><td>M-120TK</td><td>2-speed + turbo-super-charger</td><td>1,400/1,600</td><td>950kg (2,094lb)</td></tr>
<tr><td>M-120UV</td><td>2-speed</td><td>1,600/1,800</td><td>–</td></tr>
</table>

[2] according to some sources 6.5:1
[3] power rating with the jet engine turned on, 2,800 equivalent hp (3,000ehp according to some sources)
[4] according to some sources, 1,800/2,075hp

Table 22
Part 2, Chapter 25 Gnome-Rhône – the last attempt

<table>
<tr><th colspan="2">Engine type</th><th>Number of cylinders</th><th>Layout</th><th>Type of cooling</th><th>Gear</th><th>Super-charging</th><th>Power rating, hp</th><th>Bore</th><th>Stroke</th><th>Volume</th><th>Comp-ression ratio</th><th>Weight</th></tr>
<tr><td colspan="2">M-75</td><td>9</td><td>Radial</td><td>Air</td><td>Yes</td><td>1-speed</td><td>650/700</td><td>146mm (5.76in)</td><td>165mm (6.50in)</td><td>–</td><td>–</td><td>–</td></tr>
<tr><td colspan="2">M-76</td><td>9</td><td>Radial</td><td>Air</td><td>Yes</td><td>1-speed</td><td>700/800</td><td>146mm (5.76in)</td><td>165mm (6.50in)</td><td>–</td><td>–</td><td>440kg (970lb)</td></tr>
<tr><td colspan="2">M-85</td><td>14</td><td>Two-row radial</td><td>Air</td><td>Yes</td><td>1-speed</td><td>720/800</td><td>146mm (5.76in)</td><td>165mm (6.50in)</td><td>38.68litres (2,360cu in)</td><td>5.5:1</td><td>600kg (1,323lb)</td></tr>
<tr><td colspan="2">M-86</td><td>14</td><td>Two-row radial</td><td>Air</td><td>Yes</td><td>1-speed</td><td>800/950</td><td>146mm (5.76in)</td><td>165mm (6.50in)</td><td>38.68litres (2,360cu in)</td><td>5.5:1</td><td>610kg (1,345lb)</td></tr>
<tr><td colspan="2">M-87</td><td>14</td><td>Two-row radial</td><td>Air</td><td>Yes</td><td>1-speed</td><td>800/950</td><td>146mm (5.76in)</td><td>165mm (6.50in)</td><td>38.65litres (2,359cu in)</td><td>6.1:1</td><td>640kg (1,411lb)</td></tr>
<tr><td rowspan="6">M-88</td><td>M-88b/r</td><td rowspan="6">14</td><td rowspan="6">Two-row radial</td><td rowspan="6">Air</td><td>No</td><td rowspan="5">2-speed</td><td>1,000/1,090</td><td rowspan="6">146mm (5.76in)</td><td rowspan="6">165mm (6.50in)</td><td rowspan="6">38.65litres (2,359cu in)</td><td rowspan="6">6.1:1</td><td>660kg (1,455lb)</td></tr>
<tr><td>M-88</td><td rowspan="5">Yes</td><td>1,000/1,100</td><td>684kg (1,508lb)</td></tr>
<tr><td>M-88NV</td><td>1,050/1,150</td><td>–</td></tr>
<tr><td>M-88A</td><td>1,100/1,100</td><td>650kg (1,433lb)[1]</td></tr>
<tr><td>M-88B</td><td>950/1,100</td><td>684kg (1,508lb)</td></tr>
<tr><td>M-88TK</td><td>2-speed + turbo-super-charger</td><td>900/1,100</td><td>–</td></tr>
<tr><td rowspan="3">M-89</td><td>M-89</td><td rowspan="3">14</td><td rowspan="3">Two-row radial</td><td rowspan="3">Air</td><td rowspan="3">Yes</td><td rowspan="3">3-speed</td><td>1,250/1,300</td><td rowspan="3">146mm (5.76in)</td><td rowspan="3">165mm (6.50in)</td><td rowspan="3">35.7litres (2,179cu in)</td><td>6.4:1</td><td>800kg (1,765lb)</td></tr>
<tr><td>M-89[2]</td><td>1,380/1,550</td><td>7.0:1</td><td>815kg (1,797lb)</td></tr>
<tr><td>M-89NV</td><td>1,150/1,300</td><td>–</td><td>760kg (1,676lb)</td></tr>
<tr><td colspan="2">M-90</td><td>18</td><td>Two-row radial</td><td>Air</td><td>Yes</td><td>2-speed</td><td>1,550/1,750</td><td>146mm (5.76in)</td><td>165mm (6.50in)</td><td>–</td><td>–</td><td>–</td></tr>
<tr><td colspan="2">M-92</td><td>18</td><td>Two-row radial</td><td>Air</td><td>Yes</td><td>2-speed</td><td>1,850/2,150</td><td>146mm (5.76in)</td><td>165mm (6.50in)</td><td>–</td><td>–</td><td>–</td></tr>
<tr><td colspan="2">BKM</td><td>18</td><td>Two-row radial</td><td>Air</td><td>Yes</td><td>2-speed</td><td>1,850/2,150</td><td>146mm (5.76in)</td><td>165mm (6.50in)</td><td>–</td><td>–</td><td>900kg (1,985lb)</td></tr>
<tr><td colspan="2">M-95</td><td>27</td><td>Three-row radial</td><td>Air</td><td>Yes</td><td>1-speed</td><td>2,000/3,000</td><td>146mm (5.76in)</td><td>165mm (6.50in)</td><td>–</td><td>6.1:1</td><td>1,400kg (3,090lb)</td></tr>
</table>

[1] weight of first prototypes 640kg (1,411lb)
[2] an improved version

Table 23
Part 2, Chapter 26 The engines of M.A. Kossov, and other attempts to create a low-powered engine based on the M-11

Engine type		Number of cylinders	Layout	Type of cooling	Gear	Super-charging	Power rating, hp	Bore	Stroke	Volume	Comp-ression ratio	Weight
MG-11	MG-11	5	Radial	Air	No	1-speed	150/180	125mm (4.92in)	140mm (5.51in)	8.6litres (525cu in)	5.0:1	175kg (386lb)
	MG-11F						165/–					–
MG-21	MG-21	7	Radial	Air	No	1-speed	200/220	125mm (4.92in)	140mm (5.51in)	12.05litres (735cu in)	5.0:1	214kg (472lb)
	MG-21A						210/250					–
MG-31	MG-31	9	Radial	Air	No	1-speed	270/320[1]	125mm (4.92in)	140mm (5.51in)	15.5litres (946cu in)	5.0:1	247kg (544lb)
	MG-31F						270/335					250kg (551lb)[2]
MG-40		4	Inverted I	Air	No	No	145	120mm (4.72in)	140mm (5.51in)	6.33litres (386cu in)	6.35:1[3]	155kg (342lb)
MG-50		18	Two-row radial	Air	Yes	–	800/950	125mm (4.92in)	140mm (5.51in)	31.0litres (1,891cu in)	–	–
M-12		5	Radial	Air	No	No	190/200	125mm (4.92in)	140mm (5.51in)	8.6litres (525cu in)	6.2:1	215kg (474lb)
M-12 (M-11Ya)		5	Radial	Air	No	No	–	125mm (4.92in)	140mm (5.51in)	8.6litres (525cu in)	–	–
M-13 (M-13K)		9	Radial	Air	No	1-speed	300	125mm (4.92in)	140mm (5.51in)	–	–	–
M-13 (of E.V. Urmin)		9	Radial	Air	No	1-speed	300	125mm (4.92in)	140mm (5.51in)	–	–	–
M-13 (of Aksyutin)		7	Radial	Air	No	No	210/250	–	–	–	–	–

[1] according to the test results, 270/310hp
[2] according to some sources 255kg (562lb)
[3] first prototype, 5.2:1

Table 24
Part 2, Chapter 27 Voronezh-built Renault engines

Engine type		Number of cylinders	Layout	Type of cooling	Gear	Super-charging	Power rating, hp	Bore	Stroke	Volume	Comp-ression ratio	Weight
MV-4		4	Inverted I	Air	No	No	140/152	120mm (4.72in)	140mm (5.51in)	6.33litres (386cu in)	5.75:1	147kg (324lb)
MV-6	MV-6	6	Inverted I	Air	No	No	250/270	120mm (4.72in)	140mm (5.51in)	9.5litres (579cu in)	6.2:1	235kg (518lb)[2]
	MV-6[1]					2-speed	225/275					–
	MV-6[1]					2-speed + turbo-super-charger	230/300					–
MV-12	MV-12	12	Inverted V	Air	No	1-speed	390/450	114mm (4.49in)	122mm (4.8in)	14.93litres (911cu in)	6.2:1[3]	350kg (772lb)[4]
	MV-12F				No	No	440/500					405-420kg (893-926lb)
	MV-12R				Yes	No	700/750	120mm (4.72in)	140mm (5.51in)	19.0litres (1,159cu in)	–	460kg (1,014lb)
	MV-12[1]				Yes	2-speed	500/600	–	–	–	–	–
	MV-12[1]				Yes	2-speed + turbo-super-charger	500/650	–	–	–	–	–

[1] project for an improved version
[2] according to some sources 250kg (551lb)
[3] according to some sources 6.4:1
[4] according to some sources 419kg (924lb)

Table 25
Part 2, Chapter 28 The last piston engines developed at the TsIAM

Engine type	Number of cylinders	Layout	Type of cooling	Gear	Super-charging	Power rating, hp	Bore	Stroke	Volume	Comp-ression ratio	Weight
SM	12	Inverted V	Liquid	Yes	1-speed	1,750/2,000	180mm (7.08in)	200mm (7.87in)[1]	62.0litres (3,783cu in)	–	950kg (2,094lb)
M-200	6	I[2]	Liquid	–	No	650-700	100mm (3.94in)	100mm (3.94in)	9.42litres (574cu in)	–	370kg (816lb)
M-300	36	Six blocks in radial	Liquid	Yes	–	3,000/3,500	140mm (5.51in)	160mm (6.30in)	88.5litres (5,400cu in)	–	1,600kg (3,530lb)[3]

[1] in cylinders with articulated connecting rods, 209.95mm (8.27in)
[2] two opposed pistons in each cylinder
[3] according to some sources 1,626kg (3,585lb)

Table 26
Part 2, Chapter 29 Diesel aero-engines

Engine type		Number of cylinders	Layout	Type of cooling	Gear	Super-charging	Power rating, hp	Bore	Stroke	Volume	Comp-ression ratio	Weight
N-2		12	V	Liquid	–	Piston-type	1,500	–	–	–	–	1,300kg (2,870lb)
AD-1 (N-3)		12	V	Liquid	No	No	500[1]	150mm (5.91in)	165mm (6.50in)	–	–	650kg (1,433lb)
N-4		–	–	Liquid	–	–	500-600	–	–	–	–	500-600kg (1,100-1,320lb)
N-5 (FED-8)		24	X	Liquid	–	–	2,000/2,400	–	–	–	–	3,000kg (6,600lb)
N-6 (MSK)		6	Radial	Air	–	Piston-type	500	–	–	–	–	380kg (838lb)
BD-2A		12	V	Liquid	–	1-speed	600	–	–	–	–	–
N-9		9	Radial	Air	–	–	500	–	–	–	–	600kg (1,320lb)
M-87D		14	Two-row radial	Air	Yes	1-speed	750/800	146mm (5.76in)	165mm (6.50in)	–	–	750kg (1,653lb)
M-20		48	Rhombic[2]	Liquid	Yes	–	3,000	–	–	–	–	–
AN-5		24	Rhombic[2]	Liquid	Yes	–	1,500/1,750[3]	–	–	–	–	800-850kg (1,764-1,874lb)
D-11		5	Radial	Air	No	No	100/120	125mm (4.92in)	140mm (5.51in)	8.6litres (524cu in)	15.0:1	180kg (397lb)[4]
AN-1	AN-1	12	V	Liquid	No	1-speed	750/800[5]	180mm (7.09in)	200mm (7.87in)[6]	61.04litres (3,724cu in)	13.5:1	1,003kg (2,211lb)[7]
	AN-1A				No	1-speed	850/900					1,040kg (2,293lb)
	AN-1R				Yes	1-speed	850/900					1,000kg (2,200lb)
	AN-1RTK				Yes	Turbo-super-charger	1,000/1,250					1,100kg (2,430lb)
	AN-1M				Yes	No	850/950					1,350kg (2,976lb)
	MN-1				Yes	No	1,000					1,500kg (3,300lb)

[1] in fact 437hp was registered
[2] two opposed pistons in each cylinder
[3] according to some sources 1,500/1,700hp
[4] according to some sources 200kg (440lb)
[5] 814hp was registered during the tests
[6] in cylinders with articulated connecting rods, 209.95mm (8.27in)
[7] after improvement 1,021kg (2,251lb)

Table 26 *continued*

<table>
<tr><th colspan="2">Engine type</th><th>Number of cylinders</th><th>Layout</th><th>Type of cooling</th><th>Gear</th><th>Super-charging</th><th>Power rating, hp</th><th>Bore</th><th>Stroke</th><th>Volume</th><th>Comp-ression ratio</th><th>Weight</th></tr>
<tr><td rowspan="6">M-30 (ACh-30)</td><td>M-30</td><td rowspan="6">12</td><td rowspan="6">V</td><td rowspan="6">Liquid</td><td>Yes</td><td>Turbo-super-charger</td><td>1,250/1,500</td><td rowspan="6">180mm (7.09in)</td><td rowspan="6">200mm (7.87in)[6]</td><td rowspan="6">61.04litres (3,724cu in)</td><td rowspan="6">13.5:1</td><td>1,200kg (2,645lb)[8]</td></tr>
<tr><td>M-30F</td><td>Yes</td><td>Turbo-super-charger</td><td>1,500/1,750</td><td>–</td></tr>
<tr><td>ACh-30B</td><td>Yes</td><td>1-speed + turbo-super-charger</td><td>1,250/1,500</td><td>1,290kg (2,844lb)[9]</td></tr>
<tr><td>M-30D</td><td>Yes</td><td>–</td><td>1,750/2,000</td><td>–</td></tr>
<tr><td>ACh-30BF</td><td>Yes</td><td>1-speed + turbo-super-charger</td><td>1,250/1,900</td><td>1,280kg (2,822lb)</td></tr>
<tr><td>ACh-30B with moto-compressor jet engine</td><td>Yes</td><td>1-speed + turbo-super-charger</td><td>4,500[10]</td><td>1,700kg (3,750lb)</td></tr>
<tr><td rowspan="2">M-40</td><td>M-40</td><td rowspan="2">12</td><td rowspan="2">V</td><td rowspan="2">Liquid</td><td rowspan="2">Yes</td><td rowspan="2">Turbo-super-charger</td><td>1,000/1,250</td><td rowspan="2">180mm (7.09in)</td><td rowspan="2">200mm (7.87in)[6]</td><td rowspan="2">61.04litres (3,724cu in)</td><td rowspan="2">13.5:1</td><td>1,150kg (2,535lb)</td></tr>
<tr><td>M-40F</td><td>1,250/1,500</td><td>1,200kg (2,645lb)</td></tr>
<tr><td colspan="2">ACh-31</td><td>12</td><td>V</td><td>Liquid</td><td>Yes</td><td>1-speed + turbo-super-charger</td><td>1,500/1,900[11]</td><td>180mm (7.09in)</td><td>200mm (7.87in)[6]</td><td>61.04litres (3,724cu in)</td><td>13.5:1</td><td>1,387kg (3,058lb)</td></tr>
<tr><td colspan="2">ACh-32</td><td>12</td><td>V</td><td>Liquid</td><td>Yes</td><td>1-speed + turbo-super-charger</td><td>1,500/2,300[12]</td><td>180mm (7.09in)</td><td>200mm (7.87in)[6]</td><td>61.04litres (3,724cu in)</td><td>13.5:1</td><td>1,350kg (2,976lb)</td></tr>
<tr><td colspan="2">M-501</td><td>42</td><td>Seven blocks in radial</td><td>Liquid</td><td>Yes</td><td>1-speed + turbo-super-charger</td><td>4,750/6,205</td><td>160mm (6.30in)</td><td>170mm (6.69in)</td><td>143.55litres (8,760cu in)</td><td>–</td><td>2,950kg (6,503lb)[13]</td></tr>
<tr><td colspan="2">DN-200</td><td>3</td><td>Horizontal[2]</td><td>–</td><td>–</td><td>–</td><td>160/200</td><td>–</td><td>–</td><td>1.758litres (107cu in)</td><td>–</td><td>165kg (364lb)</td></tr>
</table>

[2] two opposed pistons in each cylinder
[6] in cylinders with articulated connecting rods, 209.95mm (8.27in)
[8] according to some sources 1,150kg (2,535lb)
[9] weight of the prototypes 1,280kg (2,822lb), weight of the later series engines 1,310kg (2,888lb)
[10] with the jet engine turned on
[11] from 1946, 1,500/2,000hp
[12] according to some sources 1,600/2,400hp
[13] with turbo-supercharger 3,400kg (7,500lb)

Table 27
Part 2, Chapter 30 Projects for H-shaped engines by A.P. Ro

Engine type	Number of cylinders	Layout	Type of cooling	Gear	Super-charging	Power rating, hp	Bore	Stroke	Volume	Comp-ression ratio	Weight
M-130	24	H	Liquid	Yes	2-speed	2,300/2,400[1]	148mm (5.83in)	170mm (6.69in)	70.0litres (4,272cu in)	6.8:1	1,000kg (2,205lb)

[1] according to some sources 2,300kg/2,500hp

Table 28
Part 2, Chapter 31 The engines of A.M. Dobrotvorskiy

Engine type	Number of cylinders	Layout	Type of cooling	Gear	Super-charging	Power rating, hp	Bore	Stroke	Volume	Comp-ression ratio	Weight
MB-100	24	X	Liquid	Yes	1-speed	2,100/2,200	148mm (5.83in)	170mm (6.69in)	70.0litres (4,272cu in)	6.6:1	1,325kg (2.921lb)
MB-102	24	X	Liquid	Yes	2-speed	2,370/2,450	148mm (5.83in)	170mm (6.69in)	70.0litres (4,272cu in)	6.6:1	1,400kg (3,090lb)

Table 29
Part 2, Chapter 32 The engines of S.D. Kolosov

Engine type	Number of cylinders	Layout	Type of cooling	Gear	Super-charging	Power rating, hp	Bore	Stroke	Volume	Comp-ression ratio	Weight
M-16	4	O	Air	No	No	60/65	100mm (3.94in)	100mm (3.94in)	3.14litres (192cu in)	5.5:1	80kg (176lb)
M-1	12	V	Liquid	Yes	2-speed	1,300/1,500	150mm (5.91in)	170mm (6.69in)	36.0litres (2,197cu in)	6.6:1	660kg (1,455lb)

Table 30
Part 2, Chapter 33 The conrod-free engines of S.S. Balandin

Engine type		Number of cylinders	Layout	Type of cooling	Gear	Super-charging	Power rating, hp	Bore	Stroke	Volume	Comp-ression ratio	Weight
OMB		4	X[1]	Air	No	No	83/90	125mm (4.92in)	140mm (5.51in)	6.88litres (420cu in)	5.0:1	195kg (430lb)
MB-4		4	X[1]	Air	No	No	140	125mm (4.92in)	140mm (5.51in)	6.86litres (419cu in)	5.8:1	156kg (344lb)
MB-8		8	Two-row X[1]	Air	No	No	280	125mm (4.92in)	140mm (5.51in)	13.73litres (838cu in)	5.8:1	248kg (545lb)
MB-4b		4	X[1]	Air	No	No	200	146mm (5.75in)	140mm (5.51in)	9.37litres (572cu in)	5.8:1	210kg (463lb)
MB-8b		8	Two-row X[1]	Air	No	No	400	146mm (5.75in)	140mm (5.51in)	18.74litres (1,144cu in)	5.8:1	354kg (761lb)
OM-127o		12	Four blocks in X[1]	Liquid	Yes	1-speed[2]	1,750/2,100[3]	160mm (6.30in)	170mm (6.69in)	41.0litres (2,502cu in)	7.2:1	950kg (2,094lb)[4]
OM-127RN		8	Four blocks in X[1]	Liquid	Yes	1-speed	3,200[5]	155mm (6.10in)	146mm (5.75in)	22.0litres (1,342cu in)	7.5:1[6]	2,030kg (4,475lb)[7]
M-127	M-127	24	Four blocks in X[1]	Liquid	Yes	Yes	8,000/9,000	160mm (6.30in)	170mm (6.69in)	82.0litres (5,004cu in)	6.9:1[8]	–
	M-127K						8,000/ 10,000					3,450kg (7,606lb)

[1] cylinder pairs were placed perpendicular to each other in different planes
[2] the second variant had a GCS and a turbo-supercharger
[3] with turbo-supercharger, 2,150/2,800hp
[4] with turbo-supercharger, 1,200kg (2,645lb)
[5] with impulse turbines, 3,500hp
[6] initially 5.5:1
[7] with impulse turbines, 2,150kg (4,740lb)
[8] later increased to 7.1:1

Table 31
Part 2, Chapter 34 Lesser-known projects of 1939-47

Engine type	Number of cylinders	Layout	Type of cooling	Gear	Super-charging	Power rating, hp	Bore	Stroke	Volume	Comp-ression ratio	Weight
PB	24	Coupled V	Liquid	Yes	No	850/900	–	–	–	–	420kg (926lb)
M-32	9	Radial	Air	No	No	400	–	–	–	–	330kg (727lb)
Circular engine of I.A. Uvarov	6	Circular	–	Yes	No	1,600	127mm (5.0in)	127mm (5.0in)	–	8.0:1	300kg (660lb)
M-Sh	12	Radial with inclined cylinders	–	–	–	1,450/1,850	–	–	–	–	800kg (1,760lb)
M-111TK	36	–	Liquid	–	Turbo-super-charger	4,700/5,500	–	–	–	–	–

Table 32
Part 2, Chapter 35 The engines of G.S. Skubachevskiy and I.V. Dobrynin

Engine type	Number of cylinders	Layout	Type of cooling	Gear	Super-charging	Power rating, hp	Bore	Stroke	Volume	Comp-ression ratio	Weight
M-250	24	Six blocks in radial	Liquid	Yes	3-speed	2,200/2,500	140mm (5.51in)	138mm (5.43in)	51.0litres (3,112cu in)	6.2:1	1,280kg (2,822lb)
VD-3TK	24	Six blocks in radial	Liquid	Yes	1-speed + turbo-super-charger	2,500/3,500	148mm (5.83in)	144mm (5.67in)	59.43litres (3,626cu in)	6.6:1	1,520kg (3,351lb)[1]
VD-4K	24	Six blocks in radial	Liquid	Yes	1-speed + turbo-super-charger	3,250/4,300	148mm (5.83in)	144mm (5.67in)	59.43litres (3,626cu in)	7.0:1	2,065kg (4,552lb)[2]

[1] according to some sources 1,620kg (3,572lb)
[2] without turbo-supercharger

Table 33
Part 2, Chapter 36 The engines of A.G. Ivchenko and their evolution

Engine type		Number of cylinders	Layout	Type of cooling	Gear	Super-charging	Power rating, hp	Bore	Stroke	Volume	Comp-ression ratio	Weight
	M-26						–					395kg (871lb)
	M-26GR						420/500*					–
M-26 (AI-26)	M-26GR (f)	7	Radial	Air	Yes	1-speed	420/550	155.5mm (6.12in)	155mm (6.10in)	20.6litres (1,257cu in)	6.4:1	–
	M-26GRF						420/575					–
	AI-26V						460/574					450kg (992lb)

[1] power rating of the first variant, 400/500hp

Table 33 *continued*

Engine type		Number of cylinders	Layout	Type of cooling	Gear	Super-charging	Power rating, hp	Bore	Stroke	Volume	Comp-ression ratio	Weight
M-27		5	Radial	Air	Yes	1-speed	300/350	155.5mm (6.12in)	155mm (6.10in)	–	6.4:1	300kg (660lb)
M-29		9	Radial	Air	Yes	1-speed	625/750[2]	155.5mm (6.12in)	155mm (6.10in)	–	6.4:1	–
M-4GR		4	0	Air	Yes	No	50/55	–	–	–	–	–
M-10		5	Radial	Air	No	No	80/90	105mm (4.13in)	105mm (4.13in)	4.627litres (282cu in)	5.5:1	105kg (231lb)
M-12		7	Radial	Air	No	1-speed	155/180	105.5mm (4.14in)	115mm (4.53in)	–	6.0:1	145kg (319lb)
	M-14R						260					–
	AI-14RA						217/256					200kg (441lb)
	AI-14RF				Yes		300					–
	AI-14VF						235/280					238kg (525lb)
	M-14P						360					214kg (472lb)
	M-14PM				No		315					208kg (459lb)
	M-14PM1						360					–
	M-14PT						360					216kg (476lb)
M-14 (AI-14)	M-14PF	9	Radial	Air		1-speed	360	105mm (4.13in)	130mm (5.12in)	10.16litres (620cu in)	5.9:1	214kg (472lb)
	M-14PR						360					214kg (472lb)
	M-14Kh						360					214kg (472lb)
	M-14PS				Yes		360					214kg (472lb)
	M-14SKh						360					221kg (487lb)
	M-14V26						275/325					252kg (556lb)
	M-14V26V1						370					255kg (562lb)
	M-14V1						360					254kg (560lb)
	M-14V2						400					254kg (560lb)
M-3		3	Radial	Air	Yes	–	105	105mm (4.13in)	130mm (5.12in)	–	–	–

[2] registered power rating 615hp

Table 34
Part 2, Chapter 37 The engines of the Voronezh Engine Design Bureau

Engine type		Number of cylinders	Layout	Type of cooling	Gear	Super-charging	Power rating, hp	Bore	Stroke	Volume	Comp-ression ratio	Weight
M-16		8	X	Air	–	–	300	–	–	–	–	150kg (331lb)
M-17	M-17	4	0	Air	–	–	175	–	–	–	–	118kg (260lb)
	M-17F						250					163kg (359lb)
M-18	M-18-01	2	0	Air	–	–	40	–	–	–	–	13.7kg (30lb)
	M-18-02						55					–
M-25		9	Radial	Air	Yes	1-speed	450	–	–	–	–	215kg (474lb)
M-29		4	0	Air	Yes	No	75	–	–	–	–	53kg (119lb)
M9F		9	Radial	Air	Yes	1-speed	420	105mm (4.13in)	130mm (5.12in)	10.16litres (620cu in)	–	220kg (485lb)
M7		7	Radial	Air	Yes	1-speed	270	105mm (4.13in)	130mm (5.12in)	–	–	170kg (375lb)
M5		5	Radial	Air	–	1-speed	170	105mm (4.13in)	130mm (5.12in)	–	–	135kg (298lb)
M-6		6	0	Liquid	–	–	340	105mm (4.13in)	82mm (3.22in)	4.3litres (262cu in)	9.0:1	270kg (595lb)

Table 35
Part 2, Chapter 38 Wankel-type engines

Engine type		Number of sections	Type of cooling	Gear	Super-charging	Power rating, hp	Volume	Weight
VAZ-1187		1	Liquid	No	No	40[1]	0.365litres (22cu in)	–
VAZ-1188		1	Liquid	No	No	60	0.365litres (22cu in)	–
VAZ-416	without turbo-supercharger	2	Liquid	Yes	No	180/200	1.308litres (80cu in)	110kg (242lb)
	with turbo-supercharger				Turbo-super-charger	240		125kg (275lb)
VAZ-426	with gear, without turbo-supercharger	3	Liquid	Yes	No	240/300	1.962litres (120cu in)	130kg (287lb)
	with gear and turbo-supercharger			Yes	Turbo-super-charger	400		150kg (331lb)
	VAZ-4265			No	No	270		130kg (287lb)
VAZ-526		4	Liquid	No	No	400	2.616litres (160cu in)	175kg (386lb)
D-200		2	Liquid	Yes	No	220	–	145kg (320lb

[1] several engines were boosted to 55hp

Table 36
Part 2, Chapter 39 The engines of the Samara Machine-Building Design Bureau

Engine type		Number of cylinders	Layout	Type of cooling	Gear	Super-charging	Power rating, hp	Bore	Stroke	Volume	Comp-ression ratio	Weight
P-020		2	0	Air	No	No	20	66mm (2.60in)	–	0.274litres (17cu in)	7.3:1	9.9kg (22lb)[1]
P-032	P-032	2	0	Air	No	No	32	72mm (2.83in)	–	0.44litres (27cu in)	7.0:1	13.1kg (29lb)[2]
	P-032MR				Yes		38					–
	P-032-71				Yes		23/33					25kg (55lb)
P-033		2	0	Air	No	No	38	72mm (2.83in)	–	0.44litres (27cu in)	7.0:1	–
P-065		4	H	Air	Yes	No	65	72mm (2.83in)	–	0.88litres (54cu in)	7.0:1	–
SB-039		2	0	Air	–	–	67	–	–	–	–	75kg (165lb)
B-32		2	0	Air	–	–	32	72mm (2.83in)	–	0.44litres (27cu in)	–	–

[1] according to some sources 9.76kg (21lb)
[2] according to some sources 12.5kg (28lb)

Table 37
Part 2, Chapter 40 The engines of the Kazan Engine-Building Production Enterprise (KMPO)

Engine type	Number of cylinders	Layout	Type of cooling	Gear	Super-charging	Power rating, hp	Bore	Stroke	Volume	Comp-ression ratio	Weight
P-800	4	0	Air	Yes	No	65	62mm (2.44in)	66mm (2.60in)	0.8litres (49cu in)	9.5:1	48kg (106lb)
P-1000	4	0	Air	Yes	No	80	72mm (2.83in)	66mm (2.60in)	1.075litres (66cu in)	9.5:1	55kg (121lb)

Table 38
Part 2, Chapter 41 The engines developed at the Rybinskie Motory enterprise during the 1980s-1990s

Engine type		Number of cylinders	Layout	Type of cooling	Gear	Super-charging	Power rating, hp	Bore	Stroke	Volume	Comp-ression ratio	Weight
RMZ-320MR		1	I	Air	Yes	No	20	–	–	0.3175litres (19cu in)	8.0:1	30kg (66lb)
RMZ-640	RMZ-640MR	2	I	Air	Yes	No	38	–	–	0.635litres (39cu in)	8.0:1	45kg (99lb)
	RMZ-640MR-2											49kg (108lb)

Table 39
Part 2, Chapter 42 Engines for ultralight aircraft, based on motorcycle engines

Engine type	Number of cylinders	Layout	Type of cooling	Gear	Super-charging	Power rating, hp	Bore	Stroke	Volume	Comp-ression ratio	Weight
A-170	1	I	Air	Yes	No	14/16	62mm (2.44in)	57.2mm (2.25in)	0.1733litres (11cu in)	10.5:1	12.2kg (27lb)
DSh-2	2	I	Liquid	Yes	No	60	76mm (2.99in)	75mm (2.95in)	0.68litres (41cu in)	–	30.5kg (67lb)
DSh-700	2	I	Liquid	Yes	No	60	–	–	–	–	–
IZh-MOTIV-700	2	I	Liquid	Yes	No	60	76mm (2.99in)	76mm (2.99in)	0.68litres (41cu in)	9.0:1	45kg (99lb)[1]
DD-700/45R	2	0	Air	Yes	No	45	72mm (2.83in)	86mm (3.39in)	0.7litres (43cu in)	9.0:1	50kg (110lb)

[1] according to some sources 50kg (110lb)

Russian Aircraft and Their Piston Engines

This table shows aircraft types that were in series production in Russia, and their piston engines (Russian series-built types only).

Aircraft type	Engine type
A-4 (small series)	M-26
A-7-3a	M-22
AIR-6 (Ya-6)	M-11V
An-2	ASh-62IR/M
An-14	AI-14R
Anasal	Salmson-150
ANT-9	M-26
ANT-25 (RD, DB-1)	M-34RD
Ar-2 (SB-RK)	M-105
Be-6	ASh-73
Che-2 (MDR-6)	M-63
DB-3	M-85
DB-3	M-86
DB-3B	M-87A/B
DB-3F (Il-4)	M-87A/B
DB-3F (Il-4)	M-88A/B
DB-A	M-34FRNV
DI-6	M-25V
Dux-Farman IV	*Gnom-50*
Dux-Farman IX	*Gnom-70*
Dux-Farman XV	*Gnom-80*
Dux-Farman XV	*Gnom-100*
Er-2	M-105R/RA
Er-2	ACh-30B
Farman VII	*Gnom-50*
Farman VII	*Kalep-50*
Farman XVI	*Gnom-80*
Farman XVI	*Kalep-80*
Farman ??	*Gnom-80*
Farman ??	*Gnom-100*
Farman ??	Gnome Monosoupape-100
G-4 (small series)	M-26GRF
GST (MP-7)	M-62R
I-2bis	M-5
I-3	M-17
I-5	M-22
I-7	M-17
I-14	M-25
I-15	M-22
I-15bis	M-25A/V
I-16	M-22
I-16 type 4/5	M-25
I-16 type 6/10	M-25A
I-16 type 17	M-25V
I-16 type 18/24	M-62
I-16 type 24/28/29	M-63
I-153 (small series)	M-25V
I-153	M-62
I-28 (small series)	M-87A
I-180 (small series)	M-88
I-250 ('N')	VK-107R
I-Zet	M-22
Il-2	AM-38/AM-38F
Il-10	AM-42
Il-12	ASh-82FN
Il-14	ASh-82T
Ilya Muromets type V	RBVZ-6
Ilya Muromets type V	MRB-6
Ilya Muromets type G	RBVZ-6
Ilya Muromets type G	*Reno-220*
Ilya Muromets type E	*Reno-220*
IP-1	M-25A
K-5	M-15
K-5	M-17
K-5	M-22
Ka-15	AI-14VF
Ka-18	AI-14VF
Ka-26	M-14V-26
KhAI-1 (small series)	M-22
KhAI-5 (small series)	M-63
KOR-1 (Be-2)	M-25A
KOR-2 (Be-4)	M-62IR
KR-6	M-17F
KR-6a	M-17F
La-5	ASh-82F/FN
La-7	ASh-82FN
La-9	ASh-82FN
La-11	ASh-82FN
LaGG-3	M-105P/PA/PF
Lebed-XII	Salmson-150
LK-1 (small series)	M-11V
M-5	Gnome Monosoupape-100
M-5	*Ron-110*
M-9	Salmson-150
M-11	*Ron-110*
MB	*Gnom-50*
MB bis	*Ron-110*
MBR-2	M-17B
MBR-2	M-34NA/NB
Mi-1	AI-26V

Aircraft type	Engine type
Mi-4	ASh-82V
MiG-1	AM-35A
MiG-3	AM-35A
Morane J	*Gnom-80*
MR-1	M-5
MTB-1	M-34R
MU-1	M-2
Nieuport IV	*Gnom-50*
Nieuport IV	*Gnom-70*
Nieuport IV	Gnome Monosoupape-100
P-2	M-6
Pchela-1T	P-032
Pe-2	M-105R/RA/PF
Pe-2	ASh-82F
Pe-2I (small series)	VK-107A
Pe-3	M-105RA
Pe-3bis	M-105RA/PF
Pe-3 of 1944	M-105PF
PS-9	M-17B/M-17F
PS-35 (ANT-35)	M-62IR
PS-84 (Li-2)	M-62IR
PS-89 (ZiG-1) (small series)	M-17F
R-1	M-5
R-3	M-5
R-5	M-17/M-17B/M-17F
R-5a	M-17B
R-5T	M-17F
R-6 (PS-7)	M-17/M-17B
R-6a (MP-6)	M-17/M-17B
R-10	M-25A/V
R-Zet	M-34NA/NB
S-XVI	*Gnom-80*

Aircraft type	Engine type
S-XVI	*Kalep-80*
S-??	*Ron-120*
SAM-5bis	M-11D
SB	M-100/100A/100AU
SB	M-103/103A/103U
SB	M-104
SB	M-105
Sh-2	M-11V/G/D
Shche-2	M-11D
SL-90	M-3
SPB ('D')	M-105
SSS (3S)	M-17F
Stal-2	MG-31
Stal-2	M-26
Stal-3	M-22
Su-2 (BB-1)	M-87A
Su-2	M-88A/B
Su-2	M-82A
Su-26	M-14PF
Su-29	M-14PF
Su-31	M-14PF
TB-1	M-17/M-17B
TB-3	M-17/M-17B/M-17F
TB-3	M-34
TB-3	M-34R/RD/RB
TB-3	M-34RN/RNA/RNB
TB-3	M-34FRNV
TB-7 (Pe-8) first series	M-34FRNV + M-103A as part of ATsN-2
TB-7 (Pe-8)	AM-35A
TB-7 (Pe-8)	M-30
TB-7 (Pe-8)	M-40

Aircraft type	Engine type
TB-7 (Pe-8)	ASh-82FN
Tu-2	ASh-82FN
Tu-4	ASh-73TK
Tu-10 (small series)	AM-39
U-1	M-2
U-2 (Po-2)	M-11A/B/V/G/D/K
UT-1	M-11D
UT-2	M-11D
UT-3 (small series)	MV-6/6A
UTB	ASh-21
Yak-1	M-105P/PA/PF
Yak-1 (small series)	M-106-1sk
Yak-2 (BB-22)	M-103A
Yak-3	M-105PF/PF2
Yak-3	VK-107A
Yak-4 (BB-22)	M-105
Yak-6	M-11D
Yak-7	M-105P/PA/PF
Yak-8 (small series)	M-11D
Yak-9	M-105P/PA/PF/PV/PF2
Yak-9	VK-107A
Yak-10	M-11FR
Yak-11	ASh-21
Yak-12	AI-14R
Yak-18	M-11FR
Yak-18A	AI-14R
Yak-18P/PM/T	M-14P
Yak-24	ASh-82V
Yak-50	M-14P
Yak-52	M-14P
Yak-53	M-14P
Yak-55	M-14PF

Select Bibliography

Aviamotory M-105PA, M-105RA, M-105PF, M-105RF (Oborongiz, 1943)

Aviamotory VK-107A, VK-108 (Oborongiz, 1946)

Aviatsionnie dvigateli (Mashgiz, 1951)

Aviatsionnie, raketnie, morskie, promishlennie dvigateli, 1944-2000 (AKS-Konversalt, 2000)

Aviatsionnie motory AM-34RB i AM-34NB (Voenizdat, 1939)

Aviatsionnie motory AM-38 i AM-38F (Oborongiz, 1943)

Aviatsionnie motory ASh-82F i ASh-82FN (Oborongiz, 1944)

Aviatsionnie motory M-17 i M-17B (OGIZ, 1933)

Aviatsionnie motory M-100, M-100A, M-103 (Katalogizdat, 1938)

Aviatsionniy dvigatel AI-26V (Oborongiz, 1957)

Aviatsionniy dvigatel ASh-82T (Mashinostroenie, 1965)

Aviatsionniy dvigatel ASh-82V (Mashinostroenie, 1957)

Aviatsionniy motor AM-35A (Voenizdat, 1941)

Aviatsionniy motor AM-42 (Oborongiz, 1946)

Aviatsionniy motor ASh-21 (RIO Aeroflota, 1948)

Aviatsionniy motor ASh-73TK (Oborongiz, 1953)

Aviatsionniy motor ASh-82FN (Oborongiz, 1947)

Aviatsionniy motor M-5 (OGIZ, 1931)

Aviatsionniy motor M-11 (Voenizdat, 1939)

Aviatsionniy motor M-11 tipa G (Osoaviakhim, 1939)

Aviatsionniy motor M-11D (Oborongiz, 1943)

Aviatsionniy motor M-15 (OGIZ, 1933)

Aviatsionniy motor M-22 (OGIZ, 1932)

Aviatsionniy motor M-26 (OGIZ, 1933)

Aviatsionniy motor M-63 (Voenizdat, 1940)

Aviatsionniy motor VK-107A (GIOP, 1945)

Balandin, S.S., *Besshatunnie porshnevie dvigateli vnutrennego sgoraniya* (Mashinostroenie, 1968)

Bazhanov, A. and Medved, A., *MMPP 'Salyut' – stranitsi istorii* (Vostochniy gorizont, 2002)

Berne, L.P., Boev, D.A. and Ganshin, N.S., *Otechestvennie aviatsionnie dvigateli – XX vek* (Avico Press, 2003)

Bogdanov, D.A., Bondarenko, P.D. and Stepanov, Yu.A., *Aviatsionniy dvigatel ASh-82V* (Transport, 1974)

Borisov, G.P., *et al*, *Aviatsionnie motory AM-38 i AM-38F* (Oborongiz, 1944)

Boykov, B.V., *Aviatsionnie dvigateli* (Izdatelstvo DOSAAF, 1954)

Brusyanov, B.E., *Ispitanie aviatsionnikh dvigateley* (GIOP, 1945)

Duz', P.D., *Istoriya vozdukhoplavaniya i aviatsii v Rossii (period do 1914 g.)* (Mashinostroenie, 1979)

Dvigatel AI-14VF (Mashinostroenie, 1964)

Dvigatel ASh-62IR (Mashinostroenie, 1962)

Dyomin, A.A., *Khodinka* (Rusavia, 2002)

Gunston B. *The Development of Piston Aero Engines* (Patrick Stephens Ltd, 1993)

Kalistratov, N., *Aviatsionniy motor M-100A* (Voenizdat, 1939)

Konstruktivnie izmeneniya motora M-105PF (Voenizdat, 1943)

Kratkoe opisanie motora M-105 (Oborongiz, 1942)

Labazin, P.S., *Aviatsionniy motor ASh-62IR* (Mashinostroenie, 1972)

Lapshin, A.M. and Anokhin, P.I., *Aviatsionniy dvigatel M-14P* (Mashinostroenie, 1976)

Lobach-Zhurchenko, B.M., *Aviatsionnie dvigateli* (Gosudarstvennoe izdatelstvo, 1921)

Lobach-Zhurchenko, B.M., *Aviamotory, ikh ustroystvo, rabota i proizvodstvo* (Gosudarstvennoe izdatelstvo, 1928)

Motor M-34 (RNA, RNB, NB) (Gosudarstvennoe voennoe izdatelstvo, 1936)

Motor M-82 (Oborongiz, 1943)

Motor M-85 (Voenizdat, 1937)

Motory M-86 – M-87 (Voenizdat, 1938)

Opisanie motora M2-120 (ONTI NKTP, 1931)

Orlin, A.S. and Kruglov, M.G., *Kombinirovannie dvukhtaktnie dvigateli* (Mashinostroenie, 1968)

Ot 'Russkogo Reno' – k 'Rybinskim motoram' (Rostov Velikiy, 1993)

Permskiy motorostroitelniy (Permskoe knizhnoe izdatelstvo, 1978)

Ponomaryov, A., *Aviatsionnie dvigateli* (Gosudarstvennoe voennoe izdatelstvo, 1933)

Pugachyov, N.S., *Aviatsionnie dvigateli* (Oborongiz, 1948)

Razvitie aviatsionnoy nauki i tekhniki v SSSR (Nauka, 1980)

Rodzevich, Styorkin and Efimov, *Sovetskiy aviamotor (1917-1932)* (ONTI NKTP)

Rukovodstvo po remontu aviatsionnikh motorov tipa M-25 (Voenizdat, 1939)

Rukovodstvo po remontu aviatsionnikh motorov M-103 i M-105 (Oborongiz, 1941)

Samolyotostroenie v SSSR (1917-1945), in two volumes (TsAGI, 1992-94)

Senichkin, G.V., *Konstruktsiya i ekspluatatsiya dvigatelya M-11FR* (Voenizdat, 1958)

Shavrov, V.B., *Istoriya konstruktsiy samolyotov v SSSR*, in two volumes (Mashinostroenie, 1978)

Shest' desyatiletiy progressa i traditsiy (TsIAM, 1991)

Spravochnik po aviamotoram (Oborongiz, 1942)

Spravochnik po aviamotoram proizvodstva zavoda im. Stalina (Oborongiz, 1946)

Spravochnik po aviatsionnim motoram (Oborongiz, 1943)

Tekhnicheskoe opisanie motora M-25 (NKTP, 1935)

Tkachyov, S.F., Aviatsionniy motor M-100 (Voenizdat, 1936)

Tkachyov, S.F. and Kasyanov, N.A., *Aviatsionniy motor M-17F* (Voenizdat, 1936)

TsIAM 50 let: obzor osnovnikh napravleniy nauchnoy deyatelnosti (TsIAM, 1980)

Velizhev, A.A., *Dostizheniya sovetskoy aviapromishlennosti za 15 let* (OGIZ, 1932)

Votintsev, A.S. and Ivanov, V.A., *Aviatsionniy motor M-11* (Oborongiz, 1941)

Zaikin, A.E., *et al*, *Aviatsionnie dvigateli* (GIOP, 1941)

Zdes' nachinalas' Moskva (MOSP RF, 1997)

Periodicals

Aviatsiya i Kosmonavtika

Dvigatel'

Samolyot

Teknika Vozdushnogo Flota

Archives

The author has used materials from the N.E. Zhukovskiy Scientific Memorial Museum, the museum of the Salyut factory, the Russian State Archive of Economics, and the Russian State Military Archive.

Index

2GM-13: 60-61, 242
2M-15: 83-85, 246

3M-11: *see* M-50 (3M-11)

A-170: 215
AB-20: *see* M-7 (AB-20)
AB-55: 94
ACh-30: *see* M-30
ACh-30B(M-30B): 22, 171, 176-178, 259
ACh-30BF: 177, 178, 259
ACh-31: 171, 179, 259
ACh-31A: 180
ACh-32: 171, 180, 252
AD-1: *see* N-3
AD-3: 169
ADU-4: 35
Agapov's engine: 91
AI-10: *see* M-10 (AI-10)
AI-12: *see* M-12 (AI-12)
AI-14: *see* M-14 (AI-14)
AI-20: 197
AI-26: *see* M-26 (AI-26)
AI-226: 198
Allison V-1710: 112, 231-234
Alvis Leonides: 231
AM-3: 101
AM-20: *see* M-20
AM-34(M-34): *see* M-34
AM-35: 8, 26, 99, 109, 249
AM-35A: 99, 100, 109-111, 249
AM-35ANV: 109, 249
AM-35A-TR: 110, 249
AM-35G: 109
AM-35NV: 109
AM-35TK: 109, 249
AM-36 (M-36): 26, 110, 192, 249
AM-37 (M-37): 110, 112, 249
AM-37A: 110, 249
AM-37P: 111
AM-37TK: 110
AM-37u/v: 111
AM-38: 8, 99-111, 171, 249, 250
AM-38F: 100-114, 177,250
AM-39: 100, 101, 112, 113, 250
AM-39A: 112, 250
AM-39A-TK: 112
AM-39B: 112
AM-39B-TK: 112
AM-39FK: 112, 250
AM-39FN (FNV): 112, 250
AM-39FN2: 112, 250
AM-40: 112, 113
AM-41 (AM-39UV): 112, 113, 250
AM-42: 32, 100, 114, 115, 250
AM-42B-TK: 115, 250
AM-42FB-TK: 115
AM-42FNV: 114, 250
AM-42TK: 114
AM-42V: *see* AM-44
AM-43: 115, 250
AM-43NV: 115, 250
AM-43TK: 115
AM-43TR: 115, 250
AM-44 (AM-42V): 115, 250
AM-44B-TK: 116, 250
AM-45 (M-45, MF-45): 116, 250
AM-45D: 116, 250
AM-45Sh: 116, 250
AM-46 (M-46): 116, 250
AM-46TK: 116, 250
AM-47 (M-47): 116, 250
AMB-20 (Bolshevik): 63, 243
AMB-500 (Bolshevik II): 63, 243
AMB-700 (M-24, Bolshevik I): 63, 243
AMBS (AMBS-1): 24, 40, 98
AMRD-03: 101
AM-TRD-02: 101
AN-1 (N-1): 26, 169, 170, 172, 175, 176, 230, 258
AN-1A: 170, 175, 258
AN-1M: 176, 258
AN-1R: 169, 170, 175, 176, 258
AN-1RTK: 170, 175, 176, 178, 258
AN-5: 174, 258
AN-20: 171
Antoinette: 36
Anzani: 36
Argus: 36, 38
Argus As 10C: 231
Argus As 411TA-1: 237
Armstrong Siddley Cheetah: 229
Armstrong Siddley Genet Major: 228-230
ASh-2: 124, 132, 252
ASh-2K: 118, 132, 252
ASh-2TK: 132, 252
ASh-3K: 132, 252
ASh-21: 118, 124, 130-132, 195, 252
ASh-62: *see* M-62
ASh-62IR: *see* M-62IR
ASh-62M: 122
ASh-62N: 122, 251
ASh-73: 118, 130, 251
ASh-73TK: 32, 118, 130,131, 235, 251
ASh-73TKF: 130, 251
ASh-73TKFN: 130, 251
ASh-82: *see* M-82
ASh-82FN: *see* M-82FN
ASh-82M: 127, 251
ASh-82MF: 127
ASh-82T: 118, 122, 124, 126, 127, 251
ASh-82V: 118, 123, 128, 251
ASh-83: 118, 127-129, 252
ASh-84 (ASh-84TK):118, 129, 252
ASh-93: 132
ASz-62IR-M18: 122
ASz-62IR-M18/DHC3: 122
Asso: *see* Isotta-Fraschini Asso

BD-2A: 167, 173, 258
Beardmore: 37, 38
Bentley B.R.2: 219
Benz: 38, 41
BKM: 151,156, 255
BMW III: 73
BMW IIIa: 219,220
BMW IV: 73, 220, 236
BMW IVa: 220
BMW VI: 7, 29, 73, 76, 102, 204, 225, 226
BMW VIaE6,0: 73
BMW VIaE7,3: 73
BMW VIb: 74
BMW IX: 226, 230
BMW 003: 135, 183, 238
BMW 132: 229, 237
BMW 801: 236
Bolshevik : *see* AMB-20
Bolshevik I (M-24): *see* AMB-700
Bolshevik II: *see* AMB-500
Bramo 323A Fafnir
Bristol Centaurus: 235
Bristol Hercules: 231, 232, 234
Bristol Lucifier: 220, 221
Bristol Mercury: 226, 230
Bristol Pegasus: 230, 232, 234
Bristol Taurus: 231
Buchet: 32
Buran-Avia: *see* RMZ-320MR/RMZ-640MR

Chenu: 34
Clement-Bayard: 34
Clerget: 40
Curtiss D.12: 55-57, 221, 223
Curtiss OX: 36
Curtiss V-1650 Conqueror: 221, 223, 224, 234
Curtiss V-1800 Conqueror: 8, 134, 227
Curtiss VX: 41

D-11 (MD-11): 26, 171, 174, 258
D-200: 207, 209, 264
Daimler: 33, 49
Daimler-Benz DB 601A: 232, 236
Daimler-Benz DB 603: 236
Daimler-Benz DB 605: 236
Daimler-Benz DB 606: 236
Dancelle: 34
DD-700/45R: 215, 216
De Dion-Bouton: 34
De Havilland Gipsy III: 228
De Havilland Gipsy Major: 228
De Havilland Gipsy Minor: 158, 163
De Havilland Gipsy Six: 230
DEKA M-100 (M-101): 24, 40
DN-200: 172, 180, 258
DSh-2: 215, 216
DSh-700: 215, 216

EN-1: 167
ENV: 34

FED-1: 86, 87,246
FED-3 (M-28): 86, 87, 246
FED-8: 86, 170, 172, 173
FED-10: 86, 87, 246
Fiat A.10: 41
Fiat A.12: 41
Fiat A.12bis: 219
Fiat A.20: 222, 223
Fiat A.30RAbis: 229, 231
Ford A12-400 Liberty: *see* Liberty

GAM-34: *see* GM-34
GAM-35: 110, 249
GAM-35FN: 110, 249
GAM-38F: 112, 250
Gantman's engine: 92, 247
GAZ-11: 97, 247
GAZ-Avia-60 (MGAZ-60): 97, 247
GM-13: 25, 59, 61, 223, 242
GM-27: 56, 58, 242
GM-34 (GAM-34): 99, 106, 107, 249
GM-34F: 106, 249
GM-34FN: 108, 249
GM-34BP: 108, 249
GM-34BS: 108, 249
GM-34BT: 108, 249
GM-44: 89, 90, 246
Gnom-50: *see* Gnome Omega

Gnome Lambda: 34, 35
Gnome Monosoupape: 36, 41
Gnome Rhône 9A Jupiter: 7, 25, 77, 81, 82, 133
Gnome Rhône 9Ad: 79, 225
Gnome Rhône 9Akx: 81
Gnome Rhône 9Aq: 7, 25, 79, 225
Gnome Rhône 9As: 79, 225
Gnome Rhône 7K: 80, 81
Gnome Rhône 9K Mistral: 8, 147, 151, 227
Gnome Rhône 14K Mistral Major: 147, 151, 227
Gnome Rhône 14Krsd: 80, 148, 150, 152, 227, 228
Gnome Rhône 14M: 149
Gnome Rhône 14N50: 8, 149
Gnome Rhône 18L: 151
Gnome Rhône 18P: 231
Grizodubov's engine: 36

Harleu: 34
Hirth 2703: 239
Hirth HM 60R: 231
Hirth XM 500UL: 239
Hispano Suiza 8Ab: 45,46, 48
Hispano Suiza 8Fb: 45,46,48, 219, 221, 236
Hispano Suiza 12H51: 221
Hispano Suiza 12Hb: 223
Hispano Suiza 12Xbrs: 227
Hispano Suiza 12Y: 133, 145
Hispano Suiza 12Ybrs: 8, 75, 133, 134, 136, 181, 227
Hispano Suiza 12Ycrs: 133, 136, 227, 229
Hispano Suiza 12Ydrs: 227
Hispano Suiza 12Y51: 8
HS5: 122
HS6: 203
HS6A: 203
HS7: 127
HS8: 127
Hypocycle: 36

Isotta-Fraschini: 41
Isotta-Fraschini Asso: 52, 221, 226
Isotta-Fraschini Delta RC.35JDS: 231
Isotta-Fraschini 180 RT.CC.45: 231
Ispano I: 47,240
Ispano W: 45,47
Izh-Motiv-700: 215, 216

Jumo 004: 135, 238
Jumo 4: 170, 226
Jumo 205: 167, 170, 230
Jumo 207: 236
Jumo 210: 222
Jumo 211: 231, 236
Jumo 213: 236
Jumo 222: 236
Jumo 224: 171, 236
Junkers L-4: 220
Junkers L-5: 220-222
Jupiter VI: 78, 81
Jupiter VII: 79, 230
Jupiter VIII: 79

K9: 118, 122
K9-AA: 122
K9-VS: 122
K9-VV: 122
Kalep-80: 34, 35, 37
Kerting: 34
Kertis I: 55-57, 242
Kertis V: *see* V12
Kertis W: *see* M-14 (W18, M-18)
KIM: *see* M-26 (KIM)
Kivi's engine: 94
Kostovich's engine: 33
Kotobuki: 230

Liberty (Ford A12-400): 7, 15, 49, 51, 56, 59, 206, 219-221
Le Rhone J/Jb (M-2): 24, 36, 37, 42-44, 50, 64, 94, 147, 240
Liliput: 94
Limbach: 239
LiT-3: 198
Lorraine-Dietrich 12E/Eb/Ed: 50, 219-221, 223

M-1: *see* RBVZ-6
M-1 (M-116P): 183, 184, 260
M-2: *see* Le Rhône J/Jb
M-3: *see* Renault WC
M-3 (Nitchenko's engine): 118, 124, 131, 252
M-3 (Bakanov's engine): 197, 203, 204, 262
M-4 (Russkiy Ispano): 45, 46, 221, 240
M-4 (AI-4): 196
M-4G (AI-4V): 196, 262
M-5: 7,15, 24, 25, 48-53, 56, 59, 62, 221, 241
M-5 with a magneto: 50, 54, 241
M5: 204, 206, 263
M-6: 45-47, 50, 221, 240
M-6A: 45, 46, 240
M-6T12: 46, 240
M-6 (TsIAM): 206, 263
M-7 (NRB, NRB-100): *see* NRB
M-7 (AB-20): 55, 242
M7: 204, 206, 263
M-8 (RAM): 48, 241
M-9 (Liberty X): 50-52, 241
M-9 (Starostin's engine): 24, 91, 92, 247
M9: 204-206
M9F: 24, 204-206, 263
M9FS: 206
M9X: 205
M-10 (1924): 50, 51, 241
M-10 (auxiliary): 237, 238
M-10 (diesel): 171, 174
M-10 (AI-10): 196, 198, 262
M-11: 7, 8, 25, 29, 32, 48, 64, 65, 67, 69, 84, 117, 149, 157-159, 162, 163, 171, 183, 190, 206, 220, 225, 244
M-11A (M-11a, M-11/A): 25, 66, 69, 185, 186, 244
M-11B: 25, 69, 244
M-11D: 25, 69, 70, 158, 162, 244
M-11E: 67, 69, 244
M-11FM: 158, 162
M-11FR: 70, 71, 158, 162, 244
M-11FR-1: 68, 70, 244
M-11G: 22, 25, 69, 185, 244
M-11I: 70, 244
M-11K: 70, 244
M-11L: 70, 244
M-11V: 25, 69, 244
M-12 (NAMI-100): 47, 65-67, 69, 98, 244
M-12 (Kossov's engine): 158, 162, 256
M-12 (M-11Ya): 158, 162, 256
M-12 (AI-12): 196, 198, 262
M-12R: *see* MV-12R (M-12R)
M-13 (M-600): 55, 56, 59-61, 98, 223, 242
M-13M: 60, 61, 242
M-13 (M-13K): 158, 256
M-13 (Urmin's engine): 15, 162, 256
M-13 (Muzhilov's engine): 158, 162, 256
M-13FN: 21
M-14 (1924): 50-53, 241
M-14P: 50, 54, 241
M-14 (Liberty W18, V18-I): *see* V18-I
M-14 (Kertis W, W18, M-18): *see* M-18
M-14 (AI-14): 10, 26, 196, 198, 199, 201, 204, 217, 262
M-14Kh: 199, 203, 262
M-14N: 199
M-14P: 197, 199, 202-206, 262
M-14PA: 199
M-14PF: 199, 202, 262
M-14PM: 199, 262
M-14PM1: 199, 262
M-14PR: 199, 262
M-14PS: 199, 262
M-14PT: 199, 262
M-14R (AI-14R): 197, 199-201, 262
M-14RA (AI-14RA): 199, 201, 203, 262
M-14RD: 203
M-14RDP: 203
M-14RF (AI-14RF): 197, 199, 262
M-14RFP: 199
M-14RS: 199
M-14V (AI-14V):
M-14V1: 197, 203, 262
M-14V2: 197, 203, 262
M-14V26: 197, 203
M-14V26V1: 203, 262
M-14VF (AI-14VF): 197, 199, 200, 262
M-15: 25, 74, 81, 83, 84, 197, 246
M-15a: 85, 88, 246
M-16 (Liberty I): 50, 54, 241
M-16 (1939): 183, 260
M-16 (1990): 204, 263
M-17: 7, 8, 22, 25, 28, 29, 56, 73-76, 84, 102, 133, 134, 173, 190, 228, 245
M-17B: 74, 77, 245
M-17 coupled: 77
M-17E7,3: 75, 76, 245
M-17F: 77, 245
M-17L: 76, 77, 245
M-17T: 76, 77, 245
M-17 (1990): 204, 263
M-17F: 204, 263
M-18 (Kertis W, W18, M-14): 55-58, 242
M-18 (Bakanov's engine): 204
M-18-01: 205, 263
M-18-02: 205, 263
M-19: 56-58, 242
M-19a: 58, 88, 242
M-19K: 56
M-20 (diesel): 171, 174, 258
M-20 (AM-20, NAMI-500): 25, 60, 61, 192, 242
M-20A: 60,61, 242
M-21: 46, 47, 240
M-21 (czech ASh-21)
M-22: 7, 25, 28,78-82, 84, 133, 147, 149, 190, 225, 245
M-22 arctic: 80, 81
M-22N: 79-81, 245
M-22R: 79-81, 245
M-22U: *see* M-58
M-23 (NAMI-65): 25, 66-68, 244
M-25: 25, 79, 80, 117-119, 124, 148, 172, 227, 228, 251
M-25A: 117, 119, 251
M-25B: 118
M-25D14: 124
M-25D18: 25, 129
M-25R: 119
M-25V: 29, 117, 119, 251
M-25V-TK: 119
M-25 (Bakanov's engine): 205, 263
M-25-01: 205
M-26 (KIM): 83-85, 197, 245
M-26 (AI-26): 131,196, 261
M-26GR: 196-198, 261
M-26GR(f): 198, 261
M-26GRF: 198, 261
M-27: 56-58,242
M-27 coupled: 58
M-27N: 56, 88
M-27R: 25, 58, 242
M-27RN: 58, 88, 242
M-27 (Ivchenko's engine): 196, 198, 262
M-27GR: 196
M-28: *see* FED-3
M-29: 83, 85, 88, 245
M-29 (Ivchenko's engine): 196, 198, 199, 262
M-29GR: 196, 198, 262
M-29 (Bakanov's engine): 205, 213, 263
M-30 (AD-5, ACh-30): 9,26, 170, 171, 176, 177, 178, 259
M-30B: *see* ACh-30B
M-30D: 177, 259
M-30F: 177, 259
M-31: 93
M-32: 16, 88, 89, 190, 246
M-32RN: 88, 89, 246
M-32 (1940): 190, 261
M-33: 108, 249
M-34 (AM-34): 7, 8, 16, 26, 60, 88, 98, 99, 101, 102, 108, 109, 133, 147, 175, 181, 182, 192, 226, 227, 248
M-34 coupled: 102
M-34F: 102, 248
M-34FRGN: 106
M-34FRN: 99, 105, 106, 192, 248
M-34FRNA: 106
M-34FRNB: 106, 248
M-34FRNV: 25, 99, 106, 107, 109, 181, 248
M-34FRNV-TK: 106, 248
M-34FRN with vapour cooling: 106
M-34N: 99, 102, 248
M-34NA: 105, 248
M-34NB: 104, 105, 248
M-34NF: 105, 248

M-34NV: 104, 105, 248
M-34N with PTK: 105
M-34P: 105
M-34R: 102, 103, 248
M-34RA: 105, 248
M-34RB: 106, 107
M-34RD (RSP): 99, 100, 101, 103, 248
M-34RN: 25, 29, 103, 105, 167, 173, 248
M-34RNA: 104, 105, 248
M-34RNB: 105, 174, 248
M-34RNFT: 106
M-34RNV: 105
M-34RNV-TK: 105, 248
M-34N2B: 106
M-34RSO: 105, 248
M-34TK: 105
M-35 (1932): 108, 181, 249
M-35 (diesel): 180
M-36: 93
M-37: 93
M-38: 16, 88-90, 246
M-39: 93
M-40 (not diesel): 93
M-40: 9, 26, 29, 170, 171, 176, 178, 179, 259
M-40F: 179, 259
M-41: 93
M-42: 167
M-43: 93, 100
M-44: 16, 88-90, 100, 246
M-45: 93, 100
M-46: 93, 100
M-47: 93, 100, 101
M-48: 66, 67, 72, 157, 159, 244
M-49: 66, 67, 70, 72, 157,159, 244
M-50 (3M-11): 66, 67, 72, 175, 244
M-50 (diesel): 171, 176
M-50R: 171, 176
M-51: 66, 67, 72, 157, 159, 244
M-52: 108, 249
M-52 (diesel): 171, 180
M-55: 109, 249
M-56: 95, 167, 247
M-58: 80-82, 245
M-58MN: 80, 82, 245
M-58N: 82, 245
M-62 (ASh-62): 8, 26, 118-120, 251
M-62R: 120, 251
M-62IR: 118-122, 130, 234, 251
M-62V: 122
M-63: 118, 122-124, 251
M-63R: 123
M-63TK: 123, 251
M-64: 118, 123, 251
M-64R: 123, 251
M-65: 118, 123, 251
M-70: 25, 118, 129, 252
M-71: 118. 129, 252
M-71F: 129, 252
M-71F-TK: 129
M-71TK: 129, 252
M-72: 118, 130, 252
M-72TK: 130
M-75: 80, 147, 148, 151, 227, 255
M-76: 148, 151, 255
M-80: 118, 124, 251
M-80R2: 124
M-81: 118, 124, 251
M-81R: 124
M-82 (ASh-82): 9, 118, 124. 127, 151, 251
M-82A: 125, 251
M-82F: 125, 251
M-82FN (ASh-82FN): 26, 31, 119, 124-128, 130-132, 196, 235, 251
M-82FN-TK: 126
M-82NV: 127
M-82T (czechoslovakian): 127
M-85: 24, 147-149, 151, 152, 227, 228, 255
M-85F: 149
M-85V: 149
M-86: 24, 149, 152, 153, 255
M-87: 8, 24, 149, 152, 171, 174, 255
M-87A: 149, 150, 152, 153
M-87B: 152
M-87D: 25, 153, 170, 174, 258
M-88: 24, 149-151, 155, 196, 255
M-88A: 150, 154, 255
M-88B: 150, 151, 154, 155, 255
M-88B-NV: 154
M-88BR (M-88b/r): 154, 255
M-88F: 150, 155
M-88F-NV: 155
M-88R: 154
M-88TK: 154, 255
M-88V: 155
M-89: 24, 150, 151, 155, 156, 255
M-89NV: 156, 255
M-90: 151, 156, 255
M-92: 151, 156, 255
M-95: 151, 156, 255
M-100 (Motor M-100, M-11): *see* M-11
M-100: 75, 133, 134, 136, 148, 181, 228, 253
M-100A: 134-136, 253
M-100AU: 134, 136
M-100 cannon: 136
M-100 coupled: 136
M-100SO: 136, 253
M-103: 134, 137, 138, 184, 253
M-103A: 8, 137, 138, 181, 182, 253
M-103A-TK: 137, 253
M-103G: 137, 253
M-103SP: 137
M-103P: 137, 253
M-103U: 138
M-104: 134, 138, 253
M-105 (VK-105): 9, 20, 26, 29, 31, 134, 135, 138, 139, 142, 177, 181, 183, 233, 253
M-105 coupled: 142
M-105DT: 141
M-105F: 140
M-105P: 31, 136,139, 140, 183, 184, 253
M-105PA: 139-141, 253
M-105PD: 139-141, 253
M-105PF: 9, 139, 141, 142, 183, 184, 253
M-105PF-2: 134, 139, 141, 142, 253
M-105P-TK: 140
M-105PV: 142, 253
M-105R: 22, 139, 253
M-105RA: 139, 140, 253
M-105REN: 141
M-105RF: 141, 253
M-105S: 138
M-105TK: 140
M-106: 134, 142, 254
M-106-1sk (M-106P): 162
M-106PV: 142
M-106TK: 142
M-107 (VK-107): 134, 142, 143, 254
M-107A (VK-107A): 143, 145, 183, 184, 254
M-107 coupled: 143
M-107P: 142
M-107R (VRDK): 143, 254
M-110: 145, 254
M-110A: 145, 254
M-111TK: 191, 261
M-120: 145, 192, 254
M-120TK: 145, 146, 254
M-120UV: 146, 254
M-120UV-TK: 146
M-127: 186, 188, 189, 260
M-127K: 186, 187, 189, 260
M-130: 181, 182, 192
M-170 (M-170/44): 89, 90
M-200: 89, 92, 167, 168, 257
M-222: 236
M-224: 171, 236, 237
M-250: 167, 183, 192, 193, 261
M-251TK: *see* VD-3TK
M-253K: *see* VD-4K
M-300: 167, 168, 192, 257
M-332: 238, 239
M-337: 238, 239
M-362RF: 203
M-436: 239
M-462: 203
M-462RF: 203
M-501: 171, 180, 259
M-501M: 171, 180
M-600 (M-13): *see* M-13
Maybach: 34, 41
MB-4: 185-187, 260
MB-4b: 185, 187, 260
MB-8: 185, 187, 260
MB-8b: 185, 187, 260
MB-100: 181, 182, 192, 260
MB-102: 182, 260
MD-11: *see* D-11
Mercedes: 39-41, 218, 220
MG-11: 26, 67, 72, 157-159, 162, 256
MG-11A: 159
MG-11F: 159, 256
MG-11FN: 159
MG-11N: 159
MG-21: 26, 67, 72, 157, 159, 256
MG-21A: 159, 256
MG-31: 67, 72, 157-161, 256
MG-31A: 160
MG-31F: 161, 162, 183, 196, 256
MG-31F2: 160
MG-31FN: 160
MG-31N: 160
MG-40: 158, 161, 256
MG-50: 157, 158, 161, 256
MGAZ-60: *see* GAZ-Avia-60
MGM: 95, 167, 247
MK (MK-14): 25, 62, 243
MM-1: 96, 247
MM-2: 96, 247
MN-1: 176, 258
Morgulin's engine: 94
MRB-6: 24, 27, 38
M-Sh: 191, 261
MSK: *see* N-6
MV-4: 163-166, 183, 228, 257
MV-6: 163-165, 183, 196, 228, 257
MV-6A: 164, 166, 183
MV-12: 163, 164, 166, 183, 257
MV-12F: 164, 166, 183
MV-12R (M-12R): 164, 166, 183, 257

N-1: *see* AN-1
N-2: 26, 170, 172, 258
N-3 (AD-1): 167, 169, 170, 258
N-4: 170, 172, 258
N-5: *see* FED-8
N-6 (MSK): 167, 170, 173, 258
N-9: 170, 174, 258
NAG: 34
Nakajima Ha-8: 230
Nakajima Ha-115: 237
NAMI-65: *see* M-23
NAMI-100: *see* M-12 (NAMI-100)
Napier Dagger: 231, 235
Napier Lion: 50, 219, 222, 223
Napier Sabre: 235
NRB (NRB-100, M-7): 91,92

Oerlikon: 36
OM-127: 185-187, 260
OM-127o:185-187, 260
OM-127RN: 185-187, 189, 260
OMB: 185, 186, 260

P-020: 26, 210, 211, 264
P-032: 26, 210-212, 264
P-032-71: 211, 264
P-032MR: 210, 211, 264
P-033: 212, 264
P-065: 210, 212, 264
P-800: 205, 213, 264
P-1000: 205, 213, 264
Packard 2A-1500: 221, 222
Packard 3A-2500: 221
PB: 20, 190, 261
Piaggio P.XIIRC.35: 224
Pratt & Whitney Hornet: 83, 221, 229, 230
Pratt & Whitney R-975-AN-1: 196
Pratt & Whitney R-1340: 232
Pratt & Whitney R-1830: 232-235
Pratt & Whitney R-2800: 232, 234, 238

Pratt & Whitney Wasp: 229
PZL-3S: 198

RAM: *see* M-8 (RAM)
RAM-2: 48
RBVZ-6 (M-1): 24, 27, 38, 39, 42, 44, 218, 240
RD-3M: 101
RD-10: 135, 238
RD-20: 135, 183, 238
RD-45: 136
RD-500: 172
Renault: 36
Renault 4Pei: 163, 164, 228
Renault 6Q03: 163, 228
Renault 12O01: 163, 164
Renault 12R01: 164
Renault 12R03: 164, 231, 236
Renault WC (M-3): 38, 42, 44, 240
REP: 36
RMZ-320MR Buran-Avia: 214, 264
RMZ-640MR Buran-Avia: 32, 214, 264
RMZ-640MR-2: 214, 264
Rolls-Royce Condor: 59, 221, 223
Rolls-Royce Dervent 5: 136, 172, 186
Rolls-Royce Eagle: 41, 219
Rolls-Royce Kestrel: 223, 226
Rolls-Royce Merlin: 231, 232, 234, 235
Rolls-Royce Nene 1: 136
Rolls-Royce Vulture: 235
Rotax: 239
Rotax 582: 239
Rotax 912: 239
Ron-80: 40, 41
Russkiy Ispano: *see* M-4

Salmson: 41, 218, 221
Salmson M.9: 37
Salmson P.9: 37
Salmson R.9: 37
SB-039: 210, 212, 264
Siddley Puma: 49, 220, 236
Siemens Sh, 20: 221
SM: 167, 257
SM coupled: 167
SPA 6A: 41, 219
Stulov's engine: 94
Sunbeam: 24, 40, 44, 218

Teledyne Continental IO-360ES: 239
TKRD-1(AM-TKRD-01): 101
TND-1: 217
Tuzhkut: 94

Uvarov's engine: 191

V12 (Kertis V): 52, 55, 58, 242
V18-I (Liberty W18, M-14): 51, 54, 241
V-32: 212
VAD-2: 96, 247
VAD-3: 96, 247
VAZ-311: 207
VAZ-413: 207
VAZ-416: 207, 208, 263
VAZ-426: 207-209, 263
VAZ-4265: 207, 209
VAZ-430: 26, 207
VAZ-4305: 207
VAZ-526: 207, 209, 263
VAZ-1187: 207, 208, 263
VAZ-1188: 207, 208, 263
VD-3TK: 193-195, 261
VD-4K: 132, 193-195, 261
VD-7: 193
VK-1: 136
VK-1A: 136
VK-1F: 136
VK-2: 136
VK-3: 136
VK-5: 136
VK-7: 136
VK-105: *see* M-105
VK-107: *see* M-107
VK-107VRDK: 135
VK-108: 20, 134, 144, 145, 254
VK-108F: 145
VK-109: 134, 136, 145, 254
VK-110: 136, 145, 254
VK-150: 136, 146
VyaK: 169

W18 (Bessonov's engine): 25, 55
Walter Castor III: 229
Walter Junior: 228, 230
Walter Micron: 228
Walter Minor 4-III: 238
Walter Minor 6-III: 238
Walter Pollux: 229
Weslake: 239
Wright R-1820 Cyclone: 9, 28, 79, 117, 227, 234
Wright R-1820-F3: 80. 118
Wright R-1820-F52: 229
Wright R-1820- F53: 229
Wright R-1820-G2: 229, 234
Wright R-1820-G3: 229
Wright R-1820-G7: 229
Wright R-1820- G103: 8,119
Wright R- 1820-G202: 234
Wright R-2600: 231-234
Wright R-3350: 231, 235
Wright-Riga: 34
Wright T3 Tornado: 50, 59, 221, 223
Wright T4 Typhoon: 60, 220, 221, 223